PHILIP'S

STREET ATLAS
South Essex

First published in 1999 by

Philip's, a division of
Octopus Publishing Group Ltd
2–4 Heron Quays, London E14 4JP

Second edition 2003
First impression 2003

ISBN 0-540-08283-X (spiral)

© Philip's 2003

Ordnance Survey®

This product includes mapping data licensed
from Ordnance Survey® with the permission of
the Controller of Her Majesty's Stationery Office.
© Crown copyright 2003. All rights reserved.
Licence number 100011710.

Printed and bound in Spain
by Cayfosa-Quebecor

Contents

III	**Key to map symbols**	
IV	**Key to map pages**	
VI	**Route planning**	
VIII	**Administrative and Postcode boundaries**	
1	**Street maps** at 3½ inches to 1 mile	
183	**Index** of towns and villages	
184	**Index** of streets, hospitals, industrial estates, railway stations, schools, shopping centres, universities and places of interest	

Digital Data

The exceptionally high-quality mapping found in this atlas is available as digital data in TIFF format, which is easily convertible to other bitmapped (raster) image formats.

The index is also available in digital form as a standard database table. It contains all the details found in the printed index together with the National Grid reference for the map square in which each entry is named.

For further information and to discuss your requirements, please contact Philip's on 020 7644 6932 or james.mann@philips-maps.co.uk

(22a) Motorway with junction number		◆	Ambulance station
Primary route – dual/single carriageway		◆	Coastguard station
A road – dual/single carriageway		◆	Fire station
B road – dual/single carriageway		◆	Police station
Minor road – dual/single carriageway		✚	Accident and Emergency entrance to hospital
Other minor road – dual/single carriageway		Ⓗ	Hospital
Road under construction		✛	Place of worship
Tunnel, covered road		*i*	Information Centre (open all year)
Rural track, private road or narrow road in urban area		Ⓟ	Parking
Gate or obstruction to traffic (restrictions may not apply at all times or to all vehicles)		P&R	Park and Ride
Path, bridleway, byway open to all traffic, road used as a public path		PO	Post Office
Pedestrianised area		Ⅹ	Camping site
Postcode boundaries DY7		🚐	Caravan site
County and unitary authority boundaries		▶	Golf course
Railway, tunnel, railway under construction		⊠	Picnic site
Tramway, tramway under construction		Prim Sch	Important buildings, schools, colleges, universities and hospitals
Miniature railway		River Medway	Water name
Railway station Walsall			River, weir, stream
Private railway station			Canal, lock, tunnel
London Underground station			Water
Tram stop, tram stop under construction			Tidal water
Bus, coach station			Woods
			Built up area
		Church	Non-Roman antiquity
		ROMAN FORT	Roman antiquity

Acad	**Academy**	Inst	**Institute**	Recn Gd	**Recreation Ground**
llot Gdns	**Allotments**	Ct	**Law Court**		
Cemy	**Cemetery**	L Ctr	**Leisure Centre**	Resr	**Reservoir**
C Ctr	**Civic Centre**	LC	**Level Crossing**	Ret Pk	**Retail Park**
CH	**Club House**	Liby	**Library**	Sch	**School**
Coll	**College**	Mkt	**Market**	Sh Ctr	**Shopping Centre**
Crem	**Crematorium**	Meml	**Memorial**	TH	**Town Hall/House**
Ent	**Enterprise**	Mon	**Monument**	Trad Est	**Trading Estate**
Ex H	**Exhibition Hall**	Mus	**Museum**	Univ	**University**
Ind Est	**Industrial Estate**	Obsy	**Observatory**	W Twr	**Water Tower**
IRB Sta	**Inshore Rescue Boat Station**	Pal	**Royal Palace**	Wks	**Works**
		PH	**Public House**	YH	**Youth Hostel**

87

58

Adjoining page indicators

The small numbers around the edges of the maps identify the 1 kilometre National Grid lines

■ The dark grey border on the inside edge of some pages indicates that the mapping does not continue onto the adjacent page

The scale of the maps on the pages numbered in blue is 5.52 cm to 1 km • 3½ inches to 1 mile • 1: 18103

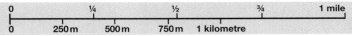

0		¼		½		¾		1 mile
0	250 m		500 m		750 m	1 kilometre		

Key to map pages

122	Map pages at 3½ inches to 1 mile

Buntingford

Stansted Mountfitchet

Stansted Airport

Great Dunmow

A120

A130

Bishop's Stortford

Ware

Hertford

A414

A119

A602

A10

A1184

Spellbrook **1**

Little Hallingbury

Hatfield Broad Oak **2** **3**

Hatfield Heath

Sawbridgeworth

Taverners Green **4** **5**

Aythorpe Roding

6 **7** Pleshey

High Easter

Hunsdonbury **8** **9**

Stanstead Abbotts Roydon

Gilston **10** **11**

Eastwick

Sheering **12** **13**

Matching

Matching Green

Harlow

White Roding **14** **15**

Abbess Roding

Leaden Roding

Good Easter **16** **17**

Mashbury

Great Waltham **18**

A1060

Hoddesdon

21

Lower Nazeing

Tye Green **22** **23**

Roydon Hamlet

Tilegate Green **24** **25**

Hastingwood

High Laver **26** **27**

Moreton

Fyfield

28 **29**

Cooksmill Green

Willingale

Roxwell **30**

31 Writtle

A1060

Cheshunt

Cuffley

Aimes Green

43

Bumble's Green **44** **45**

Epping Green

Epping

North Weald Bassett **46** **47**

Toot Hill

Bobbingworth **48** **49**

High Ongar

Chipping Ongar

50 **51**

Norton Heath

A414

Edney Common

Loves Green

52 **53**

A414

Waltham Abbey **65**

Holdbrook

Ivy Chimneys Upshire **66** **67**

Theydon Bois

Fiddlers Hamlet **68** **69**

Stapleford Tawney

Kelvedon Hatch

Stanford Rivers **70** **71**

Blackmore **72** **73** Mill Green

Doddinghurst

Margaretting **74** **75**

Stock

Ingatestone

A113

A128

A12

Forty Hill

Enfield

M25

A1005

A110

A111

A112

High Beach **88** **89**

Loughton

Sewardstonebury **87**

Chingford

Abridge **90** **91**

Stapleford Abbotts

Navestock Heath

Bentley **92** **93**

Mountnessing **94** **95**

Pilgrims Hatch

Shenfield

96 **97**

Havering's Grove

Billericay

A104

A121

M11

A129

Chingford Hatch

Buckhurst Hill

Chingford **110** **111**

Woodford **109**

Chigwell

Chigwell Row

Havering-atte-Bower **112** **113**

South Weald

Brentwood **116** **117**

Ingrave

Great Warley

114 **115**

Harold Hill

South Green

Little Burstead **118** **119**

Dunton Wayletts

A1009

A1113

A123

A1112

A12

A128

Barkingside **132** **133**

Wanstead

Ilford

A12

Romford **134** **135**

Goodmayes

Hornchurch

Upminster

136 **137**

Cranham

West Horndon **138** **139**

Laindon **140** **141**

Langdon Hills

A118

A1083

A124

A127

A127

A13

Becontree

Barking **152** **153**

Dagenham

Elm Park **154** **155**

Rainham

Corbets Tey

North Ockendon **156** **157**

Bulphan **158** **159**

Horndon on the Hill

160

Stanford-le-Ho

A125

A13

A128

M25

Wennington **170** **171**

Aveley

South Ockendon **172** **173**

Orsett **174** **175**

Linford

Chadwell St Mary

169 Belvedere

Erith

Purfleet

Little Thurrock

A13

A1306

A1013

Woolwich

Plumstead

Greenwich

Deptford

Lewisham

Crayford

Dartford

Swanscombe

Northfleet

Grays **178** **179**

Tilbury

East Tilbu

180

A282

A126

A1089

A205

A206

A207

A208

A2

A220

A2

A296

City of London

Bermondsey

Westminster

Chelsea

Battersea

Clapham

Camberwell

Brixton

London City

Eltham

Bexley

Sidcup

Chislehurst

Bromley

Beckenham

West Kent STREET ATLAS

Swanley

Hartley

Gravesend

A227

A226

London STREET ATLAS

Streatham

Penge

Mitcham

Catford

176 **177**

Hertfordshire STREET ATLAS

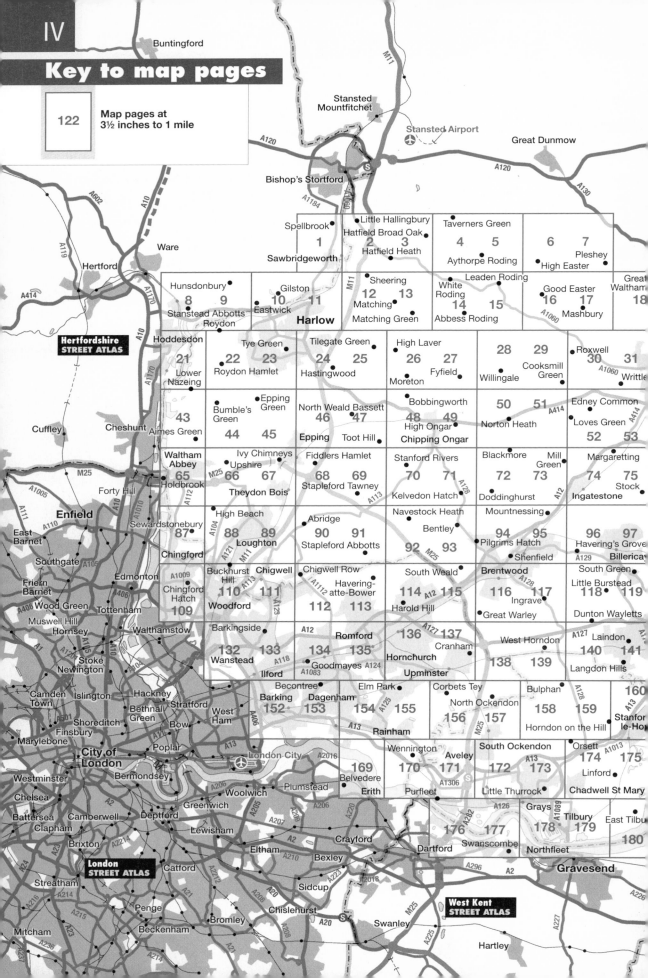

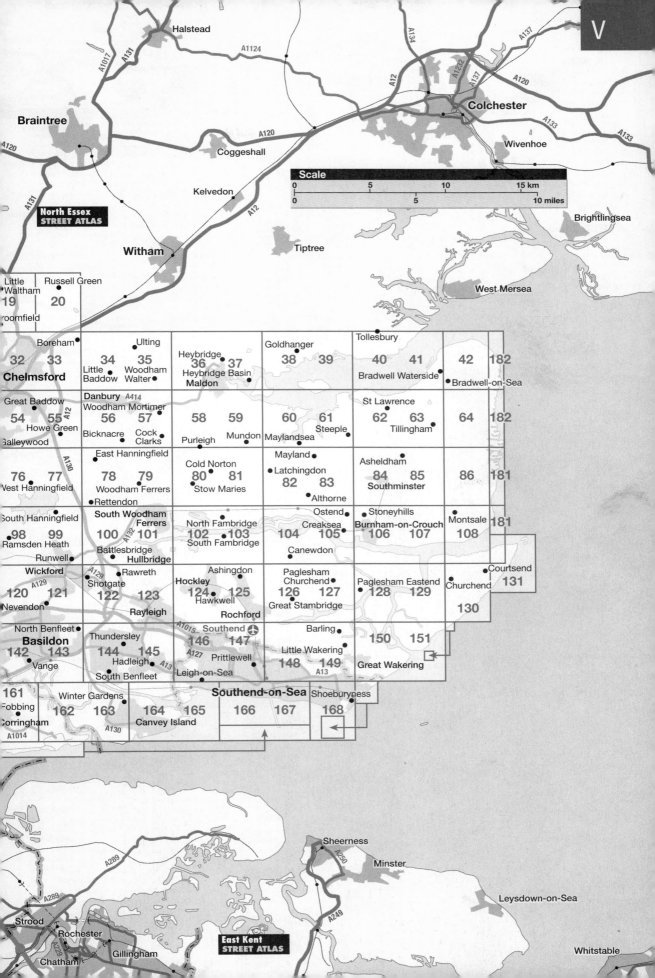

Halstead

A1124

Braintree

A1017 A131

Coggeshall

A120

Kelvedon

A12

A131

North Essex
STREET ATLAS

Witham

A134

A12

A137

A1292

A137

Colchester

A120

A133

Wivenhoe

A133

Brightlingsea

Scale

| 0 | 5 | 10 | 15 km |

| 0 | 5 | 10 miles |

West Mersea

Little Waltham
19

Russell Green
20

Broomfield

Boreham
32 | **33**

Chelmsford

Ulting
34 | **35**
Little Baddow | Woodham Walter

Heybridge
36 | **37**
Heybridge Basin
Maldon

Goldhanger
38 | **39**

Tollesbury
40 | **41**
Bradwell Waterside

42 | **182**

Bradwell-on-Sea

Great Baddow
54 | **55**
Howe Green
Galleywood

A12 A130

Danbury A414
Woodham Mortimer
56 | **57**
Bicknacre | Cock Clarks

58 | **59**
Purleigh | Mundon

60 | **61**
Steeple
Maylandsea

St Lawrence
62 | **63**
Tillingham

64 | **182**

West Hanningfield
76 | **77**

East Hanningfield
78 | **79**
Woodham Ferrers
Rettendon

Cold Norton
80 | **81**
Stow Maries

Mayland
Latchingdon
82 | **83**
Althorne

Asheldham
84 | **85**
Southminster

86 | **181**

South Hanningfield
98 | **99**
Ramsden Heath
Runwell

South Woodham Ferrers
100 | **101**
Battlesbridge
Hullbridge

North Fambridge
102 | **103**
South Fambridge

104 | **105**
Ostend
Creaksea
Canewdon

Stoneyhills
Burnham-on-Crouch
106 | **107**

Montsale
108 | **181**

Wickford
A129
120 | **121**
Nevendon

A129
Shotgate
122 | **123**
Rayleigh
Rawreth

Ashingdon
Hockley
124 | **125**
Hawkwell
Rochford

Paglesham
Churchend
126 | **127**
Great Stambridge

Paglesham Eastend
128 | **129**

Courtsend
Churchend
131

130

North Benfleet
Basildon
142 | **143**
Vange

Thundersley
144 | **145**
Hadleigh A13
South Benfleet

A1015 Southend
146 | **147**
A127 Prittlewell
148 | **149**
Leigh-on-Sea A13

Barling
Little Wakering

150 | **151**

Great Wakering

161
Fobbing
Corringham
A1014

Winter Gardens
162 | **163**
A130

164 | **165**
Canvey Island

Southend-on-Sea
166 | **167**

Shoeburyness
168

Sheerness
A250
Minster

A289

A289

A249

Leysdown-on-Sea

Strood
Rochester
A229
Chatham
Gillingham

A249

East Kent
STREET ATLAS

Whitstable

Major administrative and Postcode boundaries

County and unitary authority boundaries

District boundaries

Postcode boundaries

Area covered by this atlas

Scale

0   5   10   15 km

0   5   10 miles

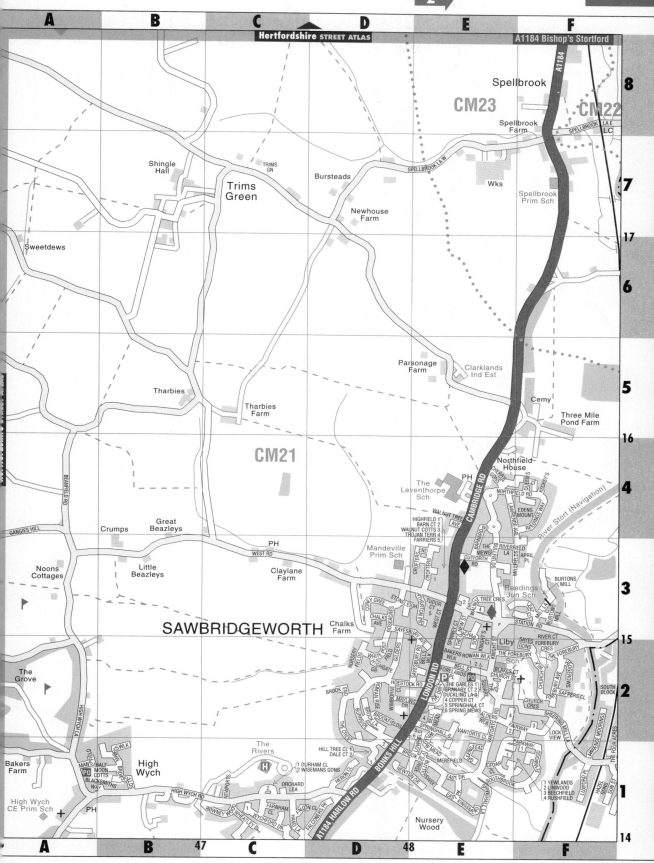

Hertfordshire STREET ATLAS

A1184 Bishop's Stortford

Spellbrook

CM23

CM22

Spellbrook LA E
LC

Shingle
Hall

TRIMS
GN

Bursteads

Spellbrook
Farm

Wks

Spellbrook
Prim Sch

Trims
Green

Newhouse
Farm

SPELLBROOK LA W

Sweetdews

Parsonage
Farm

Clarklands
Ind Est

Cemy

Tharbies

Three Mile
Pond Farm

CM21

Tharbies
Farm

Northfield
House

BEANFIELD RD

The
Leventhorpe
Sch

PH

Crumps

Great
Beazleys

PH

WEST RD

NORTHFIELD RD

CAMBRIDGE RD

River Stort (Navigation)

GANGIES HILL

HIGHFIELD 1
BARN CT 2
WALNUT COTTS 3
TROJAN TERR 4
FARRIERS 5.

WALNUT TREE
AVE

EDENS
MOUNT

Noons
Cottages

Little
Beazleys

Claylane
Farm

Mandeville
Prim Sch

The
Mews

Riverfield
LA

April
PL

BURTONS
X MILL

Reedings
Jun Sch

SAWBRIDGEWORTH

Chalks
Farm

TUDOR CT

STONELEIGH

TREE CRES

STATION RD

River Ct
FOREBURY
CRES

Liby

SAYES
GDNS

The
Grove

The Forebury
Sch

SOUTH
BLOCK

The
Rivers

HILL TREE CL 1
DALE CT 2

THE GABLES 1
GRANARY CT 2
DUCKLING LA 3
COPPER CT 4
SPRINGHALL CT 5
SPRING MEWS 6

BLAKES CT
CHURCH ST

CHURCH
CRES

SHEERING MILL LA

LOCK
VIEW

Bakers
Farm

High
Wych

PO

BLACKSMITHS
WAY

The
Rivers

H

1 DURHAM CL
2 WISEMANS GDNS

PARKWAY

1 YEWLANDS
2 LINWOOD
3 BEECHFIELD
4 RUSHFIELD

High Wych
CE Prim Sch

PH

HIGH WYCH RD

ORCHARD
LEA

FARNHAM
CL

FALCON CL

A1184 HARLOW RD

Nursery
Wood

BONKS HILL

LONDON RD

STADDLES

Wallbury

BARKERS MEAD 1
GEORGE GREEN VILLAS 2
REDBRICK ROW 3

HATCH GN

BEADLES

Beadle
Common

POST
OFFICE
COTTS

Little
Hallingbury
CE Prim
Sch

Monksbury
Farm

Little
Hallingbury

Nursery

Sewage
Works

Lock
Farm

Millhide
Common

LOWER RD

GOOSE LA

WRIGHT'S GREEN LA

SUTTON ACRES

PO

Gaston
House

Gaston
Common

Wright's
Green

Gaston
Green

BACK LA

OLD MILL LA

PADDOCKS

WRIGHTS GREEN LA

River Stort (Navigation)

Mill
(dis)

GRINSTEAD LA

Mott's
Green

CM23

Tednambury
Farm

CM22

Little
Bursteads

Little
Hallingbury
Park

SAWBRIDGEWORTH RD

South
House
Farm

Harcamlow Way

Little
Hallingbury
Hall

PH

Broadcroft

Spill
Timbers
Wood

Stone
Hall

STORTFORD RD

Kecksy's
Bridge

Camp
Farm

HALLINGBURY RD

MILL LA

A1060

THE
STABLES

GREAT
HYDE
HALL

THE
GARDEN
HOS

Oak
Spring

Round
Spring

Eighteenacre
Spring

CHESTNUT DR

Sawbridgeworth

LOWER
SHEERINGS

Little
Hyde
Hall

Wren's
Spring

FORGE
COTTS

STATION
RD

LC

Cowick

SAWBRIDGEWORTH RD

1 PRIORS CT
2 WATERSIDE PL

CM21

THE MEADOWS

IRISH GROVES

THE FOUR
ACRES

BANKS TIMBER RD

MEADOW
WAY

Quickbury
Farm

Stort Valley Way

B1

SHEERING MILL LA

Lower
Sheering

Gladwyns

LADY FELL
PROS

THE STREET

Shrubbs

MOORLANDS REACH

BACK LA

M11

PRIMLEY LA

PLASH

Sheering
CE Prim
Sch

B183 THE STREET

PO

49 | A | B | 50 | C | D | 51 | E | F

North Essex STREET ATLAS

A B C D E F

8

Woodfold

Wallis's Spring

Forest Hall

Forest Farm

Footpath Common

The Marsh

Monk's Wood

Harcamlow Way

Child's Common

The Park

7

RYES LA

17

Three Forests Way

B183

Ryes Farm

Forest Way

Copperfields

Lang Bridge

PO PH

HIGH ST

DUNMOW RD

6

FEATHERS HILL

BROAD ST

DUKES ORCH

St Mary's CE Prim Sch

MEDLARS MEAD

The Round Lodge

Liby

CAGE END

CAGE END CL

CANNONS VILLAS

CANNONS LA

OLD STREET HILL

CM22

Town Farm

Mus Brook

NEW BURY MDW

Hatfield Broad Oak

5

Corringales

Town Farm

Pincey Brook

16

Town Grove

4

Lea Green

LEA HALL BGLWS

Ongars

Lea Hall

3

Hatfield Heath Com Prim Sch

CLIPPED HEDGE

THE CLOSE

TLE HEATH

BROADMERE US

COX LEY

WEST HAYES

THE SHAW

WAGON

Hatfield Heath

15

STORTFORD RD

BEEHIVE CT

PO PH

B183

CHELMSFORD RD

B183

POND LA

Stone Bridge

Lancasters

PARK DR

MATCHING RD

2

Peggerells

BENTLEY VILLAS

Bentley Common

Muchfield Common

Lancaster's Spring

Hill Farm

BARLEY CT

The Paddocks

CM6

Heath Common

POLES CRES

FRIARS LA

Friars

Ardley End

Pooles Cottages

Grange Farm Riding Stables

SPARROW'S LA

1

Sewage Works

Gibsons

Hatfield Grange

A1060

14

A B 53 C D 54 E F

North Essex STREET ATLAS

BOXLEY LA

Taverners Green

Cannons

Barrington Hall

B183

Benningtons

Aldburys Farm

Change Common

Great Common

8

Braintris

7

Woolard's Ash

DUNMOW RD

B183

17

Crabbs Green Farm

6

Broomshawbury

Broad Street Green

Waters Villas

Waters Farm

HAMMONDS RD

BARNFIELD

CM22

Stanways

5

Broomshawbury Wood

Poplars Shaw

16

Anthonys

Anthonys

4

Sparrow Hall Farm

Needham Green

Philpotts

Poplars Wood

Poplars Farm

Pierce Williams

Cammasshall Wood

Cammas Hall

3

Row Wood

15

Three Forests Way

2

Prows Farm

Walkers Farm

CM6

1

Norrington

Pages Cottages

Marks Hall

14

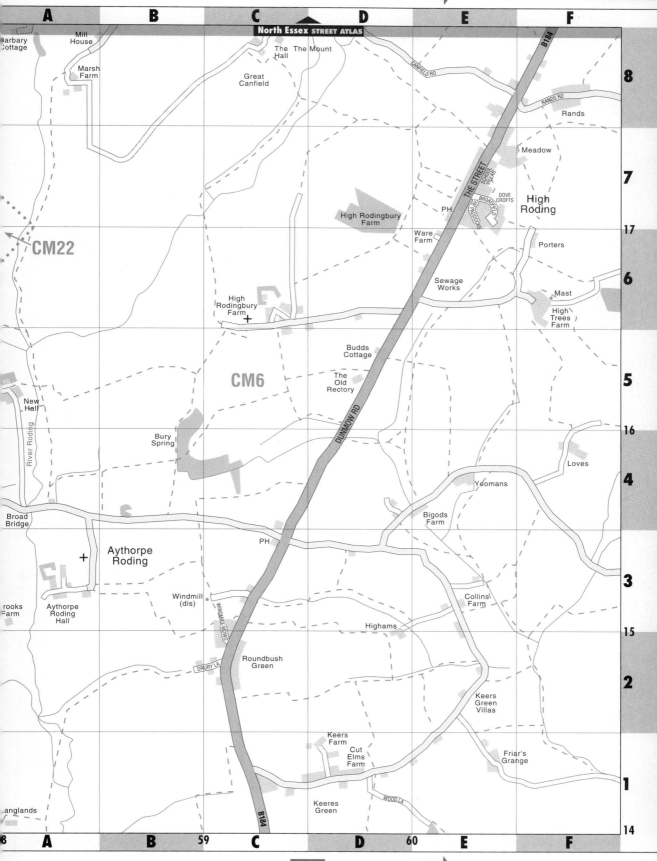

North Essex STREET ATLAS

A B C D E F

8

Barbary Cottage
Mill House

The Hall
The Mount

Marsh Farm

Great Canfield

CANFIELD RD

B184

RANDS RD

Rands

Meadow

7

THE STREET

SCHOOL LA

BROADFIELD

DOVE CROFTS

High Roding

PH

THE PADDOCKS

High Rodingbury Farm

Ware Farm

17

Porters

6

CM22

Sewage Works

Mast

High Trees Farm

High Rodingbury Farm

Budds Cottage

CM6

The Old Rectory

5

New Hall

River Roding

Bury Spring

DUNMOW RD

16

Loves

4

Yeomans

Broad Bridge

PH

Bigods Farm

Aythorpe Roding

Collins Farm

3

Windmill (dis)

WINDMILL MEWS

Highams

15

Brooks Farm

Aythorpe Roding Hall

DRURY LA

Roundbush Green

Keers Green Villas

2

Keers Farm

Cut Elms Farm

Friar's Grange

Langlands

B184

Keeres Green

WOOD LA

1

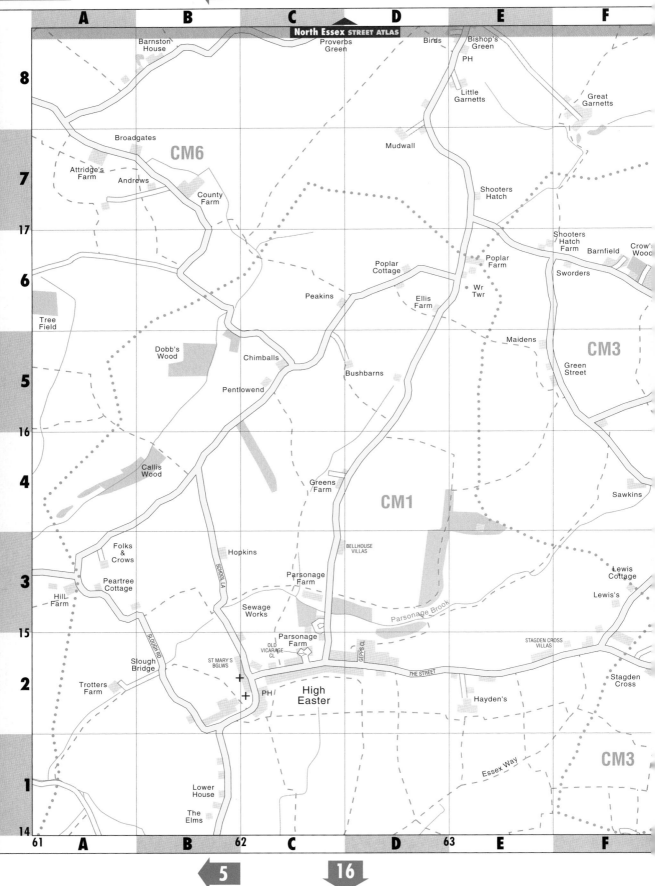

A B C D E F

8

7

17

6

5

16

4

3

15

2

1

14

61 A B 62 C D 63 E F

Barnston House
Proverbs Green
Birds
Bishop's Green
PH
Little Garnetts
Great Garnetts
CM6
Mudwall
Broadgates
Attridge's Farm
Andrews
County Farm
Shooters Hatch
Shooters Hatch Farm
Barnfield
Crow' Wood
Poplar Cottage
Poplar Farm
Sworders
Peakins
Ellis Farm
Wr Twr
Tree Field
Maidens
CM3
Dobb's Wood
Chimballs
Bushbarns
Green Street
Pentlowend
Callis Wood
Greens Farm
CM1
Sawkins
Folks & Crows
Hopkins
BELLHOUSE VILLAS
Lewis Cottage
Peartree Cottage
Parsonage Farm
Lewis's
Hill Farm
SCHOOL LA
Sewage Works
Parsonage Brook
SLOUGH RD
Parsonage Farm
OLD VICARAGE CL
STAGDEN CROSS VILLAS
GEPPS CL
Slough Bridge
ST MARY'S BGLWS
THE STREET
Stagden Cross
Trotters Farm
PH
High Easter
Hayden's
Essex Way
CM3
Lower House
The Elms

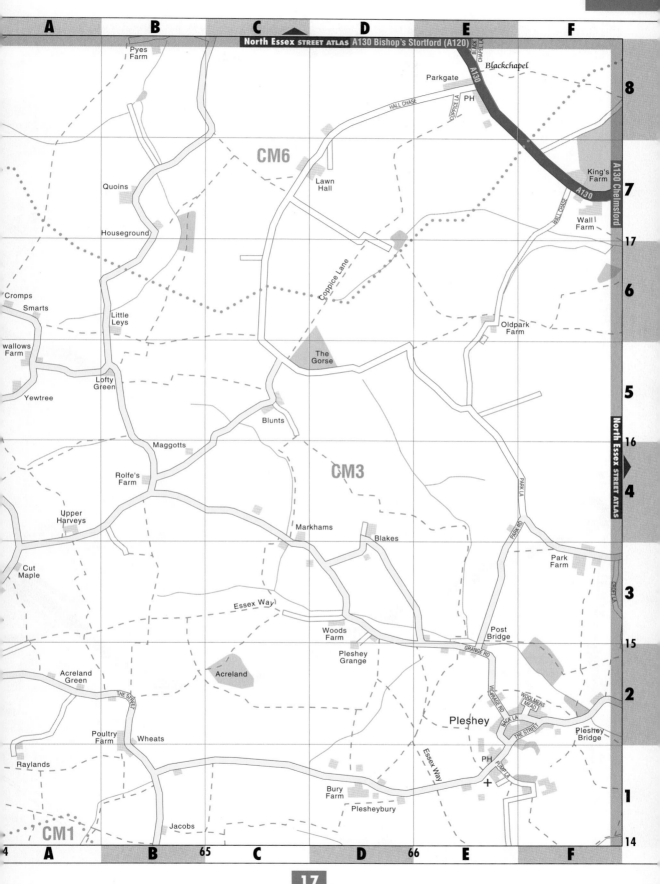

A B C D E F

Blackchapel

Pyes Farm

Parkgate

PH

HALL CHASE

COPPICE LA

BLACK CHAPEL LA

A130

A130 Chelmsford

8

CM6

Lawn Hall

King's Farm

A130

7

Quoins

WALL CHASE

Wall Farm

17

Houseground

Coppice Lane

6

Cromps

Smarts

Little Leys

Oldpark Farm

wallows Farm

The Gorse

5

Yewtree

Lofty Green

Blunts

16

Maggotts

CM3

PARK LA

4

Rolfe's Farm

Upper Harveys

Markhams

PARK RD

Blakes

Park Farm

CROFT LA

Cut Maple

Essex Way

3

Woods Farm

Post Bridge

15

Pleshey Grange

GRANGE RD

Acreland Green

Acreland

VICARAGE RD

WOOLMERS MEAD

2

THE STREET

Pleshey

BACK LA

THE STREET

Pleshey Bridge

Poultry Farm

Wheats

Essex Way

Raylands

PH

PUMP LA

+

1

Bury Farm

Plesheybury

CM1

Jacobs

14

4 A B 65 C D 66 E F

B1
1 WESTERN TERR
2 SOUTHERN TERR
3 PARKLAND CL
4 ESTFELD CL
5 CHITTENDEN CL

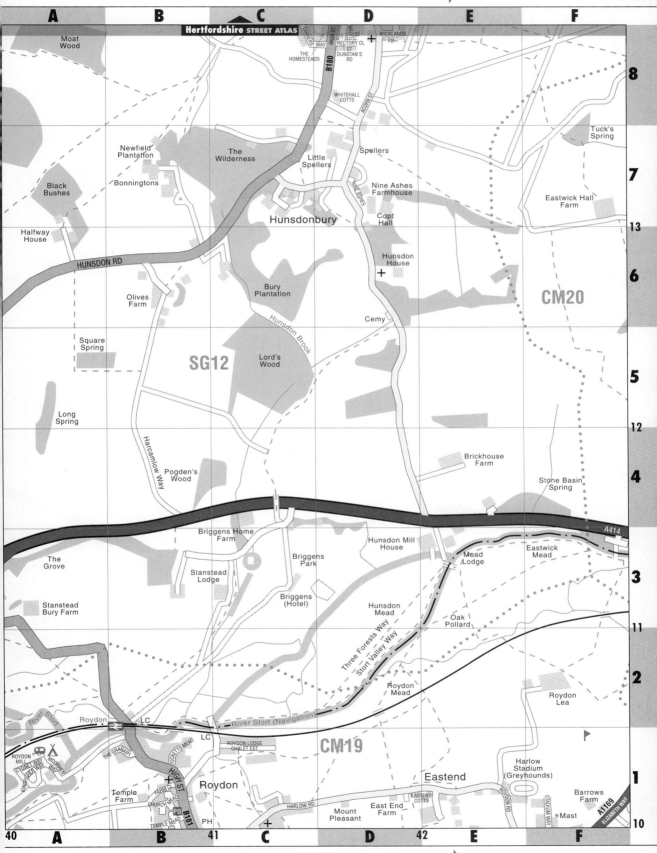

Moat Wood

Newfield Plantation

The Wilderness

Little Spellers

Spellers

Tuck's Spring

Black Bushes

Bonningtons

Hunsdonbury

Nine Ashes Farmhouse

Eastwick Hall Farm

Halfway House

HUNSDON RD

Olives Farm

Bury Plantation

Copt Hall

Hunsdon House

CM20

Square Spring

SG12

Hunsdon Brook

Lord's Wood

Cemy

Long Spring

Harcamlow Way

Pogden's Wood

Brickhouse Farm

Stone Basin Spring

A414

Briggens Home Farm

Hunsdon Mill House

Mead Lodge

Eastwick Mead

The Grove

Stanstead Lodge

Briggens Park

Briggens (Hotel)

Hunsdon Mead

Oak Pollard

Stanstead Bury Farm

Three Forests Way

Stort Valley Way

Roydon Mead

Roydon Lea

River Stort

Roydon

LC

LC

River Stort (Navigation)

CM19

Roydon Lodge CHALET EST

Roydon Mill

Temple Farm

HIGH ST

Roydon

HARLOW RD

Mount Pleasant

East End Farm

Eastend Cotts

Eastend

Harlow Stadium (Greyhounds)

Barrows Farm

B181

Temple Mead

PH

Mast

A1169

ELIZABETH WAY

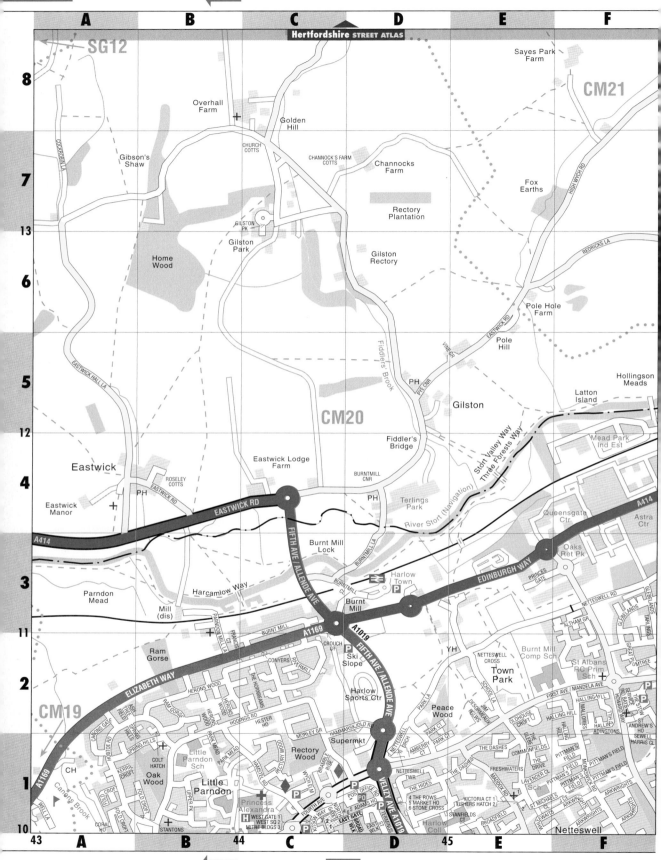

Hertfordshire STREET ATLAS

SG12

CM21

Sayes Park Farm

Overhall Farm

Golden Hill

CHURCH COTTS

Channock's Farm Cotts

Channocks Farm

Gibson's Shaw

Fox Earths

GILSTON PK

Rectory Plantation

REDRICKS LA

Gilston Park

Home Wood

Gilston Rectory

EASTWICK RD

Pole Hole Farm

HIGH WYCH RD

VINE GR

PYE CNR

Pole Hill

Fiddlers' Brook

PH

Gilston

Hollingson Meads

Latton Island

CM20

Mead Park Ind Est

Fiddler's Bridge

Eastwick

EASTWICK HALL LA

ROSELEY COTTS

Eastwick Lodge Farm

BURNTMILL CNR

Terlings Park

Stort Valley Way
Three Forests Way

Queensgate Ctr

A414

Astra Ctr

Eastwick Manor

PH

EASTWICK RD

BURNTMILL LA

PH

River Stort (Navigation)

Oaks Ret Pk

A414

EDINBURGH WAY

PRINCES GATE

Burnt Mill Lock

Harcamlow Way

Parndon Mead

Mill (dis)

BURNTMILL CL

Harlow Town

P

Burnt Mill

PRINCES GATE

NETTESWELL RD

GLEBELANDS
TATLINGS

Ram Gorse

PARNDON MILL LA

FRANCIS RD

BURNT MILL

A1169

A1019

CROUCH CT

P

Ski Slope

FIFTH AVE / ALLENDE AVE

YH

NETTESWELL CROSS

Burnt Mill Comp Sch

St Albans RC Prim Sch

P

GLEBELANDS

GREAT PLUMTREE

Elizabeth Way

CONYERS
RIVERMILL

HODINGS RD

THE HORNBEAMS

HESTER HO

MORLEY GR

HAMMARSKJOLD RD

Harlow Sports Ctr

Town Park

SCHOOL LA

Peace Wood

PARK LA

JIM DESORMEAUX BELLWS

FIRST AVE
MANDELA AVE

OLDHOUSE CROFT

HALLING HILL

MALLORIES

THE DRIVE

P

ST ANDREW'S HO
SEWELL HARRIS CL

CM19

CANONS GATE

RAM GORSE

HERONS WOOD

HERONS
PARK MEAD

HODINGS RD

COOMB MEAD

HANSEL HO

BRAMBLE RISE

Supermkt

AMBERRY CT

PARK CT

THE GLEBE

COMMONFIELDS

THE DASHES

FRESHWATERS

THE DASHES

LAVENDER CL

PITTMAN'S FIELD

MONKSWICK RD

PITTMAN'S FIELD

PITTMAN'S FIELD

ARKWRIGHTS

CH

HIGHBIDE RD

KERRIL CROFT

SPRING HILLS

FOLD CROFT

COLT HATCH

Oak Wood

Little Parndon Sch

Little Parndon

PARK MEAD

UPPER PK

WYCH ELM

Rectory Wood

A1169

P

POST OFFICE RD
PO

VELIZY AVE A1019

NETTESWELL TWR

THE HIDES

P

P

THE ROWS

Victoria Ct 1
Fishers Hatch 2

ST MICHAELS

MARSH GATE

CANONS BROOK

VELLA

CORAL HO

FOLD CROFT

STANTONS

Princess Alexandra
H

WEST GATE 1
WEST SQ 2
MITRE BLDGS 3

NETSON WAY

FOURTH AVE

1 2
EAST GATE
BROAD WALK

4 & 5 ADAMS HO

EAST GATE
EAST WLK

4 THE ROWS
5 MARKET HO
6 STONE CROSS

VICTORIA CT 1
J CL

STANFIELDS CT

BROADFIELD

Harlow Coll

ARKWRIGHTS

Netteswell

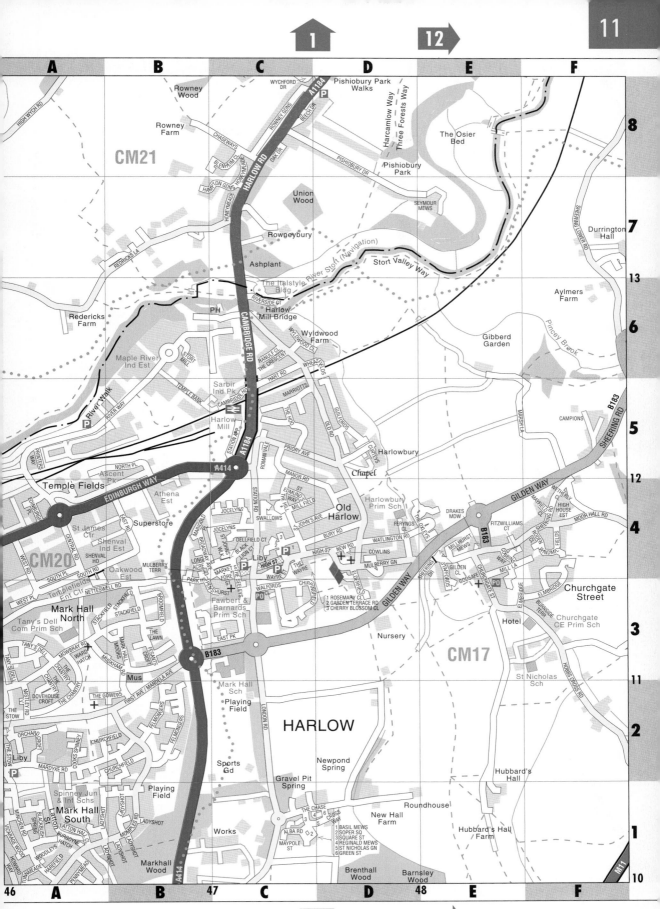

A B C D E F

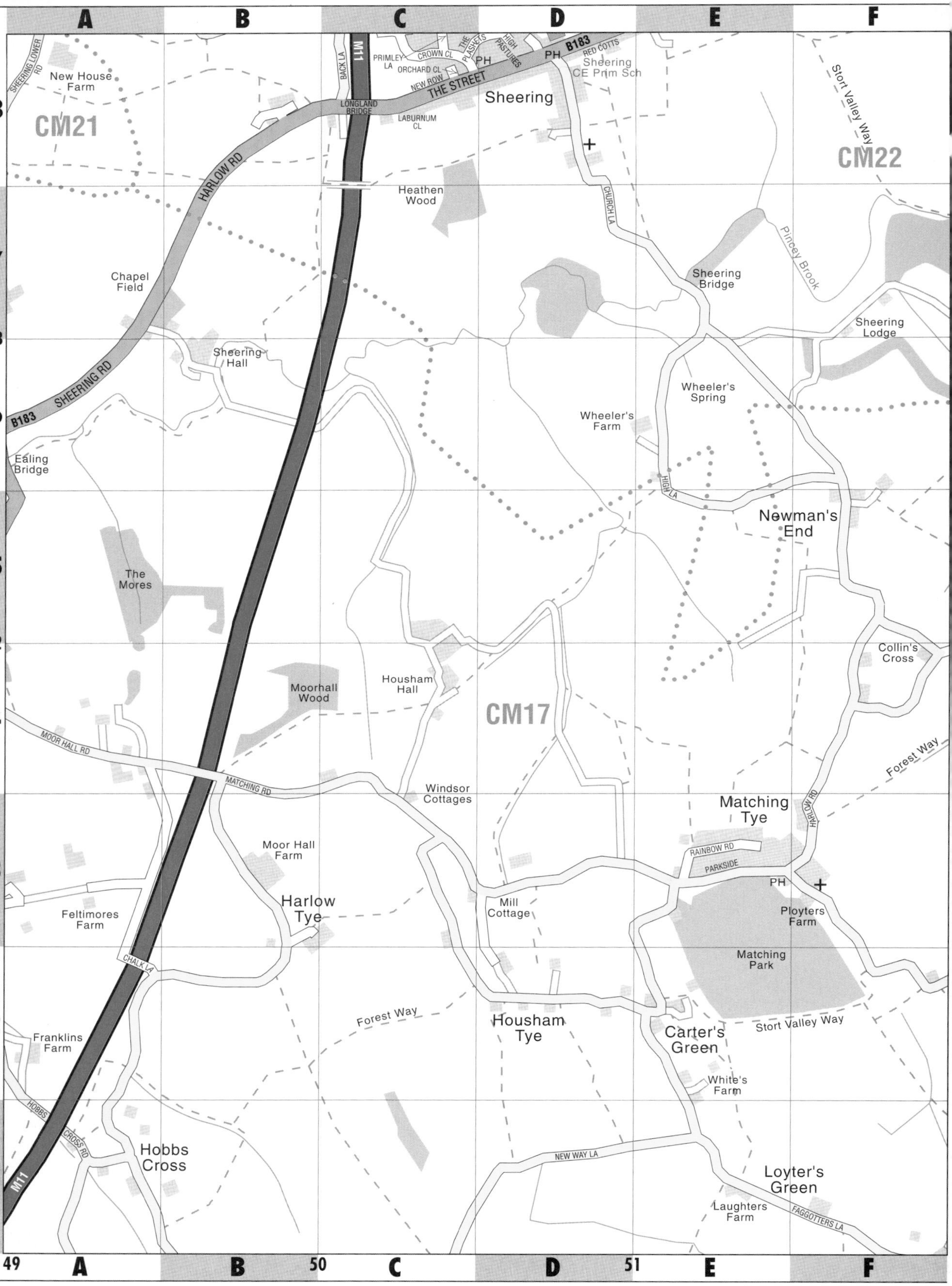

8

New House Farm

CM21

SHEERING LOWER RD

BACK LA

M11

LONGLAND BRIDGE

PRIMLEY LA

CROWN CL

ORCHARD CL

THE PLASHETS

HIGH PASTURES

PH

PH

B183

RED COTTS

Sheering CE Prim Sch

THE STREET

NEW ROW

Sheering

LABURNUM CL

Stort Valley Way

CM22

7

Chapel Field

HARLOW RD

Heathen Wood

CHURCH LA

Sheering Bridge

Pincey Brook

13

Sheering Hall

Wheeler's Spring

Sheering Lodge

6

B183

SHEERING RD

Wheeler's Farm

HIGH LA

Ealing Bridge

5

The Mores

Newman's End

12

Moorhall Wood

Housham Hall

CM17

Collin's Cross

4

MOOR HALL RD

MATCHING RD

Windsor Cottages

Forest Way

Matching Tye

3

Moor Hall Farm

Feltimores Farm

Harlow Tye

Mill Cottage

RAINBOW RD

PARKSIDE

PH

Ployters Farm

11

CHALK LA

Matching Park

2

Franklins Farm

Forest Way

Housham Tye

Carter's Green

White's Farm

Stort Valley Way

M11

HOBBS CROSS RD

Hobbs Cross

NEW WAY LA

Loyter's Green

Laughters Farm

FAGGOTTERS LA

1

10

49 A B 50 C D 51 E F

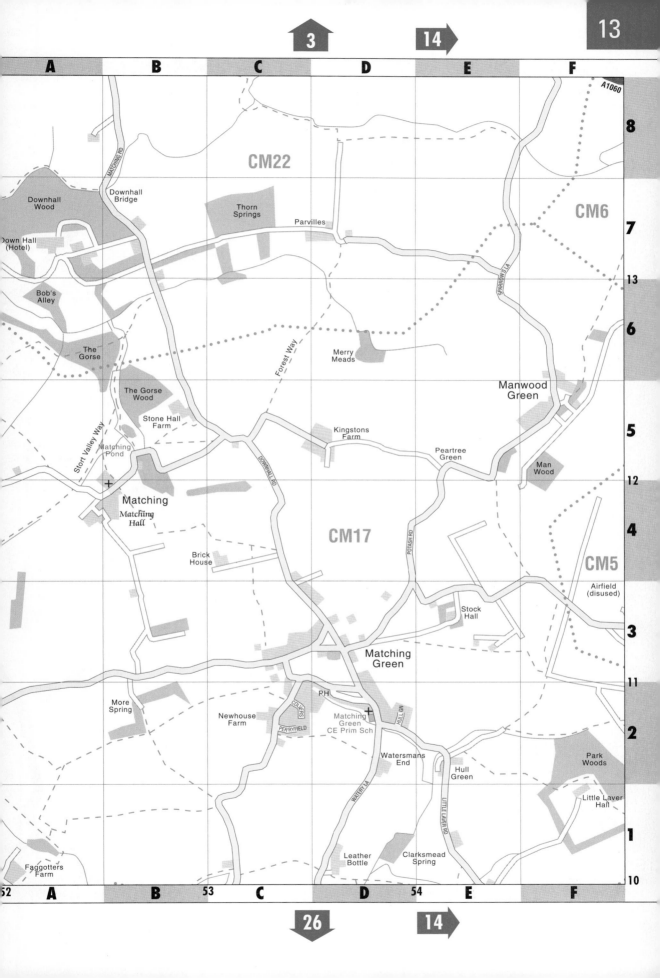

13 **4**

	A	B	C	D	E	F

A1060

8

White Roothing
or
White Roding

BRETT'S VILLAS

PH

Sewage Works

Lucas Farm

Colville Hall

St Martins Cl

Gatehouse Farm

The Elms

CM6

7

Colvillehall Wood

CHURCH LA

Windmill (disused)

Three Forests Way

STORTFORD RD   A1060

Uptrees

13

New House Farm

6

Kingstons

MATCHING LA

Mascallsbury Farm

CM17

Snows Farm

Waterloo Farmhouse

Three Forests Way

5

Berwick Hall

12

ANCHOR LA

Anchor House

Green Hill Farm

The Rectory

4

Abbess Hall Farm

Abbess Roding

Fairlands

Abbess End

THE BUNGALOWS

SCHOOL LA

3

CM5

Rookwood Hall

Sewage Works

Longbarns

B184

11

Camp Site (disused)

HORSECROFT

2

Rookwoodhall Wood

Rookwood Hall Cottages

CM17

DUNMOW RD

1

Brickles Wood

Woodend

Wood House

SCHOOL LA

Cobbler's Pieces

B184

10

55	A		B	56	C		D	57	E		F

13 **27**

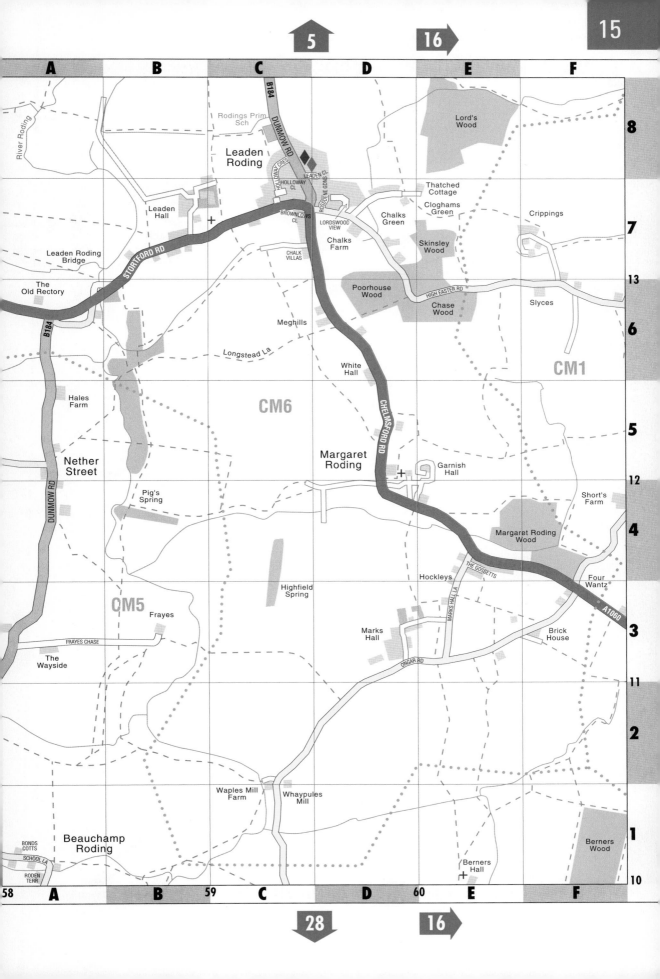

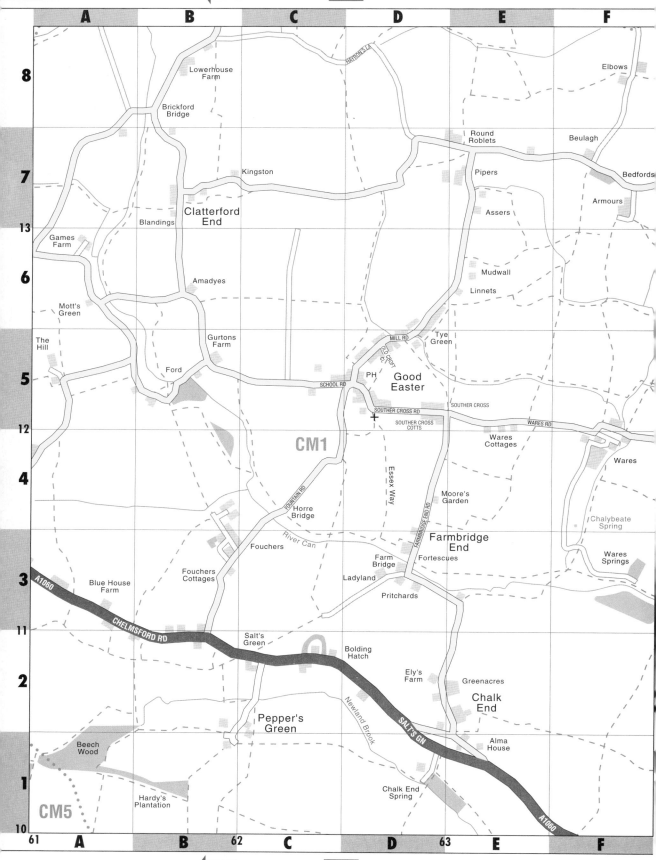

A   B   C   D   E   F

8

7

13

6

5

12

4

3

11

2

1

10

Lowerhouse Farm
Brickford Bridge
Kingston
Clatterford End
Blandings
Games Farm
Amadyes
Mott's Green
The Hill
Gurtons Farm
Ford
Round Roblets
Pipers
Assers
Mudwall
Linnets
Elbows
Beulagh
Bedfords
Armours
HAYRON'S LA.
MILL RD
OLD CROFT CL.
Tye Green
SCHOOL RD
PH
Good Easter
SOUTHER CROSS RD
SOUTHER CROSS
SOUTHER CROSS COTTS
WARES RD
Wares Cottages
Wares
CM1
Essex Way
Horre Bridge
FOUNTAIN RD
River Can
Fouchers
Fouchers Cottages
Blue House Farm
Moore's Garden
FARMBRIDGE END RD
Farmbridge End
Fortescues
Farm Bridge
Ladyland
Pritchards
Chalybeate Spring
Wares Springs
A1060
CHELMSFORD RD
Salt's Green
Bolding Hatch
Ely's Farm
Greenacres
Chalk End
Pepper's Green
Newland Brook
SALT'S GN
Alma House
Chalk End Spring
A1060
Beech Wood
Hardy's Plantation
CM5

17

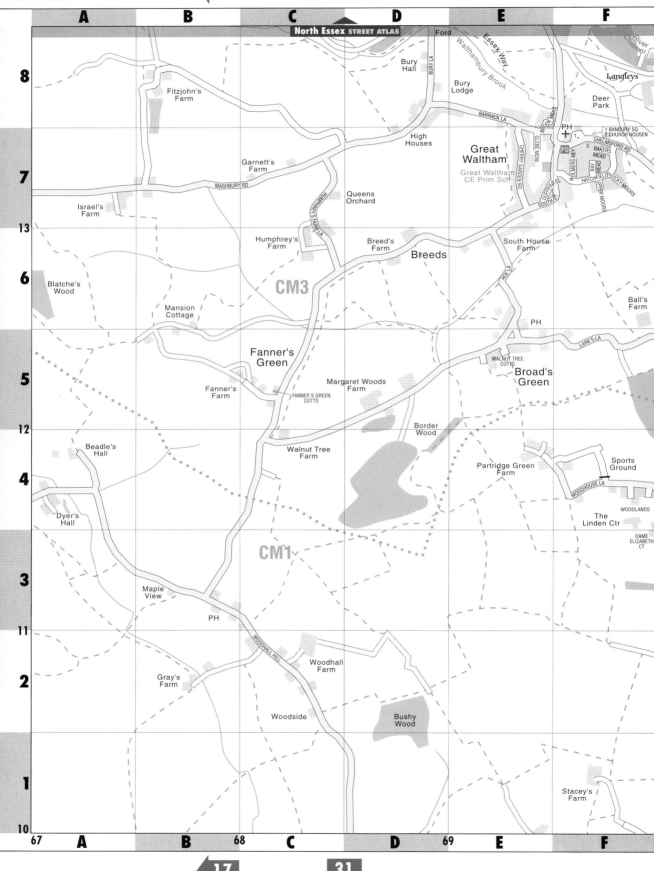

North Essex STREET ATLAS

A **B** **C** **D** **E** **F**

8

Ford
Bury Hall
Bury Lodge
Fitzjohn's Farm
BURY LA
Walthambury Brook
Essex Way
Langleys
Deer Park
BARRACK LA
BROOK MEAD
7
High Houses
Garnett's Farm
MASHBURY RD
Queens Orchard
Great Waltham
Great Waltham CE Prim Sch
CHERRY GARDEN RD
GLEBE MDW
WOLMERS HEY
CHELMSFORD RD
1 BANBURY SQ
2 CHURCH HOUSEN
BAKERS MEAD
PH
PO
RAY
HATCHFIELD
QUEENS
UPPER MOORS
DICKY MOORS

Israel's Farm
HUMPHREY'S FARM LA
DUFFERS CL
SOUTH'S
13
Humphrey's Farm
Breed's Farm
Breeds
South House Farm

6
Blatche's Wood
CM3
HOE LA
Ball's Farm

Mansion Cottage
PH
LARK'S LA

Fanner's Green
Margaret Woods Farm
WALNUT TREE COTTS
Broad's Green

5
Fanner's Farm
FANNER'S GREEN COTTS
Border Wood
Partridge Green Farm
Sports Ground
12
WOODHOUSE LA
WOODLANDS

Beadle's Hall
Walnut Tree Farm
The Linden Ctr
DAME ELIZABETH CT

4
Dyer's Hall
CM1

3
Maple View
PH

11
WOODHALL HILL
Woodhall Farm

2
Gray's Farm
Woodside
Bushy Wood
Stacey's Farm

1

10
67 **A** 68 **B** **C** 68 **D** 69 **E** **F**

River Channel
Chelmsford

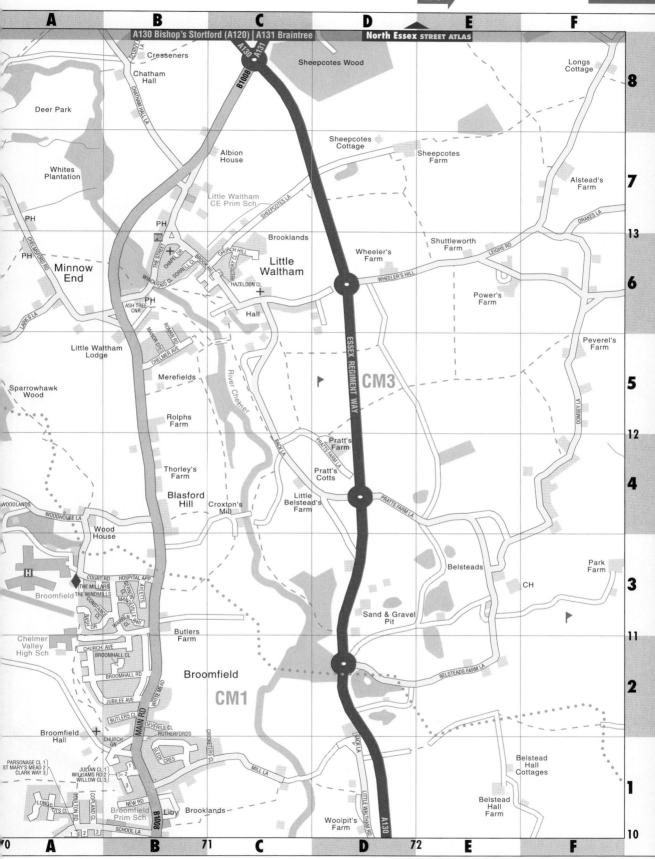

A | B | C | D | E | F

A130 Bishop's Stortford (A120) | A131 Braintree

North Essex STREET ATLAS

Cresseners

Chatham Hall

Deer Park

Whites Plantation

Albion House

Sheepcotes Wood

Sheepcotes Cottage

Sheepcotes Farm

Longs Cottage

Alstead's Farm

8

7

PH

Minnow End

PH

PH

Little Waltham CE Prim Sch

THE STREET

PO

CHAPEL DR

PH

ASH TREE CNR

WINCKFORD CL

SORRELL CL

BROOK HILL

CHURCH HILL

RECTORY CL

HAZELDON CL

Brooklands

Little Waltham

Hall

Wheeler's Farm

Shuttleworth Farm

LEIGHS RD

DRAKES LA

Power's Farm

Peverel's Farm

13

6

Little Waltham Lodge

MANOR CRES

ROMAN RD

CHELMER AVE

Merefields

Rolphs Farm

River Chelmer

ESSEX REGIMENT WAY

CM3

Sparrowhawk Wood

5

Thorley's Farm

BACK LA

Pratt's Farm

PRATTS FARM LA

Pratt's Cotts

DOMSEY LA

12

WOODLANDS

WOODHOUSE LA

Blasford Hill

Croxton's Mill

Little Belstead's Farm

PRATTS FARM LA

4

Wood House

Belsteads

Park Farm

CH

3

H

Broomfield

COURT RD

THE MILLARS

THE WINDMILLS

HOSPITAL APP

VERNON CL

JUVILLE WAY

MANVILLE CL

CONSTANCE CL

WARREN CL

NASH DR

AYLETTS

Butlers Farm

Sand & Gravel Pit

BELSTEADS FARM LA

11

Chelmer Valley High Sch

CHURCH AVE

BROOMHALL CL

BROOMHALL RD

JUBILEE AVE

Broomfield

CM1

WHITE MEAD

MAIN RD

2

Broomfield Hall

CHURCH GN

BUTLERS RD

DEVERILL CL

RUTHERFORDS

GLEBE CRES

CRICKETERS CL

MILL LA

LITTLE WALTHAM RD

BACK LA

Belstead Hall Cottages

PARSONAGE CL 1
ST MARY'S MEAD 2
CLARK WAY 3

JULIAN CL 1
WILLIAMS RD 2
WILLOW CL 3

NEW RD

Brooklands

Woolpit's Farm

Belstead Hall Farm

1

LONGS COTS CL

MOULTON CL

COPLAND CL

B1008

Liby

Broomfield Prim Sch

SCHOOL LA

A130

10

A | B | C | D | E | F

70 | 71 | 72

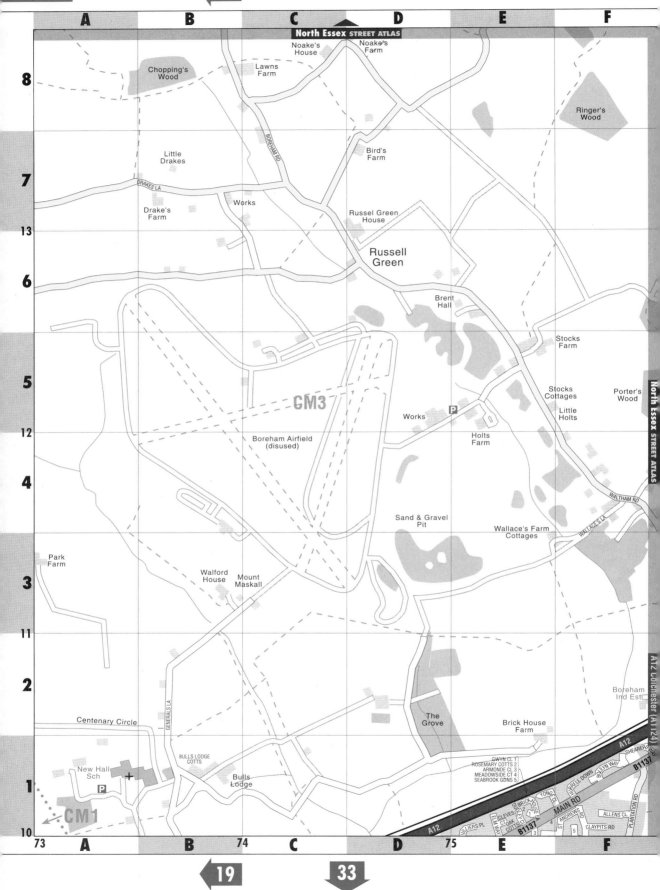

North Essex STREET ATLAS

A B C D E F

8

7

13

6

5

12

4

3

11

2

1

10

Chopping's Wood

Noake's House

Noake's Farm

Lawns Farm

Ringer's Wood

Little Drakes

BOREHAM RD

Bird's Farm

DRAKES LA

Drake's Farm

Works

Russel Green House

Russell Green

Brent Hall

Stocks Farm

Stocks Cottages

Porter's Wood

Little Holts

CM3

Works

P

Holts Farm

Boreham Airfield (disused)

WALTHAM RD

WALLACE'S LA

Sand & Gravel Pit

Wallace's Farm Cottages

Park Farm

Walford House

Mount Maskall

Boreham Ind Est

The Grove

Brick House Farm

A12

SHEAREROP

B1137

Centenary Circle

GENERALS LA

GWYN CL 1
ROSEMARY COTTS 2
ARMONDE CL 3
MEADOWSIDE CT 4
SEABROOK GDNS 5

BOLEYN WAY

BRICK HOUSE

YON

SPELL DOWN

New Hall Sch

P

Bulls Lodge Cotts

Bulls Lodge

CM1

A12

ULLIERS PL

ELM WAY

CLEVES
CT
OAK
COTTS

BRICK
RD
BY

MAIN RD

ST ANDREWS RD

B1137

ALLENS CL

CLAYPITS RD

PLANTATION RD

73 A B 74 C D 75 E F

North Essex STREET ATLAS

A12 Colchester (A1124)

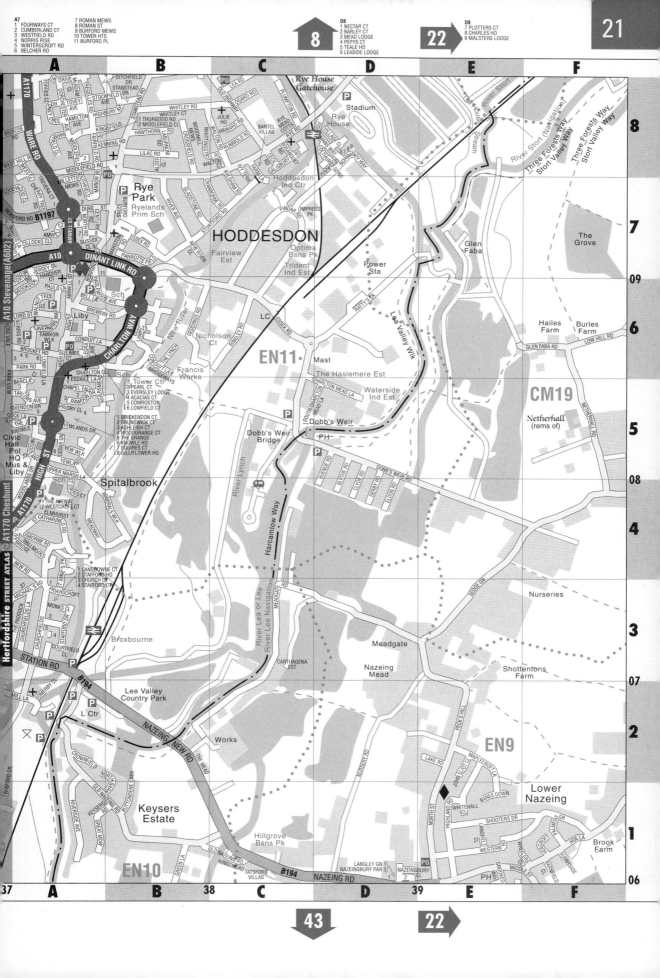

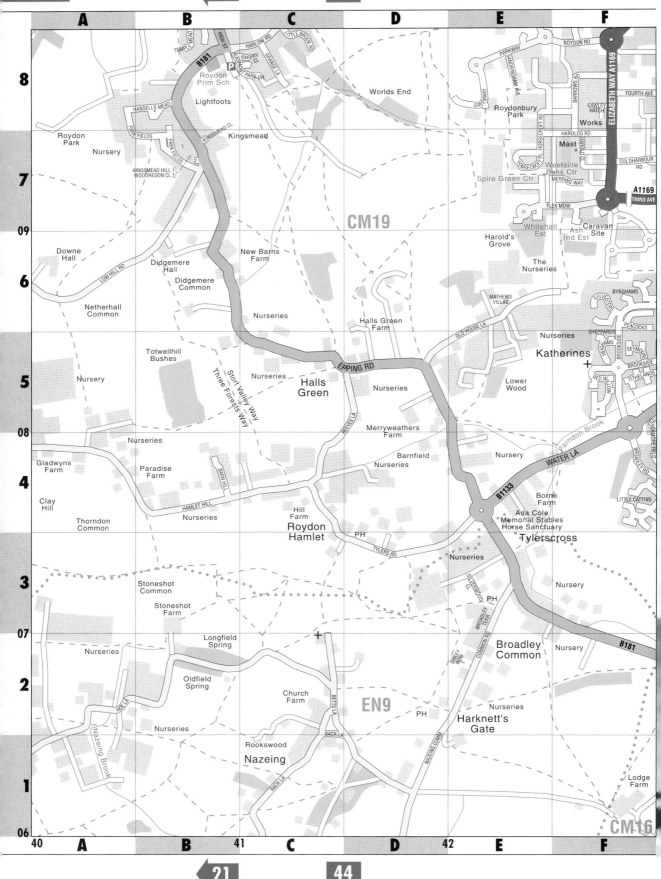

A B C D E F

8

7

09

6

5

08

4

3

07

2

1

06

CM19

CM16

EN9

Roydon Prim Sch

Lightfoots

Roydon Park

Nursery

Hansells Mead

Park Fields

Kingsmead Hill 1
Woodredon Cl 2

Kingsmead

New Barns Farm

Worlds End

Downe Hall

Didgemere Hall

Didgemere Common

Low Hill Rd

Netherhall Common

Nurseries

Halls Green Farm

Totwellhill Bushes

Nursery

Nurseries

Halls Green

Epping Rd

Nurseries

Stort Valley Way
Three Forests Way

Merryweathers Farm

Barnfield Nurseries

Gladwyns Farm

Nurseries

Paradise Farm

Clay Hill

Barn Hill

Hamlet Hill

Thorndon Common

Nurseries

Hill Farm

Roydon Hamlet

PH

Tylers Rd

Reeves La

Nurseries

Stoneshot Common

Stoneshot Farm

Longfield Spring

Nurseries

Oldfield Spring

Hoe La

Nazeing Brook

Nurseries

Church Farm

Betts La

Back La

Rookswood

Nazeing

Back La

Nazeing Comm

PH

Harknett's Gate

Broadley Common

Silverwood Cl

PH

Broadley Terr

Common Rd

Shirley Row

Nursery

Nursery

Nursery

Nurseries

B181

Tylerscross

B1133

Borne Farm

Ada Cole
Memorial Stables
Horse Sanctuary

Water La

Parndon Brook

Nursery

Little Cattins

Lower Wood

Old House La

Mathews Villas

The Nurseries

Harold's Grove

Nurseries

Katherines

Red Willow

Sheppards

Bynghams

Sylvesters

Peacocks

Seymours

Brookside

Tithelands

Brookside

Broadley Rd

Sycamorefield

Lodge Farm

Roydon Rd

Parkway

Greyway

Sandringham Ave

Roydonbury Park

Works

Mast

Spire Green Ctr

Westside Bsns Ctr

Horsecroft Rd

Horsecroft Pl

Merrig Way

Flex Mdw

Whitehall Est

Harold's Grove

Ash Ind Est

Caravan Site

Barrons Rd

Harolds Rd

Harold Cl

Cawley Hatch

Fourth Ave

Coldharbour Rd

Elizabeth Way A1169

A1169

Third Ave

B181

High St

Temple Mead

B181

Harlow Rd

Little Brook Rd

Bakery Cl

Grange La

Beaumont Pk Dr

Park Dr

Kingsmead Cl

Park Fields

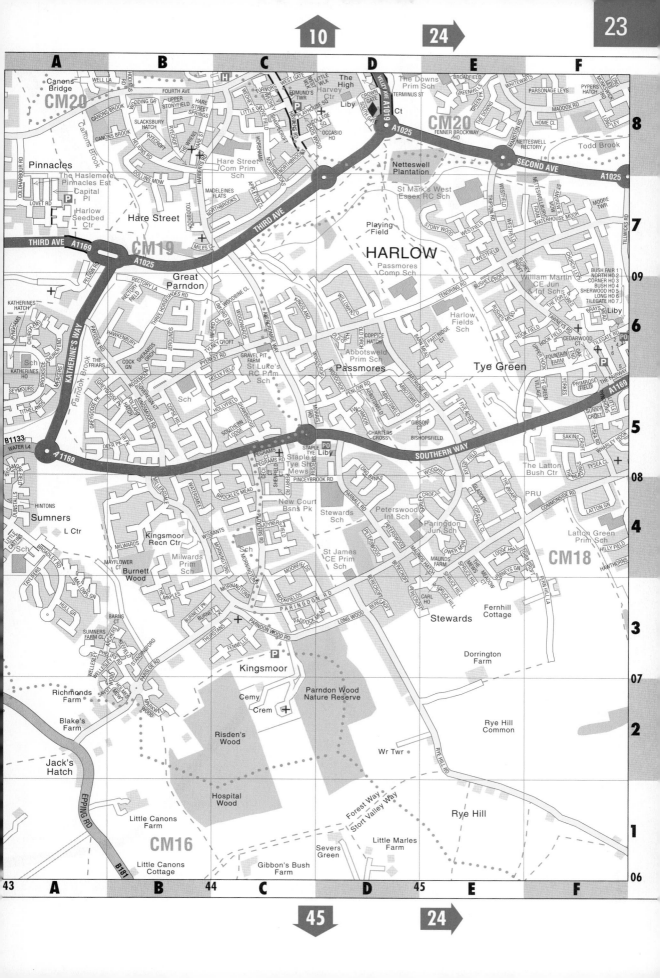

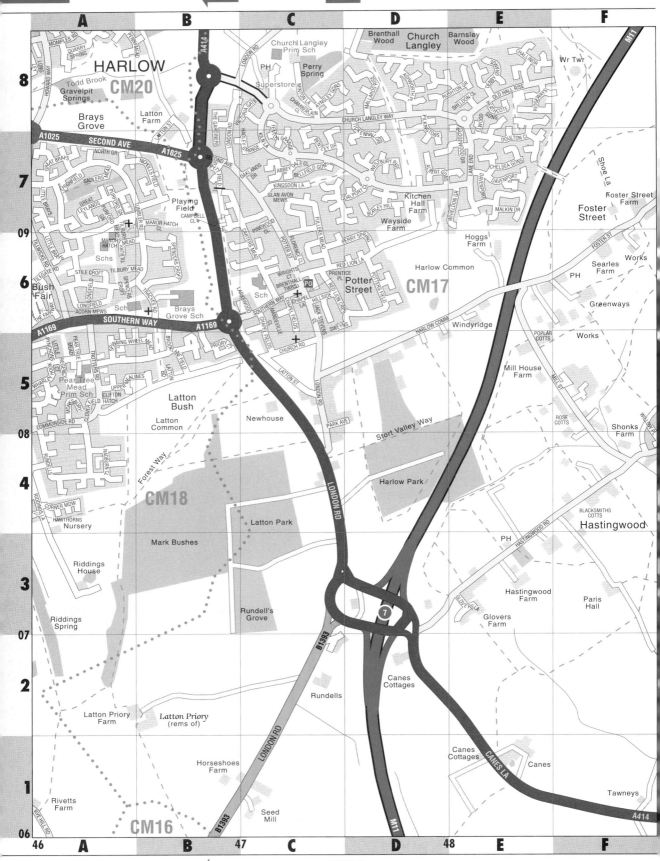

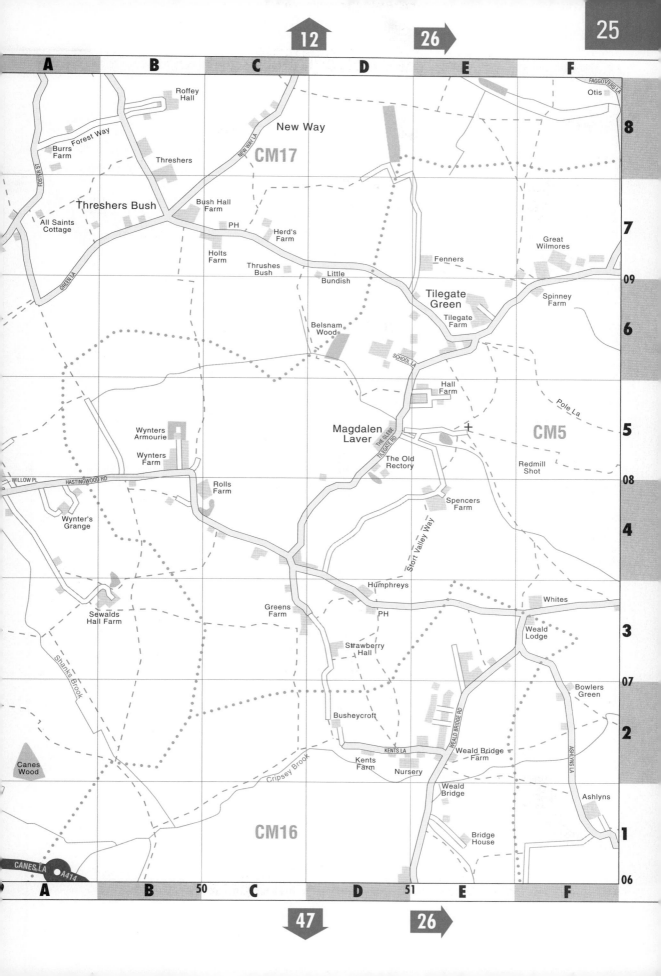

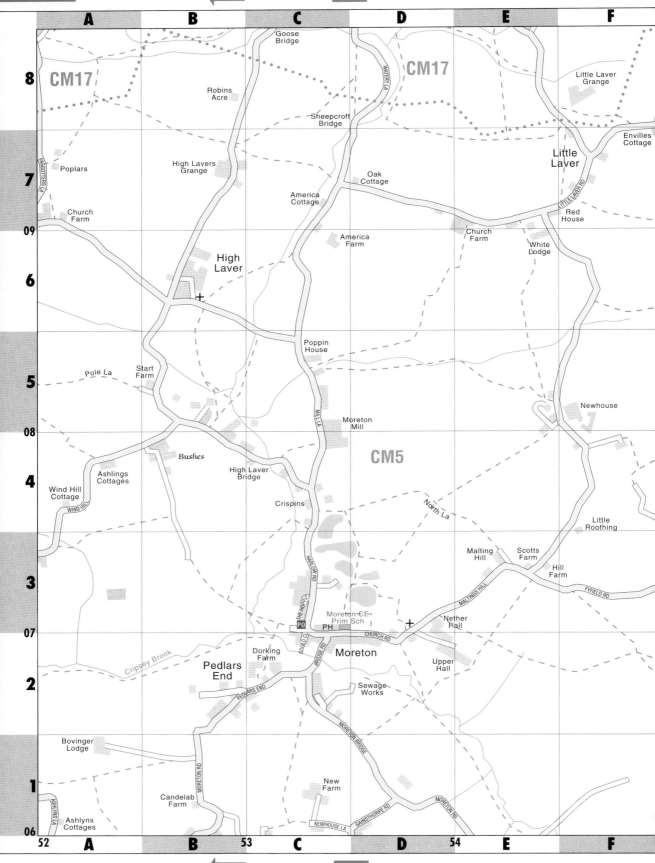

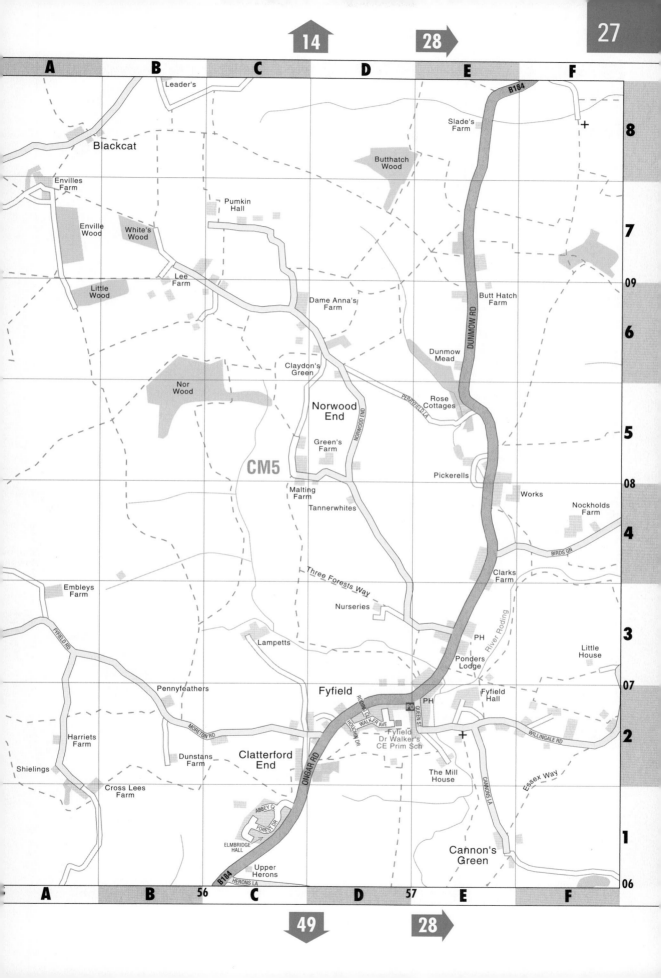

27
15

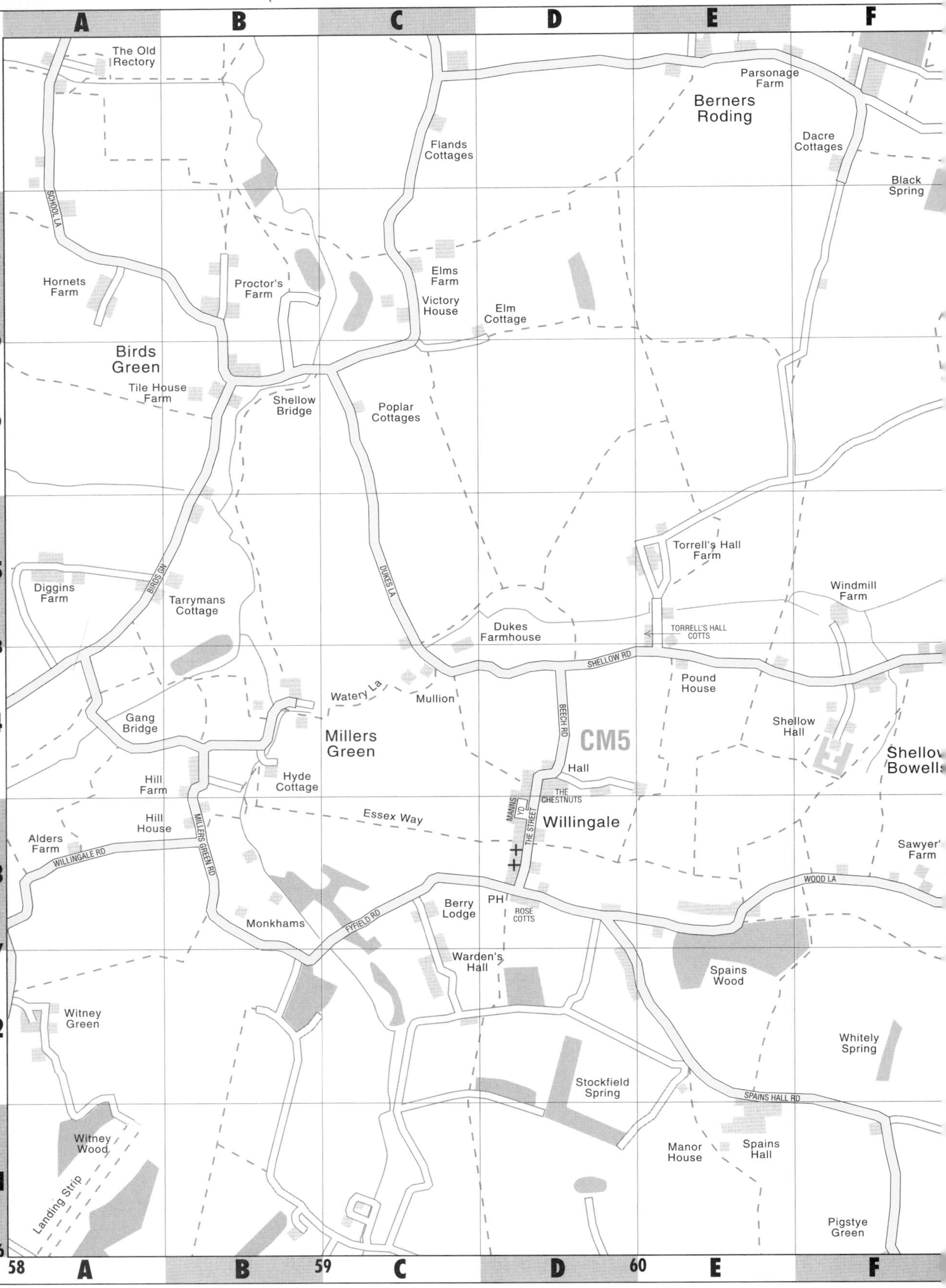

A B C D E F

8

The Old Rectory

Berners Roding

Parsonage Farm

Dacre Cottages

Flands Cottages

Black Spring

7

SCHOOL LA

Hornets Farm

Proctor's Farm

Elms Farm

Victory House

Elm Cottage

09

Birds Green

Tile House Farm

Shellow Bridge

Poplar Cottages

6

BIRDS GN

5

Torrell's Hall Farm

Windmill Farm

Diggins Farm

Tarrymans Cottage

DUKES LA

Dukes Farmhouse

TORRELL'S HALL COTTS

08

SHELLOW RD

Pound House

Shellow Hall

4

Gang Bridge

Millers Green

Watery La

Mullion

BEECH RD

CM5

Shellow Bowells

Hall

Hill Farm

Hyde Cottage

THE CHESTNUTS

THE STREET

MAINS RD

Willingale

Sawyer's Farm

3

Alders Farm

Hill House

WILLINGALE RD

MILLERS GREEN RD

Essex Way

PH

ROSE COTTS

WOOD LA

Monkhams

EYFIELD RD

Berry Lodge

Spains Wood

07

Warden's Hall

2

Witney Green

Whitely Spring

Stockfield Spring

SPAINS HALL RD

Witney Wood

Manor House

Spains Hall

1

Landing Strip

Pigstye Green

06

58 A B 59 C D 60 E F

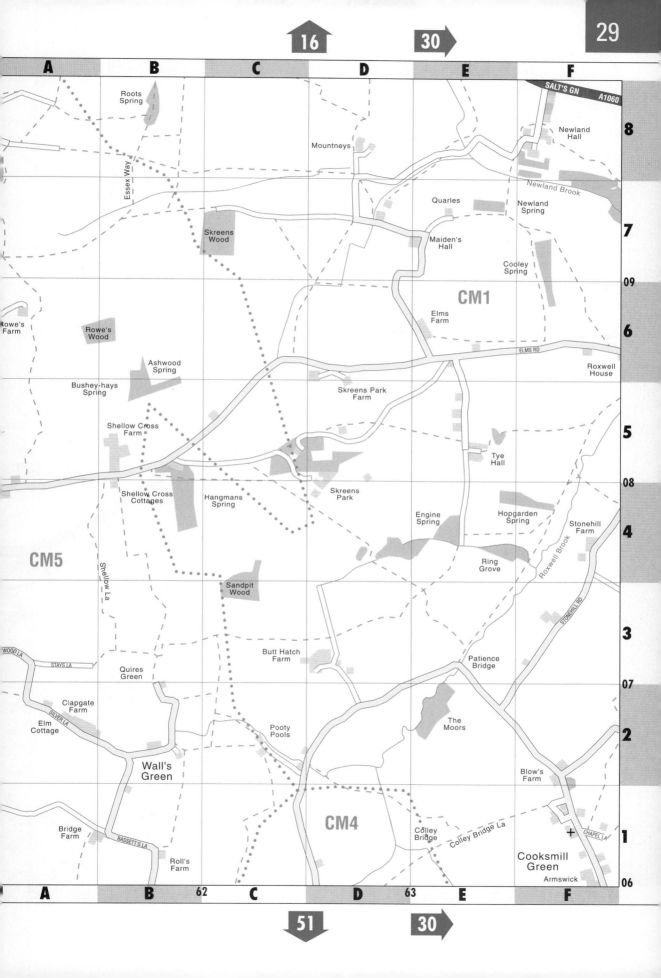

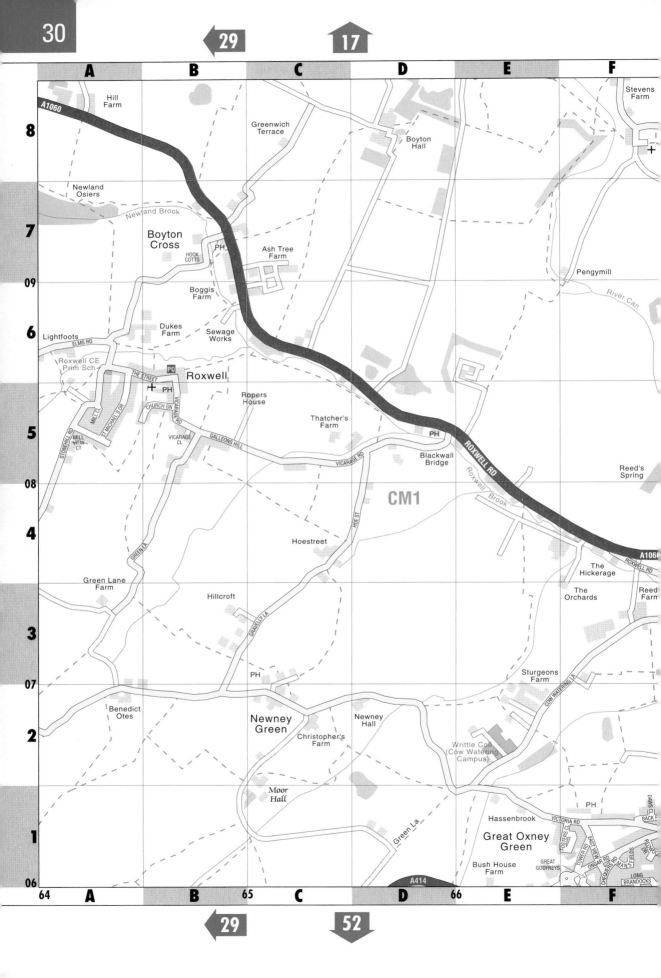

31
19

CM1

CHELMSFORD

Springfield

CM2

31
54

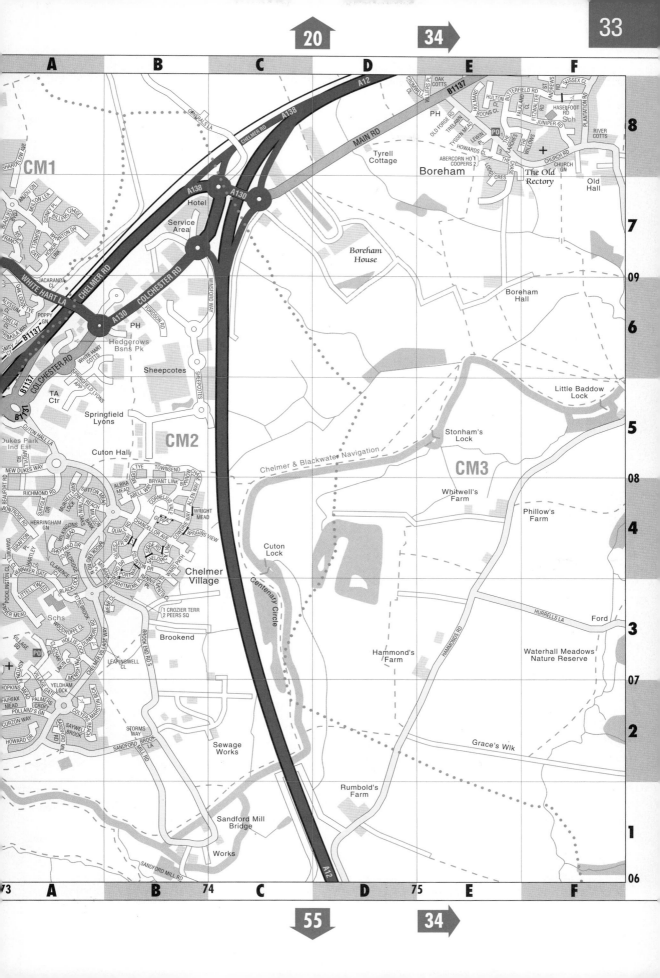

North Essex STREET ATLAS

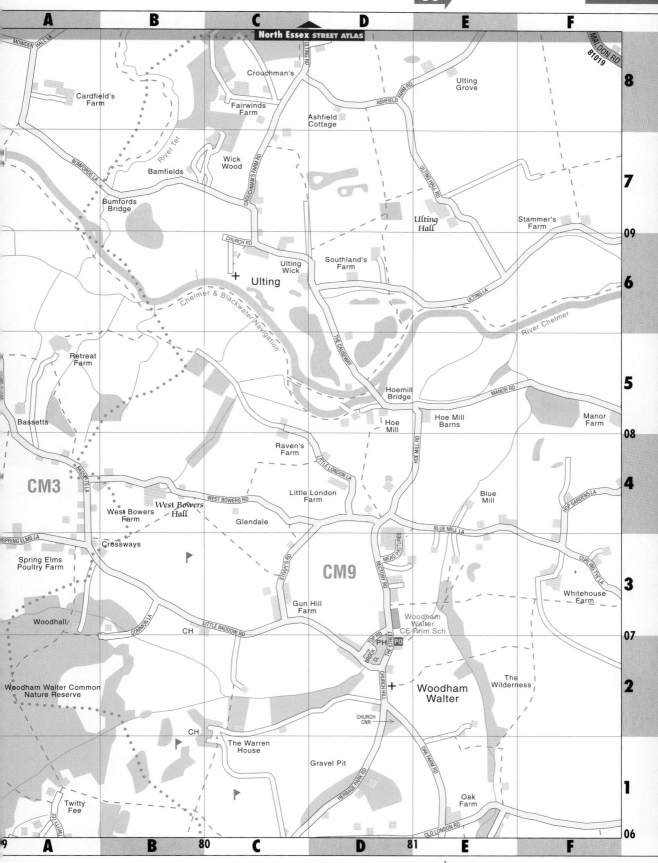

North Essex STREET ATLAS

A   B   C   D   E   F

MOWDEN HALL LA

Cardfield's Farm

Crouchman's

ULTING RD

Fairwinds Farm

Ashfield Cottage

ASHFIELD FARM RD

Ulting Grove

8

River Ter

Wick Wood

CROUCHMAN'S FARM RD

ULTING HALL RD

BUMFORDS LA

Bamfields

7

Bumfords Bridge

CHURCH RD

Ulting Hall

Stammer's Farm

09

Ulting Wick

Southland's Farm

ULTING LA

Ulting

6

Chelmer & Blackwater Navigation

River Chelmer

Retreat Farm

5

Hoemill Bridge

MANOR RD

Bassetts

Hoe Mill

Hoe Mill Barns

Manor Farm

08

Raven's Farm

LITTLE LONDON LA

HOE MILL RD

CM3

BASSETTS LA

West Bowers Farm

WEST BOWERS RD

West Bowers Hall

Little London Farm

Blue Mill

HOP GARDENS LA

4

Glendale

Crossways

SPRING ELMS LA

BLUE MILL LA

CURLING TYE LA

Spring Elms Poultry Farm

STIVY'S RD

RECTORY RD

MEAD PASTURES

CM9

Whitehouse Farm

3

COMMON LA

Woodhall

CH

LITTLE BADDOW RD

Gun Hill Farm

Woodham Walter CE Prim Sch

TOP RD

BROOK CL

PH

THE STREET

PO

07

Woodham Walter Common Nature Reserve

CHURCH HILL

Woodham Walter

The Wilderness

2

CH

CHURCH CNR

The Warren House

Gravel Pit

HERBAGE PARK RD

OAK FARM RD

1

Twitty Fee

TWITTY FEE

Oak Farm

OLD LONDON RD

06

A   B   80   C   D   81   E   F

B1019

MALDON RD

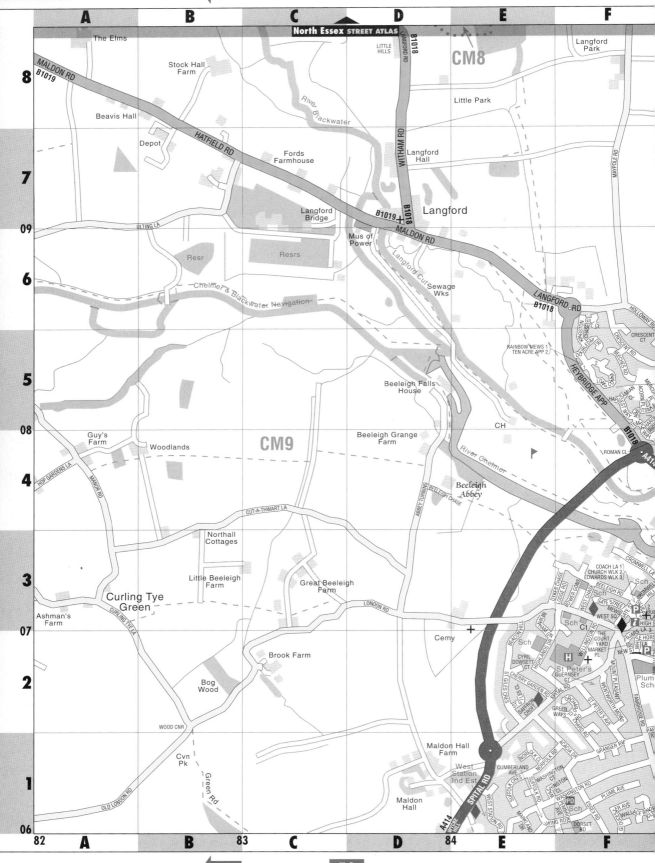

North Essex STREET ATLAS

CM8

The Elms
MALDON RD
B1019
Stock Hall Farm
Little Hills
LANGFORD RD
B1018
Langford Park
Little Park
Beavis Hall
River Blackwater
Langford Hall
Depot
HATFIELD RD
Fords Farmhouse
WITHAM RD
MAYPOLE RD
ULTING LA
Langford Bridge
B1019
B1018
MALDON RD
Langford
09
Resr
Resrs
Mus of Power
Langford Cut
Sewage Wks
LANGFORD RD
B1018
6
Chelmer & Blackwater Navigation
RAINBOW MEWS 1
TEN ACRE APP 2
CRESCENT CT
HOLLOWAY RD
HEYBRIDGE APP
B1018
Beeleigh Falls House
CH
5
Guy's Farm
Woodlands
CM9
Beeleigh Grange Farm
River Chelmer
ROMAN CL
A41
08
HOP GARDENS LA
MANOR RD
ABBEY TURNING
BEELEIGH CHASE
Beeleigh Abbey
4
CUT-A-THWART LA
Northall Cottages
CROMWELL LA
COACH LA 1
CHURCH WLK 2
EDWARDS WLK 3
Sch
3
Curling Tye Green
CURLING TYE LA
Little Beeleigh Farm
Great Beeleigh Farm
LONDON RD
DYKES CHASE
LODGE RD
WEST CHASE
BEELEIGH RD
GATE STREET
Sch
HIGH ST
P
Ashman's Farm
Cemy
BEACON HILL
Sch
Ct
THE COURT YARD
MARKET PL
NEW ST
P
2
Brook Farm
CYRIL DOWSETT CT
H
St Peter's
GUERNSEY CT
Plum Sch
Bog Wood
WOOD CNR
Cvn Pk
Maldon Hall Farm
West Station Ind Est
SPITAL RD
PO
1
Green Rd
OLD LONDON RD
Maldon Hall
A414
06

North Essex STREET ATLAS

A B C D E F

8

7

09

6

08

5

4

3

07

2

1

06

SHEEPCOATES LA
CHURCH LA

Sains Hall

Northlands Farm

Furzelands Farm

Howell's Farm

Poplar Grove Farm

PH

Broad Street Green

Slough House Farm

Lofts

Chigborough Farm

Grapnells Farm

Heybridge

Woodfield Cotts

WILLOW WLK

Sand & Gravel Pit

Saltcote Hall

Cvn Pk

B1026

PH

B1018

Heybridge Prim Sch

Cemy

B1026

Galliford Road Ind Est

A414

Quayside Ind Est

Heybridge House Ind Est

Middle Farm

CM9

GOLDHANGER RD

Canterbury Farm

Heybridge Hall

1 COATES CL
2 SWAN CT
3 HALL BRIDGE RISE

1 CROMWELL CT
2 MARKET HILL CT
3 SAXON CT
4 BULL LA

RIVER BLACKWATER CHALET SITE

Heybridge Basin

Colliers Reach

Heybridge Creek

River Chelmer

MALDON

Chelmer & Blackwater Navigation

Lock Hill

PH

Chandlers Quay

Liby

Chequers LA

White Horse

Liby Fields

Friary

The Hythe

Maldon District Mus

Promenade Park

Recn Gd

L Ctr

Northey House

River Blackwater

A B C D E F

A1
1 LESLIE NEWNHAM CT
2 NIGHTINGALE CNR
3 SASSOON WAY
4 DRAYTON CL

5   86   87

North Essex STREET ATLAS

A **B** **C** **D** **E** **F**

CHURCH LA

LITTLE TOTHAM RD

B1026

8

Little London
Farm

Folly Faunts
House

Falcons Hall
Farm

TUBBANS CHASE

7

BLIND LA

Brick
Cottages

Goldhanger
House

PO

MALDON RD

HALL EST

SORREL CL

PH

CHURCH ST

Agricultural/Domestic
Mus

Chappel
Farm

WASH LA

Goldhanger

09

PEARTREE CL

ST PETERS CL

HEAD ST

6

Rook
Hall

PH

Cobb's
Farm

FISH ST

THISTLEY CL

5

CM9

Gardener's
Farm

Bound's
Farm

08

BARROW
MARSH

Vaulty
Manor

Wash
Bridge

4

B1026

GOLDHANGER RD

Cvn
Pks

OSEA RD

Sewage
Works

Mill
Beach

3

Collier's Reach

Hilly Pool
Point

07

Decoy
Point

Causeway

2

River Blackwater

West Point

Osea
Island

Northey
Island

1

06

88 **A** **B** **89** **C** **D** **90** **E** **F**

North Essex STREET ATLAS

B1026

A **B** **C** **D** **E** **F**

Lower Grove

8

New Barn

Wycke Farm

Highams Farm

Longwick Farm

Bowstead Brook

7

09

Joyce's Farm

Lauriston Farm

6

LAURISTON BGLWS

Gore Saltings

CM9

5

08

Goldhanger Creek

4

River Blackwater

The Stumble

3

07

2

Osea Island

Works

Osea Farm

THE CHASE

East Point

1

Wr Twr

06

A **B** 92 **C** **D** 93 **E** **F**

North Essex STREET ATLAS

Bohuns
Hall

Thistly Rd

Tollesbury

Mell
Farm

Wick
Farm

MELL RD

MONKS WLK

WYCKE LA

CM9

Boreham & Profits
Farm

PRENTICE HALL LA

Decoy
Farm

Mill Farm
Marshes

Mill Creek

Rolls
Farm

Left Decoy
Marshes

Mill
Point

River Blackwater

The
Stone

CM0

SEA VIEW PROM

MOUNTVIEW
CRES

PH

OYSTER
COTTS

RIVERTON DR

TINNOCKS LA

ST LAWRENCE DR

MAIN RD

SEA VIEW
PAR

P

North Essex STREET ATLAS

A B C D E F

8

7

09

6

CM9

River Blackwater

Jetty

Pewet
Island

5

08

B1021

PARKER
CT.

PD

Bradwell
Waterside

OLD
COASTGUARD
COTTS

PH

4

Marina

TRUSSES RD

Bradwell Creek

Westwick
Farm

WATERSIDE RD

WOODYARDS

3

07

Down
Westwick

CMO

2

Orplands

ORPLANDS
COTTS

Kennel
Barn

MALDON RD

B1021 MALDON RD

1

06

97 A B 98 C D 99 E F

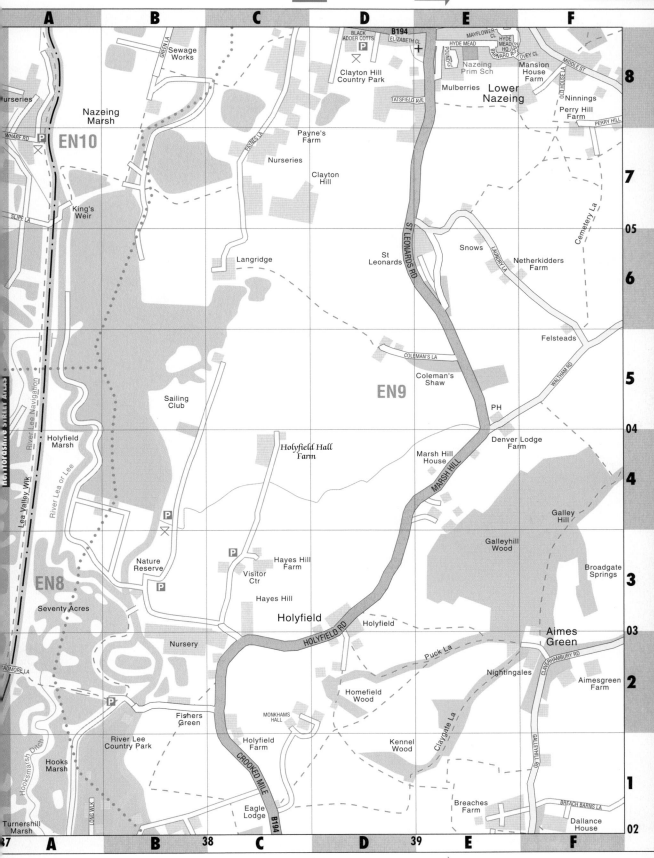

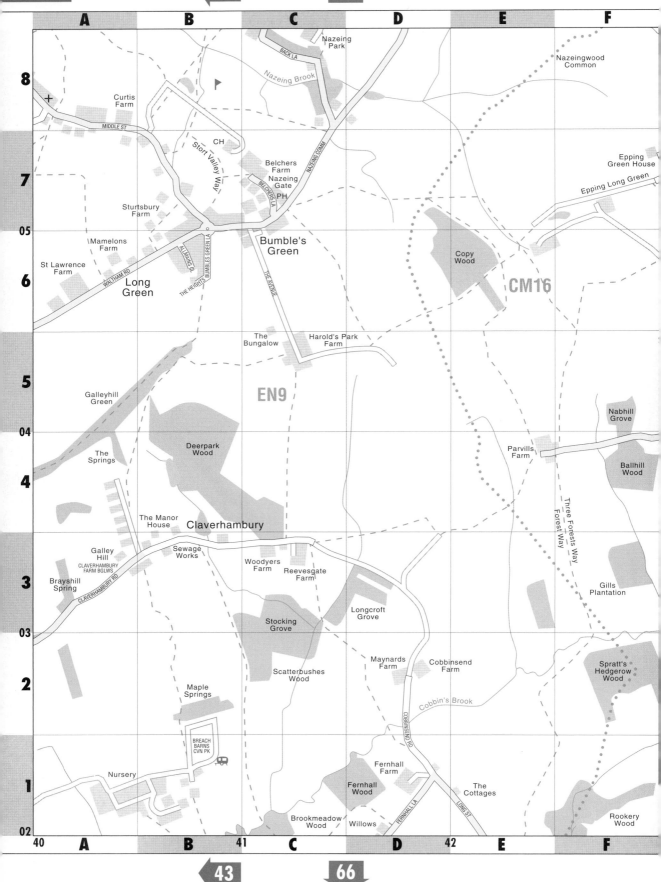

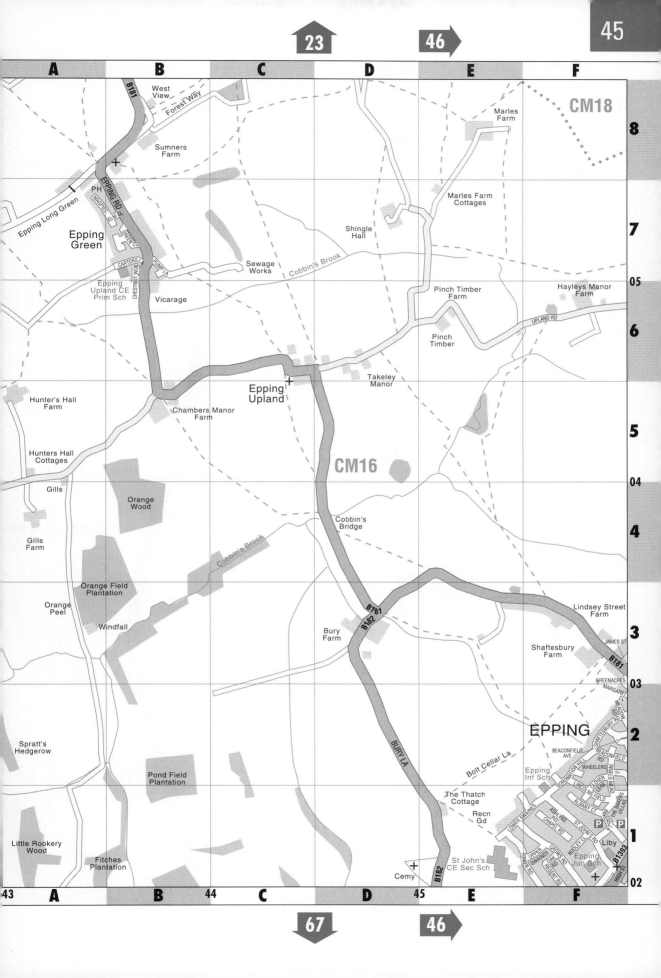

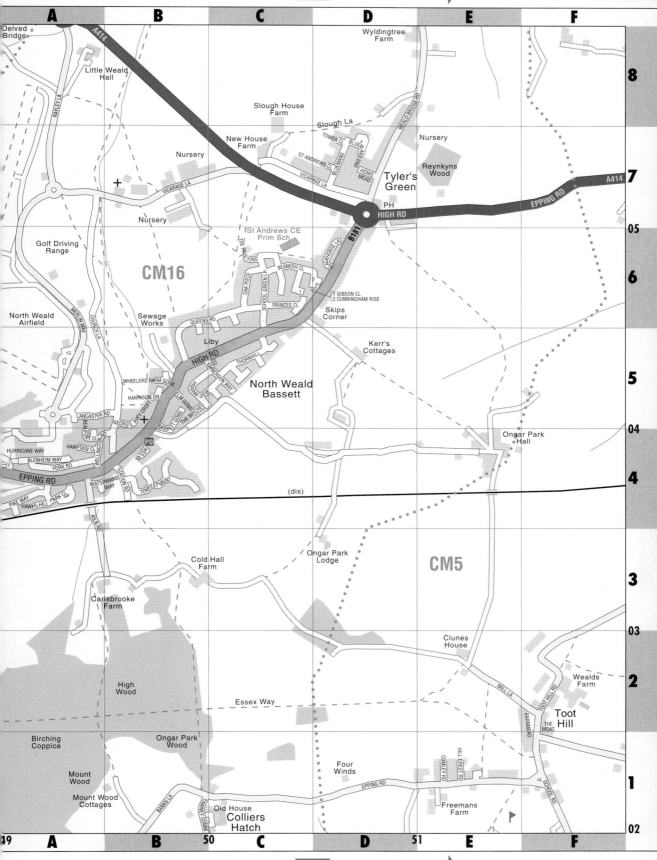

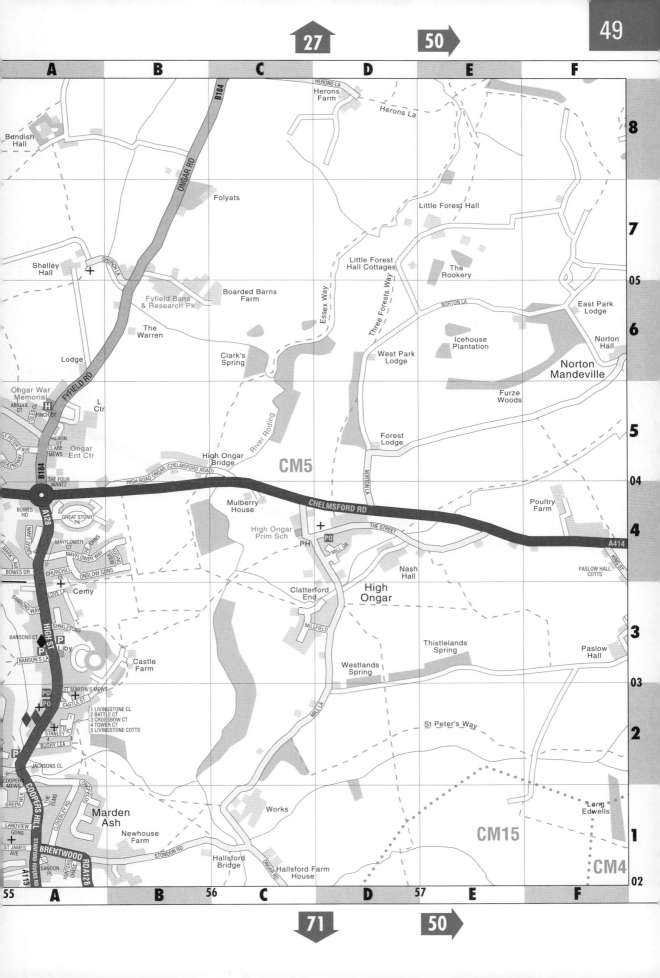

49
28

	A	B	C	D	E	F

8

Hedge Rows

Rockhills

Hodgkins Farm

NORTON HEATH RD

Bonsgrove

Hulke's Farm

7

Rockhill Cottages

Spriggs

Offin's Cottages

05

Long Spring

WILLINGALE RD

6

Norton Glebe House

NORTON LA

Dodd's Farm

+ Norton Mandeville

Ladylands

Norton Manor

Tyler's Farm

Readings Farm

A414

5

Norton Heath

PH

CM5

Chevers Hall

Dovefields Farm

FINGRITH HALL LA

CM4

04

Spurriers

The Orchard

4

Cozen's Farm

A414

A414

CHELMSFORD RD

Blewgates Farm

Old Wythers Farm

The Manor House

KING ST

ROOKERY RD

Fingrith Hall Cotts

SPRIGGS LA

3

Lodge

King Street Farm

Rookery Farm

FINGRITH HALL LA

Saybridge Lodge

03

PH

Saybridge Cottage

NINE ASHES FARM COTTS

2

Nine Ashes Farm

Nine Ashes

Sparks Farm

Larkins Farm

NINE ASHES RD

NINE ASHES RD

Orchard Manor

1

St Peter's Way

Wells Farm

Redrose Farm

REDROSE LA

Blackmore Prim Sch

WOOLARD WAY

WOOLARD WAY

ORCHARD PIECE

CHELMSFORD RD

02

58	A		B	59	C		D	60	E		F

49
72

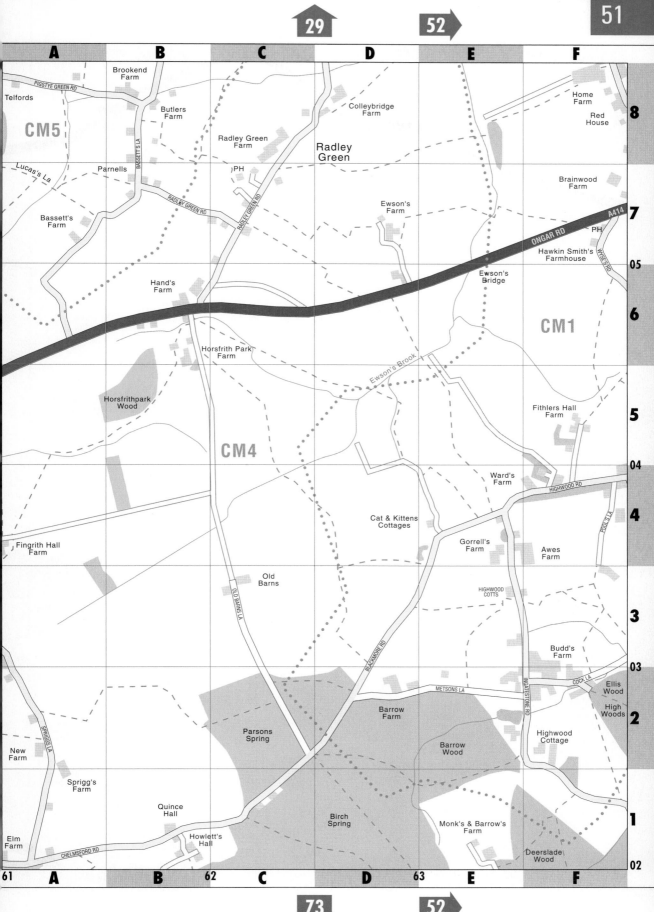

A   B   C   D   E   F

8

Pigstye Green Rd
Telfords

Brookend Farm

CM5

Butlers Farm

Radley Green Farm

Colleybridge Farm

Home Farm
Red House

Lucas's La

Parnells

PH

Radley Green

Brainwood Farm

7

Bassett's Farm

Radley Green Rd

Ewson's Farm

A414
ONGAR RD
PH

Hawkin Smith's Farmhouse

05

Hand's Farm

Ewson's Bridge

CM1

6

Horsfrith Park Farm

Ewson's Brook

Horsfrithpark Wood

Fithlers Hall Farm

5

CM4

Ward's Farm

Highwood Rd

04

Fingrith Hall Farm

Cat & Kittens Cottages

Gorrell's Farm

Awes Farm

Pool's La

4

Old Barns

Old Barns La

Highwood Cotts

3

Budd's Farm

Blackmore Rd

Ingatestone Rd

Cock La

Ellis Wood

03

Metsons La

High Woods

Barrow Farm

Highwood Cottage

2

New Farm

Spriggs La

Parsons Spring

Barrow Wood

Sprigg's Farm

Quince Hall

Birch Spring

Monk's & Barrow's Farm

1

Elm Farm

Howlett's Hall

Deerslade Wood

Chelmsford Rd

02

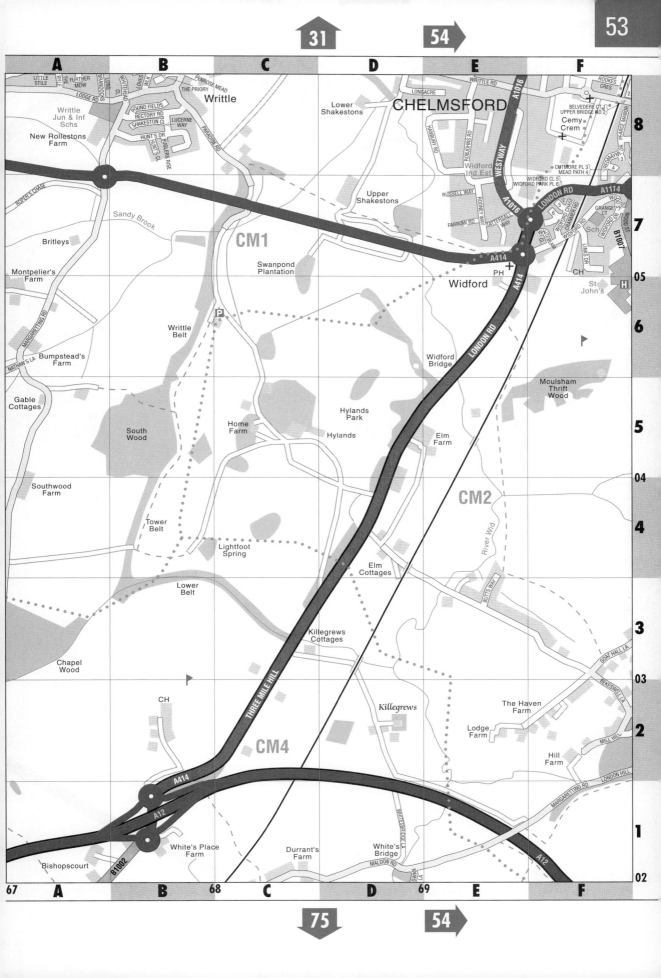

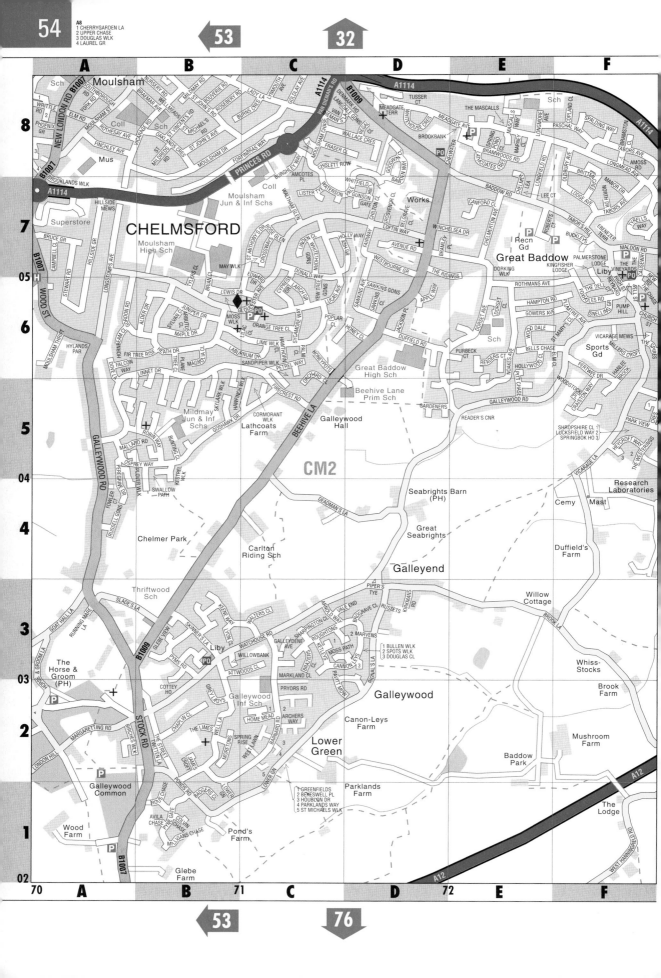

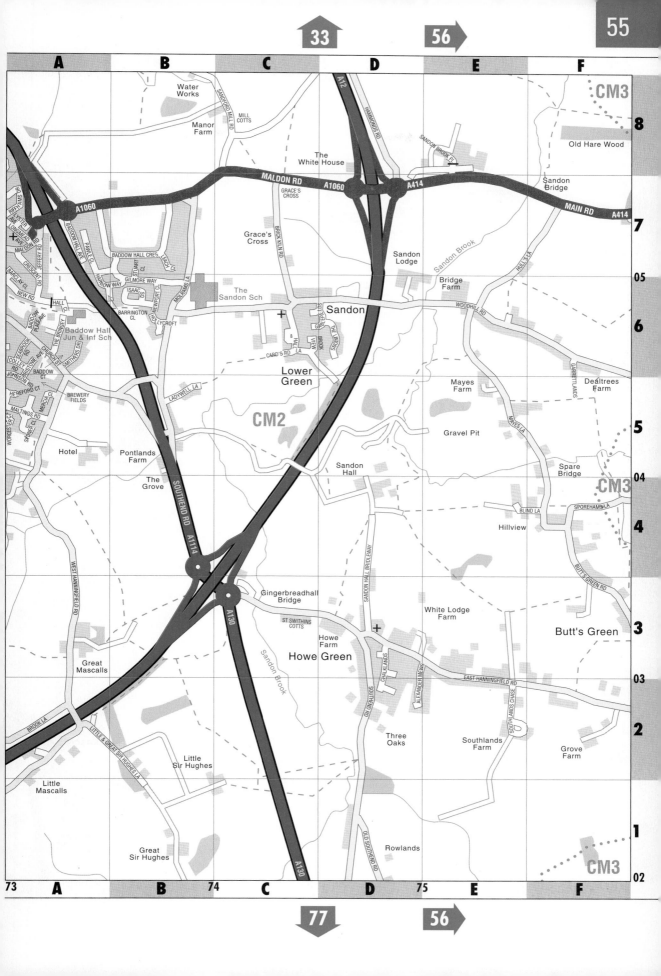

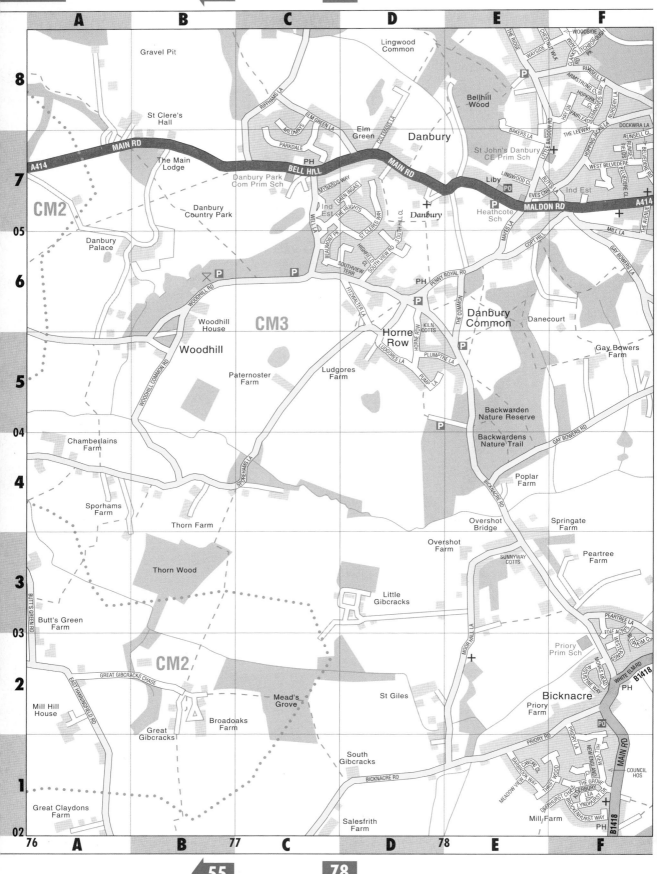

55
34

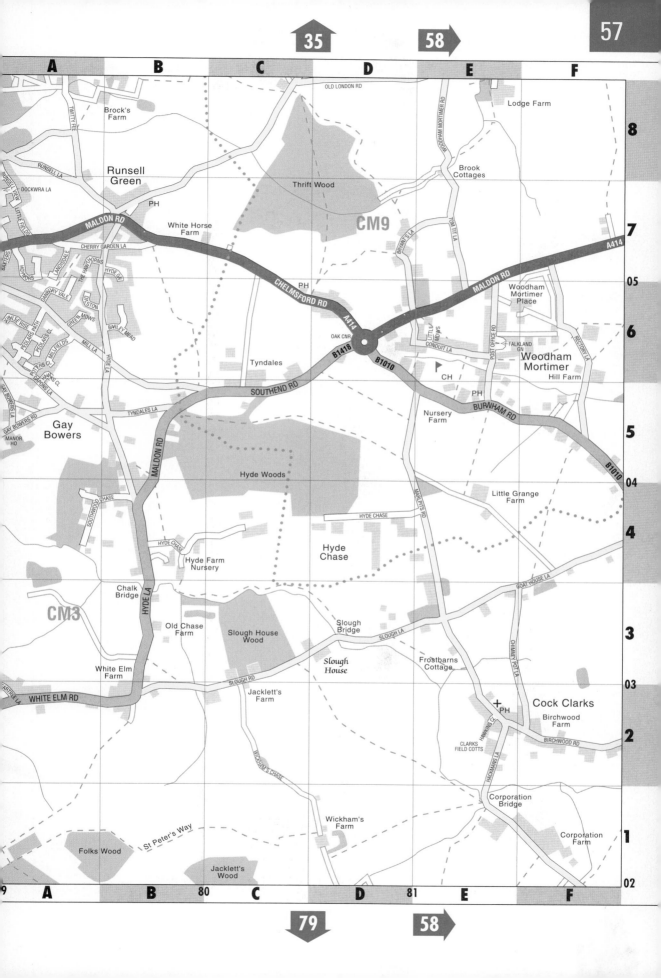

A B C D E F

8

7

05

6

5

04

4

3

03

2

1

02

00

Bradwell Marshes

Glebe Farm

POCKLEY LA

Sandbeach

St Peter's Way

Weatherwick

Packards Grove

Packards

MARK RD

Shingleford

Dots & Melons

CMO

Marshhouse Decoy Pond

MARSH RD

Leggatts

MARSH RD

Marsh House

Bridgemans Farm

Tillingham Marshes

Jerry's Farm

Midlands

Howe Farm

Crosby

Howe Outfall

GRANGE RD

BRIDGEWICK RD

Grange Farm

Small Gains

Bradwell Brook

01 02

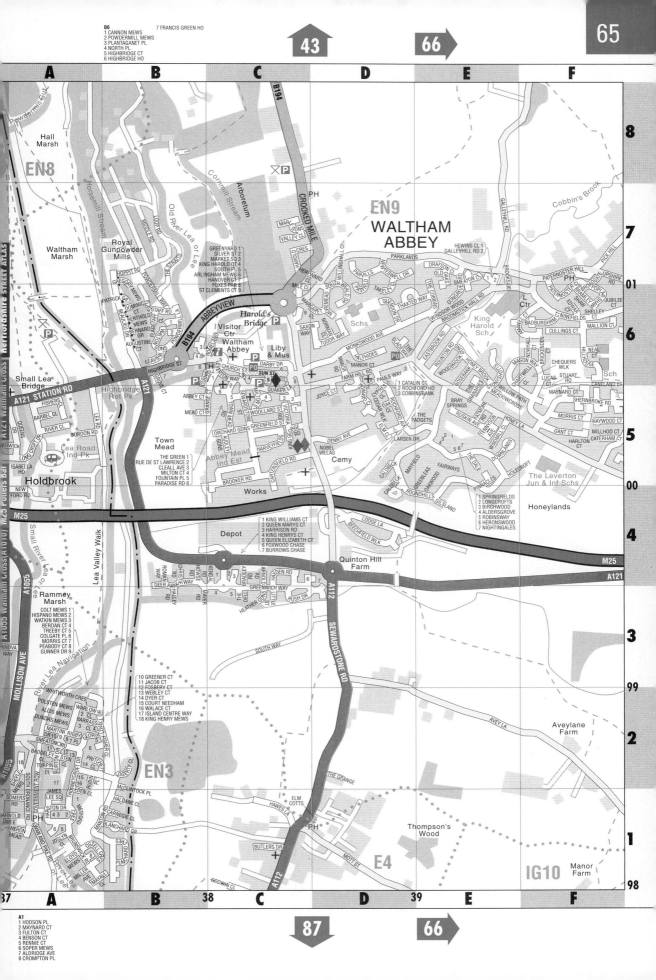

65
44

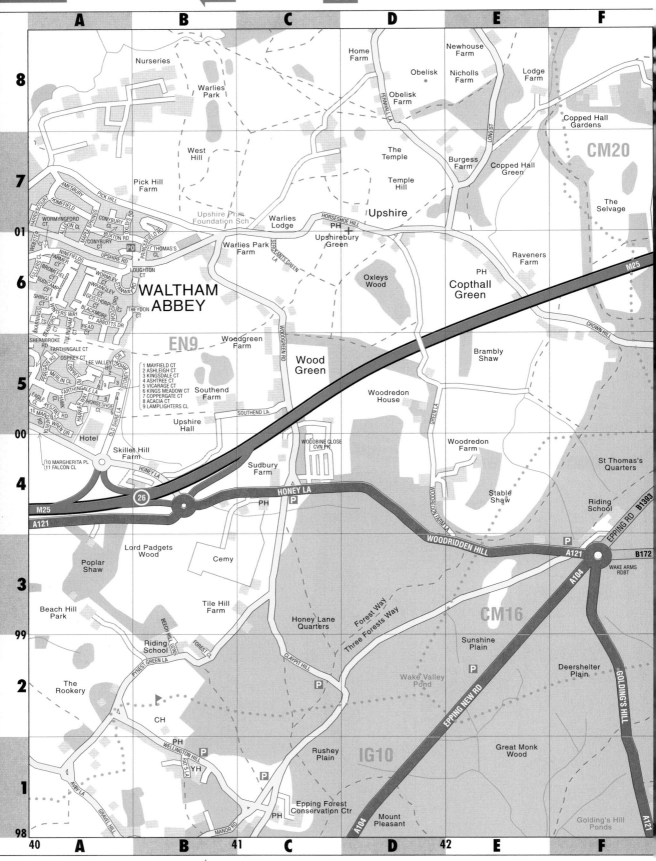

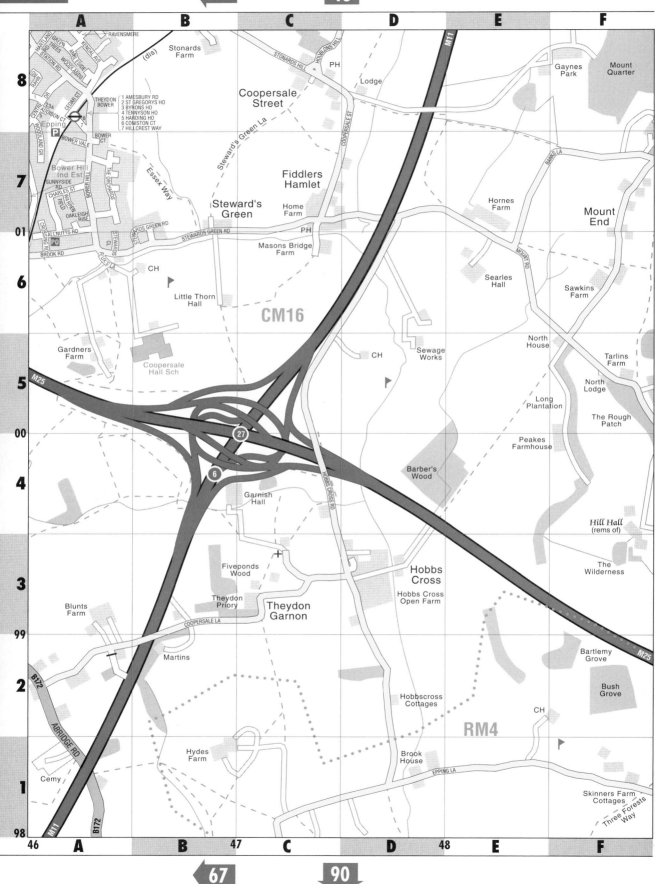

Coopersale
Street

Fiddlers
Hamlet

Steward's
Green

Home Farm
PH

Masons Bridge
Farm

Little Thorn
Hall

CM16

Gardners
Farm

Coopersale
Hall Sch

Garnish
Hall

Fiveponds
Wood

Theydon
Priory

Theydon
Garnon

Blunts
Farm

Martins

Coopersale La

Hydes
Farm

Cemy

Hobbs
Cross

Hobbs Cross
Open Farm

Hobbscross
Cottages

Brook
House

Epping La

RM4

Stonards
Farm

(dis)

Theydon
Bower

Bower
Ct

Bower Hill
Ind Est

Sunnyside
Rd

The Orchards

Epping

CH

Essex Way

Stewards Green Rd

PH

Steward's Green La

Coopersale St

Stonards Hill

Youblong Hill

PH

Lodge

M11

Banks La

Hornes
Farm

Searles
Hall

Mount Rd

North
House

Long
Plantation

Peakes
Farmhouse

Barber's
Wood

Sewage
Works

CH

Gaynes Park

Mount
Quarter

Mount
End

Sawkins
Farm

Tarlins
Farm

North
Lodge

The Rough
Patch

Hill Hall
(rems of)

The
Wilderness

Bartlemy
Grove

Bush
Grove

CH

Skinners Farm
Cottages

Three Forests Way

M25

27

6

Hobbs Cross Rd

M25

M11

B172

Abridge Rd

B172

1 AMESBURY RD
2 ST GREGORYS HO
3 BYRONS HO
4 TENNYSON HO
5 HARDING HO
6 CONISTON CT
7 HILLCREST WAY

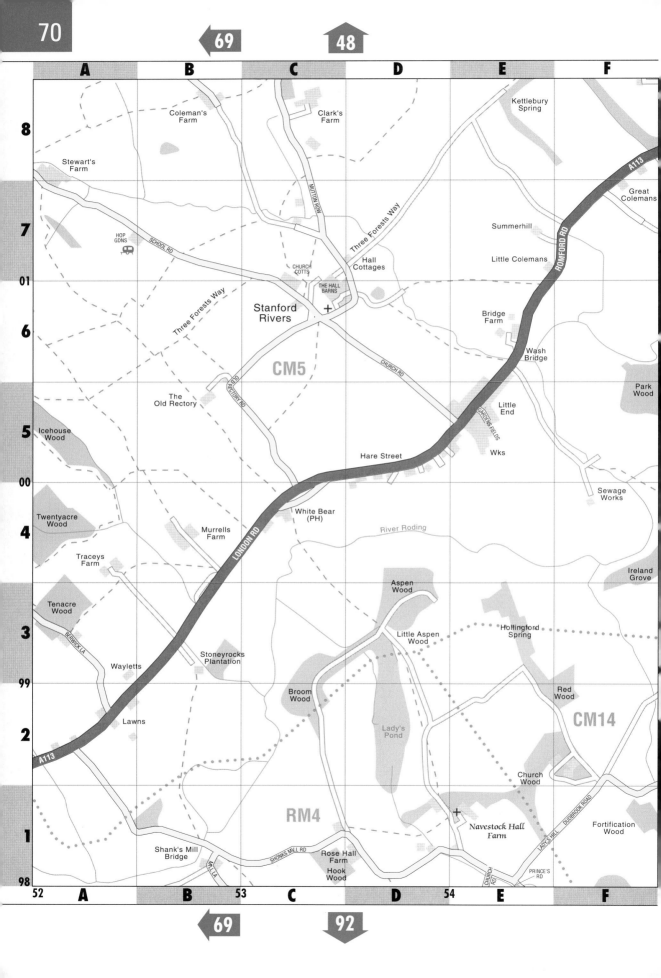

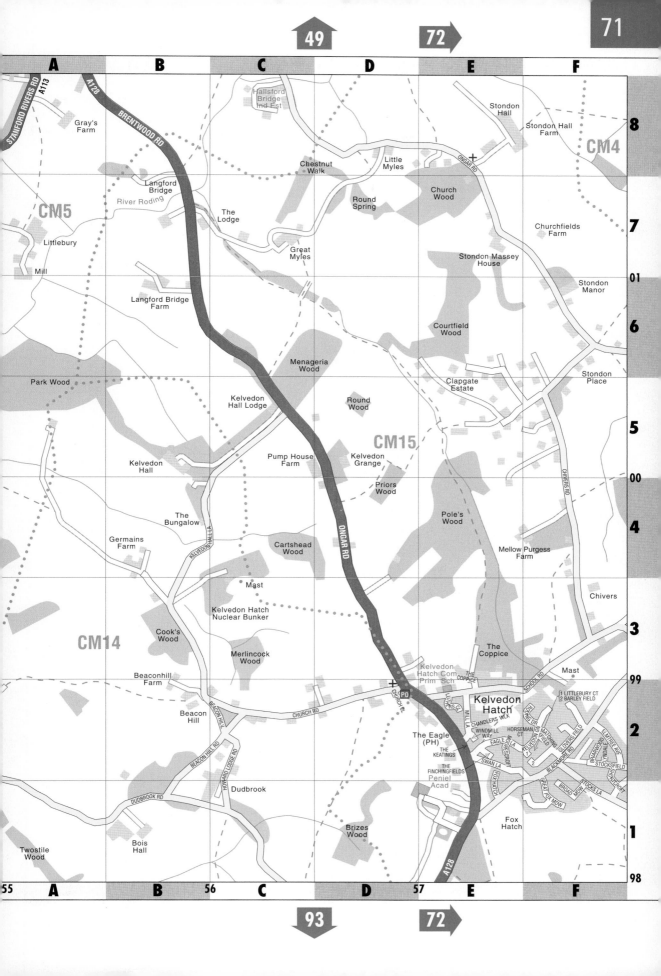

A B C D E F

8

Mill Green Rd
Ivy Barns La
Box Wood
Well Wood
Dawes Farm
Handley Green
Marshalls Farm
Wantfield Cotts
Ewelend Hall
A12
B1002
Margaretting CE Prim Sch
Penny's La
Millgreen Common
Potter Row Farm
Mast
PH
BROOKSIDE

7

Harding's La
Harding's Farm
Handley Barnes
Dog Kennel La
St Peter's Way
Osborne's Wood
Canterburys
Church La

01

Millgreen Wood
The Grove
Little Hyde La
Margaretting Hall

6

Mill Green Rd
Mill La
Back La
The Grange
The Grange
Little Hyde Farm
LC

Fryerning
Maisonetts
CM4
LC

5

Murcock's Farm
BEGGARHILL
Woodfield Cotts

00

Ingatestone Inf Sch
INGATESTONE BY-PASS
Kingfishers
New Rd
Willon Gn
Ray Farm
Rook Wood

Fryerning La
Thimble Cl
Disney Cl
Rectory Cl
Waltham Cl
Anglo-European Sch
Woodland Cl
Haslings La
Docklands Ave
Park Dr
Pine Dr
Pine Cl

4

Ingatestone & Fryerning CE Jun Sch
Pemberton Ave
Mellor Steen Cl
Eley
Bakers La
Bakers Mews
Market Pl
3
2 The Hop
P
1 CLIFTON TERR
2 SPREAD EAGLE PL
3 MILLERS MEWS
Spring Wood

The Meads
Meads Cl
Chapel
Croft
Star La
Fairy Cl
Norton Rd
The Limes
CHEQUERS
Fairfield
Fairacres
STOCK LA

The Furlongs
Cameron Cl
Deepdene
High St
Bell Mead
SUMMERFIELDS
Ingatestone
Fairacres
Barrington
Post Office Rd
Liby
STONEGATE

3

The Belvoir
Wakelin Chase
Maltings Chase
Almhouses
The Paddocks
Hashleigh Cl
P
Ingatestone
Sewage Works

Whadden Chase
The Heythrop
The Quorn
Chapentry
Station La
Gateford
Mews
LC

99

A12
Petre Cl
Tor Bryan
Ingatestone Hall Farm
Buttsbury Hall Farm
INGATESTONE RD

2

B1002
Tudor Cl
The Leas
Hunter La
Rye Wlk
Heybridge Rd
Rogeway
Heybridge
Hill La
Ingatestone Hall
White Tyrrell

1

Bacons Farm
Elmbrook Farm
BUTTSBURY

Tilehurst

98

64 A B 65 C D 66 E F

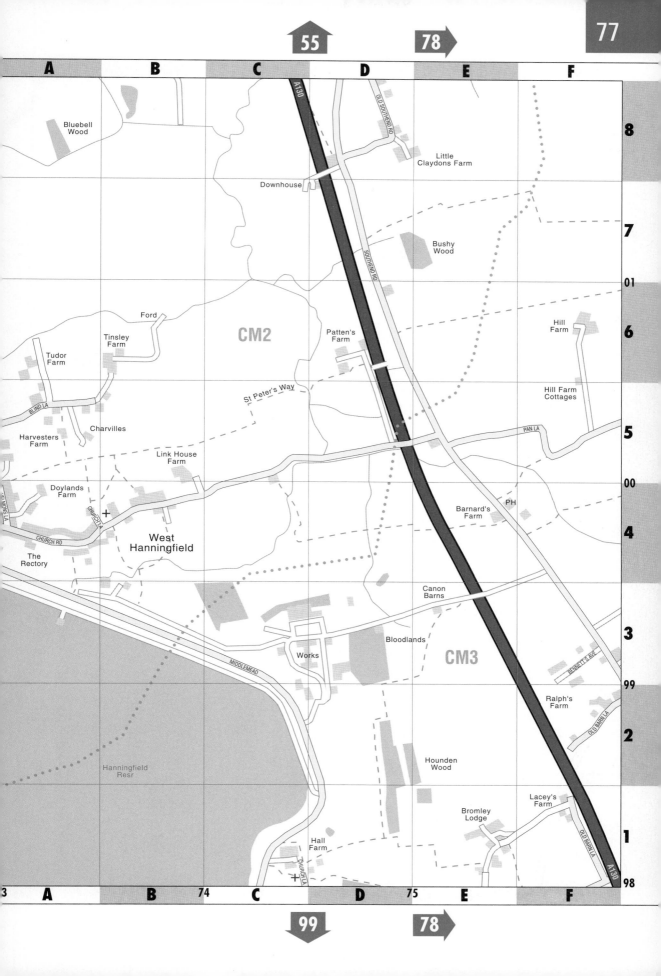

A   B   C   D   E   F

8

7

01

6

Bluebell
Wood

Little
Claydons Farm

Downhouse

OLD SOUTHEND RD

A130

SOUTHEND RD

Bushy
Wood

Hill
Farm

CM2

Ford

Patten's
Farm

Tinsley
Farm

Hill Farm
Cottages

5

Tudor
Farm

St Peter's Way

BLIND LA

Charvilles

PAN LA

00

Harvesters
Farm

Link House
Farm

4

Doylands
Farm

Barnard's
Farm

PH

CHURCH LA

West
Hanningfield

CHURCH RD

The
Rectory

Canon
Barns

3

MIDDLEMEAD

Bloodlands

CM3

BENNETT'S AVE

Works

99

Ralph's
Farm

OLD BARN LA

2

Hanningfield
Resr

Hounden
Wood

Lacey's
Farm

1

Bromley
Lodge

Hall
Farm

OLD BARN LA

A130

CHURCH LA

98

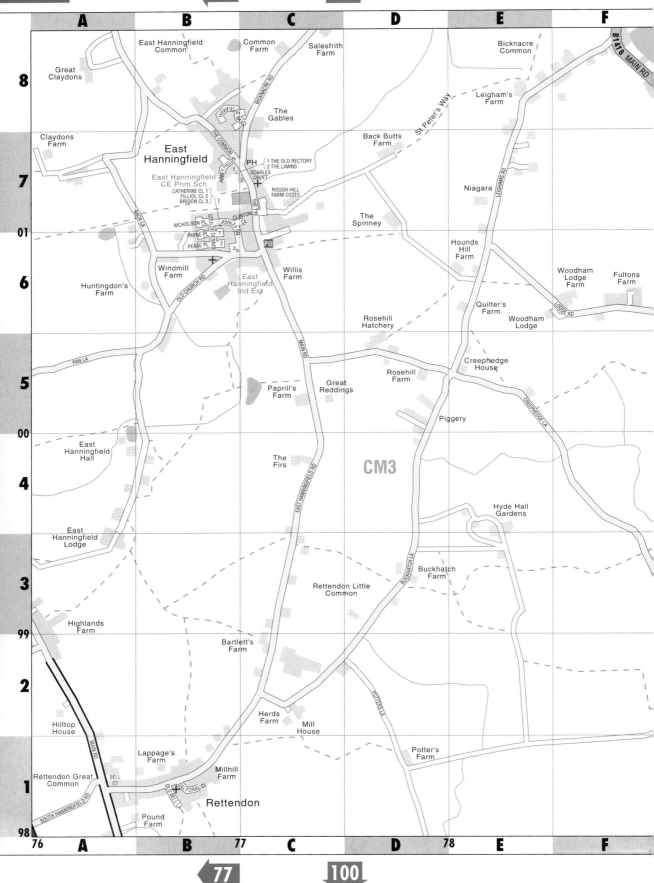

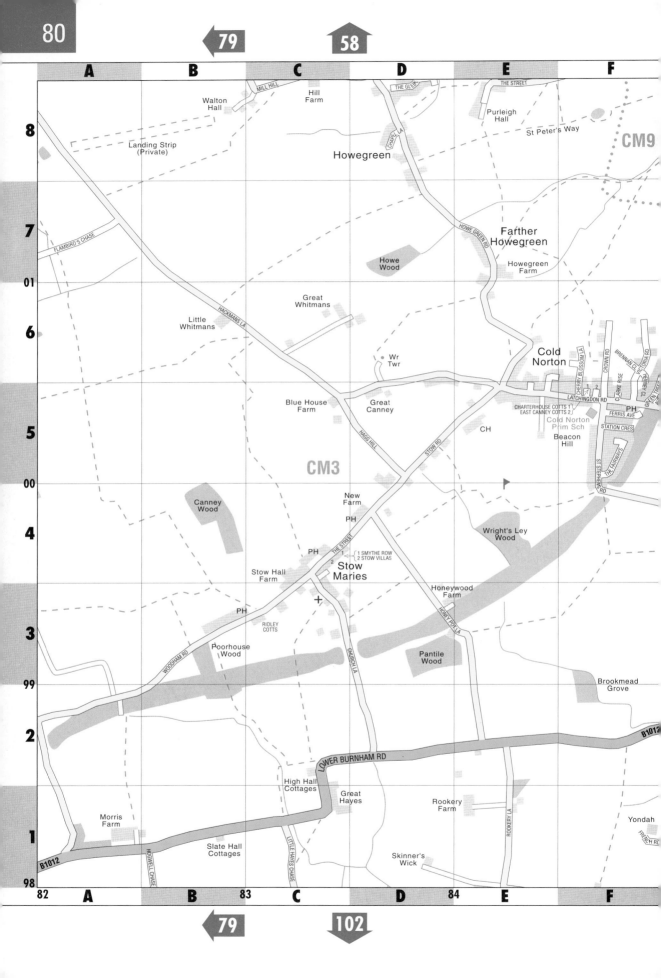

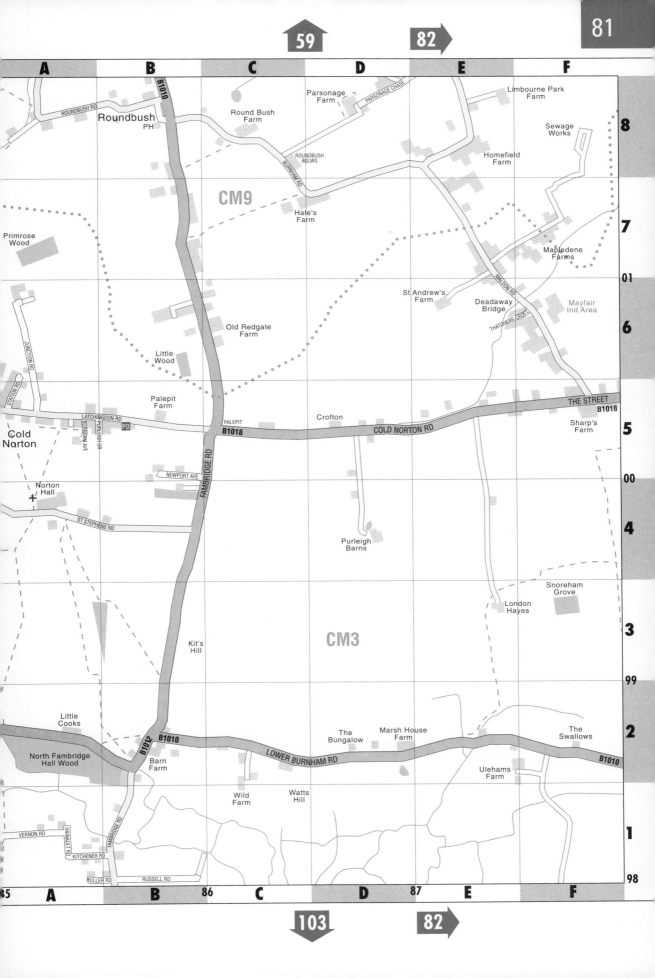

A   B   C   D   E   F

ROUNDBUSH RD

B1010

Roundbush
PH

Round Bush
Farm

Parsonage
Farm

PARSONAGE CHASE

Limbourne Park
Farm

Sewage
Works

8

ROUNDBUSH
BGLWS

BURNHAM RD

Homefield
Farm

CM9

Hale's
Farm

7

Primrose
Wood

Mapledene
Farms

01

St Andrew's
Farm

MALDON RD

Deadaway
Bridge

Mayfair
Ind Area

6

Old Redgate
Farm

THATCHERS CROFT

JUNCTION RD

Little
Wood

STATION RD

Palepit
Farm

THE STREET

B1018

Sharp's
Farm

LATCHINGDON RD

PURLEIGH GR

BURNHAM AVE

PO

PALEPIT

B1018

Crofton

COLD NORTON RD

5

Cold
Norton

FAMBRIDGE RD

NEWPORT AVE

00

Norton
Hall

ST STEPHENS RD

4

Purleigh
Barns

Snoreham
Grove

London
Hayes

3

CM3

Kit's
Hill

99

Little
Cooks

B1012

B1010

The
Bungalow

Marsh House
Farm

The
Swallows

2

North Fambridge
Hall Wood

Barn
Farm

LOWER BURNHAM RD

B1010

Ulehams
Farm

FAMBRIDGE RD

Wild
Farm

Watts
Hill

1

VERNON RD

HAINAULT RD

KITCHENER RD

BULLER RD

RUSSELL RD

98

35   A   B   86   C   D   87   E   F

A B C D E F

8

7

01

6

5

00

4

3

99

2

1

98

88 A 89 C 90 E F
B D

KATONIA AVE
THE DRIVE
Maylandsea
Prim Sch
BAKERSFIELD

Butterfields

Lawling
Hall

STEEPLE RD
Tideway
Farm

Lawling
Cottages

Brook
Hall

Greenlane
Farm

Latchingdon

Latchingdon
CE Prim Sch

PH
GREEN LA

BRIDGEMANS BN
CHASE
MEADOW WY
LUDGROVE
RANNOCH

B1018
THE STREET
PO PH

GRANARY CL
BUSHMAN WAY
CLEAR
CT
LAWLING RD

Good
Hares

Warden's
Farm

ST MICHAELS CL
SNOREHAM GDNS
HERITAGE WAY

Arley
Grange

BURNHAM RD

Snoreham
Hall

The
Beeches

Red Lyons
Farm

PH

GARDEN CL
PO

B1018

CM3

LOWER CHASE
Nursery
BURNHAM RD

RECTORY LA

Surridges

Rosedale
Farm

Scatterbrook
Farm

Barnes
Farm

UPPER CHAS

Latchingdon
Hall

Tyle
Hall

Grange
Farm

SUNNINGDALE RD
CHESTNUT FARM DR
BARNES FARM DR

FAMBRIDGE RD
B1010

Cemy
LOWER BURNHAM RD

B1010

Wr
Twr

RIVER VIEW
EAST AVE
CENTRAL AVE
WEST AVE

Althorne
Hall

Stamfords Hill
Cottages

Riverview
Park

STATION RD

Stamfords
Farm

Viking
Cottage

A **B** **C** **D** **E** **F**

WEMBLEY AVE

PRINCES AVE

TUDOR PL

TEAL CT

SMITHS AVE

SMITHS AVE

DURLEY AVE

TEAL CT

WALLACE AVE

THE DRIVE

GREB

HERON WK

DRAKE AVE

MAYLAND CL

Mayland
1 ST STEPHENS CT
2 ST JOHNS CT
3 WHITEFIELD CT

NIPSELLS CHASE

MILL RD

MALDON RD

Lower
Farm

Ashtree
Farm

Steeple
Hill

PH

MAYLAND BR

STEEPLE RD

Little Ashtree
Farm

WOODLAND PARK CHASE

Firth View
Farm

GRANGE AVE

8

Foxhall
Farm

7

Bicknacre Lodge
Farm

Highlands

HIGHLANDS HILL

FOXHALL RD

01

CM0

GREEN LA

6

Mayland
Hall

Bovill
Uplands

Hemmells

CM3

MAYLAND HILL

Mayland
Court

5

00

Button's Hill
Farm

Button's
Hill

Mayland Hall
Farm Cottages

The
Moat House

B1018

4

BUTTON'S HILL

SOUTHMINSTER RD

Ewenny
Farm

Scott's
Farm

Medway
Farm

Joyce's
Farm

Dairy
Farm

DAIRY FARM RD

Petersville

OLD HEATH RD

3

HIGHFIELD RISE

SUMMERDALE

STANFIELD HILL

WOODLANDS

AUSTRAL WAY

OAKWOOD CT

UPPER CHASE

BURNHAM RD

Althorne

Austral
Farm

PH

Poultry
Houses

THE ENDWAY

High House
Farm

99

2

Mansfield
Poultry
Farm

St Helier

Althorne
Lodge

BURNHAM RD

Hill
Farm

The
Wrekin

Andrews
Farm

Stoke's
Hall

B1010

1

98

'1 **A** **B** **92** **C** **D** **93** **E** **F**

63
86

A B C D E F

Asheldham Pits Nature Reserve

B1021

TILLINGHAM RD

END WAY COTTS

SOUTHMINSTER RD

Asheldham

Asheldham Hall

HALL RD

New Hall Farm

MANOR RD

Dengie Manor

Keelings

KEELINGS LA

KEELINGS RD

Cemy

Landwick Farm

LANDWICK LA

Irrigation Resr

01

Asheldham Brook

CMO

North Wycke

00

Wraywick Farm

99

Wraywick Cottage

Broadward Farm

Turncole Farm

8

7

6

5

4

3

2

1

98

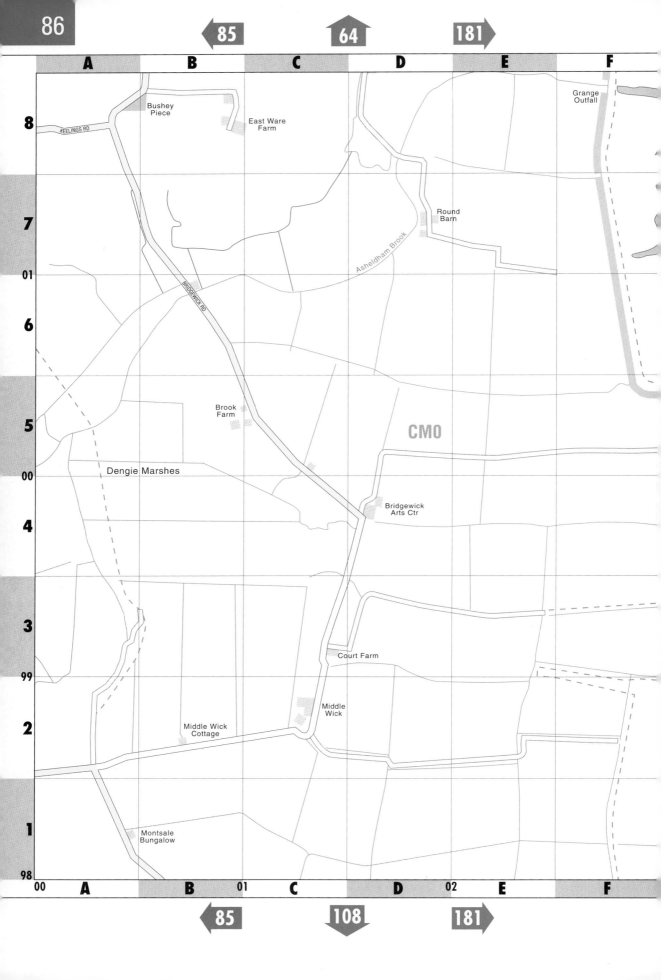

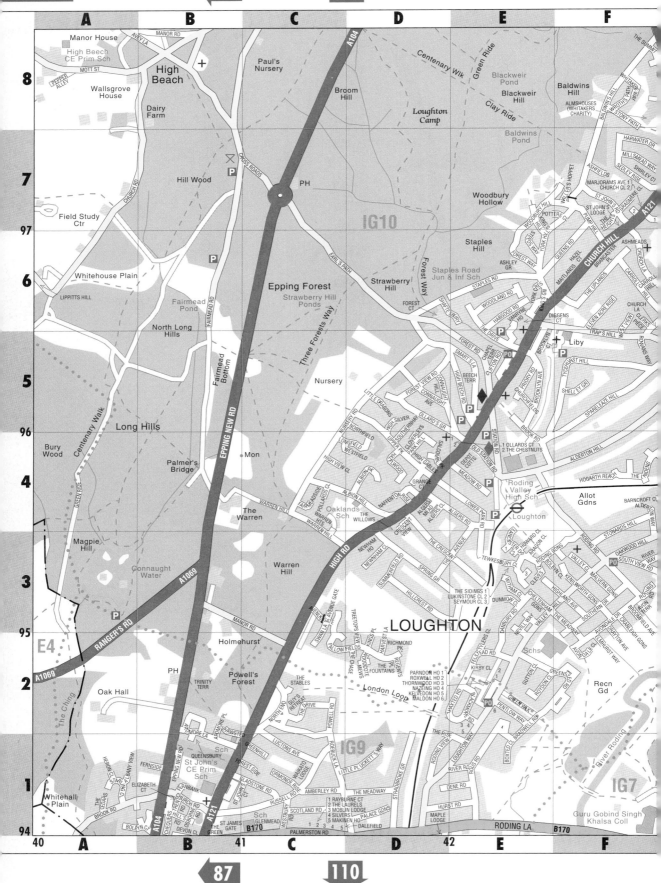

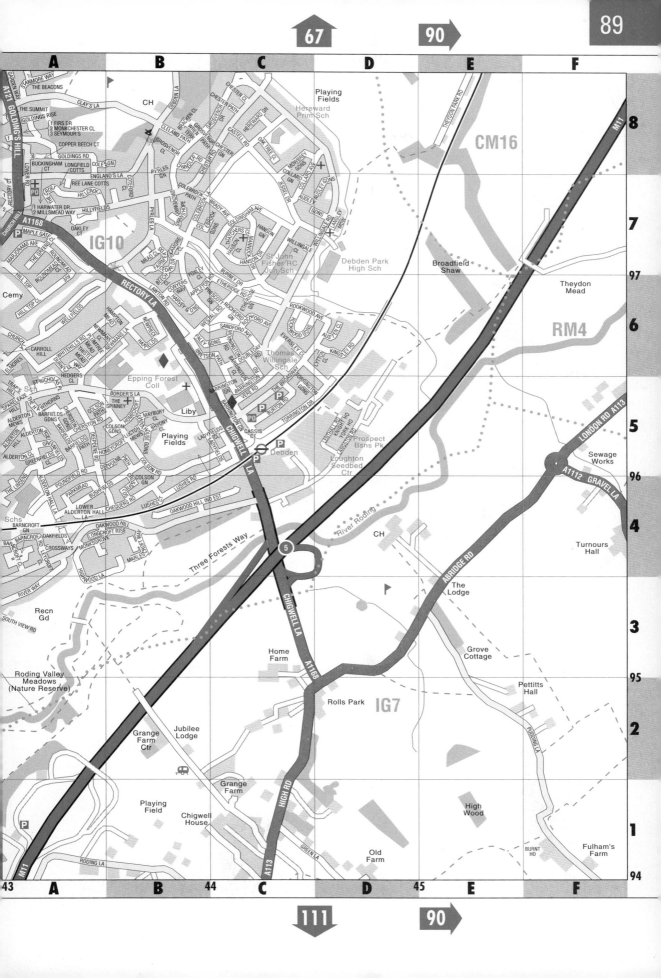

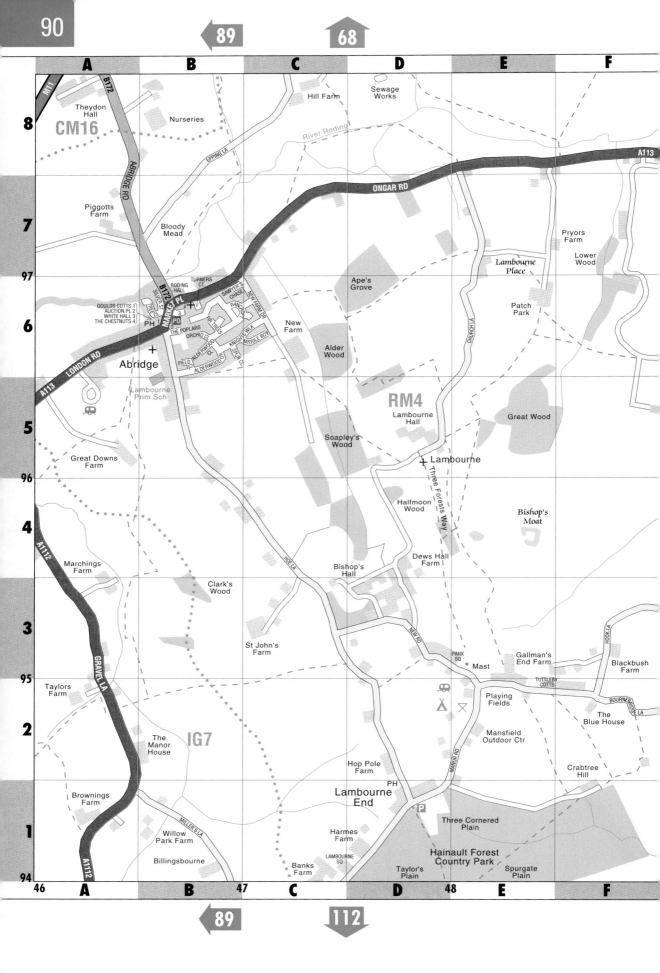

A **B** **C** **D** **E** **F**

8

CM16

Theydon Hall

Nurseries

Hill Farm

Sewage Works

River Roding

A113

ONGAR RD

7

Piggotts Farm

Bloody Mead

EPPING LA

Ape's Grove

Pryors Farm

Lambourne Place

Lower Wood

97

TURNERS CT

RODING HALL

SAWYER'S CHASE

Patch Park

Church La

6

GOULDS COTTS 1
AUCTION PL 2
WHITE HALL 3
THE CHESTNUTS 4

PH

SILVER ST

MARKET PL

PO

THE POPLARS

ORCHID CL

FIR TREES

PAN CROFT

NEW FARM DR

New Farm

Alder Wood

FIELD

KNIGHTS WLK

ALDERWOOD CL

MIDDLE BOY

SPUR CT

ALDERWOOD

Abridge

LONDON RD

A113

Lambourne Prim Sch

RM4

Lambourne Hall

Great Wood

5

Great Downs Farm

Soapley's Wood

Lambourne

Three Forests Way

96

Halfmoon Wood

Bishop's Moat

4

A1112

Marchings Farm

Clark's Wood

HOE LA

Bishop's Hall

Dews Hall Farm

3

GRAVEL LA

St John's Farm

NEW RD

PARK SQ

Mast

Gallman's End Farm

HOOK LA

Blackbush Farm

95

Taylors Farm

TUTTLEBY COTTS

BOURNEBRIDGE LA

The Blue House

2

IG7

The Manor House

Playing Fields

Mansfield Outdoor Ctr

MANOR RD

Crabtree Hill

1

Brownings Farm

MILLER'S LA

Willow Park Farm

Billingsbourne

Hop Pole Farm

PH

Lambourne End

P

Harmes Farm

LAMBOURNE SQ

Banks Farm

Three Cornered Plain

Hainault Forest Country Park

Taylor's Plain

Spurgate Plain

94

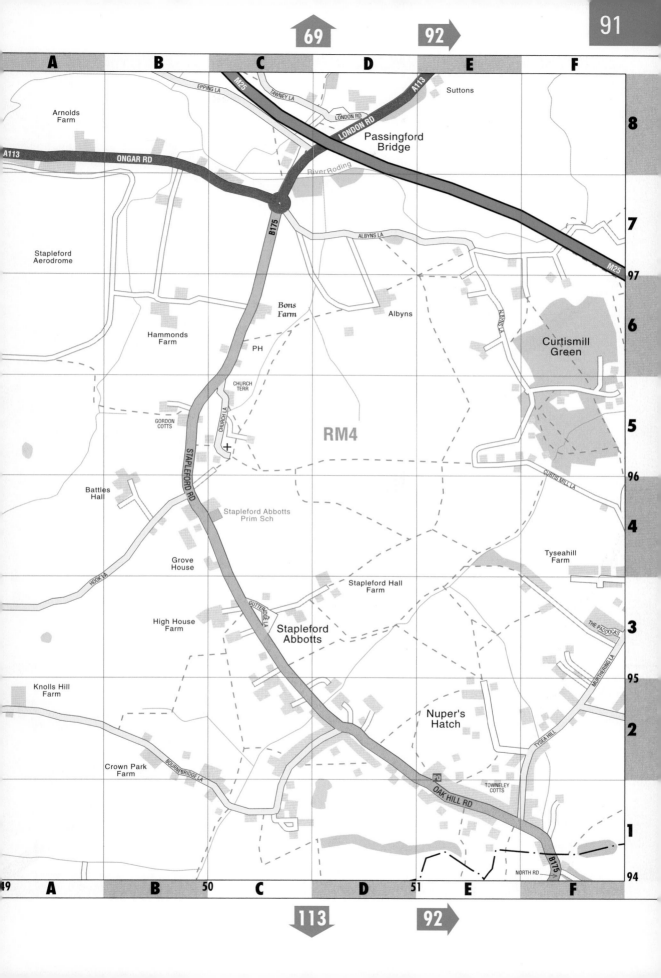

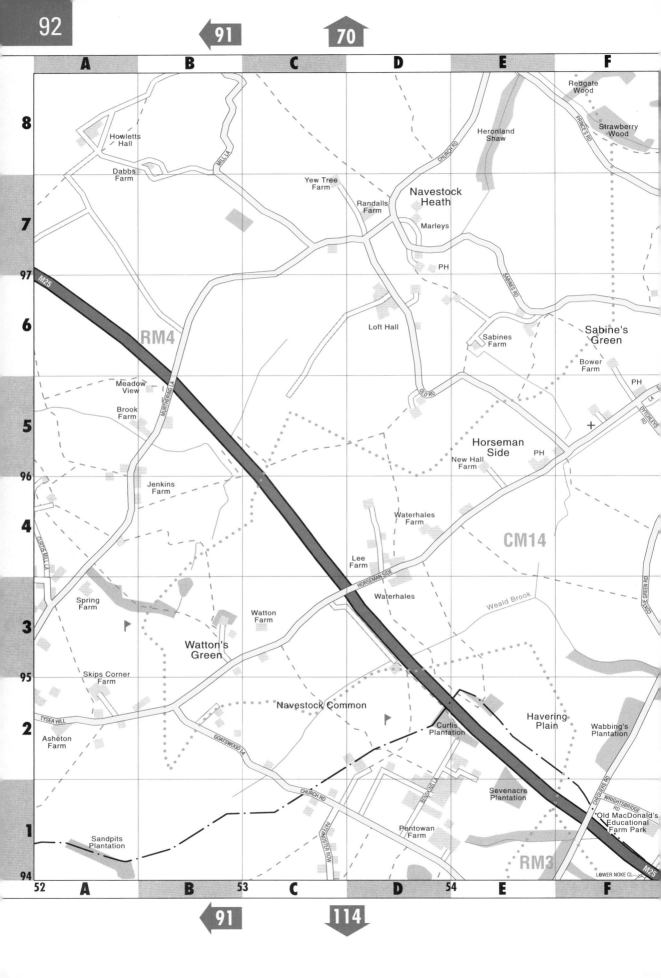

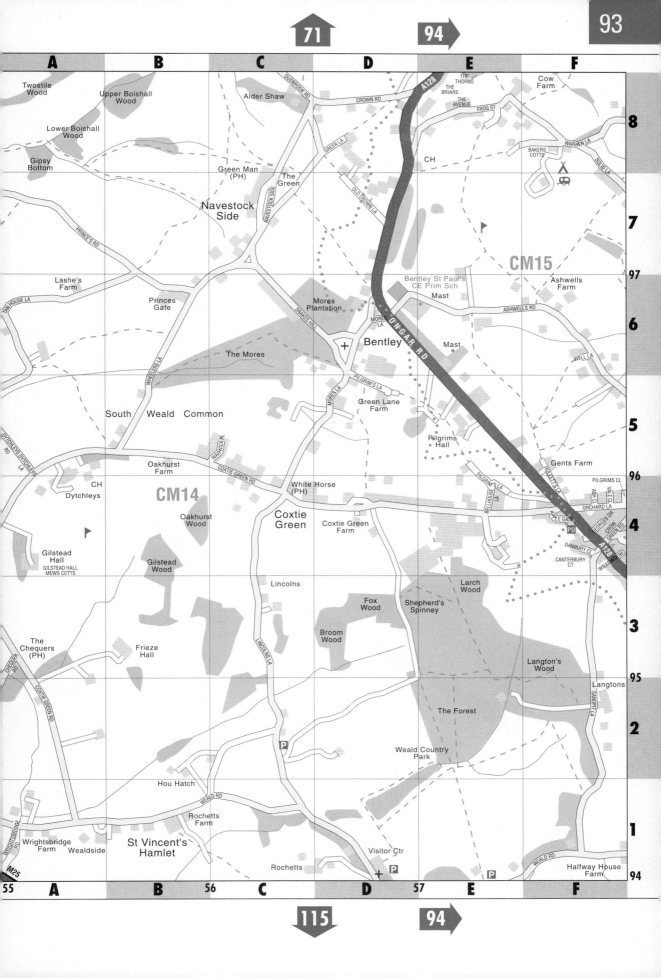

A B C D E F

8

7

97

6

5

96

4

3

95

2

1

94

Twostile Wood
Upper Boishall Wood
Lower Boishall Wood
Gipsy Bottom
PRINCE'S RD
Lashe's Farm
TAN HOUSE LA
Navestock Side
Princes Gate
Green Man (PH)
The Green
NAVESTOCK SIDE
Alder Shaw
DUDBROOK RD
CROWN RD
GREEN LA
OLD CROWN LA
A128
THE THORNS
THE BRIARS
THE AVENUE
FROG ST
Cow Farm
WARREN LA
BAKERS COTTS
SOLID LA
CH
CM15
Bentley St Paul's CE Prim Sch
Mast
Ashwells Farm
ASHWELLS RD
Mores Plantation
SNAKE'S HILL
MORES LA
Bentley
MORES LA
Mast
WELL LA
The Mores
WHEELERS LA
South Weald Common
PILGRIM'S LA
Green Lane Farm
Pilgrims Hall
ONGAR RD
Gents Farm
PILGRIM'S LA
PILLETT'S LA
PILGRIMS CL
ASH CL
VALE CL
ORCHARD LA
96
WARWICK PL
Oakhurst Farm
COXTIE GREEN RD
White Horse (PH)
BELLHOUSE LA
GEORGES DR
CROW GREEN RD
DYTCHLEYS RD
DYTCHLEYS LA
CH
Dytchleys
CM14
Oakhurst Wood
Coxtie Green
Coxtie Green Farm
AXE GATE
PO
DANBURY CL
CANTERBURY CT
A128
WILLOWMERE
Gilstead Hall
GILSTEAD HALL MEWS COTTS
Gilstead Wood
Lincolns
Fox Wood
Shepherd's Spinney
Larch Wood
Langton's Wood
The Chequers (PH)
GREGORY RD
Frieze Hall
LINCOLNS LA
Broom Wood
The Forest
Langton's Wood
SANDPIT LA
Langtons
95
Weald Country Park
Hou Hatch
WEALD RD
Rochetts Farm
Wrightsbridge Farm
WRIGHTSBRIDGE RD
Wealdside
St Vincent's Hamlet
COXTIE GREEN RD
M25
Rochetts
Visitor Ctr
WEALD RD
Halfway House Farm

A B C D E F

8

Cowes Farm

Park Wood

America Farm

SOLD LA

7

Wishfields Farm

Heard's Farm

DAYS LA

97

Sumner's Farm

Rosecroft

Palmers Farm

Bennett's Farm

HEARD'S LA

6

Howe's Farm

HALL LA

Days Farm

CROW GV

Brickhouse Farm

CM15

DODDINGHURST RD

Crow Green

Brickhouse Wood

Canterbury Tye Hall

CROW GREEN RD

5

96

CROW GREEN LA

BEADS HALL LA

ASGELLES CL

ALDERTON CL

MARCONI RD

A12

CATHERINE CL

HATCH RD

HONEYSUCKLE CL

DAFFODIL AVE

MINOSA CL

TULIP CL

POPPY CL

LILAC CL

MANOR AVE

WISTERIA

Bishop's Hall Park

Shenfield Hall Farm

HALL LA

4

PRIORY CL

LANCASTER CL

GLOUCESTER RD

STUART CL

CORNWELL

IRIS CL

HEATHER CL

1 PEONY CL
2 ELIZABETH HO
3 MEADOW VIEW
4 WEALDEN HO

Pilgrims Hatch

MAYEV

HAZELMEAD

DANES WAY

BALMORAL RD

PO

IVER RD

LANCER AVE

PRIMR

 GUARDIANS

GREEN CL

P

The Brentwood Ctr

Shenfield Hall

A1023

CHELMSFORD RD

THE FIRS

A128

BROOMWOOD GDNS

ONGAR RD

LARCHWOOD GDNS

BLENHEIM RD

KING GEORGE'S RD

HAREWOOD RD

LAWRENCE

CARISBROOKE RD

ALBANY RD

ELIZABETH RD

HIGHGROVE

P

Hall Wood

St Mary's CE Prim Sch

SAWYERS CT

3

DOUNSELL CT

DARLINGTON CT

MARLBOROUGH RD

OSBORNE RD

BISHOP'S HALL LA

KENSINGTON RD

WINDSOR RD

VIKING WAY

THURSTWOOD AVE

HUTTON RD

95

High Wood

WARESCOT RD

ST KILDA'S RD

RUSHFORE RD

ST HELENS RC JUN SCH

KIMPTON AVE

Shenfield

A129

2

Calcott Hall Farm

ST GEORGE'S CL

CHURCHILL

ROBIN HOOD RD

PO

1 DRUMMOND CT
2 GEARY CT

The Hedley Walter High Sch

DODDINGHURST RD

FARROW HO

Convent of Mercy
St Thomas of Canterbury CE Jun & Inf Schs

3 DUKE'S PL
4 INVERMAY CT
5 LAVENHAM CT
6 BURGESS CT
7 HIGHMEAD CT
8 ARGYLL CT
9 RAVENSCOURT

HALLWOOD CRES

GLENDALE HO

TROTWOOD CL

GLENDALE

MILL HILL

BERRY HILL

CLIVEDEN CL

COOMBE RISE

PARK WAY

PRIEST'S LA

GREENGHAM

GEORGE'S CL

UPPER RYLE

THORNRIDGE

CLEVE AVE

BRO

MONTBAZON

H High Wood

GEARY DR

MELFORD PL

TREE TOPS

HIGHLAND AVE

SAWYERS GR

MERRYMEAD CHASE

HOLLY HO

SHEN PLACE ALMSHOUSES

The Essex Nuffield

YORK RD

HALLWOOD

1

PORTERS CL

COSTEAD MANOR RD

TYLER WAY

CALCOTT CL

COPP

MAYFIELD GDNS

WATERLOO

WESTERN AVE

BURLAND RD

BRENTWOOD

PENDAYS CT

HOMEHURST HO

LIMES CT

MIDDLETON HALL

Middleton Hall (Brentwood Prep Sch)

H Brentwood Com

WARRIN RD

LONGMER

MIDDLETON RD

CRESCENT DR

WARRIN CL

CM14

THE RETREAT

COSTEAD MANOR RD

THE RODING

ST CHARLS

CAPON CL

THE VALE

VINEWAY

PARK VALE CT

SHENFIELD RD

A1023

94

58 59 60

A B C D E F

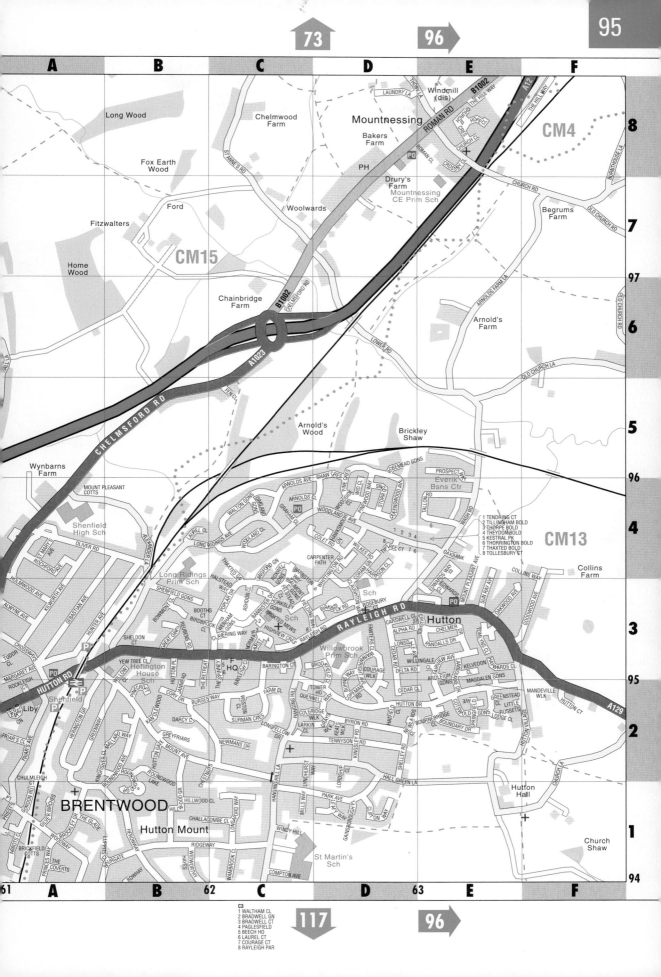

A   B   C   D   E   F

8

Stock Brook

CM4

Stockbrook
Orchard
Farm

King's
Head
Farm

MARIGOLD
LA

Greenacre
Farm

Greenacre

PETER ST
BRITTONS CL

Stock
Farm

PH

SMALLGAINS LA

Nurseries

7

Little
Blunts

Brook Farm
Riding
Stables

97

CH

Great
Blunts
Farm

Oakland Farm
Ind Est

BUCKWYNS
CHASE

Hillside
Farm

THE VALE

VALE
GT

PRINCES MEWS 1
PRINCES CT 2
ARUNDEL CE 3
ARUNDEL MEWS 4

Springfield
Farm

GOATSMOOR LA

PREACHING
CROSS

6

LAMPERN CL 1
LAMPERN MEWS 2

BROOKSIDE

1 KILBARRY WLK
2 FOXHUNTER WLK
3 TALISMAN WLK

Queen's Park
Country Park

LAMPERN CRES
ARUNDEL WAY

BROOKSIDE

FENWOOD DR
ROBIN CL

GLENCREE

BRIDLEWAY

POTASH RD

Forty Acre
Plantation

BOLEYN CL 1
GLOUCESTER PL 2
BROMPTON CL 3
DORCHESTER RD 4
BERKELEY DR 5
WELLINGTON MEWS 6

MARLOWE CL 1
BLACKSMITH CL 2
PEMBROKE CL 3
WESTBOURNE GDNS 4

NORSEY VIEW DR
SUSSEX CT
LISA CL
CENTRAL AVE
THE PRIORY

STOCK RD

LONGTAIL
DUNLIN
HOLLYROD

BROOME RD
MOORE CL
DERBY CL

CHEPSTOW

MARTINGALE RD
SMYTHE RD

5

ROSEBAY AVE
HORSESHOE CL

PAGET DR
ANVIL WAY

BURLEIGH CL
GINGHAM WAY

TYLERS AVE

ORCHARD
AVE

OXWOOD DR
DUBLET MEWS

GOACH MEWS
MERCER RD
MEADE

SADLERS

HOLLYFORD 1
BROOME CL 2
EPSOM CL 4
MARTINGALE CL 5

Sch

PERRY ST

BUSH HALL RD

CANSON

Mayflower
High Sch

WR
TWR

96

OLD
FARM CT
MOAT EDGE
LAKESIDE

CM12

HILLHOUSE RD

HILLHOUSE DR

THE GROVE
DUKES FARM RD

LILFORD RD

JUNIPER
CL

Lodge
Farm

HEATH RD

4

1 ST PAULS GDNS
2 THE PANTILES
3 KENSINGTON CL
4 BUTTERCUP CL
5 PEARTREE WLK

Lake Meadows

St John's
Sch

St John's
Sch
SYLVA

THE SPINNEY

HEADLEY RD

HORACE RD

LITTLE NORSEY RD

NORSEY RD

Norsey Wood
Nature Reserve

Info
Ctr

Tylde Hall
Farm

Ramsden Hall
Sch

Great Fox Hill

CM11

3

RADFORD CRES

RUSKIN DENE
LAKE AVE

CATER WOOD

ST JOHN'S RD

LANGDON
MEWS

PARK
LANDS

DEERBANK RD

NORSEY DR

BREAK EGG HILL

OUTWOOD COMMON RD

BRACKENDALE

THE MOUNT

3

RADFORD WAY

Billericay

DAWSON
MEWS

RADFORD HO 1
RADSTOCKS 2

CROMWELL AVE

ANDREWS DR
COUNTY PK

NORSEY RD

NEEDHAM CL

1 KELVEDON CL
2 JACKSONS MEWS
3 MEADOW CT
4 DAVID'S WLK
5 NORTHFIELD CL
6 ABBOTS RIDE

THE
CROSSWAY

WHITENAYS

Poplar
Plantation

95

WEST PARK AVE

WEST PARK CRES

HOLLEY
GDNS

GRO CL

HIGHLAND GR

KINGSWOOD CL

FEERING RD

COPFORD RD

MEADOW RISE

DEDHAM RD

FELSTED

SHALFORD
RD

HATFIELD
RD

HOLBROOK
CL

GLENSIDE

MOUNT
VIEW

2

THE AVENUE
WEST PARK DR
SUMMERDALE

WESTERN RD
WAKEFIELD
STANDLING

CRESCENT
CT

CROWN RD

LOWER CLOISTER

DANES ST

PRINCE EDWARD RD

STANSTED
CL

HILLWAY

BROWNE CL

FLETCHER
CL

GASCOIGNE
WAY

SALESBURY

OUTWOOD FARM CL

ELM GDN

Outwood
Farm

Devil's
Wood

WESTERN RD
ST JAMES MEWS
ROSE LA
LION LA

CHANDLERS
CHASE

HIGH ST

VICARAGE
CT

HIGH CLOISTER

CHANTRY WAY

SAFRON
WLK

PILGRIMS

5

4

HEATHER
WAY

THE
CHASE

PO

SHAKESPEARE

HAYNNE RD

THE MEADOW WAY

GREENWAY

MONS AVE

HARRODS

MONOUX CL
JAMES SQ

BALMORAL

1

CHESTNUT AVE

ST EDITHS LA
ST EDITH'S CT

Mus

CHAPEL CT

HILLSIDE LA

HILLSIDE

PROWER CL

WEST
CROFT

GREENS FARM LA

WREN
CL

THE MEADOW

CAVELL RD

DARELL WAY

MARRIS AVE

STUART
WAY

HUNTS MEAD
TENSING RD
HILLARY MOUNT

Liby

THE
WALK

ALMA LINK

GAINSBOROUGH

MARTIN CL

WHEATACRE

BUNTING
LA

THE RISING

Sunnymede
Inf Sch

OAK GDN

1

LONDON RD
Ct

A176

Gooseberry
Green

SUN ST

PO

SOUTHEND RD A129

ALBION RD

1 IRVINE WAY
2 MALLORY WAY
3 BURGHSTEAD CL
4 STANLEY TERR
5 FAIRVIEW

GOLDCREST DR

BEVERLY RISE

Sunnymede

Sewage
Works

Quilters
Inf & Jun Schs

LANDON RD

BILLERICAY

94

67   A   B   68   C   D   69   E   F

B2
1 LANGTHORNES
2 WEAVERS CL
3 MIDDLE CLOISTER
4 PILGRIMS WLK
5 MAYFLOWER RD
6 GANLEY CL

CM3

Hanningfield
Resr

WHITE'S
HILL

THE CHASEWAY

Bishop's
Farm

BRITTONS
LA

Great Bishop's
Wood

Kiln
Common

Whitelilies
Farm

Downham
RD

Fremnells

CM4

Broom
Wood

Crowsheath
Farm

HAWKSWOOD RD

97

Common
Farm

Hilltop
Nursery

Little
Abbott's

CROWSHEATH LA

6

Cock
Wood

Thrift
Wood

DOWSETTS LA

Ramsden Back
Common

MILL LA

5

Works

PH

SCHOOL RD

TIPLERS
BRIDGE

Nursery

Downham RD

ALLENS RD

BIRDS CL

STONEY HILLS

RECREATION WLK

WILLOWMEAD

DOWNHAM RD

OAK RD

WINDSOR RD

Downham

96

Windsor
Trad Est

PH

POST JOHNS PL

PH

FARRIER SQ

CM11

DOWNDALE CL

Greenacres
Farm

Hunt's
Farm

HEATH RD

MILL LA

PH

LINDHURST DR

CANES CL

Rectory
Wood

Ramsden
Heath

HOMELANDS GR

BRABNER GDNS

Downham
CE Prim Sch

Chitham's
Farm

The
Orchard Farm

CASTLEDON RD

3

Meepshole
Wood

SHORT LA

MANOR CL

Cox
Green

De Beauvoir
House

DE BEAUVOIR CHASE

95

PARK LA

CHURCH RD

2

Crays
Wood

Pump
Hill

PH

Kent
Hill

Barrenleys
Wood

RAMSDEN PARK RD

ORCHARD AVE

Claypitshills
Wood

Ramsden
Park Farm

1

Ramsden
Bellhouse

GLEBE RD

94

E7
1 AKENFIELD CL
2 WOODHAM CT
3 GUILD WAY
4 QUEEN ELIZABETH II SQ
5 CHIPPING ROW

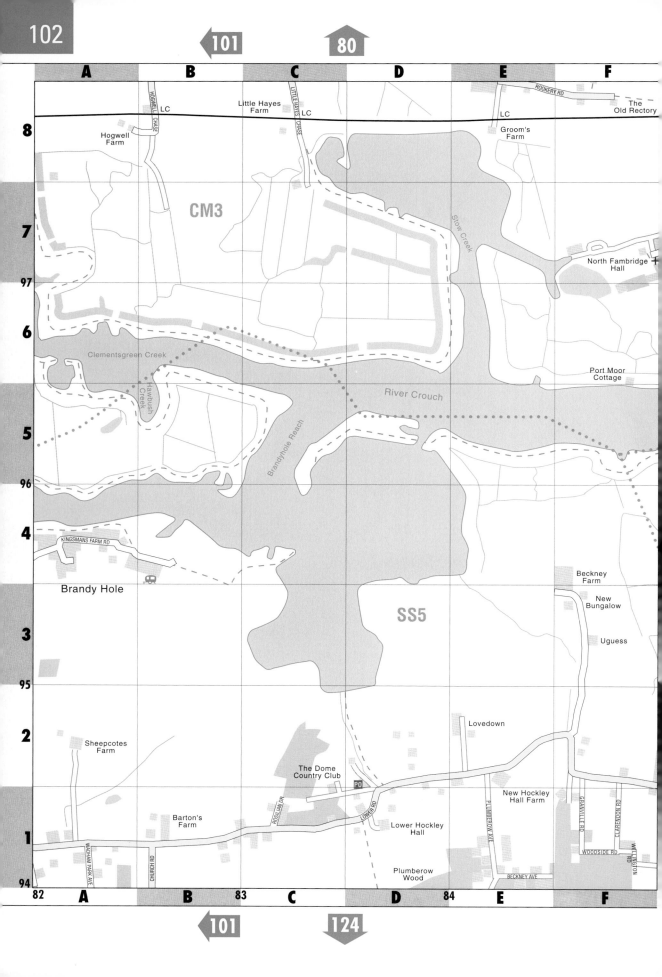

A B C D E F

8
7
97
6
5
96
4
3
95
2
1
94

North Fambridge

CM3

Fambridge

RECTORY RD
FRANKLIN RD
STEPHENSON RD
STRATHMORE RD
FAMBRIDGE RD
STATION APP

Fleet Farm

THE AVENUE
CHURCH RD
BRABANT RD
ROBERTS RD
RUTLAND RD
BLUE HOUSE FARM CHASE
FERRY RD
PO

Manor Farm

Blue House Farm

Whitehouse Farm

Ferry Boat Inn (PH)

RIVERSIDE COTTS

Kennett's Farm

Slipway

Longpole Reach

River Crouch

Bridgemarsh Creek

Works

PEMBERTON FIELD
ST THOMAS RD

The Anchor Hotel

South Fambridge

Brickhouse Farm

South Fambridge Hall

Brenham Farm

FAMBRIDGE RD

SS4

SS5

Rectory Farm House

Rectory Farm

Camp Farm

Scaldhurst Farm

Lowlands Farm

NEW HALL RD
VINCENT RD

Newhall House

CAVENDISH RD
OAKFIELD RD
NEW PARK RD
LOWER RD
ASHINGDON RD

Ashingdon Sch

ARUNDEL RD
MANOR RD
ULVERSTON RD
LYNDHURST RD
ELLESMERE RD
ETHELBERT RD

Moon's Farm

LARK HILL RD

A   B   C   D   E   F

8

CM3

→ STATION RD
Althorne LC
LC

BRIDGEMARSH LA

7
Bridgemarsh Creek

Althorne Creek

97
Bridgemarsh Island

6
Shortpole Reach
Raypits Reach

Landsend Point

5
River Crouch
Easter Reach

Old Fleet

96
Upper Raypits Farm

4

3
Pudsey Hall
SS4

Market Hill

95
Butts Hill

New Hall Farm

2
Bolt Hall
Beacon Hill
Canewdon Hall Farm
BUTTS PADDOCK
BUTTS MEAD
CANEWDON HALL
HIGH ST
GAVS LA
CAUTE CL
ALTHORNE WAY
Crouch View VILLAS
LAMBOURNE HALL RD

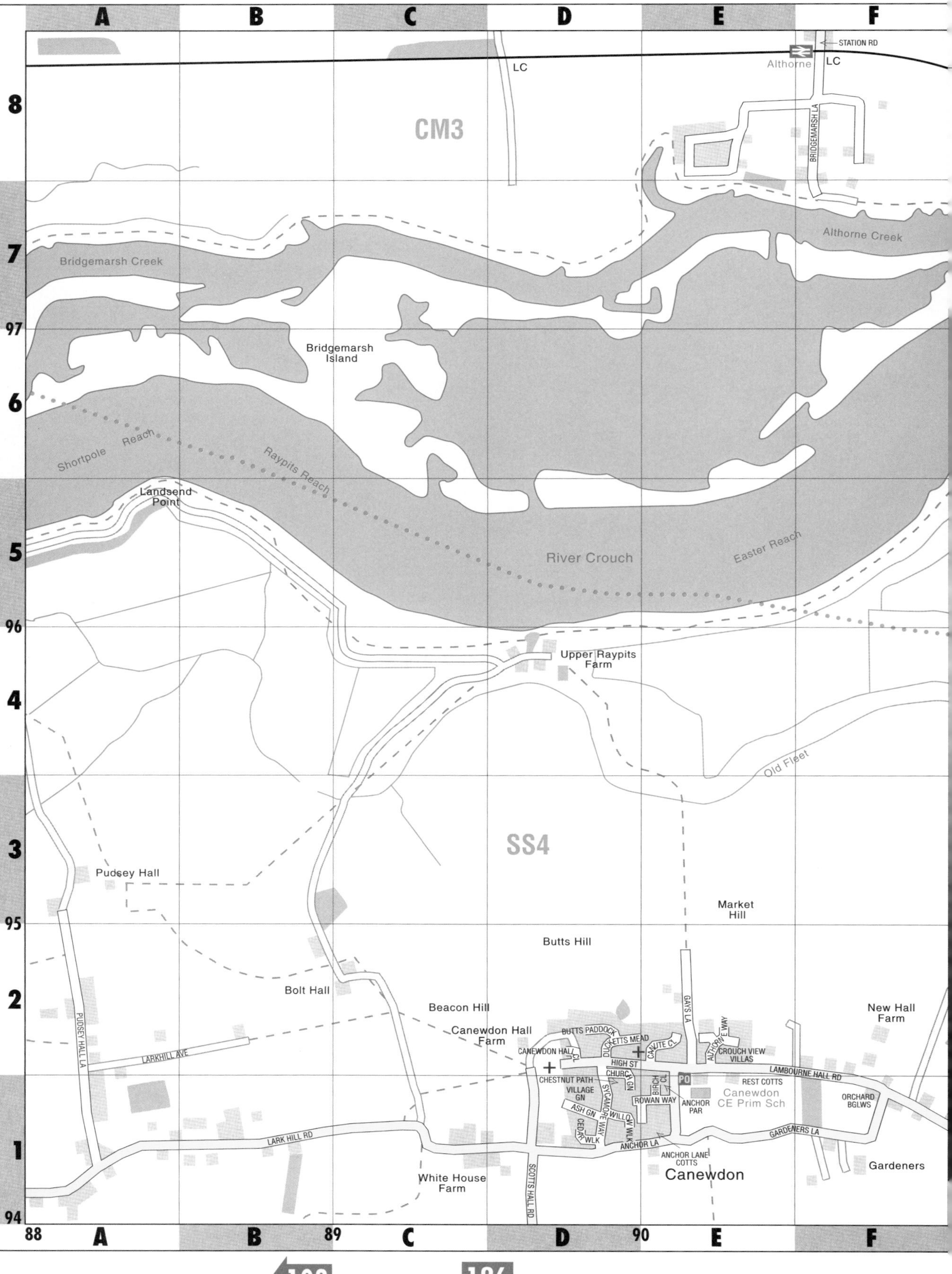

PUDSEY HALL LA
LARKHILL AVE
CHESTNUT PATH
VILLAGE GN
CHURCH GN
SYCAMORE WAY
BIRCH CL
PO
REST COTTS
Canewdon CE Prim Sch
ORCHARD BGLWS

ASH GN
CEDAR WLK
WILLO WY
ROWAN WAY
ANCHOR PAR

1
LARK HILL RD
ANCHOR LA
GARDENERS LA
Gardeners

SCOTTS HALL RD
ANCHOR LANE COTTS

White House Farm
Canewdon

94

88   A   B   89   C   D   90   E   F

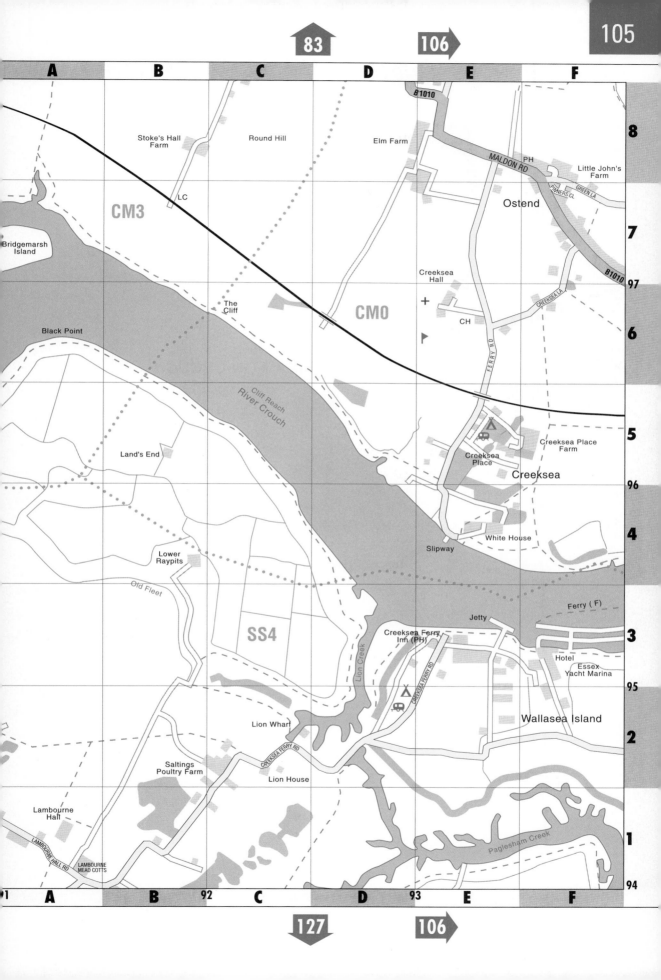

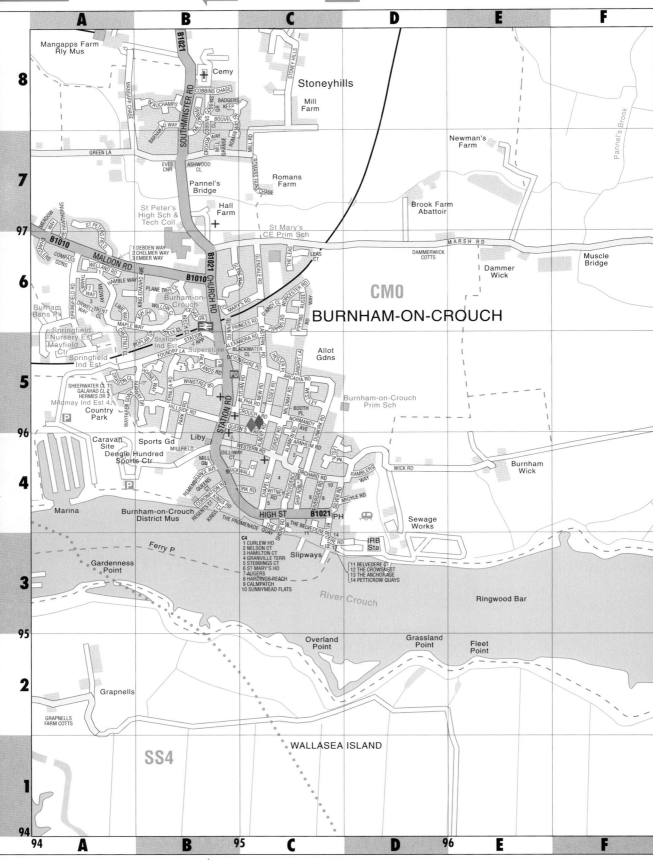

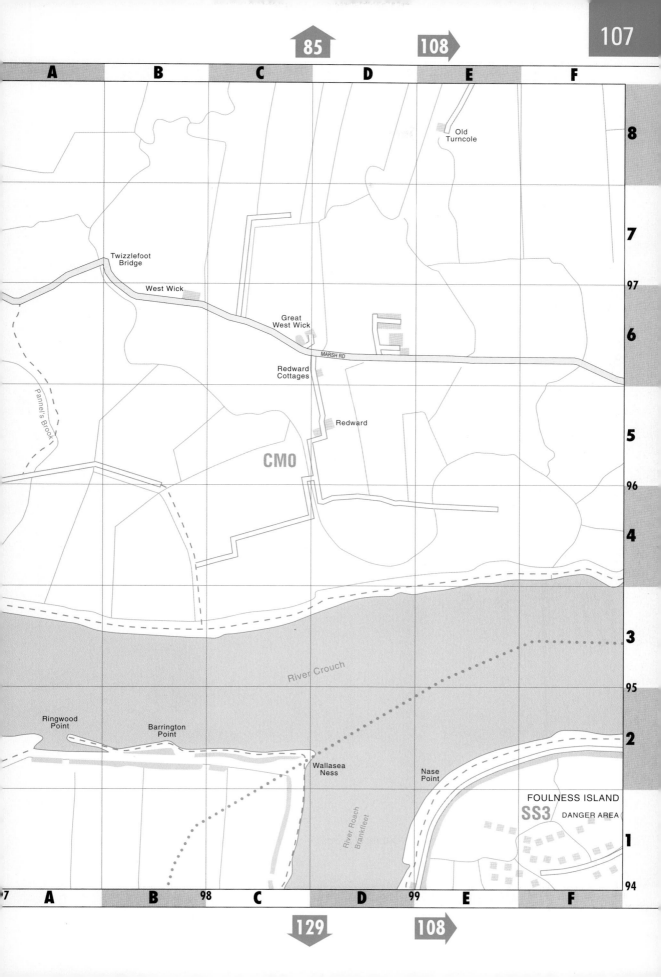

85
108
129
108

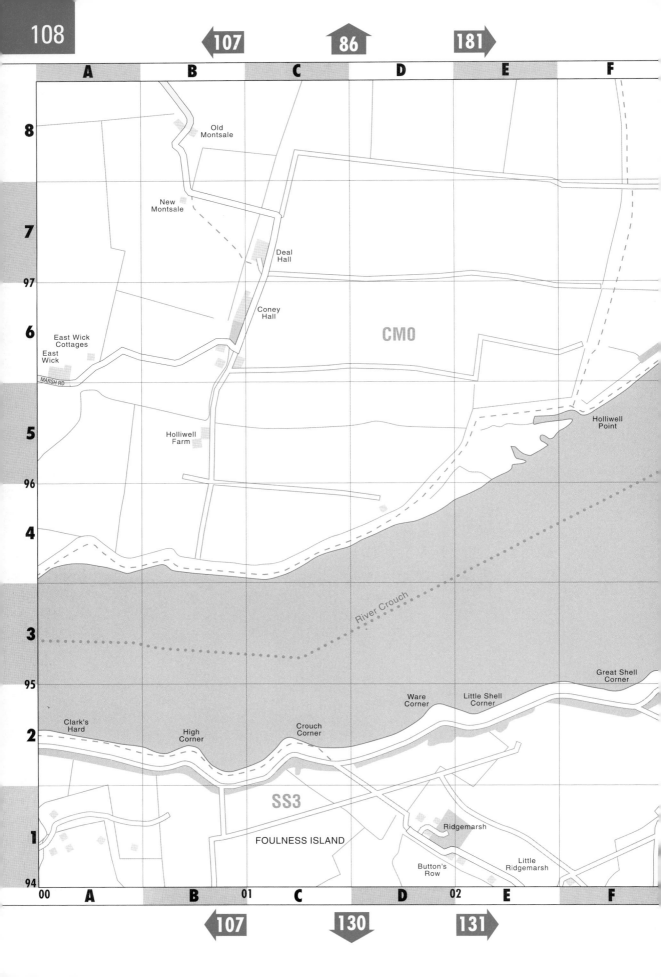

A　B　C　D　E　F

8

Old
Montsale

New
Montsale

7

Deal
Hall

97

Coney
Hall

CMO

6

East Wick
Cottages

East
Wick

MARSH RD

5

Holliwell
Farm

Holliwell
Point

96

4

River Crouch

3

Great Shell
Corner

95

Little Shell
Corner

Ware
Corner

Clark's
Hard

2

High
Corner

Crouch
Corner

SS3

FOULNESS ISLAND

Ridgemarsh

1

Button's
Row

Little
Ridgemarsh

94

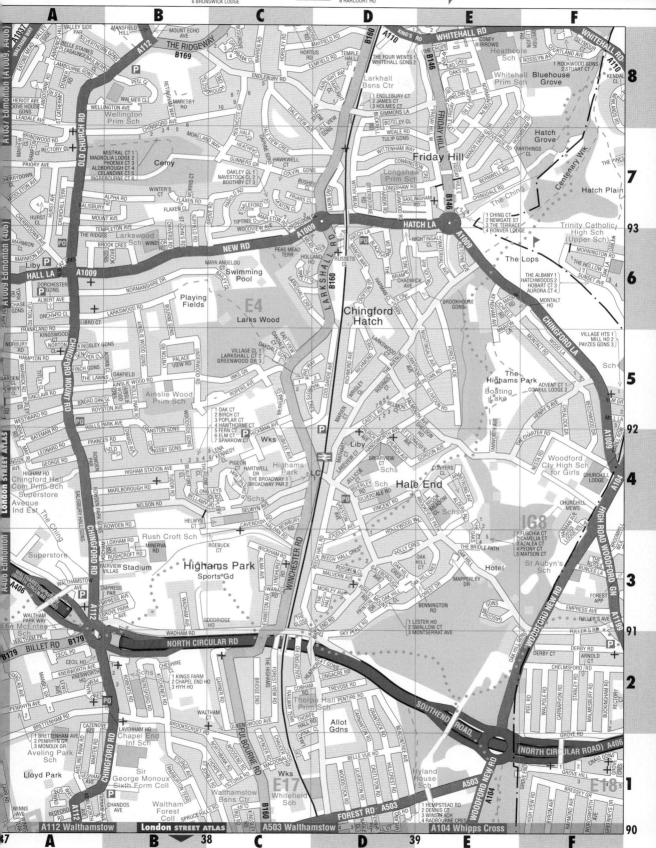

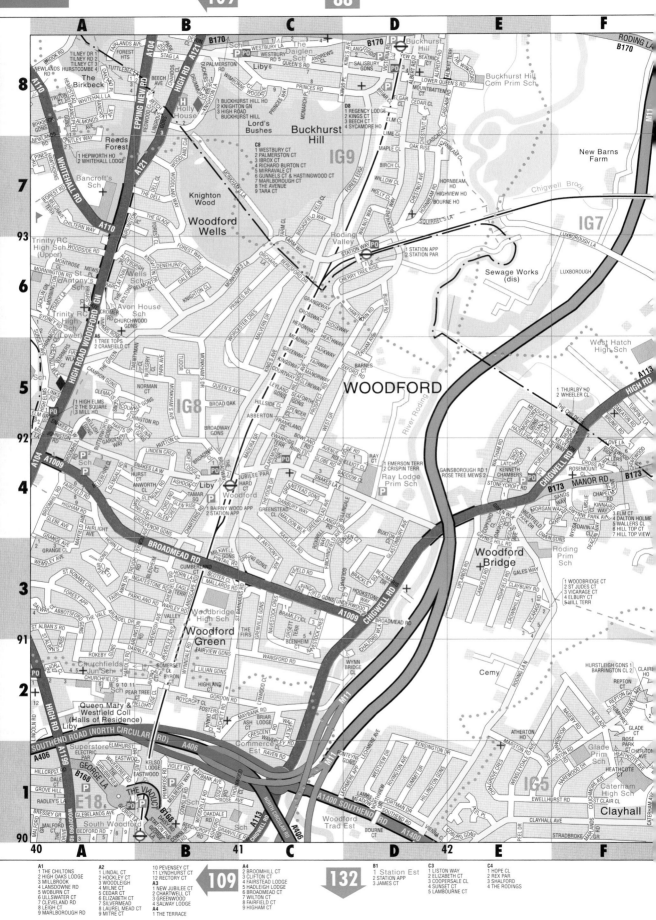

A1
1 THE CHILTONS
2 HIGH OAKS LODGE
3 MILLBROOK
4 LANSDOWNE RD
5 WOBURN CT
6 ULLSWATER CT
7 CLEVELAND RD
8 LEIGH CT
9 MARLBOROUGH RD

A2
1 LINDAL CT
2 HOCKLEY CT
3 WOODLEIGH
4 MILNE CT
5 CEDAR CT
6 ELIZABETH CT
7 SILVERMEAD
8 LAUREL MEAD CT

10 PEVENSEY CT
11 LYNDHURST CT
12 RECTORY CT

A3
1 NEW JUBILEE CT
2 CHARTWELL CT
3 GREENWOOD
4 SALWAY LODGE

A4
1 THE TERRACE

A4
2 BROOMHILL CT
3 CLIFTON CT
4 FAIRSTEAD LODGE
5 HADLEIGH LODGE
6 BROADMEAD CT
7 WILTON CT
8 FAIRFIELD CT
9 HIGHAM CT

B1
1 Station Est
2 STATION APP
3 JAMES CT

C3
1 LISTON WAY
2 ELIZABETH CT
3 COOPERSALE CL
4 SUNSET CT
5 LAMBOURNE CT

C4
1 HOPE CL
2 REX PAR
3 SHALFORD
4 THE RODINGS

111 90

A B C D E F

8

RM4

Chigwell
Row

Cabin
Hill

Chigwell Row
Inf Sch

Weddrell's Plain

MANOR RD

COOPERS CL

MILLERS STA

MILLERS CL

FAVERSHAM CL

MARDEN CL

LAMBOURNE CRES

JOHNNYMEDE

Hainault Forest
(Country Park)

GRAVEL LA

A1112

PUDDING LA

GRAVEL CL

ORCHARD WAY

WHITEHALL CL

LAMBOURNE RD

RAYMOND BERE AT WAY

RAYMOND GDNS

GLEBELANDS

ASTRA

SYLVAN WAY

DALTON

WOOLHAMPTON

ALL SAINTS CL

7

WILLOWMEAD

CHASE LA

CROSBY CL

MAYPOLE CL

B173 LAMBOURNE RD

B173

LODGE

Three Forests Way

Fox
Burrows
Farm

93

IG7

Fox
Burrows

Fox Burrow Rd

6

CROSSBOW RD

BROCKET WAY

BEARING WAY

MANFORD CL

GREENWOOD RD

BAYWOOD

LAKELAND

YELLOWPINE WAY

COPPICE PATH

The
Ridings

LITCHFORD PL

The Lake

IG7

Dog Kennel
Hill

5

VERDERERS RD

NORTH BURROW RD

LOWE CL

ALGISTER RD

REEDWORTH

NEW NEWTON

HAMMARDS WAY

MARLYON RD

MERLIN RD

KESTREL CL

FALCONER

SYLVESTER GDNS

PEREGRINE CL

BEAKER

FOWLER CL

ROMFORD RD

Coppice
Prim Sch

MANFORD
CROSS

ARROWSMITH RD

THE LOWE

BRANCH RD

HARBOURER RD

HUNTSMAN RD

Hainault Forest
High Sch

FIVE OAKS LA

92

BOAR

FERNIE CL

HURSLEY RD

POLLARD

1 MANFORD CT
2 MARIAN LAWSON CT

CROMWELL
CTR

Burnside
Ind Est

Works

CH

Hainault
Cottages

4

BURSLEM
AVE

STOKE AVE

LONGCROFT

TUNSTALL AVE

NEWCASTLE AVE

ELMBRIDGE RD

The Acorn
Ctr

ROEBUCK RD

Roebuck
Trad Est

IG6

Works

Works

Hog
Hill

John Bramston Prim Sch

FOREST RD

North View Caravan Site

PENNYLANDS RD

Forest
Farm

B174

Cold Blow
Farm

FRINTON RD

ROMFORD RD

WATTON RD

BROWNING
CL

B174

HOG HILL RD

3

HAINAULT RD

Crown
Cotts

91

RM5

2

Works

WHALEBONE LA N

COLLIER ROW RD

PROVIDE CT

Northgate
Ind Est

Hainault Farm

Fairlop
Plain

Seven Kings Water

RM6

Marks Gate

Whites
Farm

FURZE FARM CL

1

Furze House
Farm

BILLET RD

KINGSTON HILL AVE

A1112

IG2

90

46 A B 47 C 48 D E F

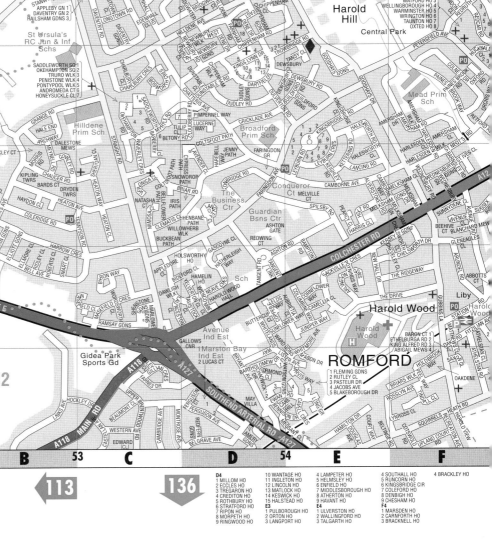

← 113   ↑ 92

D5
1 ANGMERING HO
2 AMPTHILL HO
3 THORNBURY HO
4 CARDIGAN HO
5 UPTON HO
6 DEVIZES HO

D5
7 BARNSTAPLE PATH
8 OUNDLE HO
9 KIRKHAM HO
10 ACCRINGTON HO
11 RADSTOCK HO
12 STROUD HO

13 SOUTHSEA HO
14 ALCESTER HO
15 NORTHALLERTON WAY
16 DARLINGTON PATH
17 ABERCROMBIE HO
18 THE ARCADE

E5
1 WOLVERTON HO
2 NEWMARKET HO
3 NELSON HO
4 NANTWICH HO
5 MORECAMBE HO
6 MINEHEAD HO

7 MACCLESFIELD HO
8 LYNMOUTH HO
9 LUTON HO
10 THRAPSTON HO
11 HASLINGDEN HO
12 HALIFAX HO
13 GLOSSOP HO

14 GILLINGHAM HO
15 EPSOM HO
E6
1 CAMELFORD HO
2 PORTMADOC HO
3 WILMSLOW HO
4 NORTHAMPTON HO

CM14

RM4

RM3

RM1

RM2

ROMFORD

Harold Wood

1 FLEMING GDNS
2 RUTLEY CL
3 PASTEUR DR
4 JACOBS AVE
5 BLAKEBOROUGH DR

D4
1 MILLOM HO
2 ECCLES HO
3 TREGARON HO
4 CREDITON HO
5 ROTHBURY HO
6 STRATFORD HO
7 RIPON HO
8 MORPETH HO
9 RINGWOOD HO

10 WANTAGE HO
11 INGLETON HO
12 LINCOLN HO
13 MATLOCK HO
14 KESWICK HO
15 HALSTEAD HO
E3
1 PULBOROUGH HO
2 ORTON HO
3 LANGPORT HO

4 LAMPETER HO
5 HELMSLEY HO
6 ENFIELD HO
7 MIDDLESBOROUGH HO
8 ATHERTON HO
9 HAVANT HO
E4
1 ULVERSTON HO
2 WALLINGFORD HO
3 TALGARTH HO

4 SOUTHALL HO
5 RUNCORN HO
6 KINGSBRIDGE CIR
7 COLEFORD HO
8 DENBIGH HO
9 CHESHAM HO
F4
1 MARSDEN HO
2 CARNFORTH HO
3 BRACKNELL HO

4 BRACKLEY HO

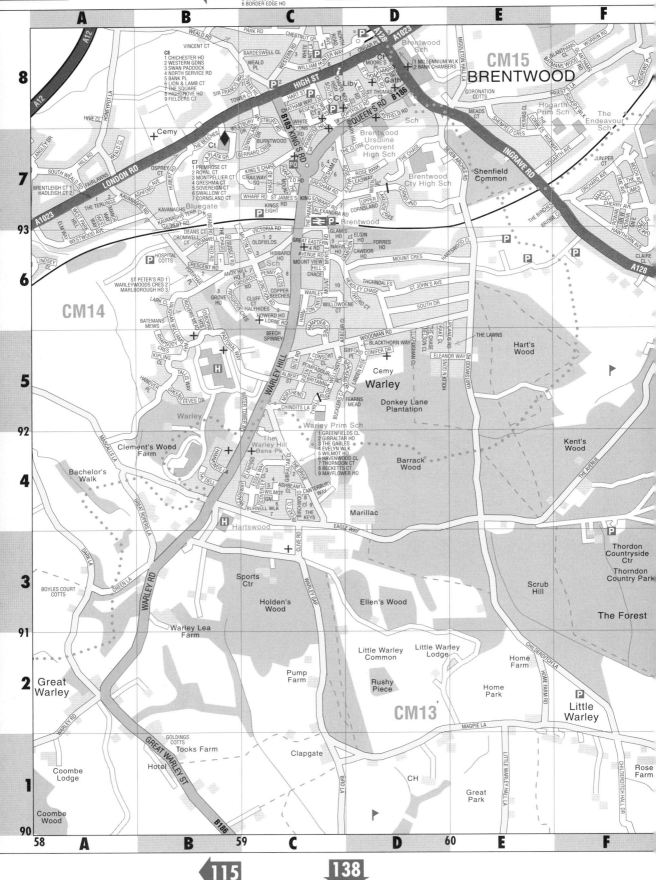

115

C6
1 VICTORIA CT
2 MASEFIELD CT
3 WHEATFIELDS
4 GAINSBOROUGH CT
5 MAURICE HO
6 BORDER EDGE HO

94

C6
7 COPELAND HO
8 BARTON CT
9 TYLERS CT
10 HIGHTREES CT

CM15
BRENTWOOD

CM14

CM13

Great
Warley

Warley

Little
Warley

The Forest

115

138

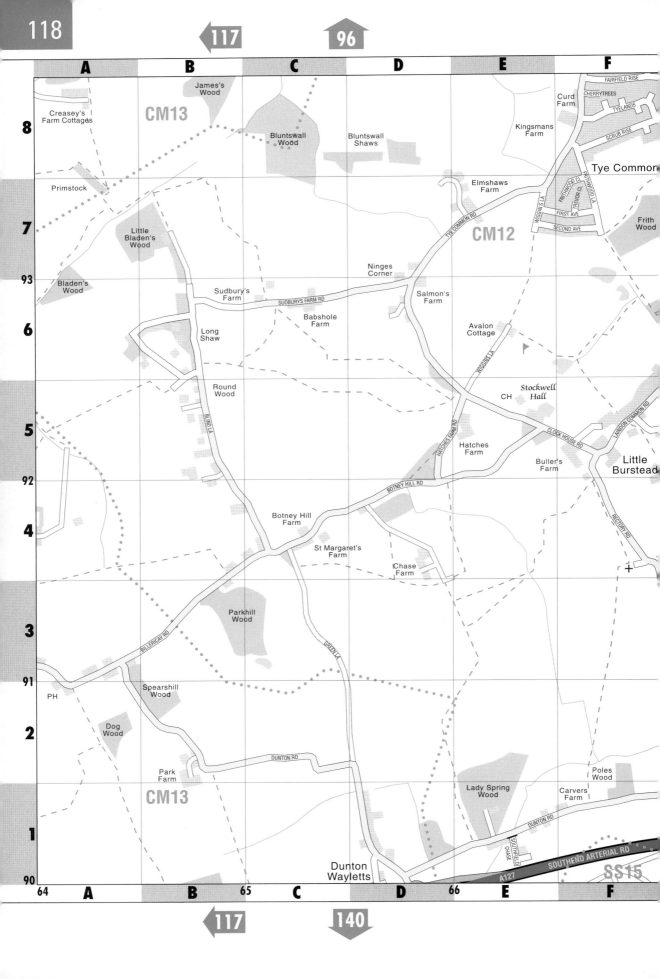

117
96

A B C D E F

8

CM13

James's
Wood

Creasey's
Farm Cottages

Bluntswall
Wood

Bluntswall
Shaws

Curd
Farm

FAIRFIELD RISE

CHERRYTREES

TYELANDS

SCRUB RISE

Kingsmans
Farm

Tye Common

7

Primstock

Little
Bladen's
Wood

Elmshaws
Farm

TYE COMMON RD

CM12

FRITHWOOD CL

TREVOR CL

FRITHWOOD LA

WIGGIN'S LA

FIRST AVE

SECOND AVE

Frith
Wood

93

Bladen's
Wood

Sudbury's
Farm

SUDBURYS FARM RD

Babshole
Farm

Ninges
Corner

Salmon's
Farm

6

Long
Shaw

Avalon
Cottage

WIGGINS LA

Stockwell
Hall

CH

Round
Wood

BLIND LA

5

HATCHES FARM RD

Hatches
Farm

CLOCK HOUSE RD

Buller's
Farm

LANGDON COMMON RD

Little
Burstead

92

BOTNEY HILL RD

4

Botney Hill
Farm

St Margaret's
Farm

Chase
Farm

RECTORY RD

Parkhill
Wood

3

BILLERICAY RD

GREEN LA

91

PH

Spearshill
Wood

2

Dog
Wood

DUNTON RD

Park
Farm

Lady Spring
Wood

Carvers
Farm

Poles
Wood

CM13

DUNTON RD

SOUTHFIELD CHASE

SOUTHEND ARTERIAL RD

1

Dunton
Wayletts

A127

SS15

90

64 A B 65 C D 66 E F

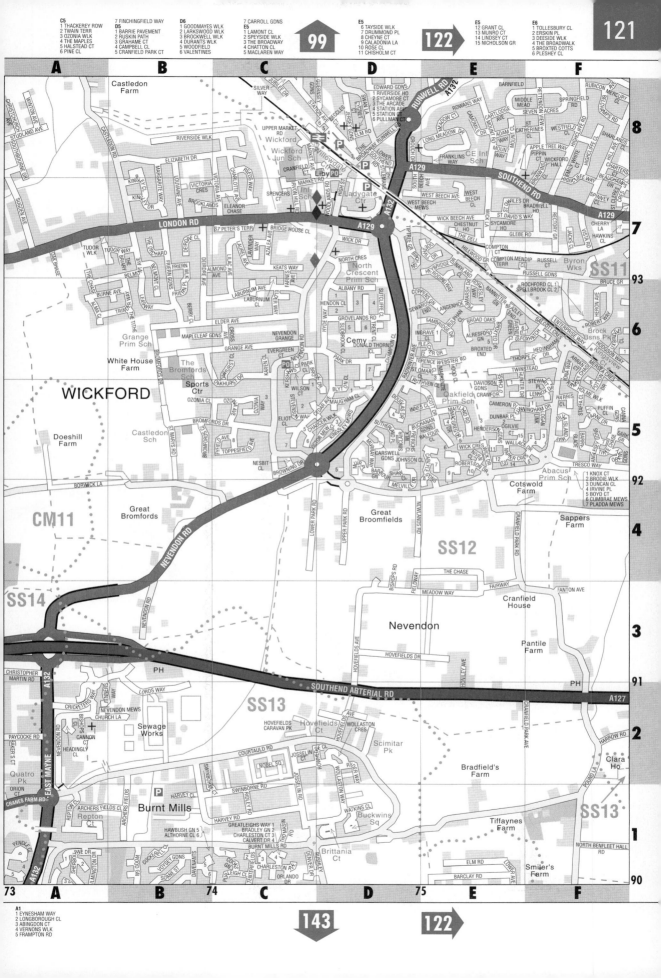

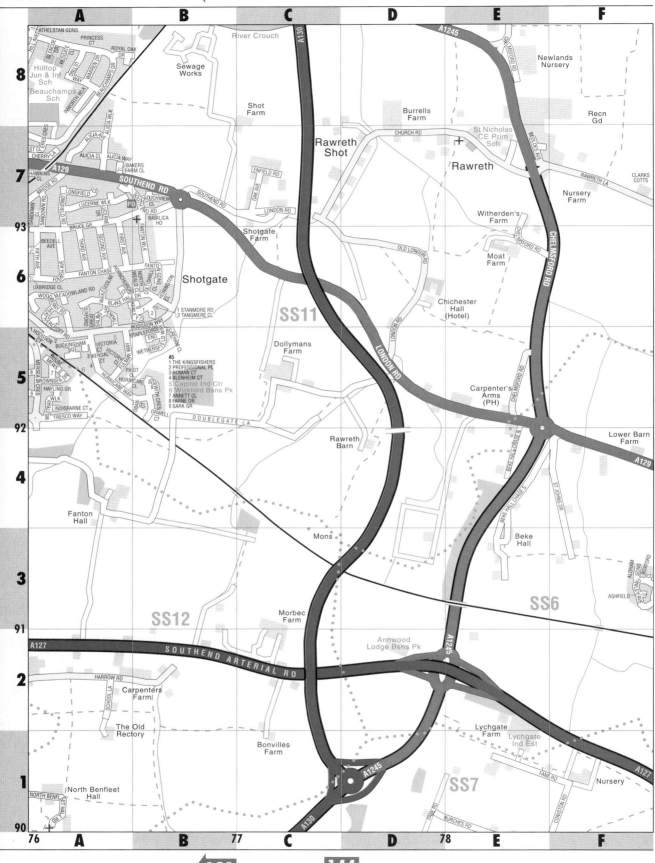

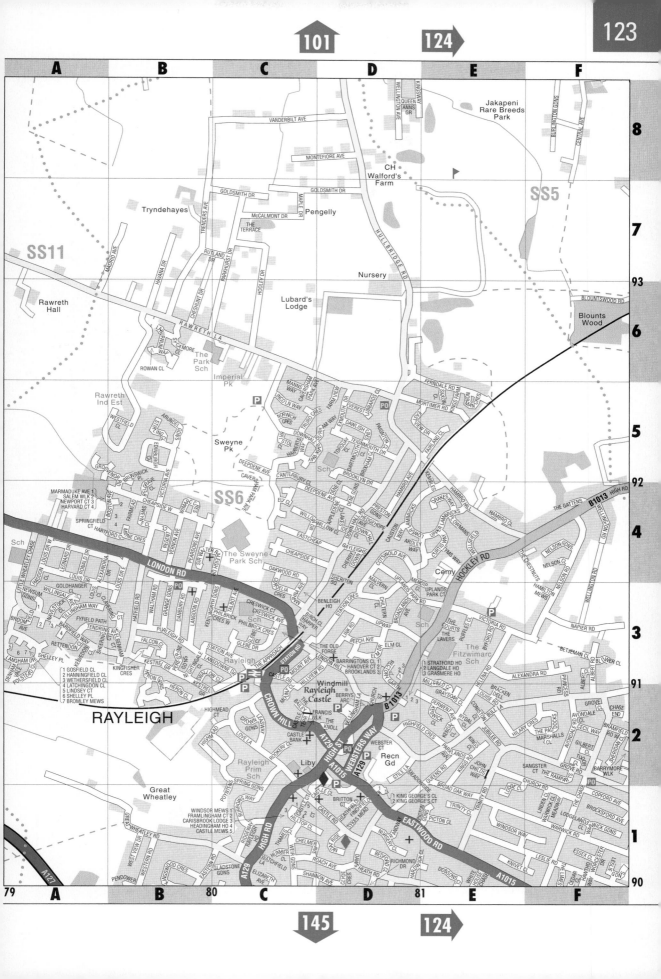

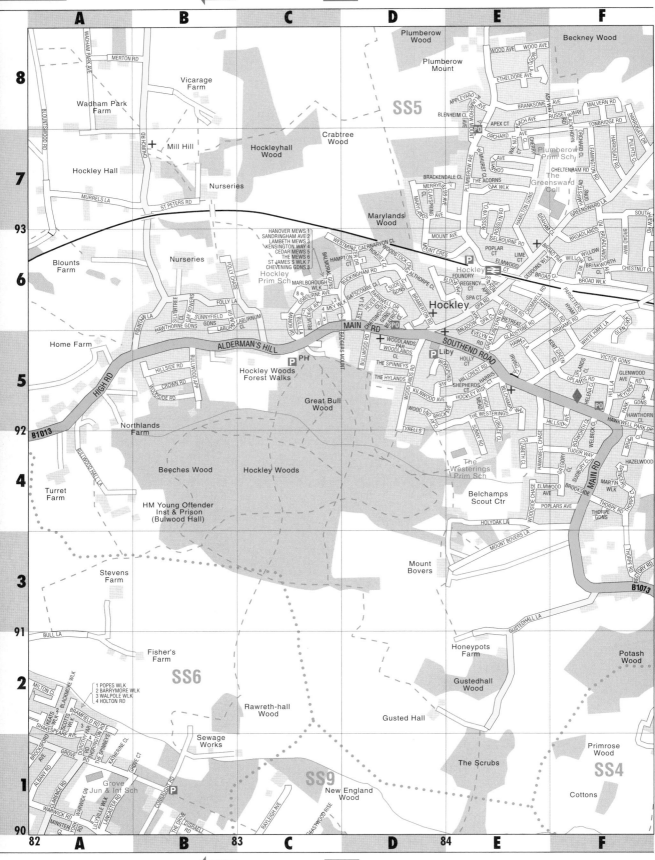

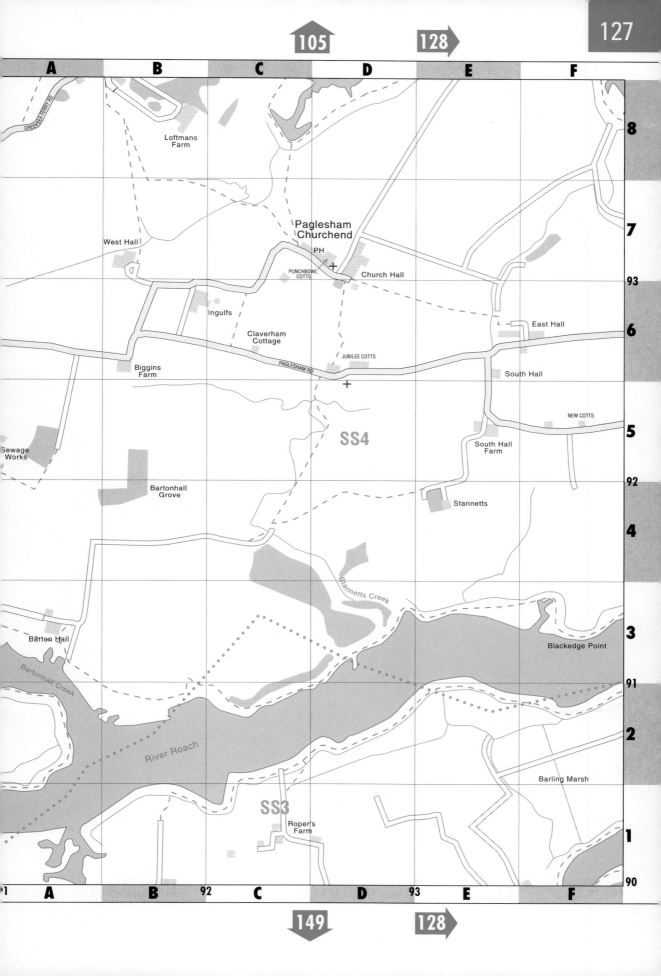

127
106

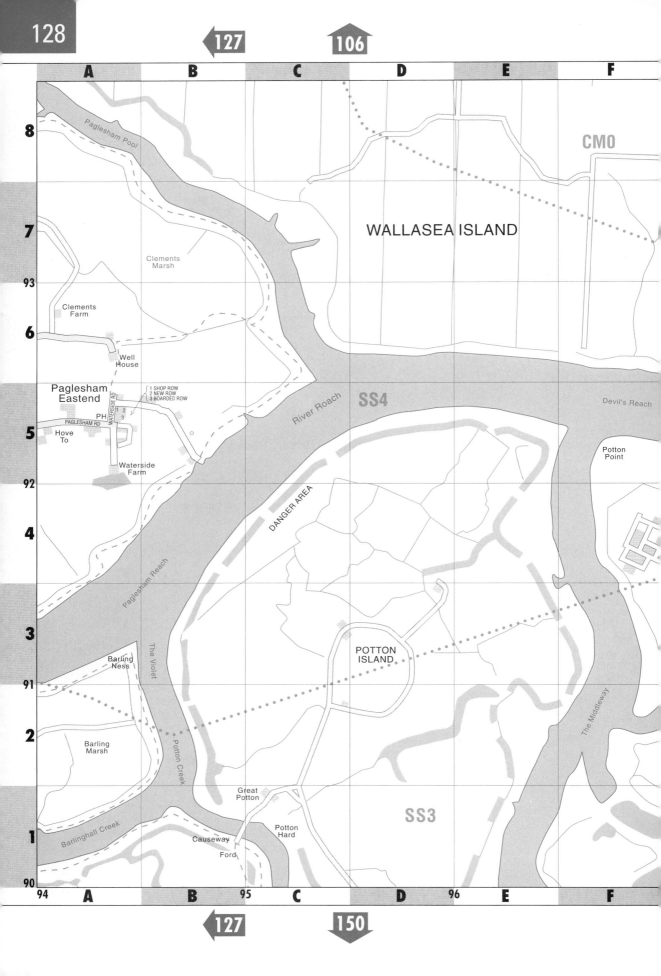

A **B** **C** **D** **E** **F**

Paglesham Pool

8

7 WALLASEA ISLAND CMO

93

Clements
Marsh

Clements
Farm

6

Well
House

Paglesham
Eastend

1 SHOP ROW
2 NEW ROW
3 BOARDED ROW

River Roach SS4 Devil's Reach

PH
PAGLESHAM RD
WATERSIDE RD

5 Hove
To

Waterside
Farm

Potton
Point

92

DANGER AREA

4

Paglesham Reach

Potton
Island

3 POTTON
ISLAND

Barling
Ness

91

The Violet

2 Barling
Marsh

Potton Creek

The Middleway

Great
Potton

SS3

1 Potton
Hard

Causeway

Barlinghall Creek

Ford

90

94 **A** **B** 95 **C** **D** 96 **E** **F**

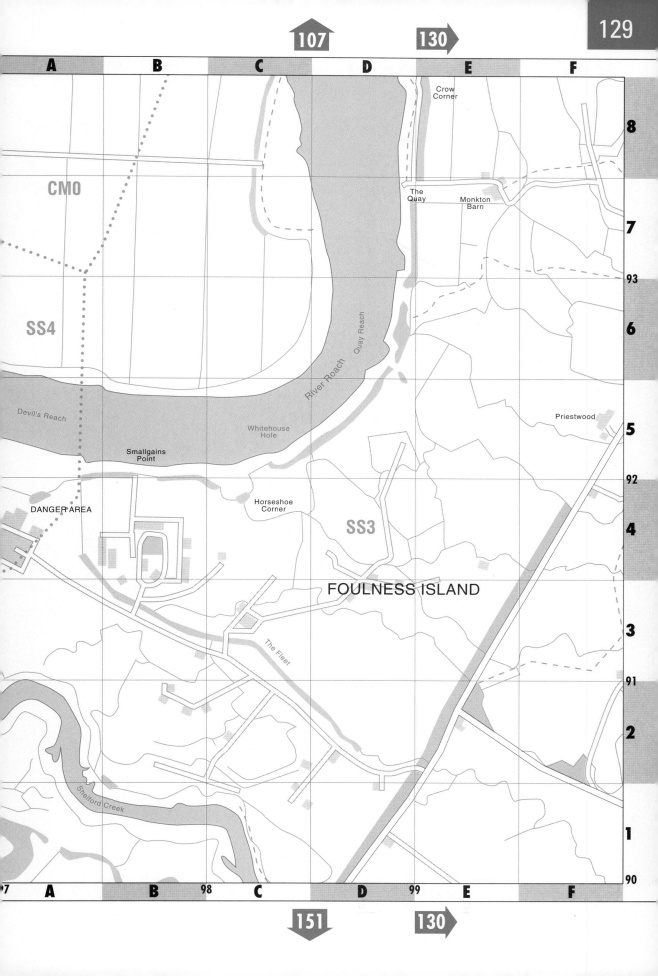

107
130
151
130

A B C D E F

8 7 93 6 5 92 4 3 91 2 1 90

CMO

SS4

Crow
Corner

The
Quay

Monkton
Barn

Priestwood

River Roach

Quay Reach

Devil's Reach

Whitehouse
Hole

Smallgains
Point

Horseshoe
Corner

SS3

DANGER AREA

FOULNESS ISLAND

The Fleet

Shelford Creek

7 A B 98 C D 99 E F

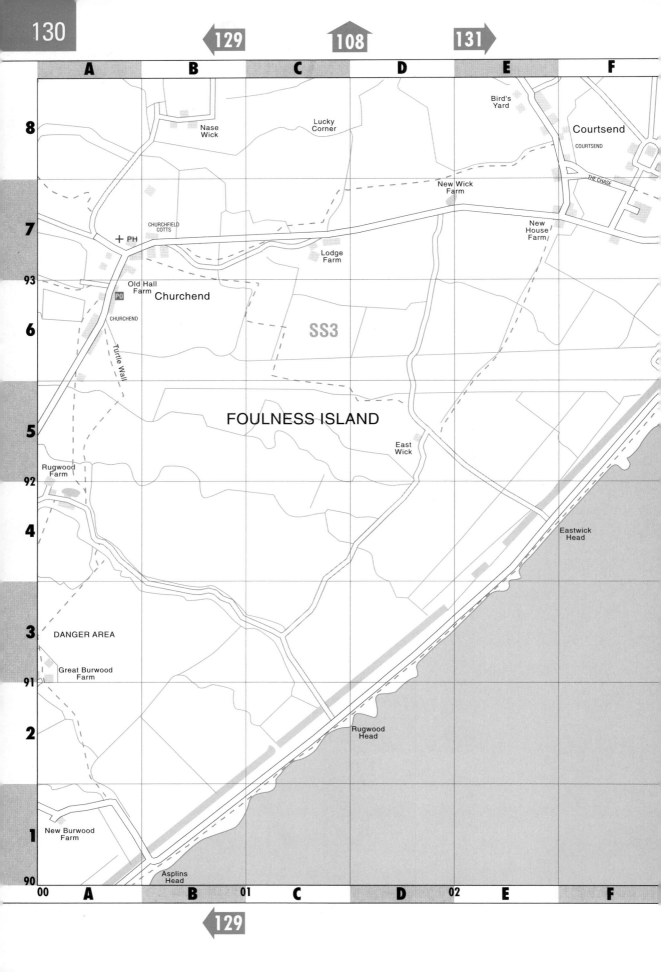

108

River Crouch

Foulness Point

East
Newlands

The Drift
(dis)

SS3

DANGER AREA

Northern
Corner

Fisherman's
Head

130

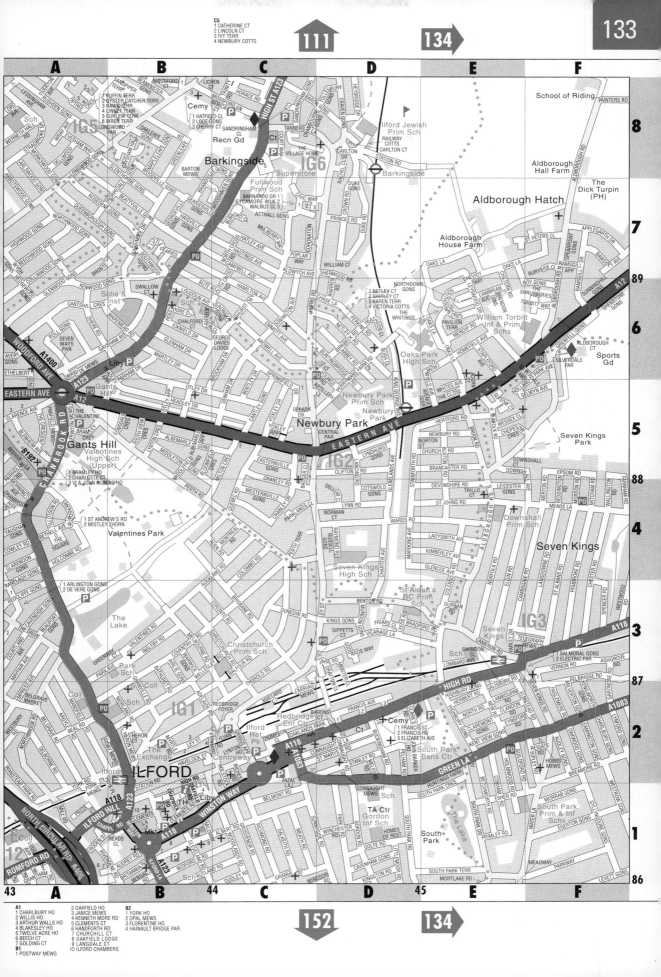

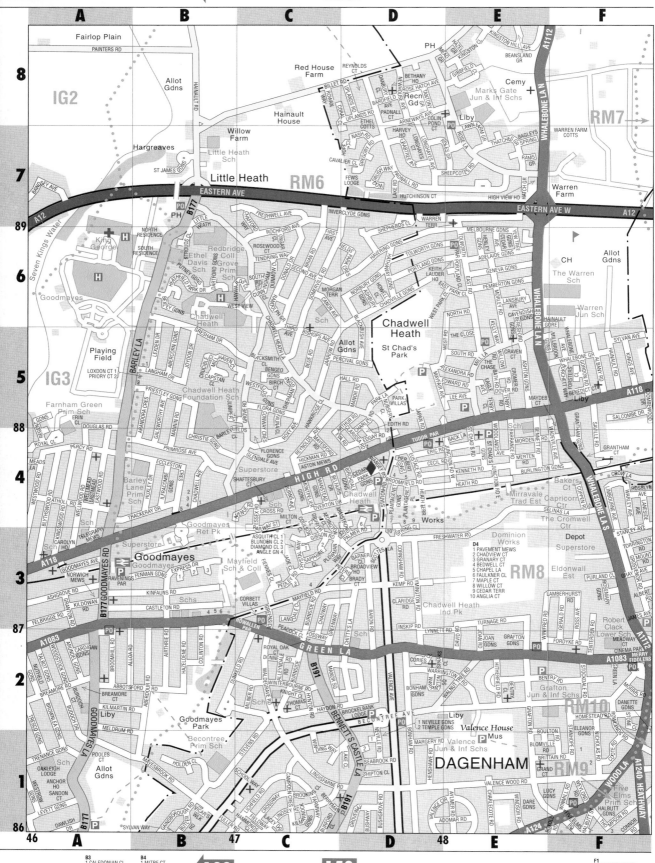

B3
1 CALEDONIAN CL
2 TALISMAN CL
3 NORSEMAN CL
4 FRANK SLATER HO
5 BROOK'S MANS
6 BROOK'S PAR

B4
1 MITRE CT
2 THE COPPINS
3 STANETTA CT
4 WILNETT CT
5 WILNETT VILLAS

F1
1 STANHOPE GDNS
2 COOTE GDNS
3 NORTHFIELD PATH

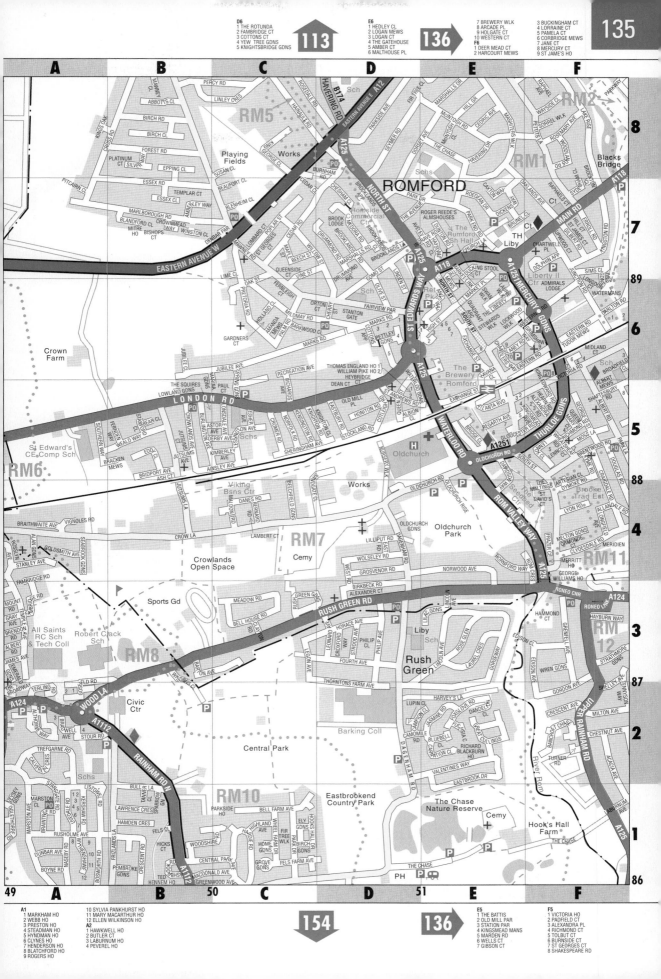

D6
1 THE ROTUNDA
2 FAMBRIDGE CT
3 COTTONS CT
4 YEW TREE GDNS
5 KNIGHTSBRIDGE GDNS

E6
1 HEDLEY CL
2 LOGAN MEWS
3 LOGAN CT
4 THE GATEHOUSE
5 AMBER CT
6 MALTHOUSE PL

7 BREWERY WLK
8 ARCADE PL
9 HOLGATE CT
10 WESTERN CT
F6
1 DEER MEAD CT
2 HARCOURT MEWS

3 BUCKINGHAM CT
4 LORRAINE CT
5 PAMELA CT
6 CORBRIDGE MEWS
7 JANE CT
8 MERCURY CT
9 ST JAMES HO

113

136

ROMFORD

RM5

RM2

RM1

Playing Fields

Works

Crown Farm

RM6

St Edward's CE Comp Sch

LONDON RD

EASTERN AVENUE W

Oldchurch

Works

RM7

Cemy

Crowlands Open Space

Sports Gd

All Saints RC Sch & Tech Coll

Robert Clack Sch

RM8

Civic Ctr

Central Park

RM10

Eastbrookend Country Park

Rush Green

Barking Coll

The Chase Nature Reserve

Cemy

Hook's Hall Farm

Oldchurch Park

RM11

RM12

UPPER RAINHAM RD

RAINHAM RD N

8

7

89

6

5

88

4

3

87

2

1

86

154   136

A1
1 MARKHAM HO
2 WEBB HO
3 PRESTON HO
4 STEADMAN HO
5 HYNDMAN HO
6 CLYNES HO
7 HENDERSON HO
8 BLATCHFORD HO
9 ROGERS HO

10 SYLVIA PANKHURST HO
11 MARY MACARTHUR HO
12 ELLEN WILKINSON HO
A2
1 HAWKWELL HO
2 BUTLER CT
3 LABURNUM HO
4 PEVEREL HO

E5
1 THE BATTIS
2 OLD MILL PAR
3 STATION PAR
4 KINGSMEAD MANS
5 MARDEN RD
6 WELLS CT
7 GIBSON CT
F6

F5
1 VICTORIA HO
2 PADFIELD CT
3 ALEXANDRA PL
4 RICHMOND CT
5 TOLBUT CT
6 BURNSIDE CT
7 ST GEORGES CT
8 SHAKESPEARE RD

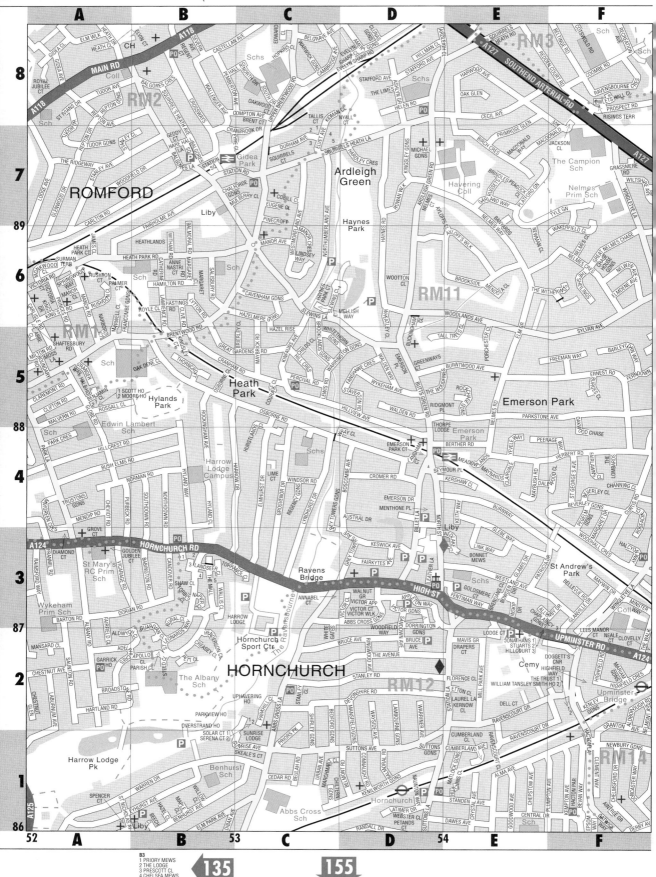

137
116

A B C D E F

8

Sewage Works

Hole Farm

Normans

B186 GREAT WARLEY ST

BRD LA

Childerditch Ind Pk

CHILDERDITCH HALL

Parker's Shaw

7

M25

CODHAM HALL LA

CM13

St Peter's Rectory

RECTORY CHASE

Woodlands Prep Sch

LITTLE WARLEY HALL LA

89

Codham Hall Wood

Codham Hall

Hotel

A12

6

FOLKES LA

Folkes Farm

SOUTHEND ARTERIAL RD

Great Warley Hall

Little Warley Hall

Hall Lane Farm

A127

29

WARLEY ST

CHURCH LA

Prettigate Farm

5

Hobbs Hole

Abattoir

88

FAIRHOLME GDNS

ACACIA GDNS

LABURNHAM GDNS

SAXON HO

WARLEY HALL LA

4

LABURNHAM CL

Upminster Trad Pk

Playing Field

Franks Wood

Monks Farm

Old England

3

Franks Farm

RM14

Puddle Dock

Westbury Farm

FRANKS COTTS

B187

ST MARY'S LA

Nursery

BURY FARM COTTS

87

B187

CLAY TYE RD

Clay Tye Wood

Sewage Works

2

Bury Farm

Broadfields Farm

Clay Tye Farm

1

M25

B186

Fairplay Farm

86

58 A B 59 C D 60 E F

117

140

A B C D E F

The Old Shop

Old Hall Pond

Octagon Plantation

P

Hill Farm

CHILDERDITCH ST

Mill Wood

Thorndon Country Park

8

Halfway House Motel

CHILDERDITCH LA

Jury Hill

Thick Shaw

7

Childerditch Hall

CHILDERDITCH HALL DR

Barrett's Shaw

SOUTHEND ARTERIAL RD

Hollow Bottom Shaw

East Horndon

TILBURY RD

89

Round Shaw

6

BRENTWOOD RD

A128

A127

Nuttys Farm

THORNDON AVE

West Horndon Prim Sch

West Horndon

CADOGAN AVE

Old Mill Cottages

5

Horndon Ind Pk

SANDERSON CL

PETRESFIELD WAY

STATION RD

CLAYFIELD GDNS

DUNMOW GDNS

PO

2

3

4

PYFIELD CL

FRESHWELL GDNS

1 CHAFFORD GDNS
2 WITHAM GDNS
3 BURNTWOOD CL
4 SAFFRON CL

TILBURY RD

PH

BYFIELD CL

PETRE CHASE

LOMBARDS

West Horndon

88

CM13

Barnards

4

ST MARY'S LA

Little Tillingham Hall

Field House

Blue House Farm

BRENTWOOD RD

Middleton Hall

BULPHAN BY-PASS

3

Tillingham Hall

DUNNINGS LA

87

A128

2

Slough House

CHINA LA

CM14

PEARTREE LA

1

86

A B 62 C D 63 E F

158

140

139
118

8 **7** **89** **6** **5** **88** **4** **3** **87** **2** **1** **86**

A B C D E F

Dunton Wayletts

A127

CM12

Eastlands Spring

Friern Manor Wood

SOUTHEND ARTERIAL RD

A127

Green Meadows Nurseries

B148

Automobile Research Ctr

SS15

Brookman's Farm

COMMERCIAL WAY

CHRISTY CT

CHRISTY CT

SYLVAN CT

SABLE WAY

SEAX WAY

SEAX CT

MYLLAS WAY

ARGENT CT

FENTON WAY

Friern Manor

MERRYLANDS CHASE

CHRISTY WAY

HORNSBY SQ

HORNSBY WAY

Southfields

1 BROADWATER GN
2 WOODSTOCK CRE
3 WOODSTOCK GDN
4 PRESIDENTS CT
5 HELMORE CT

WEST MAYNE

BRAMSTON LINK

BRAMSTON WAY

DUNTON LINK

SAFFRON CT

B14

B1036

CM13

The Old Rectory

Westmayne Ind. Pk

SUMPNERS LINK

KENNEDY CL

BROOKLANDS PK

PALATINE CL

DURHAM RD

FRASER CL

BLACKMORES

PARFORDS

ROWENHALL

HELMORE

Dunton Hills Farm

CHURCH RD

Dunton Park CVN PK

MANDEVILLE WAY

B1036

FLINT

KENTON WAY

NOTTINGHAM WAY

CHORLEY CL

READING

MARCE TREE

Dunton Hall

WORCESTER CL 1
SHREWSBURY CL 2
OSTERLEY DR 3
AMERSHAM AVE 4
MAHONIA DR 5
IPSWICH MEWS 6
ALNWICK CL 7
OXFORD CL 8
CAMBRIDGE CL 9
MONMOUTH MEWS 10

AYLESBURY DR

APPLEBY

OAKHAM CL

LOWER DUNTON RD

EGERTON DR

BURR

FERN WLK

DENEHURST GDNS

WOODVIEW

GLENWOOD GDNS

WEST AVE

NORTHAMPTON DR

MILLTOW AVE

WICK PL

STAFFORD GN

Great Berry

MIMOSA

JASMINE CL

FOREST GLADE

FIRST AVE

HIGH BANK 1
REEVES CL 2

MEADOWS

HILL TOP RISE

TORNEY CL

COBURG LA

KILOWAN CL

Great Ber Prim Sc

SUNNYSIDE

SECOND AVE

CENTRAL AVE

LAKE VIEW

Plotlands Mus

THIRD AVE

Plotlands Nature Reserve

FOURTH AVE

SS16

Poultry Farm

Langdon Conservation Ctr

Dunton Poultry Farm

A128

RM14

Lower Dunton Hall

Balgownie Farm

BRENTWOOD RD

Motel

Garlesters

BULPHAN BY-PASS

BRENTWOOD RD

Noke Hall Farm

Doesgate Farm

Bentley Farm

OLD CHURCH HILL

DOESGATE LA

A128

Manor House

Little Malgraves

Little Malgraves Ind Est

64 A B 65 C D 66 E F

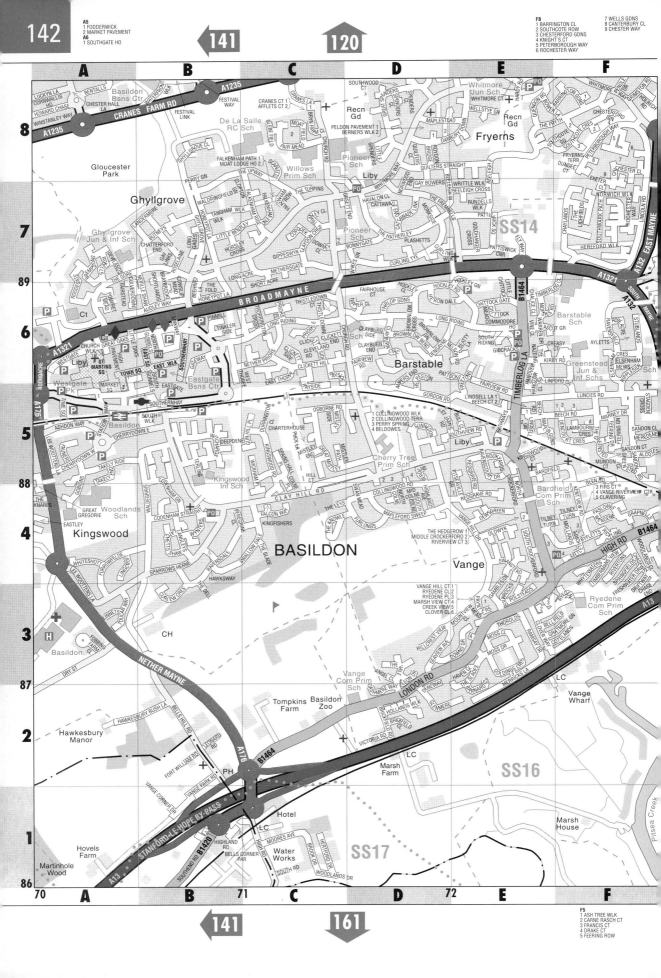

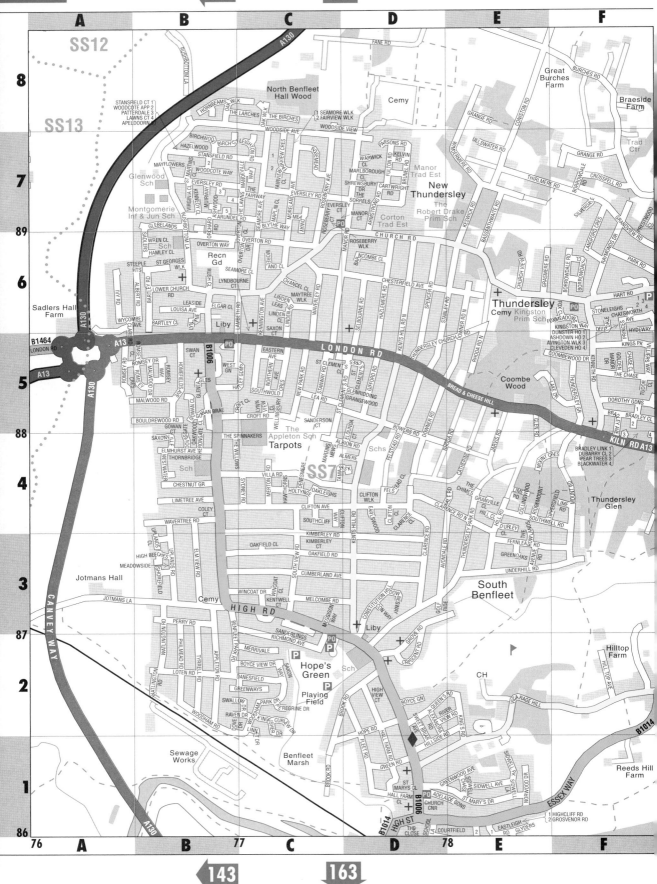

143
122

SS12

SS13

A130

FANE RD

North Benfleet
Hall Wood

Cemy

Great
Burches
Farm

BURCHES RD

Braeside
Farm

Trad
Ctr

STANSFIELD CT 1
WOODCOTE APP 2
PATTERDALE 3
LAWNS CT 4
APELDOORN 5

HORNBEAMS

THE LARCHES

THE BIRCHES

1 SEAMORE WLK
2 FAIRVIEW WLK

WOODSIDE VIEW

WOODSIDE AVE

GRANGE RD

ULLSWATER RD

GRANGE RD

BIRCHWOO

BIRCH

LEIGHTON RD

OAK WLK

PARSONS RD

CONISTON RD

HAZELWOOD

STANSFIELD RD

WOODCOTE WAY

FAIRVIEW CRES

WARWICK
CL

MARLBOROUGH

KELVIN
RD

FULTON RD

BRUNEL RD

Manor
Trad Est

WINDERMERE RD

MAYFLOWERS

EVERSLEY RD

ROSEBERRY AVE

SHREWSBURY
RD

CARTWRIGHT
RD

New
Thundersley

The
Robert Drake
Prim Sch

THIRLMERE RD

BORROWDALE

CROSSFELL RD

Glenwood
Sch

VIRGINIA CL

KENNETH CL

THE
FAIRWAY

MURRAY

THE LAWNS

MAPLIN

MORELAND

THE
SORRELS

EVERSLEY
CT

Manor
Trad Est

PO

Corton
Trad Est

KESWICK RD

CHURCH VIEW RD

GRASMERE RD

SILVERDALE

LANGFORD CL

RAYMONDS DR

GRANDVIEW RD

PRESTWOOD

PARK RD

Montgomerie
Inf & Jun Sch

ORCHARD

ARUNDEL

SEAMORE WLK

BLYTHE WAY

GLEBELANDS

OVERTON WAY

OVERTON DR

OVERTON RD

WELLING

ROSEBERRY
WLK

NCOMBE CL

CHURCH RD

BASSENTHWAITE RD

Thundersley
Cemy

Kingston
Prim Sch

HART RD

P

STONELEIGHS

CHATSWORTH

WREN CL

SADLERS

HAMLEY CL

Recn
Gd

SEAMORE CL

LYNDBOURNE
CT

CHANCEL CL

LINDEN
LEAS

CHESTERFIELD AVE

HAZLEMERE RD

SPENCER RD

STANLEY RD

THUNDERSLEY CHURCH RD

DOWNER RD N

CHURCH VIEW RD

FOXMEADOW

Kingston Way
DUNSTER HO 1
ASHDOWN HO 2
CLEVEDEN HO 3

HYDEWAY

KINGS PK

Sch

STEEPLE
HTS

IVY RD

ALBERT RD

LARCH

ST GEORGES
WLK

RUSH CL

LOWER CHURCH
RD

LEASIDE

ELGAR CL

LAMBETH RD

KENINGTON AVE

LINDEN

WAVERLEY RD

KENTS HILL RD N

RHODA RD N

GOLDEN
MANOR

KENNETH
DR

CHASE AVE

VILLIERS WAY

THE CHASE

TUDOR

Sadlers Hall
Farm

A130

WYCOMBE
AVE

BARTLEY CL

LOUISA AVE

Liby

MAYTREE
WLK

SAXON
CT

SELBOURNE RD

COOMBEWOOD DR

DOROTHY GDNS

B1464
LONDON RD

A13

A13

ROMSEY DR

ROMSEY

MALWOOD RD

HOMEFIELDS AVE

GLENA

GLES

PO

SWAN
CT

B1006

WEST
GN

EASTERN
AVE

ST CLEMENTS
CL

LONDON RD

ST CLEMENTS

GIFFORD RD

BREAD & CHEESE HILL

Coombe
Wood

THUNDERSLEY GR

GLEN RD

LAKE DR

THUNDERSLEY PARK RD

BRADLEY CL

KILN RD A13

BRADLEY LINK 1
DUBARRY CL 2
PEAR TREES 3
BLACKWATER 4

ROMSEY CRES

MALWOOD RD

BOULDREWOOD RD

GOWAN

SAXON

GOWAN BRAE

OAKWOOD

HERONGATE

NORTHERN
AVE

SOUTHWOLD

NEW PARK RD

STANWAY RD

GLENRIDDING

GRANGEWOOD

ELOUNDA

BOWERS RD

DOWNER RD

BRONIA RD

CATHERINE RD

JARVIS RD

MOUNT CRES

Thundersley
Glen

ELMHURST AVE

THORNBRIDGE

THE WILLOWS

THE SPINNAKERS

The
Appleton Sgh
Tarpots

MARTINS
MEWS

ALBION RD

Schs

FELSTEAD RD

LEAD CL

THE
CHIMES

GRANVILLE
RD

LIME
RD

COLLINGWOOD

RIDGEMONT

SOUTHWELL RD

WESTWATER

Sch

CHESTNUT GR

SWALLOW

SYDNEY RD

VILLA RD

MERTON RD

HAWTHORNS

HOLTYNGE

DENESMERE

OAKLEIGHS

SS7

TAMA

TAMA

CLIFTON
WLK

FELS

CLARENCE RD

CLARENCE
RD

HILL CL

DURLEY
CL

THE
AVENUE

FERNLEA RD

GREENOAKS

LIMETREE AVE

COLEY
CT

ELM VIEW RD

CLIFTON AVE

SOUTHCLIFF

NETFORD

KENTS HILL RD

CLIFTON

EARLSWOOD

AVONDALE RD

UNDERHILL RD

WAVERTREE RD

UPLANDS

High Beeches

THORNFIELD

KIMBERLEY RD

KIMBERLEY
CT

SOUTH VIEW RD

OAKFIELD RD

South
Benfleet

Jotmans Hall

MEADOWSIDE

UP LANDS RD

OAKFIELD CL

CUMBERLAND AVE

CONSTITUTION HILL

GOLF
RIDE

Cemy

WINCOAT DR

WINCOAT
CL

KENTWELL

MELCOMBE RD

MEADOW

MCGRISON WAY

BROOK RD

CRESCENT RD

CH

Hilltop
Farm

HIGH RD

JOTMANS LA

PERRY RD

BENFLEET PARK RD

SANDERLINGS

RICHMOND AVE

PO
P

Liby

VICARAGE HILL

HILL TOP AVE

CANVEY WAY

PHILMEAD RD

THIRELL RD

APPLETON RD

MERRIVALE

BOYCE VIEW DR

SAXON

Hope's
Green

Sch

BROOK RD

B1014

WOODHAM RD

LOTEN RD

DANESFIELD

GREENWAYS

SWALLOW

PARK RD

PEREGRINE DR

P

Playing
Field

HIGH
VIEW
CT

BOYCE GN

QUEEN'S RD

RIVER
VIEW RD

KING'S RD

RAVEN AVE

KINGS

ESSEX

CURLEW DR

LINN

DOVE

HOPE RD

FLEET RD

HALL FARM RD

GREEN RD

HILLSIDE RD

SWEET BRIAR

ALEXANDRA RD

B1014

Reeds Hill
Farm

Sewage
Works

Benfleet
Marsh

BROOK RD

ST
MARYS CL

HALL FARM RD

B1006

PO
CHURCH
CNR

ADELAIDE GDNS

GREENWOOD AVE

ST MARY'S DR

SIDWELL AVE

SIDWELL PK

NORWOOD DR

SIDWELL CHASE

ESSEX WAY

1 HIGHCLIFF RD
2 GROSVENOR RD

A130

HIGH ST

B1014

HIGH ST

THE
CLOSE

SCHOOL
LA

COURTFIELD

2

EASTLEIGH

GLYDERS

143
163

145 124

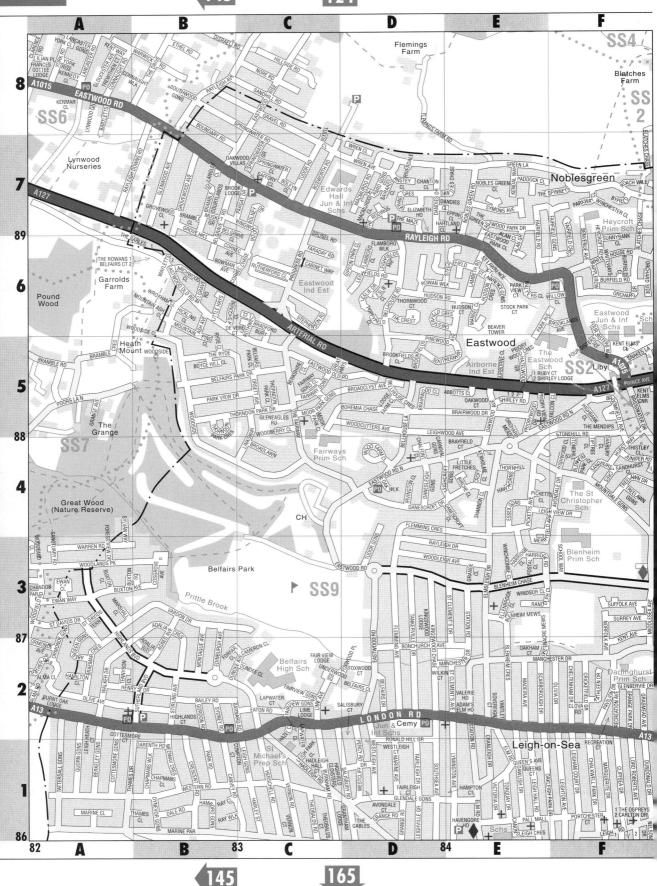

147
126

147
167

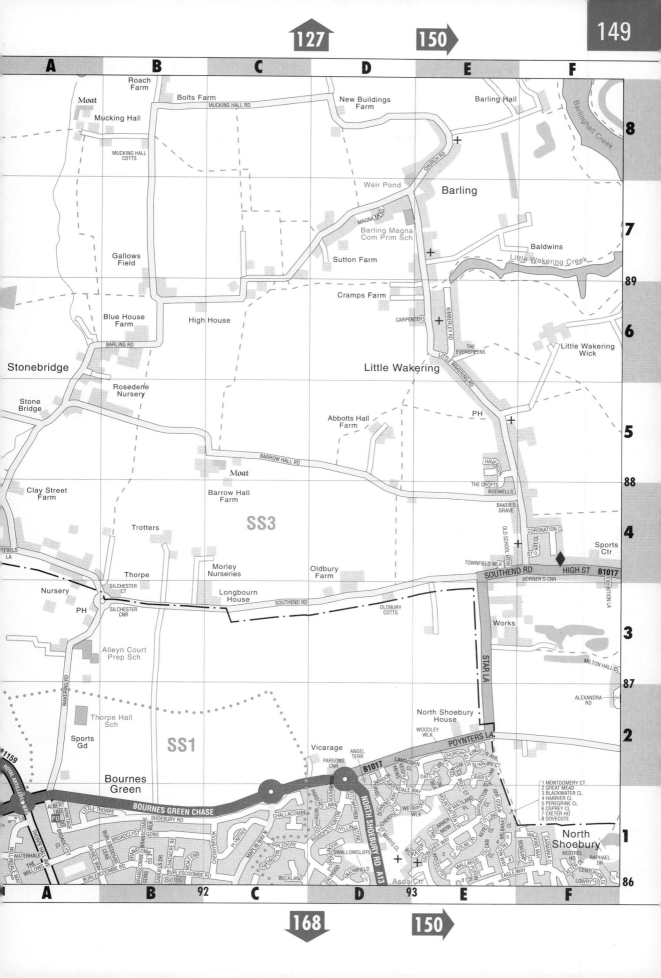

149
128

A **B** **C** **D** **E** **F**

DANGER AREA

Farm Cottages

The Middleway

Narrow Guts

8

Brimstone Hill

Fleethead Creek

Fleet Head

Swing Bridge

POTTON ISLAND

Wakering Creek

7

Rushley Island

89

Halfway House Farm

Mill Head

6

Rushley Farm

Little Wakering Hall

Millhead Cottages

Ford

Oxenham Farm

Havengore Creek

5

Millhead Villas

Sewage Works

88

Great Wakering

SS3

BRIDGE RD

LITTLE WAKERING HALL LA

4

THE MALLARDS

RUSHLEY CL

LEE LOTTS

TWYFORD AVE

MERCER AVE

CRES

ULVERS CL

NORTHFIELD

NORTH ST

CHAPEL LA

LINDSEY RD

NEWSTEAD

WHITE HALL RD

HAVERING CL

HOME FARM CL

WEDDS WAY

Great Wakering Common

LANDWICK COTTS

STAIRS RD

BROUGHAM CL

MORELAND CL

OLD HALL CT

ORCHARD CL

Liby

B1017

B1017

HIGH ST

ALP CT

BELL HO

CONWAY AVE

GOODMANS

NEW RD

GLEBE CL

MORRINS CL

SAMUEL'S CNR

PO

FAIRFIELD

Great Wakering Prim Sch

CROUCHMANS AVE

ST JOHN'S RD

1 LION FIELDS
2 SOUTHGATE MEWS
3 ST JOHN'S CL
4 THE ANCHORAGE
5 RODING CL
6 THE CEDARS

3

ALEXANDRA RD

MILTON HALL CL

SHOEBURY RD

LC

MORRIN'S CHASE

Shoeburyness New Ranges

87

Crouchmans Farm

MARINERS CT

BEACH CT

BROOMWAYS

HAVENGORE CL

SEAVIEW DR

BROOKSIDE AVE

ESTUARY GDNS

GOLDSWORTHY DR

NEW ENGLAND CRES

DANGER AREA

Crouchmans Cottage

VICTORIA DR

2

The Lansdowne

CUPIDS CHASE

Morrin's Point

POYNTERS LA

CUPID'S CNR

Black Grounds

WAKERING RD

SUTTONS RD

CHERRYTREE CHASE

1

Poynter's Point

PICASSO WAY

RAPHAEL DR

BRODIE RD

BUTTS RD

86

94 **A** **B** 95 **C** **D** 96 **E** **F**

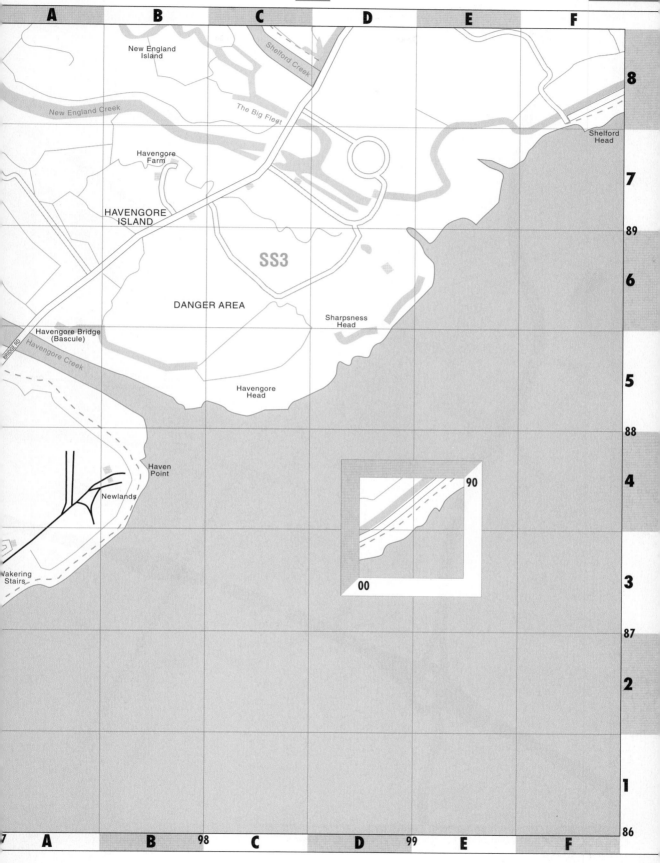

A   B   C   D   E   F

New England
Island

Shelford Creek

New England Creek

The Big Fleet

Shelford
Head

Havengore
Farm

HAVENGORE
ISLAND

SS3

DANGER AREA

Sharpsness
Head

Havengore Bridge
(Bascule)

Havengore Creek

BRIDGE RD

Havengore
Head

88

Haven
Point

Newlands

Wakering
Stairs

90

00

8

7

89

6

5

88

4

3

87

2

1

86

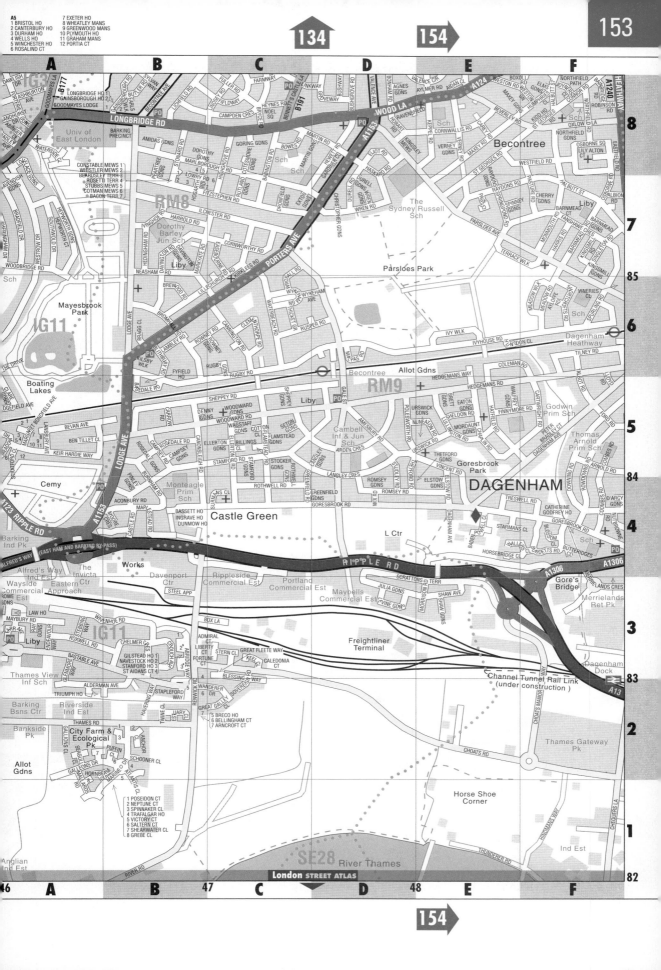

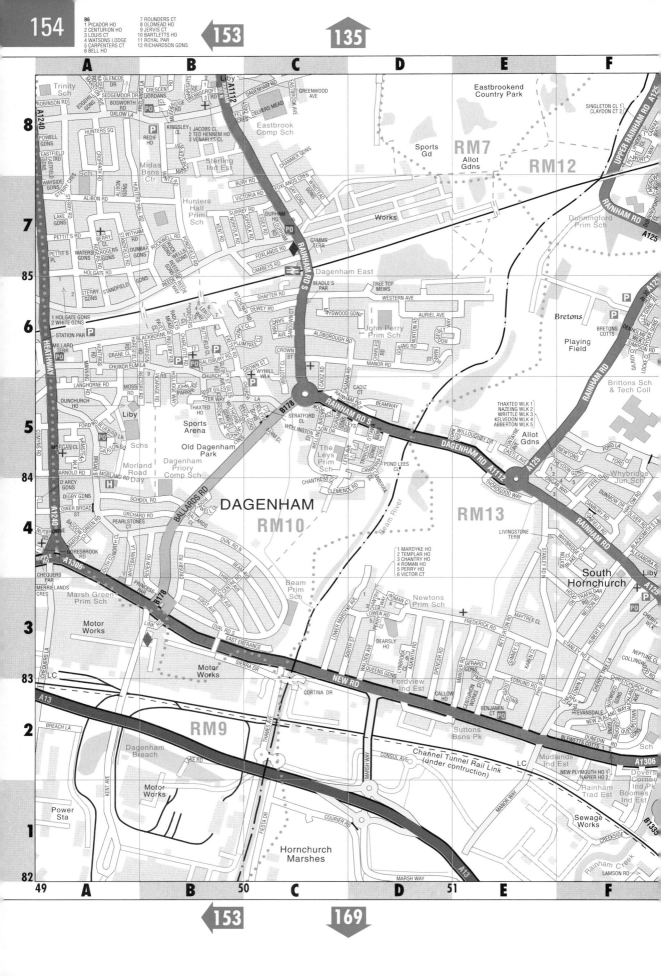

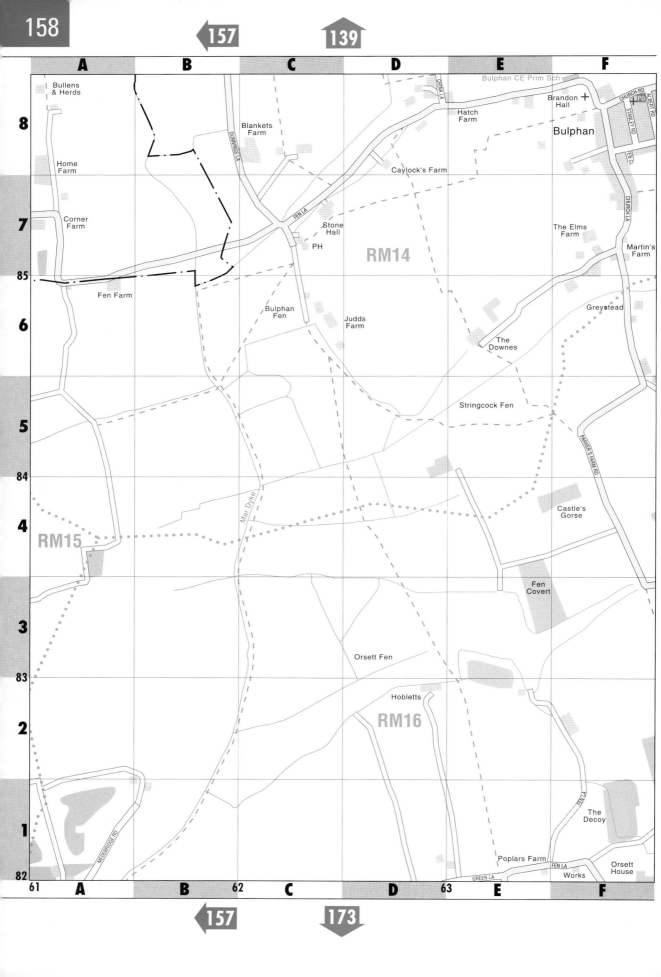

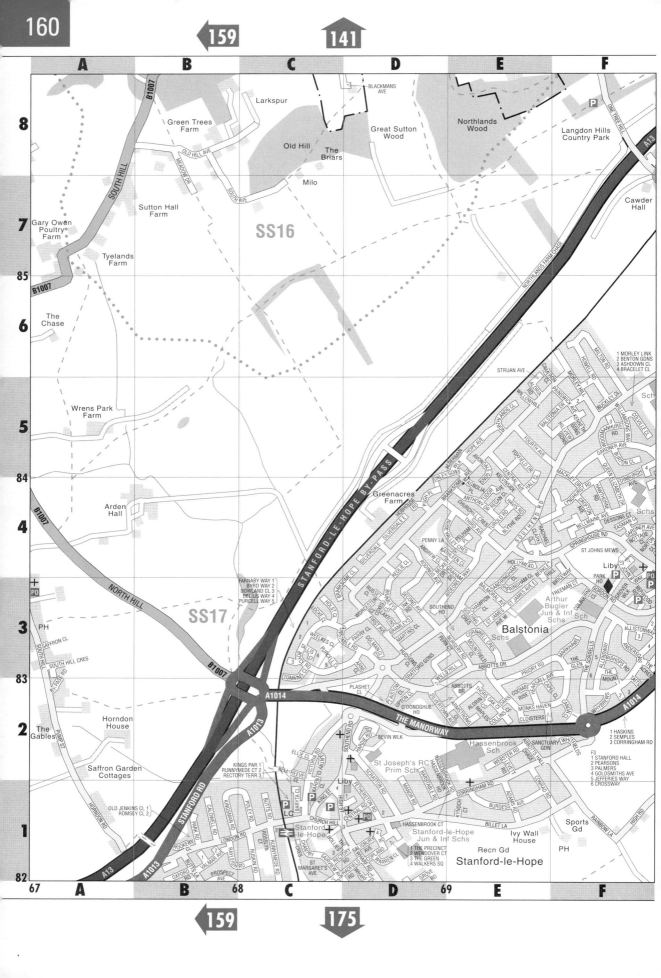

159
141

SS16

SS17

Balstonia

Stanford-le-Hope

159
175

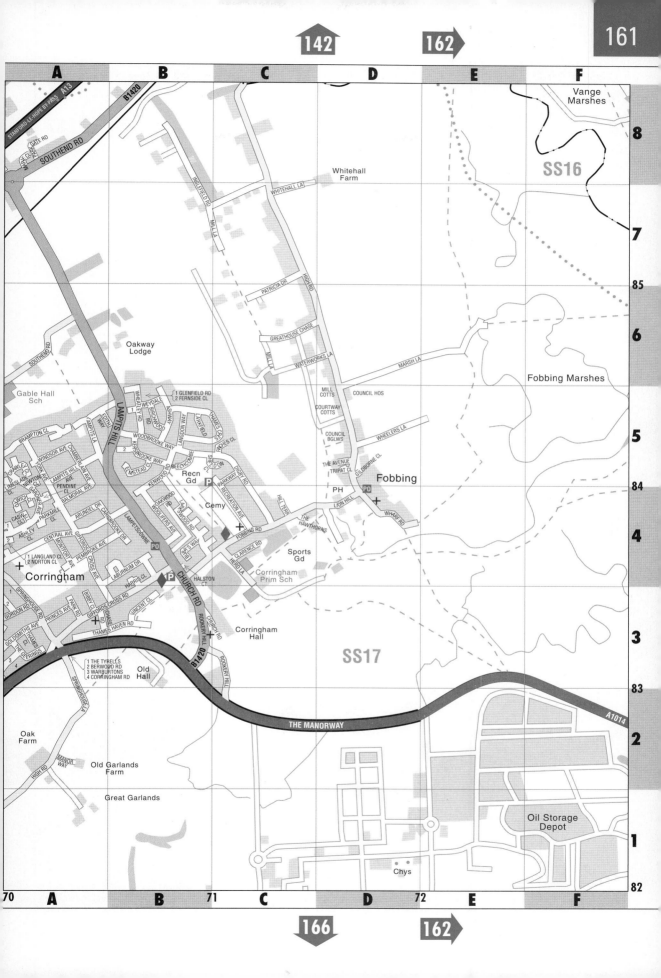

A   B   C   D   E   F

SS16

Vange
Marshes

8

Whitehall
Farm

7

85

6

Oakway
Lodge

Fobbing Marshes

Gable Hall
Sch

5

84

Recn
Gd

Cemy

Fobbing

PH   PO

4

Corringham

Sports
Gd

Corringham
Prim Sch

SS17

Corringham
Hall

3

1 THE TYRELLS
2 BERWOOD RD
3 WARBURTONS
4 CORRINGHAM RD

Old
Hall

83

THE MANORWAY

A1014

Oak
Farm

Old Garlands
Farm

2

Great Garlands

Oil Storage
Depot

1

Chys

82

70   A   B   71   C   D   72   E   F

SOUTHEND RD
A13
B1420
STANFORD-LE-HOPE BY-PASS

WHITEHALL LA
INGLEFIELD RD
MILL LA
HIGH RD

PATRICIA DR

GREATHOUSE CHASE
MILL LA
WATERWORKS LA
MARSH LA

MILL
COTTS
COURTWAY
COTTS
COUNCIL
BGLWS
COUNCIL HOS
WHEELERS LA

THE AVENUE
TRIPAT CL
GILBORNE CL

LION HILL
WHARF RD

1 GLENFIELD RD
2 FERNSIDE CL

LAMPITS HILL
WHEATLEY RD
WEYDALE
BIRCHWOOD
ASHWAY
EDITH WAY
WOODBROOKE WAY
LARKFIELD
LANGDON WAY
THAMES CRES
RICHES CL
KERSBROOKE WAY
KENWOOD RD
SHELDON
PARKWAY
DIGBY RD

BRAMPTON CL
WINDSOR AVE
CHAMBERLAIN AVE
LAMPITS LA
YORK AVE
PENDINE AVE
CHAMBERLAIN AVE
BALMORAL AVE
EMSTEAD
OAKWOOD RD
WOOLIFERS AVE
PARKS WAY
FOBBING RD
CLARENCE RD
HEIDA LA
HILL TERR
THE HAWTHORNS

FORSWELL
LIMESLADE
NEWTON
CL
CASEY CL
ASHLEY CL
PARKMILL
CENTRAL AVE
MONTFORT AVE
ARUNDEL DR
CARISBROOKE DR
LAMPETSDOWNE
GIFFORDS CROSS AVE
PEMBROOKE AVE
LABURNUM DR
HARRIS CL
HALSTON CT
VINCENT CL

1 LANGLAND CL
2 NORTON CL

SPRINGHOUSE RD
GORDON AVE
PRINCES AVE
PARK RD
BIBBY CL
GIFFORDS CROSS RD
GIFFORDS CHASE
THAMES HAVEN RD
GOLDSMITHS AVE
THAMES
THE RINGS

CHURCH RD
B1420
ROOKERY HILL

RECREATION AVE

SPRINGHOUSE LA
MANOR WAY
HIGH RD

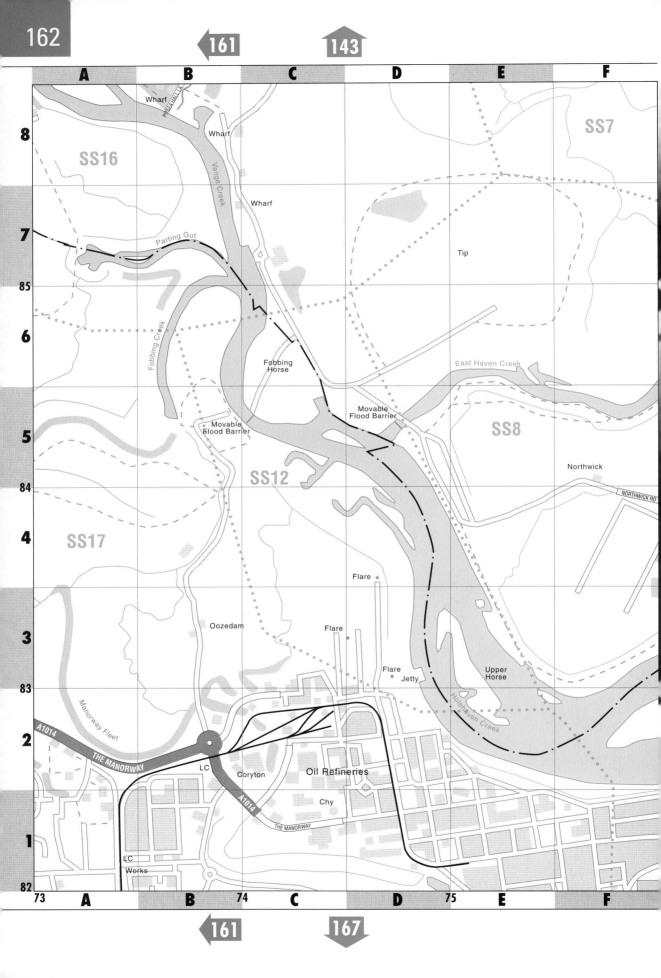

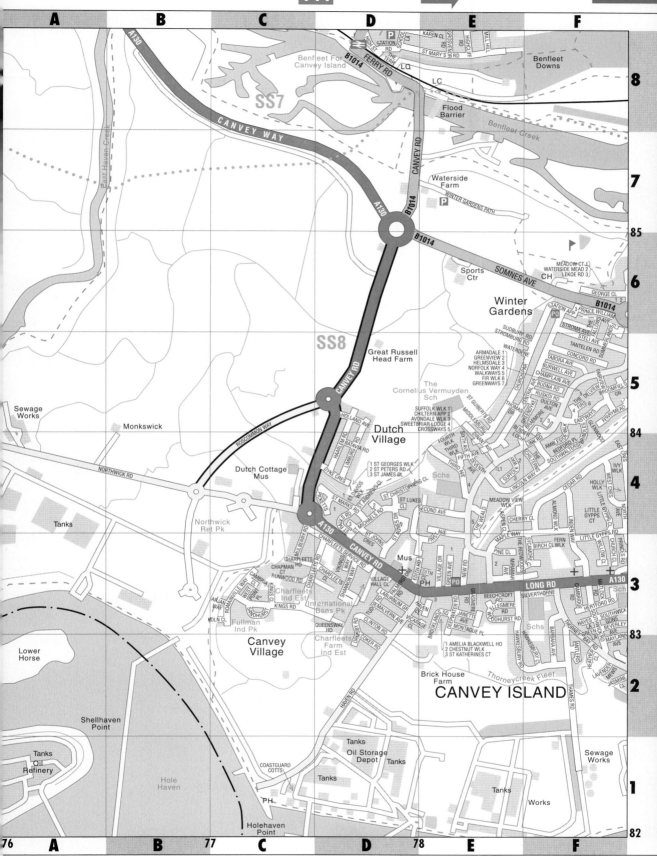

A B C D E F

8

SS7

Hadleigh
Marsh
SS9

7

Benfleet Creek

85

1 WOODBERRY CL
2 THE LEES
3 ASHWORTHS
4 ASHLEIGH CL
5 BADGERS RISE
6 ASHLEIGH CT
7 HANNAH CL
8 LEIGE AVE
9 CENTRAL WALL

Hadleigh Ray

6

ELSINOR
AVE
HARDYS
WAY

AMELAND RD

CASTLE VIEW RD
BEECROFT
CRES
HAASE RD

Castle
View
Sch

Sunken
Marsh

Tewkes Creek

10 DORSET WAY
11 CASTLE WLK
12 STAFFORD WLK

B1014 SOMNES AVE

1 CAMPERDOWN RD
2 GEESH RD
3 LINNE RD

Holmswood

Newlands

5

Sch

Schs

LAKEVIEW

LAKESIDE PATH

The Lake

CENTRAL WALL RD

GENNEP
ROAD S

LAKESIDE CRES

STRASBOURG RD
ABENSBURG RD
BERG AVE
HEESWYK RD
NEWLANDS RD
CORONA RD
HEIDEBURG RD
STANLEY RD
HINDLES RD

KELLINGTON RD

HELSINBURG RD
LANDSBURG RD
TEWKES RD
MUNSTERBURG RD

EASTFIELD RD

MILLS OWE
RAVENDALE

84

EAST CRES
DENHAM RD

TILBURG RD
SURG RD
DELFT RD
THELEN RD
METZ AVE
DELFZUL RD
LETZEN RD
URMOND RD

WAARDEN RD

PAARL RD
WAAREM AVE

Hotel
Liby

B1014
KNIGHTSWICK RD

ELDER TREE WAY

LILAC AVE

GOIRLE AVE

CREEK RD

MITCHELLS
WLK

CANVEY ISLAND

4

KINGSROAD WLK

FAIRLOP AVE
RODERICK AVE
PENNIAL RD

ROLAND LA
MERLIN CT

Sch

KNIGHTSWICK
CTR

P0

RAINBOW

GILS AVE

BARNARDS
AVE

HIGH ST

1 ROSBERG RD
2 BARNEVELD AVE

SMALLGAINS AVE
GEYLEN RD
LIMETREE RD
WAMBURG RD

Smallgains Creek

3

A130
JONES
CNR
Sch

TILBURG RD
DALEN AVE
DOLLANT
AVE
BREWSTER CL

BULOW AVE

LONG RD

LARUP GDNS 1
MORNINGTON CRES 2
AYLETT CL 3
KEEGAN PL 4
HOLMES CT 5

B1014

SS8

P0

POINT RD

B1014

Mus

82

79 A B 80 C D 81 E F

A3
1 FRED LEACH HO
2 FLORENCE NEALE HO
3 SUSAN FIELDER COTTS
4 CLAIRE JAMES COTTS
5 REMBRANDT CL
6 THAMESIDE CRES

Deadman's
Point

Thorney Bay
Camp

Thorneycreek Fleet

Thorney Bay

THE ANCHORAGE 1
CHERRY CT 2
ST JAMES CT 3
ELM HO 4
THAMES CT 5
KENT VIEW CT 6

River Thames

Leigh
Beck

1 KOLBURG RD
2 MAYFLOWER CT
3 MAURICE CT
4 BRUSSUM R
5 HAARLE RD

A B C D E F

SS9

BELTON WAY W
CASTLE DR

Belton Hills

Belton Gardens

MARINE PAR

BELTON WAY E
BELTON GDNS

SANS SOUCI 1
LEIGH PARK CT 2

ST CLEMENT'S CT

HADLEIGH CT

LAURO

NEW RD

RECTORY GR
ST
Schs

BROADWAY W

PO
NORTH ST
WEST ST

ELM RD
EAST ST

ALEXANDRA RD
SEA REACH

MAPLE AVE
VICTOR DR

HIGH CLIFF DR
SOMERVILLE GDNS

Playing
Field

Leigh-on-Sea

COCKLE SHEDS

BELTON
BRIDGE

HIGH ST

ALLEY DOCK

LEIGH PARK RD
UTTOLISE

Liby

LEIGH
HO
6 4
5

CHURCH HILL
LEIGH HILL
CL
CL

SEAVIEW RD

VICTORIA RD

AVENUE RD

BROADWAY

ASHLEIGH DR
REDCLIFF DR

GRAND DR

QUEENS RD

CLIFF PAR

LEIGHCLIFF RD

HAMPTON CT

WOODFIELD RD

8

P

P

P

P

P

P

Mus

LEIGH
THE
GARDENS

Leigh Cliffs

QUEENS
CT

GRAND PAR
REGATTA
CT
UNDERCLIFF GDNS

Leigh Creek

Sewage
Works

Leigh Marsh

Two Tree Island
Nature Reserve

SOUTHEND-ON-SEA

1 BARYTA CT
2 THE TERRACE
3 PLEASANT TERR
4 NORMAN PL
5 NORMAN TERR
6 HILLSIDE RD

ESTUARY CT 1
RICHMOND CT 2
GRAND COURT W 3
SOUTHDOWN CT 4

85

7

6

Slipway

P

Hadleigh Ray

5

84

Oyster Creek

SS8

Canvey Point

4

Smallgains Creek

SILVERPOINT MARINE
POINT RD
BOMMEL RD
BEVELAND RD
CHAPMAN RD
MARINE PAR

Leighbeck
Point

3

83

2

1

82

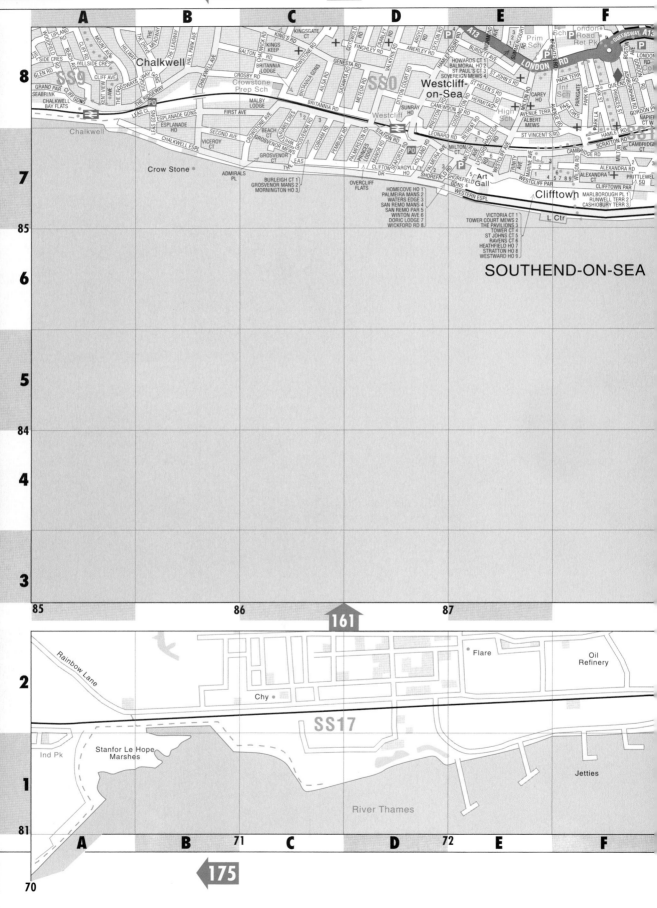

165
147
161
175

Chalkwell

SS9

Crowstone
Prep Sch

Westcliff-
on-Sea

SSO

Westcliff

Clifftown

SOUTHEND-ON-SEA

Crow Stone

ADMIRALS
PL

BURLEIGH CT 1
GROSVENOR MANS 2
MORNINGTON HO 3

OVERCLIFF
FLATS

HOMECOVE HO 1
PALMEIRA MANS 2
WATERS EDGE 3
SAN REMO MANS 4
SAN REMO PAR 5
WINTON AVE 6
DORIC LODGE 7
WICKFORD RD 8

Art
Gall

WESTERN ESPL

MARLBOROUGH PL 1
RUNWELL TERR 2
CASHIOBURY TERR 3

L Ctr

VICTORIA CT 1
TOWER COURT MEWS 2
THE PAVILIONS 3
TOWER CT 4
ST JOHNS CT 5
RAVENS CT 6
HEATHFIELD HO 7
STRATTON HO 8
WESTWARD HO 9

Rainbow Lane

Flare

Oil
Refinery

Chy

SS17

Ind Pk

Stanfor Le Hope
Marshes

Jetties

River Thames

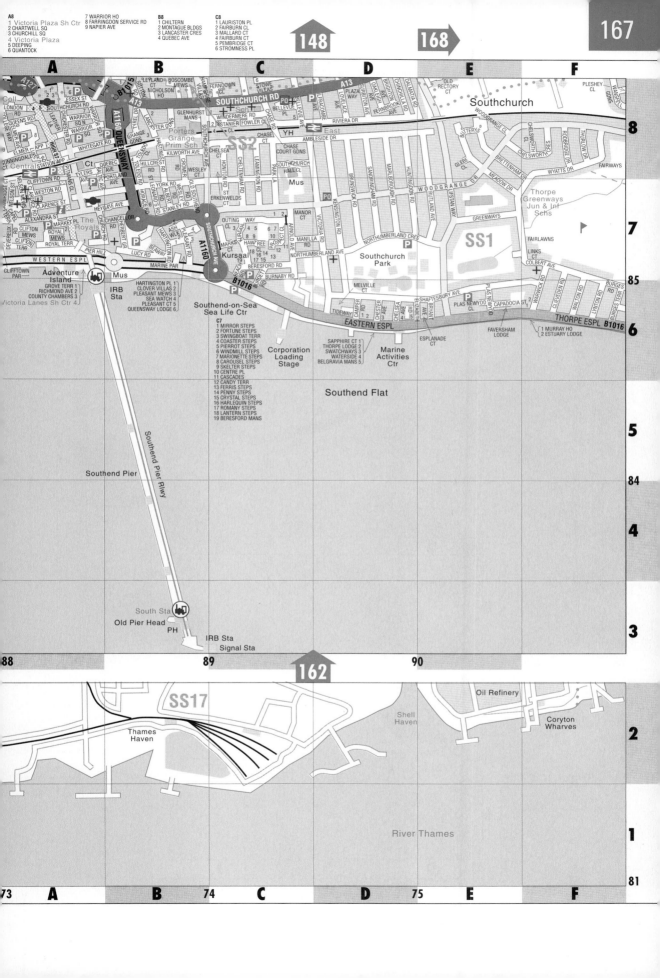

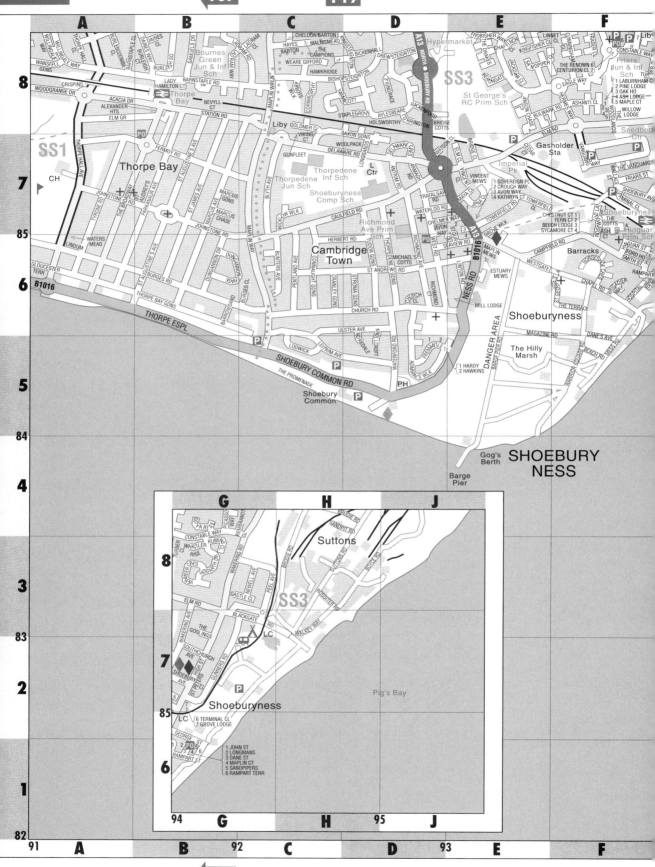

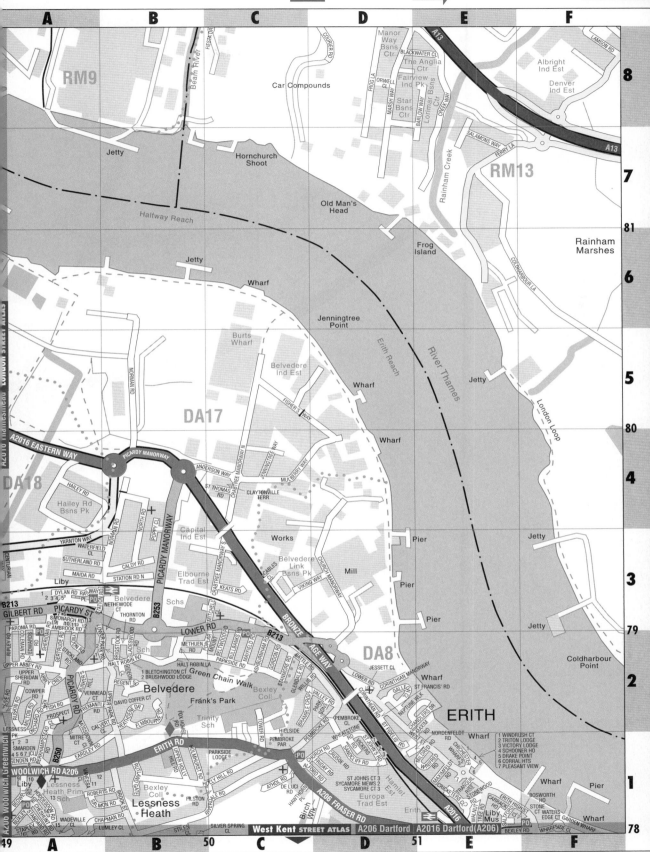

A1
1 STEVANNE CT
2 TOLCAIRN CT
3 CHALFONT CT
4 ALONSO HO
5 ARIEL CT
6 MIRANDA HO
7 PROSPERO HO
8 THE LAURELS
9 WINCHESTER CT

10 CAMDEN CT
11 NEWNHAM LODGE
12 COURT LODGE
13 FLAXMAN CT
14 HERTFORD WLK
15 RIVERVIEW CT
16 LESSNESS RD
A3
1 CRESSINGHAM CT
2 TELFORD HO

3 KELVIN HO
4 FARADAY HO
5 JENNER HO
6 KEIR HARDY HO
7 LENNOX HO
8 MARY MACARTHUR HO
9 ELIZABETH GARRETT ANDERSON HO
10 WILLIAM SMITH HO
11 BADEN POWELL HO
12 BAIRD HO

13 BOYLE HO

8

81

7

6

5

80

4

79

3

2

1

78

FERRY LA
LC
LAMSON RD
BUCKLEYS YD
P
PALLISER DR
WILFRED AVE
ELLIS AVE
FINDON GDNS
LINETTE CT
WANTZ LA
LAMBS LANE S
B1335
INGREBOURNE
DERI AVE
BROOKWAY
ELIZABETH RD
PENERLEY RD
BEECHWOOD GDNS
HUNTLAND CL
ROTHBURY GDNS
EASTWOOD DR
SOUTH HALL DR
SOUTH HALL
RIVER CL
THAMES CL
MANSTEAD GDNS

The Chafford Sch

Brady Prim Sch

South Hall Farm

Southall Bridge

East Hall Farm

New Cotts

A1306

LAUNDERS LA

NEW RD

East Hall La

CHURCH LA
CHURCH LANE COTTS

Wennington Hall Farm

The Willows

Rainham Marshes

RM13

Silt Lagoons

WENNINGTON RD

Channel Tunnel Rail Link (under construction)

A13

LAUNDRY COTTS
MARINE COTTS
KENT VIEW
THE GREEN

Wennington

B1335

PH

B1335
SANDY LA

A1306
A13

Wennington Marshes

COLDHARBOUR LA

JULIETTE WAY
Purfleet Ind Pk
LONDON RD
Thurrock Commercial Ctr
KERRY AVE
JULIETTE WAY

RM15

Aveley Marshes

Purfleet Rifle Ranges

Freightmaster Est

RM19

River Thames

MARINE CT
MARINE DR
RAPIER CL
CENTURION WAY
RIVER CT
LAMB CL RD

Crayford Ness

TANK HILL RD
LONDON ROAD PURFLEET
Hotel

Erith Rands

DA8
Darent Ind Pk
LANDAU WAY
BURNETT RD
DAYTON DR

A   B   C   D   E   F

8

Bretts
Farm

PH

Oak Wood

M25

Long Pond

Ash
Plantation

ERRIFF DR

HAMBLE LA

IRVINE GDNS

HUMBER AVE

LOMAN PATH

Moor
Hall

ROMFORD RD

RAVEL
GDNS

SEVERN RD

RAVEL RD

USK RD

7

Dilkes
Prim
Sch

GALVERN
PATH

NORTH HILL DR

GARRON LA

Belhus Park

CH

GATEHOPE DR

FRANCES
GDNS

TEESDALE WAY

P.O.

Kenningtons
Prim Sch

TEVIOT AVE

TAMAR DR

PINFOLDS
WAYMANS
MERESMANS
HAYWARDS
FRANKLINS

SWALE CL

81

GROVES
CL

FIELDOR DR

FULBROOK

SHANNON WAY

WARE RD

PERRY
WAY

MONNOW
CH

GDNS

NETHAN DR

The
Aveley
Sch

Park La

Sports
Gd

B1335

6

SANDY LA

ST PAUL
ST PL

MILL RD

AVELEY BY-PASS

RM15

STIFFORD RD

Hangman's
Wood

Sandy
Lane
Farm

Aveley

MONNOW GN

ST PAUL'S
ST PAUL'S

ST MICHAELS

IRON RD

BUCHANAN
CL

MARTIN RD

PARK
VIEW

Park La

BROOME PL
COMPLEX

STANFORD CT

STIFFORD RD

5

Ponds
Farm

PURFLEET RD

TOPLANDS AVE

GRANGE RD

BLENHEIM GDNS

HANFORD RD

ALFRED
RD

Liby

ELM RD

DACRE AVE

HESTER CL

CRESCENT WAY

DACRE CRES

HIGH ST

BROOME PL

BLOWS
COTTS

P.O.

AVELEY CL

LENNARD ROW

Aveley
Prim Sch

A13

80

MANOR CT S

THE
ROWANS

LOWLAN

MANOR CL

MANNING CL

FIELD RD

P
THE SYCAMORES

NEW
MALTINGS

30

4

Sports
Gd

LONDON RD

Thurrock
Management
Ctr

ARNHEM AVE

BEECH

EASTERN AVE

HALL AVE

CHURCH VIEW

Oak
Wood

MYRTLE GR

CRESCENT
RD

LOVE LA

CENTRAL AVE

HALL TERR

SHIP LA

KENT VIEW

HALL CRES

1 2 3

HALL RD

CRESCENT WLK

BEVIN HO 1
THE PARADE 2
LEEHOLM HO 3

Thurrock
Service
Area

i

3

Fann's
Farm

LC

A1090

THE CARAVAN SITE

Causeway
Bridge

A1306

ARTERIAL ROAD (WEST

(THURROCK)

WEST THURROCK WAY

79

Mar Dyke

SOUTH WAY

BACK LA

31

B186

TANK HILL RD

WATER LA

FANS RISE

CORNWALL
GATE

Watt's Wood

CARTEL CL

Broomhill

A1306

STONEHOUSE LA

A1090

WESTON AVE

2

MARKET WAY

MALFORDS

HAMLEY
TERR

ST CLEMENTS

CORNWALL
MEWS

ARTERIAL ROAD PURFLEET

THE QUADRANT

WATTS CRES

WOOD AVE

SOUTH GATE CRES

NORTH RD

BACON
CL

BRUNFIELD RD

GABION
RD

ARMOR RD

BAILEY CL

VEXIL CL

A1090

A282

Tunnel
Est

RM20

Tunnel
Est

CENTRAL AVE

BARCLAY WAY

EUCLID WAY

Purfleet
Prim Sch

TANK LA

1 CRUSADER CL
2 GARRISON PAR

Purfleet

HIGH ST

BOTANY WAY

Channel Tunnel Rail Link
(under construction)

PURFLEET BY-PASS

RM19

DOLPHIN WAY

JODRELL WAY

HUDSON CL

BEACON HILL
IND EST

Beacon Hill

Purfleet

Beacon Hill

CON HILL

OAKHILL RD

LINNET WAY

18 19 20
15
16 17

Dolphin
Mtorway
Est

JOSLIN RD

High House

A1090

EASTERN AVE

The
Glade
Bsns Ctr

ARRISONS
WHARF

LONDON ROAD PURFLEET

LC

Jetty

BOTANY
COTTS

A1090

1

78

B1
1 RIVERVIEW TERR
2 SUSSEX TERR
3 SOUTHLAND TERR
4 DUNCOMBE CT
5 HEBERDEN CT
6 WINGROVE DR
7 HOWBURGH CT
8 TRAYFORD CT
9 STORAS CT

10 SAWSTON CT
11 KYRKLY CT
12 BRADFIELD CT
13 RIVERVIEW FLATS
14 WROXALL CT
15 ROOKLEY CT
16 DUNNOSE CT
17 BRANSTONE CT
18 SHORWELL CT
19 BRIGHSTONE CT

20 BONCHURCH CT

A13 STANFORD RD A1013

Singlewell

Mayland

St Cleres Hall

CH

St Clere's Comp Sch

Cemy

The Grove

King Edward's Rd

Sewage Works

Thames Haven Junction

The Warren

Mucking

Stanford Marshes

Bluehouse Farm

LC

MUCKING WHARF RD

SS17

Sluice

Mucking Creek

Golden Cottages

WALTON'S HALL RD

Mucking Marshes

Travelling Crane

Jetty

Walton Hall Farm Mus

Walton's Hall

Turner's Farm

Sutton's Farm

Linford

HAMPSHIRE GDNS

PH

RM18

Sewage Works

East Tilbury

Alexandra Way

Coronation Ave

River Thames

East Tilbury Prim Sch

Thames Ind Pk

PO

Liby

East Tilbury

East Tilbury Marshes

Sand & Gravel Pit

B1
1 DONNINGTON CT
2 DENNY CT
3 BROUGHAM CT
4 BEESTON CT
5 ORFORD CT
6 ALNWICK CT
7 BRAMBER CT
8 KENILWORTH CT
9 WARDOUR CT
10 BERWICK CT
11 STOKESAY CT
12 CONISBOROUGH CT
13 PICKERING CT
14 MIDDLEHAM CT
15 PRUDHOE CT
16 NORHAN CT
17 BOWES CT
18 BARNARD CT
19 TATTERSHALL CT
20 CARISBROOKE CT
21 LONGTOWN CT
22 CLIFTON WLK
23 CALSHOT CT
24 DUNSTER CT
25 LYDFORD CT
26 PEVERIL CT
27 HARDWICK CRES
28 GRANGE CRES

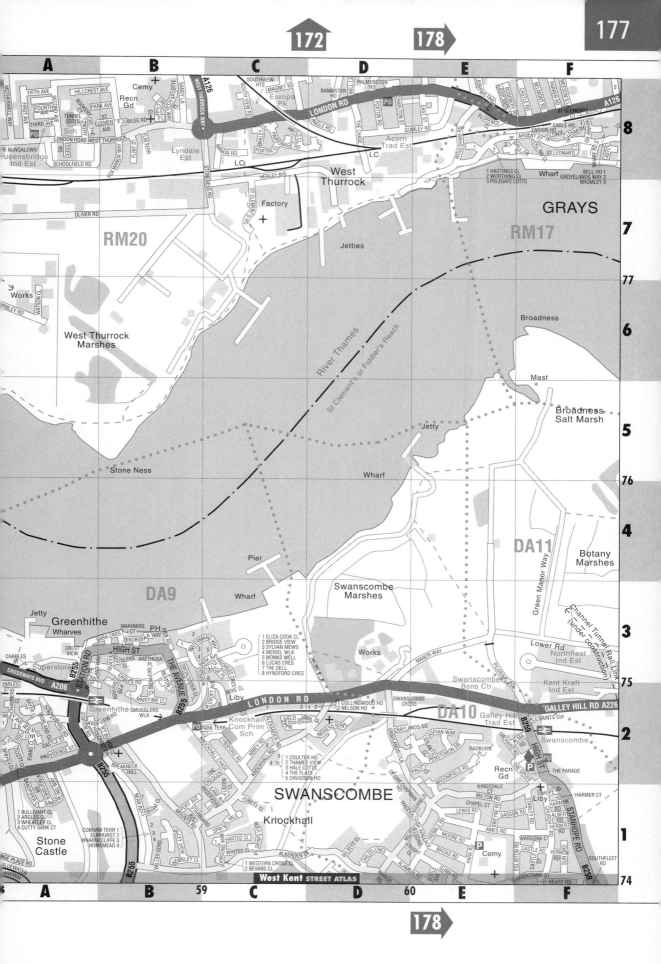

A B C D E F

MOTHERWELL WAY
FIFTH AVE
FIRST AVE
SECOND AVE
FOURTH AVE
THIRD AVE
TUNNEL COTTS
PO
Sch
HILLCREST AVE
ROWERY
PARK AVE
CREDON WAY
CHARLOTTE CL
Cemy
Recn Gd
JUBILEE CT
ST CLEMENT'S AVE
LONDON ROAD WEST THURROCK
ESSEX
SCHOOLFIELD RD
The Bungalows
Queensbridge Ind Est
FOX MANOR WAY
ELM TERR
FLINT ST
Lyndale Est
MANOR RD
STONENESS RD
WEST THURROCK WAY
SANDY LA
SOUTH VIEW RD
SOUTHVIEW HTS
MAGNET RD
Europa Pk
ANGLE RD
OAKLEY CL
HAYS CL
PARSONAGE RD
PORTER AVE
HEDLEY AVE
LC
BANNISTER HO
CHARLTON ST
FOXTON RD
THE CHASE
EAST ST
PALMERSTON RD
PO
GUMLEY RD
Acorn Trad Est
LC
West Thurrock
Factory
WOUDHAM RD
FLORENCE CL
ASKEW'S FLD
ROSEBERY RD
GRAYLANDS
CASTLE RD
BELMONT RD
PARKER RD
MEESON'S CL
ST CLEMENTS
ENSIGN HO
ARGENT ST
BELL HILL RD
EAGLE HO
CALDALE
GRIMSBY
ST LEONARD
1 HASTINGS CL
2 WORTHING CL
3 POLEGATE COTTS
Wharf
GROVELANDS WAY
WHARF RD
BELL HO 1
BROMLEY 3
GRAYS

Oliver Rd

RM20

West Thurrock Marshes

WATSON CL
Works
BRINLEY RD

RM17

77

Broadness

6

River Thames

St Clement's or Fiddler's Reach

Mast

Broadness Salt Marsh

Jetties

Jetty

5

76

Stone Ness

Wharf

4

DA11

Botany Marshes

Pier

DA9

Swanscombe Marshes

Green Manor Way

Channel Tunnel Rail Link (under construction)

3

Jetty
Greenhithe
Wharves
MARINERS CT
SARA CRES
CREST VIEW
FROBISHER
PH
PIER RD
R WAY
HIGH ST
ARETHUSA CT
QUAY LA
FIDDLERS CL
SKIPPERS CL
WATERMANS WAY
PARK AVE
PRINCESS RD
JONES CL
Works
Lower Rd
Northfleet Ind Est

CHARLES ST
CROSSWAYS BLVD
Superstore
A206
STATION RD
B255
The Avenue
WORCESTER CL
BEADY CL
MARITIME CL
ADMIRAL'S WALK
EAGLES RD
1 ELIZA COOK CL
2 BRIDGE VIEW
3 SYLVAN MEWS
4 MERIEL WLK
5 MONKS WELL
6 LUCAS CRES
7 THE DELL
8 HYNDFORD CRES
MANOR WAY
PILGRIMS RD
Swanscombe Bsns Ctr
Kent Kraft Ind Est
75

CHARLES ST
Greenhithe
RIVER VIEW RD
Smugglers WLK
Liby
PO
PARK TERR
KNOCKHALL CHASE
ALEXANDER RD
Knockhall Com Prim Sch
NGRES GDNS
LONDON RD
1 2 1 2
1 COLLINGWOOD HO
2 NELSON HO
Swanscombe Cross
DA10
Galley Hill Trad Est
GALLEY HILL RD A226
ALL SAINTS CL
B259
Swanscombe
2

WINDSOR RD
FIELD RD
DIAL CL
ABBEY RD
1 COULTER HO
2 THAMES VIEW
3 HALE COTTS
4 THE FLATS
5 DAVIDSON HO
CRAYLANDS SQ
PLANTATION RD
PENSTEMON DR
CASPIAN WAY
PACIFIC
RADBURN PL
ORCHARD RD
ALMA RD
HIGH ST
PO
P
Recn Gd
THE PARADE

Stone Castle
1 BULLIVANT CL
2 ARGLES CL
3 WHEATLEY CL
4 CUTTY SARK CT
BREAKNECK HILL
COBHAM TERR 1
ELMHURST 2
WHARNECLIFFE 3
HOMEMEAD 4
BEAN RD
COBHAM CL
SPORT AVE
STARBOARD AVE
JUBILEE CL
SPRINGS VALE
SWANSCOMBE
Knockhall
BROOMFIELD RD
DE LORE CHAPMAN RD
MAYFIELD RD
LEWIS RD
GASSON RD
MILTON RD
CHAPEL CT
KINGSDALE
Liby
HOPE RD
HARMER CT
ALBERT RD
STANLEY RD
HERBERT RD
1

VALLEY GDNS
KEMSLEY CL
SALEY VIEW
MOUNT RD
WHITES CL
HASTED CL
ALKERDEN LA
1 WESTERN CROSS CL
2 BEVANS CL
CHILDS CRES
GILBERT RD
ALAMEIN RD
MILTON RD
WALLACE RD
TREBLE RD
MOORE RD
BROAD RD
BODLE AVE
BUNN RD
PARK RD
P
Cemy
KINGSDALE
WARDONA CT
CASTLE RD
VERNON RD
EGLINTON RD
STANHOPE RD
SOUTHFLEET RD
B259
KEARY RD

A 59 B C D 60 E F

74

8 7 6 5 4 3 2 1

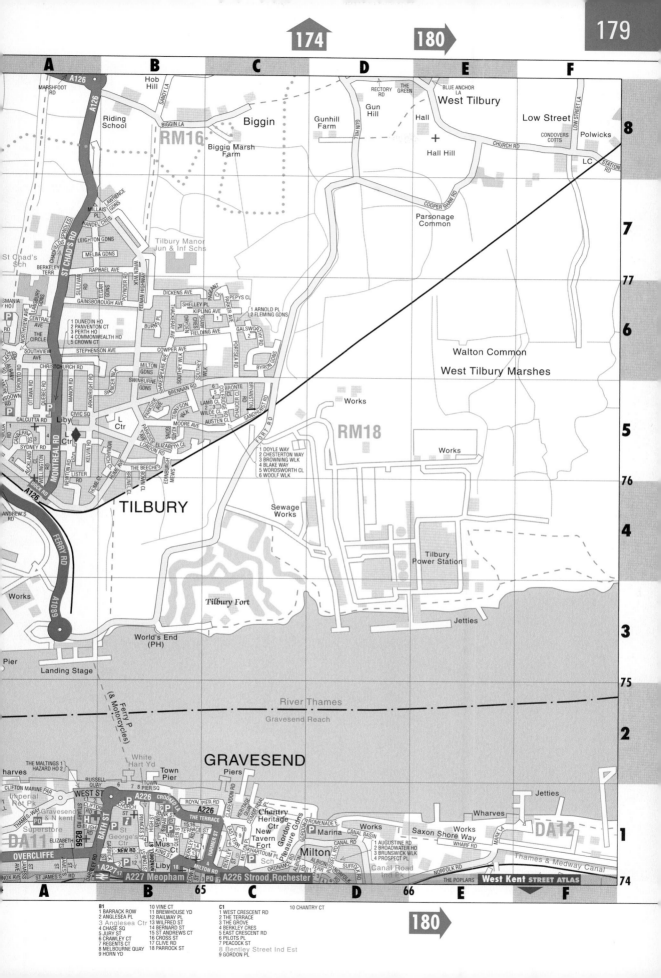

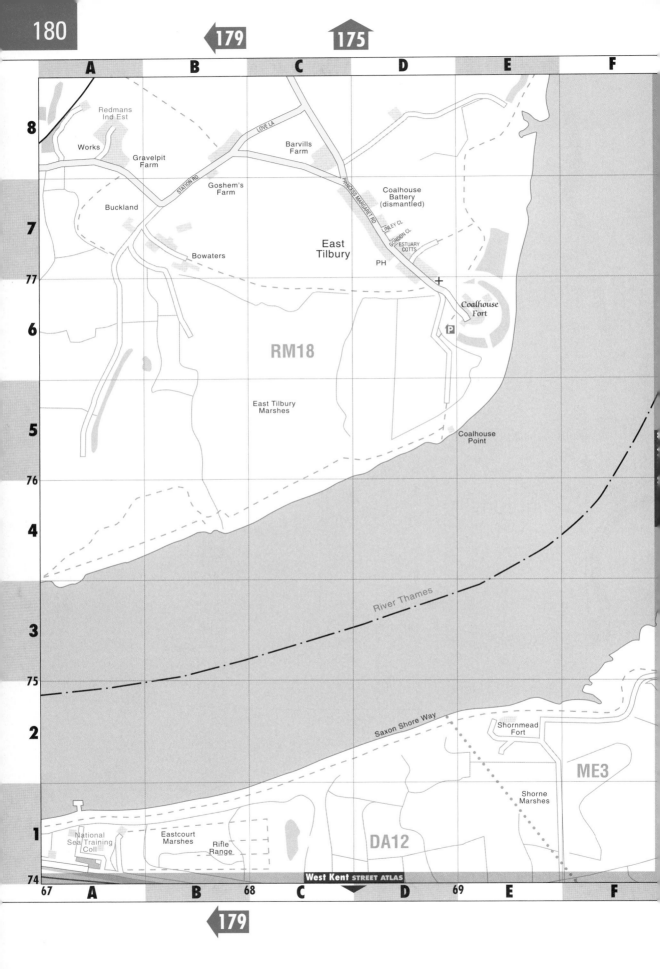

A   B   C   D   E   F

8

Redmans
Ind Est

LOVE LA

Barvills
Farm

Works

Gravelpit
Farm

Goshem's
Farm

STATION RD

PRINCESS MARGARET RD

Coalhouse
Battery
(dismantled)

7

Buckland

East
Tilbury

LINLEY CL

GORDON CL

ESTUARY
COTTS

Bowaters

PH

77

Coalhouse
Fort

6

P

RM18

East Tilbury
Marshes

Coalhouse
Point

5

76

4

River Thames

3

75

Saxon Shore Way

Shornmead
Fort

2

ME3

Shorne
Marshes

National
Sea Training
Coll

Eastcourt
Marshes

Rifle
Range

DA12

1

74

West Kent STREET ATLAS

67   A   B   68   C   D   69   E   F

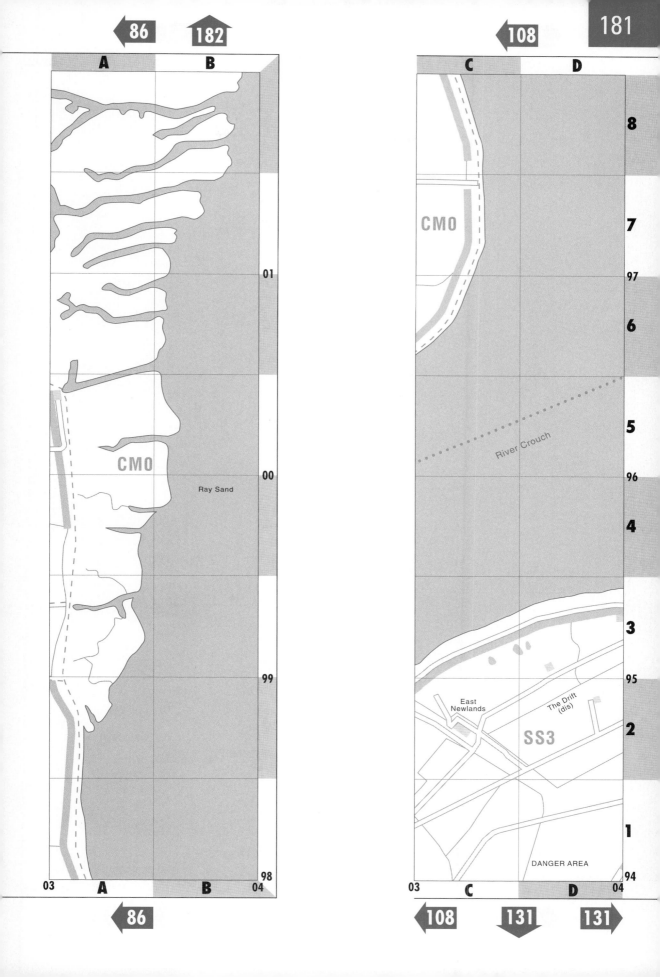

A   B

C   D

8

CMO

7

97

01

6

00

5

CMO

River Crouch

Ray Sand

96

4

3

95

East
Newlands

The Drift
(dis)

99

SS3

2

1

DANGER AREA

98

03   A   B   04

03   C   D   04

94

Sales Point

Tip Head

St Peter's Flat

Community Settlement

St Peter's Chapel

St Peter's Flat Nature Reserve

Gunner's Creek

CMO

St Peter's Way

St Peter's Way

Dengie Flat

Marshhouse Outfall

CMO

Church Rd 6 Beckenham BR2..........**53** C6

Place name	Location number	Locality, town or village	Postcode district	Page and grid square
May be abbreviated on the map	Present when a number indicates the place's position in a crowded area of mapping	Shown when more than one place has the same name	District for the indexed place	Page number and grid reference for the standard mapping

Public and commercial buildings are highlighted in magenta   **Places of interest** are highlighted in blue with a star★

Abbreviations used in the index

Acad	**Academy**	Comm	**Common**	Gd	**Ground**
App	**Approach**	Cott	**Cottage**	Gdn	**Garden**
Arc	**Arcade**	Cres	**Crescent**	Gn	**Green**
Ave	**Avenue**	Cswy	**Causeway**	Gr	**Grove**
Bglw	**Bungalow**	Ct	**Court**	H	**Hall**
Bldg	**Building**	Ctr	**Centre**	Ho	**House**
Bsns, Bus	**Business**	Ctry	**Country**	Hospl	**Hospital**
Bvd	**Boulevard**	Cty	**County**	HQ	**Headquarters**
Cath	**Cathedral**	Dr	**Drive**	Hts	**Heights**
Cir	**Circus**	Dro	**Drove**	Ind	**Industrial**
Cl	**Close**	Ed	**Education**	Inst	**Institute**
Cnr	**Corner**	Emb	**Embankment**	Int	**International**
Coll	**College**	Est	**Estate**	Intc	**Interchange**
Com	**Community**	Ex	**Exhibition**	Junc	**Junction**

L	**Leisure**	Prom	**Prom**
La	**Lane**	Rd	**Road**
Liby	**Library**	Recn	**Recreation**
Mdw	**Meadow**	Ret	**Retail**
Meml	**Memorial**	Sh	**Shopping**
Mkt	**Market**	Sq	**Square**
Mus	**Museum**	St	**Street**
Orch	**Orchard**	Sta	**Station**
Pal	**Palace**	Terr	**Terrace**
Par	**Parade**	TH	**Town Hall**
Pas	**Passage**	Univ	**University**
Pk	**Park**	Wk, Wlk	**Walk**
Pl	**Place**	Wr	**Water**
Prec	**Precinct**	Yd	**Yard**

Index of localities, towns and villages

Abbess Roding 14 E4
Abridge 90 A6
Althorne 83 A3
Asheldham 85 A7
Aveley 171 C6
Aythorpe Roding 5 B3
Barking 152 D5
Barling 149 E7
Basildon 142 C4
Battlesbridge 100 D1
Beauchamp Roding ...15 A1
Belvedere 169 B2
Bicknacre 56 F2
Billericay 97 B1
Blackmore 72 F8
Boreham 33 E8
Bradwell-on-Sea 42 B2
Bradwell Waterside ...41 F4
Brentwood 116 E8
Broomfield 19 B2
Buckhurst Hill 110 C8
Bulphan 158 F8
Burnham-on-Crouch ..106 D6
Canewdon 104 E1
Canvey Island 164 E4
Chadwell St Mary ...174 B1
Chelmsford 32 C4
Chigwell 111 B8
Chingford 87 E1
Chipping Ongar 48 F4
Cock Clarks 57 F2
Cold Norton 80 E6
Coopersale 46 C2
Corringham 161 A4
Dagenham 154 C4
Danbury 56 D7
Dartford 176 B2

Dengie 63 D1
Doddinghurst 72 B3
Downham 98 F4
East Hanningfield ...78 B7
East Tilbury 175 C1
Eastwick 10 A4
Edney Common 52 D5
Epping 46 A3
Epping Green 45 A7
Erith 169 E2
Fobbing 161 D5
Foulness Island 130 C5
Fyfield 27 D2
Galleywood 54 D2
Gilston 10 E5
Goldhanger 38 F5
Gravesend 179 C2
Grays 178 A7
Great Baddow 54 E4
Great Wakering 150 A4
Great Waltham 18 E7
Great Warley 116 A2
Greenhithe 177 A3
Hadleigh 145 E3
Harlow 11 C2
Hastingwood 24 F4
Hatfield Broad Oak ...3 F5
Hatfield Heath 3 B3
Havering-atte-Bower .113 E7
Hawkwell 125 A4
Heybridge 37 B6
Heybridge Basin 37 D3
High Beach 88 B8
High Easter 6 C2
High Ongar 49 D3
High Roding 5 F7
High Wych 1 B1

Hockley 124 E6
Hoddesdon 21 C7
Holdbrook 65 A5
Hook End 72 C4
Hornchurch 136 C2
Horndon-on-the-Hill .159 E3
Howe Green 55 D3
Hullbridge 101 D2
Hunsdonbury 9 C7
Ilford 133 B2
Ingatestone 74 C3
Ingrave 117 D5
Kelvedon Hatch 71 E2
Langford 36 D7
Latchingdon 82 A6
Leaden Roding 15 C8
Linford 175 A4
Little Baddow 34 D4
Little Burstead 118 F5
Little Hallingbury ...2 D8
Little Ilford 152 A7
Little Wakering 149 D6
Little Waltham 19 C6
Little Warley 116 F2
Loughton 88 D3
Lower Nazeing 21 F1
Maldon 37 B3
Margaret Roding ...15 D5
Margaretting 75 A8
Mashbury 17 C4
Matching Green 13 D3
Mayland 83 B8
Moreton 26 D2
Mountnessing 95 D8
Mundon 59 E2
Navestock Heath ...92 D7
Navestock Side 93 C7

North Benfleet 121 F8
North Fambridge ...103 A8
Northfleet 178 C2
North Ockendon 157 B6
North Weald Bassett ..47 C5
Orsett 174 B8
Paglesham Eastend .128 A5
Pilgrims Hatch 94 A4
Pleshey 7 E2
Purfleet 171 B1
Purleigh 58 C1
Rainham 155 A2
Ramsden Heath 98 B4
Rawreth 122 E7
Rayleigh 123 B2
Redbridge 132 C5
Rettendon 78 B1
Rochford 125 E1
Romford 135 E7
Roxwell 30 B6
Roydon 9 C1
St Lawrence 62 B8
Sawbridgeworth 1 C3
Sewardstone 87 C8
Sheering 12 D8
Shenfield 94 E7
South Benfleet 144 E3
Southend-on-Sea ...166 F6
South Hanningfield .99 C8
Southminster 84 E4
South Ockendon 172 C7
South Woodham
Ferrers 101 E8
Spellbrook 1 E8
Stanford-le-Hope ..160 E1
Stanstead Abbotts ...8 E4
Stapleford Abbotts ...91 C3

Stapleford Tawney 69 C3
Steeple 61 E3
Stock 75 F3
Stondon Massey 72 A6
Stow Maries 80 C4
Swanscombe 177 D1
Taverners Green 4 C8
Theydon Bois 67 D3
Theydon Mount 69 A3
Thornwood 46 C7
Threshers Bush 25 B7
Thundersley 144 E6
Tilbury 179 B4
Tilgate Green 25 E6
Tillingham 63 F4
Tollesbury 40 E8
Toot Hill 47 F2
Ulting 35 C6
Upminster 137 D2
Wallend 152 A4
Waltham Abbey 65 D7
Wanstead 132 C5
Wennington 170 E6
West Hanningfield ...77 B4
West Horndon 139 C5
West Tilbury 179 E8
White Roding 14 D8
Wickford 121 A5
Willingale 28 D3
Woodford 110 D5
Woodham Ferrers 79 B4
Woodham Mortimer ..57 F6
Woodham Walter 35 E2
Writtle 31 A2
Wyatts Green 72 D4

A

Aalten Ave SS8 164 F3
Abacus Prim Sch SS12 121 F5
Abberton IG8 110 C5
Abberton Wlk RM13 154 F4
Abbess Cl CM1 31 E2
Abbey Cl Fyfield CM5 27 C1
Hullbridge SS5 101 D2
Romford RM1 136 A5
Abbey Cres DA17 169 A2
Abbey Ct EN9 65 B5
Abbey Dale Cl CM17 24 C7
Abbey Fields CM3 78 B7
Abbey Mead Ind Est EN9 65 C5
Abbey Park Ind Est IG11 152 C4
Abbey Rd Barking IG11 152 B4
Barking IG11 152 C3
Billericay CM12 96 F1
Greenhithe DA9 177 C2
Hullbridge SS5 101 D1
Ilford IG2 133 D6
Abbey Turning CM9 36 D4
Abbey Wood La RM13 155 D3
Abbeyview EN9 65 C6
Abbots Cl Brentwood CM15 95 A1
Rainham RM13 155 C3
Abbots Ct SS15 119 E1
Abbots Hall Jun & Inf Schs SS17 160 E3
Abbots Ride CM11 97 C2
Abbots Wlk SS3 168 C8
Abbotsford Gdns IG8 110 A3
Abbotsford Rd IG3 134 B2
Abbotsleigh Rd CM3 101 E7
Abbotsmead CM9 36 F5
Abbotsweld CM18 23 D5
Abbotsweld Prim Sch CM18 23 D6
Abbotswood SS7 145 C5
Abbotswood Gdns
Ilford IG5 133 A8
Redbridge IG5 132 F8
Abbotts Cl Romford RM7 135 B8
Southend-on-S SS9 146 E5
Abbotts Cres E4 109 D6
Abbotts Ct Romford RM3 114 F2
Stanstead Abbotts SG12 8 D4
Abbotts Dr
Stanford-le-H SS17 160 D2
Waltham Abbey EN9 66 A6
Abbotts Hall Chase SS17 160 E2
Abbotts Pl CM2 32 D3
Abbotts Rise SG12 8 D4
Abbotts Way SG12 8 D4
Abbs Cross Gdns RM12 136 D3
Abbs Cross La RM12 136 C2
Abbs Cross Sch RM12 136 C1
Abell Way CM2 33 B4
Abenberg Way CM13 117 B8
Abensburg Rd SS8 164 D5
Abercorn Gdns RM6 134 B5
Abercorn Ho CM3 33 E8
Abercrombie Ho 17 RM3 114 D5
Abercrombie Way CM18, CM19 23 C6
Aberdeen Gdns SS9 146 A2
Aberdour Rd IG3 134 B2
Abigail Ct CM5 49 A5
Abigail Mews RM3 114 F1
Abingdon Ct 3 SS13 121 A1
Abinger Cl IG11 153 A8
Abington Ct RM14 137 C3
Abraham Ct RM14 137 A2
Abreys SS7 145 A7
Abridge Gdns RM5 113 A4
Abridge Rd Chigwell IG7 89 E4
Theydon Bois CM16 68 A1
Abridge Way IG11 153 B3
Acacia Ave RM12 135 F2
Acacia Ct EN9 66 A5
Acacia Dr Maldon CM9 36 F1
Southend-on-S SS1 168 A8
Upminster RM14 156 A8
Acacia Gdns RM14 137 F4
Acacia Rd Basildon SS13 143 E8
Greenhithe DA9 176 E1
Acacias Ct EN11 21 A6
Accrington Ho 10 RM3 114 D5
Acer Ave RM13 155 D2
Acer Gr CM1 32 D4
Acle Cl IG6 111 B3
Aconbury Rd RM9 153 B4
Acorn Cl E4 109 B5
Acorn Ct IG2 133 E6
Acorn Ctr The IG6 112 B4
Acorn Mews CM18 24 A6
Acorn Pl Basildon SS16 141 B5
Maldon CM9 36 F5
Acorn St SG12 9 D8
Acorn Trad Est RM20 177 D8
Acorns The Chigwell IG7 111 E6
Hockley SS5 124 E7
Acre Rd RM10 154 B5
Acres Ave CM5 48 F5
Acres End CM1 31 E4
Acres The SS17 160 F3
Ada Cole Meml Stables Horse Sanctuary★ CM19 22 E4
Adalia Cres SS9 146 B3
Adalia Way SS9 146 B2
Adam Bsns Ctr SS14 120 F1
Adam Way SS11 121 E8
Adam's Elm Ho SS9 146 E2
Adams Glade SS4 125 D6
Adams Ho CM20 10 D1
Adams Rd SS17 160 E1
Addison Ct CM16 68 A8
Addison Gdns RM17 173 C2
Addison Rd
Redbridge IG6 111 C2
Wanstead E11 132 A5
Adelaide Gdns
Dagenham RM6 134 E6
South Benfleet SS7 144 D1
Adelaide Rd Ilford IG1 133 B2
Tilbury RM18 178 F6
Adeliza Cl IG11 152 C5
Adelphi Cres RM12 136 B2
Adelsburg Rd SS8 164 C4
Aden Rd IG1 133 C4
Adingtons CM20 10 F2
Admiral Ct IG11 153 C3
Admirals Cl E18 132 B7
Admirals Lodge RM1 135 F6
Admirals Pl SS0 166 C7
Admirals Wlk
Chelmsford CM1 31 F3
Greenhithe DA9 177 B2
Hoddesdon EN11 21 B4
Southend-on-S SS3 168 D5
Adnams Wlk RM12 155 A7
Adomar Rd RM8 134 E1
Adstock Way RM17 172 F2
Advent Ct IG8 109 F5
Advice Ave RM16 173 A4
Afflets Ct SS14 142 C8
Afton Dr RM15 172 B7
Agister Rd IG7 112 A5
Agnes Ave Ilford IG1 152 B8
Southend-on-S SS9 146 B2
Agnes Gdns RM8 153 D8
Agricultural/Domestic Mus★ CM9 38 E7
Aidan Cl RM8 153 E8
Ailsa Rd SS0 166 C8
Ainsley Ave RM7 135 C5
Ainslie Wood Cres E4 109 B5
Ainslie Wood Gdns E4 109 B5
Ainslie Wood Prim Sch E4 109 B5
Ainslie Wood Rd E4 109 B5
Aintree Cres IG6 111 C1
Aintree Gr RM14 136 F1
Airborne Cl SS9 146 E5
Airborne Ind Est SS9 146 E5
Aire Dr RM15 157 B1
Airey Neave Ct RM16 173 A4
Airfield Way RM12 155 C6
Airlie Gdns IG1 133 B3
Airport Ret Pk SS2 147 E6
Airthrie Rd IG3 134 B2
Akenfield Cl 1 CM3 101 E7
Al-Noor Muslim Prim Sch IG3 134 B3
Alamein Gdns DA2 176 D1
Alamein Rd
Burnham-on-C CM0 106 C4
Chelmsford CM1 31 F6
Swanscombe DA10 177 D1
Alan Cl SS9 146 E6
Alan Gdns RM7 135 A4
Alan Gr SS9 146 E6
Alba Rd CM17 11 C1
Albany Ave SS0 147 E1
Albany Cl CM1 31 E5
Albany Ct Chingford E4 87 B3
Epping CM16 45 F1
Albany Rd
Dagenham RM6 134 F5
Hornchurch RM12 136 A2
Pilgrims Hatch CM15 94 B3
Rayleigh SS6 124 A1
Tilbury RM18 179 A6
Wickford SS12 121 D6
Albany Sch The RM12 136 B2
Albany The IG8 109 F6
Albany View IG9 88 A1
Albemarle App IG1 133 B5
Albemarle Cl RM17 173 A4
Albemarle Gdns IG2 133 B5
Albemarle Link CM2 32 F8
Albert Ave E4 109 A6
Albert Cl Grays RM16 173 C3
Rayleigh SS6 123 F3
Rochford SS4 125 C6
Albert Cres E4 109 A6
Albert Dr SS15 141 C6
Albert Gdns CM17 24 D7
Albert Ho 5 E18 132 B8
Albert Mews
Romford RM1 135 F5
Southend-on-S SS0 166 E8
Albert Rd
Buckhurst Hill IG9 110 D8
Bulphan RM14 158 F8
Burnham-on-C CM0 106 C4
Dagenham RM8 135 A3
Ilford IG1 133 C1
Rayleigh SS6 123 F3
Rochford SS4 125 C7
Romford RM1 135 F5
South Benfleet SS7 144 B6
South Woodham Ferrers CM3 101 D7
Southend-on-S SS1 167 B7
Albert Rd *continued*
Southend-on-S,Bournes Green SS1 149 A1
Swanscombe DA10 177 F1
4 Wanstead E18 132 B8
Albert St CM14 116 C5
Albert Terr IG9 110 E8
Albion Cl RM7 135 D5
Albion Ct Billericay CM12 97 A1
Chelmsford CM2 32 B1
Albion Hill IG10 88 D4
Albion Pk IG10 88 D4
Albion Rd
Gravesend DA12 179 D1
South Benfleet SS7 144 D4
Southend-on-S SS0 147 E1
Albion Terr
Gravesend DA12 179 D1
Sewardstone E4 87 B5
Albra Mead CM2 33 B4
Albright Ind Est RM13 169 F8
Albury Mews E12 132 C2
Albyns SS16 141 C4
Albyns Cl RM13 155 A5
Albyns La RM4 91 D7
Alcester Ho 14 RM3 114 D5
Alcotes SS14 142 F5
Aldborough Ct
Chingford E4 109 B7
Ilford IG2 133 F6
Aldborough Rd
Dagenham RM10 154 C6
Ilford IG2 133 F8
Upminster RM14 137 A2
Aldborough Rd N IG2 133 F6
Aldborough Rd S IG3 133 E4
Aldeburgh Pl IG8 110 A6
Aldeburgh Way CM1 32 D5
Alder Ave RM14 155 F8
Alder Cl Basildon SS15 119 D1
Hoddesdon EN11 21 B8
Alder Dr Chelmsford CM2 54 B6
South Ockendon RM15 157 C1
Alder Wlk IG1 152 D7
Alderbury Lea CM3 56 F1
Aldergrove Wlk RM12 155 C6
Alderleys SS7 145 A6
Alderman Ave IG11 153 A2
Alderman Wlk SS17 160 E5
Alderman's Hill SS5 124 C5
Alderney Gdns SS11 99 C2
Alders Ave IG8 109 E4
Alders Cl E11 132 B2
Alders Wlk CM21 1 E2
Aldersbrook House Coll of Railway Tech E12 133 A1
Aldersbrook La E12 132 F1
Aldersbrook Prim Sch E12 132 C2
Aldersbrook Rd E12 132 C2
Aldersey Gdns IG11 152 D6
Aldersgrove EN9 65 E5
Alderton Cl Loughton IG10 89 A5
Pilgrims Hatch CM15 94 B4
Alderton Hall La IG10 89 A5
Alderton Hill IG10 88 F4
Alderton Jun & Inf Schs The IG10 89 A4
Alderton Mews IG10 89 A5
Alderton Rd RM16 174 E7
Alderton Rise IG10 89 A5
Alderton Way IG10 88 F4
Alderwood Cl RM4 90 B6
Alderwood Dr RM4 90 B6
Alderwood Way SS7 145 C3
Aldham Dr RM15 172 C8
Aldham Gdns SS6 122 F3
Aldham Hall 1 E11 132 A5
Aldingham Ct RM12 155 B7
Aldingham Gdns RM12 155 A7
Aldington Cl RM8 134 C3
Aldis Mews EN3 65 A2
Aldria Rd SS17 160 E5
Aldriche Way E4 109 C4
Aldridge Ave 7 EN3 65 A1
Aldridge Cl CM2 33 A4
Aldrin Cl SS17 160 E2
Aldrin Way SS9 147 A6
Aldwych Ave IG6 133 C7
Aldwych Cl RM12 136 B2
Alexander Ct
1 Chelmsford CM1 32 E7
Romford RM7 135 D3
Alexander Hts SS1 168 A8
Alexander La CM15 95 B4
Alexander Mews CM2 55 D2
Alexander Rd
Basildon SS16 141 B4
Greenhithe DA9 177 C2
Alexandra Cl RM16 174 C4
Alexandra Ct
7 Southend-on-S SS2 147 F1
Southend-on-S,Clifftown SS1 166 F7
Alexandra Ho 15 IG8 111 A3
Alexandra Pl 3 RM1 135 F5
Alexandra Rd
Brentwood CM14 116 C7
Burnham-on-C CM0 106 C5
Dagenham RM6 134 E5
Great Wakering SS3 150 A3
Rainham RM13 154 F4
Rayleigh SS6 123 F3
Rochford SS4 125 C7
Romford RM1 135 F5
South Benfleet SS7 144 D2
Southend-on-S,Clifftown SS1 166 F7
Alexandra Rd *continued*
Southend-on-S,Leigh Cliffs SS9 165 E8
Tilbury RM18 178 F5
Wallend E6 152 A2
Wanstead E18 132 B8
Alexandra St SS1 167 A7
Alexandra Way RM18 175 B3
Alexandria Dr SS6 123 A4
Alf Lowne Ct RM16 174 A3
Alford Rd DA8 169 C1
Alfred Gdns SS11 99 D1
Alfred Prior Ho 7 E12 152 A8
Alfred Rd Aveley RM15 171 C5
Brentwood CM14 116 D8
Buckhurst Hill IG9 110 D8
Alfred St RM17 178 C8
Alfred's Gdns IG11 152 E3
Alfred's Way (East Ham & Barking By-Pass) IG11 152 D3
Alfred's Way Ind Est IG11 153 A4
Alfreda Ave SS5 101 D3
Algars Way CM3 101 D8
Algers Cl IG10 88 D4
Algers Mead IG10 88 D4
Algers Rd IG10 88 E4
Alibon Gdns RM10 154 A7
Alibon Rd RM10 154 A7
Alicia Ave SS11 122 A7
Alicia Cl SS11 122 A7
Alicia Way SS11 122 A7
Alicia Wlk SS11 122 A7
Alkerden La DA10 177 C1
All Saints CE Prim Sch
Maldon CM9 36 E2
Maldon CM9 36 F3
All Saints Cl
Chelmsford CM1 32 E4
Chigwell IG7 112 A7
Doddinghurst CM15 72 B3
Swanscombe DA10 177 F2
All Saints RC Sch & Tech Coll RM8 135 A3
Allandale SS7 145 A7
Allandale Rd RM11 135 F4
Allen Rd RM13 155 C2
Allen Way CM2 33 B4
Allenby Cres RM17 173 C1
Allenby Dr RM11 136 F3
Allens Cl CM3 20 F1
Allens Rd CM11 98 C5
Allensway SS17 160 F3
Allerton Cl SS4 125 C6
Alley Dock SS9 165 D8
Alleyn Court Prep Sch SS3 149 A3
Alleyn Court Sch SS0 147 C1
Alleyn Pl SS0 147 C1
Alleyndale Rd RM8 134 C2
Allington Ct CM11 119 C7
Allison Cl EN9 66 A7
Allistonway SS17 160 F3
Allmains Cl EN9 44 B6
Allnutts Rd CM16 68 A6
Alloa Rd IG3 134 A2
Allysum Wlk CM12 96 F5
Alma Ave Chingford E4 109 C3
Hornchurch RM12 136 E1
Alma Cl
South Benfleet SS7 146 A2
Wickford SS12 121 A6
Alma Dr CM1 32 A2
Alma Link CM12 97 A1
Alma Rd
South Benfleet SS7 146 A2
Swanscombe DA10 177 F2
Almere SS7 144 D4
Almond Ave SS12 121 C7
Almond Cl RM16 174 A3
Almond Wlk SS8 163 F4
Almonds Ave IG9 110 A8
Almshouses
Brentwood CM14 115 E8
Ingatestone CM4 74 B3
Almshouses (Whitakers Charity) IG10 88 F8
Almshouses The IG11 152 C6
Alnwick Cl SS16 140 F5
Alnwick Ct 6 DA2 176 B1
Alonso Ho 4 DA17 169 A1
Alp Ct SS3 150 A3
Alpha Cl SS13 143 F6
Alpha Rd Basildon SS13 143 F6
Brentwood CM13 95 D3
Burnham-on-C CM0 106 C5
Chingford E4 109 B7
Alracks SS15 141 E6
Alresford Gn SS12 121 E6
Alston Ct SS0 147 C1
Altar Pl SS15 141 C7
Altham Gr CM20 10 F3
Althorne Cl SS13 121 B1
Althorne Sta CM3 104 F8
Althorne Way
Canewdon SS4 104 E2
Dagenham RM10 135 A2
Althorpe Cl SS5 124 D6
Alton Gdns SS2 147 E5
Aluric Cl RM16 174 B2
Alverstoke Rd RM3 114 E3
Alverstone Rd E12 152 A8
Alwen Gr RM15 172 B8
Alwyne Ave CM15 95 A3
Alyssum Cl CM1 33 A6
Amanda Cl IG7 111 D4
Amanda Mews RM7 135 C6
Amber Ct 5 RM1 135 E6
Amber La IG6 111 B3
Amberden SS15 141 D5
Amberley Rd IG9 88 C1
Amberley Way RM7 135 B7
Amberry Ct CM20 10 D1
Ambleside CM16 68 A8
Ambleside Ave RM12 155 B7
Ambleside Dr SS1 167 D8
Ambleside Gdns
Hullbridge SS5 101 D2
Redbridge IG4 132 E6
Ambleside Wlk SS8 163 F5
Ambrook Rd DA17 169 A3
Amcotes Pl CM2 54 C8
Ameland Rd SS8 164 A6
Amelia Blackwell Ho SS8 163 E3
America St CM9 37 A2
Amersham Ave SS16 140 F5
Amersham Cl RM3 114 F4
Amersham Dr RM3 114 F4
Amersham Rd RM3 114 F4
Amersham Wlk RM3 114 F4
Amery Gdns RM2 136 D8
Ames Rd DA10 177 E1
Amesbury EN9 66 A7
Amesbury Cl CM16 67 F8
Amesbury Dr E4 87 B3
Amesbury Rd
Dagenham RM9 153 D5
Epping CM16 67 F8
Amid Rd SS8 164 C5
Amidas Gdns RM8 153 B8
Amoss Rd CM2 54 F8
Ampers End SS14 142 D6
Ampthill Ho 2 RM3 114 D5
Amwell Ct
Hoddesdon EN11 21 A7
Waltham Abbey EN9 65 E6
Amwell La SG12 8 B5
Amwell St EN11 21 A7
Amwell View Sch SG12 8 B4
Anchor Bvd DA2 176 D3
Anchor Cl IG11 153 B2
Anchor Dr RM13 155 B2
Anchor Ho IG3 134 A1
Anchor La
Abbess Roding CM5 14 C4
Canewdon SS4 104 E1
Heybridge CM9 37 A5
Anchor Lane Cotts SS4 104 E1
Anchor Par SS4 104 E1
Anchor Reach CM3 101 E5
Anchor St CM2 32 B1
Anchorage Hill CM9 37 A3
Anchorage The
Burnham-on-C CM0 106 C3
Canvey Island SS8 164 B1
Great Wakering SS3 150 B4
Anders Fall SS9 147 A6
Anderson Ave CM1 31 F5
Anderson Ho IG11 152 D3
Anderson Rd IG8 132 D8
Anderson Way DA17 169 C4
Andersons SS17 160 F3
Andrea Ave RM16 173 A4
Andrew Cl Redbridge IG6 111 D3
Stanford-le-H SS17 160 D4
Andrews Cl IG9 110 C8
Andrews Pl CM1 31 F3
Andromeda Ct RM3 114 C4
Andy Hill Ho CM14 116 B6
Andyk Rd SS8 164 E3
Anerley Rd SS0 166 D8
Angel Cl SS16 142 D3
Angel Terr SS3 149 D2
Angel Way RM1 135 E6
Angle Gn RM8 134 C3
Angle Rd RM20 177 D8
Anglesea Ctr 3 DA11 179 B1
Anglesea Pl 2 DA11 179 B1
Anglesey Dr RM13 155 A1
Anglesey Gdns SS12 121 F5
Anglia Ct 10 RM8 134 D4
Anglia Ctr The RM13 169 E8
Anglia Poly Univ
Chelmsford CM1 32 B2
Chelmsford CM1 32 B4
Anglia Wlk E6 152 A4
Anglian Ind Est IG11 153 A1
Anglo-European Sch CM4 74 C4
Angmering Ho 1 RM3 114 D5
Anjou Gn CM1 33 A7
Ann Boleyn Dr SS4 147 F7
Annabel Ct RM12 136 C3
Annabell Ave RM16 174 D7
Annalee Gdns RM15 172 B8
Annalee Rd RM15 172 B8
Annan Way RM1 113 E2
Anne Boleyn Mans 4 SS13 143 B5
Anne Heart Cl RM16 172 D2
Anne Nastri Ct RM2 136 B6
Anne Way IG6 111 C4
Annett Cl 7 SS12 122 A5
Annie Taylor Ho 2 E12 152 A8
Annifer Way RM15 172 B8
Annonay Wlk 7 CM2 32 C2
Annwood Lodge Bsns Pk SS6 122 D2
Anson Chase SS3 168 E8
Anson Cl Romford RM7 113 B1
South Woodham Ferrers CM3 101 F6
Anstead Dr RM13 155 A3
Anstey Cl SS9 146 D7

Antelope Ave RM16 173 A3
Anthony Cl CM11 119 D6
Anthony Dr SS17 160 E4
Antlers SS8 163 F2
Antlers Hill E4 87 B4
Anton Rd RM15 157 B1
Antony Cl SS8 164 B5
Antrim Rd SS3 168 D7
Anvil Way Billericay CM12 97 B5
Chelmsford CM1 32 E8
Anworth Cl IG8 110 B4
Apeldoorn SS7 144 B7
Apex Ct SS5 124 E8
Apollo Cl RM12 136 B2
Apple Gate CM14 93 F4
Apple Tree Cl CM15 72 D1
Apple Tree Cres CM15 72 C1
Apple Tree Way SS11 121 F8
Apple Way CM2 54 D6
Appleby Cl E4 109 C4
Appleby Dr
Basildon SS16 140 F5
Romford RM3 114 C5
Appleby Gn RM3 114 C5
Appledene Cl SS6 123 D4
Appledore SS3 149 C1
Appledore Cl RM3 114 C2
Appleford Ct 8 SS13 143 C6
Applegarth Dr IG2 133 F7
Applerow SS9 146 F6
Appleton Cl CM19 23 C7
Appleton Rd
Loughton IG10 89 B6
South Benfleet SS7 144 B2
Appleton Sch The SS7 144 C5
Appleton Way RM11 136 D3
Appletree Cl SS2 148 E3
Appleyard Ave SS5 124 E8
Approach Rd
Basildon CM11 120 D5
Canvey Island SS8 164 F3
Approach The
Rayleigh SS6 123 C3
Upminster RM14 137 B1
April Pl CM21 1 F3
Apton Hall Rd SS4 126 C6
Arabia Cl E4 87 D2
Araglen Ave RM15 172 B8
Aragon Cl Loughton IG10 88 E3
Romford RM5 113 B4
Southend-on-S SS2 147 E4
Aragon Ct IG6 111 C4
Aragon Dr IG6 111 C3
Arandora Cres RM6 134 B5
Arbor Rd E4 109 D7
Arbour Cl CM14 116 C5
Arbour La CM1 32 D4
Arbour Way RM12 155 B7
Arbutus Cl CM2 54 B6
Arcade Pl 8 RM1 135 E6
Arcade The
Wickford SS12 121 D8
18 Romford RM3 114 D5
Arcadia Rd
Burnham-on-C CM0 106 C5
Canvey Island SS8 164 D3
Arcadian Gdns SS7 145 D4
Arcany Rd RM15 157 B1
Archates Ave RM16 173 A3
Archer Ave SS2 148 E3
Archer Cl SS2 148 E3
Archer Rd SS15 141 B8
Archers CM19 23 B3
Archers Cl CM12 119 A8
Archers Ct RM15 172 B8
Archers Fields SS13 121 B1
Archers Fields Cl SS13 121 A1
Archers Way CM2 54 C2
Archibald Rd RM3 115 A1
Archibald Terr SS15 141 B7
Archway RM3 114 B4
Arden Cres RM9 153 D5
Ardleigh SS16 141 E5
Ardleigh Cl RM11 136 D8
Ardleigh Ct CM15 94 F2
Ardleigh Gdns CM13 95 E3
Ardleigh Green Jun & Inf Schs RM3 136 D8
Ardleigh Green Rd RM11 136 D7
Ardley Cres CM22 3 B2
Ardley Way SS6 123 D4
Ardmore La IG9 88 B2
Ardmore Pl IG9 88 B2
Ardmore Rd RM15 157 B1
Ardwell Ave IG6 133 C6
Arethusa Pl DA9 177 B3
Argent Ct SS15 140 F7
Argent St RM17 178 A8
Argles Cl DA9 177 A2
Argus Cl RM7 113 B2
Argyle Gdns RM14 137 D1
Argyle Rd
Burnham-on-C CM0 106 D4
Ilford IG1 133 A2
Argyll Ct CM15 94 D1
Argyll Ho SS0 166 D7
Argyll Rd Chelmsford CM2 33 A5
Grays RM17 173 A1
Southend-on-S SS0 147 D1
Ariel Ct 5 DA17 169 A1
Arisdale Ave RM15 157 B1
Arjan Way SS8 163 C3
Ark Ave RM16 173 A4
Ark La SS4 125 A1
Arkwright Rd RM18 179 B5
Arkwrights CM20 10 F1
Arlingham Mews EN9 65 C6
Arlington Gdns
Ilford IG1 133 A3
Redbridge IG1 132 F4
Romford RM3 114 E2
Arlington Ho 14 IG8 111 A3
Arlington Rd
Southend-on-S SS2 148 E1
Woodford IG8 110 B3
Arlington Sq CM3 101 C4
Arlington Way CM12 96 F5
Armada Cl SS15 141 D5
Armada Ct RM16 173 A3
Armadale SS8 163 F5
Armagh Rd SS3 168 D7
Armath Pl SS16 140 F4
Armitage Rd SS1 149 A1
Armonde Cl CM3 20 E1
Armor Rd RM19 171 D2
Armstead Wlk RM10 154 A5
Armstrong Ave IG8 109 E4
Armstrong Cl
Dagenham RM8 134 D4
Danbury CM3 56 F8
Stanford-le-H SS17 160 E2
Armstrong Rd SS7 144 D7
Arncroft Ct IG11 153 B2
Arne Cl SS17 160 D3
Arne Ct SS15 141 C8
Arne Mews SS15 141 C8
Arneways Ave RM6 134 D8
Arnheim Rd CM0 106 C4
Arnhem Ave RM15 171 C5
Arnhem Rd CM1 31 E6
Arnold Ave
Basildon SS16 141 A5
Southend-on-S SS1 167 C7
Arnold Ave E EN3 65 A1
Arnold Ct E18 109 F2
Arnold Ho CM2 32 A1
Arnold Pl RM18 179 C6
Arnold Rd
Dagenham RM9 153 F5
Waltham Abbey EN9 65 C4
Arnold Way CM2 54 C3
Arnolds Ave CM13 95 C4
Arnolds Cl CM13 95 C4
Arnolds Farm La CM13 95 E6
Arnolds Way SS4 125 D7
Arnside Ho 2 RM3 115 A4
Arran Ct SS12 121 F6
Arran Dr E12 132 D2
Arrowsmith Cl IG7 111 F5
Arrowsmith Path IG7 111 F5
Arrowsmith Rd IG7 111 F5
Arterial Ave RM13 155 C1
Arterial Rd
Southend-on-S SS6,SS9 146 C6
Thundersley SS6 145 B8
Arterial Rd North Stifford RM16 172 E4
Arterial Rd West Thurrock RM20 172 A3
Arterial Road Purfleet RM19 171 C2
Artesian Cl RM11 135 F4
Arthur Barnes Ct RM16 174 C3
Arthur Bugler Jun & Inf Schs SS17 160 E3
Arthur Ct CM1 31 F5
Arthur Rd RM6 134 D5
Arthur St RM17 178 C8
Arthur Toft Ho RM17 178 B8
Arthur Walls Ho 3 E12 133 A1
Artillery Cl IG2 133 C5
Arun RM18 175 C2
Arun Cl CM1 32 C5
Arundel Cl CM12 97 C6
Arundel Dr
Corringham SS17 161 A4
Woodford IG8 110 A3
Arundel Gdns Ilford IG3 134 A2
Rayleigh SS6 123 B5
Southend-on-S SS0 147 A3
Arundel Mews CM12 97 C6
Arundel Rd Rochford SS4 103 C1
Romford RM3 114 F2
South Benfleet SS7 144 B7
Wickford SS11 99 C1
Arundel Way CM12 97 C6
Arwen Gr CM3 101 C6
Asbaston Terr IG11 152 C6
Ascension Rd RM5 113 C4
Ascent Pk CM20 11 B5
Ascham Dr E4 109 A3
Ascot Cl Redbridge IG6 111 E4
Thundersley SS7 145 B7
Ascot Gdns RM12 155 E8
Ascot Gr SS14 142 E6
Ascot Mews CM0 84 E4
Asda Ctr SS3 149 D1
Ash Cl Pilgrims Hatch CM15 93 F4
Romford RM5 113 B3
Ash Ct Chingford E4 87 D2
Romford RM7 135 B5
Southend-on-S SS3 168 F7
Woodford E18 110 C2
Ash Gn Billericay CM11 97 E2
Canewdon SS4 104 D1
Ash Gr
Burnham-on-C CM0 106 B6
Chelmsford CM2 54 D7
Heybridge CM9 37 C6
Ash Groves CM21 2 A2
Ash Ind Est CM19 22 F7
Ash Lodge SS3 168 F8
Ash Rd Canvey Island SS8 164 C3
Hadleigh SS7 145 E2
Ash Tree Cl CM1 31 F2
Ash Tree Cnr CM3 19 B6
Ash Tree Cres CM1 31 F2
Ash Tree Ct SS4 126 D4
Ash Tree Field CM20 10 A2
Ash Tree Wlk 1 SS14 142 F5
Ash Way SS5 124 F8
Ash Wlk
South Ockendon RM15 157 D2
Southend-on-S SS1 167 B7
Ashanti Cl SS3 168 F8
Ashbeam Cl CM13 116 C4
Ashbourne Ave E18 132 B7
Ashbourne Rd RM3 114 D6
Ashbrook Rd RM10 135 B1
Ashburnham Gdns RM14 137 C3
Ashburnham Rd
Belvedere DA17 169 C2
Southend-on-S SS1 166 F8
Ashburton Ave IG3 152 F8
Ashbury Gdns RM6 134 D6
Ashby Cl
Hornchurch RM11 137 A3
Orsett RM16 174 E7
Ashcombe SS4 125 D4
Ashcombe Cl SS9 146 B6
Ashdene Cl SS5 101 E2
Ashdon Cl
Brentwood CM13 95 C3
South Ockendon RM15 172 C7
Woodford IG8 110 B4
Ashdon Way SS16 142 A5
Ashdown Cl SS17 160 F5
Ashdown Cres SS7 145 E4
Ashdown Ho SS7 144 F6
Ashdown Wlk RM7 113 B2
Asheldham Pits Nature Reserve* CM0 85 A8
Ashfield SS6 122 F3
Ashfield Farm Rd CM9 35 D8
Ashfields Basildon SS13 143 C8
Loughton IG10 88 F7
Ashford Ave CM14 116 B7
Ashford Ct RM17 173 D1
Ashford Rd
Chelmsford CM1 31 E2
Wallend E6 152 A5
Woodford E18 110 B1
Ashgrove Rd IG3 134 A3
Ashingdale Cl SS8 164 C2
Ashingdon Cl E4 109 C7
Ashingdon Hts SS4 125 B7
Ashingdon Rd SS4 125 D6
Ashingdon Sch SS4 103 B1
Ashlands Ct RM18 175 C2
Ashleigh Cl SS8 164 A6
Ashleigh Ct
Canvey Island SS8 164 A6
Hoddesdon EN11 21 A5
Ingatestone CM4 74 B3
Waltham Abbey EN9 66 A5
Ashleigh Dr SS9 165 F8
Ashleigh Gdns RM14 137 D1
Ashley Ave IG6 111 B1
Ashley Cl SS17 161 A4
Ashley Gdns RM16 173 D5
Ashley Gn CM3 78 B7
Ashley Gr IG10 88 E6
Ashley Rd E4 109 A4
Ashlyn Gr RM11 136 D8
Ashlyns SS13 143 B7
Ashlyns La CM5 25 F2
Ashlyns Rd CM16 45 F1
Ashmans Row CM3 101 D6
Ashmeads IG10 88 F6
Ashmour Gdns RM1 113 D1
Ashton Gate RM3 114 D3
Ashton Gdns RM6 134 E5
Ashton Pl CM2 33 A3
Ashton Rd RM3 114 D2
Ashtree Ct EN9 66 A5
Ashurst Ave SS2 148 F2
Ashurst Dr
Chelmsford CM1 32 D7
Ilford IG6 133 C6
Ashvale Dr RM14 137 E2
Ashvale Gdns
Romford RM5 113 D5
Upminster RM14 137 F2
Ashway SS17 161 B5
Ashwells Rd CM15 93 E6
Ashwood SS7 144 B7
Ashwood Ave RM13 155 B1
Ashwood Cl CM0 106 B7
Ashwood Rd E4 109 D7
Ashworth Pl CM17 24 D8
Ashworths
Canvey Island SS8 164 A6
Rochford SS4 125 C6
Askews Farm Rd RM17 172 E1
Askwith Rd RM13 154 D3
Aspen Cl SS8 163 E4
Aspen Ct Basildon SS15 119 C1
Brentwood CM13 117 A7
Dartford DA1 176 A1
Aspen Gr RM14 156 A8
Aspen Way RM15 157 D2
Asquith Ave SS7 145 B7
Asquith Cl RM8 134 C3
Asquith Gdns SS7 145 C7
Assandune Cl SS4 125 D7
Aster Cl 4 CM1 32 F6
Asthall Gdns IG6 133 C7
Astley RM17 177 F8
Aston Mews RM6 134 C4
Aston Rd SS15 141 B6
Astor Ave RM7 135 C5
Astra Cl RM12 155 B6
Astra Ct E 3 RM12 155 B6
Astra Ct W 2 RM12 155 B6
Astra Ctr CM20 10 F4
Athelstan Cl RM3 114 F1
Athelstan Ct E6 152 A3
Athelstan Gdns
Wickford SS11 122 A8
Wickford, Runwell SS11 99 D1
Athelstan Rd RM3 114 F1
Athena Est CM20 11 B4
Atherstone Cl SS8 164 C2
Atherstone Rd SS8 164 C2
Atherton End CM21 1 E3
Atherton Gdns RM16 174 C2
Atherton Ho
8 Romford RM3 114 E3
Woodford IG5 110 E1
Atherton Rd IG5 110 F1
Athol Cl SS8 164 E2
Athol Rd DA17 169 C1
Atholl Rd Chelmsford CM2 32 F5
Ilford IG3 134 A4
Athos Rd SS8 164 C5
Atlanta Bvd RM1 135 E5
Atlantic Cl DA10 177 E2
Atlantis Cl IG11 153 B2
Atridge Chase CM12 97 A4
Attlee Ct RM17 173 A3
Attlee Dr DA1 176 A2
Attwoods Cl CM2 54 C3
Aubrey Cl CM1 32 B7
Aubrietia Cl RM3 114 E2
Auckland Ave RM13 154 F2
Auckland Cl
Chelmsford CM1 31 E5
Tilbury RM18 179 A5
Auckland Rd IG1 133 C4
Auction Pl RM4 90 B6
Audleigh Pl IG7 111 A4
Audley Gdns Ilford IG3 133 F2
Loughton IG10 89 D7
Waltham Abbey EN9 65 C5
Audley Way SS14 142 B6
Audleys Cl SS2 147 E5
Audrey Rd IG1 133 B1
Augers 7 CM0 106 C4
Augustine Ct EN9 65 B6
Augustine Rd DA12 179 D1
Augustine Way CM3 56 F2
Aukingford Gdns CM5 48 F5
Aukingford Gn CM5 48 F4
Auriel Ave RM10 154 D6
Aurora Ct IG8 109 F6
Austen Cl
Greenhithe DA9 177 C1
Loughton IG10 89 D6
Tilbury RM18 179 C5
Austen Dr CM4 75 D2
Austral Dr RM11 136 D4
Austral Way CM3 83 A3
Avcoca Terr SS0 147 D2
Avebury Rd SS0 147 E2
Aveley By-Pass RM15 171 D6
Aveley Cl RM15 171 D5
Aveley Mans 1 IG11 152 B5
Aveley Prim Sch RM15 171 E5
Aveley Rd Romford RM1 135 E7
Upminster RM14 156 C4
Aveley Sch The RM15 171 D6
Aveley Way CM9 58 F8
Aveling Park Rd E17 109 A1
Aveling Park Sch E17 109 A1
Avelon Rd
Rainham RM13 155 A4
Romford RM5 113 D4
Avenue Cl RM3 114 F3
Avenue Ct IG5 132 E8
Avenue Gate IG10 88 C3
Avenue Ind Est
Chingford E4 109 A4
Romford RM3 114 D2
Avenue Rd
Brentwood CM14 116 C6
Chelmsford CM2 54 D7
Hoddesdon EN11 21 D5
Ilford RM6 134 C4
Ingatestone CM4 74 B3
Romford RM3 114 F3
South Benfleet SS7 144 E3
Southend-on-S,Clifftown SS0 166 F8
Southend-on-S,Leigh Cliffs SS9 165 E8
Theydon Bois CM16 67 D3
Woodford IG8 110 C4
Avenue Terr Ilford IG2 133 E5
Southend-on-S SS0 166 E8
Avenue The
Billericay CM12 97 A2
Brentwood CM13 116 F4
8 Buckhurst Hill IG9 110 C8
Canvey Island SS8 164 B2
Chingford E4 109 D5
Danbury CM3 56 F7
Fobbing SS17 161 D5
Greenhithe DA9 177 B2
Hadleigh SS7 145 E3
Hoddesdon EN11 21 A4
Hornchurch RM12 136 D2
Hullbridge SS5 101 D3
Kelvedon Hatch CM15 93 E8
Loughton IG10 88 E3
Lower Nazeing EN9 44 C6
North Fambridge CM3 103 A7
Romford RM1 135 D7
Wanstead E11 132 B6
Avery Gdns Ilford IG2 133 A6
Redbridge IG2 132 F6
Avey La High Beach IG10 88 A8
Waltham Abbey EN9 65 E2
Aviation Way SS2 147 B7
Avila Chase CM2 54 B1
Avington Wlk SS7 144 F6
Avocet Way CM9 37 C5
Avon Cl SS4 125 C5
Avon Gn RM15 172 B7
Avon House Sch IG8 110 A6
Avon Rd
Canvey Island SS8 164 A3
Chelmsford CM1 31 C5
Upminster RM14 137 D5
Avon Terr IG10 88 F3
Avon Way
Southend-on-S SS3 168 E7
Wanstead E18 132 A8
Avondale Cl
Loughton IG10 88 F2
Rayleigh SS6 123 F2
Avondale Cres IG4 132 D6
Avondale Ct
Southend-on-S SS9 146 D1
Woodford E18 110 B2
Avondale Dr
Loughton IG10 88 F3
Southend-on-S SS9 146 F4
Avondale Gdns SS17 160 E5
Avondale Rd
Basildon SS16 143 A4
Rayleigh SS6 123 F2
South Benfleet SS7 144 D3
Avondale Wlk SS8 163 E4
Avontar Rd RM15 157 B1
Avril Way E4 109 C5
Avro Rd SS2 147 D6
Axe St IG11 152 C4
Aylesbeare SS3 168 D8
Aylesbury Dr SS16 140 F5
Aylesbury Mews SS15 119 F2
Aylets Field CM18 23 E5
Aylett Cl SS8 164 C4
Aylett Rd RM14 137 C2
Ayletts Basildon SS14 142 F6
Broomfield CM1 19 B3
Aylmer Rd RM8 134 E1
Ayloff Prim Sch RM12 155 B8
Ayloff's Wlk RM11 136 E6
Ayloffe Rd RM9 153 F6
Ayloffs Cl RM11 136 E6
Aylsham La RM3 114 D6
Aylsham Rd EN11 21 C8
Aynsley Gdns CM17 24 C8
Ayr Gn RM1 113 E2
Ayr Way RM1 113 E2
Ayron Rd RM15 157 B1
Azalea Ave SS12 121 C7
Azalea Cl IG1 152 B7
Azalea Ct
8 Chelmsford CM1 32 F6
Chingford IG8 109 E3
Azalea Mews SS8 164 A2

B

Baardwyk Ave SS8 164 E3
Babbacombe Gdns IG4 132 E7
Babington Rd
Dagenham RM8 153 C8
Hornchurch RM12 136 B3
Back La Broomfield CM1 19 D1
Dagenham RM6 134 E4
East Hanningfield CM3 78 B7
Grays RM20 172 B4
Ingatestone CM4 74 A6
Little Hallingbury CM22 2 B7
Little Waltham CM3 19 C4
Lower Nazeing EN9 22 C1
Pleshey CM3 7 E2
Purfleet RM19 171 E3
Rochford SS4 125 F1
Sheering CM22 2 B1
South Ockendon RM16 172 C5
Stock CM4 75 D2
Back Rd CM1 31 A1
Backnang Sq 1 CM2 32 C2
Backwarden Nature Reserve* CM3 56 E5
Backwardens Nature Trail* CM3 56 E4
Bacon Link RM5 113 B4
Bacon Terr RM8 153 B7
Bacons Chase CM0 42 B2
Badburgham Ct EN9 65 F6
Baddeley Cl EN3 65 A2
Baddow Cl
Dagenham RM10 154 A4
Woodford IG8 110 D4
Baddow Ct CM2 55 A6
Baddow Hall Ave CM2 55 A7
Baddow Hall Cres CM2 55 B7
Baddow Hall Jun & Inf Sch CM2 55 A6
Baddow Place Ave CM2 55 A6
Baddow Rd
Chelmsford CM2 32 C1
Great Baddow CM2 54 E7
Baden Powell Cl RM9 153 E4
Baden Powell Ho 11 DA17 169 A3
Baden Rd IG1 152 B7
Bader Way RM13 155 B6
Badger Cl IG2 133 C4
Badger Hall Ave SS7 145 A4

Badgers Cl
Galleywood CM2 ....54 B1
Southend-on-S SS0 ...147 B4
Badgers Keep CM0 ...106 B8
Badgers Mount
Chadwell St M RM16 ...173 F4
Hockley SS5 ....124 D5
Badgers Rise SS8 ...164 A6
Badgers The SS16 ...141 B4
Badgers Way SS7 ...145 B4
Bag La CM4 ....73 E4
Bagleys Spring RM6 ...134 E7
Bailey Cl Chingford E4 ...109 C6
Purfleet RM19 ...171 D2
Bailey Ct 4 E4 ...109 C5
Bailey Rd SS9 ...146 B2
Baillie Cl RM13 ...155 B1
Bainbridge Rd RM9 ...153 D6
Baird Ho 12 DA17 ...169 A3
Bairny Wood App IG8 ...110 A6
Baker Mews CM9 ...37 A2
Baker St Chelmsford CM2 ...32 A1
Orsett RM16 ...173 F6
Baker's Ct SS14 ...121 A2
Baker's Grave SS3 ...149 E4
Bakers Cl CM3 ...101 D8
Bakers Ct RM8 ...134 F4
Bakers Farm Cl SS11 ...122 A7
Bakers Field CM4 ...75 E2
Bakers La Danbury CM3 ...56 C3
Epping CM16 ...45 F1
Ingatestone CM4 ...74 B4
West Hanningfield CM2 ...76 B3
Bakers Mdw CM15 ...72 C2
Bakers Mead CM3 ...18 F7
Bakers Mews CM4 ...74 B4
Bakers Villas The CM16 ...45 F1
Bakers Wlk CM21 ...1 E2
Bakersfield CM3 ...82 F8
Bakery Cl Roydon CM19 ...22 C8
Tillingham CM0 ...63 E3
Baldocks Rd CM16 ...67 E4
Baldwin's Hill IG10 ...88 F8
Balfour Cl SS12 ...121 E5
Balfour Rd Grays RM17 ...173 C2
Ilford IG1 ...133 C3
Balgonie Rd E4 ...87 D1
Balgores Cres RM2 ...136 B8
Balgores La RM2 ...136 B7
Balgores Sq RM2 ...136 B7
Ballards Cl RM10 ...154 B4
Ballards Rd RM10 ...154 B3
Ballards Wlk SS15 ...141 E7
Balliol Ave E4 ...109 E6
Balmerino Ave SS7 ...145 C6
Balmoral Ave
Corringham SS17 ...161 A4
Stanford-le-H SS17 ...160 E3
Balmoral Cl CM11 ...97 C1
Balmoral Ct CM2 ...32 C2
Balmoral Gdns
Hockley SS5 ...124 C6
Ilford IG3 ...133 F3
Balmoral Ho SS0 ...166 E8
Balmoral Rd
Hornchurch RM12 ...136 D1
Mayland CM3 ...61 A2
Pilgrims Hatch CM15 ...94 B4
Romford RM2 ...136 B6
Southend-on-S SS0 ...147 E1
Balmoral Terr SS0 ...147 D2
Balstonia Dr SS17 ...160 F5
Baltic Ave SS1 ...167 A8
Bamber Ho 3 IG11 ...152 C4
Bamford Cl IG11 ...152 C6
Bamford Way RM5 ...113 B5
Bampton Rd RM3 ...114 F2
Bancroft Ave IG9 ...110 A8
Bancroft Chase RM12 ...135 F2
Bancroft's Sch IG8 ...110 A7
Bancrofts Rd CM3 ...101 D8
Bandhills Cl CM3 ...101 D8
Banes Down EN9 ...21 E1
Bank Chambers CM15 ...116 D8
Bank End Cotts CM4 ...75 A8
Bank Pl 5 CM14 ...116 C8
Bank St DA11,DA12 ...179 B1
Bankart La CM2 ...32 F4
Bankfoot RM17 ...173 A1
Banks La Epping CM16 ...68 F7
Stapleford Tawney CM16 ...69 A8
Banks Way E12 ...152 A8
Bankside DA11 ...178 C1
Bankside Cl CM3 ...79 E1
Bankside Pk IG11 ...153 C4
Bankside Rd IG1 ...152 D7
Bann Cl RM15 ...172 B6
Banner Cl RM11 ...171 D2
Bannister Dr CM13 ...95 C3
Bannister Gn SS12 ...121 E6
Bannister Ho RM20 ...177 D8
Banson's La CM5 ...49 A3
Bansons Ct CM5 ...49 A3
Bansons Way CM5 ...49 A3
Bantel Villas EN11 ...21 C8
Banyards RM11 ...136 F2
Banyardway SS4 ...125 C4
Barbara Ave SS8 ...163 F2
Barbara Cl SS4 ...125 E2
Barbary Lodge CM2 ...32 A2
Barbel Cl EN8 ...65 A5
Barber Cl RM3 ...114 C3
Barbour Gn SS12 ...121 D5

Barbrook Way CM3 ...56 E1
Barclay Cl CM2 ...55 A6
Barclay Ct EN11 ...21 A5
Barclay Oval IG8 ...110 A6
Barclay Rd SS13 ...121 E1
Barclay Way RM20 ...171 F1
Bardell Cl CM1 ...31 F6
Bardenville Rd SS8 ...164 E3
Bardeswell Cl CM14 ...116 C8
Bardfield Com Prim Sch
SS16 ...142 E4
Bardfield Way SS6 ...123 A3
Bards Ct RM3 ...114 B3
Barfields IG10 ...89 A5
Barfields Gdns IG10 ...89 A5
Barfields Path IG10 ...89 A5
Barge Pier Rd SS3 ...168 E5
Barham Cl RM7 ...113 B1
Barington Ct CM3 ...95 C3
Bark Burr Rd RM16 ...172 F4
Barkers Mead CM22 ...2 B8
Barking Abbey Comp Sch & Sports Coll IG11 ...152 F6
Barking Abbey Comp Sch (Lower Sch) IG11 ...152 E7
Barking Coll RM7 ...135 D2
Barking Hospl IG11 ...152 F5
Barking Prec RM8 ...153 B8
Barking Rd E6 ...152 A4
Barking Sta IG11 ...152 C6
Barkingside Sta IG6 ...133 D8
Barkis Cl CM1 ...31 D7
Barkwood Cl RM7 ...135 C6
Barle Gdns RM15 ...172 B7
Barley Cl Basildon SS16 ...141 A3
Hatfield Heath CM22 ...3 E2
Barley Croft CM18 ...23 E4
Barley Ct 2 EN11 ...21 D8
Barley Field CM15 ...71 F2
Barley La IG3,RM6 ...134 B5
Barley Lane Prim Sch
RM6 ...134 B4
Barley Mead CM3 ...57 B6
Barleycorn Way RM11 ...136 F5
Barleyfields Cl RM6 ...134 C4
Barleylands Farm Mus ✱
CM11 ...119 E5
Barleylands Rd CM11,
SS15 ...119 F4
Barling Magna Com Prim Sch
SS3 ...149 D7
Barling Rd SS3 ...149 B6
Barlow Way RM13 ...169 E8
Barlow's Reach CM2 ...33 A4
Barn Ct CM21 ...1 E3
Barn Gn CM1 ...32 E8
Barn Hill CM19 ...22 B4
Barn Mead
Doddinghurst CM15 ...72 C3
Harlow CM17 ...23 E6
Theydon Bois CM16 ...67 E3
Barn The RM17 ...173 B2
Barnaby Rudge CM1 ...31 F7
Barnaby Way
Basildon SS15 ...141 D7
Chigwell IG7 ...111 B7
Barnard Acres EN9 ...43 E8
Barnard Cl SS16 ...142 E2
Barnard Ct 18 DA2 ...176 B1
Barnard Rd
Galleywood CM2 ...54 C2
Sawbridgeworth CM21 ...1 E4
Southend-on-S SS2 ...146 C2
Barnardo Dr IG6 ...133 C7
Barnards Ave SS8 ...164 D4
Barncombe Cl SS7 ...144 D6
Barncroft Cl IG10 ...89 A4
Barncroft Gn IG10 ...89 A4
Barncroft Rd IG10 ...89 A4
Barnes Ct IG8 ...110 D5
Barnes Farm Dr CM3 ...82 F7
Barnes Farm Jun & Inf Schs
CM2 ...33 A4
Barnes Ho 8 IG11 ...152 D4
Barnes Mill Rd CM2 ...32 F2
Barnes Rd IG1 ...152 C7
Barnet Park Rd SS11 ...99 F2
Barnett Ct RM17 ...173 C1
Barneveld Ave SS8 ...164 E3
Barnfield Epping CM16 ...46 A3
Hatfield Broad Oak CM22 ...4 A5
Wickford SS11 ...121 E8
Barnfield Cl
Greenhithe DA9 ...176 F1
Hoddesdon EN11 ...21 A8
Lower Nazeing EN9 ...21 F1
Barnfield Cotts CM9 ...37 B5
Barnfield Mews CM1 ...32 A6
Barnmead CM5 ...47 F2
Barnmead Ct RM9 ...153 F7
Barnmead Gdns RM9 ...153 F7
Barnmead Rd RM9 ...153 F7
Barnmead Way CM0 ...106 B8
Barns Ct CM19 ...23 B3
Barnsley Rd RM3 ...114 B5
Barnstaple Cl SS1 ...168 A8
Barnstaple Path 7 RM3 ...114 D5
Barnstaple Rd
Romford RM3 ...114 C5
Southend-on-S SS1 ...168 B8
Barnston Way SS13 ...95 D4
Barnwell Dr SS5 ...124 D6
Barnyard The SS16 ...141 A4
Baron Ct Romford RM3 ...114 F2

Baron Ct *continued*
Southend-on-S SS2 ...147 F5
Baron Gdns IG6 ...133 C8
Baron Rd Dagenham RM8 ...134 D3
South Woodham Ferrers CM3 ...101 E7
Barons Court Inf Sch
SS0 ...166 F8
Barons Ct IG1 ...133 C2
Barons Way SS16 ...141 B4
Barra Glade SS12 ...121 F5
Barrack La CM3 ...18 E4
Barrack Rd CM1 ...17 B5
Barrack Row 1 DA11 ...179 B1
Barrack Sq 10 CM2 ...32 B2
Barrass Ct EN3 ...65 A2
Barrett Cl RM3 ...114 B3
Barrie Pavement 1
SS12 ...121 D5
Barrington Cl
1 Basildon SS14 ...142 F8
Great Baddow CM2 ...55 A6
Loughton IG10 ...89 C5
Southend-on-S SS3 ...149 E1
Woodford IG5 ...110 F2
Barrington Gdns SS14 ...142 F8
Barrington Gn IG10 ...89 C5
Barrington Pl CM4 ...74 B3
Barrington Rd
Little Ilford E12 ...152 A6
Loughton IG10 ...89 C5
Barringtons Cl SS6 ...123 C3
Barron's Ct CM5 ...48 F4
Barrow Chase CM2 ...33 B4
Barrow Hall Rd SS3 ...149 C5
Barrow Marsh CM9 ...38 A4
Barrows Rd CM19 ...22 F8
Barrowsand SS1 ...168 B6
Barry Cl RM16 ...174 A3
Barry Ct RM5 ...113 D5
Barrymore Wlk SS6 ...124 A3
Barstable Rd SS17 ...160 D1
Barstable Sch SS14 ...142 F6
Bartholomew Dr RM3 ...114 D1
Bartholomew Ho 16
E1 ...111 A3
Bartlett Cl CM3 ...60 D7
Bartletts SS6 ...146 A8
Bartletts Ho 19 RM10 ...154 B6
Bartley Cl SS7 ...144 B6
Bartley Rd SS7 ...144 B6
Bartlow End SS13 ...143 B8
Bartlow Gdns RM5 ...113 D2
Bartlow Side SS13 ...143 B8
Barton Cl Chigwell IG7 ...111 C6
South Woodham F CM3 ...79 D1
Barton Ct 8 CM14 ...116 C6
Barton Friars IG7 ...111 C6
Barton Mdws IG6 ...133 C7
Barton Rd RM12 ...136 A3
Baryta Ct SS17 ...160 C1
Baryta Ct SS9 ...165 E3
Basedale Rd RM9 ...153 B5
Basil Mews CM17 ...11 C1
Basildon Ave IG5 ...111 A2
Basildon Bsns Ctr SS14 ...142 A8
Basildon Dr SS15 ...141 C8
Basildon Hospl SS16 ...142 A3
Basildon Rd SS15 ...141 E8
Basildon Rise SS15 ...141 E8
Basildon Sta SS14 ...142 A5
Basildon Trad Ctr SS14 ...141 F8
Basildon Zoo ✱ SS16 ...142 C6
Basilica Ho SS11 ...122 B7
Basin Rd CM9 ...37 D3
Basing Ho 7 IG11 ...152 D4
Bassenthwaite Rd SS7 ...144 F1
Bassett Bsns Units CM16 ...46 F4
Bassett Gdns CM16 ...47 B5
Bassett Ho RM9 ...153 B4
Bassett's La CM5,CM9 ...35 A4
Bassetts La CM3,CM9 ...35 A4
Bastable Ave IG11 ...153 A3
Bata Ave RM18 ...175 D4
Batavia Rd SS8 ...163 D4
Bate-Dudley Dr CM0 ...42 B3
Bateman Cl IG11 ...152 C6
Bateman Rd E4 ...109 A4
Batemans Mews CM14 ...116 B6
Bates Ind Est RM3 ...115 A3
Bates Rd Maldon CM9 ...37 B4
Romford RM3 ...115 A3
Bath Rd RM6 ...134 E5
Bath St DA11 ...179 B1
Bathurst Rd IG1 ...133 B3
Baton Cl RM19 ...171 D2
Batt's Rd CM0 ...84 A8
Battis The 1 RM1 ...135 E5
Battle Ct CM5 ...49 A4
Battle Rd DA17 ...169 C2
Battles Bridge Motorcycle Mus ✱ SS11 ...100 D2
Battlesbridge Craft Ctr ✱
CM3 ...100 E2
Battlesbridge Sta SS11 ...100 D2
Battleswick SS14 ...120 E1
Bawden Way CM2 ...54 D8
Bawdsey Ave IG2 ...133 F7
Baxter Ave SS2 ...147 F1
Baxter Gdns RM3 ...114 D8
Baxter Rd IG1 ...152 B7
Baxters CM3 ...57 A7
Bay Cl SS8 ...164 B2
Bay Manor La RM20 ...176 F8
Bay Tree Cl IG6 ...111 B3
Bay View CM0 ...106 C8

Bayleys Mead CM13 ...117 C8
Bayly Rd DA1 ...176 A1
Baymans Wood CM15 ...116 F8
Baytree Ho E4 ...87 B2
Baywood Sq IG7 ...112 B6
Beach Ave SS9 ...166 A8
Beach Ct
Great Wakering SS3 ...150 C3
Southend-on-S SS0 ...166 C7
Beach House Gdns SS8 ...164 E2
Beach Rd
Canvey Island SS8 ...164 D4
Southend-on-S SS1 ...167 C7
Southend-on-S, Shoeburyness SS1 ...168 F5
Beach's Dr CM1 ...31 D3
Beaches Cl SS5 ...125 A6
Beachway SS8 ...164 B2
Beachy Dr CM0 ...62 C8
Beacon Hill
Kelvedon Hatch CM14 ...71 C2
Maldon CM9 ...36 E2
Purfleet RM19 ...171 B1
Beacon Hill Ind Est
RM19 ...171 B1
Beacon Hill Rd CM14 ...71 B2
Beaconfield Ave CM16 ...46 A2
Beaconfield Rd CM16 ...46 A2
Beaconfield Way CM16 ...46 A2
Beacons The IG10 ...67 A1
Beacontree Ave E17 ...109 D1
Beadle's Par RM10 ...154 C6
Beadles The CM22 ...2 B8
Beads Hall La CM15 ...94 B4
Beal High Sch IG4 ...132 E2
Beal Rd IG1 ...133 A2
Beam Ave RM10 ...154 B6
Beam Prim Sch RM10 ...154 C3
Beambridge SS13 ...143 A6
Beambridge Ct 2 SS13 ...143 A6
Beambridge Mews
SS13 ...143 A6
Beambridge Pl 1 SS13 ...143 A6
Beaminster Gdns
Ilford IG6 ...133 B8
Redbridge IG6 ...111 B1
Beamish Cl CM16 ...47 C6
Beams Cl CM11 ...119 C8
Beams Way CM11 ...119 C8
Beamway RM10 ...154 D5
Bean Rd DA9 ...177 B1
Beanfield Rd CM21 ...1 A4
Beansland Gr RM6 ...134 E8
Bear Cl RM7 ...135 B5
Bearblock Cotts RM14 ...156 C6
Beardsley Dr CM1 ...32 F7
Beardsley Terr RM8 ...153 B7
Bearing Cl IG7 ...112 A6
Bearing Way IG7 ...112 A6
Bearsted Dr SS13 ...143 C5
Beaton Cl DA9 ...177 B2
Beatrice Ave SS8 ...164 B4
Beatrice Cl SS5 ...124 D6
Beatrice Ct IG9 ...110 D8
Beatty La SS4 ...142 E6
Beatty Rise CM3 ...101 F6
Beattyville Gdns IG6 ...133 B7
Beauchamps CM0 ...106 B8
Beauchamps Cl CM1 ...32 E8
Beauchamps Dr SS11 ...122 A8
Beauchamps Sch SS11 ...122 A8
Beaufort Cl Chingford E4 ...109 B4
Grays RM16 ...172 F3
North Weald Bassett CM16 ...47 A4
Romford RM7 ...135 C2
Beaufort Gdns IG1 ...133 A3
Beaufort Rd
Billericay CM12 ...96 F2
Chelmsford CM2 ...33 A4
Beaufort St SS2 ...148 D1
Beaulieu Bvd CM1 ...33 A7
Beaulieu Dr EN9 ...65 B6
Beauly Way RM1 ...113 C2
Beaumaris Dr IG8 ...110 D3
Beaumont Cl RM2 ...114 C1
Beaumont Cres RM13 ...155 A6
Beaumont Gdns CM13 ...95 C3
Beaumont Park Dr CM19 ...22 B8
Beaumont Pk CM3 ...56 C6
Beaumont Way CM9 ...59 B8
Beaumont Wlk CM1 ...31 D5
Beaver Rd IG6 ...112 C5
Beaver Twr SS9 ...146 E6
Beazley End SS12 ...121 E6
Bebington Cl CM12 ...97 A3
Beccles Ct SS11 ...121 D8
Beccles Dr IG11 ...152 F6
Beck Farm Cl SS8 ...164 F3
Beck Rd SS8 ...164 F3
Becket Ave E6 ...152 A2
Becket Cl
Brentwood CM13 ...116 C4
Rochford SS4 ...125 D5
Becket Way CM3 ...101 F6
Beckett Dr SS17 ...160 D4
Becketts SS15 ...141 A6
Becketts Ct
Brentwood CM13 ...116 C4
Chelmsford CM1 ...32 A3
Beckney Ave SS5 ...102 C1
Beckton Alps Ski Ctr ✱
E6 ...152 A1
Becontree Ave RM8 ...134 D2
Becontree Prim Sch
RM8 ...134 B1
Becontree Sta RM9 ...153 D6
Bedale Rd RM3 ...115 A5
Beddington Rd IG3 ...133 F4

Bede Rd RM6 ...134 C5
Bedford Cl SS6 ...123 D1
Bedford Gdns RM12 ...136 C2
Bedford Ho 1 RM3 ...115 A4
Bedford Pl SS8 ...163 F4
Bedford Rd
Basildon SS15 ...141 B6
Chingford E17 ...109 A1
Grays RM17 ...173 B1
Ilford IG1 ...133 B1
Wallend E6 ...152 A4
Woodford E18 ...110 A1
Bedfords Pk Nature Trails ✱
RM4 ...113 F4
Bedloes Ave SS11 ...122 E7
Bedwell Ct 4 RM6 ...134 D4
Bedwell Rd DA17 ...169 A1
Beech Ave
Brentwood CM13 ...116 F7
Chigwell IG9 ...110 B8
Rayleigh SS6 ...123 D3
Upminster RM14 ...156 B8
Beech Cl
Burnham-on-C CM0 ...106 B6
Hornchurch RM12 ...136 B1
Loughton IG10 ...89 B6
Beech Ct Basildon SS14 ...142 F5
3 Buckhurst Hill IG9 ...110 D8
Dartford DA1 ...176 A1
6 Ilford E12 ...133 A1
Beech Dr CM21 ...11 C8
Beech Gdns RM10 ...154 C5
Beech Gr Aveley RM15 ...171 C4
Redbridge IG6 ...111 E4
Beech Hall Cres E4 ...109 D3
Beech Hall Rd E4 ...109 D3
Beech Hill Gdns EN9 ...66 B2
Beech Ho 5 CM13 ...95 C3
Beech La IG9 ...110 B8
Beech Lodge SS3 ...168 F7
Beech Pl CM16 ...67 F8
Beech Rd Basildon SS14 ...142 F5
Hadleigh SS7 ...145 E2
Hullbridge SS5 ...101 C3
Willingale CM5 ...28 D4
Beech Spinney CM14 ...116 C5
Beech St RM7 ...135 C2
Beech Terr IG10 ...88 E5
Beech Tree Glade E4 ...87 F1
Beecham Ct SS15 ...141 C8
Beechcombe SS17 ...161 B5
Beechcroft Ave SS17 ...175 A2
Beechcroft Rd
Canvey Island SS8 ...163 E3
Woodford E18 ...110 B1
Beeches Cl CM1 ...31 E6
Beeches Rd
Chelmsford CM1 ...31 E2
Heybridge CM9 ...36 F5
Rawreth SS11 ...101 A2
Beeches The
Brentwood CM14 ...116 B7
Tilbury RM18 ...175 D3
Beechfield Hoddesdon EN11 ...8 A2
Sawbridgeworth CM21 ...1 F2
Beechfield Gdns RM7 ...135 C4
Beechfield Wlk EN9 ...65 D4
Beechmont Gdns SS2 ...147 A4
Beechwood Dr IG8 ...109 F5
Beechwood Gdns
Ilford IG5 ...133 A7
Rainham RM13 ...170 B8
Redbridge IG5 ...132 F6
Beechwood Pk E18 ...132 A8
Beecroft Cres SS8 ...164 A6
Beedell Ave
Southend-on-S SS0 ...147 D2
Wickford SS11 ...122 A6
Beehive Chase CM15 ...72 D4
Beehive Ct
Hatfield Heath CM22 ...3 A3
Romford RM3 ...114 F3
Beehive La Basildon SS14 ...142 B4
Chelmsford CM2 ...54 C5
Ilford IG1 ...133 A5
Redbridge IG1 ...132 F6
Beehive Lane Prim Sch
CM2 ...54 D5
Beeleigh Ave SS16 ...141 C3
Beeleigh Chase CM9 ...36 D4
Beeleigh Cl SS2 ...147 C3
Beeleigh Cross SS14 ...142 E7
Beeleigh E SS14 ...142 E8
Beeleigh Link CM2 ...32 F3
Beeleigh Rd CM9 ...36 F3
Beeleigh W SS14 ...142 E7
Beeston Ct 4 DA2 ...176 B1
Beggarhill CM4 ...73 E6
Begonia Cl CM1 ...32 F6
Beke Hall Chase N SS6 ...122 E4
Beke Hall Chase S SS6 ...122 E4
Bekeswell La CM2 ...53 F2
Bekeswell Pl CM2 ...54 C2
Belchamps Rd SS11 ...121 F8
Belchamps Way SS5 ...124 C5
Belcher Rd 6 EN11 ...21 A7
Belchers La EN9 ...44 C7
Belfairs Cl SS9 ...146 C2
Belfairs Ct SS9 ...146 B6
Belfairs Dr
Dagenham RM6 ...134 C4
Southend-on-S SS9 ...146 C2
Belfairs High Sch SS9 ...146 C2
Belfairs Park Cl SS9 ...146 B5
Belfairs Park Dr SS9 ...146 B5
Belgrave Ave RM2 ...114 D1
Belgrave Cl
Chelmsford CM2 ...54 D7

Belgrave Cl *continued*
Rayleigh SS6 ....123 B4
Southend-on-S SS9 ....146 B7
Belgrave Market IG1 ....133 A2
Belgrave Rd
Billericay CM12 ....97 A4
Ilford IG1 ....133 F2
Redbridge IG1 ....132 F3
Southend-on-S SS9 ....146 B7
Wanstead E11 ....132 A3
Belgrave Terr IG8 ......110 A7
Belgravia Mans SS1 ...167 D6
Belhus Woods Ctry Pk★
RM15 ....156 D2
Bell Ave RM3 ....114 B2
Bell Cl DA9 ....176 F2
Bell Cnr RM14 ....137 C2
Bell Comm CM16 ......67 E7
Bell Ct CM3 ....78 A1
Bell Farm Ave RM10 ...135 C1
Bell Farm Gn CM12 ...119 B8
Bell Hill CM3 ....56 C7
Bell Hill Cl CM12 .....119 B8
Bell Ho
6 Dagenham RM10 .....154 B6
Great Wakering SS3 ....150 A3
Bell House Rd RM7 ....135 C3
Bell La EN11 ....21 A6
Bell Mead
Ingatestone CM4 ......74 B3
Sawbridgeworth CM21 ...1 E2
Bell St Great Baddow CM2 .54 F6
Sawbridgeworth CM21 ....1 E2
Bell Wlk SS2 ....147 D4
Bell-Reeves Cl SS17 ...160 C2
Bellamy Rd E4 ....109 B4
Belle Staines Pleasaunce
E4 ....109 A8
Belle Vue CM2 ....32 A1
Belle Vue Rd
Chingford E17 ....109 D1
Romford RM5 ....113 C4
Bellevue Ave SS1 .....167 C8
Bellevue Mews SS2 ....148 C1
Bellevue Pl SS1 ....167 C8
Bellevue Rd
Billericay CM12 ....96 F2
Hornchurch RM11 ......136 F4
Southend-on-S SS2 ....148 C1
Bellfield SS16 ....142 E3
Bellfield Gdns CM17 ...24 C7
Bellflower Path RM3 ...114 C3
Bellhouse Cres SS9 ....146 D5
Bellhouse La
Pilgrims Hatch CM14 ...93 E4
Southend-on-S SS9 ....146 D5
Bellhouse Rd SS9 .....146 D6
Bellhouse Villas CM1 ....6 D3
Bellingham Ct IG11 ....153 B2
Bellingham La SS6 .....123 D2
Bellmaine Ave SS17 ...160 F4
Bellmead CM1 ....32 B2
Bells Chase CM2 ......54 E6
Bells Corner Par SS17 .142 B1
Bells Hill SS16 ....142 B2
Bells Wlk CM21 ....1 E2
Belmonde Dr CM1 ......32 E7
Belmont Ave
Upminster RM14 ......136 F2
Wickford SS12 ....121 B7
Belmont Cl
Chelmsford CM1 ....32 E7
Chingford E4 ....109 D5
Wickford SS12 ....121 B7
Woodford IG8 ....110 B6
Belmont Rd Grays RM17 ..177 F8
Hornchurch RM12 .....136 D1
Ilford IG1 ....133 C1
Belsteads Farm La CM3 ..19 E2
Belstedes SS15 ....141 D6
Beltinge Rd RM3 ......136 F8
Belton Bridge SS9 ....165 D8
Belton Gdns SS9 ......165 C8
Belton Way E SS9 .....165 C8
Belton Way W SS9 ....165 B8
Beltwood Rd DA17 .....169 C2
Belvawney Cl CM1 ......31 E6
Belvedere Ave
Hockley SS5 ....124 C6
Redbridge IG5 ....111 B1
Belvedere Cl CM3 ......56 F7
Belvedere Ct
Burnham-on-C CM0 ....106 C3
Chelmsford CM2 ....53 F8
Maldon CM9 ....58 F8
Belvedere Ind Est DA17 .169 C5
Belvedere Jun & Inf Schs
DA17 ....169 B3
Belvedere Link Bsns Pk
DA8 ....169 C3
Belvedere Pl CM9 ......58 F8
Belvedere Rd
Brentwood CM14 ......115 F7
Burnham-on-C CM0 ....106 C3
Danbury CM3 ....56 F7
Belvedere Sta DA17 ....169 B3
Belvedere The CM0 ....106 C4
Belvoir The CM4 ....74 A3
Ben Tillet Cl IG11 ......153 A5
Benbow Dr CM3 ....101 E6
Benderloch SS8 ....163 E4
Benedict Ct RM6 ......134 F5
Benedict Dr CM1 ......31 E2
Benets Rd RM11 ....137 A4
Benfleet For Canvey Island
Sta SS7 ....163 D8
Benfleet Park Rd SS7 ..144 E6
Benfleet Rd SS7 ......145 B2

Bengal Rd IG1 ....133 B1
Bengeo Gdns RM6 .....134 C5
Benham Wlk SS13 ......143 C8
Benhurst Ave RM12 ....136 B1
Benhurst Prim Sch
RM12 ....136 B1
Benjamin Cl RM11 .....136 A5
Benjamin Ct RM13 .....154 E2
Benleigh Ho SS6 ......123 C3
Bennett Rd RM6 ....134 C4
Bennett's Ave E4 ....77 F3
Bennett's Castle La
RM8 ....134 D1
Bennington Rd IG8 .....109 E3
Bennions RM12 ....155 D6
Bennison Dr RM3 ......114 E1
Benrek Cl IG6 ....111 C2
Benskins La RM4 ....92 D1
Benson Ct **4** EN3 ......65 A1
Benson Rd RM17 ......178 C8
Bentalls SS14 ....120 A1
Bentalls Cl SS14 ......148 A4
Bentalls Complex The
CM9 ....37 B3
Bentley Dr Harlow CM17 ..24 C7
Ilford IG2 ....133 C5
Bentley St DA12 ......179 C1
Bentley St Paul's CE Prim Sch
CM15 ....93 D6
Bentley Street Ind Est **8**
DA12 ....179 C1
Bentley Villas CM22 .....3 B2
Bentley Way IG8 ......110 A7
Bentleys The SS2 ......147 A7
Benton Gdns SS17 .....160 F5
Benton Rd IG1 ....133 D3
Bentonwood SS7 ......145 C5
Bentry Cl RM8 ....134 E2
Bentry Rd RM8 ....134 F2
Benvenue Ave SS9 .....146 F6
Benyon Ct RM15 ......157 C3
Benyon Path RM15 ....157 C3
Benyon Prim Sch RM15 .157 C3
Berberis Cl SS16 ......140 F4
Berberis Ct IG11 ......152 B6
Berdan Ct EN3 ....65 A2
Berdens SS16 ....142 D5
Bere Cl DA9 ....177 C2
Berecroft CM18 ......23 D3
Beredens La CM13 .....115 F1
Berens Cl SS11 ......99 F1
Beresford Cl SS7 ......145 D4
Beresford Ct
Billericay CM12 ....96 F5
Hadleigh SS7 ....145 D4
Beresford Dr IG8 .....110 C6
Beresford Gdns
Dagenham RM6 ......134 E6
Hadleigh SS7 ....145 D4
Beresford Mans **19** SS1 .167 C7
Beresford Rd
Chingford, Chingford Green
E4 ....87 D1
Chingford, Highams Park
E17 ....109 B2
Gravesend DA11 ......178 E1
Southend-on-S SS1 ....167 C7
Berg Ave SS8 ....164 D5
Bergen Ct RM6 ....58 E8
Bergholt Ave IG4 ......132 E4
Berica Ct IG6 ....133 C8
Berkeley Ave
Redbridge IG5 ....111 B1
Romford RM5 ....113 C1
Berkeley Cl RM11 .....137 B2
Berkeley Ct SS4 ......147 F7
Berkeley Dr
Billericay CM12 ....97 A5
Hornchurch RM11 .....137 A2
Berkeley Gdns SS9 ....146 A1
Berkeley La SS8 ......164 A3
Berkeley Terr RM18 ...179 A7
Berkely Dr CM2 ....32 F2
Berkhampstead Rd
DA17 ....169 A1
Berkley Cres **4** DA12 .179 C1
Berkley Ct SS0 ....147 E2
Berkley Hill SS17 ......160 E4
Berkley Rd DA12 ......179 B1
Berkshire Cl SS9 ......146 A3
Berkshire Way RM11 ...137 A7
Berman's Cl CM13 .....117 B8
Bermuda Rd RM18 .....179 A5
Bernard Gr EN9 ....65 B6
Bernard Rd RM7 ......135 C4
Bernard St **14** DA12 ...179 B1
Bernards IG6 ....111 D3
Berners Wlk SS14 .....142 D8
Bernice Ct RM13 ......155 C1
Bernwell Rd E4 ....109 E7
Berry Cl Basildon SS16 .141 B4
Dagenham RM10 .....154 A7
Hornchurch RM12 .....155 D7
Wickford SS12 ....121 B6
Berry La SS16 ....141 B4
Berry Vale CM3 ....101 C6
Berrybank Cl **4** E4 ....109 C8
Berryman Rd RM8 .....134 C1
Berrymore Wlk SS6 ....123 F2
Berrys Arc SS6 ....123 E4
Bersham La RM17 .....172 F2
Berther Rd RM11 .....136 E4
Berwick Ave CM1 ......32 B7
Berwick Cl EN8 ....65 A5
Berwick Ct **10** DA2 ....176 B1
Berwick La CM5 ....69 C6
Berwick Pond Cl RM13 .155 D3

Berwick Pond Rd RM13 .155 F5
Berwick Rd RM13 .....155 D3
Berwood Rd SS17 .....160 F3
Betchworth Rd IG3 ....133 E1
Bethany Ho RM6 ......134 D8
Bethell Ave IG1 ....133 A4
Betjeman Cl SS6 ......123 F3
Betjeman Way CM5 .....48 F5
Betjemen Mews SS2 ...148 A2
Betony Cres CM12 .....96 F5
Betony Rd RM3 ....114 D4
Betoyne Ave E4 ......109 E6
Betoyne Cl CM11 .....97 D2
Bett's La SS5 ....124 D6
Betterton Rd RM13 ....154 E3
Betts La EN9 ....22 C2
Betula Wlk RM13 .....155 D2
Beulah Rd Epping CM16 .46 A2
Hornchurch RM12 .....136 C1
Bevan Ave IG11 ....153 A5
Bevan Ho RM16 ......173 A6
Bevan Way RM12 .....136 F1
Bevans Cl DA9 ....177 C1
Beveland Rd SS8 ......165 A3
Beverley Ave SS8 .....164 A3
Beverley Cl
Hornchurch RM11 .....136 F4
Orsett RM16 ....174 D7
Beverley Cres IG8 .....110 B3
Beverley Gdns
Hornchurch RM11 .....136 F4
Southend-on-S SS2 ....147 A6
Beverley Rd
Chingford E4 ....109 D4
Dagenham RM9 ......153 E8
Beverley Rise CM11 ....97 C1
Bevil Ct EN11 ....8 A1
Bevile Ho RM17 ......178 B7
Bevin Cl RM15 ....171 C4
Bevin Ho RM15 ......171 C4
Bevin Wlk SS17 ......160 D2
Bevis Cl DA2 ....176 C1
Bewley Ct SS2 ....148 E2
Bexhill Dr RM17 ......177 F8
Bexley Coll DA17 .....169 C2
Bexley Coll Erith Rd Campus
DA17 ....169 B1
Bexley Gdns RM6 .....134 B6
Bexley Rd DA8 ....169 F1
Beyers Gdns EN11 ......8 A1
Beyers Prospect EN11 ...8 A1
Beyers Ride EN11 ......8 A1
Bibby Cl SS17 ....161 A3
Bickenhall SS3 ....168 D8
Bickerton Point CM3 ...101 F6
Bicknacre Rd
Danbury CM3 ....56 F4
East Hanningfield CM3 ..78 C8
Biddenden Ct **9** SS13 .143 C6
Bideford Cl
Romford RM3 ....114 C2
Southend-on-S SS0 ....147 A5
Biggin La RM16 ......179 B8
Bight The CM3 ....101 C5
Billericay Rd
Ingrave CM13 ....117 F3
Little Burstead CM12,
CM13 ....118 B3
Billericay Sch The
CM12 ....119 B8
Billericay Sta CM12 ....97 A3
Billers Chase CM1 .....33 A7
Billet La
Hornchurch RM11 .....136 D4
Stanford-le-H SS17 ....160 E1
Billet Rd Chingford E17 .109 A2
Ilford RM6 ....134 C8
Billings Cl RM9 ....153 C5
Bilton Rd Chelmsford CM1 .31 F1
Hadleigh SS7 ....145 E3
Bingham Cl RM11 .....172 B7
Bingley Rd EN11 ......21 C6
Binley Rd CM2 ....32 F2
Birch Cl
Buckhurst Hill IG9 ....110 D7
Canewdon SS4 ....104 E1
Canvey Island SS8 ....163 F3
Rayleigh SS6 ....123 C3
Romford RM7 ....135 B8
South Benfleet SS7 ...144 B7
South Ockendon RM15 .157 C1
Birch Cres
Hornchurch RM11 .....136 F4
South Ockendon RM15 .157 D2
Birch Ct Chingford E4 ...109 B4
Dagenham RM6 ......134 B6
Birch Gdns
Dagenham RM10 .....135 C1
Tillingham CM0 ....63 E4
Birch Gn SS12 ....121 C7
Birch La CM4 ....75 F3
Birch Pl DA9 ....176 E1
Birch Rd Romford RM7 .135 B8
Tillingham CM0 ....63 E4
Birch View CM16 ......46 B2
Bircham Rd SS2 ......148 A2
Birchdale SS5 ....101 D3
Birchdale Gdns RM6 ...134 D4
Birche Cl SS9 ....146 E4
Birches The
Brentwood CM13 ......116 E7
North Weald Bassett CM16 .47 B5
South Benfleet SS7 ...144 C8
Birches Wlk CM2 ......54 A2
Birchmores SS15 .....141 A7
Birchwood
South Benfleet SS7 ....144 B7
Waltham Abbey EN9 ....65 E5
Birchwood Cl CM13 ...116 C4

Birchwood Dr SS9 .....147 A2
Birchwood Rd
Cock Clarks CM3 ....57 C7
Corringham SS17 .....161 B5
Bird La
Great Warley CM13 ....138 D8
Little Warley CM13 ....116 C1
Upminster RM14 .....137 D6
Birdbrook Cl
Brentwood CM13 ......95 B3
Dagenham RM10 .....154 C5
Birds Cl CM11 ....98 C5
Birds Farm Ave RM5 ...113 B2
Birds Gn CM5 ....28 A5
Birk Beck CM1 ....32 C5
Birkbeck Gdns IG8 ....110 A8
Birkbeck Rd
Brentwood CM13 ......95 D3
Ilford IG2 ....133 D6
Romford RM5 ....135 D3
Birkdale Ave RM3 .....115 A3
Birs Cl SS11 ....99 D1
Biscay SS2 ....147 D6
Bishop Hall La CM1 ....32 B4
Bishop Rd CM1 ....32 B3
Bishop's Ct SS8 ......164 D3
Bishop's Hall Rd CM15 ..94 B3
Bishops Ave RM6 .....134 C5
Bishops Cl SS13 ......121 A2
Bishops Court Gdns CM2 .32 E4
Bishops Ct
Greenhithe DA9 ......176 E2
Romford RM7 ....135 B7
Bishops Rd
Stanford-le-H SS17 ....160 F3
Wickford SS12 ....121 D3
Bishops Wlk CM15 ....116 F8
Bishops' CE & RC Prim Sch
The CM1 ....32 E6
Bishopsfield CM18 .....23 E5
Bishopsteignton SS3 ...149 E6
Bittern Ct E4 ....87 D2
Black Adder Cotts EN9 ..43 D8
Black Bush La SS17 ...159 D3
Black Chapel La CM6 ....7 E8
Black Lion Ct CM17 ....11 C4
Black Smiths SS12 ......8 A7
Blackall Ind Est CM3 ...79 E1
Blackberry Gr CM0 .....42 B3
Blackborne Rd RM10 ...154 B6
Blackbush Ave RM6 ....134 D6
Blackbush Spring CM20 .11 A1
Blackdown SS0 ......147 E1
Blackgate Rd SS3 .....168 G7
Blackhorse La CM16 ....47 D6
Blackmore Ave SS8 ....164 B2
Blackmore Ct EN9 .....66 A6
Blackmore Mead CM2 ..72 F8
Blackmore Prim Sch
CM4 ....50 E1
Blackmore Rd
Blackmore CM1 ....51 D3
Buckhurst Hill IG9 ....88 E2
Grays RM17 ....173 C1
Hook End CM15 ......72 C5
Ingatestone CM4 .....73 D6
Kelvedon Hatch CM15 ..71 F2
Blackmore Wlk SS6 ....124 A2
Blackmores SS15 .....140 F6
Blackshots La RM16 ...173 C5
Blacksmith Cl
Billericay CM12 ....97 D5
Chelmsford CM1 ......32 C6
Dagenham RM10 .....154 B6
Blacksmith's La RM13 ..154 F4
Blacksmiths Alley CM4 ..72 E8
Blacksmiths Cotts CM17 .24 C4
Blacksmiths Way CM21 ...1 B1
Blackthorn Cl CM1 .....31 A1
Blackthorn Rd
Grays RM16 ....173 B5
Hockley SS5 ....124 F8
Blackthorn Way CM14 ..116 C3
Blackthorne Dr E4 .....109 D6
Blackthorne Rd SS8 ....164 C3
Blackwater SS7 ......144 F4
Blackwater Cl
Burnham-on-C CM0 ....106 C5
Chelmsford CM1 ......32 C6
Heybridge Basin CM9 ...37 E3
Rainham RM13 ......169 E8
Southend-on-S SS3 ...149 E1
Blackwood Chine CM3 ..101 E6
Blake Ave IG11 ....152 F4
Blake Cl RM13 ....154 F4
Blake Ct CM3 ....101 E6
Blake Hall Cres E11 ...132 A3
Blake Hall Dr SS11 ....122 A6
Blake Hall Gdns★ CM5 ..48 D7
Blake Hall Rd
Chipping Ongar CM5 ...48 A5
Wanstead E11 ....132 A4
Blake Way RM18 .....179 C5
Blakeborough Dr RM3 ..114 E1
Blakes Ct CM21 ....1 E1
Blakesley Ho **4** E12 ...133 A1
Blanchard Gr EN3 .....65 B1
Blanchard Mews RM3 ..114 F3
Blandford Cl RM7 .....135 B7
Blandford Cres E4 .....87 C2
Blaney Cres E6 ......152 B2
Blatches Chase
Rayleigh SS2 ....147 F7
Southend-on-S SS2 ...147 A6
Blatchford Ho **8** RM10 .135 A1

Blenheim Ave IG2 .....133 A5
Blenheim Chase SS9 ...146 E3
Blenheim Cl
Bicknacre CM3 ....56 F2
Hockley SS5 ....124 E8
Romford RM7 ....135 C7
Sawbridgeworth CM21 ..11 C8
Upminster RM14 .....137 E3
Blenheim Cres SS9 ....146 E2
Blenheim Ct
Hornchurch RM12 .....155 C7
4 Wickford SS11 .....122 A5
Woodford IG8 ....110 B3
Woodford IG8 ....110 C2
Blenheim Gdns
Aveley RM15 ....171 B5
Mayland CM3 ....61 A1
Blenheim Mews SS9 ...146 E3
Blenheim Park SS9 ....146 F4
Blenheim Prim Sch SS9 .146 F3
Blenheim Rd CM15 ....94 A3
Blenheim Way CM16 ...47 A4
Blessing Way IG11 ....153 C3
Bletchington Ct DA17 ..169 A2
Blewetts Cotts RM13 ..154 F2
Bligh Rd DA11 ....179 A1
Blind La Goldhanger CM9 .38 C7
Howe Green CM2 .....55 F4
Little Burstead CM12 ..118 A3
Mundon CM9 ....59 C2
West Hanningfield CM2 ..76 F5
Blithbury Rd RM9 .....153 B6
Blockhouse Rd RM17 ..178 C8
Blomville Rd RM8 .....134 E1
Bloomfield Cres IG2 ...133 B5
Bloomfields The IG11 ..152 C6
Blossom Cl RM9 ......153 F4
Blountswood Rd
Hockley SS5 ....124 A8
Hullbridge SS5 ......123 F6
Blower Cl SS6 ....123 E3
Blows Cotts RM15 ....171 D5
Blue Anchor La RM18 ..174 E1
Blue House Farm Chase
CM3 ....103 B7
Blue Mill La CM9 ......35 C4
Bluebell Cl RM7 ......135 C2
Bluebell Gn **5** CM1 ....32 E7
Bluebell Way IG1 .....152 B6
Bluebell Wood CM12 ..96 E4
Blueberry Cl IG8 ......110 A4
Bluebird La RM10 .....154 A5
Bluegate Pk CM4 .....116 B7
Bluehouse Rd E4 ......109 E7
Bluemans CM16 ....47 D7
Bluemans End CM16 ...47 D7
Blunden Cl RM8 ......134 C3
Blunts Wall Rd CM12 ...96 E1
Blyth Ave SS3 ....168 C2
Blyth Wlk RM14 ......137 E5
Blythe Rd
Hoddesdon EN11 ......21 D5
Stanford-le-H SS17 ....160 E4
Blythe Way Maldon CM9 .59 A8
South Benfleet SS7 ...144 C5
Blythswood Rd IG3 ....134 A4
Blyton Cl SS12 ....121 D5
Boar Cl IG7 ....112 A5
Boarded Row SS4 .....128 A5
Boardman Ave E4 .....87 B4
Bobbing Cl SS4 ....125 F2
Bobbingworth Mill CM5 .48 A7
Bockingham Gn SS13 ..143 A8
Bodell Cl RM16 ....173 B3
Bodiam Cl SS13 ......143 B6
Bodle Ave DA10 ......177 C1
Bodley Cl CM16 ......45 F1
Bodmin Rd CM1 ......32 C5
Bohemia Chase SS9 ...146 D5
Boiler Ho The SS4 ....125 E2
Boleyn Cl Billericay CM12 .97 A5
Grays RM16 ....172 F3
Loughton IG10 ....88 E3
Southend-on-S SS9 ...146 C7
Boleyn Ct IG9 ....88 B1
Boleyn Gdns
Brentwood CM13 ......117 A7
Dagenham RM10 .....154 C5
Redbridge IG6 ....111 C4
Boleyn Way
Brentwood CM13 ......117 A7
Dagenham RM10 .....154 C5
Bolney Dr SS9 ....146 C7
Boltons The IG8 ......110 A6
Bommel Ave SS8 .....165 A3
Bonchurch Ave SS9 ...146 D2
Bonchurch Ct **20** RM19 .171 B1
Bond St Chelmsford CM2 .32 C2
Grays RM17 ....178 C8
Bonds Cotts SS15 .....15 A1
Bonet Mews RM11 ....136 E3
Bonham Gdns RM8 ....134 D2
Bonham Rd RM8 ......134 D1
Bonington Chase CM1 ..32 E8
Bonington Rd RM12 ...155 D7
Bonks Hill CM21 ....1 D1
Bonner Wlk RM16 ....172 F3
Bonnetions CM13 .....117 B7
Bonnygate SS14 .....142 D7
Bonnygate Prim Sch
RM15 ....172 B8
Boomes Ind Est RM13 .154 F1
Boons Cl RM3 ....33 E8
Booth Pl CM0 ....106 C5
Bootham Cl CM12 ....96 F1
Bootham Rd CM12 ....96 F1
Boothby Ct E4 ....109 C7

Booths Ct CM13 ....95 B3
Borda Cl CM1 ....32 A5
Border Edge Ho **6**
CM14 ....116 C6
Border's La IG10 ....89 B5
Boreham Cl SS15 ....122 B5
Boreham Ind Est CM3 ...20 F2
Boreham Prim Sch CM3 .33 F8
Boreham Rd CM3 ....20 F2
Borland Rd DA9 ....177 A2
Borley Ct RM16 ....174 D7
Borman Cl SS7 ....147 A6
Borough The CM5 ....48 F2
Borrett Ave SS8 ....164 A4
Borrowdale Cl
  Redbridge IG4 ....132 E7
  Thundersley SS7 ......144 F6
Borrowdale Rd
  Thundersley SS7 ......144 F6
  Thundersley SS7 ......144 F7
Borwick La
  Basildon CM11 ....120 F4
  Wickford CM11,SS12 ..121 A4
Bosanquet Rd EN11 .....21 C8
Boscombe Ave
  Grays RM17 ....173 D2
  Hornchurch RM11 .....136 D4
  Wickford SS12 ....120 F8
Boscombe Mews SS2 ...167 B8
Boscombe Rd SS2 .....148 B1
Bosgrove E4 ....109 C8
Boston Ave Rayleigh SS6 .123 B4
  Southend-on-S SS1 ...147 F1
Boston Lofts **2** SS2 ..147 F1
Boswell Ave SS4 ......125 D5
Boswells Dr CM2 ....32 C2
Boswells Sch The CM1 ..32 D6
Bosworth Cl SS5 ......124 F4
Bosworth Cres RM3 ...114 C4
Bosworth Ho DA8 .....169 E1
Bosworth Rd
  Dagenham RM10 ......135 A1
  Southend-on-S SS9 ...146 C7
Botany Cotts RM19 ....171 A1
Botany Terr RM19 .....171 A1
Botany Way RM19 .....171 B1
Botelers SS16 ....141 E4
Boteley Cl E4 ....109 D8
Botney Hill Rd CM12 ..118 D4
Bouchers Mead CM1 ....32 F7
Bouchier Wlk **3** RM3 .155 A6
Boulderwood Rd SS7 ..144 B5
Boulevard The
  3 Redbridge IG8 ...111 A3
  Rochford SS4 ....125 F3
Boult Rd SS15 ....141 C8
Boulter Gdns RM13 ...155 A7
Boulton Rd RM8 ......134 F2
Boundary Cl IG3 ......152 E8
Boundary Dr CM13 .....95 C3
Boundary Rd
  Barking IG11 ....152 C3
  Barking IG11 ....152 D4
  Romford RM1 ....136 A5
  Southend-on-S SS9 ..146 B8
  Upminster RM14 .....137 B2
Bounderby Gr CM1 .....31 E7
Bourne Ave SS15 .....141 A8
Bourne Cl SS15 ......141 A8
Bourne Ct Wanstead E11 132 A6
  Woodford IG8 ....110 D1
Bourne End RM11 ....137 A4
Bourne Gdns E4 ......109 B6
Bourne Ho IG9 ....110 D7
Bournebridge Cl CM13 .95 E2
Bournebridge La RM4 ..91 B2
Bournemouth Park Prim Sch
SS2 ....148 B2
Bournemouth Park Rd
SS2 ....148 B2
Bournes Green Chase
SS3 ....149 B1
Bournes Green Jun & Inf Sch
SS1 ....168 B8
Bouvel Dr CM0 ....106 A8
Bouverie Rd CM2 ......54 B8
Bovey Way RM15 .....172 B8
Bovinger Way SS1 ....148 F1
Bow Arrow La
  Dartford DA1 ....176 A1
  Dartford DA1 ....176 B1
Bowbank Cl SS3 .....149 F1
Bowden Dr RM11 ....136 E3
Bower Cl RM5 ....113 D3
Bower Ct CM16 ....68 A7
Bower Farm Rd RM4 ..113 D7
Bower Gdns CM9 ......36 F3
Bower Hill CM16 ......68 A7
Bower Hill Ind Est CM16 .68 A7
Bower La SS14 ....142 E8
Bower Park Sch RM1 .113 E4
Bower Vale CM16 .....68 A7
Bowerman Rd RM16 ..174 A2
Bowers Court Dr SS13 .143 F5
Bowers Ho **5** IG11 ..152 B5
Bowers Rd SS7 ......144 D5
Bowes Ct **7** DA2 ...176 B1
Bowes Dr CM5 ....49 A4
Bowes Ho CM5 ....49 A4
Bowes Rd RM8 ......153 C8
Bowfell Cl SS16 .....141 A5
Bowfell Dr SS16 .....141 A5
Bowhay CM13 ....117 B8

Bowland Rd IG8 ......110 C4
Bowlers Croft SS14 ..120 F2
Bowls The IG7 ....111 F7
Bowman Ave SS9 ....146 B6
Bowmont Cl CM13 .....95 B3
Bown Cl RM18 ....179 B5
Bowness Way RM12 ..155 A7
Bowyer Ct **4** E4 ....87 C1
Box Cl SS15 ....119 D1
Box La IG11 ....153 C3
Boxford Cl SS6 ......122 F3
Boxley La CM22 ....4 D8
Boxmoor Rd RM5 ....113 C5
Boxoll Rd RM9 ......134 F1
Boxted Cl IG9 ....88 E1
Boyce Gn SS7 ....144 D2
Boyce Hill Cl SS9 ....146 B5
Boyce Rd
  Southend-on-S SS3 ..168 H8
  Stanford-le-H SS17 ..160 C3
Boyce View Dr SS7 ..144 C2
Boyd Ct SS12 ....121 F5
Boyden Cl SS2 ......148 F2
Boyle Ho **13** DA17 .169 A3
Boyles Court Cotts
CM14 ....116 A3
Boyne Dr RM1 ....32 D6
Boyne Rd RM10 .....135 A1
Boyton Cl SS7 ......145 A5
Boytons SS15 ....141 E6
Brabant Rd CM3 .....103 A7
Brabner Gdns CM11 ...98 C4
Brace Wlk CM3 ......101 E5
Bracelet Ct SS17 ....160 F5
Bracken Cl IG10 ......89 B8
Bracken Dell SS6 ....123 E2
Bracken Dr IG7 .....111 C4
Bracken Ind Est IG6 ..111 F2
Bracken Mews
  Chingford E4 ....87 C1
  Romford RM7 ....135 B5
Bracken Way SS7 ....145 A6
Brackendale CM11 .....97 D3
Brackendale Ave SS13 143 C3
Brackendale Ct SS5 ..124 E7
Brackendale Gdns
RM14 ....156 C8
Brackenden Dr CM1 ...32 D7
Brackens Dr CM14 ...116 D5
Brackley Cres SS13 ..143 A8
Brackley Ho **4** RM3 .114 F4
Brackley Sq IG8 .....110 D3
Bracknell Ho **3** RM3 114 F4
Bradbourne Rd RM17 .178 B8
Bradbourne Way SS13 143 C5
Bradd Cl RM15 ......157 C2
Braddock Cl RM5 ....113 C4
Bradfield Ct **12** RM19 171 B1
Bradfield Dr IG11 ....153 A7
Bradfield Ho IG8 ....111 A4
Bradford Bury SS9 ..146 C6
Bradford Rd IG1 ....133 E3
Bradford St CM2 ......32 A1
Brading Cres E11 ....132 B2
Bradleigh Ave RM17 .173 C4
Bradley Ave SS7 ....144 F5
Bradley Cl
  Canvey Island SS8 ..164 A5
  Thundersley SS7 ...144 F5
Bradley Gn SS13 ....121 C1
Bradley Link SS7 ....144 F5
Bradley Rd EN9 ......65 C4
Bradley Way SS4 ....125 F1
Bradshaw Rd RM16 ..173 A5
Bradwell Ave RM10 ..135 A2
Bradwell Cl RM12 ...155 B6
Bradwell Ct **3** CM3 .95 C3
Bradwell Gn **2** CM13 95 C3
Bradwell Ho SS11 ...121 F7
Bradwell Power Sta Visitor
Ctr ★ CM0 ....42 A6
Bradwell Rd
  Buckhurst Hill IG9 ....88 E1
  St Lawrence CM0 .....62 E6
  Steeple CM0 ....62 A3
  Tillingham CM0 ......63 C6
Brady Ave IG10 ....89 C7
Brady Ct RM8 ....134 D3
Brady Prim Sch RM13 170 C8
Braemar Ave CM2 .....54 B8
Braemar Cres SS9 ..146 A2
Braemar Gdns RM11 .137 A5
Braemar Wlk SS13 ..143 B6
Braemore SS8 ......163 F5
Braeside Sch
  Buckhurst Hill IG9 ...110 A4
  Buckhurst Hill IG9 ....88 B1
Bragg Cl RM8 ....153 B6
Braintree Ave IG4 ...132 E7
Braintree Rd RM10 ..135 A1
Brairwood Cl SS9 ...146 D5
Braiswick Pl SS15 ..141 B8
Braithwaite Ave RM7 .135 A4
Bramber Ct **7** DA2 .176 B1
Bramble Cl SS9 .....146 B7
Bramble Cres SS7 ..146 A5
Bramble Croft DA8 ..169 C2
Bramble La RM14 ...156 D4
Bramble Rd
  Canvey Island SS8 ..164 C3
  Hadleigh SS7 ....145 F6
  Southend-on-S SS9 .146 B7
Bramble Rise CM20 ...10 C1
Bramble Tye SS15 ...119 F1
Brambles The
  Basildon SS15 ......141 A8
  Chigwell IG7 ....111 C4

Brambles The continued
  Southminster CM0 ....84 D3
  Steeple CM0 ....84 A7
Bramblings The E4 ...109 D6
Bramerton Rd SS5 ..124 C6
Bramfield Rd E SS6 .124 A2
Bramfield Rd W SS6 .123 F2
Bramley Cl **3** IG8 ..110 C3
Bramley Cres IG2 ...133 A5
Bramley Ct
  7 Chingford E4 ....87 C1
  Hadleigh SS7 ....145 E2
Bramley Gdns SS15 .141 C8
Bramley Ho IG2 .....133 A6
Bramley Pl CM2 ......54 D7
Bramley Shaw EN9 ...65 F6
Bramley Way CM3 ....61 A1
Bramleys SS17 ......160 D3
Bramleys The SS4 ..125 D5
Brampstead **5** SS15 141 A6
Brampton Cl
  Great Baddow CM2 ...54 F8
  Redbridge IG6 ......111 F4
Bramshill Cl IG7 ....111 E5
Bramston Cl
  Great Baddow CM2 ..54 F8
  Redbridge IG6 ......111 F4
Bramston Link SS15 .140 E6
Bramston Way SS15 .140 E6
Bramwoods Rd CM2 ..54 E8
Brancaster Pl IG10 ...88 F6
Brancaster Rd IG2 ..133 E6
Brancepeth Gdns IG9 110 A8
Branch Rd Hadleigh SS7 145 E2
  Redbridge IG6 ......112 B3
Brandenburg Rd IG9 .164 D5
Brandesbury Sq **4** IG8 111 A3
Brandon Cl
  Billericay CM12 ......97 A5
  Grays RM16 ....172 F4
Brandon Groves Ave
RM15 ....157 D2
Brandville Gdns IG6 .133 B8
Branfil Inf Sch RM14 .137 A1
Branfil Jun & Inf Schs
RM14 ....156 A8
Branfil Rd RM14 ....137 B2
Branksome Ave
  Hockley SS5 ....124 E8
  Stanford-le-H SS17 .160 E4
  Wickford SS12 ......120 F7
Branksome Cl SS17 .160 E4
Branksome Rd SS2 ..148 C1
Branscombe Gdns SS1 149 B5
Branscombe Sq SS1 149 B5
Branscombe Wlk SS1 149 B5
Branstone Ct **17** RM19 171 B1
Branton Rd DA9 ....176 F1
Brantwood Gdns IG4 132 E7
Brathertons Ct CM12 ..96 F3
Braxted Cl SS4 .....125 C4
Braxteds **10** SS15 ..141 A6
Bray Ct SS3 ....149 E2
Bray Springs EN9 ....65 E5
Braybrooke SS14 ...142 B6
Brayburn Ct SS0 ....147 A1
Brayers Mews SS4 ..125 F1
Brayfield Ct SS9 ....146 B6
Brays Grove Sch CM18 .24 B6
Brays La SS4 ....125 E5
Brays Mead RM18 ....23 F6
Braziers Cl CM2 ......54 C3
Breach Barns Cvn Pk
EN9 ....44 B1
Breach Barns La EN9 .43 F1
Breach La RM9 .....154 A2
Breach Rd RM20 ....176 F8
Bread & Cheese Hill
SS7 ....144 E5
Break Egg Hill CM11 ..97 D3
Breakneck Hill DA9 .177 B2
Bream Gdns E6 .....152 A2
Breamore Ct IG3 ....134 A2
Breamore Rd IG3 ...133 F2
Breams Field SS16 ..141 C4
Breco Ho IG11 .....153 B2
Brecon SS0 ....147 E1
Brecon Cl SS13 ....143 C8
Brede Cl E6 ....152 A2
Bree Hill CM3 ......101 C6
Brempsons SS14 ...142 A7
Brendans Cl RM11 ..136 E3
Brendon SS15 ......141 D5
Brendon Gdns IG2 ..133 E6
Brendon Pl CM1 .....31 E1
Brendon Rd RM8 ...135 A3
Brendon Way SS0 ..147 A5
Brennan Cl CM3 .....80 F6
Brennan Rd RM18 ..179 B5
Brennan Cl CM3 .....80 F6
Brent Ave CM3 ......79 D1
Brent Cl DA2 ....176 B1
Brent Ct RM2 ......136 D3
Brent Way IG2 .....133 A2
Brentfield Rd DA1 ..176 A1
Brenthall Twrs CM17 ..24 C6
Brentleigh Ct CM14 .116 A7
Brentwood Cathedral ★
CM14 ....116 D8
Brentwood Com Hospl
CM14 ....94 E1
Brentwood Ctr The ★
CM15 ....94 C3
Brentwood Cty High Sch
CM14 ....116 D7
Brentwood Pl CM15 ..94 D1
Brentwood Rd
  Bulphan CM14 ......139 F3
  Chipping Ongar CM5,CM15 .71 B8

Brentwood Rd continued
  Grays RM16 ....174 C4
  Ingrave CM13 ......117 D4
  Orsett RM16,RM14 ..159 B4
  Romford RM1,RM2 ..136 B5
  West Horndon CM13 .139 E8
Brentwood Sch CM15 116 D8
Brentwood Sta CM14 116 C7
Brentwood Ursuline Convent
High Sch CM14 .....116 D8
Bressey Gr E18 .....109 F1
Bressingham Gdns CM3 101 C7
Bretons SS15 ......141 E6
Bretons Cotts RM13 .154 E6
Brett Gdns RM9 ....153 E5
Brettenham Ave E17 .109 A2
Brettenham Dr SS1 .167 E8
Brettenham Rd E17 .109 A2
Bretts Villas CM6 .....14 C8
Brevet Cl RM19 ....171 D2
Brewers Yd CM0 .....84 D4
Brewery Fields CM2 ..55 A5
Brewery Rd EN11 .....21 B6
Brewery The RM1 ...135 E6
Brewery Wlk **7** RM1 135 E6
Brewhouse Yd **11** DA11 179 B1
Brewood Rd RM8 ...153 B6
Brewster Cl SS8 ....164 A3
Brian Cl Chelmsford CM2 .54 B8
  Hornchurch RM12 ..155 B8
Brian Rd RM6 ......134 C6
Briar Cl Billericay CM11 119 D7
  Buckhurst Hill IG9 ..110 D8
  Hockley SS5 ....124 F4
Briar Lodge E18 ....110 C2
Briar Mead SS15 ...141 B8
Briar Rd RM3 ......114 D3
Briar View CM11 ...119 D7
Briarleas Gdns RM14 137 E4
Briars The Harlow CM18 .23 A4
  Kelvedon Hatch CM15 .93 E8
Briars Wlk RM3 ....114 F1
Briarswood
  Canvey Island SS8 ..164 A5
  Chelmsford CM1 .....32 D7
Briarview Ct E4 .....109 D4
Briarwood CM15 .....71 F2
Briarwood Dr SS9 ..146 E5
Briary The SS12 ....121 B7
Briceway SS17 .....160 F4
Brick Ct RM17 .....178 A8
Brick House La CM3 ..20 D1
Brick Kiln Rd CM2 ....55 C7
Brickenden Ct EN9 ...65 F6
Brickenden Ct EN11 ..21 A5
Brickfield Cl SS16 ..142 D2
Brickfield Cotts
  Brentwood CM15 .....95 A1
  Epping CM16 ....46 B3
Brickfield Rd
  Basildon SS16 ......142 D2
  Coopersale CM16 ....46 D2
Brickfields Rd CM3 ..101 C3
Brickfields Way SS4 .148 A8
Brickwall Cl CM0 ...106 C4
Bridge Ave RM14 ...137 A1
Bridge Cl
  Brentwood CM13 ...116 F7
  Dartford DA2 ....176 D4
  Romford RM7 ......135 E5
  Southend-on-S SS3 .168 E7
Bridge Cotts
  South Woodham F CM3 .79 B1
  Southend-on-S SS3 .168 D8
Bridge Ct Grays RM17 178 B8
  Maldon CM9 ....37 A3
Bridge End E17 .....109 A2
Bridge Hill CM16 .....67 F6
Bridge House Cl SS12 121 C7
Bridge Par CM2 ......96 F3
Bridge Rd Grays RM17 178 B8
  Great Wakering SS3 .150 F4
  Moreton CM5 ....26 C2
  Rainham RM13 .....155 A1
  Wickford SS12 .....122 A7
Bridge St Basildon SS15 119 F2
  Writtle CM1 ....31 C1
Bridge View DA9 ...177 B3
Bridge View Ind Est
RM20 ....176 F8
Bridgecote La SS15 .119 F2
Bridgemans Gn CM3 ..82 A6
Bridgemarsh La CM3 .104 F8
Bridgend Cl CM3 ....101 E8
Bridges Dr DA1 .....176 B2
Bridgeview Ct IG6 ..111 D4
Bridgeway IG11 ....152 F5
Bridgeways EN11 .....21 B6
Bridgewick Rd CM0 ..86 B6
Bridgwater Cl RM3 .114 C5
Bridgwater Dr SS0 .147 A4
Bridgwater Rd RM3 .114 C5
Bridgwater Wlk RM3 114 D5
Bridle Cl EN11 ....8 A2
Bridle Path The IG8 .109 E3
Bridle Way SG12 ......8 A6
Bridle Way (N) EN11 ..8 B2
Bridle Way (S) EN11 ..8 A1
Bridleway CM11 .....97 D6
Bridon Cl CM3 ....78 B6
Bridport Ave RM7 ..135 B5
Bridport Rd SS17 ...160 C5
Brierley Cl RM11 ...136 C5
Brigadier Way SS3 ..168 F6
Brighstone Ct **19** RM19 171 B1
Brighten Rd SS1 ....166 F8
Brighton Ave SS1 ..167 D8
Brighton Rd E6 .....152 A2

Brights Ave RM13 ...155 B1
Brightside CM12 ......96 F4
Brightside Cl CM12 ...96 F4
Brightside Prim Sch
CM12 ....96 F5
Brightwell Rd SS0 ..147 D2
Brigstock Rd DA17 ..169 B2
Brimfield Rd RM19 .171 D2
Brimsdown Ave SS15 141 B6
Brindles
  Canvey Island SS8 ..163 F5
  Hornchurch RM11 ..136 E7
Brindles Cl
  Brentwood CM13 ...117 C8
  Linford SS17 ....175 A2
Brindwood Rd E4 ...109 A7
Bringey The CM2 .....55 A6
Brinkworth Cl SS15 .124 F6
Brinkworth Rd IG5 ..132 E8
Brinsmead Rd RM3 .115 A1
Brisbane Ho RM18 ..178 F6
Brisbane Rd IG1 ....133 E5
Briscoe Prim Sch SS13 143 B8
Briscoe Rd Basildon SS13 143 B7
  Hoddesdon EN11 ....21 A8
  Rainham RM13 .....155 D1
Bristol Cl SS6 ......123 C5
Bristol Ho **1** IG11 .153 A5
Bristol Rd SS2 .....147 D6
Bristowe Ave CM2 ...55 A6
Bristowe Dr RM16 ..177 F8
Britannia Bsns Pk SS2 147 B7
Britannia Cl CM11 ...97 B2
Britannia Cl SS13 ..121 D1
Britannia Gdns SS0 .166 C8
Britannia Lodge SS0 166 C8
Britannia Rd
  Brentwood CM14 ...116 C5
  Ilford IG1 ....133 B1
  Southend-on-S SS0 ..166 C8
British Legion Rd E4 .109 F8
Brittain Rd RM8 ....134 F1
Britten Cl SS16 .....141 A5
Britten Cres CM2 .....54 F8
Britton Cl SS6 .....123 D1
Brittons Sch & Tech Coll
RM13 ....154 F5
Brixham Cl SS6 .....123 C6
Brixham Gdns IG3 ..152 F2
Broad Cl SS5 ....124 E6
Broad Mdw CM15 ....71 F1
Broad Oak IG8 .....110 B5
Broad Oak Cl E4 ...109 A5
Broad Oak Way SS6 123 E1
Broad Oaks SS12 ..121 E6
Broad Par SS5 .....124 F6
Broad Rd CM10 ....177 E1
Broad St
  Dagenham RM10 ...154 A5
  Hatfield Broad Oak CM22 .3 F6
Broad Street Green Rd
CM9 ....37 C7
Broad Way SS5 .....124 F6
Broad Wk N The CM13 117 A7
Broad Wk S The CM13 117 A6
Broad Wlk Harlow CM20 .10 D1
  Hockley SS5 ....124 F6
Broadclyst Ave SS9 .146 F6
Broadclyst Cl SS1 ..149 A1
Broadclyst Gdns SS1 149 A1
Broadfield Harlow CM20 .10 E1
  High Roding CM6 .....5 E7
Broadfield Cl RM1 ..135 F6
Broadfield Way IG9 .110 C7
Broadfields CM21 .....1 B1
Broadfields Prim Sch
CM20 ....10 E1
Broadford Prim Sch
RM3 ....114 D4
Broadgate EN9 ......65 F7
Broadhope Ave SS7 .175 C8
Broadhurst Ave IG3 .152 F8
Broadhurst Gdns IG7 111 C6
Broadhurst Wlk **3**
RM13 ....155 A6
Broadlands Grays RM17 177 F8
  Thundersley SS7 ...145 A6
Broadlands Ave
  Hockley SS5 ....124 F6
  Rayleigh SS6 ....123 D3
Broadlands Rd SS5 .124 F6
Broadlawn SS9 ....146 C4
Broadley Rd CM19 ...23 A4
Broadley Terr EN9 ...22 F4
Broadmayne SS14,SS15 142 C6
Broadmead Ct **6** IG8 110 A4
Broadmead Rd
  Woodford IG8 ......110 B3
  Woodford IG8 ......110 B3
Broadoaks CM16 .....67 F6
Broadstone Rd RM12 136 A2
Broadstrood IG10 ....67 A1
Broadview Ave RM16 173 A4
Broadview Ho RM8 .134 D3
Broadwalk E18 .....132 A8
Broadwalk The **4** SS12 121 E6
Broadwater Gn SS12 140 F6
Broadwater Ho DA12 179 D1
Broadway
  Barking IG11 ....152 C4
  Grays RM17 ....178 C8
  Rainham RM13 .....155 A1
  Romford RM2 ......114 A1
  Southend-on-S SS9 .165 E8
  Tilbury RM18 ......178 F5
Broadway Ave CM11 ..11 A4
Broadway Chambers **5**
SS13 ....143 B5

Broadway Cl IG8 .....110 B4
Broadway Gdns IG8 ...110 B4
Broadway Link SS13 ..143 B5
Broadway Mkt IG6 ....111 D1
Broadway N **7** SS13 ..143 B5
Broadway Par
 Chingford E4 ....109 C4
 Hornchurch RM12 ...155 B8
Broadway The
 8 Basildon SS13 ...143 B5
 Chingford E4 ....109 D4
 Dagenham RM8 .....135 A1
 Hornchurch RM12 ...155 B8
 Loughton IG10 ....89 C5
 Southend-on-S SS1 ..168 A7
 Wickford SS11 ......121 D8
 9 Wickford SS12 ...121 C8
 Woodford IG8 ....110 B4
Broadway W SS9 .....165 B4
Brock Gn RM15 ......172 B4
Brock Hill SS11 ......99 C4
Brock Hill Dr SS11 ....99 C3
Brockdish Ave IG11 ..152 F7
Brockbank Lodge
 RM8 ....134 D2
Brockenhurst Dr SS17 .175 C8
Brockenhurst Gdns IG1 152 C7
Brockenhurst Way CM3 .56 F1
Brocket Cl IG7 ....111 F6
Brocket Rd EN11 ......21 A6
Brocket Way IG7 .....111 F6
Brockett Rd RM16 ....174 B3
Brockham Dr IG2 ....133 C6
Brockles Mead CM19 ..23 C4
Brockley Cres SS11 ...113 C3
Brockley Gr CM13 ....95 A1
Brockley Rd CM2 ......32 D2
Brocksford Ave SS6 ..123 F1
Brocksparkwood CM3 .117 B7
Brockton Cl RM1 .....135 F7
Brockwell Wlk **3** SS12 .121 D6
Brodie Rd Chingford E4 ..109 C8
 Southend-on-S SS3 ..168 H8
Brodie Wlk SS12 .....121 F5
Brograve Cl CM2 ......54 D3
Bromefield Ct EN9 ....66 A6
Bromfelde Rd CM11 ..120 C5
Bromfords Cl SS12 ...121 B5
Bromfords Dr SS12 ...121 B5
Bromfords Sch The
 SS12 ....121 B6
Bromhall Rd RM8 ....153 B6
Bromley RM17 ....177 F8
Bromley Mews SS6 ..123 A3
Brompton Cl CM12 ....97 A5
Brompton Gdns CM9 ..58 E8
Brompton Wlk RM2 ..172 B2
Bronte Cl Ilford IG2 ..133 B7
 Tilbury RM18 ....179 C6
Bronte Mews SS2 ....148 A3
Bronze Age Way DA17 .169 C2
Brook Ave RM10 .....154 B5
Brook Cl Rochford SS4 .148 A8
 Romford RM2 ....113 F2
 Woodham Walter CM9 .35 D2
Brook Cres E4 ....109 B6
 Great Waltham CM3 ...18 E8
 Wickford SS12 ......121 C6
Brook Dr Basildon SS17 .142 C1
Brook End CM21 ......1 D2
Brook End Rd N CM2 ..33 A4
Brook End Rd S CM2 ..33 B3
Brook Gdns E4 ....109 B6
Brook Hill CM3 ....101 C3
Brook La Chelmsford CM2 .33 B2
 Doddinghurst CM15 ...72 D2
 Doddinghurst CM15 ...72 E2
 Galleywood CM2 ......54 E3
 Sawbridgeworth CM21 ..1 D2
Brook Lodge
 Romford RM7 ......135 D7
 Southend-on-S SS9 ..146 B7
Brook Mead
 Basildon SS15 ......141 B7
 Great Waltham CM3 ...18 E8
Brook Meadow Cl IG8 .109 E4
Brook Par IG7 ....111 B7
Brook Rd
 Brentwood CM14 ....115 D5
 Brentwood,Brook Street
 CM14 ....115 F7
 Buckhurst Hill IG9 ....88 A1
 Epping CM16 ....68 A6
 Ilford IG2 ....133 E5
 Loughton IG10 ....88 E4
 Rayleigh SS6 ....145 D8
 Romford RM2 ....113 F2
 Sawbridgeworth CM21 ..1 E1
 South Benfleet SS7 ..144 C1
 St Lawrence CM0 .....63 E5
 Tillingham CM0 ....63 B5
Brook Rise IG7 ......111 A7
Brook Road Ind Ctr 145 D8
Brook St Belvedere DA17 .169 B1
 Brentwood CM14 ....115 E6
 Chelmsford CM1 ......32 B4
Brook St Rdbt CM14 ..115 D5
Brook View
 CM2 ....55 C6
Brook Way IG7 ......111 B7
Brook's Mans **5** SS13 .134 B3
Brook's Par **6** IG3 ..134 B3
Brookbank CM2 ....54 E8
Brookdale Ave RM14 ..137 D5
Brookdale RM14 CM14 .137 D5
Brooke Rd RM17 .....173 A1
Brooke Sq IG7 ....37 A1
Brooke Trad Est RM1 .135 F4
Brooker Rd EN9 ......65 C5

Brookfield CM16 ......46 C6
Brookfield Cl CM13 ...95 D3
Brookfield House Sch
 IG8 ....109 E4
Brookfield Path IG8 ..109 E4
Brookfields
 Chipping Ongar CM5 ..48 F6
 Sawbridgeworth CM21 ..1 D2
 Southend-on-S SS9 ..146 D5
Brookfields Cl SS9 ...146 D5
Brookhouse Gdns E4 .109 E6
Brookhurst Cl CM2 ...32 D3
Brooking Cl RM8 .....134 C1
Brooklands Rayleigh SS6 .123 D3
 Wickford SS12 ......121 B7
Brooklands App RM1 ..135 D7
Brooklands Ave SS9 ..146 F6
Brooklands Cl RM7 ...135 D7
Brooklands Gdns RM11 .136 C5
Brooklands La RM7 ...135 D7
Brooklands Pk SS15 ..140 F6
Brooklands Rd RM7 ..135 D7
Brooklands Sq SS7 ...163 E3
Brooklane Field IG18 .24 B5
Brooklyn Ave IG10 ....88 E5
Brooklyn Cl IG10 .....88 E5
Brooklyn Dr SS6 .....123 D5
Brookman's Ave RM16 .173 D5
Brookmans RM14 ....137 E4
Brookmans Rd CM4 ...75 D2
Brookscroft Rd E17 ..109 B2
Brookside Billericay CM11 .97 C6
 Canvey Island SS8 ..164 A5
 Harlow CM19 ....23 A5
 Hockley SS5 ....124 F4
 Hoddesdon EN11 .....21 A6
 Hornchurch RM11 ...136 F6
 Margaretting CM4 .....74 F7
 Redbridge IG6 ......111 C4
 Waltham Abbey EN9 ..65 C7
Brookside Ave SS3 ..150 C2
Brookside Cl CM11 ...97 C6
Brookside Ctr SS2 ...147 F5
Brookside Jun & Inf Schs
 RM3 ....114 E5
Brookway RM13 .....170 B8
Broom Rd SS5 ....101 E2
Broome Cl CM11 ......97 D5
Broome Pl RM15 .....171 D5
Broome Pl Complex
 RM15 ....171 D5
Broome Rd CM11 .....97 D5
Broomfield Hadleigh SS7 145 D4
 Harlow CM20 ....11 B3
Broomfield Ave
 Loughton IG10 ....88 F3
 Rayleigh SS6 ....123 A3
 Southend-on-S SS9 ..146 F5
Broomfield Cl RM5 ...113 D3
Broomfield Gn SS8 ..163 F5
Broomfield Hospl CM1 .19 A3
Broomfield Prim Sch
 CM1 ....19 B1
Broomfield Rd
 Chelmsford CM1 ......32 A5
 Dagenham RM6 .....134 D4
 Swanscombe DA10 ..177 E2
Broomfields
 Basildon SS13 ......143 A6
 Hatfield Heath CM22 ..3 A3
Broomfields Ct **6** SS13 .143 A6
Broomfields Mews **4**
 SS13 ....143 A6
Broomfields Pl **5** SS13 .143 A6
Broomhall Cl CM1 .....19 B2
Broomhall Rd CM1 ....19 B2
Broomhill Ct **7** IG8 ...110 A4
Broomhill Rd Ilford IG3 .134 A2
 Woodford IG8 ....110 A4
Broomhill Wlk IG8 ...109 F3
Broomhills Chase CM12 119 A5
Broomstick Hall Rd EN9 .65 E6
Broomways SS3 .....150 A4
Broomwood Gdns CM15 .94 A3
Broomwood La CM11 ..98 B8
Broseley Gdns RM3 ..114 E6
Broseley Rd RM3 ....114 E6
Brougham Cl SS3 ....150 A4
Brougham Ct **3** DA2 ..176 B1
Broughton Rd
 Hadleigh SS7 ....145 F2
 South Woodham Ferrers
 CM3 ....101 C6
Browne Cl
 Brentwood CM14 .....94 B3
 Romford RM5 ....113 B5
Browning Ave SS2 ...148 B2
Browning Cl RM5 ....112 F3
Browning Dr SS12 ...121 C5
Browning Rd
 Dartford DA1 ....176 A3
 Maldon CM9 ....59 A8
Browning Wlk RM18 ..179 C5
Brownings Ave CM1 ..32 A5
Brownlea Gdns IG3 ..134 A2
Brownlow Bend SS14 .142 D6
Brownlow Cross SS14 .142 D6
Brownlow Gn SS14 ..142 D6
Brownlows Cl CM6 ...15 C7
Browns Ave SS11 ....99 F3
Browns Cotts RM16 ..172 E5
Brownsea Dr SS12 ...122 A5
Broxbourne Ave E18 ..132 B7
Broxbourne Rd E7 ...132 A1
Broxbourne Sta EN10 ..21 A3
Broxburn Dr RM15 ...172 B6
Broxburn Par RM15 ..172 B6

Broxhill Rd
 Havering-atte-B RM4 ..114 B7
 Romford RM4 ....113 F7
Broxted Cotts **5** SS12 .121 E6
Broxted Dr SS12 .....121 E6
Broxted End SS12 ...121 E6
Broxted Mews CM13 ..95 C3
Bruce Ave RM12 .....136 D2
Bruce Gr Chelmsford CM2 .54 A7
 Wickford SS11 ......122 A7
Bruce Rd E3 ....31 B1
Bruces Wharf Rd RM17 .178 A8
Bruges Rd SS8 ......164 C3
Brundish SS13 ......143 A5
Brunel Cl Romford RM1 .135 E7
 Tilbury RM18 ....179 B5
Brunel Rd Chigwell IG8 .110 B1
 South Benfleet SS7 ..144 D7
 Southend-on-S SS9 ..146 C7
Brunel Way CM3 ......101 C7
Brunswick Ave RM14 .137 E4
Brunswick Ct
 Hoddesdon EN11 .....21 A5
 Upminster RM14 ....137 E4
Brunswick Gdns IG6 ..111 C3
Brunswick Lodge **6** E4 109 C8
Brunswick Pl SS6 ...123 B5
Brunswick Rd
 Holdbrook EN3 ....65 A1
 Southend-on-S SS1 ..167 D7
Brunswick Wlk DA12 ..179 D1
Brunwins Cl SS11 ...121 F8
Brushwood Lodge DA17 169 A2
Brussum Rd SS8 .....164 D2
Bryanston Rd RM8 ...179 C5
 Southend-on-S SS1 ..167 E6
Bryant Ave Romford RM3 .114 D1
Bryant Link CM2 .....33 B4
Bryant Row RM3 ....114 C8
Bryant's La CM9 ......57 D7
Bryce Rd RM8 ......153 C8
Bryn Farm Cl SS14 ..142 C8
Bryony Cl IG10 ......89 B5
Buchanan Cl RM15 ..171 C5
Buchanan Gdns SS12 .121 E5
Buchanan Way CM3 ...82 B5
Buckbean Path RM3 ..114 C3
Buckeridge Way CM0 ..42 B3
Buckerills SS13 ......143 A6
Buckhatch La CM3 ....78 D3
Buckhurst Hill Com Prim Sch
 IG9 ....110 E8
Buckhurst Hill Ho IG9 .110 B8
Buckhurst Hill Sta IG9 .110 D8
Buckhurst Way IG9 ..110 D7
Buckingham Cl RM11 .136 D6
Buckingham Ct
 2 Chelmsford CM2 ..32 F4
 Loughton IG10 ....89 A7
 3 Romford RM1 ...135 E6
Buckingham Hill Rd
 Linford SS17,RM16 ..174 F5
 Stanford-le-H SS17 ..175 A7
Buckingham Rd
 Basildon SS15 ......141 B8
 Hockley SS5 ....124 D6
 Ilford IG1 ....133 D2
 Wanstead E11 ......132 C6
 Woodford E18 ......109 F2
Buckinghamshire Sq
 SS11 ....122 A5
Buckland SS3 ....149 C1
Buckland Gate SS3 ..101 C6
Bucklebury Heath CM3 .101 D6
Bucklers Ct CM14 ...116 C5
Buckles La SS12 ....172 D8
Buckley Cl SS17 .....160 F5
Buckleys CM2 ....54 F7
Buckleys Yd RM13 ...170 A8
Bucknells Mead CM1 ..52 A4
Buckrell Rd E4 ......109 D8
Buckwins Sq SS13 ..121 D1
Buckwyns Chase CM12 .96 F6
Buckwyns Ct CM12 ...96 F4
Budna Rd SS8 ......163 F5
Budoch Ct IG3 ......134 A2
Budoch Dr IG3 ......134 A2
Buglers Rise CM14 ...53 B8
Bull Cl Basildon SS16 .142 E5
 Grays RM20 ....172 F4
Bull La Dagenham RM10 .135 B1
 Hockley SS5 ....124 C6
 Maldon CM9 ....37 A3
 Rayleigh SS6 ....123 E2
Bullbanks Rd DA17 ..169 C2
Bullen Ct IG6 ....111 E4
Bullen Wlk CM2 ......54 C3
Buller Rd Barking IG11 .152 E5
 Basildon SS15 ......141 B7
 North Fambridge CM3 ..81 A1
Bullfields **21** 1 E3
Bullivant Cl DA9 ....177 A2
Bulls Lodge Cotts CM3 .20 B1
Bullwood App SS5 ...124 B5
Bullwood Hall La SS5 .124 A4
Bullwood Rd SS5 ....124 D5
Bulmers Wlk RM13 ..155 C3
Bulow Ave SS8 ......164 B3
Bulphan By-Pass RM14 .140 A1
Bulphan CE Prim Sch
 RM14 ....158 F8
Bulphan Cl SS12 ....121 E6
Bulwark Rd SS3 .....168 E8
Bumbles Green La EN9 .44 B6
Bumfords La CM3,CM9 ..35 A7
Bunces La IG8 ....109 F3

Bundick's Hill CM1 ...31 F3
Bungalows The
 Abbess Roding CM5 ..14 E3
 Grays RM20 ....177 A8
 Redbridge IG6 ......111 E2
Bunker's Hill DA17 ..169 A2
Bunters Ave SS3 ....168 C6
Bunting Cl CM2 ......54 B5
Bunting La CM11 .....97 C1
Buntingbridge Rd IG2 .133 D6
Burch Rd DA11 .....178 F1
Burches SS14 ....119 E1
Burches Mead SS7 ..145 A7
Burches Rd SS7 ....144 F8
Burchett Way RM6 ..134 C3
Burchwall Cl RM5 ...113 C3
Burden Way E11 ....132 B2
Burdett Ave SS0 ....166 E8
Burdett Rd SS1 .....167 C7
Burdetts Rd RM9 ...153 F4
Bure RM18 ....175 D3
Buren Ave SS8 ......164 E3
Burfield Cl SS9 .....146 F6
Burfield Rd SS9 ....146 F6
Burford Cl
 Dagenham RM8 ....134 C1
 Ilford IG6 ....133 C7
Burford Gdns EN11 ..21 A7
Burford Mews **9** EN11 .21 A7
Burford Pl **11** EN11 ..21 A7
Burford St EN11 .....21 A7
Burges Ct
 Hornchurch RM11 ...136 F5
 Southend-on-S SS1 ..168 C6
Burges Rd
 Southend-on-S SS1 ..168 B6
 Wallend E6 ....152 A8
Burges Terr SS1 .....167 F6
Burgess Ave SS17 ..160 E4
Burgess Ct
 Brentwood CM15 .....94 D1
 Wallend E12 ....152 A5
Burgess Field CM2 ...32 F4
Burghley Rd RM16 ..172 C3
Burghley Way CM2 ...54 C8
Burghstead Cl CM12 ..97 A1
Burgoyne Hatch CM20 ..11 A1
Burgundy Ct CM2 ....32 C2
Burgundy Way CM0 ..42 B3
Burgundy Gdns **6** SS13 143 B8
Burham Bsns Pk CM0 .106 A6
Burham-on-Crouch Sta
 CM0 ....106 B6
Burland Rd
 Brentwood CM15 .....94 D1
 Romford RM5 ....113 C4
Burleigh Cl CM12 ....97 B5
Burleigh Ct
 Southend-on-S SS0 ..166 C8
 Southend-on-S, Thorpe Bay
 SS1 ....168 B8
Burleigh Sq SS1 ....168 B8
Burleigh St SS13 ...143 B8
Burlescoombe Cl SS1 .168 A8
Burlescoombe Leas
 SS1 ....149 B1
Burlescoombe Rd SS1 .149 A1
Burley Cl E4 ....109 A5
Burley Hill CM17 .....24 D7
Burlington Ave RM7 .135 E5
Burlington Cl SS13 ..143 B8
Burlington Gdns
 Dagenham RM6 .....134 C4
 Hadleigh SS7 ......145 F3
 Hullbridge SS5 .....123 F8
Burlington Pl IG8 ...110 A7
Burnaby Rd
 Gravesend DA11 ....178 E1
 Southend-on-S SS1 ..167 E4
Burne Ave SS3 .....121 A6
Burnell Gate CM1 ....33 A4
Burnell Wlk CM13 ...116 C4
Burnels Ave E6 .....152 A2
Burnett Pk CM19 ....23 B3
Burney Dr IG10 ......89 C6
Burnham Ave CM3 ...81 A5
Burnham Cres E11 ..132 C4
Burnham Rd Althorne CM3 83 B1
 Battlesbridge SS11 ..100 E3
 Chelmsford CM1 ......32 D5
 Dagenham RM9 .....153 B4
 Hullbridge SS5 .....101 D1
 Latchingdon CM3 ....82 D5
 Mundon CM9 ....81 C8
 Romford RM7 ....135 D8
 South Woodham F CM3 .79 D1
 Southend-on-S SS1 ..146 C1
 Southminster CM0 ...84 C2
 Southminster CM0 ...84 D3
 Woodham Mortimer CM9,
 CM3 ....57 E5
Burnham-on-Crouch District
 Mus★ CM0 ....106 B4
Burnham-on-Crouch Prim
 Sch CM0 ....106 C5
Burnley Rd RM20 ...177 A6
Burns Ave Basildon SS13 .143 B5
 Dagenham RM6 .....134 C4
Burns Cl Billericay CM11 .97 B3
 Maldon CM9 ....37 A1
Burns Cres CM2 ......54 C8
Burns Pl RM18 .....179 B6
Burns Way CM13 .....95 D2
Burnside
 Canvey Island SS8 ..164 A5
 Dagenham RM8 ....134 C2
 Sawbridgeworth CM21 ..1 D2
Burnside Ave E4 ....109 A4
Burnside Cres CM1 ...32 B5

Burnside Ct **6** RM1 ..135 F5
Burnside Ind Est IG6 .112 B5
Burnside RM8 ......134 C3
Burnside Terr CM17 ..11 F3
Burnt Ho IG7 ....89 F1
Burnt Mill CM20 .....10 C3
Burnt Mill Comp Sch
 CM20 ....10 E2
Burnt Mills Rd SS13 ..121 C1
Burnt Oak Lodge SS9 .146 A2
Burnthouse La
 Ingatestone CM4 .....73 F1
 Mountnessing CM4,CM13 .96 A8
Burntmill Cl CM20 ...10 C3
Burntmill Cnr CM20 ..10 D4
Burntmill La CM20 ...10 D3
Burntwood CM14 ...116 C2
Burntwood Ave RM11 .136 E5
Burntwood Cl
 Billericay CM12 ......96 F2
 West Horndon CM13 .139 D5
Burnway RM11 ......136 E4
Burr Cl SS16 ....140 E5
Burr Hill Chase SS2 .147 E3
Burr's Way SS17 ....161 B4
Burrow Cl IG7 ......111 F5
Burrow Gn IG7 .....111 F5
Burrow Rd IG7 .....112 A5
Burrows Chase EN9 ..65 D4
Burrows Way SS6 ..123 C1
Burrswood Pl CM9 ...37 E3
Burses Way CM13 ...95 C2
Burslem Ave IG6 ....112 A4
Burstead Dr CM11 ..119 D7
Burstead Grange CM11 119 D6
Burstead Cl SS17 ...160 F5
Burton Dr EN3 ......65 A2
Burton Pl CM2 ......32 F4
Burton Rd Loughton IG10 .89 C5
 Wanstead E18 ......132 B8
Burtons Mill CM21 ....1 F3
Burts Wharf DA17 ...169 C5
Burwell Ave SS8 ....163 F5
Burwood Ct CM2 ....32 C1
Burwood Gdns RM13 .154 F2
Bury Farm Cotts RM14 .138 E2
Bury Farm La CM11 ..120 D3
Bury La Epping CM16 ..45 D2
 Great Waltham CM3 ..18 D8
Bury Rd Chingford E4 ..87 E4
 Dagenham RM10 ...154 C7
 Epping CM16 ....67 E8
 Harlow CM17 ....11 D4
Buryside Cl IG3 .....133 F7
Bush Cl IG2 ....133 D6
Bush Elms Rd RM11 .136 A4
Bush Fair CM18 ......23 F6
Bush Hall Rd CM12 ..97 C5
Bush Ho CM18 ....23 F6
Bush Rd Wanstead E11 .132 A4
 Woodford IG9 ......110 D6
Bushey Cl Chingford E4 .109 C7
 South Woodham Ferrers
 CM3 ....101 C7
Bushey Croft CM18 ..23 E7
Bushfields IG10 .....89 A4
Bushgrove Rd RM8 ..134 D1
Bushway RM8 ......134 D1
Bushwood E11 .....132 A3
Bushy Lea CM5 ......49 C8
Bushy Mead SS13 ..141 B8
Business Ctr The RM3 .114 D3
Busway SS16 ......141 A5
Bute Rd IG6 ....133 B6
Butler Ct **2** RM8 ...135 A2
Butler Ho RM17 ....178 B8
Butler Rd RM8 .....153 B8
Butler Wlk RM21 ...173 D2
Butlers Cl CM1 ......19 B4
Butlers Dr E4 ....65 C1
Butlers Gr SS16 ....141 B3
Butneys SS14 ......142 B7
Butt La CM9 ....37 A3
Butt's Green Rd CM2 ..55 F3
Buttell Cl RM17 ....173 D1
Butterbur Chase CM3 .101 C6
Buttercross La CM16 ..46 A1
Buttercup Cl
 Billericay CM12 ......97 A4
 Romford RM3 ......114 D2
Buttercup Way CM0 ..84 C3
Butterfield Rd CM3 ..33 E8
Butteridges Cl RM9 ..153 F4
Buttersweet Rise CM21 ..1 E1
Butterworth Gdns IG8 .110 A5
Butterys SS1 ....167 E8
Buttfield Cl RM10 ..154 B6
Button Rd RM17 ....172 F2
Button's Hill CM3 ...83 B4
Buttondene Cres EN10 ..21 B1
Butts Green RM11 ..136 D5
Butts La Danbury CM3 ..56 F7
 Stanford-le-H SS17 ..175 C8
Butts Paddock SS4 ..104 D2
Butts Rd SS17 .....160 C1
Butts Way CM2 .....53 E3
Buttsbury CM4 ......74 E1
Buttsbury Inf Sch CM12 .97 B5
Buttsbury Jun Sch The
 CM12 ....97 B5
Buttsbury Rd IG1 ...152 C2
Buttsbury Terr CM4 ..75 E2
Buxton Ave SS9 ....146 A3
Buxton Cl
 Southend-on-S SS9 ..146 A3

Buxton Cl *continued*
Woodford IG8 ....110 D4
Buxton Link SS15 ....140 E6
Buxton Lodge E11 ....132 B2
Buxton Rd Chingford E4 ..87 D2
Grays RM16 ....173 E4
Ilford IG2 ....133 E5
Theydon Bois CM16 ....67 E3
Waltham Abbey EN9 ....66 A6
Buxton Sq SS9 ....146 A3
Buyl Ave SS8 ....164 B5
By-Pass Rd SS17 ....160 A2
Byfield SS9 ....146 F7
Byfield Ct CM13 ....139 C5
Byfletts SS16 ....142 F4
Byford Rd SS6 ....123 E3
Bynghams CM19 ....22 F6
Byrd Ct SS15 ....141 C8
Byrd Mead CM15 ....72 A6
Byrd Way SS17 ....160 C3
Byrne Dr SS2 ....147 E5
Byron Ave
Southend-on-S SS2 ....148 B2
Woodford E18 ....109 F1
Byron Cl SS8 ....164 C4
Byron Ct Basildon SS15 ..141 B6
11 Wanstead E11 ....132 A7
Woodford E18 ....110 B2
Byron Gdns RM18 ....179 C6
Byron Mans RM14 ....137 C1
Byron Rd Brentwood CM13 95 D2
Chelmsford CM2 ....32 D2
Dartford DA1 ....176 B3
Byron Way RM3 ....114 C2
Byron Wks SS11 ....121 F7
Byrons Ho CM16 ....68 A8
Bysouth Cl IG5 ....111 B2
Bywater Rd CM3 ....101 C6

C

Cabborns Cres SS17 ..175 D8
Cabinet Way SS9 ....146 C6
Cables Cl DA8 ....169 C3
Cadiz Ct RM10 ....154 D5
Cadiz Rd RM10 ....154 C6
Cadmore La EN8 ....43 A2
Cadogan Ave CM13 ....139 D5
Cadogan Gdns E18 ....132 B8
Cadogan Ho 17 IG8 ....111 A3
Cadogan Terr SS13 ....143 C7
Caernarvon Cl
Hockley SS5 ....124 D6
Hornchurch RM11 ....137 A3
Caernarvon Dr IG5 ....111 A2
Cage End CM22 ....3 F5
Cage End Cl CM22 ....3 F5
Cage Field Cotts SS4 ..126 D4
Cagefield Rd SS4 ....126 E4
Caidge Row CM0 ....42 A2
Cairns Ave IG8 ....110 F4
Caister Dr SS13 ....143 B6
Caladonia La 9 SS12 ..121 E5
Calbourne Ave RM12 ..155 B7
Calcott Cl CM14 ....94 B1
Calcroft Ave DA9 ....177 B2
Calcutta Rd RM18 ....178 F5
Caldbeck EN9 ....65 D5
Calder RM18 ....175 C2
Caldwell Rd SS17 ....160 B1
Caldy Rd DA17 ....169 B3
Caledon Rd E6 ....152 A5
Caledonia Ct IG11 ....153 C3
Caledonian Cl 1 IG3 ....134 B3
Callan Gr RM15 ....172 B6
Callow Ho RM13 ....154 D2
Callowood Croft CM3 ..58 D1
Calmore Cl RM12 ....155 C7
Calmpatch 9 CM0 ....106 C4
Calne Ave IG5 ....111 B2
Calshot Ave RM16 ....172 F4
Calshot Ct 23 DA2 ....176 B1
Calverley Cres RM10 ..135 A2
Calvert Cl DA17 ....169 B2
Calvert Dr SS13 ....121 C1
Calverton Rd E6 ....152 A4
Calvina Cl SS15 ....119 F2
Cam Gn RM15 ....172 B7
Cambell Jun & Inf Sch
RM9 ....153 D5
Cambeys Rd RM10 ....154 C7
Camborne Ave RM3 ....114 E3
Camborne Cl CM1 ....32 E5
Camborne Way RM3 ....114 E3
Cambria Cl SS8 ....163 C3
Cambrian Ave IG2 ....133 E6
Cambridge Ave RM2 ..136 C8
Cambridge Cl
Basildon SS16 ....140 F5
Stock CM4 ....75 D2
Cambridge Ct SS1 ....166 F7
Cambridge Gdns
Grays RM16 ....174 B2
Rochford SS4 ....125 C5
Cambridge Ho CM17 ....11 C5
Cambridge Park Rd
E11 ....132 A4
Cambridge Pk E11 ....132 A5
Cambridge Rd
Barking IG11 ....152 C5
Canvey Island SS8 ....163 F3
3 Chingford E4 ....87 D1
Harlow CM20 ....11 C6
Ilford IG3 ....133 E3

Cambridge Rd *continued*
Sawbridgeworth CM21 ....1 E4
Southend-on-S SS1 ....166 F7
Wanstead E11 ....132 A4
Camden Cl RM16 ....174 B2
Camden Ct 9 DA17 ....169 A1
Camden Rd Grays RM16 .172 F3
Wanstead E11 ....132 B5
Camelford Ho 1 RM3 ....114 E6
Camelia Ct IG8 ....109 E4
Camellia Cl
2 Chelmsford CM1 ....32 F6
Romford RM3 ....114 E2
Camelot Cl CM1 ....31 F5
Camelot Gdns SS13 ....143 C8
Cameron Cl
Brentwood CM14 ....116 D6
Ingatestone CM4 ....74 B3
Southend-on-S SS9 ....146 C2
Stanford-le-H SS17 ....160 E6
Cameron Pl SS12 ....121 E5
Cameron Rd IG3 ....133 E3
Camms Terr RM10 ....154 C7
Camomile Dr SS11 ....121 E8
Camomile Rd RM7 ....135 D2
Campbell Ave IG6 ....133 C7
Campbell Cl
Chelmsford CM2 ....54 A7
Harlow CM17 ....24 B7
Romford RM1 ....113 E4
4 Wickford SS12 ....121 D5
Campden Cres RM8 ....153 C8
Camper Rd SS1 ....167 D6
Camperdown Rd SS8 ..164 C5
Campfield Rd SS3 ....168 E6
Campion Cl RM7 ....135 D2
Campion Ct RM17 ....178 D8
Campion Gdns IG8 ....110 A5
Campion Sch The RM11 136 F7
Campions Harlow CM17 ....11 F5
Loughton IG10 ....67 A1
Campions The SS1 ....168 C8
Cample La RM15 ....172 A6
Campsey Gdns RM9 ....153 B5
Campsey Rd RM9 ....153 B5
Can Bridge Way CM2 ....32 C1
Canal Basin DA12 ....179 D1
Canal Rd DA12 ....179 D1
Canal Road Ind Pk
DA12 ....179 D1
Canberra Cl
Chelmsford CM1 ....31 E5
Dagenham RM10 ....154 D5
Hornchurch RM12 ....155 C8
Canberra Cres RM10 ..154 D5
Canberra Sq RM18 ....179 A5
Cander Way RM15 ....172 B6
Candlemakers The SS2 .148 A5
Candover Rd RM12 ....136 B3
Candy Terr 12 SS1 ....167 C7
Candytuft Rd CM1 ....32 F6
Cane Hill RM3 ....114 D1
Caneland Ct EN9 ....65 F5
Canes La CM17 ....24 E1
Canewdon CE Prim Sch
SS4 ....104 E1
Canewdon Cl SS11 ....99 D2
Canewdon Gdns SS11 ..99 D2
Canewdon Hall Cl SS4 .104 D2
Canewdon Rd
Rochford SS4 ....125 D8
Southend-on-S SS0 ....166 D8
Canewdon View Rd
SS4 ....125 F6
Canfield Rd
High Roding CM6 ....5 E8
Rainham RM13 ....154 F4
Woodford IG8 ....110 E3
Canford Ave SS12 ....120 F8
Canford Cl CM2 ....54 E7
Canna Gdns SS12 ....121 F5
Canney Rd CM0 ....61 D4
Cannington Rd RM9 ....153 C6
Cannon Ct SS13 ....121 A2
Cannon Leys CM2 ....54 D3
Cannon Mews 1 EN9 ....65 B6
Cannons La Fyfield CM5 ..27 E1
Hatfield Broad Oak CM22 ....3 F5
Cannons Mead CM15 ....72 A6
Cannons Villas CM22 ....3 F5
Canon Ave RM6 ....134 C6
Canon Cl SS17 ....160 F2
Canon Palmer RC High Sch
IG3 ....133 E3
Canons Brook CM19 ....23 B8
Canons Cl CM3 ....56 E1
Canons Gate CM20 ....10 A2
Canonsleigh Cres SS9 ..146 E1
Canonsleigh Rd RM9 ..153 B5
Canterbury Ave
Redbridge IG1 ....132 E4
Southend-on-S SS2 ....148 E3
Upminster RM14 ....137 F2
Canterbury Cl
8 Basildon SS14 ....142 F8
Chigwell IG7 ....111 F7
Rayleigh SS6 ....123 C5
Canterbury Ct CM15 ....93 F4
Canterbury Ho 2 IG11 ..153 A5
Canterbury Par RM15 ..157 C2
Canterbury Pl RM17 ....173 D1
Canterbury Way
Brentwood CM13 ....116 C4
Chelmsford CM1 ....31 E4
Dartford DA2 ....176 D5
Canters The SS7 ....145 B5
Cantley Gdns IG2 ....133 C5
Canuden Rd CM1 ....31 E2

Canute Cl SS4 ....104 E2
Canvey Jun & Inf Schs
SS8 ....163 F3
Canvey Rd Basildon SS13 143 F6
Canvey Island SS8 ....163 D5
Southend-on-S SS9 ....146 B1
Canvey Way SS7 ....144 A3
Canvey Wlk CM1 ....32 E6
Capadocia St SS1 ....167 E6
Cape Cl IG11 ....152 B5
Capel Cl Chelmsford CM1 ..32 B7
Stanford-le-H SS17 ....160 E2
Capel Gdns IG3 ....152 F8
Capel Terr SS1 ....167 A7
Capelston SS15 ....141 F6
Capital Ind Est DA17 ..169 B3
Capital Pl CM19 ....23 A7
Capitol Ind Ctr 5 SS11 .122 A5
Capon Cl CM14 ....94 B1
Capons La CM3 ....57 A5
Cappell La SG12 ....8 D5
Capricorn Ctr
Basildon SS14 ....120 F1
Dagenham RM8 ....134 F4
Capstan Cl RM6 ....134 B5
Capstan Ct DA2 ....176 C3
Capstan Ctr RM18 ....178 D7
Caravan Site The RM15 .171 D3
Caravel Cl RM16 ....172 F3
Carbis Cl E4 ....87 D1
Carbury Cl RM12 ....155 C6
Card's Rd CM2 ....55 C6
Cardamon Ct 1 E12 ....152 A8
Cardigan Ave SS0 ....147 C3
Cardigan Gdns IG3 ....134 A2
Cardigan Ho 4 RM3 ....114 D5
Cardinal Dr IG6 ....111 C4
Cardinal Rd RM16 ....172 E3
Cardinal Way RM13 ....155 D3
Carew Cl RM16 ....172 E3
Carey Ho SS0 ....166 E8
Carey Rd RM9 ....153 E8
Carfax Rd RM12 ....154 F8
Carisbrook Lodge SS6 .123 C1
Carisbrooke Cl
Basildon SS13 ....143 B6
Hornchurch RM11 ....137 A3
Carisbrooke Ct 20 DA2 .176 B1
Carisbrooke Dr
Corringham SS17 ....161 B4
South Woodham Ferrers
CM3 ....101 C7
Carisbrooke Rd
Pilgrims Hatch CM15 ....94 B3
Southend-on-S SS0 ....147 E1
Carl Ho CM18 ....23 E3
Carlina Gdns IG8 ....110 B5
Carlingford Dr SS0 ....147 C3
Carlisle Gdns IG1 ....132 E5
Carlisle Ho IG1 ....132 E5
Carlisle Rd Dartford DA1 176 A1
Romford RM1 ....136 A6
Carlisle Way SS13 ....143 B6
Carlton Ave
Greenhithe DA9 ....176 E1
Southend-on-S SS0 ....147 C4
Carlton Cl RM14 ....137 B2
Carlton Ct Ilford IG6 ....133 D8
Southend-on-S SS2 ....148 A1
Carlton Dr Hadleigh SS7 .145 C4
Ilford IG6 ....133 D8
Southend-on-S SS9 ....146 F1
Carlton Rd Basildon SS13 143 E8
Grays RM16 ....173 F3
Romford RM2 ....136 A7
Wickford SS13 ....99 C2
Carlton Terr E11 ....132 B6
Carlton Villas SS2 ....148 A1
Carlyle Gdns
Billericay CM12 ....96 F5
Wickford SS12 ....121 E5
Carmania Cl SS3 ....149 F1
Carmelite Way CM9 ....36 F2
Carnach Gn RM15 ....172 B6
Carnanton Rd E17 ....109 D2
Carnarvon Rd
Southend-on-S SS2 ....147 F1
Woodford E18 ....109 F2
Carnation Cl
Chelmsford CM1 ....32 F5
Romford RM7 ....135 E2
Carne Rasch Ct 2 SS14 142 F5
Carnegie Cl EN3 ....65 B1
Carnforth Gdns RM12 ..155 A7
Carnforth Ho 2 RM3 ....114 F4
Carnival Cl SS14 ....120 B1
Carnival Gdns SS9 ....146 D4
Caro Rd SS8 ....164 C3
Carol Cl SS15 ....141 D7
Carol Ct SS15 ....141 D7
Caroline's Cl SS2 ....147 E5
Carolyn Ho IG3 ....134 A3
Carousel Stps 8 SS1 ....167 C7
Carpenter Cl CM12 ....96 F3
Carpenter Path CM13 ....95 D4
Carpenters SS3 ....149 E6
Carpenters Arms La
CM16 ....46 C6
Carpenters Ct 5 RM10 .154 B6
Carr Rd E17 ....109 A1
Carrack Ho DA8 ....169 E1
Carriage Dr CM1 ....32 E7
Carriage Mews IG1 ....133 C2
Carrick Dr IG6 ....111 C2
Carrington Rd DA1 ....176 A1
Carroll Gdns 7 SS12 ....121 D6
Carroll Hill IG10 ....88 F6
Carron Mead CM3 ....101 F6

Carrow Rd RM9 ....153 B5
Carruthers Cl SS11 ....99 D1
Carruthers Dr SS11 ....99 D1
Carsey Cl CM11 ....98 C4
Carson Rd CM11 ....97 D5
Carstone Pl CM1 ....31 F2
Carswell Cl
Brentwood CM13 ....95 D3
Redbridge IG4 ....132 D7
Carswell Gdns SS12 ....121 D5
Cart La Chingford E4 ....87 E1
Grays RM17 ....173 B1
Carte Pl SS16 ....141 A5
Cartel Cl RM19 ....171 D2
Carter Cl RM5 ....113 B3
Carter Dr RM5 ....113 B4
Carters La CM16 ....45 B7
Carters Mead CM17 ....24 C6
Cartersfield Rd EN9 ....65 C5
Carthagena Est EN9 ....21 C3
Cartlodge Ave SS11 ....121 E8
Cartwright Rd
Dagenham RM9 ....153 F5
South Benfleet SS7 ....144 D7
Cartwright Wlk CM2 ....32 F2
Carvers Wood CM11 ....119 C7
Cascade Cl IG9 ....110 D8
Cascade Rd IG9 ....110 D8
Cascades 11 SS1 ....167 C7
Casey La CM0 ....63 E4
Cashiobury Terr SS1 ....166 F7
Cashmere Way SS16 ....142 D2
Caspian Way DA10 ....177 E2
Cassel Ave SS8 ....164 C5
Cassino Rd CM1 ....31 E6
Cassis Ct IG10 ....89 C5
Castell Rd IG10 ....89 C8
Castellan Ave RM2 ....136 B8
Castle Ave Chingford E4 .109 D5
Hadleigh SS7 ....145 D1
Rainham RM13 ....154 E5
Castle Bank SS6 ....123 C2
Castle Cl Hoddesdon EN11 ..8 C1
Rayleigh SS6 ....123 D2
Romford RM3 ....114 C7
Southend-on-S SS3 ....168 G8
Castle Cotts RM14 ....157 C6
Castle Ct Hadleigh SS7 ..145 E2
Rayleigh SS8 ....123 C1
Castle Dr Rayleigh SS6 ..123 C3
Redbridge IG4 ....132 E5
Southend-on-S SS9 ....165 B8
Castle Ho 3 E4 ....109 D5
Castle La SS7 ....145 D1
Castle Mews SS6 ....123 C1
Castle Point Transport Mus*
SS8 ....164 E3
Castle Rd Dagenham RM9 153 B4
Grays RM17 ....177 F8
Hadleigh SS7 ....145 E2
Hoddesdon EN11 ....8 C1
Rayleigh SS6 ....123 D1
Swanscombe DA10 ....177 F1
Castle St
Chipping Ongar CM5 ....49 A2
Greenhithe DA9 ....177 A2
Swanscombe DA10 ....177 F1
Castle Terr SS6 ....123 C2
Castle View Gdns IG1 ..132 F5
Castle View Rd SS8 ....164 A6
Castle View Sch SS8 ..164 B6
Castle Wlk
11 Basildon SS13 ....143 C6
Canvey Island SS8 ....164 A5
Castledon Rd CM11,SS12 .99 A2
Castledon Sch SS12 ....121 B5
Castleton Rd
Chingford E17 ....109 D1
Ilford IG3 ....134 B3
Southend-on-S SS2 ....148 E1
Caswell Cl SS17 ....161 A4
Caswell Mews CM2 ....32 F2
Catalin Ct EN9 ....65 D6
Catalina Ave RM16 ....172 F4
Cater Mus The* CM12 ..97 A2
Cater Wood CM12 ....97 B3
Caterham Ave IG5 ....111 A1
Caterham Ct EN9 ....65 F5
Caterham High Sch IG5 110 F1
Catharine Cl RM16 ....172 F4
Cathedral CE Prim Sch The
CM1 ....32 C3
Cathedral Dr SS15 ....141 C7
Cathedral Wlk CM1 ....32 B3
Catherine Cl
East Hanningfield CM3 ....78 B7
Pilgrims Hatch CM15 ....94 A4
Catherine Ct 1 IG2 ....133 C5
Catherine Godfrey Ho
RM9 ....153 F4
Catherine Lodge 4 SS2 147 F1
Catherine Rd
Romford RM2 ....136 B6
South Benfleet SS7 ....144 E4
Cattawade End SS14 ....142 D7
Cattawade Link SS14 ..142 D7
Caulfield Rd
Southend-on-S SS3 ....168 D7
Wallend E6 ....152 A5
Causeway Cotts CM1 ....52 E8
Causeway The
Edney Common CM1 ....52 D7
Great Baddow CM2 ....54 F7
Maldon CM9 ....37 A4
Ulting CM9 ....35 D5
Causton Sq RM10 ....154 A5
Causton Way SS6 ....123 D4
Cautherly La SG12 ....8 A5

Cavalier Cl RM6 ....134 D7
Cavell Cres Dartford DA1 176 B3
Romford RM3 ....114 E1
Cavell Rd CM11 ....97 C1
Cavendish Ave
Hornchurch RM12 ....155 B6
Woodford IG8 ....110 B3
Cavendish Cres RM12 ..155 B6
Cavendish Ct E4 ....87 E2
Cavendish Gdns
Barking IG11 ....152 F7
Chelmsford CM2 ....32 E3
Dagenham RM6 ....134 E6
Ilford IG1 ....133 A3
Southend-on-S SS0 ....147 B2
Cavendish Rd
Chingford E4 ....109 C4
Hockley SS5 ....103 A1
Rochford SS5 ....103 A1
Cavendish Way SS15 ..119 D1
Cavenham Gdns
Hornchurch RM11 ....136 C6
Ilford IG1 ....133 D1
Caversham Ave SS3 ....149 E2
Caversham Park Ave
SS6 ....123 C4
Cawdor Ave RM15 ....172 B6
Cawdor Ho CM14 ....116 D6
Cawkwell Cl CM2 ....33 A4
Cawley Hatch CM19 ....22 F8
Caxton Rd EN11 ....8 B2
Caxton Way RM1 ....135 E7
Cazenove Rd E17 ....109 A2
Cecil Ave Barking IG11 ..152 D5
Grays RM16 ....172 F4
Hornchurch RM11 ....136 E8
Cecil Ct Harlow CM18 ....23 C5
Southend-on-S SS2 ....147 E3
Cecil Ho E17 ....109 A2
Cecil Jones High Sch
SS2 ....148 D3
Cecil Jones High Sch (Lower
Sch) SS2 ....148 B3
Cecil Rd Chingford E17 ..109 A2
Dagenham RM6 ....134 D4
Hoddesdon EN11 ....21 C8
Ilford IG1 ....152 B8
Cecil Way SS6 ....123 F2
Cedar Ave
Chelmsford CM1 ....32 A3
Dagenham RM6 ....134 E6
Upminster RM14 ....156 A8
Wickford SS12 ....121 D5
Cedar Ave W CM1 ....32 A3
Cedar Chase CM9 ....37 C5
Cedar Cl Brentwood CM13 .95 D2
Buckhurst Hill IG9 ....110 D8
Rayleigh SS6 ....123 F1
Romford RM7 ....135 C7
Sawbridgeworth CM21 ....1 E1
Southend-on-S SS2 ....148 A2
Cedar Ct Epping CM16 ....68 A8
Southend-on-S SS3 ....168 E7
6 Wanstead E11 ....132 B6
5 Woodford E18 ....110 A2
Cedar Dr Hullbridge SS5 ..101 E2
Loughton IG10 ....89 B7
Cedar Gdns RM14 ....137 C1
Cedar Gn EN11 ....21 A5
Cedar Gr CM0 ....106 B6
Cedar Hall Gdns SS7 ..145 A6
Cedar Hall Sch SS7 ..145 B6
Cedar Mews SS5 ....124 C6
Cedar Park Cl SS7 ....145 A6
Cedar Park Gdns RM6 ..134 D4
Cedar Pk IG7 ....111 A5
Cedar Rd Brentwood CM13 95 D3
Canvey Island SS8 ....163 F4
Grays RM16 ....174 B3
Hornchurch RM12 ....136 C1
Romford RM7 ....135 C7
Thundersley SS7 ....145 A6
Cedar Rise RM15 ....157 D1
Cedar Terr 9 RM8 ....134 D4
Cedar Wlk
Canewdon SS4 ....104 D1
Waltham Abbey EN9 ....65 D5
Cedars SS17 ....160 E2
Cedars The
Buckhurst Hill IG9 ....88 A1
Great Wakering SS3 ....150 B4
South Woodham Ferrers
CM3 ....101 D8
Cedarwood Ct CM18 ....23 F6
Cedric Ave RM1 ....135 E8
Celandine Cl
Billericay CM12 ....96 F4
South Ockendon RM15 ..157 C1
Celandine Ct E4 ....109 B7
Celeborn St CM3 ....101 B6
Celedon Cl RM16 ....172 E4
Cement Block Cotts
RM17 ....178 C8
Centaur Way CM9 ....59 A8
Central Ave Althorne CM3 .82 E2
Aveley RM15 ....171 C4
Basildon SS16 ....140 E4
Billericay CM12 ....97 C6
Canvey Island SS8 ....163 F5
Corringham SS17 ....161 A4
Grays RM20 ....171 F1
Hadleigh SS7 ....145 E5
Hullbridge SS5 ....101 F1
Rochford SS4 ....125 D5
Southend-on-S SS2 ....148 C1
Stanford-le-H SS17 ....160 E4
Tilbury RM18 ....179 A6
Central Cl SS7 ....145 E4

Central Dr RM12 136 E1
Central Par IG2 133 D5
Central Park Ave RM10 135 C1
Central Rd Harlow CM20 11 A4
Stanford-le-H SS17 160 D1
Central Sq 7 CM1 32 B2
Central Wall SS8 164 A6
Central Wall Cotts SS8 164 B5
Central Wall Rd SS8 164 B5
Centre Ave CM16 67 F7
Centre Dr CM16 67 F7
Centre Gn CM16 67 F7
Centre Pl 10 SS1 167 C7
Centre Rd
Dagenham RM10 154 B3
Wanstead E11 132 A2
Centre Reach SS2 148 A1
Centreway IG1 133 C2
Centurian Way DA18 169 A3
Centurion Cl SS3 168 F8
Centurion Ho 2 RM10 154 B6
Centurion Way RM19 170 F2
Centurion Works RM13 154 E2
Century Rd EN11 21 A7
Ceylon Rd SS0 166 D8
Chadacre Ave
Redbridge IG5 132 F8
Woodford IG5 110 F1
Chadacre Rd SS1 149 B1
Chadfields RM18 179 A7
Chadview Ct 2 RM6 134 D4
Chadville Gdns RM6 134 D6
Chadway RM8 134 C3
Chadwell Ave RM6 134 B4
Chadwell By-Pass
RM16 174 A1
Chadwell Heath RM6 134 D4
Chadwell Heath Foundation
Sch RM6 134 B5
Chadwell Heath Hospl
RM6 134 B6
Chadwell Heath Ind Pk
RM8 134 D3
Chadwell Heath La RM6 134 C5
Chadwell Heath Sta
RM6 134 D4
Chadwell Hill RM16 174 B1
Chadwell Prim Sch
RM6 134 C4
Chadwell Rd RM16,
RM17 173 D2
Chadwell St Mary Prim Sch
RM16 174 B2
Chadwick Ave E4 109 D6
Chadwick Dr RM3 114 D1
Chadwick Rd Ilford IG1 133 B1
South Woodham F CM3 79 E1
Southend-on-S SS0 166 C8
Chaffinch Cl SS3 168 E8
Chafford Gdns CM13 139 D5
Chafford Hundred Sta
RM16 172 B2
Chafford Sch The RM13 170 C8
Chafford Way
Grays RM16 173 B5
Ilford RM6 134 C7
Chafford Wlk RM13 155 C3
Chaingate Ave SS2 148 E2
Chale Ct SS17 175 C8
Chalfont Cl SS9 146 D4
Chalfont Ct 3 DA17 169 A1
Chalford Ct IG2 133 B6
Chalford Wlk IG8 110 D3
Chalforde Gdns RM2 136 B7
Chalgrove Cres IG5 110 E1
Chalice Cl SS14 142 E6
Chalice Way DA9 176 F2
Chalk Ct RM17 178 A8
Chalk End SS13 143 A7
Chalk La CM17 12 A2
Chalk Rd SS8 164 A6
Chalk St CM3 99 F7
Chalk Villas CM6 15 C7
Chalklands CM2 55 D3
Chalks Ave CM21 1 D3
Chalkwell Ave SS0 166 B8
Chalkwell Bay Flats
SS9 166 A8
Chalkwell Espl SS0 166 B7
Chalkwell Hall Jun & Inf Sch
SS0 147 A1
Chalkwell Lodge SS0 147 C1
Chalkwell Park Dr SS9 146 F1
Chalkwell Sta SS9 166 A8
Challacombe SS1 149 C1
Challacombe Cl CM13 95 C1
Challinor CM17 24 E8
Challock Lees SS13 143 C5
Chalvedon Ave SS13 143 B7
Chalvedon Sch SS13 143 B6
Chalvedon Sq 3 SS13 143 A6
Chamberlain Ave
Canvey Island SS8 164 C4
Corringham SS17 161 A5
Chamberlain Cl CM17 24 C8
Chamberlains Ride
CM3 101 D6
Chambers Cl DA9 177 A2
Champion Cl
Stanford-le-H SS17 160 E3
Wickford SS12 121 D6
Champion Rd RM14 137 B2
Champions Gn EN11 8 A1
Champions Way
Hoddesdon EN11 8 A1
South Woodham Ferrers
CM3 101 C8
Champlain Ave SS8 163 F5
Champness Rd IG11 152 F5
Chance Cl RM16 172 F3
Chancel Cl Basildon SS15 141 C7
South Benfleet SS7 144 C6
Tillingham CM0 63 E4
Chancellor Ave CM2 33 B4
Chancellor Rd SS1 167 B7
Chancery Pl CM1 31 B1
Chandler Rd IG10 89 B8
Chandlers CM0 106 A6
Chandlers Chase CM12 97 A2
Chandlers Cnr RM13 155 C1
Chandlers Dr DA8 169 E2
Chandlers Quay CM9 37 A3
Chandlers Way
Romford RM1 135 E6
South Woodham Ferrers
CM3 101 E7
Southend-on-S SS2 148 A5
Chandlers Wlk CM15 71 E2
Chandos Ave E17 109 A1
Chandos Cl IG9 110 B8
Chandos Par SS7 146 A3
Chanlock Path RM15 172 B6
Channing Cl RM11 136 F4
Channock's Farm Cotts
CM20 10 C7
Chanton Cl SS9 146 D7
Chantress Cl RM10 154 C4
Chantreywood CM13 117 B7
Chantry Cres SS17 160 C1
Chantry Ct 10 DA12 179 C1
Chantry Dr CM4 74 B3
Chantry Heritage Ctr*
DA12 179 C1
Chantry Ho RM13 154 D3
Chantry La SS15 141 C7
Chantry Prim Sch DA12 179 C1
Chantry The
3 Chingford E4 87 C1
Harlow CM20 11 A2
Chantry Way
Billericay CM11 97 B2
Rainham RM13 154 D3
Chapel Cl RM20 177 B8
Chapel Croft CM4 74 B4
Chapel Ct Billericay CM12 97 B2
Swanscombe DA10 177 E1
Chapel Dr CM3 19 B6
Chapel End EN11 21 A5
Chapel End Ho E17 109 B2
Chapel End Inf Sch
Chingford E17 109 B1
Chingford E17 109 B2
Chapel End Jun Sch
E17 109 B2
Chapel Fields CM17 24 C6
Chapel High CM14 116 C8
Chapel La Chigwell IG7 111 F7
5 Dagenham RM6 134 D4
Great Wakering SS3 150 B4
Hadleigh SS7 145 C3
Harlow CM17 24 C6
Heybridge Basin CM9 37 E2
Little Baddow CM3 34 B3
Purleigh CM3 80 D8
Roxwell CM1 29 F1
Tillingham CM0 63 E4
Chapel Lodge RM13 155 A1
Chapel Mews IG8 111 A4
Chapel Rd
Burnham-on-C CM0 106 C4
Epping CM16 45 F1
Ilford IG1 133 B1
Southend-on-S SS3 168 F6
Chapel St CM12 97 A2
Chapel Terr IG10 88 E5
Chapel The 5 RM11 136 B3
Chapelfields SG12 8 D4
Chaplaincy Gdns RM11 136 E3
Chaplemount Rd IG8 110 F4
Chaplin Cl Basildon SS15 119 E1
Galleywood CM2 54 B2
Chaplin Rd RM9 153 E5
Chapman Ct SS8 163 C3
Chapman Rd
Belvedere DA17 169 B1
Canvey Island SS8 165 A3
Chapmans Cl SS9 146 B1
Chapmans Wlk SS9 146 B1
Charfinch Cres CM11 97 C1
Charfleets Cl SS8 163 D3
Charfleets Farm Ind Est
SS8 163 D3
Charfleets Ho SS8 163 C3
Charfleets Ind Est SS8 163 D3
Charfleets Rd SS8 163 C3
Charfleets Service Rd
SS8 163 D3
Charity Farm Chase
CM12 96 F3
Charlbury Cl RM3 114 C4
Charlbury Cres RM3 114 C4
Charlbury Gdns IG3 133 F2
Charlbury Ho 1 E12 133 A1
Charlecote Rd RM8 134 E1
Charlemont Rd E6 152 A2
Charles Cl SS0 147 A5
Charles Ho 8 EN11 21 D8
Charles Rd
Dagenham RM10 154 D6
Ilford RM6 134 D5
Charles St Epping CM16 68 A7
Grays RM17 178 C8
Greenhithe DA9 177 A3
Greenhithe, Stone DA9 176 F2
Charleston Ave SS13 121 C1
Charleston Ct SS13 121 C1
Charlotte Ave SS12 121 C7
Charlotte Cl IG6 111 C2
Charlotte Ct Ilford IG2 133 A5
South Woodham Ferrers
CM3 101 D6
Charlotte Gdns RM5 113 B4
Charlotte Mews 5 SS2 147 F1
Charlotte Pl RM20 177 B8
Charlotte Rd RM10 154 B6
Charlton Cl
Basildon SS13 143 C7
Hoddesdon EN11 21 A6
Charlton Cres IG11 152 F3
Charlton Mead La EN11 21 D5
Charlton St RM20 177 D8
Charlton Way EN11 21 B8
Charnwood Ave CM1 31 E1
Charnwood Dr E18 132 B7
Charter Ave IG2 133 D4
Charter Ho CM9 37 A2
Charter Rd The IG8 109 F4
Charterhouse SS16 142 C5
Charterhouse Cotts CM3 80 F5
Charteris Rd IG8 110 B4
Charters Cross CM18 23 D5
Charters Ct SS11 121 F8
Chartwell Cl EN9 65 E6
Chartwell Ct 2 IG8 110 A3
Chartwell Pl PL RM1 135 F7
Chartwell Sq 2 SS1 167 A8
Chase Cl SS7 144 F5
Chase Court Gdns SS1 167 C8
Chase Cross Rd RM5 113 D3
Chase Ct SS1 167 C8
Chase Dr CM3 101 C8
Chase End Basildon SS16 142 F3
Rayleigh SS6 123 F2
Chase Gdns Chingford E4 109 A6
Southend-on-S SS0 147 D3
Chase House Gdns
RM11 136 F6
Chase La Chigwell IG7 112 A7
Ilford IG6 133 D6
Chase Nature Reserve The*
RM7 135 E1
Chase Rd
Brentwood CM14 116 C7
Corringham SS17 161 A3
Southend-on-S SS1 167 C8
Chase Sq 4 DA11 179 B1
Chase The
Basildon, Steeple View
SS15,CM12 119 B2
Basildon,Landon Hills
SS16 141 E3
Billericay CM11 97 C2
Boreham CM3 33 E8
Brentwood CM14 116 D7
Brentwood, Warley CM14 116 B6
Brentwood, Warley CM14 116 D5
Chigwell IG7 111 C6
Dagenham RM7 135 D1
Dagenham RM7,RM12 135 F1
Foulness Island SS3 130 F7
Goldhanger CM9 39 A1
Grays RM20 177 D8
Great Amwell SG12 8 A6
Great Baddow CM2 54 F6
Harlow CM17 11 C1
Ingrave CM13 117 C5
Loughton IG10 88 D2
Rayleigh SS6 123 F1
Rochford SS4 125 C8
Romford RM1 135 E8
South Woodham Ferrers
CM3 101 C8
Southminster CM0 84 D4
Thundersley SS7 145 A5
Upminster RM14 137 E1
Wickford SS11 100 A3
Wickford, Nevendon SS12 121 E4
Wickford, Runwell SS12 121 A6
Dagenham RM6 134 E5
Chaseside SS6 145 E8
Chaseside Cl RM1 113 E4
Chaseway SS16 142 F4
Chaseway The CM4 98 A8
Chaseways CM21 11 C8
Chatfield Way SS13 143 C7
Chatham Hall La CM3 19 B8
Chatham Pavement
SS13 143 C7
Chatham Rd 1 E18 109 F1
Chatham Way CM14 116 C8
Chatsworth SS7 144 F6
Chatsworth Gdns SS5 124 D6
Chatterford End SS14 142 B7
Chatteris Ave RM3 114 D4
Chatton Cl 4 SS12 121 E5
Chaucer Cl Maldon CM9 59 A8
Tilbury RM18 179 C5
Chaucer Ct EN11 8 A1
Chaucer Rd
Chelmsford CM2 32 D1
Chingford E17 109 C1
Romford RM3 114 B3
Wanstead E11 132 A5
Chaucer Way
Dartford DA1 176 A3
Hoddesdon EN11 8 A2
Chaucer Wlk SS12 121 D5
Cheapside E SS6 123 C4
Cheapside W SS6 123 B4
Cheddar Ave SS0 147 A5
Chedington SS3 149 C1
Cheelson Rd RM15 157 C3
Cheldon Barton SS1 168 C8
Chelmer Ave
Little Waltham CM3 19 B5
Rayleigh SS6 123 C1
Chelmer Cres IG11 153 B3
Chelmer Dr
Brentwood CM13 95 E3
South Ockendon RM15 172 C6
Chelmer Ho RM16 174 A1
Chelmer Lea CM2 54 E7
Chelmer Pl CM2 32 D3
Chelmer Rd
Chelmsford CM2 32 E2
Grays RM16 174 A1
Upminster RM14 137 D5
Chelmer Terr CM9 37 B2
Chelmer Valley High Sch
CM1 19 A2
Chelmer Valley Rd CM1 32 B5
Chelmer Village Ret Pk
CM2 32 E2
Chelmer Village Way
CM2 33 A3
Chelmer Way
Burnham-on-C CM0 106 A6
Southend-on-S SS3 168 D7
Chelmerton Ave CM2 54 E7
Chelmsford & Essex
Regiment Mus* CM2 54 A8
Chelmsford Ave
Romford RM5 113 D4
Southend-on-S SS2 147 F1
Chelmsford Coll
Chelmsford CM2 54 A8
Chelmsford CM2 54 C7
Chelmsford Cty High Sch for
Girls CM1 32 A4
Chelmsford Dr RM14 136 F1
Chelmsford Gdns IG1 132 F4
Chelmsford Rd
Battlesbridge SS11 100 E1
Brentwood CM15 95 B5
Great Waltham CM3 19 A6
Hatfield Heath CM22 3 C3
High Ongar CM4,CM5 49 D4
Margaret Roding CM6,CM5 15 E4
Mountnessing CM15 95 C6
Purleigh CM3 58 C3
Rawreth SS11 122 E6
Shenfield CM15 94 F3
Woodford E18 109 F2
Woodham Mortimer CM9 57 C6
Writtle CM1 31 C1
Chelmsford Sta CM1 32 B3
Chelsea Ave SS1 167 D6
Chelsea Ct
6 Chingford E4 87 C1
Rochford SS4 125 E2
Southend-on-S SS1 167 C8
Chelsea Fields EN11 8 B2
Chelsea Gdns CM17 24 E7
Chelsea Mews 4 RM11 136 B3
Chelston Ct 2 E11 132 B6
Chelsworth Cl
Romford RM3 114 F2
Southend-on-S SS1 167 F8
Chelsworth Cres SS1 167 F8
Chelsworth Dr RM3 114 F2
Cheltenham Dr
Southend-on-S SS9 146 F2
Thundersley SS7 145 B7
Cheltenham Gdns IG10 88 E3
Cheltenham Ho IG8 111 A4
Cheltenham Rd
Hockley SS5 124 F7
Southend-on-S SS1 167 C8
Chelwater CM2 54 D8
Chelwood Cl E4 87 B3
Chenies Dr SS15 119 B1
Chepstow Ave RM12 136 E1
Chepstow Cl CM11 97 D5
Chepstow Cres IG3 133 E5
Chepstow Ho RM3 115 A5
Chequers
Buckhurst Hill IG9 88 B1
Ingatestone CM4 74 B4
Chequers La
Dagenham RM9 154 A2
Maldon CM9 37 A2
Chequers Par RM9 154 A4
Chequers Rd
Brentwood CM14,RM3 92 F1
Loughton IG10 89 B4
Writtle CM1 30 F1
Chequers Wlk EN9 65 F6
Cheriton Ave IG5 111 A1
Cherries The SS8 164 B1
Cherry Ave CM13 116 F7
Cherry Blossom Cl CM17 11 C4
Cherry Blossom La CM3 80 F6
Cherry Cl
Canvey Island SS8 163 F4
Hockley SS5 124 E7
Cherry Ct
Canvey Island SS8 164 B1
Ilford IG6 133 B8
Cherry Garden La CM3 57 B7
Cherry Garden Rd
Great Waltham CM3 18 E7
Maldon CM9 36 E2
Cherry Gdns
Billericay CM12 96 E4
Dagenham RM9 153 F7
Sawbridgeworth CM21 1 E4
Cherry La SS11 122 A7
Cherry Orch CM0 84 E4
Cherry Orchard La SS4 147 B8
Cherry Orchard Way
Rochford SS4 125 B1
Cherry Orchard Way *continued*
Southend-on-S SS2, SS4 147 B8
Cherry St RM7 135 D6
Cherry Tree Cl
Grays RM17 178 D8
Rainham RM13 155 A3
Cherry Tree Ct 3 E18 109 F1
Cherry Tree Dr RM15 157 D1
Cherry Tree La RM13 154 F2
Cherry Tree Prim Sch
SS16 142 D5
Cherry Tree Rd EN11 21 A7
Cherry Tree Rise IG9 110 D6
Cherry Wlk Grays RM16 174 A3
Rainham RM13 154 F3
Cherrybrook SS1 149 C1
Cherrydene Cl SS5 101 E2
Cherrydown Grays RM16 173 D5
Rayleigh SS6 123 D4
Cherrydown Ave E4 109 A7
Cherrydown Cl E4 109 A7
Cherrydown E SS14 142 A5
Cherrydown W SS16 142 A5
Cherrydown Wlk RM7 113 B1
Cherrygarden La 1 CM2 54 A8
Cherrymeade SS7 145 A4
Cherrytree Chase SS3 150 C1
Cherrytrees CM12 118 F8
Cherston Gdns IG10 89 A5
Cherston Rd IG10 89 A5
Chertsey Cl SS3 149 D1
Chertsey Rd IG1 152 D8
Cherwell Dr CM1 31 C5
Cherwell Gr RM15 172 B6
Chesham Cl RM7 135 D7
Chesham Dr SS15 119 B1
Chesham Ho 9 RM3 114 E4
Cheshire Cl
Chingford E17 109 B2
Hornchurch RM11 137 A6
Cheshunt Dr SS6 123 B6
Cheshunt Rd DA17 169 A1
Cheshunts SS13 143 A7
Chester Ave
Southend-on-S SS1 167 D6
Upminster RM14 137 E2
Chester Cl Grays RM16 172 E3
Loughton IG10 89 C8
Chester Gn IG10 89 C8
Chester Hall La SS14 120 A1
Chester Path IG10 89 C8
Chester Pl CM1 32 A5
Chester Rd Chigwell IG7 111 A7
Ilford IG3 133 F4
Loughton IG10 89 C8
Wanstead E11 132 B5
Chester Way 9 SS14 142 F8
Chesterfield Ave SS7 144 D6
Chesterfield Cres SS9 146 D6
Chesterford Gdns 3
SS14 142 F8
Chesterford Gn SS14 142 F8
Chesterford Rd E12 152 A7
Chesterton Way RM18 179 C5
Chestnut Ave
Billericay CM12 97 A2
Buckhurst Hill IG9 110 D7
Grays RM16 173 B4
Heybridge CM9 37 C6
Hornchurch RM12 136 A2
Chestnut Cl
Buckhurst Hill IG9 110 D8
Burnham-on-C CM0 106 A5
Gravesend DA11 178 F1
Hockley SS5 124 F6
Hornchurch RM12 155 C8
Chestnut Cotts CM16 67 E2
Chestnut Ct
Basildon SS16 143 A4
Southend-on-S SS3 168 F7
Chestnut Dr
Hatfield Heath CM22 2 F3
Wanstead E11 132 A5
Chestnut Farm Dr CM3 82 E2
Chestnut Glen RM12 136 A2
Chestnut Gr
Brentwood CM14 116 C8
Redbridge IG6 111 E4
South Benfleet SS7 144 B4
Southend-on-S SS2 148 B2
Chestnut Ho
2 Basildon SS13 143 B8
Wickford SS11 121 E7
Chestnut Path SS4 104 D1
Chestnut Rd SS16 143 A4
Chestnut Wlk
Canvey Island SS8 163 E3
Chelmsford CM1 32 A5
Epping Green CM16 45 B7
Little Baddow CM3 34 E1
Woodford IG8 110 A5
Chestnuts CM13 95 B2
Chestnuts The
Rayleigh SS6 123 E4
Southminster CM0 84 D4
Willingale CM5 28 D4
Abridge RM4 90 B6
Loughton IG10 88 E4
Chestwood Cl CM12 97 B5
Chetwood Prim Sch The
CM3 101 D6
Cheveley Cl RM3 114 F2
Chevely Cl CM16 46 D2
Chevening Gdns SS5 124 C6
Chevers Pawen SS13 143 A5

Chevington Pl RM12 . . . . . . .155 D7
Chevington Way RM12 . . . . .155 D8
Cheviot Dr CM1 . . . . .31 D6
Cheviot Ho DA11 . . . . .178 D1
Cheviot Rd RM11 . . . . .136 A4
Cheviot Way IG2 . . . . .133 E2
Chevron Ho RM17 . . . . .178 B7
Cheyne Ct 8 SS12 . . . . .121 E5
Chichester Cl
Aveley RM15 . . . . .171 C5
Basildon SS14 . . . . .142 F8
Canvey Island SS8 . . . . .164 A2
Grays RM16 . . . . .172 D2
Chichester Dr CM1 . . . . .32 C4
Chichester Gdns IG1 . . . . . .132 F4
Chichester Ho 1 CM14 . . . . .116 C8
Chichester Rd
Greenhithe DA9 . . . . .176 F1
Southend-on-S SS1 . . . . . . .167 A8
Chichester Way SS9 . . . . . . .59 B8
Chichester Wharf DA8 . . . . .169 E1
Chieftan Dr RM19 . . . . .171 A2
Chigborough Rd CM9 . . . . . . .37 F6
Chignall Rd CM1 . . . . .31 D5
Chignalls The 4 SS15 . . . . .141 A6
Chigwell Cty Prim Sch
IG7 . . . . .111 C8
Chigwell La IG10 . . . . .89 C5
Chigwell Park Dr IG7 . . . . . .111 A6
Chigwell Pk IG7 . . . . .111 B6
Chigwell Rd
Wanstead E18 . . . . .132 B8
Woodford IG8 . . . . .110 D3
Chigwell Rise IG7 . . . . .111 A8
Chigwell Row Inf Sch
IG7 . . . . .112 B8
Chigwell Sch IG7 . . . . .111 C8
Chigwell Sta IG7 . . . . .111 B7
Chigwell View RM5 . . . . . . .113 A1
Childerditch Hall Dr
CM13 . . . . .139 A7
Childerditch Ind Pk
CM13 . . . . .138 F8
Childerditch La
Little Warley CM13 . . . . .116 E2
West Horndon CM13 . . . . . .139 B5
Childerditch St CM13 . . . . . .139 B8
Childers The IG8 . . . . .110 E5
Childs Cl RM11 . . . . .136 C5
Childs Cres DA10 . . . . .177 D1
Chilham Ct SS13 . . . . .143 C5
Chiltern 1 SS1 . . . . .167 B8
Chiltern App SS8 . . . . .163 E4
Chiltern Cl SS6 . . . . .123 D3
Chiltern Gdns RM12 . . . . . .136 C1
Chiltern Rd IG2 . . . . .133 E6
Chiltern Way IG8 . . . . .110 A7
Chilterns The SS8 . . . . .163 F4
Chilton Cl CM2 . . . . .54 D7
Chilton Rd RM16 . . . . .174 A3
Chiltons The 1 E18 . . . . . . .110 A1
Chimes The SS7 . . . . .144 E4
Chimney Pot La CM3 . . . . . . .57 C4
China La CM14 . . . . .139 D1
Chinchilla Rd SS1 . . . . .167 D8
Chindits La CM14 . . . . .116 C5
Chinery Cl CM1 . . . . .32 C4
Ching Ct E4 . . . . .109 E7
Chingdale Rd E4 . . . . .109 E7
Chingford Ave E4 . . . . .109 B8
Chingford CE Inf Sch E4 87 D1
Chingford CE Jun Sch
E4 . . . . .87 D1
Chingford Foundation Sch
E4 . . . . .87 B1
Chingford Hall Com Prim Sch
E4 . . . . .109 A4
Chingford La IG8 . . . . .109 F5
Chingford Mount Rd E4 109 A5
Chingford Rd
Chingford E17 . . . . .109 B1
Chingford, Highams Park
E4 . . . . .109 A3
Chingford Sta E4 . . . . .87 E2
Chippenham Cl RM3 . . . . . .114 D5
Chippenham Gdns RM3 114 D5
Chippenham Rd RM3 . . . . . .114 D5
Chippenham Wlk RM3 . . . . .114 D4
Chipperfield Ct RM14 . . . . .137 E3
Chipping Ongar Prim Sch
CM5 . . . . .48 F1
Chipping Row 5 CM3 . . . . .101 E7
Chippingfield CM17 . . . . .11 C3
Chisholm Cl 11 SS12 . . . . .121 E5
Chislett Row CM2 . . . . .54 C8
Chittenden Cl 8 EN11 . . . . . .8 B1
Chittock Gate SS14 . . . . . . .142 E6
Chittock Mead SS14 . . . . . .142 E6
Chitty's La RM8 . . . . .134 D2
Chivers Rd CM3 . . . . .109 B6
Stondon Massey CM15 . . . . . .71 F4
Choats Manor Way RM9 153 E2
Choats Rd IG11 . . . . .153 E2
Chorley Cl SS16 . . . . .140 F5
Christchurch Ave
Rainham RM13 . . . . .154 F2
Wickford SS12 . . . . .121 A8
Christchurch Prim Sch
IG1 . . . . .133 C3
Christchurch Rd
Ilford IG1 . . . . .133 C3
Southend-on-S SS2 . . . . . . .148 C1
Tilbury RM18 . . . . .179 A6
Christie Gdns RM6 . . . . . . .134 B4
Christie Rd EN9 . . . . .65 B4

Christine Ct 7 RM13 . . . . . .155 A1
Christopher Cl RM12 . . . . . .155 D8
Christopher Gdns RM9 . . . .153 D7
Christopher Martin Rd
SS14 . . . . .120 F3
Christy Ave CM1 . . . . .31 F4
Christy Cl SS15 . . . . .140 E7
Christy Ct SS15 . . . . .140 E7
Christy Way SS15 . . . . .140 E7
Chudleigh Cres IG3 . . . . . . .152 E6
Chudleigh Rd RM3 . . . . . . .114 E6
Chulmleigh Ct CM15 . . . . . . .95 A1
Church Ave
Broomfield CM1 . . . . .19 A2
Chingford E4 . . . . .109 D4
Church Chase CM3 . . . . . . .100 C5
Church Cl
Canvey Island SS8 . . . . .163 F3
Horndon-on-t-H SS17 . . . . . .159 F3
Kelvedon Hatch CM14 . . . . . .71 D2
Loughton IG10 . . . . .88 F7
Mountnessing CM15 . . . . . . .95 E8
Southend-on-S SS0 . . . . . . .168 D6
Church Cnr
South Benfleet SS7 . . . . . . .144 D1
Woodham Walter CM9 . . . . . .35 D2
Church Cotts
Chipping Ongar CM5 . . . . . . .70 C7
Gilston CM20 . . . . .10 C7
Church Cres
Mountnessing CM15 . . . . . . .95 E8
Sawbridgeworth CM21 . . . . . .1 E7
South Ockendon RM15 . . . . .157 C2
Church Ct EN10 . . . . .21 A3
Church Elm La RM10 . . . . . .154 A6
Church End CM19 . . . . .23 A6
Church End Ave SS11 . . . . . .99 E2
Church End La SS11 . . . . . . .99 E2
Church Field CM16 . . . . .46 A2
Church Gn Boreham CM3 .33 F8
Broomfield CM1 . . . . .19 B1
Canewdon SS4 . . . . .104 C3
Roxwell CM1 . . . . .30 B5
Church Hill
Basildon SS15 . . . . .141 B8
Epping CM16 . . . . .46 A2
Greenhithe DA9 . . . . .176 E2
Little Waltham CM3 . . . . .19 C6
Loughton IG10 . . . . .88 F6
Purleigh CM3 . . . . .58 E1
Southend-on-S SS9 . . . . . . .165 E8
Stanford-le-H SS17 . . . . . . .160 C1
Woodham Walter CM9 . . . . . .35 D2
Church Hollow RM19 . . . . . .171 A1
Church Housen 18 F7
Church La Abridge RM4 . . . .90 E6
Basildon, Burnt Mills SS13 121 E7
Basildon, Crays Hill CM11 . .120 B6
Brentwood CM13 . . . . .95 F2
Bulphan RM14 . . . . .158 F7
1 Chelmsford, Moulsham
CM1 . . . . .32 B2
Chelmsford, Springfield
CM1 . . . . .32 D4
Chipping Ongar CM5 . . . . . . .49 B7
Dagenham RM10 . . . . .154 A6
Doddinghurst CM15 . . . . .72 B2
Great Warley CM13 . . . . . . .138 D5
Heybridge CM9 . . . . .38 A8
Loughton IG10 . . . . .88 F6
Margaretting CM4 . . . . .74 E6
North Ockendon RM14 . . . . .157 B7
North Weald Bassett CM16 . . .47 A4
Purfleet RM19 . . . . .171 A1
Romford RM1 . . . . .135 E2
Sheering CM22 . . . . .12 D7
South Hanningfield CM3 . . . . .99 C8
Stapleford Abbotts RM4 . . . . .91 C5
Stow Maries CM3 . . . . .80 D3
Wennington RM13 . . . . .170 D7
West Hanningfield CM2 . . . . . .77 A4
White Roding CM6 . . . . .14 C7
Writtle CM1 . . . . .31 B1
Church Lane Cotts
Doddinghurst CM15 . . . . .72 B2
Rainham RM13 . . . . .170 D7
**Church Langley Com Prim
Sch** CM17 . . . . .24 C8
Church Langley Way
CM17 . . . . .24 D8
Church Leys CM18 . . . . .23 F7
Church Manorway DA8 .169 D3
Church Mead CM19 . . . . .9 B1
Church Mews SS15 . . . . . . .141 B7
Church Par SS8 . . . . .163 E5
Church Park Rd SS13 . . . . .143 B5
Church Path
Greenhithe DA9 . . . . .176 F1
Northfleet DA11 . . . . .178 C1
Wanstead E11 . . . . .132 A6
Church Rd Barking E12 . .152 C6
Barling SS3 . . . . .149 E8
Basildon, Noak Bridge
SS15 . . . . .119 E1
Basildon,Barstable SS14,
SS16 . . . . .142 C6
Basildon,Bowers Gifford
SS13 . . . . .143 F6
Basildon,Great Berry
RM14 . . . . .140 D5
Basildon,Pipps Hill SS15 . .141 E8
Buckhurst Hill IG9 . . . . .88 B1
Bulphan RM14 . . . . .158 F8
Burnham-on-C CM0 . . . . . . .106 B6
Chipping Ongar CM5 . . . . . . .70 D6
Corringham SS17 . . . . .161 B3
Erith DA8 . . . . .169 D1
Greenhithe DA9 . . . . .176 F2

Church Rd continued
Hadleigh SS7 . . . . .145 F2
Harlow CM17 . . . . .24 C5
High Beach IG10 . . . . .88 A7
Hockley SS5 . . . . .124 B7
Ilford IG2 . . . . .133 E5
Kelvedon Hatch CM14 . . . . . .71 C2
Little Baddow CM3 . . . . .34 A6
Little Ilford E12 . . . . .152 A7
Moreton CM5 . . . . .26 D2
Mountnessing CM15 . . . . . . .95 F7
Navestock Heath RM4 . . . . . .92 D8
North Fambridge CM3 . . . . .103 A7
Ramsden Heath CM11,SS14,
SS16,SS13 . . . . .98 D2
Rawreth SS11 . . . . .122 D7
Rayleigh SS6 . . . . .123 D7
Rochford SS4 . . . . .125 C7
Romford RM4 . . . . .92 C1
Romford,Harold Park RM3 115 A3
South Benfleet, New Thundersley
SS7 . . . . .144 D6
Southend-on-S SS4 . . . . . . .167 A7
Southend-on-S, Cambridge Town
SS3 . . . . .168 D6
Swanscombe DA10 . . . . . . .177 D1
Tilbury RM18 . . . . .178 F6
Ulting CM9 . . . . .35 C6
West Hanningfield CM2 . . . . . .77 A4
West Tilbury RM18 . . . . .179 D8
Church Row RM16 . . . . .159 A1
Church St
Billericay CM11 . . . . .119 C6
Blackmore CM4 . . . . .72 E8
Chelmsford CM1 . . . . .32 B2
Dagenham RM10 . . . . .154 B6
Goldhanger CM9 . . . . .38 E7
Gravesend DA11 . . . . .179 B1
Grays RM17 . . . . .178 D8
Great Baddow CM2 . . . . .55 A6
Maldon CM9 . . . . .37 B2
Rayleigh SS6 . . . . .123 D2
Sawbridgeworth CM21 . . . . . .1 E7
Waltham Abbey EN9 . . . . . . .65 C6
Church Terr RM4 . . . . .91 C5
Church View
Aveley RM15 . . . . .171 D4
Upminster RM14 . . . . .137 D2
Church View Rd SS7 . . . . . .144 E6
Church Wlk
Basildon SS14 . . . . .142 A6
Brentwood CM15 . . . . .94 B2
Maldon CM9 . . . . .36 F3
Sawbridgeworth CM21 . . . . . .1 E7
Churchall Terr IG6 . . . . .111 F5
Churchend SS3 . . . . .130 A6
Churchfield CM20 . . . . .11 B2
Churchfield Cotts SS3 . . . . .130 B7
Churchfields
Hoddesdon EN10 . . . . .21 A3
Loughton IG10 . . . . .88 E5
Southend-on-S SS3 . . . . . . .149 E2
Woodford E18 . . . . .110 A2
Churchfields Inf Sch
E18 . . . . .110 A2
Churchfields Jun Sch
E18 . . . . .110 A2
Churchfields La EN10 . . . . . .21 A3
Churchgate CE Prim Sch
CM17 . . . . .11 F3
Churchgate St CM17 . . . . . . .11 E4
Churchill Cl CM5 . . . . .49 A4
Churchill Cres SS17 . . . . . .160 E4
Churchill Ct 7 IG1 . . . . .133 E1
Churchill Lodge IG8 . . . . . . .109 F4
Churchill Mews IG8 . . . . . . .109 F4
Churchill Pk DA1 . . . . .176 A2
Churchill Rd RM17 . . . . .178 D8
Churchill Rise CM1 . . . . .32 E7
Churchill Sq 1 SS1 . . . . . . .167 A8
Churchill Terr E4 . . . . .109 A7
Churchway SS7 . . . . .145 F2
Churchwood Gdns IG8 . . . . .110 A6
Chuzzlewit Dr CM1 . . . . .31 E7
Cillocks Cl EN11 . . . . .21 A7
Cimarron Cl CM3 . . . . .101 D7
Cinema Par RM8 . . . . .134 F2
Circle The RM18 . . . . .179 A6
Civic Sq RM18 . . . . .179 A5
Civic Way IG6 . . . . .133 C7
Clachar Cl CM2 . . . . .33 A4
Claire Cl CM13 . . . . .116 F6
Claire Ho IG5 . . . . .110 F2
Clairvale RM11 . . . . .136 E4
Clandon Rd IG2 . . . . .133 E2
Claps Gate La E6 . . . . .152 B1
Clare Ave SS11 . . . . .99 D2
Clare Cswy DA2 . . . . .176 F3
Clare Gdns IG11 . . . . .153 A5
Clare James Cotts 4
SS8 . . . . .164 A3
Clare Mews CM5 . . . . .49 A5
Clare Rd SS7 . . . . .144 A4
Claremont Cl
Grays RM16 . . . . .173 C3
Southend-on-S SS0 . . . . . . .147 E1
Claremont Dr SS16 . . . . . . .143 A4
Claremont Gdns
Ilford IG3 . . . . .133 E4
Upminster RM14 . . . . .137 D3
Claremont Gr IG8 . . . . .110 C4
Claremont Rd
Basildon SS15 . . . . .141 C8
Hornchurch RM11 . . . . .136 A5
Southend-on-S SS0 . . . . . . .147 D1
Clarence Ave Ilford IG2 . . .133 A5
Redbridge IG1 . . . . .132 F5

Clarence Ave continued
Upminster RM14 . . . . .137 A2
Clarence Cl
Chelmsford CM2 . . . . .33 A4
South Benfleet SS7 . . . . . . .144 D4
Clarence Gate IG8 . . . . .111 A4
Clarence Rd
Basildon SS13 . . . . .143 F7
Corringham SS17 . . . . .161 C4
Grays RM17 . . . . .173 B1
Pilgrims Hatch CM15 . . . . . . .94 B3
Rayleigh SS6 . . . . .124 A1
South Benfleet SS7 . . . . . . .144 D3
Southend-on-S SS1 . . . . . . .167 A7
Clarence Rd N SS7 . . . . . . .144 E4
Clarence St SS1 . . . . .167 A7
Clarendon Gdns
Ilford IG1 . . . . .133 A4
Redbridge IG1 . . . . .132 F4
Clarendon Rd
Basildon SS13 . . . . .143 C7
Canvey Island SS8 . . . . .164 C4
Gravesend DA12 . . . . .179 C1
Hockley SS5 . . . . .102 F1
Wanstead E18 . . . . .132 A8
Claridge Rd IG6 . . . . .111 E4
Clarissa Rd RM6 . . . . .134 D4
Clark Way CM1 . . . . .19 A1
Clark's Rd IG1 . . . . .133 C4
Clarkbourne Dr RM17 . . . . .178 D8
Clarke Mans 8 IG11 . . . . . .152 F5
Clarke Rise CM1 . . . . .80 F5
Clarklands Ind Est CM21 . . . .1 E5
Clarks Cotts SS11 . . . . .122 F7
Clarks Farm Rd CM3 . . . . . . .56 F8
Clarks Field Cotts CM3 . . . . .57 E2
Clarks La CM16 . . . . .67 C8
Clarksons The IG11 . . . . . . .152 C3
Claters Cl SS2 . . . . .148 F1
Clatterfield Gdns SS0 . . . . .147 B3
Claudian Way RM16 . . . . . .174 B3
Claughton Way CM13 . . . . . .95 D3
Claverhambury Farm Bglws
EN9 . . . . .44 A3
Claverhambury Rd EN9 . . .44 A3
Clavering SS16 . . . . .142 F4
Clavering Ct SS6 . . . . .123 B3
Clavering Gdns CM13 . . . . .139 D5
Clavering Rd E12 . . . . .132 D2
Clavering Way CM13 . . . . . . .95 D3
Clay Hill Rd SS16 . . . . .142 C4
Clay Tye Rd
North Ockendon RM14 . . . . .157 C8
Upminster RM14 . . . . .138 C1
Clay's La IG10 . . . . .89 A8
Claybrook Ave SS5 . . . . . . .124 D5
Clayburn Circ SS14 . . . . . . .142 D6
Clayburn End SS14 . . . . . . .142 D6
Clayburn Gdns RM15 . . . . .172 B6
Clayburn Side SS14 . . . . . . .142 D6
Claybury Broadway IG5 132 E8
Claybury Rd IG8 . . . . .110 E3
Claydon Cres SS14 . . . . . . .142 C7
Claydon Ct RM12 . . . . .154 E8
Claydons La SS7 . . . . .145 C7
Claygate Cl RM12 . . . . .155 A8
Clayhall Ave
Redbridge IG5 . . . . .111 A1
Woodford IG5 . . . . .110 E1
Claypit Hill EN9 . . . . .66 C2
Claypits Rd CM3 . . . . .20 F1
Clayside IG7 . . . . .111 C5
Clayspring Cl SS5 . . . . .124 D7
Clayton Ave RM14 . . . . . .156 B7
Clayton Hill Ctry Pk★
EN9 . . . . .43 D8
Clayton Rd RM7 . . . . .135 C3
Clayton Way CM9 . . . . .36 D4
Claytonville Terr DA17 . . . . .169 C4
Cleall Ave EN9 . . . . .65 C5
Clear Ct CM3 . . . . .82 B5
Cleland Path IG10 . . . . .89 B8
Clematis Cl RM3 . . . . .114 C3
Clematis Gdns IG8 . . . . .110 A5
Clematis Tye 3 CM1 . . . . . . .32 E7
Clemence Rd RM10 . . . . . . .154 C4
Clement Way RM14 . . . . . . .136 F1
Clementhorpe Rd RM9 . . .153 C6
Clements Cl CM2 . . . . .33 B3
Clements Ct 5 IG11 . . . . . . .133 B1
Clements Gdns SS5 . . . . . . .125 A5
Clements Green La
CM3 . . . . .101 D8
Clements Hall La SS5 . . . . .125 A5
Clements Hall Sports Ctr
SS5 . . . . .125 A4
Clements Hall Way SS5 125 A4
Clements La IG1 . . . . .133 B1
Clements Pl CM3 . . . . .101 D8
Clements Rd Ilford IG1 . . . .133 B1
Wallend E6 . . . . .152 A5
Clerks Piece IG10 . . . . . . .88 F6
Cleveden Ho SS7 . . . . .144 F6
Cleveland Dr SS0 . . . . .147 E3
Cleveland Ho DA17 . . . . . . .178 C1
Cleveland Prim Sch
IG1 . . . . .133 B1
Cleveland Rd
Basildon SS14 . . . . .142 C6
Canvey Island SS8 . . . . .164 B2
Ilford IG1 . . . . .133 B1
Wanstead E18 . . . . .132 A8
7 Woodford E18 . . . . .110 A1
Clevelands The IG1 . . . . . . .152 C6
Cleves Ave CM14 . . . . .94 B1
Cleves Cl IG10 . . . . .88 E3
Cleves Ct SS13 . . . . .143 D6
Cleves Wlk IG6 . . . . .111 C3

Clevis Dr CM3 . . . . .101 E5
Clickett End SS14 . . . . .142 C6
Clickett Hill SS14 . . . . .142 C6
Clickett Side SS14 . . . . .142 C6
Clieveden Rd SS1 . . . . .167 F6
Cliff Ave
Southend-on-S SS0 . . . . . . .147 E1
Southend-on-S,Chalkwell
SS9 . . . . .166 A8
Cliff Gdns SS9 . . . . .166 A8
Cliff Par SS9 . . . . .165 E8
Cliff Pl RM15 . . . . .157 D2
Cliff Rd SS9 . . . . .166 A8
Clifford Ave IG5 . . . . .111 A3
Clifford Cl SS15 . . . . .141 D5
Clifford Rd
Chingford E17 . . . . .109 C1
Grays RM16 . . . . .172 F3
Cliffsea Gr SS9 . . . . .146 F1
Clifftown Par SS1 . . . . .166 F7
Clifftown Rd SS1 . . . . .167 A7
Clifton Ave SS7 . . . . .144 C4
Clifton Cl SS7 . . . . .144 D4
Clifton Ct 3 IG8 . . . . .110 A4
Clifton Dr SS0 . . . . .166 D7
Clifton Hatch CM18 . . . . .24 A5
Clifton Marine Par
DA11 . . . . .178 F1
Clifton Mews SS1 . . . . .166 F7
Clifton Rd Basildon SS13 .143 F7
Canvey Island SS8 . . . . .164 B3
Gravesend DA11 . . . . .179 A1
Hornchurch RM11 . . . . .136 A5
Ilford IG2 . . . . .133 D5
Loughton IG10 . . . . .88 E5
Rochford SS4 . . . . .125 C7
Clifton Terr
Ingatestone CM4 . . . . .74 C4
Southend-on-S SS1 . . . . . . .167 A7
Clifton Way
Brentwood CM15 . . . . .95 D1
South Benfleet SS7 . . . . . . .144 C4
Clifton Wlk
22 Dartford DA2 . . . . .176 B1
South Benfleet SS7 . . . . . . .144 C4
Climmen Rd SS8 . . . . .164 B5
Clinton Cl CM3 . . . . .78 B7
Clinton Cres IG6 . . . . .111 E4
Clinton Rd SS8 . . . . .164 B5
Clipped Hedge CM22 . . . . . . .3 B3
Clipper Bvd DA2 . . . . .176 E3
Clipper Bvd W DA2 . . . . . . .176 D4
Clitheroe Rd RM5 . . . . .113 C5
Clive Rd Belvedere DA17 .169 F1
Brentwood CM13 . . . . .116 C3
17 Gravesend DA11 . . . . . .179 B1
Romford RM2 . . . . .136 B6
Cliveden Cl
Chelmsford CM1 . . . . .31 E3
Shenfield CM15 . . . . .94 F3
Cliveden Rd E4 . . . . .109 E5
Clobbs Yd CM1 . . . . .32 B8
Clock Ct E11 . . . . .132 B7
Clock Ho SS15 . . . . .141 B6
Clock House Par 1 E11 132 B5
Clock House Rd CM12 . . . . .118 F5
Clockhouse Ave IG11 . . . . . .152 C3
Clockhouse Jun & Inf Sch
RM5 . . . . .113 B4
Clockhouse La
Grays RM16 . . . . .172 E3
Romford RM5 . . . . .113 C4
South Ockendon RM16 . . . . .172 E5
Clockhouse The RM14 . . . . .137 C2
Cloister Cl RM13 . . . . .155 B1
Cloisters
1 Hornchurch RM13 . . . . .155 A6
Stanford-le-H SS17 . . . . . . .160 E2
Cloisters The SS15 . . . . . . .141 E4
Clopton Gn SS14 . . . . .142 B7
Clore Tikva Sch IG6 . . . . . .111 C1
Close The
Brentwood CM14 . . . . .116 D7
Chingford E4 . . . . .109 C3
Dagenham RM6 . . . . .134 E5
Grays RM16 . . . . .173 C4
Hatfield Heath CM22 . . . . . . .3 A4
Ilford IG2 . . . . .133 E5
South Benfleet, Hope's Green
SS7 . . . . .144 D1
Thundersley SS7 . . . . .145 B8
Cloudberry Rd RM3 . . . . . . .114 D4
Clova Rd SS9 . . . . .146 F2
Clovelly Ct
Hornchurch RM11 . . . . .136 F2
Upminster RM14 . . . . .137 A2
Clovelly Gdns RM7 . . . . . . .113 B2
Clover Cl SS16 . . . . .142 E3
Clover Ct RM17 . . . . .178 D8
Clover Field CM18 . . . . .24 A5
Clover Leas CM16 . . . . .45 F2
Clover Way SS16 . . . . .142 E3
Clover Villas SS1 . . . . .167 B7
Cloverley Rd CM5 . . . . .49 A1
Cloverleys IG10 . . . . .88 D4
Cluff Ct CM14 . . . . .116 C6
Clunas Gdns RM2 . . . . .136 D8
Clunford Pl CM1 . . . . .32 F7
Cluny Sq SS2 . . . . .148 C3
Clusters The 3 SS2 . . . . . .147 F1
Clyde Rd RM18 . . . . .175 C2
Clyde Cres
Chelmsford CM1 . . . . .31 D4
Rayleigh SS6 . . . . .145 D8
Upminster RM14 . . . . .137 E5
Clyde Rd EN11 . . . . .21 D5
Clyde Way RM1 . . . . .113 E2
Clydesdale Rd RM11 . . . . . .135 F4

Clynes Ho 6 RM10 .....135 A1
Coach La CM9 ....36 F3
Coach Mews CM11 ......97 D5
Coal Ct RM17 ....178 A8
Coalhouse Fort★ RM18 .180 E6
Coalport Cl CM17 ......24 D7
Coaster Stps 4 SS1 ....167 C7
Coastguard Cotts
Bradwell-on-S CM0 ....63 E8
Canvey Island SS8 ......163 C1
Coates Cl CM9 ....37 B4
Coates Quay CM2 ....32 C2
Cobbetts Ave IG4 ......132 D6
Cobbins Chase CM0 .....106 B8
Cobbins Cl CM0 ....106 B8
Cobbins Gr CM0 ....106 B8
Cobbins The
Burnham-on-C CM0 ......106 B8
Waltham Abbey EN9 ......65 E6
Cobbins Way CM17 ....11 E4
Cobbinsbank EN9 ....65 D6
Cobbinsend Rd EN9 .....44 D2
Cobbles The
Brentwood CM15 ....116 E8
Upminster RM14 ....137 F4
Cobbs Pl CM1 ....32 D3
Cobden Wlk SS13 ......143 C7
Cobdens IG7 ....111 D4
Cobham RM16 ....173 B4
Cobham Cl DA9 ....177 B1
Cobham Ho IG11 ......152 C4
Cobham Rd
Chingford E17 ....109 C2
Ilford IG3 ....133 E1
Southend-on-S SS0 .....166 C7
Cobham Terr DA9 ......177 B1
Cobill Cl RM11 ....136 C7
Coburg Gdns IG5 .....110 E1
Coburg La SS16 ......140 F4
Coburg Pl CM3 ....101 D6
Cock Gn CM19 ....23 B6
Cock La Blackmore CM1 ...51 F2
Edney Common CM1 ....52 A3
Hoddesdon EN11 ....21 A5
Cockabourne Ct RM3 ..115 A1
Cockerell Cl SS13 ....121 B1
Cockethurst Cl SS0 ...147 A4
Cockle Sheds SS9 .....165 D8
Cockrobin La CM20 .....10 A7
Codenham Gn SS16 ....142 B5
Codenham Straight
SS16 ....142 B4
Codham Hall La CM13 ..138 C7
Cokefield Ave SS2 .....148 D3
Coker Rd SS8 ....163 D2
Colam La CM3 ....34 C3
Colbert Ave SS1 ......167 F7
Colbourne Cl SS17 ....160 F3
Colchester Ave E12 ...132 F1
Colchester Cl SS2 ....147 F2
Colchester Rd
Chelmsford CM2 ....33 A6
Heybridge CM9 ....37 B5
Romford RM3 ....114 E2
Southend-on-S SS2 .....147 F2
Cold Norton Prim Sch
CM3 ....80 F5
Cold Norton Rd CM3 ....81 D5
Coldharbour La RM13 ..170 B4
Coldharbour Rd CM19 ...23 A7
Cole Ave RM16 ....174 C2
Cole Ct RM3 ....114 D5
Colebrook Gdns IG10 ...89 B7
Colebrook La IG10 .....89 B7
Colebrook Path IG10 ...89 B7
Colebrooke Dr E11 ....132 C4
Coleford Ho 7 RM3 ...114 E4
Coleman Rd
Belvedere DA17 ....169 A2
Dagenham RM9 ....153 E6
Coleman St SS2 ....148 A1
Coleman's La EN9 ......43 E5
Colemans Ave SS0 .....147 D4
Colemans La CM3 ....56 D7
Colenso Rd IG2 ....133 E4
Coleridge Rd
Dartford DA1 ....176 B3
Maldon CM9 ....37 A1
Romford RM3 ....114 B3
Tilbury RM18 ....179 C5
Coleridge Wlk CM13 ....95 D2
Coles Cl CM5 ....49 A5
Coles Gn IG10 ....89 A8
Colet Rd CM13 ....95 D4
Coley Ct SS7 ....144 B4
Colgate Pl EN3 ....65 A2
Colin Cl DA2 ....176 B1
Colin Pond Ct RM6 ....134 D8
Colinton Rd IG3 ......134 B2
Collard Ave IG10 ......89 C7
Collard Gn IG10 ....89 C7
College Ave RM17 .....173 C2
College Cl RM17 ......173 C2
College Gdns Chingford E4 87 B2
Redbridge IG4 ....132 E6
College Pl DA9 ....177 C3
College Rd Grays RM17 .173 C2
Northfleet DA11 ....178 B2
College Sq CM20 ....23 D8
College Way SS1 ......167 A8
Colley Rd CM2 ....55 A6
Collier Row La RM5 ...113 C1
Collier Row Rd
Dagenham RM5 ....112 F2
Romford RM5 ....113 B3
Colliers The CM9 ......37 E3
Collindale Cl SS8 ....164 D4
Collingwood SS7 ......144 E4
Collingwood Ho
Greenhithe DA9 ....177 D2
Southend-on-S SS0 .....147 D2
Collingwood Prim Sch
CM3 ....101 E6
Collingwood Rd
Basildon SS16 ....142 D4
Rainham RM13 ....155 A3
South Woodham Ferrers
CM3 ....101 F6
Collingwood Terr SS16 .142 D5
Collingwood Way SS3 ..149 E1
Collingwood Wlk SS16 .142 D5
Collins Cl SS17 ......160 E2
Collins Ho 8 IG11 ...152 B5
Collins Mdw CM19 ......23 B7
Collins Way
Brentwood CM13 ....95 F4
Southend-on-S SS9 .....147 A6
Collinwood Gdns
Ilford IG5 ....133 A7
Redbridge IG5 ....132 F6
Colman Cl SS17 ....160 D3
Colne RM18 ....175 C3
Colne Cl
South Ockendon RM15 ..172 C6
South Woodham Ferrers
CM3 ....101 E7
Colne Ct RM18 ....175 C2
Colne Dr Romford RM3 ..114 F4
Southend-on-S SS3 .....149 E1
Colne Ho IG11 ....152 B6
Colne Pl SS16 ....142 C5
Colne Valley RM14 ....137 E5
Colney Rd DA1 ....176 A1
Colombo Rd IG1 ......133 C4
Colson Gdns IG10 ......89 B5
Colson Gn IG10 ....89 B4
Colson Path IG10 ......89 A5
Colson Rd IG10 ....89 B5
Colt Hatch CM20 ....10 B1
Colt Mews EN3 ....65 A2
Colthurst Gdns EN11 ...21 D8
Coltishall Cl SS11 ...122 B6
Coltishall Rd RM12 ...155 C6
Coltsfoot Ct RM17 ....178 D8
Coltsfoot Path
Romford RM3 ....114 C3
Romford RM3 ....114 D4
Columbia Wharf Rd
RM17 ....178 A8
Columbine Way RM3 ...114 E2
Colvers CM17 ....13 C2
Colville Cl SS17 .....160 F5
Colville Mews CM12 ....96 F5
Colvin Chase CM2 ......54 B1
Colvin Gdns Chingford E4 109 C7
Redbridge IG6 ....111 C3
Wanstead E11 ....132 B7
Colwall Gdns IG8 .....110 A5
Colworth Cl SS7 ......145 D4
Colyers Reach CM2 .....33 A2
Combes Rd RM9 ....153 F5
Comet Cl RM19 ....171 A2
Comet Way SS2 ....147 B6
Comfrey Ct RM17 ......178 D8
Commerce Est E18 .....110 C1
Commercial Pl DA12 ...179 C1
Commercial Rd SS0 ....147 D4
Commercial Way SS15 ..140 E7
Commodore Ho SS14 ...142 E6
Common App SS7 ....145 A7
Common La
Little Baddow CM3 ....34 E2
Stock CM4 ....75 E2
Thundersley SS7 ....145 B7
Woodham Walter CM9 ......35 B3
Common Rd
Great Wakering SS3 .....150 B4
Harlow EN9 ....22 E2
Ingrave CM13 ....117 C5
Stock CM4 ....75 E3
Common The
Danbury CM3 ....56 E6
East Hanningfield CM3 ...78 B7
Thundersley SS7 ....145 A7
Commonfields CM20 .....10 E1
Commonhall La SS7 ....145 D3
Commonside Rd CM18 ....23 F4
Commonwealth Ho
RM18 ....179 A5
Como St RM7 ....135 D7
Compass Gdns
Burnham-on-C CM0 ....106 A6
South Woodham Ferrers
CM3 ....101 F7
Compton Ave
Brentwood CM13 ....95 C1
Romford RM2 ....136 C8
Compton Ct
Canvey Island SS8 ......164 D2
Southend-on-S SS9 ......146 B1
Wickford SS11 ....121 E7
Compton Terr SS11 ....121 E7
Compton Wlk SS15 .....141 B7
Comroston EN11 ....21 A6
Comyns Pl CM1 ....31 B1
Comyns Rd RM9 ....154 A5
Con Way SS7 ....144 D3
Concord Rd SS8 ....163 F5
Concorde Ho 1 RM12 ..155 B6
Condor Wlk RM12 .....155 B5
Condovers Cotts RM18 .179 F8
Conduit La
Hoddesdon EN11 ....21 A6
Woodham Mortimer CM9 ....57 E6
Conduit La E EN11 .....21 B6
Coney Burrows E4 .....109 E8
Coney Gree CM21 ....1 D3
Conference Cl 3 E4 ..109 C8
Congreve Rd EN9 ....65 E6
Conifer Ave RM5 ......113 B5
Conifer Ct IG1 ....152 B6
Conifer Dr CM14 ......116 D5
Conifers SS7 ....145 E3
Coningsby Gdns E4 ....109 B4
Conisborough Ct 12
DA2 ....176 B1
Coniston SS2 ....147 A7
Coniston Ave
Barking IG11 ....152 E5
Upminster RM14 ....156 C8
Coniston Cl Barking IG11 152 E5
Rayleigh SS6 ....123 E2
Coniston Ct CM16 ....68 A8
Coniston Gdns IG4 ....132 E7
Coniston Rd
Canvey Island SS8 ......164 A3
South Benfleet SS7 .....144 E8
Coniston Way RM12 ....155 A7
Connaught Ave
Chingford E4 ....87 D2
Grays RM16 ....173 C3
Loughton IG10 ....88 D5
Connaught Ct E4 ....87 E2
Connaught Dr CM3 .....101 C7
Connaught Gdns SS3 ...168 C6
Connaught Hill IG10 ...88 D5
Connaught La IG1 .....133 D2
Connaught Mews IG1 ..133 D2
Connaught Rd
Chingford E4 ....87 E1
Hornchurch RM12 ....136 D1
Ilford IG1 ....133 D2
Rayleigh SS6 ....146 A8
Connaught Way CM12 ...97 A5
Connaught Wlk SS6 ....146 A8
Connington Cres E4 ...109 D7
Connor Cl IG6 ....111 C2
Connor Rd RM9 ....153 F8
Conqueror Ct RM3 .....114 D3
Conrad Cl RM16 ....173 B4
Conrad Gdns RM16 ....173 B4
Conrad Rd SS17 ....160 E1
Consort Cl CM14 ......116 C5
Constable Mews RM8 ..153 B8
Constable View CM1 ....32 F6
Constable Way SS3 ....168 G8
Constance Cl CM1 ......19 A3
Constitution Hill SS7 .144 D3
Consul Ave RM13 ......154 D2
Convent Cl SS15 ......141 C6
Convent Rd SS8 ....164 B3
Conway Ave SS3 ....150 B3
Conway Cl RM13 ....155 A5
Conway Cres RM6 ......134 C5
Conway Gdns RM17 ....178 B7
Conway's Rd RM16 ....159 A3
Conybury Cl EN9 ....66 A7
Conybury Ct EN9 ....66 A7
Conyer Cl CM9 ....58 F8
Conyers CM20 ....10 C2
Conyers Cl IG8 ....109 E4
Conyers Way IG10 ......89 B6
Cook Pl CM2 ....32 F3
Cook's Cl RM5 ....113 C2
Cooke Cl RM16 ....172 E3
Cookham Ct SS3 ......149 E2
Cooks Gn SS13 ....121 C1
Cooks Spinney CM20 ....11 A2
Coolgardie Ave
Chigwell IG7 ....111 A7
Chingford E4 ....109 D5
Coombe Dr SS16 ....141 C1
Coombe Rd
Romford RM3 ....136 F8
Southminster CM0 ....84 D5
Coombe Rise
Chelmsford CM1 ....32 B7
Shenfield CM15 ....94 F1
Stanford-le-H SS17 .....160 E2
Coombes Cl CM12 ....96 F4
Coombes Gr SS4 ......126 B3
Coombes Rd RM9 ......153 F4
Coombewood Dr
Dagenham RM6 ....134 F5
Thundersley SS7 ....144 F5
Cooper Cl DA9 ....176 F2
Cooper Shaw Rd RM18 .179 E7
Cooper's Row CM1 ......32 A5
Coopers CM3 ....33 E8
Coopers Ave CM9 ....37 D5
Coopers Cl Chigwell IG7 .112 B8
Dagenham RM10 ....154 B6
Coopers Company & Coborn
Sch The RM14 ....137 D2
Coopers Dr CM11 .....119 C6
Coopers Hill CM5 ......49 A1
Coopers Mews CM5 .....49 A2
Coopers Way SS2 .....148 A5
Coopersale & Theydon
Garnon CE Prim Sch
CM16 ....46 D2
Coopersale Cl 3 IG8 ..110 C3
Coopersale Comm CM16 46 D3
Coopersale Hall Sch
CM16 ....68 B5
Coopersale La CM16 ....68 B3
Coopersale St CM16 ....68 D7
Coopersales SS15 ....141 A6
Coote Gdns 2 RM8 ....134 F1
Coote Rd RM8 ....134 F1
Copdoek SS14 ....142 C7
Copeland Ho 7 CM14 ..116 C6
Copelands SS4 ....125 D6
Copeman Rd CM13 ....95 D2
Copford Ave SS6 ......123 F1
Copford Cl Billericay CM11 97 C2
Woodford IG8 ....110 E4
Copford Rd CM11 ....97 C2
Copland Cl
Broomfield CM1 ....19 A1
Great Baddow CM2 ....54 F8
Copland Rd SS17 .....160 D1
Coppen Rd RM8 ....134 F4
Coppens Gn SS12 .....121 E6
Copper Beech Ct IG5 ..111 A2
Copper Beech Ct IG10 ..89 A8
Copper Beech Rd RM15 157 C2
Copper Beeches
Brentwood CM14 ....116 C6
Thundersley SS7 ....145 B7
Copper Ct CM21 ....1 E2
Copperfield
Billericay CM11 ....119 D6
Chigwell IG7 ....111 D4
Copperfield Gdns CM14 .94 C1
Copperfield Rd CM1 ....31 E7
Copperfields SS15 ....141 C7
Copperfields Way RM3 .114 D2
Coppergate Ct EN9 .....66 A5
Coppice Hatch CM18 ....23 D6
Coppice La
Basildon SS15 ....119 F1
Pleshey CM6 ....7 E8
Coppice Path IG7 .....112 B6
Coppice Prim Sch IG7 .112 A5
Coppice Row CM16 .....67 D3
Coppice The CM15 ......71 E2
Coppid Hall RM16 ....172 F5
Coppings The EN11 ......8 A1
Coppins Cl CM2 ....32 E4
Coppins The 2 RM6 ...134 B4
Copse Hill CM19 ....23 B5
Copse The Billericay CM12 .97 B4
Chingford E4 ....87 F1
Copshall Cl CM18 ......23 E4
Copt Hill CM3 ....56 E6
Coptfold Cl SS1 .....148 F1
Coptfold Rd CM14 ....116 D8
Copthorne Ave IG6 ...111 B4
Copthorne Gdns RM11 .137 A6
Coral Cl Ilford RM6 ..134 D8
South Woodham Ferrers
CM3 ....101 C8
Coral Ho CM20 ....10 A1
Coram Gn CM13 ....95 D4
Corasway SS7 ....145 C5
Corbets Ave RM14 .....156 B7
Corbets Tey Rd RM14 ..156 B8
Corbets Tey Sch RM14 .156 C7
Corbett Rd E11 ....132 C5
Corbett Villas RM8 ...134 C3
Corbridge Mews 6
RM1 ....135 F6
Corcorans CM15 ....94 C3
Cordelia Cres SS6 ....123 C3
Cordwainers The SS2 ..148 A5
Corfe Cl 2 SS13 .....143 B5
Cories Cl RM8 ....134 D2
Corinthian Manorway
DA8 ....169 D2
Corinthian Rd DA8 ....169 D2
Cormorant Wlk
Chelmsford CM2 ....54 C5
8 Hornchurch RM12 .....155 B6
Cornec Ave SS9 ....146 B6
Cornec Chase SS9 .....146 C6
Cornelius Vale CM2 ....33 B4
Cornelius Vermuyden Sch
The SS8 ....163 E5
Cornell Way RM5 ......113 B5
Corner Ho CM18 ....23 F6
Corner Mdw CM18 ....24 A4
Corner Rd CM11 ....120 D6
Cornfields CM3 ....101 C8
Cornflower Dr CM1 .....32 F6
Cornflower Gdns CM12 ..96 F4
Cornflower Way RM3 ..114 E2
Cornhill 4 CM1 ....32 B2
Cornhill Ave SS5 .....124 E7
Cornhouse Bldgs SS6 .145 C8
Cornish Gr CM3 ....101 E6
Cornmill EN9 ....65 B6
Cornshaw Rd RM8 .....134 D3
Cornsland CM14 ......116 D7
Cornsland Ct 7 CM14 .116 C7
Cornwall Cl Barking IG11 152 F6
Hornchurch RM11 ....137 A7
Cornwall Cres CM1 ......32 A7
Cornwall Gate RM19 ...171 A2
Cornwall Gdns SS4 ...125 C5
Cornwall Rd
Basildon SS13 ....143 F7
Dartford DA1 ....176 A4
Pilgrims Hatch CM15 .....94 B4
Cornwallis Dr CM3 ....101 F7
Cornwallis Ho SS14 ...142 A8
Cornwallis Rd RM9 ....153 E8
Cornwell Cres SS17 ..160 E3
Cornworthy SS3 ......168 C8
Cornworthy Rd RM8 ...153 C7
Corona Rd Basildon SS16 141 B3
Canvey Island SS8 ......164 D5
Coronation Ave RM18 .175 C2
Coronation Cl
Great Wakering SS3 .....149 F4
Ilford IG6 ....133 C7
Coronation Cotts CM15 .116 E8
Coronation Ct RM18 ...175 C2
Coronation Dr RM12 ...155 B7
Coronation Hill CM16 ...45 F2
Coronation Rd CM0 ....106 B4
Corporation Rd CM1 ....32 A4
Corral Hts DA8 ....169 E1
Corran Way RM15 .....172 B6
Corringham Prim Sch
SS17 ....161 C4
Corringham Rd
Stanford-le-H SS17 .....160 E1
Stanford-le-H, Balstonia
SS17 ....160 F2
Corringham SS17 ....161 A3
Corsel Rd SS8 ....164 E3
Cortina Dr RM13 .....154 C3
Corton Trad Est SS7 ..144 D7
Corve La RM15 ....172 B6
Cory Dr CM13 ....95 B2
Cosgrove Ave SS9 ....146 B3
Cossington Rd SS0 ...166 E8
Costead Manor Rd CM14 94 B1
Coteford Cl IG10 ......89 B7
Cotelands SS16 ......142 F3
Cotesmore Gdns RM8 ..153 C8
Cotleigh Rd RM7 .....135 D5
Cotman Lodge CM1 ......32 F6
Cotman Mews RM8 ....153 B7
Cotswold Ave SS6 ....123 D4
Cotswold Cres CM1 .....31 D6
Cotswold Gdns
Brentwood CM13 ....95 E2
Ilford IG2 ....133 D4
Cotswold Rd
Romford RM3 ....114 F1
Southend-on-S SS0 ......147 D1
Cottage Pl CM1 ....32 B3
Cottages The SS3 ....168 F7
Cottesmore Ave IG5 ..111 A1
Cottesmore Cl SS8 ...164 B2
Cottesmore Ct SS9 ...146 A2
Cottesmore Gdns SS9 .146 A1
Cottey Ho CM2 ....54 B2
Cottis Cl SS16 ......141 A3
Cotton Cl RM9 ....153 C5
Cotton La DA2 ....176 C2
Cottons App RM7 .....135 D6
Cottons Ct 3 RM7 ...135 D6
Couchmore Ave IG5 ...110 F1
Coulde Dennis CM3 .....78 B7
Coulson Cl RM8 ......134 C3
Coulter Ho DA9 ......177 C2
Coulter Mews CM11 .....97 B3
Council Ave DA11 ....178 C1
Council Bglws
Fobbing SS17 ....161 D5
Steeple CM0 ....61 E2
Council Hos
Bicknacre CM3 ....56 F1
Bradwell-on-S CM0 ....63 E8
Corringham SS17 ....161 D5
County Chambers SS1 .167 A7
County Pl CM2 ....32 B1
Courage Cl RM11 .....136 C5
Courage Ct 7 CM13 ....95 C3
Courage Wlk CM13 ......95 D3
Court Ave RM3 ....115 A3
Court Gdns RM3 ....115 A3
Court Ind Est CM2 .....32 C2
Court Lodge 11 DA17 .169 A1
Court Mews DA11 .....178 B1
Court Needham EN3 .....65 A2
Court Rd CM1 ....19 A3
Court View CM4 ....73 F1
Court Way Ilford IG6 .133 C8
Romford RM3 ....114 E1
Courtauld Rd SS13 ...121 C2
Courtenay Dr RM16 ...172 F3
Courtenay Gdns RM14 .137 C3
Courtfield SS7 ......144 D1
Courtfield Cl EN10 ....21 A3
Courtland Ave
Chingford E4 ....109 F8
Ilford IG1 ....133 A3
Redbridge IG1 ....132 F2
Courtland Dr IG7 ....111 C7
Courtland Mews CM9 ....58 F8
Courtland Pl CM9 ......58 F8
Courtlands Billericay CM12 96 E2
Chelmsford CM1 ....32 A6
Southend-on-S SS9 .....146 B7
Courtney Park Rd SS16 .141 B5
Courtney Rd RM16 ....174 C4
Courts The SS6 ......123 E3
Courtsend SS3 ....130 F8
Courtway IG8 ....110 C5
Courtway Cotts SS17 ..161 D5
Courtyard The
Brentwood CM15 ....94 B2
Maldon CM9 ....36 F2
Coval Ave CM1 ....32 A3
Coval La CM1 ....32 A2
Coval Wells CM1 ....32 A2
Covenbrook CM13 .....117 B7
Coventry Cl SS5 .....101 F1
Coventry Hill SS5 ...101 E1
Coventry Rd IG1 .....133 B3
Coverdales The IG11 ..152 D3
Coverley Cl CM13 ....116 C4
Covert Rd IG6 ....111 F4
Coverts The
Brentwood CM13 ....95 A1
Writtle CM1 ....31 B1
Cow Watering La CM1 ...30 E2
Cowbridge La IG11 ...152 B5
Cowdray Way RM12 ....155 A8
Cowdrie Way CM2 ....33 B4
Cowell Ave CM1 ....31 E5
Cowell Lodge IG8 ....109 F5
Cowley Ave DA9 ......177 A2

Cowley Rd Ilford IG1 . . . . .133 A4
Redbridge IG1 . . . . .132 F4
Romford RM3 . . . . .114 B3
Wanstead E11 . . . . .132 B6
Cowlins CM17 . . . . .11 D4
Cowper Ave RM18 . . . . . .179 B6
Cowper Rd
Belvedere DA17 . . . . .169 A2
Rainham RM13 . . . . .155 A1
Cowslip Mead SS14 . . . . .142 B6
Cowslip Rd E18 . . . . .110 B1
Cox Ley CM22 . . . . .3 A3
Coxbridge Ct CM12 . . . . . . .97 A2
Coxes CI SS17 . . . . .160 D3
Coxes Farm Rd CM11 . . . .119 E7
Coxon Dr RM16 . . . . .172 E3
Coxs CI CM3 . . . . .101 E8
Coxtie Green Rd
Pilgrims Hatch CM14 . . . . . .93 C5
South Weald CM14 . . . . . . .93 A2
Crabtree Ave RM6 . . . . . . .134 D7
Crabtree Manorway N
DA17 . . . . .169 C5
Crabtree Manorway S
DA17 . . . . .169 C3
Craftsmans Sq SS2 . . . . . .148 A5
Craig Gdns CM12 . . . . .109 F1
Craigdale Rd RM11 . . . . . .135 F4
Craiston Way CM2 . . . . .54 F5
Crammavill St RM16 . . . . .173 A5
Crammerville Wlk **2**
RM13 . . . . .155 B1
Cramphorn Wlk CM1 . . . .31 F3
Cranborne Gdns RM14 . . .137 B2
Cranborne Rd
Barking IG11 . . . . .152 D4
Hoddesdon EN11 . . . . .21 C7
Cranbourne Ave E11 . . . .132 B7
Cranbourne Dr EN11 . . . . . .8 C2
Cranbourne Gdns IG6 . . .133 C8
Cranbourne Ho EN61 . . . . . .8 C2
Cranbourne Prim Sch The
EN11 . . . . .8 B2
Cranbrook Ave SS7 . . . .145 C4
Cranbrook Coll (Boys)
IG1 . . . . .133 A2
Cranbrook Dr RM2 . . . . . .136 C7
Cranbrook Rd IG1,IG2 . . .133 A5
Cranbrook Rise
Ilford IG1 . . . . .133 A4
Redbridge IG1 . . . . .132 F5
Crane CI RM10 . . . . .154 A6
Cranell Gn RM15 . . . . .172 A5
Cranes CI SS13 . . . . .120 F1
Cranes Ct SS14 . . . . .142 C8
Cranes Farm Rd SS14 . . .120 D1
Cranes La SS14 . . . . .142 C8
Cranfield Ct
Wickford SS12 . . . . .121 C8
2 Woodford IG8 . . . . . . .110 A6
Cranfield Park Ave
SS12 . . . . .121 F2
Cranfield Park Ct **5**
SS12 . . . . .121 D5
Cranfield Park Rd SS12 . .121 E4
Cranham Gdns RM14 . . . .137 F4
Cranham Pl RM14 . . . . . . .157 A7
Cranham Rd RM11 . . . . . .136 B5
Cranleigh Dr SS9 . . . . .146 E1
Cranleigh Gdns
Barking IG11 . . . . .152 D6
Hullbridge SS5 . . . . .101 D1
Loughton IG10 . . . . .88 F3
Cranley Ave SS0 . . . . .147 D1
Cranley Dr IG2 . . . . .133 C4
Cranley Gdns SS3 . . . . . . .168 C6
Cranley Rd Ilford IG2 . . . .133 C4
Southend-on-S SS0 . . . . . .147 D1
Cranmer CI CM12 . . . . .97 B6
Cranmer Gdns RM10 . . . .154 C8
Cranmer Ho CM2 . . . . .53 F7
Cranston Ave SS0 . . . . . . .147 D1
Cranston Gdns E4 . . . . . . .109 A4
Cranston Park Ave
RM14 . . . . .156 C8
Cranworth Cres **7** E4 . . .87 D1
Craven Ave SS4 . . . . .164 A3
Craven CI SS4 . . . . .125 D5
Craven Ct RM6 . . . . .134 E5
Craven Gdns
Barking IG11 . . . . .152 E3
Ilford IG6 . . . . .133 D8
Redbridge IG6 . . . . .111 D1
Romford, Willoughby's Hill
RM5 . . . . .113 A5
Romford,Harold Park RM3 115 C4
Crawford Rd RM16 . . . . . .173 B5
Crawford Chase SS12 . . . .121 C5
Crawford CI CM12 . . . . .97 C5
Crawley CI **6** DA11 . . . .179 B1
Craword Compton CI
RM12 . . . . .155 C6
Crayford CI CM9 . . . . .58 E8
Craylands SS14 . . . . .142 F7
Craylands La DA10 . . . . . .177 D2
Craylands Sq DA10 . . . . . .177 D2
Crays Hill CM11 . . . . .120 C5
Crays Hill Prim Sch
CM11 . . . . .120 D6
Crays Hill Rd CM11 . . . . . .120 D4
Crays View CM12 . . . . .119 B8
Crealock Gr IG8 . . . . .109 F5
Creance Ct CM2 . . . . .32 A4
Creasen Butt CI CM9 . . . . .37 A4

Creasey CI RM11 . . . . .136 B2
Creasy Ct SS14 . . . . .142 E6
Crediton Ho **4** RM3 . . .114 D4
Credo Way RM20 . . . . . . .177 B8
Cree Way RM1 . . . . .113 A3
Creeds Cotts CM16 . . . . . . .67 E2
Creek Rd Barking IG11 . . .152 F2
Canvey Island SS8 . . . . . .164 D4
Creek The DA11 . . . . .178 B2
Creek View SS16 . . . . .142 E3
Creek View Ave SS5 . . . . .101 D3
Creekmouth Ind Pk
IG11 . . . . .152 F1
Creeksea Ferry Rd SS4 . .105 C3
Creeksea La CM0 . . . . . . .105 F6
Creekside RM13 . . . . .154 F1
Creekview Rd CM3 . . . . . .101 F7
Creephedge La CM3 . . . . . .78 E5
Crescent Ave
Grays RM17 . . . . .178 D8
Hornchurch RM12 . . . . . . .135 F2
Crescent CI CM12 . . . . .96 F4
Crescent Ct
Billericay CM12 . . . . .97 A2
Grays RM17 . . . . .173 D1
Heybridge CM9 . . . . .36 F5
Crescent Dr CM15 . . . . .94 E1
Crescent Gdns CM12 . . . . .96 F4
Crescent Rd
Aveley RM15 . . . . .171 C4
Billericay CM12 . . . . .96 F4
Brentwood CM14 . . . . . . .116 B6
Canvey Island SS8 . . . . . .164 D2
Chingford E4 . . . . .87 E2
Dagenham RM10 . . . . . . .135 B1
Great Baddow CM2 . . . . . . .55 A7
Heybridge CM9 . . . . .36 F5
South Benfleet SS7 . . . . . .144 D2
Southend-on-S SS9 . . . . . .146 B1
Woodford E18 . . . . .110 C2
Crescent The Epping CM16 67 F4
Greenhithe DA9 . . . . .177 C2
Hadleigh SS7 . . . . .145 F3
Harlow CM17 . . . . .11 C6
Ilford IG2 . . . . .133 A5
Loughton IG10 . . . . .88 D3
Upminster RM14 . . . . .137 F4
Crescent View IG10 . . . . . .88 D4
Crescent Way RM15 . . . . .171 D5
Crescent Wlk RM15 . . . . .171 C4
Cressells SS14 . . . . .141 F6
Cresset CI SG12 . . . . .8 C3
Cressingham Ct **1**
DA17 . . . . .169 A3
Crest Ave Basildon SS13 . .143 C6
Grays RM17 . . . . .178 B7
Crest The
Sawbridgeworth CM21 . . . . .1 D2
Southend-on-S SS9 . . . . . .146 D6
Crest View DA9 . . . . .177 A3
Cresthill Ave RM17 . . . . . .173 C2
Creswick Ave SS6 . . . . . . .123 C3
Creswick St SS6 . . . . .123 C3
Crete Hall Rd DA11 . . . . . .178 E1
Cricketers CI
Broomfield CM1 . . . . .19 C1
Erith DA8 . . . . .169 E1
Cricketers La CM13 . . . . . .117 D3
Cricketers Row CM13 . . . .117 D3
Cricketers Way SS13 . . . .121 A2
Cricketfield Gr SS9 . . . . . .146 F2
Crickhollow CM3 . . . . .101 C5
Cricklade Ave RM3 . . . . . .114 D4
Cringle Lock CM3 . . . . . . .101 E5
Cripplegate CM0 . . . . .84 E5
Cripsey Ave CM5 . . . . .48 F5
Crispe Ho IG11 . . . . .152 D3
Crispin Terr IG8 . . . . .110 D4
Crispins SS1 . . . . .168 A8
Critchett Terr **1** CM1 . . .32 A3
Crocus Way CM1 . . . . .32 E7
Croft
South Benfleet SS7 . . . . . .144 C5
Southend-on-S SS9 . . . . . .146 E4
Croft Ct CM1 . . . . .32 E8
Croft La CM3 . . . . .7 F3
Croft Lodge CI IG8 . . . . . . .110 B4
Croft Rd SS7 . . . . .144 C5
Croft The Chingford E4 . . .109 E8
Loughton IG10 . . . . .89 A7
Rayleigh SS6 . . . . .145 F8
Crofters CM21 . . . . .1 E3
Crofters End CM21 . . . . .1 E3
Crofton Ave SS17 . . . . . . .160 F4
Crofton Gr E4 . . . . .109 D6
Crofton Rd RM16 . . . . . . .173 E3
Crofts The SS3 . . . . .149 E4
Cromar Way CM1 . . . . .31 F1
Crombie CI IG4 . . . . .132 F6
Cromer Ave SS15 . . . . . . .141 B8
Cromer CI SS15 . . . . .141 B8
Cromer Rd
Dagenham RM6 . . . . .134 E5
Hornchurch RM11 . . . . . . .136 D4
Romford RM7 . . . . .135 C5
Southend-on-S SS1 . . . . . .167 B8
Woodford IG8 . . . . .110 A6
Crompton CI SS14 . . . . . . .141 F4
Crompton Pl **8** EN3 . . . .65 A1
Crompton St CM1 . . . . .31 F1
Cromwell Ave CM12 . . . . . .97 A3
Cromwell CI CM3 . . . . .33 D8
Cromwell Ct
Brentwood CM14 . . . . . . .116 B6
Maldon CM9 . . . . .37 F4
Cromwell Ctr IG6 . . . . .112 B5
Cromwell Ctr The RM8 . . .134 F4

Cromwell Hill CM9 . . . . .36 F3
Cromwell La CM9 . . . . .36 F3
Cromwell Lodge IG11 . . . .152 E7
Cromwell Rd
Brentwood CM14 . . . . . . .116 B6
Grays RM17 . . . . .173 A1
Hockley SS5 . . . . .124 E6
Southend-on-S SS2 . . . . . .148 B3
Cromwells Mere RM5 . . . .113 D4
Crondon Park La CM4 . . . . .75 E4
Crooked La DA11,DA12 . . .179 B1
Crooked Mile EN9 . . . . .65 C7
Crooked Way EN9 . . . . .65 C7
Cropenburg Wlk SS8 . . . .164 B5
Croppath Rd RM10 . . . . . .154 A8
Crosby Ct IG7 . . . . .112 A7
Crosby Rd
Dagenham RM10 . . . . . . .154 B4
Southend-on-S SS0 . . . . . .166 C8
Cross Ave SS12 . . . . .121 C6
Cross Gn SS16 . . . . .141 B4
Cross Rd Basildon SS13 . .143 F7
Chingford E4 . . . . .87 E1
Dagenham RM6 . . . . .134 C4
Gravesend DA11 . . . . .178 F1
Hadleigh SS7 . . . . .145 B4
Maldon CM9 . . . . .37 A1
Romford RM7 . . . . .135 B8
Woodford SS8 . . . . .110 F4
Cross Roads IG10 . . . . .88 C7
Cross St **16** DA11 . . . . . .179 B1
Cross Way CM17 . . . . .11 D1
Crossbow Ct CM5 . . . . .49 A2
Crossbow Rd IG7 . . . . .111 F5
Crossby CI CM15 . . . . .95 E8
Crossfell Rd SS7 . . . . .144 F7
Crossfield Rd
Hoddesdon EN11 . . . . .21 B8
Southend-on-S SS2 . . . . . .148 D2
Crossfields IG10 . . . . .89 A4
Crossing Rd CM16 . . . . . . .68 A6
Crossness Rd IG11 . . . . . .152 F1
Crossfield Rd
6 Stanford-le-H SS17 . . .160 F3
Woodford IG8 . . . . .110 C6
Crossway The CM11 . . . . . .97 D3
Crossways
Canvey Island SS8 . . . . . .163 E4
Chelmsford CM2 . . . . .54 C7
Loughton IG10 . . . . .89 A4
Romford RM2 . . . . .136 B8
Shenfield CM15 . . . . .95 A3
Crossways Bvd DA2 . . . . .176 C3
Crossways The SS0 . . . . . .166 A8
Crouch Ave Barking IG11 .153 B3
Hullbridge SS5 . . . . .101 E7
Crouch Beck CM3 . . . . . . .101 E7
Crouch Ct CM20 . . . . .10 C3
Crouch Cvn Pk SS5 . . . . . .101 F4
Crouch Dr SS11 . . . . .121 D8
Crouch Mdw SS5 . . . . .101 E4
Crouch Rd
Burnham-on-C CM0 . . . . . .106 C5
Grays RM17 . . . . .174 A1
Crouch St SS15 . . . . .119 E2
Crouch Valley RM14 . . . . .137 E4
Crouch View Cotts CM3 . .100 C5
Crouch View Cres SS5 . . .125 A4
Crouch View Gr SS5 . . . . .101 D3
Crouch View Villas SS4 . .104 E2
Crouch Way SS3 . . . . .168 E7
Crouchman CI RM16 . . . . .173 C4
Crouchman's Farm Rd
CM9 . . . . .35 C7
Crouchmans Ave SS3 . . . .150 A4
Crouchview CI SS11 . . . . .122 B7
Crow Gn CM15 . . . . .94 A5
Crow Green La CM15 . . . . .94 A4
Crow Green Rd CM15 . . . . .94 A5
Crow La RM7 . . . . .135 B4
Crowborough Rd SS2 . . . .148 A2
Crowlands Ave RM7 . . . . .135 B5
Crowlands Jun & Inf Schs
RM7 . . . . .135 C5
Crown Ave SS13 . . . . .143 C7
Crown Bldgs **4** E4 . . . . .87 D1
Crown CI Basildon SS13 . .143 C6
Sheering CM22 . . . . .12 C3
Crown Ct RM18 . . . . .179 A5
Crown Gate CM20 . . . . .23 D8
Crown Hill Loughton CM16 67 A5
Rayleigh SS6 . . . . .123 C2
Crown Par RM13 . . . . .155 B1
Crown Rd Billericay CM11 . .97 B2
Cold Norton CM3 . . . . .80 F5
Grays RM17 . . . . .178 A8
Hockley SS5 . . . . .124 B5
Ilford IG6 . . . . .133 D7
Kelvedon Hatch CM14 . . . . .93 D8
Crown St
Brentwood CM14 . . . . . . .116 C8
Dagenham RM10 . . . . . . .154 C6
Crown Way CM0 . . . . .84 C4
Crownfield EN10 . . . . .21 A4
Crownfield Ave IG2 . . . . . .133 E6
Crownfields Jun & Inf Schs
RM7 . . . . .113 A1
Crownhill Rd IG8 . . . . .110 E8
Crownmead Way RM7 . . . .135 B7
Crows Field Cotts CM2 . . . .76 F4
Crows La CM3 . . . . .79 D4
Crows Rd Barking IG11 . . .152 B6
Epping CM16 . . . . .45 F1
Crowsheath La CM11 . . . . .98 E6
Crowsnest The CM0 . . . . .106 C3

Crowstone Ave SS0 . . . . . .166 C8
Crowstone CI SS0 . . . . . . .147 D1
Crowstone Prep Sch
Rochford SS4 . . . . .148 B8
Southend-on-S SS0 . . . . . .166 C8
Crowstone Rd
Grays RM16 . . . . .173 C4
Southend-on-S SS0 . . . . . .166 C4
Croxford Way RM7 . . . . . .135 D3
Croxon Way CM0 . . . . .106 B7
Crozier Terr CM2 . . . . .33 B4
Crucible CI RM6 . . . . .134 B5
Cruick Ave RM15 . . . . .172 C6
Crusader CI RM17 . . . . . . .171 A2
Crushes CI CM13 . . . . .95 E3
Crushton Pl CM1 . . . . .31 F6
Crusoe Rd DA8 . . . . .169 D1
Crystal Ave CM12 . . . . . . .136 E1
Crystal Ct **1** RM13 . . . .155 A1
Crystal Stps **15** SS1 . . .167 C7
Crystal Way RM4 . . . . .134 C3
Cuckoo Cnr SS2 . . . . .147 E4
Cuckoo La RM16 . . . . .172 F5
Culford Rd RM16 . . . . .173 C4
Cullen Sq RM15 . . . . .172 C5
Cullings Ct EN9 . . . . .65 F6
Culpepper CI IG6 . . . . .111 B4
Culver Rise CM3 . . . . .101 E6
Culverdown SS14 . . . . .142 A6
Cumberland Ave
Hornchurch RM12 . . . . . . .136 E1
Maldon CM9 . . . . .36 E1
South Benfleet SS7 . . . . . .144 C3
Southend-on-S SS2 . . . . . .148 D2
Cumberland CI
Hornchurch RM12 . . . . . . .136 E1
Redbridge IG6 . . . . .111 C2
Cumberland Cres CM1 . . . .32 A7
Cumberland Ct
2 Hoddesdon EN11 . . . .21 A7
Woodford IG8 . . . . .110 B3
Cumberland Dr SS15 . . . . .141 A6
Cumberland Ho
Romford RM7 . . . . .113 A1
Southend-on-S SS2 . . . . . .147 F1
Cumberland Rd RM16 . . . .172 E4
Cumbrae Mews SS12 . . . .121 F5
Cumley Rd CM5 . . . . .47 C1
Cumming Rd CM11 . . . . . . .99 A2
Cummings Hall La RM3 . . .114 D7
Cunningham CI
Ilford RM6 . . . . .134 C6
Southend-on-S SS3 . . . . . .168 F3
Cunningham Dr SS12 . . . .121 C5
Cunningham Rise CM16 . . .47 D6
Cupid's Cnr SS3 . . . . .150 C2
Cupids Chase SS3 . . . . . . .150 C2
Curlew Ave CM3 . . . . .83 A8
Curlew CI CM9 . . . . .37 C5
Curlew Cres SS16 . . . . . . .142 B3
Curlew Dr SS7 . . . . .144 C2
Curlew Ho **1** CM0 . . . . .106 C4
Curlew Terr IG5 . . . . .133 A8
Curling La RM17 . . . . .172 F1
Curling Tye SS14 . . . . .142 D7
Curling Tye La
Maldon CM9 . . . . .36 A3
Woodham Walter CM9 . . . . .35 F3
Curling Wlk SS14 . . . . .142 D7
Curteys CM17 . . . . .11 C5
Curtis Mill La RM4 . . . . . . .91 A4
Curtis Rd RM11 . . . . .136 F4
Curtis Way SS6 . . . . .123 E4
Rainham RM13 . . . . .154 F4
Curzon Cres IG11 . . . . . . .152 F2
Curzon Dr RM17 . . . . .178 C7
Curzon Way CM2 . . . . .33 A2
Cusak Rd CM2 . . . . .32 F3
Cut-A-Thwart La CM9 . . . . .36 C4
Cutforth Rd CM21 . . . . .1 E3
Cuthberga CI **2** IG11 . .152 C5
Cutlers Rd CM3 . . . . .101 E8
Cutmore Pl CM2 . . . . .53 F8
Cuton Hall La CM2 . . . . . . .33 A5
Cutty Sark Ct DA9 . . . . . . .177 A2
Cygnet CT SS12 . . . . .121 D8
Cygnet View RM20 . . . . . .171 F2
Cygnet Way CM19 . . . . . . .9 A1
Cyns Ct **6** E11 . . . . .132 A5
Cypress CI EN9 . . . . .65 D5
Cypress Dr CM2 . . . . .54 C6
Cypress Gr IG6 . . . . .111 C4
Cypress Path RM3 . . . . . .114 D3
Cyril Dowsett Ct CM9 . . . .36 E2
Czarina Rise SS15 . . . . . . .141 E8

D

D'arcy Ave CM9 . . . . .37 B1
D'arcy CI CM0 . . . . .106 C4
D'arcy Gdns RM9 . . . . . . .153 F4
Daarle Ave SS8 . . . . .164 A4
Dacre Ave Aveley RM15 . . .171 D5
Redbridge IG5 . . . . .111 A1
Dacre CI IG7 . . . . .111 C6
Dacre Cres RM15 . . . . . . .171 D5
Dacre Gdns IG7 . . . . .111 C6
Dads Wood CM20 . . . . . . .23 C8
Daen Ingas CM3 . . . . .56 D7
Daffodil Ave CM15 . . . . . . .94 B4
Daffodil Gdns IG1 . . . . . . .152 B7
Daffodil Way CM1 . . . . .32 E7
Dagenham Ave RM9 . . . . .153 E4
Dagenham Dock Sta
RM9 . . . . .153 F3
Dagenham East Sta
RM10 . . . . .154 C7

Dagenham Heathway Sta
RM9 . . . . .153 F6
Dagenham Priory Comp Sch
RM10 . . . . .154 B4
Dagenham Rd
Dagenham RM10,RM7 . . .135 D2
Rainham RM13 . . . . .154 C5
Dagmar Rd RM10 . . . . . . .154 C5
Dagnam Park CI RM3 . . . .114 F5
Dagnam Park Dr RM3 . . . .114 F5
Dagnam Park Gdns
RM3 . . . . .115 A4
Dagnam Park Sq RM3 . . .115 B4
Dagwood La CM15 . . . . . . .72 B1
Dahlia CI **2** CM1 . . . . . . .32 F5
Dahlia Gdns IG1 . . . . .152 B6
Daiglen Dr RM15 . . . . .172 B7
Daiglen Sch The IG9 . . . . .110 C8
Daines CI Little Ilford E12 .132 F1
South Ockendon RM15 . . .157 A1
Southend-on-S SS1 . . . . . .168 B8
Daines Rd RM11 . . . . .97 C2
Daines Way SS1 . . . . .168 B8
Dairy Farm Rd CM3 . . . . . .83 D3
Dairy Rd CM2 . . . . .32 F4
Daisy Ct CM1 . . . . .33 A6
Daisy Rd E18 . . . . .110 B1
Dakyn Dr CM4 . . . . .75 D3
Dale CI RM15 . . . . .172 A7
Dale Ct
Sawbridgeworth CM21 . . . . .1 D1
Woodford E18 . . . . .110 A1
Dale Gdns IG8 . . . . .110 B6
Dale Rd SS9 . . . . .146 B1
Dale The
Thundersley SS7 . . . . .145 A4
Waltham Abbey EN9 . . . . . .65 E5
Dale View Ave E4 . . . . . . .109 C8
Dale View Cres E4 . . . . . . .109 C7
Dale View Gdns E4 . . . . . .109 D7
Dalefield IG9 . . . . .88 D1
Dalen Ave SS8 . . . . .164 A3
Dales The SS4 . . . . .125 D3
Daleside Gdns IG7 . . . . . .111 C7
Dalestone Mews RM3 . . . .114 B4
Dalewood CI RM11 . . . . . .136 E4
Dalkeith Rd IG1 . . . . .133 C1
Dalmatia Rd SS1 . . . . .167 D8
Dalmeney SS16 . . . . .141 B4
Dalroy CI RM15 . . . . .172 A7
Dalrymple CI CM1 . . . . .32 D3
Dalton Holme IG6 . . . . . . .110 F4
Daltons Fen SS13 . . . . . . .143 C8
Dalwood SS3 . . . . .149 D1
Dalwood Gdns SS7 . . . . . .145 E4
Dalys Rd SS4 . . . . .125 E4
Dame Elizabeth Ct CM1 . . .18 F3
Dame Tipping CE Prim Sch
RM4 . . . . .113 E7
Dames Rd E7 . . . . .132 A1
Dammerwick Cotts
CM0 . . . . .106 D6
Danacre SS15 . . . . .141 C7
Danbury CI CM15 . . . . .94 D8
Pilgrims Hatch CM15 . . . . .93 F4
Southend-on-S SS9 . . . . . .146 F4
Danbury Cres RM15 . . . . .172 B7
Danbury Ctry Pk* CM3 . . .56 B7
Danbury Down SS14 . . . . .142 E8
Danbury Mans **3** SS2 . .152 B5
Danbury Park Com Prim Sch
CM3 . . . . .56 C7
Danbury Rd Loughton IG10 .88 C7
Rainham RM13 . . . . .154 F4
Rayleigh SS6 . . . . .123 B3
Danbury Vale CM3 . . . . . . .57 A6
Danbury Way IG8 . . . . . . .110 C6
Dandelion CI RM7 . . . . . . .135 E2
Dandies Chase SS9 . . . . . .146 E7
Dandies CI SS9 . . . . .146 D7
Dandies Dr SS9 . . . . .146 D7
Dane Rd Chelmsford CM1 . .31 E2
Ilford IG1 . . . . .152 C7
Dane St SS3 . . . . .168 G6
Dane's Ave SS3 . . . . .168 F5
Danehurst Gdns IG4 . . . . .132 F6
Danemead EN11 . . . . .8 A1
Danes Rd RM7 . . . . .135 C4
Danes Way RM15 . . . . .94 A4
Danescroft CI SS9 . . . . . . .146 E4
Danescroft Dr SS9 . . . . . . .146 E4
Danesfield SS7 . . . . .144 C2
Danesleigh Gdns SS9 . . . .146 E4
Danette Gdns RM8 . . . . . .134 F2
Dangan Rd E11 . . . . .132 A5
Daniel CI
Grays, Chafford Hundred
RM16 . . . . .172 E4
Grays, Orsett Heath RM16 .174 B3
Danyon Rd RM13 . . . . . . .155 C3
Daphne Gdns E4 . . . . .109 C7
Darby Dr EN9 . . . . .65 C6
Darcy CI CM13 . . . . .95 B2
Darcy Rise CM3 . . . . .34 E1
Dare Gdns RM8 . . . . .134 E1
Darell Way CM11 . . . . .57 D1
Darent Ind Pk DA8 . . . . . .170 D1
Darenth La RM15 . . . . .172 A7
Darenth Rd SS9 . . . . .146 B1
Dark La Brentwood CM14 . .115 F5
Great Warley CM14 . . . . . . .1 6 A3
Thundersley SS7 . . . . .145 A6
Darlinghurst Gr SS9 . . . . .147 A2
Darlinghurst Prim Sch
SS9 . . . . .146 F2
Darlington Ct CM15 . . . . . .94 A3
Darlington Gdns RM3 . . . .114 C5

Darlington Path 16 RM3 .114 D5
Darnay Rise CM1 .31 D6
Darnley Rd
Gravesend DA11 .179 B1
Grays RM17 .178 B8
Woodford IG8 .110 B2
Darrell Cl CM1 .32 B6
Dart Cl RM14 .137 D5
Dart Gn RM15 .172 B7
Dartfields RM3 .114 D4
Dartford Gdns RM6 .134 B6
Dartmouth Cl SS6 .123 D5
Dartmouth Rd CM1 .32 E6
Dartview Cl RM17 .173 E2
Darwell Cl E6 .152 A3
Darwin Rd RM18 .178 F6
Dashes The CM20 .10 E1
Datchet Dr SS3 .149 E2
Davall Ho RM17 .178 B8
Davenant Foundation Sch IG10 .67 C1
Davenants SS13 .143 B8
Davenport CM17 .24 E7
Davenport Ctr IG11 .153 B3
Daventry Gdns RM3 .114 C5
Daventry Gn RM3 .114 C5
Daventry Rd RM3 .114 C5
David Ave SS11 .99 D2
David Coffer Ct DA17 .169 B2
David Dr RM3 .115 A3
David Rd RM8 .134 E2
David Terr RM3 .115 A4
David's Wlk CM11 .97 C2
Davids Way IG6 .111 E3
Davidson Gdns SS12 .121 E5
Davidson Ho DA9 .177 C2
Davidson Way RM7 .135 E5
Davies Cl RM13 .155 C2
Davington Gdns RM8 .153 B7
Davington Rd RM8 .153 B7
Davinia Cl IG8 .110 F4
Davis Rd Aveley RM15 .171 D5
Grays RM16 .172 F3
Dawberry Pl CM3 .101 D5
Dawes Ave RM12 .136 E1
Dawes Cl DA9 .176 F2
Dawley Gn RM15 .172 A7
Dawlish Cres SS6 .123 D5
Dawlish Dr Ilford IG3 .152 F8
Southend-on-S SS9 .146 E1
Dawlish Wlk RM3 .114 C2
Dawn Cl CM9 .59 B8
Dawnings The CM3 .101 C8
Daws Cl CM1 .30 F1
Daws Heath Rd
Hadleigh SS7 .145 E6
Rayleigh SS6 .145 E8
Daws Hill E4 .87 C6
Dawson Ave IG11 .152 F5
Dawson Dr RM13 .155 B5
Dawson Gdns 9 IG11 .152 F5
Dawson Mews CM11 .97 B3
Daylop Dr IG7 .112 B7
Days Cl CM1 .32 B8
Days La
Doddinghurst CM15 .72 C1
Pilgrims Hatch CM15 .94 B7
Dayton Dr DA8 .170 D1
De Beauvoir Chase CM11 98 E3
De La Salle RC Sch SS14 .142 C8
De Luci Rd DA8 .169 C1
De Vere Ave CM9 .37 B1
De Vere Ct SS9 .146 C6
De Vere Gdns Ilford IG1 .133 A3
Redbridge IG1 .132 F3
De Warren Ho DA11 .178 D1
Deacon Dr SS15 .141 C7
Deacon Way IG8 .110 F4
Deadman's La CM2 .54 C4
Dealtree Cl CM15 .72 B4
Dean Ct RM7 .135 D5
Dean Way CM1 .31 E1
Deanes Sch The SS7 .145 C6
Deans Ct CM14 .116 B6
Deans Ind Est RM13 .155 D1
Deans Rd CM14 .116 B6
Dearsly Ho RM13 .154 D3
Debden Cl IG8 .110 D3
Debden Gn SS16 .141 C4
Debden La IG10 .67 C1
Debden Park High Sch IG10 .89 D7
Debden Rd IG10 .67 B1
Debden Sta IG10 .89 C5
Debden Way CM0 .106 A6
Debden Wlk 4 RM12 .155 B6
Deben RM18 .175 C3
Deborah Ct 7 E18 .132 B8
Dedham Cl CM11 .97 C2
Dedham Rd CM11 .97 C2
Dee Cl RM14 .137 E5
Dee Way RM1 .113 E2
Deepdale SS7 .144 F6
Deepdene Basildon SS16 .142 B5
Ingatestone CM4 .74 B3
Deepdene Ave SS6 .123 D4
Deepdene Cl E11 .132 A7
Deepdene Path IG10 .89 B5
Deepdene Rd IG10 .89 A5
Deeping 5 SS1 .167 A8
Deepwater Rd SS8 .163 E3
Deer Mead Ct 1 RM2 .135 F6
Deer Park Way EN9 .65 B4
Deer Pk CM19 .23 B5
Deerbank Rd CM11 .97 C3
Deere Ave RM13 .155 A6
Deerhurst SS7 .145 B7
Deerhurst Chase CM3 .56 F1
Deerhurst Cl SS7 .145 B7
Deerleap Gr E4 .87 B4
Deeside Wlk 3 SS12 .121 E6
Defoe Par RM16 .174 B3
Defoe Way RM5 .113 B4
Deidre Chapman Ho DA10 .177 E1
Deirdre Ave SS12 .121 B7
Deirdre Cl SS12 .121 B7
Delafield Rd RM17 .173 D1
Delamere Rd CM1 .31 E1
Delargy Cl RM16 .174 B3
Delaware Cres SS3 .168 D7
Delaware Rd SS3 .168 D7
Delder Ave SS8 .164 D2
Delft Rd SS8 .164 A4
Delfzul Rd SS8 .164 A4
Delgada Rd SS8 .164 D3
Delhi Rd SS13 .143 C6
Delimands SS15 .141 F6
Delius Way SS17 .160 C3
Dell Cl IG8 .110 B7
Dell Ct Grays RM17 .173 B2
Hornchurch RM12 .136 E2
Dell La CM22 .2 A8
Dell Rd RM17 .173 B2
Dell The Basildon SS16 .142 B3
Brentwood CM13 .116 B4
Great Baddow CM2 .54 F6
Greenhithe DA9 .177 B2
Waltham Abbey EN9 .65 C3
Wickford SS11 .121 E7
Woodford IG8 .110 B7
Dellfield Ct CM17 .11 C4
Dellow Cl IG2 .133 D4
Dells Cl E4 .87 B2
Dellwood Gdns IG5 .133 A8
Delmar Gdns SS11 .99 C2
Delmores SS16 .141 C3
Delta Rd CM13 .95 D3
Delvers Mead RM10 .154 C8
Delview SS8 .163 F5
Delvins SS13 .143 B8
Denbar Par RM7 .135 C7
Denbigh Cl RM11 .137 A7
Denbigh Ho 8 RM3 .114 E4
Denbigh Rd SS15 .141 B5
Denby Grange CM17 .24 E8
Dencourt Cres SS14 .142 F5
Dene Cl SS6 .123 D4
Dene Ct CM1 .31 D5
Dene Gdns SS6 .123 D4
Dene Path RM15 .172 A7
Dene Rd IG9 .88 E1
Denecroft Gdns RM17 .173 D3
Deneholm Prim Sch RM16 .173 C4
Denehurst Gdns
Basildon SS16 .140 E4
Woodford IG8 .110 B6
Denesmere SS7 .144 C4
Deneway SS16 .142 D2
Dengayne SS14 .142 D6
Dengie Hundred Sports Ctr CM0 .106 B4
Denham Dr IG2 .133 C5
Denham Rd SS8 .164 A4
Denham Vale SS6 .123 A3
Denham Way IG11 .152 F4
Denholme Wlk RM13 .154 F6
Denmark Ho CM2 .54 D8
Denner Rd E4 .109 A8
Dennis Ct E17 .109 D1
Dennis Rd RM15 .157 A4
Dennises La RM14 .156 E5
Denny Ave EN9 .65 D5
Denny Ct 2 DA2 .176 B1
Denny Gdns RM9 .153 B5
Dent Cl RM15 .172 A7
Denton App SS0 .147 C5
Denton Ave SS0 .147 C5
Denton Cl SS0 .147 C5
Denver Dr SS13 .121 C1
Denver Ind Est RM13 .169 F8
Denys Dr SS14 .120 F1
Depot Cotts IG10 .88 E4
Derby Ave Romford RM7 .135 C5
Upminster RM14 .137 A1
Derby Cl Basildon SS16 .140 F4
Billericay CM11 .97 D5
Mayland CM3 .61 A1
Derby Ct E18 .109 F2
Derby Rd Grays RM17 .173 B1
Hoddesdon EN11 .21 D5
Woodford E18 .109 F2
Derby Road Bridge RM17 .178 B8
Derbydale SS4 .125 C6
Dereham Pl RM5 .113 B4
Dereham Rd IG11 .152 F7
Derek Gdns SS2 .147 E5
Dereham Gdns RM14 .137 C1
Deri Ave RM13 .155 B1
Dering Cres SS9 .146 D7
Derry Ave RM15 .172 A7
Dersingham Ave E12 .152 A8
Dersingham Inf Sch E12 .152 A7
Derventer Ave SS8 .164 A6
Derwent Ave SS6 .123 E2
Derwent Gdns IG4 .132 E7
Derwent Par RM15 .172 B7
Derwent Way
Chelmsford CM1 .31 D4
Hornchurch RM12 .155 B7
Desborough Path CM2 .32 F8
Dessons Ct SS17 .160 F4
Detling Cl RM12 .155 C7
Devereux Rd Grays RM16 172 F3
Southend-on-S SS1 .167 A7
Devereux Way CM12 .97 A5
Deverill Cl CM1 .19 B2
Deveron Gdns RM15 .172 A8
Deveron Way RM1 .113 E2
Devizes Ho 6 RM3 .114 D5
Devon Cl IG9 .110 B8
Devon Gdns SS4 .125 C5
Devon Ho Romford RM7 .113 A1
5 Wanstead E11 .132 A6
Devon Rd IG11 .152 E4
Devon Way SS8 .164 B5
Devonport Gdns IG1 .132 F5
Devonshire Cl SS15 .141 A8
Devonshire Gdns SS17 .175 A3
Devonshire Ho IG6 .111 B3
Devonshire Rd
Basildon SS15 .141 A7
Burnham-on-C CM0 .106 C5
Grays RM16 .172 F3
Hornchurch RM12 .136 D2
Ilford IG2 .133 E4
Southminster CM0 .84 C4
Dewey Path RM12 .155 C6
Dewey Rd RM10 .154 C6
Dewlands SS14 .142 A7
Dewsbury Cl RM3 .114 E4
Dewsbury Gdns RM3 .114 E4
Dewsbury Rd RM3 .114 E4
Dewsgreen SS16 .142 E4
Dewyk Rd SS8 .164 C5
Dexter Cl RM17 .173 A3
Deyncourt Gdns RM14 .137 C2
Deynecourt Gdns E11 .132 C7
Dial Cl DA9 .177 D2
Diamond Cl
Dagenham RM8 .134 C3
Grays RM16 .172 F3
Diamond Ct RM11 .136 A3
Diana Cl Grays RM16 .172 F2
Woodford E18 .110 B2
Diban Ave RM12 .155 B8
Diben Ct RM12 .155 B8
Dickens Ave
Dartford DA1 .176 A3
Tilbury RM18 .179 B6
Dickens Cl SS2 .148 B2
Dickens Ct
Basildon SS15 .141 D7
10 Wanstead E11 .132 A7
Dickens Dr SS15 .141 D7
Dickens Pl CM1 .31 D7
Dickens Rise IG7 .111 B7
Dickens Way RM1 .135 E7
Dicky Moors CM3 .18 F7
Digby Gdns RM10 .154 A4
Digby Rd Barking IG11 .152 F5
Corringham SS17 .161 C5
Digby Wlk RM12 .155 C7
Diggens Ct IG10 .88 E6
Dilkes Prim Sch RM15 .171 F7
Dilliway Ct CM0 .106 B4
Dilston CM3 .57 A6
Dinant Ave SS8 .163 E4
Dinant Link Rd EN11 .21 B7
Disney Cl CM4 .74 B4
Disraeli Rd SS6,SS9 .146 B8
Ditchfield Rd EN11 .8 A1
Ditton Court Rd SS0 .166 D8
Dixon Ave CM1 .31 F4
Dixon Ct SS13 .143 B6
Dobb's Weir Rd EN11 .21 D5
Dobsons Cl SS6 .123 E1
Dock Approach Rd RM16,RM17 .173 E2
Dock Rd
Grays RM17,RM18 .178 E7
Mayland CM3 .61 B1
Tilbury RM18 .178 F5
Docklands Ave CM4 .74 C4
Dockwra La CM3 .57 A7
Doddinghurst CE Jun Sch CM15 .72 B2
Doddinghurst Ct CM15 .94 C2
Doddinghurst Inf Sch CM15 .72 B2
Doddinghurst Rd
Brentwood CM15 .94 D5
Doddinghurst CM15 .72 C1
Doesgate La RM14 .140 C1
Doeshill Dr SS12 .121 E7
Dog Kennel La CM4 .74 C7
Doggett's Cnr RM11 .136 F2
Doggetts Chase SS4 .126 A4
Doggetts Prim Sch SS4 .125 F3
Dolby Rise CM2 .32 F2
Dollant Ave SS8 .164 A3
Dolphin App RM1 .135 F7
Dolphin Gdns CM12 .96 F5
Dolphin Motorway Est RM19 .171 E1
Dolphin Way RM19 .171 E1
Dolphins SS0 .147 D4
Dombey Cl CM1 .31 F7
Dominic Ct EN9 .65 B6
Dominion Dr RM5 .113 B4
Dominion Way RM13 .155 A2
Dominion Wks RM8 .134 E3
Domsey La CM3 .19 F5
Don Way RM1 .113 E3
Donald Dr RM6 .134 C6
Donald Thorn Cl SS12 .121 D6
Donald Way CM2 .54 C7
Doncaster Way RM14 .136 F1
Doncel Ct E4 .87 D2
Doncella Cl RM16 .172 D3
Donington Ave IG6 .133 C6
Donne Rd RM8 .134 C2
Donnington Ct 1 DA2 .176 B1
Donovan's Gdn CM13 .117 E3
Dorchester Ave EN11 .21 A8
Dorchester Ct 2 E18 .109 F2
Dorchester Gdns E4 .109 A6
Dorchester Rd CM12 .97 A5
Dordells SS15 .141 E6
Dore Ave E12 .152 A7
Dorian Rd RM12 .136 A3
Doric Ave SS4 .125 D5
Doric Lodge SS0 .166 E7
Dorking Rd RM3 .114 D6
Dorking Rise RM3 .114 D6
Dorking Wlk
Great Baddow CM2 .54 E7
Romford RM3 .114 D5
Dorkins Way RM14 .137 E4
Dorothy Barley Jun Sch RM8 .153 B7
Dorothy Farm Rd SS6 .124 A1
Dorothy Gdns
Dagenham RM8 .153 B8
Thundersley SS7 .144 F5
Dorrington Gdns RM12 .136 D3
Dorset Ave
Great Baddow CM2 .54 E6
Romford RM1 .135 D8
Dorset Cl CM2 .54 E6
Dorset Gdns
Linford SS17 .175 A4
Rochford SS4 .125 C5
Dorset Rd
Burnham-on-C CM0 .106 C4
Maldon CM9 .58 F8
Dorset Way
Billericay CM12 .97 A5
Canvey Island SS8 .164 A5
Doubleday Dr CM9 .36 F5
Doubleday Rd IG10 .89 C6
Doublegate La SS11 .122 B5
Doublet Mews CM11 .97 D5
Doug Siddons Ct RM17 .178 C8
Douglas Ave
Chingford E17 .109 A2
Romford RM3 .114 E1
Douglas Cl
Galleywood CM2 .54 D3
Grays RM16 .172 E3
Douglas Dr SS12 .121 D5
Douglas Rd Chingford E4 .87 E1
Hadleigh SS7 .145 F3
Ilford IG3 .134 A5
Romford RM11 .135 F5
Douglas Wlk 3 CM2 .54 A8
Doulton Cl CM17 .24 E7
Doulton Way SS4 .125 C6
Dounsell Ct CM15 .94 A3
Dove Cl RM16 .172 E3
Dove Crofts CM6 .5 E7
Dove Dr SS7 .144 B2
Dove House Gdns E4 .109 A8
Dove La CM2 .54 A6
Dove Wlk 7 RM12 .155 B6
Dovecote SS3 .149 E1
Dovedale SS8 .164 E5
Dovedale Ave IG5 .111 A1
Dovedale Cl
Basildon SS16 .141 A4
Ramsden Heath CM11 .98 C4
Dovehouse Croft CM20 .11 A2
Dovehouse Mead IG11 .152 D3
Dover Cl RM5 .113 C1
Dover Rd Dagenham RM6 134 E5
Northfleet DA11 .178 D1
Wanstead E12 .132 C2
Dover Way SS13 .143 B6
Dovercliff Rd SS8 .164 E2
Dovers Corner Ind Pk RM13 .154 F1
Dovervelt Rd SS8 .164 C5
Doves Mews SS15 .119 D1
Dovesgate SS7 .144 B4
Dovetree Ct RM3 .114 D6
Dow Ct CM0 .84 C4
Dowding Cl RM12 .155 B5
Dowland Cl SS17 .160 C3
Dowland Wlk SS15 .141 C7
Down Hall Prim Sch SS6 .123 D5
Down Hall Rd SS6 .123 D4
Downer Rd SS7 .144 D5
Downer Rd N SS7 .144 E6
Downesway SS7 .144 D3
Downey Cl SS14 .142 C7
Downhall Cl SS6 .123 D4
Downhall Park Way SS6 .123 D5
Downhall Rd CM17 .13 C5
Downham CE Prim Sch CM11 .98 C4
Downham Cl RM5 .113 A3
Downham Rd
Canvey Island SS8 .164 A3
Ramsden Heath CM11 .98 D5
Ramsden Heath CM4,CM11 .98 D7
Stock CM4 .76 B1
Wickford SS11 .99 C3
Downing Rd RM9 .153 F5
Downlands EN9 .65 E5
Downleaze CM3 .101 E8
Downs Gr SS16 .142 E3
Downs Prim Sch The CM20 .23 E8
Downs Rd CM9 .37 B3
Downs The CM20 .23 E8
Downshall Ave IG3 .133 F5
Downshall Ct IG3 .133 E5
Downshall Prim Sch IG3 .133 E4
Downsland Dr CM14 .116 C7
Downsway CM1 .32 D6
Dowsetts La CM11 .98 C6
Doyle Way RM18 .179 C5
Dragon Cl CM0 .106 A5
Drake Ave CM3 .83 A8
Drake Cl
Brentwood CM14 .116 D5
Hadleigh SS7 .145 C5
Drake Ct 4 SS14 .142 F5
Drake Mews RM12 .155 A6
Drake Point DA8 .169 E1
Drake Rd Basildon SS15 .141 D6
Grays RM16 .172 E4
Southend-on-S SS0 .147 C1
Drakes La Boreham CM3 .20 B7
Little Waltham CM3 .19 F7
Drakes Mdw CM17 .11 E4
Drakes The SS3 .168 E8
Drakes Way SS6 .123 E4
Draper's Cnr CM5 .48 C2
Drapers Chase CM9 .37 D4
Drapers Ct RM12 .136 E2
Drapers Rd CM3 .101 E8
Draycot Rd E11 .132 B4
Drayson Cl EN9 .65 E7
Drayton Ave IG10 .88 F3
Drayton Cl Ilford IG1 .133 D3
4 Maldon CM9 .37 A1
Drewsteignton SS3 .168 D8
Driftway SS16 .142 F4
Drive The Barking IG11 .152 F5
Brentwood CM13 .116 C4
Buckhurst Hill IG9 .88 C2
Chelmsford CM1 .32 A6
Chingford E4 .87 D2
Harlow CM20 .10 E1
Hoddesdon EN11 .21 A8
Hullbridge SS5 .101 D3
Ilford IG1 .133 A3
Loughton IG10 .88 E5
Mayland CM3 .82 F8
Rayleigh SS6 .146 B8
Redbridge E18 .132 F4
Rochford SS4 .125 F3
Romford, Collier Row RM5 113 D3
Romford, Harold wood RM3 .114 F2
Sawbridgeworth CM21 .1 E2
Southend-on-S SS0 .166 B8
Wanstead E18 .132 A8
Barking IG11 .153 A6
Driveway The SS8 .164 B3
Droitwich Ave SS2 .148 D1
Dronfield Gdns RM8 .153 C7
Drood Cl CM1 .31 F7
Drovers Mead CM14 .116 B6
Droveway IG10 .89 B7
Drummond Ave RM7 .135 D7
Drummond Ct CM15 .94 C2
Drummond Pl 7 SS12 .121 E5
Drummond Rd
Romford RM7 .135 D7
Wanstead E11 .132 C5
Drummonds The
Buckhurst Hill IG9 .110 B8
Epping CM16 .46 A1
Drury La CM6 .5 C2
Dry St SS16 .141 E1
Dryden Ave SS2 .148 B2
Dryden Cl Maldon CM9 .59 A8
Redbridge IG6 .111 F4
Dryden Pl RM18 .179 B6
Dryden Twrs RM3 .114 B3
Drysdale Ave E4 .87 B3
Drywoods CM3 .101 D5
Duarte Pl RM16 .172 F3
Dubarry Cl SS7 .144 F5
Duchess Gr IG9 .110 B8
Duck La CM16 .46 C6
Ducker's La CM1 .17 C7
Ducketts Mead
Canewdon SS4 .104 D2
Roydon CM19 .9 B1
Ducking Stool Ct RM1 .135 E7
Duckling La CM21 .1 E2
Dudbrook Rd CM14 .71 B1
Dudley Cl Boreham CM3 .20 E1
Grays RM16 .172 E4
Dudley Ct 9 E11 .132 A6
Dudley Gdns RM3 .114 D4
Dudley Rd Chingford E17 109 A1
Ilford IG1 .152 B8
Romford RM3 .114 D4
Duffield Cl RM16 .172 F3
Duffield Rd CM2 .54 D6
Duffries Cl CM3 .18 E7
Duke Gdns IG6 .133 D7
Duke Pl SS15 .141 E8
Duke Rd IG6 .133 D7
Duke St Chelmsford CM1 .32 B2
Hoddesdon EN11 .21 A7
Dukes Ave Grays RM17 .173 A4
Southminster CM0 .84 D3
Theydon Bois CM16 .67 E4
Dukes Cl CM16 .47 B4
Dukes Ct E6 .152 A4
Dukes Farm Cl CM12 .97 C5
Dukes Farm Rd CM12 .97 B5
Dukes La
5 Chelmsford CM2 .32 F4

Dukes La continued
Willingale CM5 ....28 C5
Dukes Orch
Hatfield Broad Oak CM22 ..3 F6
Writtle CM1 ....31 B1
Dukes Park Ind Est CM2 .32 F4
Dukes Pl CM14 ....94 C1
Dukes Priory Hospl The
CM1 ....32 D4
Dukes Rd Billericay CM11 .97 C4
Wallend E6 ....152 A4
Dulverton Ave SS0 ......147 A5
Dulverton Cl SS0 ....147 A5
Dulverton Rd RM3 ......114 D4
Dunbar Ave RM10 ....135 A1
Dunbar Gdns RM10 .....154 B7
Dunbar Pl SS12 ....121 E5
Duncan Cl SS12 ....121 F5
Dunchurch Ho RM10 ....154 A5
Duncombe Cl 4 RM19 ..171 B1
Dundas Mews EN3 ....65 A2
Dundee Ave SS9 ....146 B2
Dundee Cl SS9 ....146 C2
Dundee Ct SS14 ....142 F8
Dundonald Dr SS9 ......146 F1
Dunedin Ho RM18 ......179 A5
Dunedin Rd Ilford IG1 ..133 C3
Rainham RM13 ....154 C7
Dunfane CM11 ....97 C5
Dungannon Chase SS1 ..168 B6
Dungannon Dr SS1 .....168 B6
Dunkeld Rd RM8 ....134 C2
Dunkellin Gr RM15 .....172 A7
Dunkellin Way RM15 ...172 A7
Dunkin Rd DA1 ....176 A3
Dunkirk Rd CM0 ....106 C5
Dunlin Cl Heybridge CM9 .37 C5
South Woodham F CM3 ..79 D1
Dunlop Rd RM18 ....178 F6
Dunmore Rd CM2 ....33 A3
Dunmow Cl Ilford RM6 ..134 C6
Loughton IG10 ....88 E3
Dunmow Dr RM13 ......154 F4
Dunmow Gdns CM13 ....139 D5
Dunmow Ho RM9 ....153 B4
Dunmow Rd Fyfield CM5 .27 E6
Hatfield Broad Oak CM22 ..3 F6
High Roding CM6 ......5 D5
Leaden Roding CM6 ....15 A4
Dunning Cl RM15 ......172 A7
Dunningford Cl RM12 ..154 F7
Dunningford Prim Sch
RM12 ....154 F7
Dunnings La CM13 .....139 B2
Dunnose Ct 16 RM19 ...171 B1
Dunspring La IG5 ......111 B1
Dunstable Cl RM3 ......114 D4
Dunstable Rd
Romford RM3 ....114 D4
Stanford-le-H SS17 ....160 D3
Dunstalls CM19 ....23 A4
Dunster Ave SS0 ....147 A5
Dunster Cl RM5 ....113 C1
Dunster Cres RM11 ....137 B2
Dunster Ct 24 DA2 .....176 B1
Dunster Ho SS7 ....144 F6
Dunton Park Cvn Pk
CM13 ....140 E5
Dunton Rd
Basildon CM12,SS15 ...119 B1
Romford RM1 ....135 E7
Dupre Cl RM16 ....172 E3
Durants Wlk 4 SS12 ...121 D6
Durban Gdns RM10 ....154 C5
Durban La SS15 ....119 C3
Durban Rd IG2,IG3 ....133 E3
Durdans The SS16 .....141 B4
Durell Gdns RM9 ......153 D7
Durell Rd RM9 ....153 D7
Durham Ave
Romford RM2 ....136 C7
Woodford IG8 ....110 D5
Durham Cl
Sawbridgeworth CM21 ..1 C1
Stansted Abbotts SG12 ..8 B5
Durham Ho
3 Barking IG11 ......153 A5
Romford RM7 ....113 A1
Durham Pl IG1 ....152 C8
Durham Rd
Basildon SS15 ....140 E6
Dagenham RM10 ......154 C7
Rochford SS4 ....125 B6
Southend-on-S SS2 ....148 D2
Durham Way SS6 ......123 D5
Duringe Wlk RM16 ....173 B6
Durley Ave SS12 ......120 F8
Durley Cl SS7 ....144 E4
Durnell Way IG10 .....89 A6
Durrants Cl RM13 .....155 C3
Durrington Cl SS16 ....142 C5
Dury Falls Cl RM11 ...137 A3
Dutch Cottage Mus★
SS8 ....163 C4
Duxford SS11 ....122 A6
Duxford Cl RM12 .....155 C6
Dycorts Sch RM3 .....115 A6
Dyer Ct EN3 ....65 A2
Dyer's Rd CM9 ....37 A2
Dyers Way RM3 ....114 B3
Dyke Cres SS8 ....163 D4
Dykes Chase CM9 .....36 F3
Dylan Rd DA17 ....169 A3
Dymchurch Cl IG5 ....111 A1
Dymoke Rd RM11 .....135 F4

Dymokes Way EN11 ....8 A1
Dynevor Gdns SS9 ....146 B1
Dytchleys La CM14 ....93 A5
Dytchleys Rd CM14 ...92 F5

E

Eagle Ave RM6 ....134 E5
Eagle Cl
Hornchurch RM12 .....155 B6
Waltham Abbey EN9 ...66 A5
Eagle Ct 6 E11 ....132 A4
Eagle Ho RM17 ....177 F8
Eagle La
Kelvedon Hatch CM15 ..71 E2
Wanstead E11 ....132 A7
Eagle Terr IG8 ....110 B3
Eagle Way
Great Warley CM13 ....116 D4
Northfleet DA11 ......178 A2
Southend-on-S SS3 ...168 B8
Eagles Rd DA9 ....177 B2
Eardley Rd DA17 .....169 A1
Earl Mountbatten Dr
CM12 ....96 F4
Earl's Path IG10 ......88 C6
Earls Hall Ave SS2 ....147 E3
Earls Hall Par SS2 ....147 E3
Earls Hall Prim Sch
SS0 ....147 D4
Earls Wlk RM8 ....153 B8
Earlsdown Ho IG11 ...152 D3
Earlsfield Dr CM2 .....32 F3
Earlswood SS7 ....144 D4
Earlswood Gdns IG5 ..133 A8
Easebourne Rd RM8 ..153 C7
Easedale Dr RM12 ....155 B7
Easington Way RM15 .172 A8
East Ave CM3 ....82 E2
East Bridge Rd CM3 ..101 E8
East Canney Cotts CM3 .80 F3
East Cl RM13 ....155 B1
East Cres SS8 ....163 F4
East Crescent Rd 5
DA12 ....179 C1
East Dene Dr RM3 ....114 D5
East Ct DA21 ....1 E1
East End Rd CM0 .....42 C3
East Entrance RM10 ..154 B3
East Gate CM20 ......10 D1
East Hall La RM13 ....170 D7
East Hanningfield CE Prim
Sch CM3 ....78 B2
East Hanningfield Ind Est
CM3 ....78 C6
East Hanningfield Rd
Howe Green CM2 .....55 E2
Rettendon CM3 ....78 C4
East Kent Ave DA11 ..178 C3
East Mayne SS13 .....121 A2
East Mill DA11 ....179 A1
East Park Cl RM6 .....134 E6
East Pk Harlow CM17 ..11 C3
Sawbridgeworth CM21 ..1 E1
East Rd
Dagenham, Chadwell Heath
RM6 ....134 E6
Harlow CM20 ....11 B4
Romford RM7 ....135 D4
East Row E11 ....132 A5
East Sq SS14 ....142 B6
East St Barking IG11 ..152 C5
Grays RM17 ....178 C8
Grays, West Thurrock
RM20 ....177 B8
Rochford SS4 ....125 F2
Southend-on-S SS2 ...147 F2
Southend-on-S,Leigh Cliffs
SS9 ....165 E8
East Terr DA12 ....179 C1
East Thorpe SS14 ....142 C6
East Thurrock Rd RM17 .178 C8
East Tilbury Prim Sch
RM18 ....175 C1
East Tilbury Rd SS17 .175 D4
East Tilbury Sta RM18 .175 B2
East View Chingford E4 .109 C5
Writtle CM1 ....30 F1
East Wlk Basildon SS14 .142 B6
Harlow CM20 ....10 D1
Eastbourne Gr SS0 ...147 C3
Eastbourne Rd E6 ....152 A2
Eastbrook Ave RM10 .154 C8
Eastbrook Comp Sch
RM10 ....154 C8
Eastbrook Dr RM7 ....135 E2
Eastbrook Rd EN9 ....65 E6
Eastbrookend Ctry Pk★
RM7 ....135 D1
Eastbrooks SS13 .....143 B7
Eastbrooks Mews SS13 .143 B7
Eastbrooks Pl SS13 ...143 B7
Eastbury Ave
Barking IG11 ....152 E4
Rochford SS4 ....125 D4
Eastbury Comp (Lower) Sch
IG11 ....152 D5
Eastbury Comp Sch
IG11 ....152 F5
Eastbury Ct IG11 ....152 F5
Eastbury Inf Sch IG11 .152 F5
Eastbury Rd
Romford RM7 ....135 D5
Wallend E6 ....152 A1
Eastbury Sq IG11 ....152 F4
Eastcheap SS6 ....123 C4
Eastcote Gr SS2 .....148 D3

Eastcourt Ind Sch IG3 .134 A3
Eastend Cotts CM19 ..9 D1
Eastern App
Barking IG11 ....153 A3
Chelmsford CM2 .....32 F5
Eastern Ave
Aveley RM15 ....171 C4
Grays RM20 ....176 F8
Ilford IG2 ....133 D5
South Benfleet SS7 ...144 C5
Southend-on-S SS2 ...148 B3
Wanstead E11 ....132 C6
Eastern Ave E RM1,RM2,
RM3 ....113 E1
Eastern Avenue W RM7 .135 E1
Eastern Cl SS2 ....148 A3
Eastern Cres CM1 ....31 F5
Eastern Espl
Canvey Island SS8 ...164 D2
Southend-on-S SS1 ...167 D6
Eastern Rd
Burnham-on-C CM0 ..106 C5
Grays RM17 ....173 D2
Rayleigh SS6 ....123 B1
Romford RM1 ....135 F6
Eastern Way
Belvedere DA18 .....169 A4
Grays RM17 ....173 A4
Easternville Gdns IG2 .133 C5
Eastfield Gdns RM10 .154 A8
Eastfield Rd
Basildon SS15 ....119 F2
Brentwood CM14 ....116 B8
Canvey Island SS8 ...164 D5
Dagenham RM9,RM10 .154 A8
Eastgate SS14 ....142 B5
Eastgate Bsns Ctr SS14 .142 B6
Eastham Cres CM13 ..117 A7
Eastleigh Rd SS7 ....144 E1
Eastley SS16 ....141 F4
Eastmead IG3 ....134 A4
Easton End SS15 .....141 A6
Eastview Dr SS6 .....123 E5
Eastway E11 ....132 B6
Eastways SS3 ....163 F5
Eastwick Hall La CM20 .10 A5
Eastwick Rd
Eastwick CM20 ......10 A5
Gilston CM20 ....10 E6
Eastwood Bvd SS0 ...147 A2
Eastwood Cl E18 .....110 A1
Eastwood Dr RM3 ....170 B7
Eastwood Ind Est SS9 .146 C6
Eastwood Jun & Inf Schs
SS9 ....146 F6
Eastwood La S SS0 ...147 B2
Eastwood Old Rd SS9 .146 B6
Eastwood Park Cl SS9 .146 E6
Eastwood Park Dr SS9 .146 E7
Eastwood Rd Ilford IG3 .134 A4
Rayleigh SS6 ....123 E1
Southend-on-S SS9 ..146 B3
Woodford E18 ....110 A1
Eastwood Rd N SS9 ..146 D4
Eastwood Rise
Rayleigh SS9 ....124 C1
Southend-on-S SS9 ..146 C8
Eastwood Sch The SS9 .146 F6
Eastwoodbury Cl SS2 .147 E6
Eastwoodbury Cres SS2 .147 E6
Eastwoodbury La SS2 .147 C6
Eaton Cl CM12 ....97 A5
Eaton Dr RM5 ....113 A3
Eaton Gdns RM9 .....153 E5
Eaton Rd
Southend-on-S SS9 ..146 C2
Upminster RM14 .....137 E2
Eaton Rise E11 ......132 C6
Eatons Mead E4 .....109 A8
Ebbsfleet Ind Est DA11 .178 A4
Ebbsfleet Wlk DA11 ..178 B1
Ebenezer Terr CM2 ..54 F7
Eccles Ho 2 RM3 ....114 D4
Eccleston Cres RM6 ..134 B4
Eccleston Gdns CM12 .97 A5
Echo Hts E4 ....87 B1
Eckersley Rd CM1 ...32 C3
Eddy Cl RM7 ....135 B5
Eden Cl EN3 ....65 A1
Eden Gn RM15 ......172 B8
Eden Way CM1 ......31 C5
Edenhall Cl RM3 ....114 C5
Edenhall Glen RM3 ..114 C5
Edenhall Rd RM3 ...114 C5
Edens Mount CM21 ..1 F4
Edgar Ho E11 ....132 A4
Edgar Rd RM6 ....134 D4
Edgecotts SS16 .....141 E4
Edgefield Ave IG11 ..152 F5
Edgefield Ct 2 IG11 .152 F5
Edgehill Gdns RM10 ..154 A8
Edinburgh Ave
Corringham SS17 ....160 F4
Southend-on-S SS9 ..146 B2
Edinburgh Cl SS6 ...123 B5
Edinburgh Ho 1 RM2 .136 C7
Edinburgh Mews RM18 .179 B5
Edinburgh Pl CM20 ..11 A4
Edinburgh Way
Basildon SS13 ....143 B6
Harlow CM20 ....10 E3
Edison Ave RM12 ....135 F3
Edison Cl RM12 .....135 F3
Edisons Pk DA2 .....176 D4
Edith Cl SS8 ....163 E3
Edith Rd
Canvey Island SS8 ...163 D3
Dagenham RM6 .....134 D4

Edith Rd continued
Southend-on-S SS2 ...147 F2
Edith Way SS17 .....161 A5
Edmund Rd Grays RM16 .172 D4
Rainham RM13 ......154 E2
Edmund's Twr CM19 .23 C8
Edridge Cl RM12 ....155 D7
Edward Ave E4 ......109 D4
Edward Bright Cl CM9 .37 A2
Edward Cl Billericay CM12 .96 F5
Grays RM16 ....172 D3
Rochford SS4 ....125 C6
Romford RM2 ....136 C8
Edward Ct EN9 ......65 F6
Edward Dr CM2 .....54 C7
Edward Francis Jun Sch
SS6 ....123 E3
Edward Gdns SS11 ..121 D8
Edward Mans 7 IG11 .152 F5
Edward Rd RM6 .....134 E6
Edwards Cl CM13 ...95 E3
Edwards Hall Jun & Inf Schs
SS9 ....146 C7
Edwards Rd DA17 ...169 A2
Edwards Way CM13 ..95 E4
Edwards Wlk CM9 ...36 F3
Edwin Ave E4 ....152 A3
Edwin Cl RM13 .....154 F2
Edwin Hall View CM3 .79 C1
Edwin Lambert Sch
RM11 ....136 A4
Edwin St DA12 ......179 B1
Edwin's Hall Rd CM3 .79 D3
Edwina Gdns IG4 ...132 E6
Egbert Gdns SS11 ...99 D1
Egerton Dr SS16 ....140 E5
Egerton Gdns IG3 ...133 F1
Egg Hall CM16 ......46 A2
Eglington Rd E4 .....87 D2
Eglinton Dr CM2 ....33 B4
Eglinton Rd DA10 ...177 F1
Eisenhower Rd SS15 .141 A6
Elan Rd RM15 ......132 D8
Elbourne Trad Est DA17 .169 B3
Elbury Ct IG11 ......110 E3
Eldan Ho RM4 ......113 E7
Eldbert Cl SS2 ......148 E2
Eldeland SS15 ......141 E7
Elder Ave SS12 .....121 C6
Elder Tree Rd SS8 ..164 C4
Elder Way
Rainham RM13 ......155 D2
Wickford SS12 ......121 C6
Elderberry Cl
Basildon SS16 ......141 B5
Redbridge IG6 ......111 B3
Elderfield CM17 .....11 D3
Elderfield Wlk E11 ..132 B6
Elderstep Ave SS8 ..164 E3
Elderton Rd SS0 ....147 D1
Eldon Rd EN11 .....21 D4
Eldon Way SS5 ......124 E6
Eldonwall Est RM8 ..134 F3
Eldred Gdns RM14 ..137 E4
Eldred Rd IG11 .....152 E4
Eleanor Chase SS12 .121 C7
Eleanor Gdns RM8 ..134 F2
Eleanor Way CM14 ..116 E5
Electric Ave SS0 ....147 C2
Electric Par Ilford IG3 .133 D2
Woodford E18 ....110 A1
Eleven Acre Rise IG10 .88 F6
Elgar Cl Basildon SS15 .141 D8
Buckhurst Hill IG9 ...110 D8
South Benfleet SS7 ..144 B6
Elgar Gdns RM18 ...179 B6
Elgin Ave Chelmsford CM1 .32 A2
Romford RM3 ....115 B4
Elgin Ho RM11 .....116 D6
Elgin Rd IG3 ....133 E4
Elham Dr SS13 .....143 C6
Eliot Cl SS12 ....121 C5
Eliot Mews SS2 .....148 A2
Eliot Rd Dagenham RM9 .153 D8
Dartford DA1 ....176 B2
Eliot Way CM9 ......37 A1
Eliza Cook Cl DA9 ..177 B3
Elizabeth Ave Ilford IG1 .133 D2
Rayleigh SS6 ....123 C1
Elizabeth Cl Hockley SS5 .124 E4
Lower Nazeing EN9 ..43 D8
Romford RM7 ....113 B2
Tilbury RM18 ....179 B5
Elizabeth Ct
Buckhurst Hill IG9 ..88 B1
Gravesend DA11 ....179 A1
6 Woodford, South Woodford
E18 ....110 A2
2 Woodford, Woodford Green
IG8 ....110 C3
Elizabeth Dr
Theydon Bois CM16 ..67 E3
Wickford SS12 ......121 B8
Elizabeth Garrett Anderson
Ho 9 DA17 ....169 A3
Elizabeth Ho
Pilgrims Hatch CM15 ..94 B3
3 Romford RM2 .....136 C7
Southend-on-S SS9 ..146 D7
Elizabeth Rd Grays RM16 .172 F4
Pilgrims Hatch CM15 ..94 B3
Rainham RM13 ......170 B8
Southend-on-S SS1 ..167 D6
Elizabeth St DA9 ....176 E2
Elizabeth Twr 6 SS2 .147 F1
Elizabeth Way
Basildon SS15 ......141 D5
Hadleigh SS7 ....145 C4

Elizabeth Way continued
Harlow CM20 ....10 B2
Heybridge CM9 .....37 A5
Elkins The RM1 .....113 E1
Ellen Cl 5 E4 ....87 C1
Ellen Wilkinson Ho 12
RM10 ....135 A1
Ellenbrook Cl SS9 ..146 E3
Ellerman Rd RM18 ..178 F5
Ellerton Gdns RM9 ..153 C5
Ellerton Rd RM9 ....153 C5
Ellesmere Gdns IG4 .132 E5
Ellesmere Rd
Canvey Island SS8 ...163 E3
Rochford SS4 ....103 C1
Ellie Cl SS17 ....160 E1
Elliot Cl
South Woodham Ferrers
CM3 ....101 F6
Woodford IG8 ....110 D4
Elliott Gdns RM3 ...114 B3
Ellis Ave RM13 .....170 A8
Ellis Cl RM16 ....174 E7
Ellmore Cl RM3 ....114 B2
Ellswood SS15 ......119 C8
Elm Ave Heybridge CM9 .37 C5
Upminster RM14 ....156 B8
Elm Bank Pl SS17 ...155 F4
Elm Cl Buckhurst Hill IG9 .110 D8
Chelmsford CM1 ....32 A8
Epping Green CM16 ..45 B7
Great Baddow CM2 ..54 F6
Rayleigh SS6 ....123 D3
Romford RM7 ....113 B1
Southend-on-S SS3 ..168 E7
Waltham Abbey EN9 ..65 D5
Wanstead E11 ......132 B5
Elm Cotts
Southend-on-S SS2 ..147 F2
Waltham Abbey EN9 ..65 D1
Elm Ct Chingford E4 ..109 C4
Theydon Bois CM16 ..67 C3
Woodford IG8 ....110 C4
Elm Dr SS6 ....123 D3
Elm Gdns CM2 ......47 B5
Elm Gn Basildon SS13 .143 A5
Billericay CM11 .....97 E2
Elm Gr Hornchurch RM11 .136 C6
Hullbridge SS5 ......101 D2
Southend-on-S SS1 ..168 A8
Woodford IG8 ....109 F5
Elm Green La CM3 ..56 C8
Elm Green Prep Sch
CM3 ....34 D3
Elm Hall Gdns E11 ..132 B5
Elm Ho RM3 ....164 B1
Elm Par RM12 ......155 B8
Elm Park Ave
Hornchurch RM12 ...155 A8
Rainham RM12 .....154 F8
Elm Park Sta RM12 ..155 A8
Elm Rd Aveley RM15 .171 D5
Basildon SS13 ......121 E1
Canvey Island SS8 ..164 C3
Chelmsford CM2 ....54 A8
Grays RM17 ....178 C8
Greenhithe DA9 ....176 E1
Hadleigh SS7 ......145 D2
Romford RM7 ......113 C6
South Woodham Ferrers
CM3 ....101 C8
Southend-on-s, Leigh-on-S
SS9 ....146 E1
Southend-on-s, Shoeburyness
SS3 ....168 E8
Wickford SS12 .....121 D8
Elm Terr RM20 .....177 B8
Elm View Rd SS7 ...144 B3
Elm Way Boreham CM3 .20 E1
Brentwood CM14 ...116 A6
Elm Wlk RM2 ......136 A8
Elmbourne Dr DA17 .169 B2
Elmbridge CM17 ....11 F3
Elmbridge Hall CM5 .27 C4
Elmbridge Rd IG6 ..112 A4
Elmbrook 2 E18 ....132 A8
Elmcroft Ave E11 ...132 B7
Elmcroft Cl E11 ....132 B7
Elmdene Ave RM11 .136 A5
Elmdon Rd RM15 ...172 A8
Elmer App SS1 .....167 A8
Elmer Ave Romford RM4 .113 E7
Southend-on-S SS1 ..167 A8
Elmer Cl RM13 .....155 A5
Elmer Gdns RM13 ..155 A5
Elmfield Rd E4 .....109 D8
Elmhurst Greenhithe DA9 .177 B1
Hoddesdon EN10 ...21 A4
Elmhurst Ave SS7 ..144 A4
Elmhurst Dr
Hornchurch RM11 ...136 C4
Woodford E18 ......110 A1
Elmhurst Way IG10 ..88 F2
Elmores IG10 ....89 A6
Elms Dr CM1 ....32 A4
Elms Farm Rd RM12 .155 C7
Elms Gdns RM9 ....153 E8
Elms Ind Est RM3 ..115 B3
Elms Rd RM1 ....29 C6
Elms The CM5 ......49 A1
Elmsleigh Dr SS9 ...146 E3
Elmslie Cl IG8 ......110 F4
Elmstead Cl SS17 ..161 B5
Elmstead Rd IG3 ...133 F2
Elmtree Ave CM15 ..71 F2
Elmtree Rd SS16 ...143 A4
Elmway RM16 ......173 C5
Elmwood CM21 ....1 F1

Elmwood Ave SS5 ....124 F4
Elmwood Ct SS5 ......124 E6
Elmwood Prim Sch CM3 101 D7
Elounda Ct SS7 ......144 D4
Elrington Rd IG8 .....110 A5
Elronds Rest CM3 ....101 C6
Elsden Chase CM0 ....84 D4
Elsenham Cres SS14 ..142 F4
Elsenham Ct SS6 .....123 B3
Elsenham Mews SS14 ..142 F4
Elsenham Rd E12 .....152 A7
Elsinor Ave SS8 ......164 A6
Elstow Gdns RM9 .....153 E4
Elstow Rd RM9 ....153 E4
Elstree Gdns IG1 .....152 B8
Eltisley Rd IG1 ......152 B8
Elverston Cl SS15 ....141 D8
Elvet Ave RM2 ....136 C7
Elvin Ct RM2 ....136 B8
Elwick Rd RM15 ......172 C7
Elwood CM17 ....24 E8
Ely Cl Rayleigh SS6 ..123 C4
  Westminster CM0 .....84 D4
Ely Gdns
  Dagenham RM10 .....135 C1
  Redbridge IG1 ......132 E4
Ely Pl IG8 ....111 A5
Ely Rd SS2 ....148 C2
Emanuel Rd SS16 .....141 B4
Embassy Ct Maldon CM9 .37 A2
  7 Wanstead E18 ....132 A8
Ember Way CM0 ......106 A6
Emberson Ct CM2 .....32 A7
Emberson Way CM16 ..47 C5
Emerald Gdns RM8 ...135 A3
Emerald Ho 2 RM13 ..155 A1
Emerson Dr RM11 ....136 C4
Emerson Park Ct RM11 136 D4
Emerson Park Sch
  RM11 ....137 B4
Emerson Park Sta RM11 136 E4
Emerson Pl RM11 .....136 D5
Emerson Rd IG1 ......133 A4
Emerson Terr IG8 ....110 A4
Emily White Ct SS11 ..121 F8
Emma's Cres SG12 ....8 A5
Emmaus Way IG7 .....111 A5
Emmott Ave IG6 ......133 C6
Empire Wlk 2 CM2 ...32 C2
Empress Ave
  Chingford E4 ....109 B3
  Ilford IG1 ....133 A2
  Redbridge IG1 ......132 F2
  Wanstead E12 ......132 D2
  Woodford IG8 ....109 F3
Empress Par SS4 .....109 A3
Emsworth Rd IG6 ....111 B1
Enborne Rd RM15 ....172 A8
End Way Cotts CM0 ..85 A7
Endeavour Sch The
  CM15 ....116 F7
Endeavour Way IG11 ..153 A3
Endlebury Cl E4 ......109 D8
Endlebury Rd E4 .....109 C8
Endsleigh Gdns IG1 ..132 F3
Endway SS7 ....145 E2
Endway The CM3 .....83 D2
Endways Ct CM15 ....94 C1
Enfield Ho 6 RM3 ...114 E3
Enfield Rd SS11 .....122 C7
Engayne Gdns RM14 ..137 B3
Engayne Prim Sch
  RM14 ....137 E5
England's La IG10 ....89 B7
Englefield Cl SS5 ....125 A4
Englefields CM0 .....63 E3
Ennerdale Ave RM12 ..155 A7
Ennerdale Ct E11 ....132 A4
Ennismore Gdns SS2 ..148 A3
Ensign Cl SS9 ....147 A1
Ensign Ho RM17 .....177 F8
Enterprise Ctr The SS14 120 E2
Enterprise Ho
  Barking IG11 ....152 F2
  Chingford E4 ....87 C2
Enterprise Way SS11 ..121 F6
Epping Cl Chelmsford CM1 31 E1
  Romford RM7 ....135 B8
  Southend-on-S SS16 ..146 E7
Epping Forest Coll IG10 .89 B5
Epping Forest Conservation
  Ctr * IG10 ....66 C1
Epping Forest District Mus*
  EN9 ....65 C6
Epping Forest YH* IG10 .66 B1
Epping Glade E4 .....87 C3
Epping Inf Sch CM16 ..45 F1
Epping Jun Sch CM16 ..45 F1
Epping La
  Chipping Ongar RM4 ..69 A1
  Stapleford Abbotts RM4 .91 B8
  Theydon Bois RM4 ..68 D1
Epping New Rd
  Buckhurst Hill IG9,IG10 .88 B4
  Loughton IG10,CM16 ..66 E2
Epping Rd
  Chipping Ongar CM5 ..48 D6
  Coopersale CM16 ....46 D4
  Epping Green CM16 ..23 A1
  Loughton CM16 .....67 A4
  Roydon CM19 ....22 D5
  Toot Hill CM5 ......47 D1
Epping Sta CM16 .....68 A8
Epping Upland CE Prim Sch
  CM16 ....45 B7
Epping Way E4 ......87 B3
Epsom Cl CM11 ......97 D5

Epsom Ho 15 RM3 ...114 E5
Epsom Mews CM0 ....84 E4
Epsom Rd IG3 ....133 F5
Epsom Way RM12 ....155 F8
Eric Clarke La IG11 ..152 C2
Eric Rd Basildon SS13 ..143 F6
  Dagenham RM6 .....134 D4
Erick Ave CM1 ....32 A5
Eridge Cl CM1 ....32 D7
Erin Cl IG3 ....134 A5
Erith Cres RM5 ......113 C2
Erith Ct RM19 ....171 A2
Erith High St DA8 ...169 E1
Erith Mus* DA8 .....169 E1
Erith Rd DA17 ......169 B1
Erith Sta DA8 ....169 E1
Ernan Cl RM15 ......172 A3
Ernan Rd RM15 ......172 A3
Ernest Rd RM11 .....136 F5
Erriff Dr RM15 ......172 A8
Errington Cl RM16 ...174 B3
Erroll Rd RM1 ....135 F7
Erskine Pl 2 SS12 ...121 E6
Esdaile Gdns RM14 ..137 D4
Esdaile La EN11 .....21 A5
Esher Ave RM7 ......135 C5
Esher Rd IG3 ....133 E1
Esk Way RM1 ....113 E3
Eskley Gdns
  South Ockendon RM15 157 B1
  South Ockendon RM15 172 B8
Esmond Cl RM13 .....155 B5
Esplanade Ct SS1 ....167 E6
Esplanade Gdns SS0 ..166 B8
Esplanade Ho SS0 ...166 B8
Esplanade The
  Hullbridge SS5 .....101 D3
  Mayland CM3 ....60 E1
Essenden Rd DA17 ...169 A1
Essex Ave CM1 ......32 A7
Essex Cl Basildon SS15 141 B6
  Canvey Island SS8 ..164 A2
  Rayleigh SS6 ....123 F2
  Romford RM7 ....135 C4
Essex County Cricket Club*
  CM2 ....32 B2
Essex Gdns
  Hornchurch RM11 ...137 B4
  Linford SS17 ....175 A4
  Southend-on-S SS9 ..146 B4
Essex Nuffield Hospl The
  CM15 ....94 E1
Essex Rd Barking IG11 ..152 C6
  Burnham-on-C CM0 ..106 C5
  Canvey Island SS8 ..164 C4
  Chingford E4 ....87 E1
  Dagenham RM10 ....154 C7
  Dagenham, Goodmayes
    RM6 ....134 C4
  Grays RM20 ....177 A8
  Hoddesdon EN11 ...21 C6
  Maldon CM9 ....36 F1
  Romford RM7 ....135 B7
  Woodford E18 ......110 B1
Essex Regiment Way
  CM3 ....19 D5
Essex St SS1 ....167 A8
Essex Way
  Brentwood CM13 ...116 C4
  South Benfleet SS7 ..144 F1
Estate Rd SS7 ....145 F3
Estella Mead CM1 ...31 E7
Estfeld Cl 4 EN11 ...8 B7
Estuary Cl IG11 .....153 B2
Estuary Cotts RM18 ..180 D7
Estuary Ct SS9 ......165 F8
Estuary Gdns SS3 ...150 C2
Estuary Lodge SS1 ..167 F6
Estuary Mews SS3 ...168 E6
Ethel Cotts RM6 .....134 D8
Ethel Davis Sch RM6 134 B6
Ethel Rd SS6 ....146 B8
Ethelbert Gdns IG2 ..133 A6
Ethelbert Rd SS4 ....103 C1
Ethelburga Rd RM3 ..114 F2
Etheldore Ave SS5 ..124 E8
Ethelred Gdns SS11 ..99 E1
Etheridge Gn IG10 ..89 C6
Etheridge Rd IG10 ..89 C6
Eton Cl SS8 ....164 B5
Eton Rd IG1 ....152 D8
Eton Wlk SS3 ....149 E2
Etton Cl RM12 ......136 E2
Euclid Way RM20 ...171 F1
Eugene Cl RM2 ......136 C7
Europa Pk RM20 ....177 C3
Europa Trad Est DA8 ..169 D1
Eustace Rd RM6 .....134 D4
Eva Rd RM6 ....134 D4
Evans Cl DA9 ....177 A2
Evansdale RM13 .....154 F2
Evanston Ave E4 ....109 C3
Evanston Gdns IG4 ..132 E5
Evelyn Pl CM1 ....31 F1
Evelyn Rd SS5 ......124 E6
Evelyn Sharp Cl RM2 136 D8
Evelyn Sharp Ho RM2 136 D8
Evelyn Wlk CM13 ...116 C4
Everard Rd SS14 ....143 A8
Everest SS15 ....123 D5
Everest Rise CM12 ..96 F5
Everest Way CM9 ...37 B5
Everglades The SS7 ..145 F2
Evergreen Ct SS12 ..121 C6
Evergreen The SS3 ..149 E6
Everik Bsns Ctr CM13 ..95 E4
Eversleigh Gdns RM14 137 D3
Eversley Cl IG10 ....89 C6

Eversley Ct SS7 .....144 C7
Eversley Lodge EN11 ..21 A6
Eversley Prim Sch SS13 143 C6
Eversley Rd
  Basildon SS13 ......143 D6
  South Benfleet SS7 ..144 C6
Eves Cnr
  Burnham-on-C CM0 ..106 B7
  Danbury CM3 ....56 E7
Eves Cres CM1 ......32 A5
Evesham Ave E17 ...109 A1
Evesham Way IG5 ...133 A8
Ewan Cl SS9 ....146 A3
Ewan Rd RM3 ....114 D1
Ewan Way SS9 ......146 A3
Ewanrigg Terr IG8 ..110 C5
Ewellhurst Rd IG5 ..110 C1
Exchange St
  Romford RM1 ....135 E5
  Romford RM1 ....135 E6
Exchange The IG1 ...133 B2
Exchange Way 5 CM1 ..32 B2
Exeter Cl Basildon SS14 142 F7
  Southend-on-S SS3 ..149 F1
Exeter Gdns IG1 ....132 F3
Exeter Ho
  7 Barking IG11 .....153 A5
  Southend-on-S SS3 ..149 F1
Exeter Rd Chelmsford CM1 32 E5
  Dagenham RM10 ...154 B6
Exford Ave SS0 .....147 B5
Exhibition La SS3 ...149 F4
Exley Cl CM4 ....74 B4
Exmoor Cl
  Chelmsford CM1 ....31 D1
  Redbridge IG6 ......111 C2
Exmouth Dr SS6 ....123 D5
Exmouth Rd RM17 ..178 B8
Express Dr IG3 .....134 B3
Exton Gdns RM8 ....153 C7
Eyhurst Ave IG2 ....136 B1
Eynesham Way 1 SS13 121 A1
Eynsford Rd
  Greenhithe DA9 ....177 C2
  Ilford IG3 ....133 E2
Eyre Cl RM2 ....136 B7

F

Factory Rd DA11 ....178 C1
Faggotters La CM17 ..12 F1
Fagus Ave RM13 ....155 D2
Fair Mead SS14 .....142 C8
Fair Oak Pl IG6 .....111 C1
Fair View Lodge SS9 ..146 C2
Fairbank Cl CM5 ....48 F2
Fairburn Cl 2 SS1 ..167 C8
Fairburn Ct 4 SS1 ..167 C8
Faircross Ave
  Barking IG11 ....152 C6
  Romford RM5 ......113 D3
Faircross Par IG11 ..152 E7
Fairfax Ave SS13 ...143 C8
Fairfax Dr SS0 .....147 D2
Fairfax Mead CM2 ..33 A2
Fairfax Rd Grays RM17 173 B1
  Tilbury RM18 ......178 F6
Fairfield
  Great Wakering SS3 ..150 A3
  Ingatestone CM4 ...74 C4
Fairfield Ave
  Grays RM16 ....173 C6
  Upminster RM14 ...137 C1
Fairfield Cl RM12 ...136 A4
Fairfield Cres SS9 ..146 F6
Fairfield Ct 8 IG8 ..110 A4
Fairfield Gdns SS9 ..146 F7
Fairfield Rd
  Brentwood CM14 ...116 C7
  Chelmsford CM1 ...32 A3
  Chipping Ongar CM5 ..48 F2
  Epping CM16 ....46 B2
  Hoddesdon EN11 ...21 B2
  Ilford IG1 ....152 B6
  Southend-on-S SS9 ..146 E7
  Woodford IG8 ......110 A4
Fairfield Rise CM12 ..118 F8
Fairfields CM3 ......58 D1
Fairford Cl RM3 .....115 B4
Fairford Way RM3 ..115 B4
Fairham Ave RM15 ..172 A6
Fairholme Ave RM2 ..136 B7
Fairholme Rd Ilford IG1 133 A4
  Redbridge IG1 .....132 F4
Fairhouse Com Jun & Inf Sch
  SS14 ....142 D6
Fairhouse Ct SS14 ..142 D6
Fairkytes Ave RM11 ..136 F3
Fairland Cl SS13 ....123 E5
Fairlands Ave IG9 ...110 A8
Fairlawn Dr IG8 ....110 A3
Fairlawn Gdns SS2 ..147 E5
Fairlawns
  Brentwood CM14 ...116 A7
  10 Chingford E4 ...109 C8
  Epping CM16 ....46 B2
  Southend-on-S SS1 ..167 B2
Fairlawns Cl RM11 ..136 F4
Fairleads CM3 ......56 F8
Fairleigh Ave SS13 ..143 D5
Fairleigh Ct SS9 ....146 D1
Fairleigh Dr SS9 ....146 D1
Fairleigh Rd SS13 ..143 D5
Fairlight Ave
  Chingford E4 ....109 D8
  Woodford IG8 ......110 A4

Fairlight Cl E4 ......109 D8
Fairlight Rd SS7 ....145 C3
Fairlight Villas RM4 ..113 C7
Fairlop Cl E4 ....109 D8
Fairlop Ct RM12 ....155 B6
Fairlop Gdns
  Basildon SS14 ......142 D6
  Redbridge IG6 ......111 C3
Fairlop Prim Sch IG6 ..111 C2
Fairlop Rd IG6 ......111 C1
Fairlop Sta IG6 .....111 D2
Fairlop Waters Ctry Pk*
  IG6 ....111 E1
Fairmead SS6 ....123 B4
Fairmead Ave
  Hadleigh SS7 ......145 E6
  Southend-on-S SS0 ..147 C2
Fairmead Ct 4 E7 ...87 E2
Fairmead Gdns IG4 ..132 E2
Fairmead Ho SS0 ...147 C2
Fairmead Rd IG10 ..88 B6
Fairmeadside IG10 ..88 C4
Fairoak Gdns RM1 ..113 C4
Fairstead SS14 .....142 F5
Fairstead Lodge 4 IG8 110 A4
Fairview Billericay CM12 .97 A1
  Canvey Island SS8 ..163 C7
Fairview Ave
  Brentwood CM13 ...95 E3
  Rainham RM13 .....155 D2
  Stanford-le-H SS17 ..160 C1
Fairview Chase SS17 ..175 C8
Fairview Cl Chigwell IG7 111 E6
  South Benfleet SS7 ..144 C4
Fairview Cres SS7 ..144 C7
Fairview Dr Chigwell IG7 111 E5
  Southend-on-S SS9 ..147 C4
Fairview Est EN11 ..21 C7
Fairview Gdns
  Southend-on-S SS9 ..146 C2
  Woodford IG8 ......110 B2
Fairview Ind Pk RM13 ..169 D8
Fairview Par RM7 ...135 D6
Fairview Rd
  Basildon SS14 .....142 F5
  Chigwell IG7 ......111 E6
Fairview Villas E4 ..109 B3
Fairview Wlk SS7 ...144 C7
Fairway Chelmsford CM2 .54 D7
  Grays RM16 ....173 B5
  Sawbridgeworth CM21 ..1 F2
  Wickford SS12 .....121 E3
  Woodford IG8 .....110 C5
Fairway Dr CM0 ....106 B5
Fairway Gardens Cl
  SS9 ....146 C5
Fairway Gdns Ilford IG1 152 C2
  Southend-on-S SS9 ..146 C5
Fairway The Harlow CM18 24 A4
  South Benfleet SS7 ..144 C7
  Southend-on-S SS9 ..146 C5
  Upminster RM14 ...137 D4
Fairways
  Southend-on-S SS1 ..167 F8
  Waltham Abbey EN9 ..65 C5
Fairways Prim Sch SS9 146 C4
Fairways The CM3 ...80 F5
Falbro Cres SS7 ....145 D4
Falcon Ave RM17 ...178 C8
Falcon Cl Rayleigh SS6 123 B3
  Sawbridgeworth CM21 ..1 C1
  Southend-on-S SS9 ..146 F5
  Waltham Abbey EN9 ..66 A5
Falcon Ct 6 E18 ....132 B8
Falcon Fields CM9 ..58 F8
Falcon Mews CM9 ..58 F8
Falcon Pk SS14 .....141 F8
Falcon Rd CM0 .....84 C4
Falcon Way
  Basildon SS16 .....142 C4
  Chelmsford CM2 ...54 A6
  Rainham RM13 .....155 A5
  Southend-on-S SS3 ..149 E1
  Wanstead E11 .....132 A7
Falconer Rd IG6 ....112 C5
Falconers Pk CM21 ..1 D1
Falcons Mead CM2 ..32 A1
Falkenham End SS14 ..142 C7
Falkenham Path SS14 142 C7
Falkenham Rise SS14 ..142 C7
Falkenham Row SS14 142 C7
Falkirk Cl RM11 ....137 A3
Falkland Cl CM3 ....33 E8
Falkland Gn CM9 ...57 E6
Falklands Rd CM0 ...106 B5
Falkner Cl CM4 .....75 F3
Fallow Cl IG7 ....111 E5
Fallow Fields IG10 ..88 C2
Fallowfield SS3 .....149 D1
Fallows The SS8 ....163 F6
Falmouth Ave E4 ...109 E5
Falmouth Gdns IG4 ..132 E6
Falmouth Rd CM1 ..32 E5
Falstaff Pl SS16 ....141 A5
Falstones SS15 .....141 B6
Fambridge Ct 2 RM7 135 D6
Fambridge Dr SS12 ..121 E6
Fambridge Rd
  Althorne SS4 ....82 F2
  Cold Norton CM9,CM3 ..81 C5
  Dagenham RM8 ....135 A3
  Maldon CM9 ....36 F1
  Rochford SS4, CM3 ..103 C3
Fambridge Sta CM3 ..103 B8
Fane Rd SS7 ....144 D8

Fanner's Green Cotts
  CM3 ....18 C5
Fanns Rise RM19 ...171 A2
Fanshawe Ave IG11 ..152 C6
Fanshawe Cres
  Dagenham RM9 ....153 F7
  Hornchurch RM11 ..136 D5
Fanshawe Rd RM16 ..174 A3
Fanton Ave SS12 ...121 F3
Fanton Chase SS11 ..122 A6
Fanton Gdns SS11 ..122 B6
Fanton Wlk SS11 ...122 B6
Faraday Ho 4 DA17 ..169 A3
Faraday Rd SS9 .....146 C6
Faringdon Ave RM3 ..114 D3
Faringdon Gr RM3 ..114 D3
Farley Dr IG3 ....133 E3
Farm Cl Brentwood CM13 95 C2
  Buckhurst Hill IG9 ..110 C7
  Dagenham RM10 ...154 C5
  Roydon CM19 ......9 B1
Farm Cres SS11 .....100 E4
Farm Dr RM16 ......173 C6
Farm End E4 ....87 E4
Farm Hill Rd EN9 ...65 D6
Farm La EN11 ......21 C8
Farm Rd
  Canvey Island SS8 ..164 B5
  Chadwell St M RM16 ..173 F4
  East Tilbury RM18 ..175 C2
  Rainham RM13 .....155 C2
Farm View SS6 .....123 D5
Farm Way
  Buckhurst Hill IG9 ..110 C6
  Hornchurch RM12 ..155 C8
  Thundersley SS7 ...145 B6
Farmbridge End Rd CM1 16 D4
Farmer Ct EN9 .....66 A6
Farmway RM8 ......134 C1
Farnaby Way SS17 ..160 C3
Farnan Ave E17 ....109 B1
Farne Dr SS12 ......121 F5
Farnes Ave SS12 ...121 C7
Farnes Dr RM2 .....114 C1
Farnham Cl CM21 ...1 C1
Farnham Green Prim Sch
  IG3 ....134 A5
Farnham Rd Ilford IG3 ..133 F4
  Romford RM3 ......114 D5
Farnley Rd E4 ......87 E2
Farnol Rd DA1 ......176 A3
Farr Ave IG11 ......153 A3
Farrance Rd RM6 ...134 E4
Farrier Sq CM11 ....98 C4
Farriers Great Amwell SG12 .8 A6
  Sawbridgeworth CM21 ..1 E3
Farriers Dr CM12 ...97 B5
Farriers Way SS12 ..147 F5
Farringdon Service Rd 8
  SS1 ....167 A8
Farrow Gdns RM16 ..173 C5
Farrow Ho CM15 ...94 C1
Farrow Rd CM1 .....53 E7
Farthingale Ct EN9 ..66 A5
Farthingale La EN9 ..66 A5
Farthings Cl E4 .....109 E7
Fastnet SS2 ....147 A7
Faulkner Cl 6 RM8 ..134 D4
Fauna Cl RM6 ......134 C5
Fauners SS16 ....142 A5
Faversham Ave E4 ..87 F1
Faversham Cl IG7 ..112 B4
Faversham Lodge IG1 152 E6
Fawbert & Barnards Prim
  Sch CM17 ....11 C3
Fawbert & Bernard Inf Sch
  CM21 ....1 E2
Fawcett Dr SS15 ....119 E1
Fawkner Cl CM2 ....32 F2
Fawkon Wlk EN11 ..21 A6
Fawn Rd IG7 ....111 F5
Fawters Cl CM11 ...95 D3
Faymore Gdns RM15 ..172 A7
Fazal Laj IG1 ....133 C2
Fearns Mead CM14 ..116 D5
Feathers Hill CM22 ..3 E6
Featherby Way SS4 ..126 A1
Feeches Rd SS2 ....147 D4
Feenan Highway RM18 179 B6
Feering Dr SS14 ....142 F5
Feering Gn SS14 ....142 F5
Feering Rd CM11 ...97 C2
Feering Row 5 SS14 ..142 F5
Felbrigge Rd IG3 ...133 F3
Felhurst Cres RM10 ..154 C8
Felicia Way RM16 ...174 B2
Felipe Rd RM16 .....172 C3
Fell Christy CM1 ....32 B5
Fellcroft 5 SS13 ....143 C6
Felmongers CM20 ..11 B2
Felmore Ct 9 SS13 ..143 B8
Felmore Prim Sch SS13 143 B8
Felmores SS13 .....143 B8
Felmores End 8 SS13 143 B8
Fels Cl RM10 ....135 B1
Fels Farm Ave RM10 ..135 C1
Felstead Ave IG5 ...111 A4
Felstead Cl
  Brentwood CM13 ...95 C3
  South Benfleet SS7 ..144 D4
Felstead Rd
  Loughton IG10 .....88 D2
  Romford RM5 ......113 C3
  South Benfleet SS7 ..144 D4
  Wanstead E11 .....132 A4

Felsted Rd CM11 ....**97** C2
Felton Gdns IG11 .....**152** E3
Felton Cl SS17 ....**161** C5
Felton Rd IG11 ....**152** E3
Fen Cl Brentwood CM15 ..**95** C5
  Bulphan RM14 ....**158** F8
Fen La Bulphan RM14 ..**158** C7
  North Ockendon RM14 ...**157** E7
  Orsett RM16 ....**173** E8
Fencepiece Rd IG7 .....**111** C3
Fengates CM3 ....**101** C8
Fenman Gdns IG3 ......**134** B3
Fenn Cl CM3 ....**101** C8
Fennells CM19 ....**23** C3
Fenner Brockway Ho
  CM20 ....**23** E8
Fenner Rd SS6 ....**172** C3
Fenners Way SS13 .....**121** A2
Fennfields Rd CM8 ....**101** B8
Fentiman Way RM11 ...**136** E3
Fenton Grange CM17 ...**24** C7
Fenton Rd RM16 ....**172** E3
Fenton Way SS15 ......**140** F7
Fenwick Way SS8 .....**164** A6
Ferguson Rd RM2 .....**114** D1
Ferguson Ct RM2 ......**114** D1
Fermoy Rd SS1 ....**168** B7
Fern Cl CM12 ....**97** B4
  Chingford E4 ....**109** C6
  Southend-on-S SS3 ....**168** F7
  Stanford-le-H SS17 ....**160** D3
Fern Hill SS6 ....**141** C4
Fern Hill La CM18 ......**23** C7
Fern Wlk Basildon SS16 **140** E4
  Canvey Island SS8 .....**163** F3
Fernbank Billericay CM12 ..**96** F1
  Buckhurst Hill IG9 ......**88** B1
Fernbrook Ave SS1 ....**167** D8
Fernbank Ave RM12 ...**155** C8
Ferndale SS15 ....**141** B6
Ferndale Cres SS8 ....**164** B2
Ferndale Rd
  Rayleigh SS6 ....**123** C5
  Romford RM5 ....**113** C1
  Southend-on-S SS2 ....**148** C2
Ferndown Way RM7 ...**135** B5
Ferndown
  Hornchurch RM11 .....**136** F5
  6 Wanstead E18 ......**132** A8
Ferndown Cl SS2 ......**167** C8
Fernhall La EN9 ....**66** D8
Fernhill Ct E17 ....**109** D1
Fernie Cl IG7 ....**112** A5
Fernlea Rd
  Burnham-on-C CM0 ...**106** B5
  South Benfleet SS7 ...**144** E3
Fernleigh Ct
  Romford RM7 ....**135** C6
  Southend-on-S SS0 ...**147** A1
Fernleigh Dr SS9 ......**147** A1
Fernways IG1 ....**152** B8
Fernwood SS7 ....**145** E4
Ferrers Rd CM3 ....**101** D6
Ferris Ave CM3 ....**80** F5
Ferris Stps **18** SS1 ...**167** C7
Ferro Rd RM13 ....**155** A1
Ferry La RM13 ....**169** E7
Ferry Rd
  Burnham-on-C CM0 ...**105** E6
  Hullbridge SS5 ....**101** D2
  North Fambridge CM3 ...**103** A6
  South Benfleet SS7 ...**163** D8
  Tilbury RM18 ....**179** A4
Ferrymead SS8 ....**163** F5
Feryby Rd RM16 ......**174** B3
Feryngs Cl CM17 ....**11** C4
Fesants Croft CM20 ....**11** D3
Festival Link SS14 ....**142** B8
Fetherston Rd SS17 ..**160** D1
Fews Lodge RM6 .....**134** D7
Fiddlers Cl DA9 ....**177** B3
Field Cl Abridge RM4 ...**90** B6
  Buckhurst Hill IG9 .....**110** C7
  Chingford E4 ....**109** B4
Field Rd RM15 ....**171** C5
Field View RM14 .....**174** A3
Field Way EN11 ....**8** C2
Fielders Cl **9** CM14 ..**116** C8
Fielders The SS8 ......**164** A6
Fieldfare CM11 ....**119** C8
Fieldhouse Cl E18 ....**110** B2
Fielding Ave RM18 ...**179** C6
Fielding Way CM13 ....**95** C3
Fields Park Cres RM6 ..**134** D6
Fieldway Basildon SS13 **143** C4
  Dagenham RM8 ....**153** C8
  Grays RM16 ....**173** A5
  Stanstead Abbotts SG12 ..**8** B4
  Wickford SS12 ....**121** D3
Fiennes Cl RM8 ....**134** C3
Fiesta Dr RM9,RM13 ..**154** C1
Fifth Ave
  Canvey Island SS8 ....**163** B6
  Chelmsford CM1 ....**32** B6
  Grays RM20 ....**177** A8
  Wickford SS11 ....**122** A6
Fifth Ave / Allende Ave
  CM20 ....**10** C3
Filey Rd CM0 ....**84** A3
Fillebrook Ave SS9 ...**147** A2
Fillebrook Ct SS9 .....**147** A2
Filliol Cl CM3 ....**78** B6

Filston Rd DA8 ....**169** C1
Finch Ct CM5 ....**49** A5
Finch Gdns E4 ....**109** A5
Finches Cl SS17 ......**161** C5
Finches The SS7 ......**145** A4
Finchfield SS6 ....**123** D1
Finchingfield Ave IG8 **110** C3
Finchingfield Way **7**
  SS12 ....**121** C5
Finchingfields WIk **7** E2
Finchley Ave CM2 ......**54** A8
Finchley Cl DA1 ......**176** A1
Finchley Rd Grays RM17 **178** B8
  Southend-on-S SS0 ...**166** D8
Finchmoor CM18 ....**23** D5
Findon Gdns RM13 ...**170** B8
Fingrith Hall Cotts CM4 ..**50** F3
Fingrith Hall La CM4 ...**50** F3
Finnymore Rd RM9 ...**153** E5
Finucane Gdns RM13 .**155** A6
Fir Pk CM19 ....**23** B8
Fir Tree Cl Grays RM17 **178** D8
  Romford RM1 ....**135** D8
Fir Tree La CM3 ....**34** E1
Fir Tree Rise CM2 ......**54** B6
Fir Tree Wlk
  Dagenham RM10 .....**135** C1
  Heybridge CM9 ....**37** C5
Fir Trees Abridge RM4 ..**90** B6
  Epping CM16 ....**46** B2
Fir Wlk SS8 ....**163** F5
Firbank RM5 ....**113** B5
Firecrest Rd CM2 ......**54** C5
Firfield Rd SS7 ....**145** C6
Firham Park Ave RM3 **115** A3
Firle The SS16 ....**141** C3
Firmans SS16 ....**141** B3
Firs Ave Basildon SS16 **140** E4
  Billericay CM12 ....**118** F7
  Canvey Island SS8 ....**163** E4
  Chelmsford CM1 ....**32** B5
  Dagenham RM10 .....**154** B3
  Grays RM20 ....**177** A8
  Hook End CM15 ....**72** C5
  Hullbridge SS5 ....**101** F1
  Ilford RM6 ....**134** C6
  Southend-on-S SS0 ...**166** B8
  Stanford-le-H SS17 ...**160** D3
  Wickford SS11 ....**122** A6
Firs Ave / Mandela Ave
  CM20 ....**10** F2
Fish St CM9 ....**38** E6
Fisher Cl EN3 ....**65** D7
Fisher's Way DA17 ...**169** C5
Fishermans Way EN11 **21** D8
Fishermen's Hill DA11 **178** B2
Fishers Cl EN8 ....**65** A5
Fishers Hatch CM20 ...**10** E1
Fiske Ct IG11 ....**152** E3
Fitches Cres CM9 ......**37** B1
Fitches Mews CM9 ....**37** B1
Fitzgerald Rd E11 ....**132** A6
Fitzilian Ave RM3 ....**114** F2
Fitzroy Cl CM12 ....**97** A4
Fitzstephen Rd RM8 .**153** C7
Fitzwalter La CM3 .....**56** D6
Fitzwalter Pl CM1 .....**31** E3
Fitzwalter Rd CM3 .....**33** F8
Fitzwarren SS3 ......**149** E1
Fitzwilliam Rd SS7 ...**145** C2
Fitzwilliams Ct CM17 ..**11** E4
Fitzwimarc Sch The
  SS6 ....**123** E3
Five Acres Bicknacre CM3 **56** F3
  Harlow CM18 ....**23** E5
Five Elms Prim Sch
  RM8 ....**134** F1
Five Elms Rd RM9 ...**134** F1
Five Oaks SS7 ....**145** B4
Five Oaks La IG7 ....**112** C5
Flagstaff Cl EN9 ......**65** B6
Flagstaff Rd EN9 .....**65** B6
Flambird's Chase
  Purleigh CM3 ....**80** A7
  Stow Maries CM3 ......**79** F6
Flamboro Cl SS9 .....**146** D6
Flamboro Wlk SS9 ...**146** D6
Flamingo Wlk **4** SS9 **155** A6
Flamstead Gdns RM9 **153** C5
Flamstead Rd RM9 ...**153** C5
Flanders Rd E6 ......**152** A3
Flats The Grays RM17 **173** D2
  Greenhithe DA9 ......**177** C2
Flaxen Cl E4 ....**109** B7
Flaxen Rd E4 ....**109** B7
Flaxman Ct **12** DA17 **169** A1
Fleet Ave RM14 ......**137** D5
Fleet Cl RM14 ....**137** D5
Fleet Hall Cotts SS4 .**148** B8
Fleet Rd SS7 ....**144** D1
Fleethall Gr RM16 ...**173** A5
Fleethall Rd SS4 ....**148** A8
Fleetwood Ave SS0 ..**147** C2
Fleming Gdns
  Romford RM3 ....**114** D1

Fleming Gdns continued
  Tilbury RM18 ....**179** C6
Fleming Rd RM16 ....**172** C3
Flemings CM13 ....**116** C4
Flemings Farm Rd SS9 **146** B8
Flemming Ave SS9 ...**146** D4
Flemming Cres SS9 ..**146** D4
Fletcher Ct CM11 ......**97** D2
Fletcher Dr SS12 .....**121** E6
Fletcher Rd IG7 ......**111** F5
Fletchers SS16 ....**141** E3
Fletchers Sq **2** SS2 ..**148** A5
Flex Mdw CM19 ....**22** C7
Flint Cl SS16 ....**140** F5
Flint St RM20 ....**177** B8
Flintwich Manor CM1 ..**31** E7
Flora Gdns RM6 .....**134** C5
Florence Cl Grays RM20 **177** E8
  Hadleigh SS7 ....**145** D3
  Harlow CM17 ....**24** C6
  Hornchurch RM12 ....**136** E2
Florence Ct E11 ......**132** C7
Florence Elson Cl E12 **152** A8
Florence Gdns
  Dagenham RM6 .....**134** C4
  Hadleigh SS7 ....**145** D3
Florence Neale Ho **2**
  SS8 ....**164** A3
Florence Rd SS8 ....**164** D3
Florence Root Ho **3**
  IG4 ....**132** F6
Florence Terr SS17 ..**159** F4
Florence Way SS16 ..**141** F5
Florentine Ho **3** IG1 **133** B2
Flux's La CM16 ....**68** A6
Fobbing Farm Cl SS16 **142** A3
Fobbing Rd SS17 ....**161** C4
Fodderwick **1** SS14 .**142** A5
Fogerty Cl EN3 ....**65** B2
Foksville Rd SS8 .....**164** C4
Fold Croft CM20 ......**10** A1
Fold The SS14 ......**142** B6
Folkes La RM4,CM13 **137** F7
Folly Chase SS5 ....**124** B6
Folly La SS5 ....**124** C5
Folly View SS12 ......**8** B4
Fontayne Ave
  Chigwell IG7 ....**111** C6
  Rainham RM13 ......**154** F5
  Romford RM1 ....**113** E1
Fonteyn Ct SS15 ....**141** C8
Fonteyne Gdns IG8 ..**110** D1
Fontwell Park Gdns
  RM12 ....**155** E8
Forbes Cl RM11 .....**136** B3
Ford Cl Basildon SS15 **141** A6
  Rainham RM13 ......**154** F5
Ford End IG8 ....**110** B4
Ford Ho SS3 ....**183** C6
Ford La RM10 ....**154** A5
Ford Rd Dagenham RM10 **154** A5
  Northfleet DA11 .....**178** B2
Fordham Cl RM11 ...**137** A4
Fordhams Row RM16 **174** B8
Fordson Rd CM2 ......**33** B6
Fordview Ind Est RM13 **154** D2
Fordyce Cl RM11 ....**137** A4
Fordyke Rd RM8 ....**134** F2
Fore St Basildon SS19 **119** E2
  Harlow CM17 ....**11** C4
Forebury Ave CM21 ....**1** F1
Forebury Cres CM21 ...**1** F1
Forebury The CM21 ....**1** F1
Forefield Gn CM1 .....**32** F7
Forelands Pl CM21 ....**1** F1
Foremans CM1 ....**31** B3
Foremark Cl IG6 .....**111** F4
Forest App Chingford E4 **87** D2
  Woodford IG8 ....**110** A3
Forest Ave Chigwell IG7 **111** A5
  Chingford E4 ....**87** D2
Forest Cl
  Waltham Abbey EN9 ...**66** B1
  Wanstead E11 ....**132** A6
  Woodford IG8 ....**110** B6
Forest Ct Chingford E4 .**87** F1
  Loughton IG10 ....**88** D6
Forest Dr Chelmsford CM1 **31** E1
  Chingford IG8 ....**109** E3
  Fyfield CM5 ....**27** C1
  Theydon Bois CM16 ...**67** E3
  Wanstead E12 ....**132** D1
Forest Edge IG8 .....**110** D7
Forest Farm Cotts IG6 **111** E2
Forest Glade
  Basildon SS16 ....**140** F4
  Chingford E4 ....**109** E5
  Epping CM16 ....**46** E4
Forest Ho E4 ....**87** E2
Forest Hts IG9 ....**110** A8
Forest Ind Pk IG6 ...**111** E2
Forest La IG7 ....**111** A5
Forest Mount Rd IG8 **109** D3
Forest Rd Chingford E17 **109** D1
  Loughton IG10 ....**88** E5
  Redbridge IG6 ....**112** B4
  Romford RM7 ....**135** B8
  Woodford IG8 ....**110** A7
Forest Side
  Buckhurst Hill IG9 .....**88** C1
  Chingford E4 ....**87** F1
  Epping CM16 ....**67** D6
Forest Terr IG8 ......**111** A5
Forest View E4 ....**87** D2
Forest View Dr SS9 .**146** C3
Forest View Rd
  Chingford E17 ....**109** C2

Forest View Rd continued
  Loughton IG10 ....**88** D5
Forest Way Loughton IG10 **88** E6
  Woodford IG8 ....**110** B6
Forester Ct CM12 .....**96** F3
Forfar Cl SS9 ....**146** B2
Forge Cotts CM22 .....**2** F7
Forres Cl EN11 ....**21** A8
Forrest Ind Est CM16 **116** D6
Forres Prim Sch EN11 ..**8** B1
Forrest Cl CM3 ......**101** C7
Forster Cl E4 ....**109** D3
Forsters Cl RM6 ....**134** F5
Forsythia Cl
  Chelmsford CM1 ......**32** E7
  Ilford IG1 ....**152** B7
Fort Rd RM18 ....**179** C5
Fort William Rd SS16 **142** B2
Forterie Gdns IG3 ...**153** E8
Fortescue Chase SS1 **148** F1
Forth Rd RM14 .....**137** D5
Fortin Cl RM15 ......**172** A6
Fortin Path RM15 ...**172** A6
Fortin Way RM15 ...**172** A6
Fortinbras Way CM2 ..**54** B8
Fortune Ct IG11 .....**153** C2
Fortune Stps **2** SS1 **167** C7
Fortunes The CM18 ...**23** F6
Forum The SS2 ......**148** A5
Fosbery Ct EN3 ....**65** A2
Fossetts Way SS2 ...**148** C4
Fossway RM8 ....**134** C2
Fostal Cl SS9 ....**146** E3
Foster St CM17 ....**25** A7
Foster Rd SS8 ......**164** C4
Fosters Cl Woodford E18 **110** B2
  Writtle CM1 ....**30** C1
Foulgar Cl CM3 ......**101** E8
Founders Rd EN11 ....**8** B1
Foundry SS5 ....**124** E6
Founes Dr RM16 ....**172** E5
Fountain Farm CM18 ..**23** F6
Fountain La SS16 ...**124** B6
Fountain Pl EN9 ......**65** C5
Fountain Rd CM1 .....**16** C4
Fountain Wlk DA11 .**178** F1
Fountains The IG10 ..**88** B7
Four Acres The CM21 ..**2** A1
Four Sisters Cl SS9 .**146** F5
Four Sisters Way SS9 **146** F5
Four Wantz The CM5 ..**49** A4
Four Wents The E4 ..**109** C6
Fourth Ave
  Basildon SS16 ....**140** E3
  Chelmsford CM1 ......**32** B5
  Harlow CM19 ....**23** B8
  Romford RM7 ....**135** D3
  Stanford-le-H SS17 ...**160** D3
  Wickford SS11 ....**122** A6
Fourth Wlk SS8 .....**163** E4
Fourways Ct **1** EN11 ..**21** A7
Fowey Ave IG4 ......**132** D6
Fowler Cl SS1 ....**167** C8
Fowler Ct CM2 ....**54** A4
Fowler Rd IG6 ......**112** C5
Fox Burrow Rd IG7 ..**112** C6
Fox Burrows La CM1 ..**31** B2
Fox Cl Romford RM5 .**113** B5
  Thundersley SS7 ....**144** B5
Fox Cres CM1 ....**31** F4
Fox Hatch CM15 ......**71** E5
Fox House Rd DA17 .**169** B1
Fox Manor Way RM20 **177** B8
Foxborough Chase CM4 ..**76** B5
Foxes Gn RM16 .....**174** A4
Foxes Gr CM13 ....**96** C2
Foxes Par EN9 ....**65** C6
Foxfield Cl SS5 ......**125** C6
Foxfield Dr SS17 ....**160** E5
Foxglove Cl EN11 ......**8** C1
Foxglove Gdns E11 ..**132** C7
Foxglove Rd
  Romford RM7 ....**135** E2
  South Ockendon RM15 **172** C5
Foxglove Way CM1 ....**32** F6
Foxgloves The CM12 ..**96** F5
Foxhall Rd Mayland CM0 **83** E7
  Steeple CM0 ....**84** B7
  Upminster RM14 .....**156** C5
Foxhatch SS12 ......**121** F6
Foxhills Rd RM16 ...**173** D5
Foxholes Rd CM2 .....**54** F6
Foxhunter Wlk CM11 ..**97** D6
Foxlands Cres RM10 **154** C7
Foxlands Rd RM10 ...**154** C7
Foxleigh CM12 ......**119** A8
Foxleigh CM12 ......**119** A8
Foxley Cl IG10 ....**89** B7
Foxmeadows SS7 ...**144** F6
Foxton Rd Grays RM20 **177** B8
  Hoddesdon EN11 ......**21** A6
Foxwood Chase EN9 ..**65** C5
Foxwood Ct SS9 ....**146** D2
Foxwood Pl SS9 ....**146** D2
Foyle Dr RM15 ......**172** A7
Foys Wlk CM11 .....**119** C2

Frances Cottee Lodge
  SS6 ....**146** A8
Frances Gdns RM15 .**171** F7
Frances Gn CM1 ......**33** A7
Frances Rd E4 ......**109** A4
Francis Ave IG1 ....**133** D2
Francis Cl SS17 .....**159** F3
Francis Ct Harlow CM20 **10** B2
  3 Basildon SS14 ...**142** E4
Francis Green Ho **7** EN9 **65** B6
Francis Mews CM9 ...**59** B8
Francis Rd IG1 ......**133** D2
Francis St IG1 ......**133** D2
Francis Wks EN11 ....**21** B6
Francis Wlk SS6 ....**123** D2
Francisco Ct RM16 ..**172** C3
Francombe Gdns RM1 **136** A5
Frank Bailey Wlk E12 **152** D2
Frank Slater Ho **4** IG3 **134** B3
Frankland Cl IG8 ....**110** C5
Frankland Rd E4 ....**109** A5
Franklin Rd
  Hornchurch RM12 ....**155** C6
  North Fambridge CM3 **103** B8
Franklins RM15 .....**171** D7
Franklins Way SS11 .**121** E8
Franklyn Gdns IG6 ..**111** D4
Franks Cotts RM14 .**138** B3
Franmil Rd RM12 ...**136** B3
Fraser Cl Basildon SS15 **140** F6
  Chelmsford CM2 ......**54** C8
  Southend-on-S SS3 ..**168** F8
Fraser Rd DA8 ......**169** D1
Frating Cres IG8 ....**110** B4
Frayes Chase CM5 ...**15** A3
Frazer Cl RM1 ......**135** E5
Fred Leach Ho **1** SS8 **164** A3
Frederica Rd E4 ......**87** D2
Frederick Andrews Ct
  RM17 ....**178** D8
Frederick Rd RM13 .**154** E3
Fredrick J French Meml
  Homes CM1 ....**32** B6
Freeborne Gdns RM13 **155** A6
Freeman Ct SS17 ...**160** F3
Freeman Way RM11 .**136** F5
Freemantle Ho RM18 **178** D4
Freightmaster Est
  RM13 ....**170** A2
Fremantle SS3 ......**168** D5
Fremantle Cl CM3 ....**79** D1
Fremantle Rd
  Belvedere DA17 .....**169** A2
  Redbridge IG6 ......**111** C1
Fremnells The SS14 .**142** D7
French Rd CM3 ....**80** F1
French's Cl SG12 ......**8** B4
French's Wlk **4** CM2 ..**32** C2
Frerichs Cl SS12 ....**121** D5
Fresh Wharf Est IG11 **152** B4
Fresh Wharf Rd IG11 **152** B4
Freshfields Ave RM14 **156** C7
Freshwater Cres CM9 ..**37** B4
Freshwater Dr SS16 .**142** F4
Freshwater Rd RM8 .**134** E3
Freshwaters CM20 ...**10** E1
Frettons SS14 ......**142** E6
Friar's Ave CM15 .....**95** A2
Friar's Cl CM15 ......**95** A2
Friars Cl Basildon SS15 **141** C6
  Chingford E4 ....**109** C7
  Ilford IG1 ....**133** D3
Friars Gate Cl IG8 ..**110** A6
Friars Jun & Inf Sch
  SS3 ....**168** F8
Friars La
  Hatfield Heath CM22 ...**3** C1
  Maldon CM9 ....**36** F2
Friars St SS3 ....**168** F7
Friars The Chigwell IG7 **111** E6
  Harlow CM19 ....**23** A6
Friars Wlk CM2 ....**32** B1
Friarscroft EN10 ......**21** A3
Friary Fields CM9 .....**37** A2
Friary La IG8 ....**110** A6
Friday Hill E4 ......**109** E7
Friday Hill E E4 ....**109** E7
Friday Hill W E4 ....**109** E8
Friday Rd DA8 ......**169** D1
Friern Gdns SS12 ...**121** B7
Friern Pl SS12 ......**121** B6
Friern Wlk SS12 ....**121** B7
Frimley Ave RM11 ..**137** A3
Frimley Rd IG3 .....**133** E1
Frinton Dr IG8 ......**109** D3
Frinton Mews IG2 ..**133** A5
Frinton Rd RM5 .....**113** A4
Friston Path **4** IG6 **111** E5
Frithwood Cl CM12 .**118** F7
Frithwood La CM12 .**118** F7
Frizlands La RM10 .**135** B1
Frobisher Cl
  Basildon SS15 ......**141** D6
  Maldon CM9 ....**59** A8
Frobisher Way
  Greenhithe DA9 .....**177** B3
  Southend-on-S SS3 ..**149** E1
Froden Brook CM11 .**119** C2
Froden Cl CM11 .....**119** C2
Froden Ct CM11 .....**119** C2
Frog La RM13 ......**169** D8
Frog St CM15 ....**93** E8
Froghall La IG7 ....**111** D6
Frogmore Est RM20 **172** A1
Frome RM18 ....**175** C2
Front La CM14 .....**137** A6

Fry Cl RM5 . . . . .113 A4
Fryerning La CM4 . . . . . .74 B4
Fryerns Terr SS14 . . . . . .142 F8
Fryth The SS14 . . . . .142 E8
Fuchsia Cl RM7 . . . . .135 E2
Fulbourne Rd E17 . . . . . .109 C1
Fulbrook La RM15 . . . . . .171 F6
Fulcher Ave CM2 . . . . . . .32 F3
Fulford Dr SS9 . . . . .147 A6
Fullarton Cres RM15 . . . .171 F7
Fullbridge CM9 . . . . .37 A3
Fuller Rd RM8 . . . . .153 C6
Fuller Terr IG1 . . . . .152 D7
Fuller's Ave IG8 . . . . . . .109 F3
Fuller's La RM5 . . . . .113 C3
Fuller's Rd E18 . . . . .109 F3
Fullers Cl Romford RM5 . .113 C3
Waltham Abbey EN9 . . . . . .66 A6
Fullers Mead CM17 . . . . . .24 C1
Fullman Ind Pk SS8 . . . . .163 C3
Fullwell Ave IG5 . . . . . . .111 B2
Fullwell Ct IG5 . . . . .111 A2
Fullwell Par IG5 . . . . . . .111 A2
Fullwood Prim Sch IG6 . .133 C7
Fulmar Rd CM2 . . . . .155 B6
Fulmar Way SS11 . . . . . .122 A5
Fulton Ct 3 EN3 . . . . . . .65 A1
Fulton Rd SS7 . . . . .144 D7
Fulwich Rd DA1 . . . . .176 A1
Furlong Way SG12 . . . . . . .8 A7
Furlongs SS16 . . . . .142 D4
Furlongs The CM4 . . . . . . .74 B3
Furness Cl RM16 . . . . . . .174 B1
Furness Way RM12 . . . . .155 A7
Furrowfelde SS16 . . . . . .142 A4
Further Mdw CM1 . . . . . . .53 A8
Furtherwick Park Sch
  SS8 . . . . .164 C3
Furtherwick Rd SS8 . . . . .164 C2
Furze Farm Cl RM6 . . . . .112 C1
Furze Glade SS16 . . . . . .141 B4
Furze Inf Sch RM6 . . . . . .134 C5
Furze La CM4 . . . . .76 A1
Fuschia Ct IG8 . . . . .109 C4
Fusedale Way RM15 . . . .171 F6
Fyefields SS13 . . . . .143 C7
Fyfield Ave SS12 . . . . . . .121 C5
Fyfield Bsns & Research Pk
  CM5 . . . . .49 B6
Fyfield Cl CM13 . . . . .139 D5
Fyfield Dr RM15 . . . . . . .171 F6
Fyfield Dr Walker's CE Prim
  Sch CM5 . . . . .27 D2
Fyfield Ho RM9 . . . . .153 B6
Fyfield Path SS6 . . . . . . .123 A3
Fyfield Rd
  Chipping Ongar CM5 . . . . .49 A5
  Moreton CM5 . . . . .26 F3
  Rainham RM13 . . . . .154 F4
  Willingale CM5 . . . . .28 C3
  Woodford IG8 . . . . .110 C3

G

Gabion Ave RM19 . . . . . .171 D2
Gable Hall Sch SS17 . . . .161 A5
Gablefields CM2 . . . . .55 D6
Gables The Barking IG11 .152 C6
  Basildon SS13 . . . . .143 B8
  Sawbridgeworth CM21 . . . . .1 E2
  Southend-on-S SS9 . . . . .146 D1
  Southend-on-S, Eastwood
    SS9 . . . . .146 B6
  Brentwood CM13 . . . . . . .116 C4
Gabriel Cl Grays RM16 . . .172 C3
  Romford RM5 . . . . .113 C3
Gadsden Cl RM14 . . . . . .137 E5
Gafzelle Dr SS8 . . . . .164 E3
Gaiger Cl CM1 . . . . .32 D7
Gains Cl SS8 . . . . .164 D4
Gainsborough Ave
  Canvey Island SS8 . . . . . .164 E3
  Little Ilford E12 . . . . .152 A7
  Tilbury RM18 . . . . .179 B6
Gainsborough Cl CM11 . . .97 B1
Gainsborough Cres CM2 . .32 E3
Gainsborough Ct 4
  CM14 . . . . .116 C6
Gainsborough Dr SS0 . . . .147 E2
Gainsborough Ho
  Barking RM8 . . . . .153 B8
  Redbridge IG8 . . . . .111 B4
Gainsborough Pl
  Brentwood CM13 . . . . .95 D1
  Chigwell IG7 . . . . .111 F7
Gainsborough Rd
  Dagenham RM8 . . . . .134 B1
  Rainham RM13 . . . . .155 A4
  Woodford IG8 . . . . .110 E4
Gainsthorpe Rd CM5 . . . . .48 D8
Gaitskell Ho RM16 . . . . . .173 B5
Galadriel Spring CM3 . . . .101 C6
Galahad Cl CM0 . . . . .106 B5
Gale St RM9 . . . . .153 D5
Galeborough Ave IG8 . . . .109 D3
Gales Way IG8 . . . . .110 E3
Galey Gn RM15 . . . . .172 B8
Galleon Bvd DA2 . . . . . . .176 D3
Galleon Cl DA8 . . . . .169 D2
Galleon Rd RM16 . . . . . . .172 C2
Galleons Dr IG11 . . . . . . .153 A2
Galleons Hill CM1 . . . . . . .30 B5
Galley Cl SS3 . . . . .8 A2
Galley Hill Rd
  Northfleet DA11 . . . . .178 A2
  Swanscombe DA10 . . . . . .177 F2

Galley Hill Trad Est
  DA10 . . . . .177 E2
Galleydene SS7 . . . . .145 C3
Galleydene Ave CM2 . . . . .54 C3
Galleyhill Rd EN9 . . . . . . .65 E7
Galleywood Cres RM5 . . .113 D4
Galleywood Rd
  Chelmsford CM2 . . . . .54 A5
  Great Baddow CM2 . . . . . .54 C5
Galliford Rd CM9 . . . . .37 A4
Galliford Road Ind Est
  CM9 . . . . .37 A4
Gallions Cl IG11 . . . . .153 D7
Gallops The SS16 . . . . . . .141 B5
Gallows Cnr RM3 . . . . . . .114 C2
Galsworthy Ave RM6 . . . .134 B4
Galsworthy Rd RM18 . . . .179 C6
Galton Rd SS0 . . . . .166 C8
Gambleside SS16 . . . . . . .142 E3
Gammon Field RM16 . . . .173 D5
Gandalf's Ride CM3 . . . . .101 D6
Ganels Cl CM11 . . . . .119 C7
Ganels Rd CM11 . . . . .119 C7
Gangies Hill CM21 . . . . .1 A4
Ganley Cl 6 CM11 . . . . . . .97 B2
Gant Ct EN9 . . . . .65 E4
Gants Hill Sta IG2 . . . . . .133 B5
Gantshill Cres IG2 . . . . . .133 A6
Garbutt Rd RM14 . . . . . . .137 C2
Garden Cl Althorne CM3 . . .82 F4
  Chingford E4 . . . . .109 A5
  Steeple CM0 . . . . .61 F3
Garden Ct RM14 . . . . .137 E3
Garden End CM4 . . . . .75 F2
Garden Fields CM0 . . . . . . .61 F3
Garden Hos The CM21 . . . . .2 B3
Garden Terrace Rd CM17 . 11 C4
Garden Way IG10 . . . . .67 A1
Garden Wharf DA8 . . . . . .169 F1
Gardeners CM2 . . . . .54 D5
Gardeners La SS4 . . . . . . .104 F1
Gardenia Way IG8 . . . . . .110 A5
Gardens Fields CM5 . . . . . .70 E5
Gardens The
  Doddinghurst CM15 . . . . . .72 B3
  Southend-on-S SS9 . . . . .146 F7
Gardiner Cl RM8 . . . . .153 D8
Gardiners Cl SS14 . . . . . .120 D1
Gardiners La N CM11 . . . .120 E4
Gardiners La S SS14 . . . . .120 E2
Gardiners Link SS14 . . . . .120 D1
Gardiners The CM17 . . . . .24 B8
Gardiners Way SS14 . . . . .120 D2
Gardner Ave E11 . . . . . . .132 B5
Gardners Ct RM7 . . . . . . .135 C6
Garenne Ct 8 E4 . . . . .87 C1
Garfield Rd E4 . . . . .87 D1
Garland Way RM11 . . . . . .136 E7
Garner Ct RM8 . . . . .134 D3
Garner Rd E17 . . . . .109 C2
Garners The SS4 . . . . .125 E2
Garnon Mead CM16 . . . . . .46 D3
Garrettlands CM2 . . . . .55 F6
Garrick Ho RM12 . . . . . . .136 A2
Garrick St RM11 . . . . .179 B1
Garrison Par RM19 . . . . . .171 A2
Garry Cl RM1 . . . . .113 B3
Garry Way RM1 . . . . .113 B3
Garth Rd RM15 . . . . .157 C1
Gartmore Rd IG3 . . . . . . .133 F2
Gascoigne Gdns IG8 . . . . .109 E3
Gascoigne Prim Sch
  IG11 . . . . .152 C4
Gascoigne Rd IG11 . . . . . .152 C4
Gascoigne Way CM11 . . . . .97 D2
Gascoyne Ct RM3 . . . . . . .114 D2
Gasson Rd DA10 . . . . .177 L1
Gate Lodge Sq SS15 . . . . .119 C2
Gate Lodge Way SS15 . . . .119 F2
Gate St CM9 . . . . .36 F3
Gate Street Mews CM9 . . .36 F3
Gatehope Dr RM15 . . . . . .171 F7
Gatehouse Mews CM4 . . . .74 B3
Gatehouse The 4 RM1 . . .135 E6
Gateway SS14 . . . . .142 B6
Gateway Com Prim Sch The
  DA1 . . . . .176 B1
Gatscombe Cl SS5 . . . . . .124 D6
Gattens The SS6 . . . . .123 F4
Gatwick View CM12 . . . . .119 B8
Gatwick Way RM12 . . . . . .136 F1
Gavenny Path RM15 . . . . .171 F7
Gay Bowers
  Basildon SS14 . . . . .142 D7
  Hockley SS5 . . . . .124 B6
Gay Bowers La CM3 . . . . . .56 F7
Gay Bowers Rd CM3 . . . . . .56 F5
Gay Gdns RM10 . . . . .154 D2
Gay Links SS14 . . . . .142 B7
Gayfere Rd IG5 . . . . .132 F8
Gayleighs SS6 . . . . .123 D4
Gaylor Rd RM18 . . . . .178 F6
Gaynes Ct RM14 . . . . .156 B8
Gaynes Hill Rd IG8 . . . . . .110 E3
Gaynes Park Rd RM14 . . .156 B8
Gaynes Rd RM14 . . . . . . .137 B2
Gaynes Sch RM14 . . . . . . .156 C7
Gaynesford SS16 . . . . . . .141 E4
Gays La SS4 . . . . .104 E2
Gaysham Ave IG2 . . . . . . .133 C5
Gaysham Hall IG5 . . . . . . .133 B8
Gayton Rd SS2 . . . . .148 A5
Gaywood SS15 . . . . .141 A4
Gearies Inf Sch IG2 . . . . .133 B6
Gearies Jun Sch IG2 . . . . .133 B6

Geariesville Gdns IG6 . . .133 B7
Geary Ct CM14 . . . . .94 C1
Geary Dr CM14 . . . . .94 C1
Geddings Rd EN11 . . . . . . .21 B6
Geesh Rd SS14 . . . . .164 C5
Geisthorp Ct EN9 . . . . .66 A6
Gelsthorpe Rd RM5 . . . . .113 B3
Generals La CM3 . . . . .20 B2
Genesta Rd SS0 . . . . .166 D8
Geneva Gdns RM6 . . . . . .134 E6
Genever Cl E4 . . . . .109 A5
Genk Cl SS8 . . . . .164 B5
Gennep Rd SS8 . . . . .164 B5
Gennep Rd S SS8 . . . . . . .164 B5
Gentry Cl SS17 . . . . .160 C2
George Avey Croft .47 B5
  CM3 . . . . .60 E1
George Cl SS8 . . . . .163 F6
George Comberton Wlk 5
  E12 . . . . .152 A7
George Crooks Ho
  RM17 . . . . .178 B8
George Ct CM2 . . . . .32 B1
George Davies Lodge
  IG6 . . . . .133 C6
George Green Villas CM22 .2 B8
George La Wanstead E18 132 B4
  Woodford E18 . . . . .110 A1
George Lovell Dr EN3 . . . .65 C2
George Rd E4 . . . . .109 A4
George St Barking IG11 . . .152 C5
  Chelmsford CM2 . . . . .32 B1
  Grays RM17 . . . . .178 A8
  Romford RM1 . . . . .135 F5
  Southend-on-S SS3 . . . . .168 G6
George Tilbury Ho
  RM16 . . . . .174 B4
George Williams Ho
  RM7 . . . . .135 F4
Georges Dr CM15 . . . . . . .93 F4
Georgeville Gdns IG6 . . . .133 B7
Gepp Pl CM2 . . . . .33 B4
Gepps Cl CM1 . . . . .6 D2
Gerald Rd RM8 . . . . .134 F3
Gerard Gdns RM13 . . . . . .154 E3
Gerboa Ct 7 E4 . . . . .109 D5
Gernon Cl Broomfield CM1 . 19 B3
  Rainham RM13 . . . . .155 D3
Gernons SS14 . . . . .141 F4
Gerpins La RM14 . . . . . . .156 A4
Gerrard Cres CM14 . . . . . .116 C7
Gertrude Rd DA17 . . . . . .169 A2
Geylen Rd SS8 . . . . .164 E4
Ghyllgrove SS14 . . . . .142 E6
Ghyllgrove Cl SS14 . . . . . .142 B8
Ghyllgrove Jun & Inf Sch
  SS14 . . . . .142 A7
Gibb Croft CM18 . . . . .23 D4
Gibbards Cott 1 IG11 . . . .152 F5
Gibbfield Cl RM6 . . . . .134 E8
Gibcracks SS14 . . . . .142 E6
Gibraltar Cl CM13 . . . . . . .116 C4
Gibraltar Ho CM13 . . . . . .116 C4
Gibson Cl CM16 . . . . .47 C6
Gibson Ct Harlow CM18 . . .23 E5
  7 Romford RM1 . . . . .135 E5
Gibson Rd RM8 . . . . .134 C3
Gibson Vale CM1 . . . . .32 B8
Gidea Ave RM2 . . . . .136 A8
Gidea Cl Romford RM2 . . .136 A8
  South Ockendon RM15 . . .157 C2
Gidea Park Coll RM2 . . . . .136 A8
Gidea Park Prim Sch
  RM2 . . . . .136 A8
Gidea Park Sta RM2 . . . . .136 B7
Gideon Cl DA17 . . . . .169 B2
Gideons Way SS17 . . . . . .160 E3
Giffards Jun & Inf Schs
  SS17 . . . . .160 F4
Gifford Cl SS13 . . . . .143 B5
Gifford Pl CM14 . . . . .116 C6
Gifford Rd SS7 . . . . .144 D5
Giffords Cross Ave
  SS17 . . . . .161 A4
Giffords Cross Rd SS17 . . .161 B3
Giffordside RM16 . . . . . . .174 B1
Gifhorn Rd SS8 . . . . .164 A4
Gilbert Calvin Prim Sch
  IG5 . . . . .111 A1
Gilbert Cl Rayleigh SS6 . . .123 F2
  Swanscombe DA10 . . . . . .177 D1
Gilbert Dr SS16 . . . . .141 A5
Gilbert Rd
  Belvedere DA17 . . . . .169 A3
  Grays RM16 . . . . .172 C3
  Romford RM1 . . . . .135 F7
Gildborne Cl SS17 . . . . . .161 D5
Gilden Cl CM17 . . . . .11 E4
Gilden Way CM17 . . . . . . .11 D3
Gilders CM21 . . . . .1 D2
Giles Cl RM13 . . . . .155 D3
Gill Cl CM7 . . . . .36 F6
Gill The SS7 . . . . .145 D5
Gillam Way RM13 . . . . . . .155 A6
Gillian Cres RM2 . . . . . . .114 C1
Gilliflower Ho EN11 . . . . . .21 A5
Gillingham Ho 14 RM3 . . .114 E5
Gills Ave SS8 . . . . .164 C4
Gillwell La E4 . . . . .87 D5
Gilmore Way CM2 . . . . . . .55 B6
Gilmour Rise CM2 . . . . . . .96 F1
Gilpin's Gallop SG12 . . . . . .8 B4
Gilroy Cl RM13 . . . . .154 F6

Gilsland EN9 . . . . .65 E4
Gilson Cl SS2 . . . . .32 F2
Gilstead Hall Mews Cotts
  CM14 . . . . .93 A4
Gilstead Ho IG11 . . . . . . .153 B8
Gilston Pk CM20 . . . . .10 C7
Gilwell Cl E4 . . . . .87 B5
Gimli Watch CM3 . . . . . . .101 D6
Gippeswyk SS14 . . . . .142 C7
Gipson Park Cl SS9 . . . . . .146 D6
Gipsy La RM17 . . . . .178 C8
Girona Cl RM16 . . . . .172 C3
Gisborne Gdns RM13 . . . .154 F2
Gladden Ct CM18 . . . . .23 E4
Gladden Fields CM3 . . . . .101 C6
Glade Bsns Ctr The
  RM20 . . . . .171 F1
Glade Ct SS7 . . . . .110 F2
Glade Prim Sch IG5 . . . . .110 F1
Glade The Basildon SS16 . .95 A1
  Upminster RM14 . . . . . . .156 C7
  Brentwood CM13 . . . . .95 A1
Gladeswood Rd DA17 . . . .169 B2
Gladeway The EN9 . . . . . . .65 D6
Gladstone Cl CM2 . . . . . . .32 B1
Gladstone Gdns SS6 . . . . .123 C1
Gladstone Rd
  Buckhurst Hill IG9 . . . . . . .88 C1
  Hockley SS5 . . . . .124 E6
  Hoddesdon EN11 . . . . .21 B7
Gladwyns SS15 . . . . .141 E7
Glamis Dr RM11 . . . . .136 E3
Glamis Ho CM14 . . . . .116 C6
Glan Avon Mews CM17 . . . .24 C7
Glanmead CM15 . . . . .94 E1
Glanmire CM11 . . . . .97 D6
Glanthams Cl CM15 . . . . .116 F8
Glanthams Rd CM15 . . . . .116 F8
Glanville Dr RM11 . . . . . . .136 F3
Glasseys La SS6 . . . . .145 C8
Glastonbury Ave IG8 . . . . .110 D4
Glastonbury Chase SS0 . . .147 D8
Glebe Ave IG8 . . . . .110 A4
Glebe Cl
  Great Wakering SS3 . . . . .150 D3
  Rayleigh SS6 . . . . .123 C3
  Southend-on-S SS1 . . . . .167 E8
Glebe Cres CM1 . . . . .19 B1
Glebe Dr SS6 . . . . .123 C3
Glebe Field SS14 . . . . . . .142 C8
Glebe Gdns CM13 . . . . . . .117 C3
Glebe Jun & Inf Sch
  SS6 . . . . .123 C3
Glebe La CM0 . . . . .63 D1
Glebe Mdw CM3 . . . . .18 E7
Glebe Rd Chelmsford CM1 . .32 B3
  Chipping Ongar CM5 . . . . .48 F2
  Dagenham RM10 . . . . . . .154 B6
  Heybridge CM9 . . . . .37 C5
  Rainham RM13 . . . . .155 C1
  Wickford SS11 . . . . .121 E7
  Wickford, Ramsden Bellhouse
    CM11 . . . . .98 F1
Glebe The Harlow CM20 . . .10 E1
  Purleigh CM3 . . . . .58 D1
  Tilgate Green CM5 . . . . . . .25 D5
Glebe View CM2 . . . . .54 B3
Glebe Way
  Burnham-on-C CM0 . . . . .106 C6
  Hadleigh SS7 . . . . .145 F3
  Hornchurch RM11 . . . . . .136 E3
Glebelands Chigwell IG7 . .112 B7
  Harlow CM20 . . . . .10 F3
  South Benfleet SS7 . . . . . .144 B7
Glebelands Ave
  Ilford IG2 . . . . .133 D5
  Woodford E18 . . . . .110 A1
Glebeway IG8 . . . . .110 C6
Glen Ct SS7 . . . . .145 B4
Glen Faba Rd CM19 . . . . . .21 F6
Glen Hazel RM11 . . . . .72 D4
Glen Rd Basildon SS16 . . .142 F5
  South Benfleet SS7 . . . . . .144 E5
  Southend-on-S SS9 . . . . .166 A8
Glen Rise SS7 . . . . .110 B4
Glen The Basildon SS16 . . .143 A4
  Rainham RM13 . . . . .155 C1
  Rayleigh SS6 . . . . .124 B8
  Stanford-le-H SS17 . . . . . .160 F3
Glenarm Coll IG1 . . . . . . .133 B2
Glenavon Lodge 4 E18 132 A8
Glenbervie Dr SS9 . . . . . .146 F2
Glencoe Ave IG2 . . . . .133 E4
Glencoe Dr
  Dagenham RM10 . . . . . . .154 A8
  Wickford SS11 . . . . .122 A8
Glencree CM11 . . . . .97 D6
Glencrofts SS5 . . . . .124 F6
Glendale CM3 . . . . .79 E1
Glendale Ave RM6 . . . . . .134 C4
Glendale Cl CM15 . . . . . . .94 E1
Glendale Gdns SS9 . . . . . .146 D1
Glendale Ho CM15 . . . . . . .94 E2
Glendale Rd
  Burnham-on-C CM0 . . . . .106 C6
  Erith DA8 . . . . .169 C2
Glendower Rd E4 . . . . .87 D1
Gleneagles Cl RM3 . . . . . .114 F3
Gleneagles Gdns RM13 . .144 B5
Gleneagles Rd SS9 . . . . . .146 C5
Glenester Cl EN11 . . . . .8 A1
Glenfield Rd SS17 . . . . . . .161 B5
Glengall Rd IG8 . . . . .110 B4
Glenham Dr IG2 . . . . .133 B6

Fry – Gol **199**

Glenhurst Mans SS1 . . . . .167 B8
Glenhurst Rd SS2 . . . . . . .148 A2
Glenmead IG9 . . . . .88 C1
Glenmere SS16 . . . . .142 D2
Glenmere Park Ave SS7 145 B4
Glenmire Terr SG12 . . . . . .8 C4
Glenmore IG9 . . . . .88 C1
Glenmore Rd SS4 . . . . . . .125 C4
Glenmore St SS2 . . . . . . .148 D1
Glenmore Way IG11 . . . . .153 A3
Glenny Rd IG11 . . . . .152 C6
Glenridding SS7 . . . . .144 D5
Glenside Billericay CM11 . . .97 D2
  Chigwell IG7 . . . . .111 B4
Glenthorne Gdns IG6 . . . .133 B7
Glenton Cl RM1 . . . . .113 C3
Glenton Way RM1 . . . . . . .113 E3
Glenwood SS8 . . . . .163 F5
Glenwood Ave
  Hockley SS5 . . . . .124 F5
  Rainham RM13 . . . . .155 B5
  Southend-on-S, Eastwood
    SS9 . . . . .146 A2
  Southend-on-S, Prittlewell
    SS0 . . . . .147 D2
Glenwood Ct 5 E18 . . . . .132 A8
Glenwood Dr RM2 . . . . . . .136 A7
Glenwood Gdns
  Basildon SS16 . . . . .140 E4
  Ilford IG2 . . . . .133 A6
Glenwood Sch SS7 . . . . . .144 B7
Gleten Rd SS8 . . . . .164 C4
Globe Rd
  Hornchurch RM11 . . . . . .136 A5
  Woodford IG8 . . . . .110 C4
Glossop Ho 13 RM3 . . . . .114 E5
Gloucester Ave
  Chelmsford CM2 . . . . .54 C6
  East Tilbury RM18 . . . . . .175 D4
  Grays RM16 . . . . .173 C4
  Hornchurch RM11 . . . . . .137 A7
  Maldon CM9 . . . . .36 F1
  Rayleigh SS6 . . . . .146 A8
Gloucester Cres CM1 . . . . .32 A5
Gloucester Ct RM8 . . . . . .178 F5
Gloucester Gdns IG1 . . . . .132 E4
Gloucester Pl CM12 . . . . . .97 A5
Gloucester Rd
  Little Ilford E12 . . . . .132 F1
  Pilgrims Hatch CM15 . . . . .94 B4
  Romford RM1 . . . . .135 F5
  Wanstead E11 . . . . .132 C6
Gloucester Terr SS1 . . . . .168 A6
Glovers Field CM15 . . . . . .71 F2
Glovers La SS3 . . . . .24 E1
Glyders SS7 . . . . .144 E1
Glynde Way SS2 . . . . .148 E1
Glynn Rd CM0 . . . . .106 B5
Goat Hall La
  Chelmsford CM2 . . . . .53 F3
  Galleywood CM2 . . . . .54 A3
Goat House La CM3 . . . . . .57 F4
Goatsmoor La
  Billericay CM4,CM11 . . . . .97 F6
  Stock CM4 . . . . .98 A8
Goatswood La RM4 . . . . . .92 B2
Gobions SS15 . . . . .142 A4
Gobions Ave RM5 . . . . . . .113 D3
Goddard Rd RM16 . . . . . . .173 A5
Goddard Way CM2 . . . . . . .32 F2
Goddards Way IG1 . . . . . .133 D3
Godfreys Mews CM2 . . . . . .32 B1
Godman Rd RM16 . . . . . . .174 B3
Godsafe CM17 . . . . .11 E4
Godwin Cl E4 . . . . .65 C1
Godwin Prim Sch RM9 . . .153 E5
Goirle Ave SS8 . . . . .164 C4
Goldace RM17 . . . . .177 F8
Goldberry Mead CM3 . . . .101 C6
Goldcrest Dr CM11 . . . . . . .97 C1
Golden Cross SS4 . . . . . . .125 D4
Golden Cross Mews
  SS4 . . . . .125 D5
Golden Cross Par SS4 . . . .125 D5
Golden Cross Rd SS4 . . . .125 D6
Golden Jubilee Ct
  RM12 . . . . .136 A3
Golden Manor Dr SS7 . . . .144 F5
Goldenacres CM1 . . . . .32 F8
Goldfinch La SS7 . . . . . . .145 B4
Goldhanger Cl SS6 . . . . . .123 A3
Goldhanger Cross SS14 . .142 C7
Goldhanger Rd CM9 . . . . . .37 D4
Goldhaze Cl IG8 . . . . .110 D3
Golding Cres SS17 . . . . . .160 E3
Golding Ct 7 IG1 . . . . . . .133 A1
Golding Thoroughfare
  CM2 . . . . .32 F3
Golding's Hill IG10,CM16 . .66 F2
Goldingham Ave IG10 . . . . .89 C7
Goldings Cotts CM13 . . . .116 B1
Goldings Cres SS16 . . . . . .142 E3
Goldings Rd IG10 . . . . .89 A8
Goldings Rise IG10 . . . . . .89 A8
Goldington Cres CM12 . . . .96 F5
Goldlay Ave CM2 . . . . .32 C1
Goldlay Gdns CM2 . . . . . . .32 C1
Goldlay Rd CM2 . . . . .32 C1
Goldmer Cl SS3 . . . . .168 C8
Goldsands Rd CM0 . . . . . . .84 E2
Goldsborough Cres E4 . . .109 C4
Goldsmere Ct RM11 . . . . .136 E3
Goldsmith RM17 . . . . .177 F8
Goldsmith Ave RM7 . . . . .135 A4
Goldsmith Dr SS6 . . . . . . .123 D7
Goldsmith Ho IG8 . . . . . . .111 B4

Goldsmiths Ave
Corringham SS17 . . . . .161 A3
[4] Stanford-le-H SS17 . .160 F3
Goldsworthy Dr SS3 . . . . .150 C2
Golf Ride SS7 . . . . .144 D3
Golfe Rd IG1 . . . . .133 D1
Gooderham Ho RM16 . . . . .174 B4
Goodey Rd IG11 . . . . .152 F5
Goodier Rd CM1 . . . . .31 F4
Goodmans SS3 . . . . .150 B3
Goodmayes Ave IG3 . . . . .134 A3
Goodmayes Hospl IG3 . . . .134 A6
Goodmayes La IG3 . . . . . . .134 A4
Goodmayes Lodge RM8 . .153 A8
Goodmayes Prim Sch
  IG3 . . . . .134 B3
Goodmayes Rd IG3 . . . . . . .134 B3
Goodmayes Ret Pk IG3 . . .134 B3
Goodmayes Sta IG3 . . . . . .134 A3
Goodmayes Wlk [1]
  SS12 . . . . .121 D6
Goodridge Ho E17 . . . . . . .109 C3
Goodview Rd SS14 . . . . . . .120 A2
Goodwin Cl CM2 . . . . .54 D8
Goodwood Ave
  Brentwood CM13 . . . . .95 F3
  Hornchurch RM12 . . . . . . .155 E8
Goodwood Cl
  Hoddesdon EN11 . . . . .21 A7
  Thundersley SS7 . . . . .145 B7
Goose Cotts SS11 . . . . . . .100 E1
Goose La CM22 . . . . .2 E7
Gooseley La E6 . . . . .152 A2
Gooshays Dr RM3 . . . . . . .114 E4
Gooshays Gdns RM3 . . . . .114 E4
Gordon Ave Chingford E4 .109 E4
  Hornchurch RM12 . . . . . . .135 F2
Gordon Cl Billericay CM12 .96 F3
  East Tilbury RM18 . . . . . . .180 D7
Gordon Cotts RM4 . . . . . . .91 B5
Gordon Inf Sch IG1 . . . . . .133 D1
Gordon Pl [9]
  Gravesend DA12 . . . . .179 C1
  Southend-on-S SS1 . . . . . .166 F8
Gordon Promenade E
  DA12 . . . . .179 D1
Gordon Rd Barking IG11 . .152 E4
  Basildon SS14 . . . . .142 D5
  Belvedere DA17 . . . . .169 C2
  Brentwood CM15 . . . . .95 A1
  Chelmsford CM2 . . . . .54 A6
  Chingford E4 . . . . .87 C2
  Corringham SS17 . . . . .160 F3
  Dagenham RM6 . . . . .134 F5
  Gravesend DA11 . . . . .178 E1
  Grays RM16 . . . . .173 F3
  Holdbrook EN9 . . . . .65 A5
  Horndon-on-t-H SS17 . . . .159 F3
  Ilford IG1 . . . . .133 D1
  Southend-on-S SS9 . . . . . .146 B2
  Southend-on-S,Westcliff-on-S
    SS1 . . . . .166 F8
  Wanstead E11 . . . . .132 A5
  Woodford E18 . . . . .110 B2
Gordons SS13 . . . . .143 A4
Gore Rd SS4 . . . . .126 E6
Gore The SS14 . . . . .142 A7
Goresbrook Rd RM9 . . . . .153 D4
Goring Cl RM5 . . . . .113 C2
Goring Gdns RM8 . . . . . . .153 C8
Goring Rd RM10 . . . . .154 D6
Gorseway RM7 . . . . .135 E3
Gosfield Cl SS6 . . . . .123 A3
Gosfield Rd RM8 . . . . .135 A3
Gosford Gdns IG4 . . . . . . .132 F6
Goshawk Dr CM2 . . . . .54 B5
Goslings The SS3 . . . . .168 G7
Gosport Dr RM12 . . . . .155 C6
Gossetts The CM6 . . . . .15 E4
Gould Cl CM5 . . . . .26 C2
Goulds Cotts RM4 . . . . .90 B6
Goulton Rd CM1 . . . . .19 A1
Gourney Gr RM16 . . . . .173 B6
Government Row EN3 . . . . .65 A2
Gowan Brae SS7 . . . . .144 B5
Gowan Cl SS7 . . . . .144 B5
Gowan Ct SS7 . . . . .144 B5
Gowan Lea [4] E18 . . . . . .132 A7
Gower Ho [3] IG11 . . . . . . .152 C5
Gowers Ave CM2 . . . . .54 E6
Gowers La RM16 . . . . .174 A4
Gowers The CM20 . . . . .11 B2
Goya Rise SS3 . . . . .168 G8
Grace Cl IG6 . . . . .111 F4
Grace's Cross CM2 . . . . . . .55 C7
Graces La CM3 . . . . .34 B1
Grafton Gdns RM8 . . . . . . .134 E2
Grafton Inf Sch RM8 . . . . .134 D2
Grafton Jun Sch RM8 . . . .134 F2
Grafton Pl CM2 . . . . .33 A4
Grafton Rd
  Canvey Island SS8 . . . . . . .164 C2
  Dagenham RM8 . . . . .134 E2
Graham Cl Billericay CM12 97 C5
  Brentwood CM13 . . . . .95 C4
  Hockley SS5 . . . . .124 E7
  Stanford-le-H SS17 . . . . . .160 E4
Graham James Prim Sch
  SS17 . . . . .160 F3
Graham Mans [11] IG11 . .153 A5
Grahame Ct [3] SS12 . . . .121 D5
Grahame Ho SS2 . . . . .148 C3
Grainger Cl SS2 . . . . .148 A1
Grainger Rd SS2 . . . . .148 A1

Grainger Road Ind Est
  SS2 . . . . .148 A1
Grampian SS0 . . . . .147 E1
Granaries The EN9 . . . . . . .65 E5
Granary Cl CM3 . . . . .82 B5
Granary Ct
  [3] Dagenham RM6 . . . . . .134 D4
  Sawbridgeworth CM21 . . . . .1 E2
Granary Mdw CM15 . . . . . .72 C3
Granary The Roydon CM19 . .9 C3
  Stanstead Abbotts SG12 . . . .8 C3
Granby Rd DA11 . . . . .178 D1
Grand Court W SS9 . . . . . .165 F8
Grand Ct RM8 . . . . .134 E1
Grand Dr SS9 . . . . .165 F8
Grand Par SS9 . . . . .165 F8
Grandview Rd SS7 . . . . . . .144 F7
Grange Ave Mayland CM3 . .83 C7
  South Benfleet SS7 . . . . . .146 A5
  Wickford SS12 . . . . .121 C6
  Woodford IG8 . . . . .110 A3
Grange Cl Ingrave CM13 . .117 C5
  Southend-on-S SS9 . . . . . .146 E3
  Woodford IG8 . . . . .110 A3
Grange Cres
  Chigwell IG7 . . . . .111 D5
  [23] Dartford DA2 . . . . . . .176 B1
Grange Ct Chelmsford CM2 53 F7
  Loughton IG10 . . . . .88 D4
  Waltham Abbey EN9 . . . . . .65 C5
Grange Gdns
  Rayleigh SS6 . . . . .123 B3
  Southend-on-S SS1 . . . . . .167 B8
Grange Hill Sta IG7 . . . . . .111 D6
Grange Ho [6] IG11 . . . . . .152 D4
Grange La CM19 . . . . .22 C8
Grange Par CM11 . . . . .119 C7
Grange Park Dr SS9 . . . . . .146 F2
Grange Prim Sch SS12 . . .121 B6
Grange Rd Aveley RM15 . .171 C5
  Basildon SS13 . . . . .143 E8
  Billericay CM11 . . . . .119 D7
  Grays RM17 . . . . .178 B8
  Ilford IG1 . . . . .152 C8
  Pleshey CM3 . . . . .7 E2
  Romford RM3 . . . . .114 B4
  Southend-on-S SS9 . . . . . .146 D1
  Thundersley SS7 . . . . .144 F7
  Tillingham CM0 . . . . .64 A1
  Wickford SS11 . . . . .99 C2
Grange The
  Hoddesdon EN11 . . . . .21 A5
  Waltham Abbey EN9 . . . . . .65 D2
  [3] Wanstead E18 . . . . . . .132 A8
Granger Ave CM9 . . . . .36 F1
Granger Row CM1 . . . . .31 F6
Granger Way RM1 . . . . . . .136 A5
Grangeway
  Thundersley SS7 . . . . .145 A6
  Woodford IG8 . . . . .110 C6
Grangeway Gdns IG4 . . . .132 E6
Grangewood SS7 . . . . .144 D5
Grangewood Ave
  Grays RM16 . . . . .173 C3
  Rainham RM13 . . . . .155 C1
Grangewood Cl CM13 . . . .117 A2
Granites Chase CM11 . . . .119 F5
Grant Cl [12] SS12 . . . . . . .121 E5
Grant Ct [2] E4 . . . . .87 C1
Grantham Ct RM6 . . . . . . .134 F4
Grantham Gdns RM6 . . . . .134 F4
Grantham Lodge SS9 . . . .146 D1
Grantham Rd Ilford E12 . . .133 A1
  Little Ilford E12 . . . . .152 A8
Grantham Ware RM16 . . . .173 A5
Grantock Rd E17 . . . . .109 D2
Granton Ave RM14 . . . . . . .136 F2
Granton Rd IG3 . . . . .134 A3
Granville Cl
  Billericay CM12 . . . . .96 F5
  South Benfleet SS7 . . . . . .144 E4
Granville Gdns CM11 . . . . . .8 A2
Granville Rd Epping CM16 . .46 B2
  Hockley SS5 . . . . .102 F1
  Ilford IG1 . . . . .133 E2
  Woodford E18 . . . . .110 B1
Granville Terr [4] CM0 . . .106 C4
Grapnells SS16 . . . . .142 F4
Grapnells Farm Cotts
  SS4 . . . . .106 A2
Grasmead Ave SS9 . . . . . .146 F2
Grasmere Ave SS5 . . . . . . .101 D3
Grasmere Cl IG10 . . . . .88 F7
Grasmere Gdns IG4 . . . . . .132 F6
Grasmere Ho SS6 . . . . .123 D2
Grasmere Rd
  Canvey Island SS8 . . . . . . .163 E3
  Thundersley SS7 . . . . .144 E6
Grass Croft RM17 . . . . . . .173 B1
Grassmere Rd RM11 . . . . .136 F7
Gratmore Gn SS16 . . . . . . .142 F3
Gravel Cl IG7 . . . . .112 A8
Gravel Hill IG10 . . . . .66 A1
Gravel La IG7 . . . . .90 A3
Gravel Pit Farm CM19 . . . .23 C6
Gravel Rd SS9 . . . . .146 C8
Gravelly La CM1 . . . . .30 C3
Gravesend & North Kent
  Hospl DA11 . . . . .179 A1
Gravesend Sta DA11 . . . . .179 B1
Gravesend Mus★ DA11 . .179 B1
Gray Ave RM8 . . . . .134 F4
Gray Gdns RM16 . . . . .155 A6
Graylands RM17 . . . . .177 E8
Grays Ave SS16 . . . . .141 C1
Grays Convent High Sch
  RM17 . . . . .173 B2

Grays Cotts RM14 . . . . . . .137 D7
Grays End Cl RM17 . . . . . .173 A3
Grays Sch The RM17 . . . . .173 B3
Grays Sh Ctr RM17 . . . . . .178 A8
Grays Sta RM17 . . . . .178 A8
Grays Wlk CM13 . . . . .95 D2
Graysons Cl SS6 . . . . .123 E2
Great Baddow High Sch
  CM2 . . . . .54 D6
Great Berry Farm Chase
  SS16 . . . . .141 A4
Great Berry La SS16 . . . . .141 A5
Great Berry Prim Sch
  SS16 . . . . .140 F4
Great Brays CM18 . . . . .24 A7
Great Burches Rd SS7 . . . .145 A7
Great Cob CM1 . . . . .32 E5
Great Cullings RM7 . . . . . .135 C2
Great Eastern Ave SS2 . . .148 C5
Great Eastern Rd
  Brentwood CM14 . . . . .116 C6
  Hockley SS5 . . . . .124 E6
Great Fleete Way IG11 . . .153 C3
Great Fox Mdw CM15 . . . . .71 F1
Great Galley Cl IG11 . . . . .153 C2
Great Gardens Rd RM11 136 C5
Great Gibcracks Chase
  CM2 . . . . .56 A2
Great Godfreys CM1 . . . . . .30 F1
Great Gregorie SS16 . . . . .141 F5
Great Gregories La CM16 67 E6
Great Hays SS9 . . . . .146 C5
Great Hyde Hall CM21 . . . . .2 B3
Great Knightleys SS15 . . .141 E6
Great Lawn CM5 . . . . .49 A4
Great Leighs Way SS13 . .121 C1
Great Leylands CM18 . . . . .24 A7
Great Mdw EN10 . . . . .21 A1
Great Mead SS3 . . . . .149 E1
Great Mistley SS16 . . . . . .142 C5
Great Nelmes Chase
  RM11 . . . . .136 F6
Great Oaks
  Basildon SS14 . . . . .142 A6
  Brentwood CM13 . . . . .95 B3
  Chigwell IG7 . . . . .111 C6
Great Owl Rd IG7 . . . . .111 A7
Great Oxcroft SS15 . . . . . .141 B6
Great Plumtree CM20 . . . . .10 F2
Great Ranton SS13 . . . . . . .143 C8
Great Ropers La CM13 . . .116 B4
Great Saling SS11 . . . . .122 A6
Great Smials CM3 . . . . .101 C5
Great Spenders SS14 . . . .142 D8
Great Stony Pk CM5 . . . . . .49 A4
Great Wakering Prim Sch
  SS3 . . . . .150 A3
Great Waltham CE Prim Sch
  CM3 . . . . .18 E7
Great Warley St CM13 . . . .116 B1
Great Wheatley Rd SS6 . .123 B1
Greatfields Rd IG11 . . . . . .152 D4
Greathouse Chase SS17 . .161 C6
Greaves Cl IG11 . . . . .152 E5
Grebe Cl Barking IG11 . . . .153 A1
  Mayland CM3 . . . . .83 A4
Grebe Crest RM20 . . . . . . .172 A2
Greding Wlk CM13 . . . . . . .117 B8
Green Ave SS8 . . . . .163 E3
Green Cl Chelmsford CM1 . .32 D4
  Epping Green CM16 . . . . . . .45 B7
  Writtle CM1 . . . . .31 B1
Green Glade CM16 . . . . .67 C6
Green Glades RM11 . . . . . .137 A5
Green La
  Basildon, Steeple View
    CM12 . . . . .119 A2
  Basildon,Lee Chapel S
    SS16 . . . . .141 E4
  Brentwood CM14 . . . . .94 A1
  Burnham-on-C CM0 . . . . . .106 A7
  Canvey Island SS8 . . . . . . .163 F3
  Chigwell IG7 . . . . .111 E7
  Chigwell IG7 . . . . .89 C1
  Dagenham IG3,RM8 . . . . . .134 C2
  Dagenham RM8 . . . . .134 F4
  Great Warley CM13,CM14 .116 A3
  Hoddesdon EN10 . . . . .43 B8
  Ilford IG1,IG3 . . . . .133 E2
  Kelvedon Hatch CM14 . . . . .93 D8
  Little Burstead CM12,
    CM13 . . . . .118 C3
  Mayland CM3 . . . . .83 B6
  Orsett RM16 . . . . .173 C8
  Pilgrims Hatch CM15 . . . . . .94 C3
  Roxwell CM1 . . . . .30 A4
  South Woodham Ferrers
    CM3 . . . . .101 D8
  Southend-on-S SS9 . . . . . .146 E7
  Threshers Bush CM17 . . . . .25 A6
  Waltham Abbey EN9 . . . . . .66 D4
Green Mdws CM3 . . . . .57 B6
Green Mead CM3 . . . . .101 C8
Green Pk CM20 . . . . .23 E8
Green Rd SS7 . . . . .144 D1
Green Ride E4,IG9,IG10 . . .88 A4
Green St Harlow CM17 . . . . .11 D1
  Ingatestone CM4 . . . . .73 C4
Green The Blackmore CM4 .72 B8
  Chelmsford CM1 . . . . .31 F4
  Chingford E4 . . . . .87 D1
  Orsett RM16 . . . . .174 A8
  Southend-on-S SS9 . . . . . .146 E7
  Stanford-le-H SS17 . . . . . .160 D1
  Theydon Bois CM16 . . . . . . .67 D3
  Theydon Bois CM16 . . . . . . .67 E2
  Waltham Abbey EN9 . . . . . .65 C5
  Wanstead E11 . . . . .132 B5

Green The continued
  Wennington RM13 . . . . . . .170 E6
  West Tilbury RM18 . . . . . . .179 D8
  Woodford IG8 . . . . .110 A5
  Writtle CM1 . . . . .31 B1
  Buckhurst Hill IG9 . . . . .88 B1
  South Ockendon RM15 . . . .157 D2
Green Trees CM16 . . . . .68 A8
Green Trees Ave CM3 . . . . .80 F5
Green View CM16 . . . . .67 E2
Green Wlk
  Chipping Ongar CM5 . . . . . .49 A1
  Loughton IG10 . . . . .88 C2
  Woodford IG8 . . . . .110 E4
Green Wlk The E4 . . . . .87 D1
Greenacre La CM4 . . . . .97 E8
Greenacre Mews SS9 . . . .146 E2
Greenacres Epping CM16 . .45 F3
  Hadleigh SS7 . . . . .145 E3
Greenacres Cl RM13 . . . . . .155 E2
Greenbank Cl
  Chingford E4 . . . . .109 C8
  Romford RM3 . . . . .114 D7
Greenbanks
  Southend-on-S SS9 . . . . . .147 A2
  Upminster RM14 . . . . .137 B2
Greendyke SS8 . . . . .163 F5
Greener Ct EN3 . . . . .65 A2
Greenfield Rd RM9 . . . . . . .153 C4
Greenfield St EN9 . . . . .65 C5
Greenfields
  Billericay CM12 . . . . .119 A8
  Galleywood CM2 . . . . .54 C2
  Loughton IG10 . . . . .89 A5
Greenfields Cl
  Billericay CM12 . . . . .119 A8
  Brentwood CM13 . . . . .116 C4
  Loughton IG10 . . . . .89 A5
Greenheys Dr E18 . . . . . . .109 F1
Greenhill IG9 . . . . .88 C1
Greenhills CM20 . . . . .23 E8
Greenhithe Sta DA9 . . . . .177 A2
Greenlands SS4 . . . . .125 D4
Greenleafe Dr IG6 . . . . . . .133 B8
Greenleas
  Thundersley SS7 . . . . .145 B6
  Waltham Abbey EN9 . . . . . .65 E5
Greenoaks SS7 . . . . .144 E3
Greenock Way RM1 . . . . . .113 C3
Greens Cl The IG10 . . . . . . .89 A7
Greens Farm La CM11 . . . . .97 C1
Greenshaw CM15 . . . . .94 B2
Greenside RM8 . . . . .134 C3
Greenslade Rd IG11 . . . . . .152 D5
Greensleeves Dr CM14 . . .116 B5
Greenstead CM21 . . . . .1 E1
Greenstead Ave IG8 . . . . . .110 C4
Greenstead Cl
  Brentwood CM13 . . . . .95 C2
  Woodford IG8 . . . . .110 C4
Greenstead Cty Jun & Inf
  Schs SS14 . . . . .142 F6
Greenstead Gdns IG8 . . . .110 C4
Greenstead Cl SS14 . . . . . .142 F5
Greensted Log Church★
  CM5 . . . . .48 D2
Greensted Rd
  Chipping Ongar CM5 . . . . . .48 D2
  Loughton IG10 . . . . .88 D7
Greensted The SS14 . . . . . .142 F6
Greenstone Mews E11 . . . .132 A5
Greensward Coll The
  SS5 . . . . .124 F7
Greensward La SS5 . . . . . .124 F7
Greenview SS8 . . . . .163 F5
Greenway Billericay CM11 . .97 C8
  Brentwood CM13 . . . . .95 A4
  Harlow CM19 . . . . .22 E8
  Romford RM3 . . . . .115 B4
  Woodford IG8 . . . . .110 C6
Greenway Ct IG1 . . . . .133 B3
Greenway The SS11 . . . . . . .99 C3
Greenways
  Canvey Island SS8 . . . . . . .163 F5
  Chelmsford CM1 . . . . .32 B6
  Maldon CM9 . . . . .36 F2
  Rochford SS4 . . . . .125 F2
  [7] South Benfleet SS7 . . .144 C2
  Southend-on-S SS1 . . . . . .167 E7
Greenways Ct RM11 . . . . . .136 D5
Greenwich Way EN9 . . . . . .65 C3
Greenwood [3] IG8 . . . . . . .110 A3
Greenwood Ave
  Dagenham RM10 . . . . .154 B8
  South Benfleet SS7 . . . . . .144 E1
Greenwood Dr E4 . . . . .109 D5
Greenwood Gdns IG6 . . . .111 C5
Greenwood Ho RM17 . . . . .178 B8
Greenwood Mans [9]
  IG11 . . . . .153 A5
Greenwood Pl IG8 . . . . . . .110 A3
Greer Rd RM16 . . . . .173 B4
Gregory Cl SS5 . . . . .124 F4
Gregory Mews EN9 . . . . . . .65 B7
Gregory Rd RM6 . . . . .134 D7
Grenfell Ave RM12 . . . . . . .135 F3
Grenfell Gdns IG2 . . . . . . .133 F6
Grennan Cl CM13 . . . . .117 D4
Grenville Gdns IG8 . . . . . . .110 C4
Grenville Rd RM16 . . . . . . .173 B4
Gresham Cl CM14 . . . . .116 C7
Gresham Ct [4] CM14 . . . .116 C7
Gresham Dr RM6 . . . . .134 B5
Gresham Rd CM14 . . . . . . .116 C7
Grested Ct SS4 . . . . .125 F2
Grevatt Lodge SS13 . . . . . .143 C5

Grey Lady Pl CM11 . . . . . . .97 B3
Grey Ladys CM2 . . . . .54 B2
Grey Towers Ave RM11 . . .136 D3
Grey Towers Gdns
  RM11 . . . . .136 C3
Greyfriars CM13 . . . . .95 B2
Greygoose Pk CM19 . . . . . .23 A5
Greyhound La RM16 . . . . . .174 A4
Greyhound Pk SS2 . . . . . . .148 A1
Greyhound Way SS2 . . . . .148 A1
Greystone Gdns IG6 . . . . . .111 C1
Gridiron Pl RM14 . . . . .137 B2
Griffin Ave
  Canvey Island SS8 . . . . . . .164 C5
  Upminster RM14 . . . . .137 E5
Griffin Wlk DA9 . . . . .177 B2
Griffin's Wood Cotts
  CM16 . . . . .67 D7
Griffins The RM16 . . . . . . .173 B4
Griffith Cl RM8 . . . . .134 C3
Grifon Cl RM16 . . . . .172 C3
Grifon Rd RM16 . . . . .172 C3
Griggs App IG1 . . . . .133 C2
Griggs Gdns RM12 . . . . . . .155 C7
Grimshaw Way RM1 . . . . . .135 F6
Grimston Rd SS14 . . . . . . .142 F8
Grimstone Cl RM5 . . . . . . .113 B4
Grinstead La CM22 . . . . .2 C6
Grosvenor Cl
  Chelmsford CM2 . . . . .54 D7
  Loughton IG10 . . . . .89 B8
Grosvenor Ct
  Southend-on-S SS0 . . . . . .166 C7
  [3] Wanstead E11 . . . . . . .132 B6
Grosvenor Dr
  Hornchurch RM11 . . . . . . .136 C4
  Loughton IG10 . . . . .89 B8
Grosvenor Gdns
  Billericay CM12 . . . . .97 A4
  Upminster RM14 . . . . .137 D3
  Woodford IG8 . . . . .110 B4
Grosvenor Lodge [4]
  E18 . . . . .109 F1
Grosvenor Mans SS0 . . . . .166 C8
Grosvenor Mews SS0 . . . . .166 C7
Grosvenor Path IG10 . . . . . .89 B8
Grosvenor Rd
  Dagenham RM8 . . . . .134 F3
  Ilford IG1 . . . . .133 C1
  Orsett RM16 . . . . .174 D7
  Rayleigh SS6 . . . . .123 B5
  Romford RM7 . . . . .135 D4
  South Benfleet SS7 . . . . . .163 E8
  Southend-on-S SS0 . . . . . .166 C7
  Wanstead E11 . . . . .132 B6
Grove Ave SS16 . . . . .141 B3
Grove Cl SS6 . . . . .123 F2
Grove Cotts IG7 . . . . .111 F7
Grove Cres E18 . . . . .109 F1
Grove Ct
  Hornchurch RM11 . . . . . . .136 A3
  Rayleigh SS6 . . . . .124 B1
  Southend-on-S SS0 . . . . . .147 B3
  Upminster RM14 . . . . .156 A8
  Waltham Abbey EN9 . . . . . .65 B6
Grove End E18 . . . . .109 F1
Grove Gdns RM10 . . . . .135 C1
Grove Hill
  Southend-on-S SS9 . . . . . .146 B7
  Woodford E18 . . . . .109 F1
Grove Ho CM14 . . . . .116 B6
Grove Jun & Inf Sch
  SS6 . . . . .124 A1
Grove La Chigwell IG7 . . . .111 F7
  Epping CM16 . . . . .46 A1
Grove Lodge SS3 . . . . .168 G7
Grove Park Ave E4 . . . . . . .109 B3
Grove Park Rd RM13 . . . . .155 A4
Grove Pk E11 . . . . .132 B6
Grove Prim Sch RM6 . . . . .134 C6
Grove Rd Billericay CM12 . .96 F2
  Canvey Island SS8 . . . . . . .164 C4
  Chelmsford CM2 . . . . .32 B1
  Chingford E4 . . . . .109 C7
  Grays RM17 . . . . .178 C8
  Ilford RM6 . . . . .134 C5
  Northfleet RM17 . . . . .178 B2
  Rayleigh SS6 . . . . .123 F2
  South Benfleet SS7 . . . . . .144 D2
  Stanford-le-H SS17 . . . . . .175 D8
  Woodford E18 . . . . .109 F1
Grove Terr SS1 . . . . .167 A7
Grove The Bicknacre CM3 . .56 F1
  Billericay CM11 . . . . .97 C4
  Brentwood CM14 . . . . .115 F6
  [3] Gravesend DA12 . . . . .179 C1
  Southend-on-S SS2 . . . . . .148 C2
  Stanford-le-H SS17 . . . . . .175 D8
  Swanscombe DA10 . . . . . . .177 F2
  Upminster RM14 . . . . .156 B7
Grove Wlk SS3 . . . . .168 E2
Grovelands Rd SS12 . . . . . .121 D6
Grovelands Way RM17 . . . .172 F1
Grover Wlk SS17 . . . . .160 F3
Groves Cl RM15 . . . . .171 F6
Groveside Rd E4 . . . . .109 E7
Groveway RM8 . . . . .153 D8
Grovewood Ave SS9 . . . . . .146 B2
Grovewood Pl IG8 . . . . .110 B4
Guardian Bsns Ctr RM3 . .114 D3
Guardian Cl RM11 . . . . . . .136 B2
Guardsman Cl CM14 . . . . .116 D5
Gubbins La RM3 . . . . .114 F2
Guernsey Ct CM9 . . . . .36 F2
Guernsey Gdns SS11 . . . . . .99 D1
Guild Way [3] CM3 . . . . . . .101 E7
Guildford Ct SS2 . . . . .148 A1

Guildford Gdns RM3 ...114 E4
Guildford Rd
Chingford E17 ...109 C2
Ilford IG3 ...133 E2
Romford RM3 ...114 E4
Southend-on-S SS2 ...148 A1
Guilfords CM17 ...11 D5
Gull Wlk 1 RM12 ...155 B5
Gumley Rd RM20 ...177 E8
Gun Hill RM18 ...179 D8
Gun Hill Pl SS16 ...142 C5
Gunfleet SS3 ...168 C7
Gunn Rd DA10 ...177 E1
Gunnels Ct & Hastingwood Ct
6 IG9 ...110 C8
Gunner Dr EN3 ...65 A2
Gunners Gr E4 ...109 C7
Gunners Rd SS3 ...168 G7
Gunning Rd RM17 ...173 D1
Gunson Gate CM2 ...54 D7
Gurney Cl IG11 ...152 B6
Guru Gobind Singh Khalsa
Coll IG7 ...88 F1
Gustedhall La SS5 ...124 E3
Gutteridge La RM4 ...91 C3
Gutters La CM1 ...32 C7
Guy's Retreat IG9 ...88 C2
Guys Farm CM1 ...31 B1
Guys Farm Rd CM3 ...101 D7
Guysfield Cl RM13 ...155 A4
Guysfield Dr RM13 ...155 A4
Gwendalen Ave SS8 ...164 D4
Gwyn Cl CM3 ...20 E1
Gwynne Ho 3 E11 ...132 A6
Gwynne Park Ave IG8 ...110 F4
Gyllyngdune Gdns IG3 ...133 F1

H

Haarle Rd SS8 ...164 D2
Haarlem Rd SS8 ...163 D4
Haase Cl SS8 ...164 A6
Habgood Rd IG10 ...88 E6
Hackamore SS7 ...145 B5
Hackmans La
Cock Clarks CM3 ...57 E2
Cold Norton CM3 ...80 B6
Hacton Dr RM12 ...155 E8
Hacton La RM14 ...155 F8
Hacton Par RM12 ...136 F1
Hacton Prim Sch RM12 ...155 E8
Haddon Cl SS6 ...123 A4
Haddon Mead CM3 ...101 D5
Hadfield Rd SS17 ...160 D1
Hadleigh Castle* SS7 ...145 D1
Hadleigh Castle Ctry Pk*
SS7 ...145 B1
Hadleigh Ct
Brentwood CM14 ...116 A7
Chingford E4 ...87 E2
Hadleigh Hall Ct SS9 ...146 C1
Hadleigh Inf Sch SS7 ...145 E3
Hadleigh Jun Sch SS7 ...145 E3
Hadleigh Lodge 5 IG8 ...110 A4
Hadleigh Park Ave SS7 ...145 C3
Hadleigh Rd
Southend-on-S SS9 ...146 C1
Southend-on-S,Westcliff-on-S
SS0 ...166 E7
Hadley Grange CM17 ...24 C7
Hadrians Way CM9 ...37 A4
Hagg Hill CM3 ...80 D5
Haig Ct CM2 ...32 A1
Haig Rd RM16 ...174 A3
Haigville Gdns IG6 ...133 B7
Hailey Ave EN11 ...8 A2
Hailey La SG13 ...8 A2
Hailey Rd DA18 ...169 A4
Hailey Rd Bsns Pk DA18 ...169 A4
Hailsham Cl RM3 ...114 C5
Hailsham Gdns RM3 ...114 C5
Hailsham Rd RM3 ...114 C5
Hainault Ave
Rochford SS4 ...125 D4
Southend-on-S SS0 ...147 D2
Hainault Bridge Par 4
IG1 ...133 B2
Hainault Cl SS7 ...145 E4
Hainault Forest Ctry Pk*
IG7 ...112 C7
Hainault Forest High Sch
IG6 ...112 B5
Hainault Gore RM6 ...134 E6
Hainault Gr
Chelmsford CM1 ...31 E1
Chigwell IG7 ...111 C6
Hainault Rd Chigwell IG7 111 C6
Dagenham RM6 ...134 F5
Ilford RM6 ...134 B8
North Fambridge CM3 ...81 A1
Redbridge RM6 ...112 B2
Romford RM5 ...135 C8
Hainault St IG1 ...133 B2
Hainault Sta IG6 ...111 E3
Halbutt Gdns RM9 ...134 F1
Halbutt St RM9 ...153 F7
Halcyon Cvn Pk SS5 ...101 F4
Halcyon Way RM11 ...136 F3
Haldan Rd E4 ...109 C4
Haldane Cl EN3 ...65 B1
Haldon Cl 3 IG7 ...111 E5
Hale Cl E4 ...109 C7
Hale Cotts DA9 ...177 C2
Hale End RM3 ...114 B4
Hale End Rd E17 ...109 D2
Hale Ho RM11 ...136 A5
Hale The E4 ...109 D3
Halesworth Cl RM3 ...114 E3
Halesworth Rd RM3 ...114 E4
Half Moon Cotts CM21 ...1 B1
Half Moon La CM16 ...67 F8
Halfhides
Brentwood CM14 ...116 C6
Waltham Abbey EN9 ...65 D6
Halfway Ct RM19 ...171 A2
Halidon Rise RM3 ...115 B4
Halifax Ho 12 RM3 ...114 E5
Hall Ave RM15 ...171 C5
Hall Barns The CM5 ...70 C6
Hall Bridge Rise CM9 ...37 C4
Hall Chase CM6 ...7 D8
Hall Cl Great Baddow CM2 .55 A6
Stanford-le-H SS17 ...160 E4
Hall Cres Aveley RM15 ...171 C4
Hadleigh SS7 ...145 D3
Hall Est CM9 ...38 E7
Hall Farm Cl SS7 ...144 D1
Hall Farm Rd SS7 ...144 D1
Hall Green La CM13 ...95 D2
Hall La Brentwood CM15 ...95 A6
Chelmsford CM2 ...55 C6
Chingford E4 ...109 A6
Ingatestone CM4 ...74 C1
Romford RM14 ...115 C1
Shenfield CM15 ...94 F4
Shenfield CM15 ...94 F6
South Ockendon RM15 ...157 D3
Upminster RM14 ...137 D5
West Hanningfield CM2 ...76 D6
Hall Mead Sch RM14 ...137 D3
Hall Park Ave SS0 ...166 B8
Hall Park Rd RM14 ...156 C7
Hall Rd Asheldham CM0 ...85 C7
Aveley RM15 ...171 C4
Hockley SS5 ...125 A2
Ilford RM6 ...134 D5
Maldon CM9 ...37 B4
Rochford SS4 ...125 D1
Romford RM2 ...136 B8
Southminster CM0 ...84 E4
Hall St CM2 ...32 B1
Hall Terr Aveley RM15 ...171 D4
Romford RM3 ...115 A3
Hallam Cl CM15 ...72 B3
Hallam Ct CM12 ...96 F4
Hallet Rd SS8 ...164 E3
Halley Rd EN9 ...65 B3
Halling Hill CM20 ...10 F2
Hallingbury Rd CM21 ...2 A4
Hallmores EN10 ...21 A4
Hallowell Down CM3 ...101 E6
Hallsford Bridge Ind Est
CM5 ...71 C8
Hallwood Cres CM15 ...94 E2
Halsham Cres IG11 ...152 F7
Halstead Ct 5 SS12 ...121 C5
Halstead Ho 15 RM3 ...114 D4
Halstead Rd E11 ...132 B6
Halstead Way CM13 ...95 C3
Halston Ct SS17 ...161 B4
Halston Pl CM9 ...58 F8
Halstow Way SS13 ...143 C5
Halt Dr SS17 ...175 B2
Halt Robin La DA17 ...169 B2
Halt Robin Rd DA17 ...169 B2
Halton Rd RM16 ...174 C3
Haltwhistle Rd CM3 ...101 C8
Halyard Reach CM3 ...101 E5
Hamberts Rd CM3 ...79 E1
Hamble La RM15 ...171 F8
Hamble Way CM0 ...106 A6
Hamboro Gdns SS9 ...146 B1
Hambro Ave SS6 ...123 D4
Hambro Cl SS6 ...123 E4
Hambro Hill SS6 ...123 E4
Hambro Rd CM14 ...116 D8
Hamden Cres RM10 ...135 B1
Hamerton Rd DA11 ...178 B2
Hameway E6 ...152 A1
Hamilton Ave
Hoddesdon EN11 ...21 A8
Ilford IG6 ...133 C6
Romford RM1 ...113 D1
Hamilton Cl SS9 ...146 A2
Hamilton Cres CM14 ...116 C6
Hamilton Ct
3 Burnham-on-C CM0 ...106 C4
Chelmsford CM1 ...31 D6
Hamilton Dr RM3 ...114 E1
Hamilton Gdns SS5 ...124 E7
Hamilton Mews SS6 ...123 F3
Hamilton Rd Ilford IG1 ...152 B8
Romford RM2 ...136 B6
Hamlet Cl RM5 ...113 A3
Hamlet Court Mews
SS0 ...147 E1
Hamlet Court Rd SS0 ...166 E8
Hamlet Ct CM14 ...115 E6
Hamlet Est DA8 ...169 D1
Hamlet Hill CM19 ...22 B4
Hamlet Rd
Chelmsford CM2 ...32 B1
Romford RM5 ...113 A3
Southend-on-S SS1 ...166 F7
Hamley Cl SS7 ...144 B6
Hammarskjold Rd CM20 .10 D2
Hammond Ct RM12 ...135 F3
Hammonds Cl RM8 ...134 C1
Hammonds La
Billericay CM11 ...119 C7
Brentwood CM13 ...116 B4
Hammonds Rd
Hatfield Broad Oak CM22 ...4 A6
Little Baddow CM3 ...33 E3
Hampden Cl CM16 ...47 A4
Hampden Cres CM14 ...116 C5
Hampden Rd
Grays RM17 ...173 B1
Romford RM5 ...113 B3
Hampshire Gdns SS17 ...175 A4
Hampshire Rd RM11 ...137 A7
Hampshire Villas SS2 ...167 B8
Hampstead Ave 8 IG8 ...111 A3
Hampstead Gdns SS5 ...124 F7
Hampton Cl SS2 ...147 E4
Hampton Ct Hockley SS5 124 D6
Southend-on-S SS9 ...146 E1
Southend-on-S,Chalkwell
SS9 ...165 F8
Hampton Gdns
Sawbridgeworth CM21 ...11 C7
Southend-on-S SS2 ...147 E4
Hampton Mead IG10 ...89 B6
Hampton Rd
Chingford E4 ...109 A5
Great Baddow CM2 ...54 E6
Ilford IG1 ...152 C8
Hamstel Mews SS2 ...148 D1
Hamstel Prim Sch SS2 ...148 D2
Hamstel Rd Harlow CM20 ...10 C1
Southend-on-S SS2 ...148 D2
Hanbury Rd CM1 ...53 E8
Hand La CM21 ...1 C1
Handel Cres RM18 ...179 B7
Handel Rd SS8 ...164 D2
Handforth Rd 6 IG1 ...133 B1
Handley Gn SS15 ...141 C5
Handleys Chase SS15 ...119 F2
Handleys Ct SS15 ...119 F2
Handsworth Ave E4 ...109 D4
Handsworth Prim Sch
E4 ...109 D4
Handtrough Way IG11 ...152 B3
Hanford Rd RM15 ...171 C5
Hanging Hill CM13 ...95 C2
Hanging Hill La CM13 ...117 B8
Hanlee Brook CM2 ...54 F6
Hannah Cl SS8 ...164 A6
Hannards Way IG6 ...112 B5
Hannett Rd SS8 ...164 E3
Hanningfield Cl SS6 ...123 A3
Hanningfield Nature Trail*
CM3 ...99 B8
Hanover Cl SS14 ...142 E5
Hanover Ct
Hoddesdon EN11 ...21 A7
Rayleigh SS6 ...123 D3
Waltham Abbey EN9 ...65 C6
Hanover Dr SS14 ...142 E6
Hanover Gdns IG6 ...111 C3
Hanover Mews SS5 ...124 D6
Hanover Pl CM14 ...116 B5
Hansells Mead CM19 ...22 B8
Hanson Cl IG10 ...89 C7
Hanson Dr IG10 ...89 C7
Hanson Gn IG10 ...89 C7
Harberts Rd CM19 ...23 B8
Harberts Way SS6 ...123 C5
Harbourer Cl IG6 ...112 B5
Harbourer Rd IG6 ...112 B5
Harcourt Ave SS2 ...147 F1
Harcourt Ho 6 E4 ...109 D5
Harcourt Mews 2 RM2 ...135 F6
Hard Ct IG8 ...110 C4
Hardie Rd
Dagenham RM10 ...135 C1
Stanford-le-H SS17 ...160 D2
Harding Ho CM16 ...68 A8
Harding Rd RM16 ...174 A3
Harding's Elms Rd
CM11 ...120 B4
Harding's La CM4 ...74 A7
Hardings Reach 8 CM0 106 C4
Hardley Cres RM11 ...136 D7
Hardwick Cl SS6 ...123 D1
Hardwick Cres 27 DA2 ...176 B1
Hardwick Ct
Southend-on-S SS2 ...147 E3
9 Wanstead E11 ...132 A5
Hardwicke St IG11 ...152 C4
Hardy SS3 ...168 D5
Hardy Ct 9 E11 ...132 A7
Hardy Gr DA1 ...176 A3
Hardy Rd SS14 ...142 E8
Hardys Way SS8 ...164 A6
Hare Hall La RM2 ...136 B7
Hare St CM19 ...23 B8
Hare Street Com Prim Sch
CM19 ...23 C8
Hare Street Springs
CM19 ...23 B8
Hare Terr RM20 ...172 D1
Harebell Cl CM12 ...96 F4
Harebell Way RM3 ...114 D3
Harefield CM20 ...11 A1
Hares Chase CM12 ...96 F3
Haresfield Rd RM10 ...154 A6
Haresland Cl SS7 ...145 F6
Harewood Ave SS4 ...125 D5
Harewood Dr IG5 ...110 F1
Harewood Hill CM16 ...67 E4
Harewood Rd
Chelmsford CM1 ...31 E1
Pilgrims Hatch CM15 ...94 B3
Harford Cl E4 ...87 B2
Harford Rd E4 ...87 B2
Harfred Ave CM9 ...37 E3
Harkness Cl RM3 ...114 F5
Harlech Rd 1 SS13 ...143 B5
Harlequin Stps 16 SS1 ...167 C7
Harlesden Cl RM3 ...114 F4
Harlesden Rd RM3 ...114 F4
Harlesden Wlk RM3 ...114 F3
Harley Ct E11 ...132 A4
Harley St SS9 ...146 C1
Harlings Gr CM1 ...32 C3
Harlow Coll CM20 ...10 D1
Harlow Comm CM17 ...24 D6
Harlow Fields Sch CM18 .23 E6
Harlow Gdns RM5 ...113 C4
Harlow Mans 2 IG11 ...152 B5
Harlow Mill Sta CM20 ...11 C5
Harlow Rd Moreton CM5 ...26 C3
Rainham RM13 ...154 F4
Roydon CM19 ...9 C1
Sawbridgeworth CM21 ...11 C8
Sheering CM22,CM17 ...12 B8
Sheering,Matching Tye
CM22 ...12 F3
Harlow Seedbed Ctr
CM19 ...23 A7
Harlow Stad (Greyhounds)
CM19 ...9 E1
Harlow Town Sta CM20 ...10 D3
Harlowbury Prim Sch
CM17 ...11 D4
Harlton Ct EN9 ...65 F5
Harman Ave IG8 ...109 F4
Harman Cl E4 ...109 D6
Harmer Ct DA10 ...177 F1
Harmer Rd DA10 ...177 F1
Harmer St DA12 ...179 C1
Harness Cl CM1 ...32 E7
Harold Cl CM19 ...22 F7
Harold Court Prim Sch
RM3 ...115 A3
Harold Court Rd RM3 ...115 B3
Harold Cres EN9 ...65 C7
Harold Ct RM3 ...115 B3
Harold Gdns SS11 ...99 E1
Harold Rd Chingford E4 ...109 C7
Woodford IG8 ...110 A2
Harold Rise CM9 ...36 F5
Harold View RM3 ...114 F1
Harold Wood Hall RM3 .114 D2
Harold Wood Hospl
RM3 ...114 E2
Harold Wood Prim Sch
RM3 ...137 A8
Harold Wood Sta RM3 ...114 F2
Harolds Rd CM19 ...22 F7
Haron Cl SS8 ...164 B3
Harpenden Rd E12 ...132 C2
Harper Cl RM16 ...172 C1
Harper Way SS6 ...123 C3
Harpers La CM15 ...72 D2
Harpour Rd IG11 ...152 C6
Harrap Chase RM17 ...172 F1
Harridge Cl SS9 ...146 E3
Harridge Rd SS9 ...146 E3
Harrier Ave E11 ...132 B5
Harrier Cl
Hornchurch RM12 ...155 B6
Southend-on-S SS3 ...149 E1
Harrier Way EN9 ...66 A5
Harriescourt EN9 ...66 A7
Harris Cl Romford RM3 ...114 E3
Wickford SS12 ...121 F5
Harris Ct SS5 ...124 E5
Harris Rd RM9 ...153 F7
Harrison Cl CM13 ...95 D4
Harrison Ct CM1 ...31 F3
Harrison Dr CM16 ...47 B5
Harrison Gdns SS5 ...101 D2
Harrison Rd
Dagenham RM10 ...154 B6
Waltham Abbey EN9 ...65 C4
Harrisons Wharf RM19 ...171 A1
Harrods Ct CM11 ...97 E2
Harrogate Dr SS5 ...124 F8
Harrogate Rd SS5 ...124 F7
Harrold Rd RM8 ...153 B7
Harrow Cl SS5 ...125 A5
Harrow Cres RM3 ...114 B2
Harrow Dr RM11 ...136 C4
Harrow Gdns SS5 ...125 A5
Harrow Lodge RM11 ...136 C3
Harrow Lodge Campus
RM11 ...136 B4
Harrow Rd Barking IG11 ...152 E4
Basildon SS12 ...122 A2
Canvey Island SS8 ...164 B5
Ilford IG1 ...152 C8
North Benfleet SS12 ...121 F2
Harrow Way CM2 ...55 A6
Harston Dr EN3 ...65 A1
Hart Cl SS7 ...145 A6
Hart Cnr RM20 ...172 D1
Hart Cres IG7 ...111 F5
Hart Ct E12 ...152 A5
Hart Rd Harlow CM17 ...11 C6
Thundersley SS7 ...145 B6
Hart St Brentwood CM14 ...116 C8
Chelmsford CM2 ...32 A1
Hartford Cl SS6 ...123 B4
Hartford End SS13 ...143 A5
Hartington Pl SS1 ...167 B7
Hartington Rd SS1 ...167 B7
Hartland Cl SS9 ...146 D7
Hartland Rd Epping CM16 .46 A1
Hornchurch RM12 ...136 A2
Hartley Cl CM2 ...33 A4
Harts Gr IG8 ...110 A5
Harts La IG11 ...152 B6
Hartshorn Gdns E6 ...152 A1
Hartswood Cl CM14 ...116 E6
Hartswood Hospl CM13 ...116 B4
Hartswood Rd CM14 ...116 E5
Hartwell Dr E4 ...109 C4
Harty Cl RM16 ...173 B5
Harvard Ct SS6 ...123 B4
Harvard Wlk RM12 ...155 A8
Harvest Cl CM3 ...101 D7
Harvest La IG10 ...88 D2
Harvest Rd SS8 ...164 B5
Harvest Way CM9 ...36 F5
Harvey RM16 ...173 B4
Harvey Cl SS13 ...121 B1
Harvey Ctr CM20 ...23 D8
Harvey Gdns IG10 ...89 B6
Harvey Ho
4 Barking IG11 ...152 C5
Ilford RM6 ...134 D7
Harvey Rd Basildon SS13 121 C1
Ilford IG1 ...152 B7
Harvey's La RM7 ...135 E2
Harveyfields EN9 ...65 C5
Harwater Dr IG10 ...88 F7
Harwood Ave RM11 ...136 E8
Harwood Ct RM17 ...178 C8
Harwood Hall La RM14 .156 B6
Haselfoot Rd CM3 ...33 F8
Haskard Rd RM9 ...153 D7
Haskins SS17 ...160 F2
Haslars Ct CM4 ...74 C4
Haslemere Est The EN11 .21 D6
Haslemere Pinnacles Est The
CM19 ...23 A7
Haslemere Rd Ilford IG3 133 F2
Wickford SS12 ...99 C2
Haslewood Ave EN11 ...21 A6
Haslingden Ho 11 RM3 ...114 E5
Hassell Rd SS8 ...164 D3
Hassenbrook Ct SS17 ...160 E1
Hassenbrook Ho SS17 ...160 D1
Hassenbrook Rd SS17 ...160 E1
Hassenbrook Sch SS17 ...160 E2
Hasted Cl DA9 ...177 C1
Hastings Ave IG6 ...133 C7
Hastings Cl RM17 ...177 E8
Hastings Rd
Romford RM2 ...136 B6
Southend-on-S SS1 ...167 B8
Hastings The SS11 ...99 D1
Hastingwood Ct CM5 ...48 F5
Hastingwood Rd CM17 ...24 E4
Hatch Gn CM22 ...2 B8
Hatch Gr RM6 ...134 E7
Hatch La E4 ...109 E7
Hatch Rd CM15 ...94 B4
Hatch Side IG7 ...111 A5
Hatches Farm Rd CM12 118 D5
Hatchfields CM3 ...18 F7
Hatchwoods IG8 ...109 F6
Hatfield Cl
Brentwood CM13 ...95 D2
Hornchurch RM12 ...155 D7
Ilford IG6 ...133 B8
Redbridge IG6 ...111 B1
Hatfield Dr CM11 ...97 D2
Hatfield Gr CM1 ...31 D1
Hatfield Heath Com Prim Sch
CM22 ...3 A3
Hatfield Ho SS4 ...125 F2
Hatfield Rd
Dagenham RM9 ...153 E5
Grays RM16 ...172 D1
Langford CM9 ...36 B7
Rayleigh SS6 ...123 B3
Hatfields IG10 ...89 B6
Hathaway Cres E12 ...152 A6
Hathaway Gdns
Grays RM17 ...173 A3
Ilford RM6 ...134 D6
Hathaway Rd RM17 ...173 B2
Hatherleigh Way RM3 ...114 D2
Hatherley The SS14 ...142 D7
Hatley Ave IG6 ...133 C7
Hatley Gdns SS7 ...144 C5
Hatterill SS15 ...141 D5
Hatton Cl RM16 ...172 C3
Hatton Sch IG8 ...132 D8
Havalon Cl SS14 ...142 D7
Havana Cl RM1 ...135 E6
Havana Dr SS6 ...123 B7
Havant Ho 9 RM3 ...114 E3
Havelock St IG1 ...133 B2
Haven Cl Basildon SS16 ...142 E3
Canvey Island SS8 ...163 E3
Haven Pl RM16 ...173 C4
Haven Rd SS8 ...163 D2
Haven Rise CM11 ...119 D6
Haven The RM16 ...173 F2
Havencourt CM1 ...32 B3
Havengore
Basildon SS13 ...143 C8
Chelmsford CM1 ...32 F5
Havengore Cl SS3 ...150 C3
Havengore Ho SS9 ...146 E1
Havenside SS3 ...149 E5
Havenwood Cl CM13 ...116 C4
Haverhill Rd E4 ...87 C1
Havering Cl SS3 ...150 B4
Havering Coll of F & H Ed
Hornchurch RM11 ...136 E7
Romford, Harold Hill RM3 .114 E6
Havering Ctry Pk*
RM4 ...113 C6
Havering Dr RM1 ...135 E8
Havering Gdns RM6 ...134 D6
Havering Rd RM1 ...113 D3
Havering Sixth Form Coll
RM11 ...136 F3
Havering Way IG11 ...153 B2
Havis Rd SS17 ...160 E4
Havisham Way CM1 ...31 E7

Haward Rd EN11 ....21 C8
Hawbush Gn SS13 ....121 B1
Hawes La E4 ....65 C1
Hawfinch Wlk CM2 ....54 B5
Hawk Cl EN9 ....66 A5
Hawk Cnr RM20 ....172 D1
Hawk Hill SS11 ....100 D2
Hawk La SS11 ....100 D2
Hawk Terr IG5 ....133 A8
Hawkdene E4 ....87 C3
Hawkenbury CM19 ......23 B6
Hawkes Cl RM17 ......178 B8
Hawkesbury Bush La
  SS16 ....142 B2
Hawkesbury Cl SS8 ..163 F2
Hawkesbury Rd SS8 ..163 G2
Hawkhurst Cl CM1 .....31 E2
Hawkhurst Gdns RM5 .113 D4
Hawkinge Way RM12 ..155 C6
Hawkins SS3 ....168 D5
Hawkins Cl
  Cock Clarks CM3 .....57 E2
  Wickford SS11 ......121 F7
Hawkins Dr RM16 .....172 D4
Hawkridge SS3 ....168 C8
Hawkridge Cl RM6 ...134 C5
Hawkridge Dr RM17 ..173 D1
Hawks Cl CM3 ....57 A6
Hawks Hill CM16 ......47 A4
Hawks La SS5 ....124 E5
Hawksmoor Gn CM13 ...95 D4
Hawksmouth E4 ....87 C2
Hawksway SS16 ....142 B4
Hawkswood Rd CM11,
  SS11 ....99 A6
Hawkswood Sch E4 ....87 C4
Hawkwell Chase SS5 .124 E4
Hawkwell Ct E4 .....109 C4
Hawkwell Ho 1 RM8 ..135 A2
Hawkwell Park Dr SS5 125 A5
Hawkwell Park Rd SS5 124 F5
Hawkwell Rd SS5 ....124 F6
Hawkwood Cl CM3 .....79 E1
Hawkwood Cres E4 ....87 B3
Hawsted IG9 ....88 B2
Hawthorn Ave
  Brentwood CM13 ....116 F6
  Rainham RM13 ......155 B1
Hawthorn Cl
  Chelmsford CM2 .....54 C6
  Hockley SS5 ....124 F5
Hawthorn Pl DA8 ....169 C1
Hawthorn Rd
  Canvey Island SS8 .164 C3
  Hoddesdon EN11 .....21 B8
  Woodford IG9 ......110 D6
Hawthorn Way SS6 ...123 F1
Hawthorne Ct E4 ....109 B4
Hawthorne Gdns SS5 124 B6
Hawthorne Rd SS17 .160 F4
Hawthornes E4 ....58 C1
Hawthorns Harlow CM18 .23 F4
Hawthorns The
  South Benfleet SS7 144 C4
  Southend-on-S SS9 146 C4
  Woodford IG8 ......110 A7
Hawthorns The
  Burnham-on-C CM0 .106 A7
  Corringham SS17 ...161 C4
  Danbury CM3 ....57 A7
  Hadleigh SS7 ......145 E2
  Loughton IG10 ......89 A5
Hawtree Cl SS1 .....167 C2
Hay Gn CM3 ....56 F8
Hay Green La CM15 ....72 E4
Hay Terr RM20 ......172 D1
Hayburn Way RM12 ...135 F3
Hayden EN9 ....65 C4
Hayden Way RM5 .....113 C1
Haydens Rd CM20 .....23 C8
Haydock Cl RM12 ....155 F8
Haydon Cl RM8 ......114 B3
Haydon Rd RM8 .....134 C2
Hayes Barton SS1 ...168 C8
Hayes Chase SS11 ...101 A4
Hayes Cl Chelmsford CM2 .32 B1
  Grays RM20 ....177 C8
Hayes Dr RM13 ......155 B5
Hayes Farm Cvn Pk
  SS11 ....101 A4
Hayes Hill Farm★ EN9 .43 C3
Hayes La SS8 ....163 F3
Hayes Rd DA9 ....176 E1
Hayle RM18 ....175 C3
Hayley Cl RM15 .....172 C3
Hayling Gr SS12 ....122 A5
Haynes Park Ct RM11 136 C6
Haynes Rd RM11 ....136 D6
Hayrick Cl SS16 ....141 A4
Hayron's La CM1 .....16 D8
Haysoms Cl RM1 ....135 E7
Haystocks E18 .....132 C2
Hayward Sch The CM1 .32 A4
Haywards RM15 .....171 D7
Haywards Cl
  Brentwood CM13 ....95 E3
  Ilford RM6 ....134 C6
Haywood Ct EN9 .....65 F5
Hazard Rd DA11 ....179 A1
Hazel Cl Basildon SS15 119 F2
  Hadleigh SS7 .....145 F3
  Hornchurch RM12 ..136 B1
  Southend-on-S SS9 .146 C4
Hazel Ct 7 Chigwell IG6 111 E5
  Loughton IG10 ......88 F6

Hazel Dr RM15 ......157 D2
Hazel Gdns Grays RM16 .173 E3
  Sawbridgeworth CM21 .1 F1
Hazel Gr RM6 ....134 E8
Hazel La IG6 ....111 B3
Hazel Rise RM11 ....136 C5
Hazelbrouck Gdns IG6 .111 D3
Hazeldene Rd IG3 ..134 B2
Hazeldon Cl CM3 .....19 C6
Hazeleigh CM13 ....117 B7
Hazeleigh Gdns IG8 .110 A3
Hazeleigh Hall La CM3 .58 C4
Hazell Cres RM5 ...113 B2
Hazelmere SS13 ....143 B4
Hazelmere Gdns RM11 136 C6
Hazelwood Hockley SS5 124 B1
  Linford SS17 ......175 A2
  Loughton IG10 ......88 D4
  South Benfleet SS7 144 B7
Hazelwood Ct CM9 ...37 B6
Hazelwood Gdns CM15 .94 A3
Hazelwood Gr SS9 ..146 E5
Hazelwood Park Cl 5
  IG7 ....111 E5
Hazlemere Rd SS7 ..144 D6
Head St CM9 ....38 E6
Headcorn Cl SS13 ..143 C5
Headingham Ho SS6 .123 C1
Headingley Cl IG6 ..111 F4
Headingly Cl SS13 ..121 A2
Headley App IG2 ...133 B6
Headley Chase CM14 116 D6
Headley Dr IG2 ....133 B5
Headley Rd RM1 .....97 C4
Heard's La CM15 .....94 F6
Hearn Rd RM11 .....135 F5
Hearsall Ave
  Chelmsford CM1 .....32 B7
  Stanford-le-H SS17 160 E2
Heath Cl Billericay CM12 .96 F1
  Romford RM2 ......136 A8
Heath Dr Chelmsford CM2 .54 B6
  Romford RM2 ......114 A1
  Theydon Bois CM16 .67 E4
Heath Park Ct RM2 .136 A6
Heath Park Rd RM2 136 B6
Heath Rd Billericay CM11 .97 F4
  Chadwell St M RM16 173 E1
  Dagenham RM6 ....134 E4
  Grays RM16 ....174 A3
  Ramsden Heath CM11 .98 B4
Heath Terr RM6 ....134 D4
Heath View Gdns RM16 173 C3
Heath View Rd RM16 .173 C4
Heathcote Ave IG5 .110 F1
Heathcote Ct IG5 ..110 F1
Heathcote Gdns CM17 .24 E8
Heathcote Gr E4 ...109 C8
Heathcote Sch
  Chingford E4 .....109 E8
  Danbury CM3 ....56 E7
Heathcroft Gdns E17 109 D2
Heathdene Dr DA17 169 B2
Heather Ave RM1 ...113 D1
Heather Bank RM1 ...97 C2
Heather Cl
  Canvey Island SS8 .163 F2
  Pilgrims Hatch CM15 .94 B4
  Romford RM1 ......113 D2
Heather Dr 10 CM1 ...32 F6
Heather Dr Romford RM1 113 E1
  South Benfleet SS7 146 A2
Heather Gdns
  Romford RM1 ......113 E2
  Waltham Abbey EN9 .65 C3
Heather Glen RM1 ..113 D1
Heather Way RM1 ..113 D2
Heathercroft Rd SS13 122 A6
Heatherley Dr IG5 .132 F8
Heatherwood Cl E12 132 C2
Heathfield Chingford E4 109 C7
  Rayleigh SS6 .....123 D1
  Thundersley SS7 ..145 C6
Heathfield Ho
  3 Romford RM1 ...115 A4
  Southend-on-S SS1 166 F7
Heathfield Park Dr RM6 134 B4
Heathfield Rd CM1 ...32 B7
Heathlands RM2 ....136 B6
Heathlands Dr SS16 141 B4
Heathside Cl IG2 ...133 D6
Heathway
  Dagenham RM9,RM10 154 A6
  Woodford IG8 .....110 C5
Heaton Ave RM3 ...114 B3
Heaton Cl Chingford E4 109 C7
  Romford RM3 ......114 C3
Heaton Grange Rd RM2 113 F1
Heaton Way RM3 ...114 C3
Heberden Ct 8 RM19 171 B1
Hedge La SS7 ......145 D4
Hedge Place Rd DA9 176 F1
Hedgehope Ave SS6 123 D4
Hedgeley IG4 ......132 F7
Hedgemans Rd RM9 153 E6
Hedgemans Way RM9 153 E6
Hedgemoor Ct 1 E4 109 D5
Hedgerow Ct SS15 ..119 F2
Hedgerow The SS16 142 E4
Hedgerows CM21 .....1 F2
Hedgers Cl IG10 ....89 A6
Hedgewood Gdns IG2,
  IG5 ....133 A6
Hedingham Dr SS12 121 F6
Hedingham Pl SS4 .125 D4
Hedingham Rd
  Dagenham RM8 ....153 B7

Hedingham Rd continued
  Grays RM16 ....172 C1
  Hornchurch RM11 .137 A3
Hedley Ave RM20 ..177 C8
Hedley Cl 1 RM1 ..135 E6
Hedley Walter High Sch The
  CM15 ....94 C2
Heenan Cl IG11 ....152 C6
Heeswyk Rd SS8 ...164 D5
Heideburg Rd SS8 .164 D5
Heideck Gdns CM13 117 B8
Heighams CM19 ......22 F5
Heights The Danbury CM3 .56 D7
  Loughton IG10 .....88 B7
  Lower Nazeing EN9 .44 B6
  Theydon Bois CM16 .67 E3
Heilsburg Rd SS8 ..164 D5
Helden Ave SS8 ....164 B5
Helen Rd RM11 ....136 D8
Helena Cl SS5 .....124 F5
Helena Ct CM3 .....101 D6
Helena Rd SS6 .....123 E3
Helford Ct RM15 ...172 B6
Helford Way RM14 137 D5
Helions Rd CM19 ....23 B8
Helleborine RM17 ..172 F1
Hellendoorn Rd SS8 164 D2
Helmons La CM2 .....77 A4
Helmore Cl IG11 ...152 F5
Helmores SS15 ....140 F6
Helmsdale SS8 ....163 F5
Helmsdale Cl RM1 .113 E3
Helmsdale Rd RM1 .113 E3
Helmsley 10 E18 ..132 A8
Helmsley Ho 5 RM3 114 E3
Helpeston SS14 ...142 D6
Helston Rd CM1 .....32 E6
Helwys Ct E4 ......109 C4
Hemley Rd RM16 ...174 D7
Hemmells SS15 ....141 B8
Hemmings Ct CM9 ..58 E8
Hemnall St CM16 ....67 F8
Hempstalls SS15 ..141 F5
Hempstead Cl IG9 .110 A8
Hempstead Rd E17 109 D1
Henderson Cl RM11 136 B2
Henderson Dr DA1 176 A2
Henderson Gdns SS12 121 E5
Henderson Ho 7 RM10 135 A1
Hendon Cl SS12 ...121 D6
Hendon Gdns RM5 .113 C4
Hengist Gdns SS11 ..99 D1
Henham Cl CM11 ....97 D2
Henham Ct RM5 ...113 C1
Henley Cres SS0 ..147 D4
Henley Ct IG1 .....152 B8
Henley Gdns RM6 ..134 E6
Henley Rd IG1 ....152 B8
Henney Cl CM3 ......80 F6
Henniker Gate CM2 ..33 A4
Henry De Grey Cl RM17 172 F2
Henry Dr SS9 ......146 B2
Henry Green Prim Sch
  RM8 ....134 D2
Henry Rd CM1 ....32 B4
Henry St RM17 ....178 C8
Henry's Ave IG8 ..109 F5
Henry's Wlk IG8 ..111 D3
Henshawe Rd RM8 134 D1
Henson Ave SS14 ..164 B3
Henwood Side IG8 110 F4
Hepburn Cl RM16 .172 D2
Hepworth Ct IG11 153 A7
Hepworth Gdns IG11 153 A7
Hepworth Ho IG8 .110 A7
Heralds Way CM3 .101 E7
Herbage Park Rd CM9 35 D1
Herbert Gdns RM6 134 D4
Herbert Gr SS1 ...167 A3
Herbert Rd
  Canvey Island SS8 164 C4
  Hornchurch RM11 136 F4
  Ilford IG3 ....133 E2
  Southend-on-S SS3 168 C6
  Swanscombe DA10 177 F1
Herd La SS17 ......161 C4
Hereford Ct CM2 ...55 A5
Hereford Gdns IG1 132 E4
Hereford Rd E11 ..132 B6
Hereford Wlk SS14 142 F7
Herent Dr IG5 .....132 F8
Hereward Cl EN9 ...65 C7
Hereward Gdns SS11 .99 D1
Hereward Gn IG10 ..89 D1
Hereward Prim Sch IG10 89 C3
Herewood Lincoln Ho
  DA11 ....178 D1
Herga Hyll RM16 ..174 B8
Herington Gr CM13 .95 A2
Herington House Sch
  CM13 ....95 B3
Heriot Ave E4 .....109 A8
Heritage Ctr Mus The★
  SS8 ....163 D3
Heritage Quay DA12 179 C1
Heritage Way
  Latchingdon CM3 ...82 B5
  Rochford SS4 .....125 E2
Hermes Dr CM0 ....106 B5
Hermes Way SS3 ..168 F8
Hermitage Ave SS7 145 A4
Hermitage Cl SS7 .145 A4
Hermitage Ct 3 E18 132 A7
Hermitage Dr SS15 141 C7
Hermitage Rd SS0 .166 E8
Hermitage Wlk E18 132 A7
Hermon Hill E11 ...132 A7

Hernen Rd SS8 ....164 C5
Hernshaw CM13 ...117 D3
Heron Ave SS11 ...121 F6
Heron Chase CM13 117 E3
Heron Cl
  Buckhurst Hill IG9 ..88 A1
  Rayleigh SS6 .....123 B2
  Sawbridgeworth CM21 .1 D1
Heron Ct
  Chipping Ongar CM5 .49 A5
  Ilford IG1 ....133 B2
Heron Dale SS14 ..142 D6
Heron Dr SG12 ....8 B4
Heron Flight Ave RM12 155 B5
Heron Gdns SS6 ..123 B3
Heron Mead EN3 ...65 A1
Heron Mews IG1 ..133 B2
Heron Way Grays RM20 172 B1
  Heybridge CM9 .....37 C5
  Mayland SS8 ....83 A8
  Upminster RM14 ..137 F3
Herongate
  South Benfleet SS7 144 B4
  Southend-on-S SS3 168 E8
Herongate Rd E12 .132 C2
Herons Ct SS14 ...120 F1
Herons La CM5 .....49 D8
Herons Wood CM20 .10 B2
Heronsgate Trad Est
  SS14 ....120 F2
Heronswood EN9 ...65 G3
Heronway
  Brentwood CM13 ...95 B1
  Woodford IG8 ....110 C6
Herringham Gn CM2 33 A4
Herringham Inf Sch
  RM16 ....174 B2
Herschell Rd SS9 .146 C1
Hertford Dr SS17 .142 C1
Hertford Rd
  Barking IG11 .....152 B5
  Canvey Island SS8 163 F3
  Hoddesdon EN11 ...21 A7
  Ilford IG2 ....133 E5
Hertford Wlk 13 DA17 169 A1
Hesketh Rd E7 ....132 A1
Hesselyn Dr RM13 155 B5
Hester Ho CM20 ....10 C2
Hester Pl CM0 ....106 C5
Hetzand Rd SS8 ...164 F3
Hever Cl SS5 ......124 D6
Hewett Rd RM8 ...153 D8
Hewins Cl EN9 .....65 E7
Hewitt Rd 2 E4 ...109 D5
Heybridge App CM9 .36 F3
Heybridge Ct RM7 135 D5
Heybridge Dr Ilford IG6 133 C8
  Redbridge IG6 ....111 D1
  Wickford SS12 ....121 E7
Heybridge House Ind Est
  CM9 ....37 B4
Heybridge Prim Sch CM9 37 C5
Heybridge Rd CM4 ..74 A2
Heybridge St CM9 ..37 B5
Heycroft Prim Sch SS2 146 F7
Heycroft Rd Hockley SS5 124 F5
  Southend-on-S SS9 146 F6
Heycroft Way 54 F5
Heygate Ave SS1 .167 B2
Heymeads Ct CM9 ...37 A5
Heynes Rd RM8 ...153 D2
Heythrop The
  Chelmsford CM2 ...32 D4
  Ingatestone CM4 ...74 A3
Heywood Ct CM9 ...37 B6
Heywood Way CM9 ..37 B6
Hibbard Ho CM14 .116 C6
Hickling Cl SS9 ...146 B6
Hickling Rd IG1 ..152 B6
Hickman Ave E4 ..109 C4
Hickman Rd RM6 ..134 C4
Hicks Ct Dagenham RM10 135 B1
  Grays RM17 ....173 B1
Hickstars La CM12 119 C7
Hides The CM20 .....10 D1
High Ash Cl SS17 .175 D4
High Bank SS13 ...140 F4
High Barrets SS13 143 A5
High Beech CE Prim Sch
  IG10 ....88 A8
High Beech Rd IG10 .88 E5
High Beeches SS7 144 B3
High Bridge Rd CM2 .32 C1
High Chelmer 8 CM1 .32 B2
High Cliff Dr SS9 .165 F6
High Cloister SS7 ..97 B2
High Easter Rd CM6 .15 E6
High Elms Chigwell IG7 111 E6
  Upminster RM14 ..137 E3
  Woodford IG8 .....110 A5
High Elms Rd SS5 .101 E1
High Gables IG10 ...88 D4
High House Est CM7 .11 F4
High House La RM18 174 D1
High La CM17 ....12 E6
High Mdw CM11 ....97 C2
High Mdws IG7 ....111 C8
High Mead Chigwell IG7 111 C8
  Hockley SS5 ......124 E5
High Oaks SS16 ...141 B3
High Oaks Lodge 2
  E18 ....110 A1
High Ongar Prim Sch
  CM5 ....49 C4
High Pasture CM3 ..34 D3
High Pastures CM22 .12 D8
High Pavement SS14 142 A6

High Rd
  Basildon,Laindon SS16,
  SS15 ....141 B6
  Basildon,Pitsea SS13 143 A6
  Basildon,Westley Heights
  SS16 ....141 B2
  Chigwell IG7 ......111 B7
  Corringham SS17 ..161 C6
  Dagenham RM6,IG3 134 C4
  Epping CM16 ....67 D7
  Hockley SS5 ......124 A5
  Hoddesdon EN10 ...21 A4
  Horndon-on-t-H SS17 159 F3
  Ilford IG1 ....133 E2
  Ilford, Seven Kings IG1,
  IG3 ....133 E2
  Loughton IG9,IG10 .88 C3
  North Weald Bassett CM16 67 A5
  Orsett RM16 ......174 A8
  Rayleigh SS6 .....123 C1
  South Benfleet SS7 144 C1
  South Ockendon RM16 172 E5
  Stanford-le-H SS17 160 F1
  Thornwood CM16 ...46 C6
  Woodford E18 ....110 A2
High Rd N SS15 ...119 C1
High Road Ongar
  (Chelmsford Rd) CM5 49 B5
High Road Woodford Gn
  IG8 ....110 A6
High Silver IG10 ...88 D5
High St Aveley RM15 171 D5
  Billericay CM12 ....97 A2
  Bradwell-on-S CM0 .42 A4
  Brentwood CM14 .116 A6
  Burnham-on-C CM0 106 C4
  Canewdon SS4 ...104 D2
  Canvey Island SS8 164 D4
  Chelmsford CM1 ...32 B2
  Chipping Ongar CM5 .49 A3
  Epping CM16 ....67 F8
  Gravesend DA11 ..179 B1
  Grays RM17 ....178 A8
  Great Baddow CM2 ..54 F1
  Great Wakering SS3 150 A4
  Greenhithe DA9 ...177 B3
  Hadleigh SS7 .....145 D3
  Harlow CM17 ....11 C4
  Hatfield Broad Oak CM22 .3 A5
  Hoddesdon EN11 ...21 A5
  Hornchurch RM11,RM12 136 D3
  Ilford IG6 ....133 C8
  Ingatestone CM4 ...74 B3
  Little Wakering SS3 149 F4
  Maldon CM9 ....37 A2
  Northfleet RM17 ..178 C1
  Purfleet RM19 ....171 A1
  Rayleigh SS6 .....123 D2
  Redbridge IG6 ....111 C1
  Romford RM1 .....135 E6
  Roydon CM19 ....9 B1
  South Benfleet SS7 144 D1
  Southend-on-S SS1 167 A8
  Southend-on-S, Shoeburyness
  SS3 ....168 G7
  Southend-on-S,Leigh-on-S
  SS9 ....165 D2
  Southminster CM0 ..84 D4
  Stanford-le-H SS17 160 C1
  Stanstead Abbotts SG12 .8 A1
  Stock CM4 ....75 E3
  Swanscombe DA10 177 F2
  Wanstead E11 ....132 A6
  Wickford SS12 ....121 D7
High Trees DA2 ....176 B1
High View CM0 .....62 C8
High View Ave RM17 173 C3
High View Cl IG10 ..88 C4
High View Gdns RM17 173 C1
High View Ho RM6 134 C4
High View Par 1 IG4 132 F6
High View Rd E18 .109 F1
High View Rise CM11 120 C5
High Wood Hospl CM14 94 C1
High Wood Rd EN11 .21 B8
High Wych CE Prim Sch
  CM21 ....1 A2
High Wych La CM21 ..1 A2
High Wych Rd
  Gilston CM21 ......10 F7
  High Wych CM21 ....1 A2
Higham Ct 9 IG8 ..110 A4
Higham Ho E4 .....109 A4
Higham Rd IG8 ....110 A4
Higham Station Ave E4 109 B4
Higham View CM16 ..47 B6
Highams Chase CM9 .39 A8
Highams Park Sch E4 109 D4
Highams Park Sta E4 109 D4
Highams Rd SS5 ..124 F6
Highams The E17 .109 C2
Highbank CI SS1 ..146 F5
Highbridge Ct 5 EN9 .65 B6
Highbridge Rd 6 EN9 .65 B6
Highbridge Rd IG11 152 B4
Highbridge Ret Pk EN9 .65 B6
Highbridge St EN9 ..65 B6
Highbury Ave EN11 .21 A8
Highbury Gdns IG3 133 E2
Highcliff Cres SS4 125 C4
Highcliff Dr SS12 .120 F8
Highcliff Rd SS7 ..163 E6
Highcliffe Cl SS11 121 F8
Highcliffe Gdns IG4 132 E6
Highcliffe Rd SS11 121 F8
Highcliffe Way SS11 121 F8
Highfield Harlow CM18 .24 A7

Highfield *continued*
Sawbridgeworth CM21 1 E3
Highfield App CM11 119 D8
Highfield Ave SS7 145 C4
Highfield Cl Danbury CM3 56 D6
Romford RM5 113 C4
Southend-on-S SS0 147 D2
Highfield Cloisters
SS99 146 C1
Highfield Cres
Hornchurch RM12 136 F2
Rayleigh SS6 123 D2
Southend-on-S SS0 147 D2
Highfield Ct CM11 119 D7
Highfield Dr SS0 147 D2
Highfield Gdns
Grays RM16 173 D5
Southend-on-S SS0 147 D3
Highfield Gn CM16 67 E8
Highfield Gr SS0 147 D3
Highfield Link RM5 113 D4
Highfield Pl CM16 67 E8
Highfield Rd
Billericay CM11 119 D7
Chelmsford CM1 31 E4
Hornchurch RM12 136 F2
Romford RM5 113 C4
Woodford IG8 110 E3
Highfield Rise CM3 83 A3
Highfield Way
Hornchurch RM12 136 F2
Southend-on-S SS0 147 D3
Highfields Mead CM3 78 B8
Highfields Twrs RM5 113 D5
Highgate Gr CM21 1 D2
Highgrove CM15 94 B3
Highgrove Ho 8 CM14 116 C8
Highgrove Mews RM17 173 C1
Highgrove Rd RM8 153 C8
Highland Ave
Brentwood CM15 94 D1
Dagenham RM10 135 C1
Loughton IG10 88 F3
Highland Ct E18 110 B2
Highland Gr CM11 97 B2
Highland Rd
Basildon SS17 142 B1
Lower Nazeing EN9 21 E1
Highlands Ave SS16 142 D4
Highlands Bvd SS9 146 A2
Highlands Cres SS13 143 F6
Highlands Ct SS9 146 B2
Highlands Dr CM9 36 E2
Highlands Gdns IG1 132 F3
Highlands Hill CM3 83 D6
Highlands Prim Sch
IG1 132 F3
Highlands Rd
Basildon SS13 143 F6
Rawreth SS11 101 B2
Highmead SS6 123 B2
Highmead Ct
Brentwood CM15 94 D1
Rayleigh SS6 123 C2
Highstone Ave E11 132 A5
Highstone Ct 4 E11 132 A5
Hightrees CM4 75 D2
Hightrees Ct 10 CM14 116 C6
Highview Ave SS16 140 F5
Highview Cres CM13 95 C3
Highview Gdns RM14 137 B2
Highview Ho IG9 110 D7
Highview Rd SS7 145 A7
Highwood Cl
Brentwood CM14 94 B2
Southend-on-S SS9 146 F4
Highwood Cotts CM1 51 E3
Highwood Gdns
Ilford IG5 133 A7
Redbridge IG5 132 F7
Highwood La IG10 89 A3
Highwood Prim Sch CM1 52 A4
Highwood Rd
Edney Common CM1 52 C6
Roxwell CM1 51 F4
Hilary Cl
Hornchurch RM12 155 D7
Rochford SS4 125 E5
Hilary Cres SS6 123 E2
Hilbery Rd SS8 164 D3
Hildaville Dr SS0 147 C2
Hill Ave SS11 121 F8
Hill Cl SS7 144 E4
Hill Cres Chelmsford CM2 32 D2
Hornchurch RM11 136 C5
Hill Crest Rd CM5 47 E1
Hill Ct Basildon SS16 142 C5
Romford RM1 135 F7
Hill Gr RM1 135 E8
Hill Hall★ CM16 68 F4
Hill House Dr RM16 174 C1
Hill House Rd DA2 176 C1
Hill La SS5 124 F5
Hill Rd Brentwood CM14 116 A7
Chelmsford CM2 32 D2
South Benfleet SS7 144 E4
Southend-on-S SS2 147 F2
Theydon Bois CM16 67 E2
Hill Rd S CM2 32 D2
Hill Rise RM14 137 A2
Hill Terr
Corringham SS17 161 C4
Woodford IG8 110 E3
Hill The Harlow CM17 11 C4
Northfleet DA11 178 C1
Hill Top IG10 89 A6
Hill Top Ave SS7 144 F2
Hill Top Cl IG10 89 A6
Hill Top Ct IG8 110 F4
Hill Top Rise SS16 140 F4
Hill Top View IG8 110 F4
Hill Tree Cl CM21 1 D1
Hill View CM3 56 F1
Hill View Cres IG1 132 F5
Hill View Rd CM1 32 C4
Hill Way The
Ingatestone CM4 73 F1
Mountnessing CM15 95 F8
Hill's Chace CM14 116 C6
Hill's Rd IG9 88 B1
Hillary Cl Chelmsford CM1 32 D4
Heybridge CM9 37 B5
Hillary Mount CM12 97 A1
Hillboro Ct 1 E18 109 F2
Hillborough Mans SS0 147 D3
Hillborough Rd SS0 147 D3
Hillcourt RM11 136 F2
Hillcrest CM3 61 A1
Hillcrest Ave
Basildon SS16 140 E3
Grays RM20 177 A8
Hullbridge SS5 101 E1
Hillcrest Cl SS17 159 F4
Hillcrest Ct RM5 113 C2
Hillcrest Dr DA9 177 A2
Hillcrest Rd
Chingford E17 109 D1
Hockley SS5 124 E5
Hornchurch RM11 136 A4
Horndon-on-t-H SS17 159 F4
Loughton IG10 88 D3
South Woodham Ferrers
CM3 101 C7
Southend-on-S SS1 167 B8
Woodford E18 110 A1
Hillcrest View SS16 142 D3
Hillcrest Way CM16 68 A8
Hillcroft IG10 89 A7
Hilldene Ave RM3 114 D5
Hilldene Cl RM3 114 D5
Hilldene Prim Sch RM3 114 C4
Hillfoot Ave RM5 113 C2
Hillfoot Rd RM5 113 C2
Hillgrove Bsns Pk EN10 21 C1
Hillhouse EN9 65 F6
Hillhouse CE Prim Sch
EN9 65 F6
Hillhouse Cl CM12 97 B4
Hillhouse Dr CM12 97 B4
Hillington Gdns IG8 110 D1
Hillman Cl RM11 136 D8
Hillrise Rd RM5 113 C4
Hillside Belvedere DA8 169 C2
Grays RM17 173 D2
Harlow CM17 24 C6
Hillside Ave Hockley SS5 124 F5
Woodford IG8 110 C5
Hillside Cl Billericay CM11 97 B1
Woodford IG8 110 C5
Hillside Cres
Southend-on-S SS9 166 A8
Stanstead Abbotts SG12 8 B4
Hillside Gr CM2 54 A7
Hillside La SG12 8 A5
Hillside Mews CM2 54 A7
Hillside Rd Billericay CM11 97 B1
Burnham-on-C CM0 106 B5
Hockley SS5 124 B5
Rayleigh SS9 146 C8
South Benfleet SS7 144 D1
Southend-on-S SS9 165 E8
Southminster CM0 84 C4
Hillside Wlk CM14 115 F7
Hilltop Ave SS5 101 E1
Hilltop Cl SS6 123 C1
Hilltop Jun & Inf Sch
SS11 122 A8
Hilltop Rd Basildon SS15 141 E7
Grays RM20 177 B8
Hillview Ave RM11 136 D5
Hillview Gdns SS17 160 F5
Hillview Rd SS6 123 C3
Hillway Billericay CM11 97 D2
Southend-on-S SS0 166 A8
Hillwood Cl CM13 95 B1
Hillwood Gr
Brentwood CM13 95 B1
Wickford SS11 121 E7
Hilly Field CM18 23 F4
Hilly Rd SS15 141 D7
Hillyfields IG10 89 A7
Hilton Rd SS8 164 A5
Hilton Wlk SS8 164 A5
Hilversum Way SS8 164 B5
Hind Cl IG7 111 F5
Hind Terr RM20 172 D1
Hindles Rd SS8 164 D4
Hindmans Way RM9 153 F1
Hinguar Prim Sch SS3 168 F6
Hinguar St SS3 168 F6
Hintons CM19 23 A4
Hispano Mews EN3 65 A2
Hitchin Cl RM3 114 C6
Hitchman Ho RM5 113 B3
Hither Blakers CM3 101 D8
Hitherfield Rd RM8 134 E2
Hitherwood Cl RM12 155 D8
Hive Cl CM14 116 A8
Hive La DA11 178 B2
Hive The DA11 178 B1
Hobart Cl CM1 31 E5
Hobart Ct IG8 109 F6
Hobart Rd
Dagenham RM9 153 D8
Redbridge IG6 111 C1
Tilbury RM18 179 A6
Hobbiton Hill CM3 101 C6
Hobbs Cross Open Farm★
CM16 68 D3
Hobbs Cross Rd
Epping CM16 68 C4
Harlow CM17 11 F3
Hobbs Mews IG3 133 F2
Hobhouse Rd SS17 160 D4
Hobleythick La SS0 147 D4
Hobtoe Rd CM20 10 A1
Hockley Cl Basildon SS14 142 D6
Bradwell-on-S CM0 42 C2
Hockley Ct 2 E18 110 A2
Hockley Dr RM2 114 C1
Hockley Gn SS14 142 E6
Hockley La CM0 42 C2
Hockley Mews IG11 152 E2
Hockley Prim Sch SS5 124 C6
Hockley Rd
Basildon SS14 142 D6
Rayleigh SS6 123 E4
Hockley Rise SS5 124 E5
Hockley Sta SS5 124 E6
Hockley Woods★ SS5 124 C4
Hoddesdon Ind Ctr EN11 21 C7
Hoddesdon Rd
Belvedere DA17 169 A1
Stanstead Abbotts SG12 8 C3
Hodges Cl RM16 172 D1
Hodgson Ct SS11 122 A5
Hodgson Way SS11 122 B6
Hodings Rd CM20 10 C2
Hodson Pl 1 EN3 65 A1
Hoe La Abridge RM4 90 C4
Great Waltham CM3 18 E6
Lower Nazeing EN9 22 A2
Rettendon CM3 100 A6
Hoe Mill Rd CM9 35 E4
Hoe St CM1 30 D4
Hoe The CM12 119 B4
Hoecroft EN9 21 F1
Hoestock Rd CM21 1 D2
Hoffmanns Way CM1 32 B4
Hog Hill Rd RM5 113 A3
Hogarth Ave CM15 116 F7
Hogarth Ct CM1 32 E6
Hogarth Dr SS3 168 G8
Hogarth Prim Sch CM15 116 F7
Hogarth Rd
Dagenham RM8 153 B7
Grays RM16 173 A5
Hogarth Reach IG10 88 F4
Hogarth Way SS4 125 C6
Hogg La RM16,RM17 173 A2
Hogwell Chase
Hullbridge CM3 102 B8
South Woodham F CM3 80 B1
Holbech Rd SS14 142 F8
Holbek Rd SS8 164 E3
Holbrook Cl
Billericay CM11 97 D2
South Woodham Ferrers
CM3 101 E7
Holbrook Ho SS7 145 E3
Holcombe Rd IG1 133 A4
Holdbrook Way RM3 114 F1
Holden Cl RM8 134 B1
Holden Gdns
Basildon SS14 120 F1
Brentwood CM14 116 D5
Holden Rd SS14 120 F1
Holden Way RM14 137 D4
Holden Wlk SS14 120 F1
Holecroft EN9 65 E5
Holford Rd SS17,RM18 174 E4
Holgate SS13 143 C8
Holgate Ct 9 RM1 135 E6
Holgate Gdns RM10 154 A6
Holgate Rd RM10 154 A7
Holkham Ave CM3 101 D5
Holland Ave SS8 163 D5
Holland Cl RM7 135 C6
Holland Ho E4 109 C6
Holland Park Ave IG3 133 F6
Holland Rd
Southend-on-S SS0 166 D7
Wallend E6 152 A5
Hollands Wlk SS16 142 D2
Holley Gdns CM11 97 B3
Holliday Hill CM2 76 F4
Hollidge Way RM10 154 B5
Hollies RM14 137 B2
Hollies The
Stanford-le-H SS17 160 D1
7 Wanstead E11 132 A6
Hollis Lock CM2 33 A3
Hollis Pl RM17 173 A2
Hollow Cotts RM19 171 A1
Hollow La CM1 31 E8
Hollow The IG8 109 F6
Holloway Cl CM6 15 C7
Holloway Cres CM6 15 C8
Holloway Rd CM9 37 A5
Hollowfield Ave RM17 173 D2
Holly Cl
Buckhurst Hill IG9 110 D7
Burnham-on-C CM0 106 B6
Holly Cotts CM16 67 D7
Holly Cres IG8 109 D3
Holly Ct Billericay CM12 97 A2
Hockley SS5 124 E5
Holly Dr Chingford E4 87 B2
South Ockendon RM15 157 D1
Holly Gr SS16 140 F5
Holly Hill Rd DA17 169 B1
Holly Ho CM15 94 D1
Holly Ho Hospl IG9 110 B8
Holly Trees Prim Sch
CM14 116 C6
Holly Way CM2 54 D7
Holly Wlk SS8 163 F4
Hollybank SS16 140 F4
Hollybush Cl E11 132 A6
Hollybush Hill E11 132 A6
Hollycroft CM2 55 B6
Hollycross Rd SG12 8 B7
Hollyfield CM19 23 C5
Hollyford CM11 97 C5
Hollymead SS17 160 E4
Hollytree Gdns SS6 145 B8
Hollywood Cl CM2 54 E6
Hollywood Way IG8 109 D4
Holmans CM3 33 E8
Holme Rd RM11 137 A3
Holme Wlk SS12 121 F5
Holmes Cl SS17 159 F3
Holmes Ct
Canvey Island SS8 164 C4
Chingford E4 109 D8
Holmes Mdw CM19 23 B2
Holmhurst Rd DA17 169 B1
Holmsdale Cl SS0 147 C3
Holmswood SS8 164 E5
Holmwood Ave CM15 95 A3
Holmwood Rd IG3 133 E2
Holst Ave SS15 141 C8
Holst Cl SS17 160 C3
Holstock Rd IG1 133 C2
Holsworthy SS3 168 D8
Holsworthy Ho RM3 114 D2
Holt Cl IG7 111 F5
Holt Farm Jun & Inf Schs
SS4 125 D3
Holt Farm Way SS4 125 D4
Holt Rd RM3 114 E3
Holt The IG6 111 C4
Holt Way IG7 111 F5
Holton Rd
Canvey Island SS8 164 F3
Rayleigh SS6 124 A2
Holtynge SS7 144 C4
Holy Cross RC Prim Sch
Harlow CM18 24 A6
South Ockendon RM15 172 B7
Holy Family RC Prim Sch
SS7 144 D5
Holybread La CM3 34 C4
Holyfield Hall Farm★
EN9 43 C4
Holyfield Rd EN9 43 D2
Holyoak La SS5 124 E4
Holyrood Dr SS0 147 B2
Holyrood Gdns RM16 174 C2
Home Cl CM20 23 F8
Home Farm Cl SS3 150 B4
Home Farm Ind Pk SG12 8 F5
Home Farm Rd CM13 116 E2
Home Gdns RM10 135 C1
Home Mdws CM12 97 A2
Home Mead
Basildon SS15 141 B8
Galleywood CM2 54 C2
Writtle CM1 31 A1
Homebush Ho E4 87 B2
Homecove Ho SS0 166 D7
Homecroft Gdns IG10 89 B5
Homefield
Southminster CM0 84 E5
Waltham Abbey EN9 66 A7
Homefield Ave IG2 133 E6
Homefield Cl
Billericay CM11 119 D6
Chelmsford CM1 31 D5
Epping CM16 46 A1
Homefields Ave SS7 144 B5
Homeholly Ho SS11 99 D2
Homehurst Ho CM15 94 D1
Homelands Gr CM11 98 C4
Homemead DA9 177 B1
Homes Of Rest IG1 133 D1
Homesdale Cl E11 132 A6
Homestead CM1 32 B7
Homestead Ct SS7 145 D3
Homestead Dr SS16 141 C2
Homestead Gdns SS7 145 D2
Homestead Rd
Basildon,Bowers Gifford
SS13 143 E7
Dagenham RM8 134 F2
Hadleigh SS7 145 D2
Ramsden Heath SS13 120 D8
Homestead Way SS7 145 D3
Homesteads The SG12 9 D8
Homeway RM3 115 B4
Honey Brook EN9 65 E6
Honey Cl Chelmsford CM2 54 D6
Dagenham RM10 154 B6
Wyatts Green CM15 72 D4
Honey La EN9 65 E5
Honey Pot La CM3 80 D3
Honeycroft IG10 89 B5
Honeymeade CM21 11 C7
Honeypot La
Basildon SS14 142 B6
Brentwood CM14 116 A8
Stock CM4 75 C1
Honeypots CM2 54 C6
Honeysuckle Cl
Pilgrims Hatch CM15 94 B4
Romford RM3 114 C4
Honeysuckle Ct IG11 152 B6
Honeysuckle Path 9
CM1 32 F6
Honiley Ave SS12 121 E3
Honington Cl SS11 122 B6
Honiton Rd
Romford RM7 135 D5
Southend-on-S SS1 167 C8
Honor Link CM1 33 A7
Honywood Rd SS14 120 F2
Hoo The CM17 11 C5
Hood Cl SS12 121 E6
Hood Lodge E11 132 B2
Hood Rd RM13 154 F3
Hood Wlk RM7 113 B2
Hook Cotts CM1 30 B7
Hook End La CM15 72 C5
Hook End Rd CM15 72 C4
Hook Field CM18 23 F6
Hook La RM4 91 A3
Hooks Hall Dr RM10 135 C1
Hookstone Way IG8 110 D3
Hooley Dr SS6 123 C6
Hoover Dr SS15 140 F6
Hop Gardens La CM9 35 F4
Hop Gdns CM5 70 A7
Hope Ave SS17 160 E5
Hope Cl Ilford RM6 134 D7
Mountnessing CM15 95 E8
1 Woodford IG8 110 C4
Hope Rd Basildon CM11 120 C5
Canvey Island SS8 164 D3
South Benfleet SS7 144 D2
Swanscombe DA10 177 F1
Hope Terr RM20 172 D1
Hopewell Cl RM16 172 D1
Hopkins Cl
Chelmsford CM2 33 A3
Romford RM2 136 C8
Hopkins Mead CM2 33 A2
Hopkirk Cl CM3 56 F8
Hoppet The CM4 74 C4
Hoppett Rd E4 109 E8
Hopping Jacks La CM3 56 F7
Hoppit Rd EN9 65 B7
Hoppitt The CM5 26 C3
Horace Ave RM7 135 D3
Horace Rd Billericay CM11 97 C4
Ilford IG6 133 C8
Southend-on-S SS1 167 B7
Horkesley Way SS12 121 E6
Horksley Gdns CM13 95 C3
Horn La IG8 110 A3
Horn Yd 9 DA11 179 B1
Hornbeam Ave RM14 156 A8
Hornbeam Chase RM15 157 D2
Hornbeam Cl
Barking IG11 153 A2
Brentwood CM13 117 B7
Buckhurst Hill IG9 110 D7
Chelmsford CM2 54 A6
Ilford IG1 152 D7
Theydon Bois CM16 67 E2
Hornbeam Gr E4 109 F7
Hornbeam Ho IG9 110 D7
Hornbeam La E4 87 E4
Hornbeam Rd
Buckhurst Hill IG9 110 D7
Theydon Bois CM16 67 D2
Hornbeam Way SS15 119 D1
Hornbeams SS7 144 B8
Hornbeams The CM20 10 C2
Hornby Ave SS0 147 D5
Hornby Cl SS0 147 D5
Hornchurch Cl SS11 122 A6
Hornchurch Ctry Pk★
RM12 155 D6
Hornchurch Rd RM11 136 B3
Hornchurch Sports Stad
RM14 137 A2
Hornchurch Sta RM12 136 D1
Horndon Cl RM5 113 C2
Horndon Gn RM5 113 C2
Horndon Ind Pk CM13 139 C5
Horndon on the Hill CE Prim
Sch SS17 159 F4
Horndon Rd
Horndon-on-t-H SS17 160 A1
Romford RM5 113 C2
Horne Row CM3 56 D5
Horner's Cnr SS3 149 F4
Hornet Way CM0 106 B5
Hornford Way RM7 135 E4
Hornminster Glen
RM11 137 A2
Horns Rd IG2,IG6 133 C6
Hornsby La RM16 174 A5
Hornsby Sq SS15 140 F7
Hornsby Way SS15 140 F7
Hornsland Rd SS8 164 E3
Horse & Groom La CM2 54 A3
Horsebridge Cl RM9 153 E4
Horsecroft CM5 14 D2
Horsecroft Pl CM19 22 E7
Horsecroft Rd CM19 22 E7
Horseman Ct CM15 71 F2
Horseman Side CM14 92 D3
Horseshoe Cl
Billericay CM12 97 A5
Waltham Abbey EN9 66 A5
Horseshoe Cres SS3 168 F6
Horseshoe Ct SG12 8 D4
Horseshoe Hill EN9 66 C7
Horshams CM19 23 C8
Horsley Cross SS14 142 B7
Horsley Rd E4 109 C8
Hortus Rd E4 109 C8
Hospital App CM1 19 B3
Hospital Cotts CM14 116 B6
Hospital Rd SS3 168 F6

Houblon Dr CM2 . . . . .54 C2
Houblons Hill
  Coopersale CM16 . . . . . . .46 D1
  Epping CM16 . . . . .68 C8
Houchin Dr CM5 . . . . .27 C2
Hove Cl Brentwood CM13 117 C8
  Grays RM17 . . . . .178 A8
Hovefields Ave SS12 . . . .121 D3
Hovefields Ct SS13 . . . . . .121 D2
Hovefields Cvn Pk SS13 121 C2
Hovefields Dr SS12 . . . . . .121 D3
Hoveton Way IG6 . . . . . . .111 B3
Howard Chase SS14 . . . .142 A8
Howard Cl Loughton IG10 .88 C3
  Waltham Abbey EN9 . . . . .65 D5
Howard Cres SS13 . . . . . .143 C5
Howard Ct 12 IG11 . . . . . .152 D4
Howard Dr CM2 . . . . .33 A2
Howard Lodge Rd CM14 .71 C2
Howard Pl SS8 . . . . .164 B2
Howard Rd Barking IG11 152 C4
  Dartford DA1 . . . . .176 A1
  Grays RM16 . . . . .172 C3
  Ilford IG1 . . . . .152 B8
  Upminster RM14 . . . . . . .137 D2
Howard Way CM20 . . . . . . .10 F2
Howards Chase SS0 . . . .147 F2
Howards Cl CM3 . . . . .33 E8
Howards Ct SS0 . . . . .166 E8
Howburgh Ct 7 RM19 . . .171 B1
Howe Cl RM7 . . . . .113 A2
Howe Green Rd CM3 . . . .80 E7
Howell Cl RM6 . . . . .134 D6
Howell Rd SS17 . . . . .160 F6
Howerd Ho CM14 . . . . . . .116 C6
Howfield Gn EN11 . . . . .8 A1
Hows Mead CM16 . . . . . . .47 D7
Howse Rd EN9 . . . . .65 B4
Hoylake Gdns RM3 . . . . .115 C4
Hoynors CM3 . . . . .57 A7
Hubbards Chase RM11 .137 A6
Hubbards Cl RM11 . . . . . .137 B6
Hubert Rd
  Brentwood CM14 . . . . . .116 B7
  Rainham RM13 . . . . .154 C1
Hucknall Cl RM3 . . . . . . .114 F4
Hudson Cl RM20 . . . . . . .171 F1
Hudson Cres SS9 . . . . . .146 E6
Hudson Ct SS9 . . . . .146 E6
Hudson Rd SS9 . . . . .146 D6
Hudson Way SS8 . . . . . . .164 A6
Hudsons Cl SS17 . . . . . . .160 D3
Huggens's Coll (Almshouses)
  DA11 . . . . .178 B3
Hughes Rd RM16 . . . . . . .174 A3
Hugo Gdns 5 RM13 . . . .155 A6
Hull Gn CM17 . . . . .13 D2
Hull Gr CM19 . . . . .23 A3
Hull's La CM2 . . . . .55 E7
Hullbridge Rd
  Rayleigh SS6 . . . . .123 D7
  South Woodham Ferrers
  CM3 . . . . .101 D6
Hullett's La CM15 . . . . . . .93 F4
Hulse Ave Barking IG11 .152 E6
  Romford RM7 . . . . .113 B2
Hulton Ct CM3 . . . . .33 E8
Humber Ave RM15 . . . . .171 F7
Humber Cl SS6 . . . . .123 C1
Humber Dr RM14 . . . . . . .137 D5
Humber Rd CM1 . . . . .32 C5
Hume Ave RM18 . . . . . . .179 B5
Hume Cl RM18 . . . . .179 A4
Humphrey Cl IG5 . . . . . . .110 F2
Humphrey's Farm La
  CM3 . . . . .18 C7
Humphries Cl RM9 . . . . .153 F6
Hungerford Ho 4 RM3 .115 A4
Hunsdon Cl RM9 . . . . . . .153 E6
Hunsdon Rd SG12 . . . . . . .8 E5
Hunsdon Road Cotts SG12 8 E5
Hunt Ave CM9 . . . . .37 B5
Hunt's Cl CM1 . . . . .53 B8
Hunt's Dr CM1 . . . . .53 B8
Hunter Ave CM15 . . . . . . .95 A3
Hunter Dr
  Hornchurch RM12 . . . . .155 C8
  Wickford SS12 . . . . .121 E6
Hunter's Gr RM5 . . . . . . .113 B5
Hunters Ave CM12 . . . . . .119 B7
Hunters Chase
  Brentwood CM13 . . . . . . .96 C2
  Chipping Ongar CM5 . . . .49 A1
Hunters Hall Prim Sch
  RM10 . . . . .154 B7
Hunters Hall Rd RM10 . .154 A7
Hunters Rd IG1 . . . . .152 B7
Hunters Sq RM10 . . . . . .154 A8
Hunters Way CM1 . . . . . . .32 F2
Huntingdon Rd SS1 . . . .167 D7
Huntings Rd RM10 . . . . .154 A6
Huntland Cl RM13 . . . . . .170 A4
Huntley Ave DA11 . . . . . .178 C1
Hunts Hill Cotts RM14 . .156 C3
Hunts Mead CM12 . . . . . .97 A1
Huntsman Rd IG6 . . . . . .112 B5
Huntsmans Dr RM14 . . .156 C2
Hurlock Rd CM11 . . . . . . .97 B2
Hurrell Down CM3 . . . . . .20 F1
Hurrells La CM3 . . . . .57 B8
Hurricane Cl SS11 . . . . . .122 B5
Hurricane Way
  North Weald Bassett CM16 .47 A4
  Wickford SS11 . . . . .122 A5

Hursley Rd Chigwell IG7 .111 F5
  Redbridge IG7 . . . . .112 A5
Hurst Ave E4 . . . . .109 A7
Hurst Cl E4 . . . . .109 A7
Hurst Ct IG8 . . . . .110 B4
Hurst Ho SS7 . . . . .145 B4
Hurst Park Ave RM12 . . .155 E8
Hurst Rd IG9 . . . . .88 E1
Hurst Way Chelmsford CM2 .32 F2
  Southend-on-S SS9 . . . .146 F4
Hurstbourne Gdns IG11 152 E6
Hurstcombe IG9 . . . . .110 A8
Hurstlands Cl RM11 . . . .136 C5
Hurstleigh Gdns IG5 . . . .111 A2
Hurstwood Ave
  Pilgrims Hatch CM15 . . . .94 B2
  Wanstead E18 . . . . .132 B7
Hurstwood Ct RM14 . . . .137 C2
Huskards RM14 . . . . .137 C2
Hutchins Cl RM12 . . . . . .136 E1
Hutchinson Ct RM6 . . . . .134 D7
Hutson Terr RM19 . . . . . .176 D8
Hutton All Saints CE Prim
  Sch CM13 . . . . .95 D3
Hutton Cl IG8 . . . . .110 B4
Hutton Ct CM13 . . . . .95 F2
Hutton Dr CM13 . . . . .95 D2
Hutton Gate CM13 . . . . . .95 B2
Hutton Pl CM13 . . . . .95 B3
Hutton Rd
  Brentwood CM15 . . . . . . .95 A2
  Shenfield CM15 . . . . .94 F2
Hutton Village CM13 . . . . .95 F2
Huxley Dr RM6 . . . . .134 B4
Hyacinth Cl IG1 . . . . .152 B6
Hyacinth Ct 4 CM1 . . . . . .32 E7
Hycliffe Gdns IG7 . . . . . .111 C6
Hyde Chase Danbury CM3 .57 B4
  Woodham Mortimer CM9 . .57 C4
Hyde Gn CM3 . . . . .57 B7
Hyde La Danbury CM3 . . . .57 B4
  Danbury CM3 . . . . .57 B6
Hyde Mead EN9 . . . . .43 B8
Hyde Mead Ho EN9 . . . . .43 B8
Hyde The SS16 . . . . .141 C4
Hyde Way SS12 . . . . .121 D6
Hyde Wood La SS4 . . . . .125 F7
Hyder Rd RM16 . . . . .174 C3
Hydeway SS7 . . . . .144 F6
Hyh Ho E17 . . . . .109 B2
Hyland Cl RM11 . . . . .136 B4
Hyland Gate CM11 . . . . . .119 D6
Hyland House Sch E17 .109 D1
Hyland Way RM11 . . . . . .136 B4
Hylands Par CM2 . . . . . . .54 A8
Hylands Rd E17 . . . . .109 D1
Hylands The SS5 . . . . . . .124 D5
Hyleford Sch IG3 . . . . . . .152 E8
Hyndford Cres DA9 . . . . .177 C2
Hyndman Ho 8 RM10 . . .135 A1
Hynton Rd RM8 . . . . .134 C2
Hythe The CM9 . . . . .37 B2

I

I Butts Rd SS3 . . . . .150 C1
Ian Rd CM12 . . . . .96 F4
Ibbetson Path IG10 . . . . . .89 B6
Ibrox Ct 3 IG9 . . . . .110 C8
Ibscott Cl RM10 . . . . .154 C6
Icknield Dr IG2 . . . . .133 C6
Ilchester Rd RM8 . . . . . . .153 C7
Ilford Chambers IG1 . . . .133 B1
Ilford Cty High Sch IG6 111 B1
Ilford Hill IG1 . . . . .133 A1
Ilford Jewish Prim Sch
  IG6 . . . . .133 D8
Ilford La IG1 . . . . .152 B7
Ilford Prep Sch IG3 . . . . .134 A3
Ilford Ret Pk IG1 . . . . . . .133 C2
Ilford Sta IG1 . . . . .133 B2
Ilford Trad Est SS14 . . . .120 E2
Ilford Ursuline High Sch
  IG1 . . . . .133 B2
Ilfracombe Ave
  Basildon SS13 . . . . .143 D5
  Southend-on-S SS1 . . . .167 D8
Ilfracombe Cres RM6 . . .134 B4
Ilfracombe Gdns RM6 . . .134 B4
Ilfracombe Rd SS2 . . . . .148 C1
Ilgars Rd SS11 . . . . .99 E1
Ilmington Dr SS13 . . . . . .121 A1
Immanuel Sch RM7 . . . . .113 A3
Imperial Ave Mayland CM3 60 E1
  Southend-on-S SS0 . . . .147 C2
Imperial Bsns Pk DA11 .178 F1
Imperial Lodge CM4 . . . . .74 A3
Imperial Pk Rayleigh SS6 123 C6
  Southend-on-S SS2 . . . .148 C2
Imperial Ret Pk DA11 . . .179 A1
Imperial Trad Est RM13 .155 C1
Impress Pk EN11 . . . . . . .21 C7
Inchbonnie Rd CM3 . . . .101 D5
Ingatestone & Fryerning CE
  Jun Sch CM4 . . . . .74 A3
Ingatestone By-Pass
  CM4 . . . . .74 B5
Ingatestone Inf Sch CM4 .74 B4
Ingatestone Rd
  Blackmore CM4 . . . . .72 F7
  Edney Common CM4 . . . .52 A1

Ingatestone Rd continued
  Roxwell CM1 . . . . .51 F2
  Stock CM4 . . . . .75 B1
  Wanstead E12 . . . . .132 C3
  Woodford IG8 . . . . .110 B3
Ingatestone Sta CM4 . . . .74 B3
Ingaway SS16 . . . . .141 F5
Ingels Mead CM16 . . . . . .45 F5
Ingleby Gdns IG7 . . . . . . .112 B7
Ingleby Rd
  Dagenham RM10 . . . . . .154 B6
  Grays RM16 . . . . .174 C3
  Ilford IG1 . . . . .133 B3
Inglefield Rd SS17 . . . . . .161 B7
Ingleglen RM11 . . . . .137 A4
Inglehurst Gdns IG4 . . . .132 F6
Ingleton Ho 11 RM3 . . . .114 D4
Inglewood Cl
  Hornchurch RM12 . . . . .155 D8
  Redbridge IG6 . . . . .111 F4
Ingram Rd RM3 . . . . .173 C2
Ingrave Cl SS12 . . . . .121 E6
Ingrave Ho RM9 . . . . .153 E5
Ingrave Johnstone CE Prim
  Sch CM13 . . . . .117 C4
Ingrave Rd
  Brentwood CM13, CM15 .116 E7
  Romford RM1 . . . . .135 E7
Ingrebourne Ct E4 . . . . .109 B8
Ingrebourne Gdns
  RM14 . . . . .137 D3
Ingrebourne Prim Sch
  RM3 . . . . .114 C6
Ingrebourne Rd RM13 . .155 B1
Ingrebourne Valley ★
  RM13 . . . . .155 E7
Ingress Gdns DA9 . . . . . .177 D2
Ingress Park Ave DA9 . . .177 B1
Ingreway RM3 . . . . .115 C4
Inkerpole Pl CM2 . . . . . . .32 F4
Inks Gn E4 . . . . .109 C5
Inmans Row IG8 . . . . . . .110 A6
Innes Cl SS12 . . . . .121 E5
Innova Way EN3 . . . . .65 A3
Inskip Dr RM11 . . . . .136 E3
Inskip Rd RM8 . . . . .134 D3
Institute Rd 7 RM1 . . . . . .46 D2
Integrated Support Ctr,PRU
  CM18 . . . . .23 F4
International Bsns Pk
  SS8 . . . . .163 D3
Inverclyde Gdns RM6 . . .134 C1
Invermay Ct CM15 . . . . . .94 C1
Inverness Ave SS0 . . . . .147 D2
Inverness Dr IG6 . . . . . . .111 E4
Invicta Cl CM12 . . . . .96 E3
Invicta Ctr The IG11 . . . .153 A4
Invicta Rd DA2 . . . . .176 B1
Inworth Wlk CM11 . . . . . .122 A8
Io Ctr IG11 . . . . .152 F1
Iona Way SS12 . . . . .121 F6
Ipswich Mews SS16 . . . .140 F5
Ireton Pl RM17 . . . . .173 A2
Iris Cl Chelmsford CM1 . . .32 E7
  Pilgrims Hatch CM15 . . . .94 B4
Iris Path RM3 . . . . .114 C3
Irons Way RM5 . . . . .113 C2
Ironwell La Hockley SS5 .125 A3
  Rochford SS4 . . . . .125 E2
Irvine Gdns RM15 . . . . . .171 F7
Irvine Pl SS12 . . . . .121 F5
Irvine Way CM12 . . . . .97 A1
Irving Cl SS5 . . . . .124 E5
Irvington CM19 . . . . .23 B6
Irvon Hill Rd SS12 . . . . . .121 C7
Isaac Sq CM2 . . . . .55 B6
Isabella Ho EN8 . . . . .65 A5
Isbell Gdns RM1 . . . . . . .113 E3
Isis Dr RM14 . . . . .137 E5
Island Centre Way EN3 . .65 A2
Italstyle Bldg The CM20 . .11 C6
Iver Rd CM15 . . . . .94 B3
Ives Gdns RM1 . . . . .135 F7
Ivinghoe Rd RM8 . . . . . . .153 B7
Ivy Barns La
  Ingatestone CM4 . . . . . . .74 A8
  Margaretting CM4 . . . . . .52 C1
Ivy Bower Cl DA9 . . . . . . .177 B2
Ivy Chys CM16 . . . . .67 E7
Ivy Chys Prim Sch CM16 .67 F7
Ivy Chys Rd CM16 . . . . . .67 E7
Ivy Cl DA1 . . . . .176 A1
Ivy Cotts CM0 . . . . .62 A3
Ivy Lodge La RM3 . . . . . .115 B1
Ivy Rd SS7 . . . . .144 A6
Ivy Terr Hoddesdon EN11 .21 B1
  3 Ilford IG2 . . . . .133 C5
Ivy Wlk Canvey Island SS8 163 F4
  Dagenham RM9 . . . . . . .153 E6
Ivybridge EN10 . . . . .21 A4
Ivyhouse Rd RM9 . . . . . .153 E6

J

J Ct CM20 . . . . .10 F1
Jacaranda Cl CM1 . . . . . . .33 A6
Jack Cook Ho 9 IG11 . . .152 B7
Jack Cornwell St E12 . . .152 A8
Jack Evans Ct RM15 . . . .172 A4
Jack Lobley Prim Sch
  RM18 . . . . .178 F6
Jack Stevens Cl CM17 . . .24 C6
Jackdaw Cl
  Billericay CM11 . . . . .119 C8
  Southend-on-S SS3 . . . .168 E8
Jacklin Gn IG8 . . . . .110 A6
Jacks Cl SS11 . . . . .121 F7

Jackson Cl
  Greenhithe DA9 . . . . . . .177 A2
  Hornchurch RM11 . . . . . .136 F7
Jackson Ct E11 . . . . .132 B3
Jackson Pl CM2 . . . . .54 D6
Jackson Rd IG11 . . . . . . .152 D4
Jacksons Cl CM5 . . . . . . .49 A2
Jacksons La CM11 . . . . . .97 C2
Jacksons Mews CM11 . . .97 C2
Jacob Ct EN3 . . . . .65 A3
Jacobs Ave RM3 . . . . . . .114 E1
Jacobs Cl RM10 . . . . .154 B8
Jacqueline Gdns CM12 . .97 B5
Jade Cl RM8 . . . . .134 C3
Jade Ho 6 RM13 . . . . . . .155 A1
Jaffe Rd IG1 . . . . .133 D3
Jakapeni Rare Breeds Pk ★
  SS5 . . . . .123 E8
James Alexander Ho
  SS5 . . . . .101 D3
James Ave RM8 . . . . .134 F3
James Cl RM2 . . . . .136 A6
James Croft CM2 . . . . . . .55 A7
James Ct Chingford E4 . .109 D8
  3 Woodford IG8 . . . . . . .110 B1
James Hornsby High Sch The
  SS15 . . . . .141 D7
James Lee Sq EN3 . . . . . .65 A3
James Oglethorpe Prim Sch
  The RM14 . . . . .137 C2
James Sq CM11 . . . . .97 C2
James St Barking IG11 . .152 C5
  Epping CM16 . . . . .46 A3
Jane Ct 7 RM1 . . . . .135 F6
Janet Duke Inf Sch
  SS15 . . . . .141 D6
Janet Duke Jun Sch
  SS15 . . . . .141 D6
Janette Ave SS8 . . . . . . .163 E3
Janice Mews 3 IG1 . . . . .133 B1
Janmead CM13 . . . . .95 B2
Japan Rd RM6 . . . . .134 D5
Jardine Rd SS13 . . . . . . .143 C8
Jarndyce CM1 . . . . .31 F6
Jarrah Cotts RM19 . . . . . .176 D8
Jarrow Rd RM6 . . . . .134 C5
Jarvis Cl 1 IG11 . . . . .152 D4
Jarvis Field CM3 . . . . .34 D5
Jarvis Rd
  Canvey Island SS8 . . . . .164 A6
  South Benfleet SS7 . . . .144 E4
Jasmine Cl
  Basildon SS16 . . . . .140 F4
  Canvey Island SS8 . . . . .163 F2
  2 Chelmsford CM1 . . . . .32 E7
  Ilford IG1 . . . . .152 B7
Jasmine Rd RM7 . . . . . . .135 C2
Jason Cl
  Canvey Island SS8 . . . . .164 B5
  Orsett RM16 . . . . .174 E7
Jason Ct CM14 . . . . .115 F6
Jasons Cl CM14 . . . . .115 F6
Jeffcut Rd CM2 . . . . .32 E2
Jefferies Way 5 SS17 . . .160 F2
Jefferson Ave 3 SS15 . . .141 A6
Jefferson Cl IG2 . . . . .133 B6
Jeffery Rd CM2 . . . . .55 A7
Jellicoe Ct E4 . . . . .109 D4
Jena Cl SS3 . . . . .168 E7
Jenkins La IG11 . . . . .152 C2
Jenner Ho 6 DA17 . . . . . .169 A3
Jenner Mead CM2 . . . . . . .33 A3
Jenningham Dr RM16 . . .173 A5
Jennings Pl CM4 . . . . .75 A8
Jenningtree Way DA17 . .169 B1
Jenny Path RM3 . . . . .114 D3
Jericho Pl CM4 . . . . .72 E8
Jermayns SS15 . . . . .141 E6
Jerningham Ave IG5 . . . .111 B1
Jerounds CM19 . . . . .23 B6
Jerounds Com Jun & Inf Sch
  CM19 . . . . .23 B5
Jersey Cl EN11 . . . . .21 A5
Jersey Gdns SS13 . . . . . .121 D8
Jersey Rd Ilford IG1 . . . . .152 B8
  Maldon CM9 . . . . .37 B1
  Rainham RM13 . . . . .155 A5
Jervis Ct 9 RM10 . . . . . .154 B6
Jesmond Rd
  Canvey Island SS8 . . . . .164 B2
  Grays RM16 . . . . .173 D5
Jessel Dr IG10 . . . . .89 C7
Jessett Cl DA8 . . . . .169 D2
Jetty Wlk RM17 . . . . .178 A8
Jim Desormeaux Bglws
  CM20 . . . . .10 E2
Joan Gdns RM8 . . . . .134 E2
Joan Rd RM8 . . . . .134 E2
Jocelyns CM17 . . . . .11 C4
Jodrell Way RM20 . . . . . .171 F1
John Barker Ho IG1 . . . .133 D2
John Bramston Prim Sch
  IG6 . . . . .112 A4
John Burns Dr IG11 . . . . .152 E5
John Chilos Way SS6 . . .123 E5
John Clay Gdns RM16 . . .173 B5
John Cornwell VC Ho 6
  E12 . . . . .152 A8
John Ct EN11 . . . . .8 A1
John Eliot Cl EN9 . . . . . . .21 E2
John Henry Keene Meml
  Homes CM1 . . . . .32 A4
John Parker Rd RM10 . . .154 B6
John Perry Prim Sch
  RM10 . . . . .154 D6
John St Grays RM17 . . . .178 C8
  Southend-on-S SS3 . . . .168 G6

John Warner Sch The
  EN11 . . . . .8 B1
John William Cl RM16 . . .172 D1
John's Rd DA2 . . . . .176 C1
John's Terr RM3 . . . . .115 C4
Johns The CM5 . . . . .49 A4
Johnson Cl Rochford SS4 125 D5
  Wickford SS12 . . . . .121 D5
Johnson Ct SS4 . . . . .125 F2
Johnson Rd CM2 . . . . . . .55 A5
Johnsons Way DA9 . . . . .177 C1
Johnston Rd IG8 . . . . . . .110 C1
Johnston Way CM9 . . . . . .59 A8
Johnstone Rd SS1 . . . . . .168 A7
Jonathans RM11 . . . . . . .136 E3
Jonathon Ho RM17 . . . . .173 D2
Jones Cl SS2 . . . . .147 E3
Jones Cnr SS4 . . . . .164 A3
Jordans Cl RM10 . . . . . . .154 B8
Jordans The SS2 . . . . . . .148 A2
Jordans Way RM13 . . . . .155 D3
Joseph Clarke Sch E4 . .109 C4
Joseph Lister Lodge
  E11 . . . . .132 B3
Joslin Rd RM19 . . . . .171 D1
Josling Cl RM17 . . . . .177 F8
Joslyn Cl EN3 . . . . .65 A1
Josselin Ct SS13 . . . . . . .121 C2
Josselin Rd SS13 . . . . . . .121 C2
Jotmans Hall Prim Sch
  SS7 . . . . .144 E4
Jotmans La
  South Benfleet SS7 . . . .143 F2
  South Benfleet SS7 . . . .144 E4
Journeymans Way SS2 . .148 A5
Joyce Ct EN9 . . . . .65 D5
Joyce's Chase CM9 . . . . .39 A8
Joydon Dr RM6 . . . . .134 B5
Joyes Cl RM3 . . . . .114 D6
Joyners Cl RM9 . . . . .153 F8
Joyners Field CM18 . . . . .23 C4
Jubilee Ave
  Broomfield CM1 . . . . .19 B2
  Chingford E4 . . . . .109 C4
  Romford RM7 . . . . .135 C2
Jubilee Cl
  Greenhithe DA9 . . . . . . .177 C1
  Hockley SS5 . . . . .124 E5
  Romford RM7 . . . . .135 B6
Jubilee Cotts SS4 . . . . . .127 D6
Jubilee Ct EN9 . . . . .65 F6
Jubilee Dr SS11 . . . . .121 C8
Jubilee Par IG8 . . . . .110 C4
Jubilee Rd
  Basildon CM11 . . . . .120 C4
  Grays RM20 . . . . .177 B8
  Rayleigh SS6 . . . . .123 E2
Jubilee Rise CM3 . . . . . . .57 C6
Jubilee Terr
  Chelmsford CM1 . . . . . . .32 A4
  Woodham Ferrers CM3 . . .79 B4
Judge Rd CM2 . . . . .33 B4
Judith Anne Ct RM14 . . .137 E2
Judith Ave RM5 . . . . .113 B4
Julia Gdns IG11 . . . . .153 D3
Julian Cl CM1 . . . . .19 B1
Julie Ho EN11 . . . . .21 C8
Juliers Cl SS8 . . . . .164 C3
Juliers Rd SS8 . . . . .164 B3
Juliette Way RM15 . . . . . .170 F5
Junction Rd
  Basildon SS13 . . . . .143 B4
  Brentwood CM14 . . . . . .116 C6
  Cold Norton CM3 . . . . . . .81 A6
  Romford RM1 . . . . .135 F6
Junction Rd W RM6 . . . .134 E4
Juniper Cl CM11 . . . . .97 C4
Juniper Ct
  Brentwood CM13 . . . . . .116 F7
  Ilford RM6 . . . . .134 C5
Juniper Dr
  Chelmsford CM2 . . . . . . .54 B6
  South Ockendon RM15 . .157 E2
Juniper Rd Boreham CM3 .33 F8
  Ilford IG1 . . . . .152 B8
  Southend-on-S SS9 . . . .146 F4
Juniper Way RM3 . . . . . .114 C2
Jury St 5 DA11 . . . . .179 B1
Jutsums Ave RM7 . . . . . .135 B5
Jutsums Ct RM7 . . . . . . .135 B5
Jutsums La RM7 . . . . . . .135 B5

K

Kale Rd SS7 . . . . .144 E4
Kamerwyk Ave SS8 . . . . .164 C4
Kandlewood RM13 . . . . . .155 B8
Karen Cl Brentwood CM15 .94 C2
  Rainham RM13 . . . . .154 E3
  South Benfleet SS7 . . . .163 E4
  Stanford-le-H SS17 . . . .160 C1
  Wickford SS12 . . . . .121 C6
Karen Terr IG2 . . . . .133 D6
Karina Cl IG7 . . . . .111 E5
Katella Trad Est IG11 . . .152 E2
Katemon Ct SG12 . . . . . . .8 D4
Katherine Cl SS6 . . . . . . .124 A1
Katherine Gdns IG6 . . . .111 C3
Katherine Rd SS13 . . . . .143 E7
Katherine's Way CM19 . . .23 A6
Katherines Hatch CM19 . .23 A6
Katherines Ho CM19 . . . .23 A6
Katherines Prim Sch
  CM19 . . . . .23 A6
Kathleen Cl SS17 . . . . . . .160 E4
Kathleen Dr SS9 . . . . . . .146 F2

Kathleen Ferrier Cres
SS15 . . . .**141** D8
Kathryn Ct SS3 . . . .**168** E7
Katonia Ave CM3 . . . .**60** F1
Kavanaghs CM14 . . . .**116** B7
Kavanaghs Rd CM14 . . . . .**116** B7
Kavanaghs Terr CM14 . . . .**116** B7
Keary Rd DA10 . . . .**177** F1
Keatings The CM15 . . . . . .**71** E2
Keats Ave RM3 . . . .**114** B3
Keats CI Chigwell IG7 . . . . .**111** C4
Maldon CM9 . . . .**59** A8
Wanstead E11 . . . .**132** B6
Keats Rd RM18 . . . .**179** B5
Keats Sq DA17 . . . .**169** C3
Keats Way SS12 . . . .**121** C7
Keats Wlk
Brentwood CM13 . . . .**95** D2
Rayleigh SS6 . . . .**124** A2
Kecksy's CM21 . . . .**1** F4
Keeble Pk CM9 . . . .**58** F8
Keefield CM19 . . . .**23** B3
Keegan PI SS8 . . . .**164** C4
Keel CI IG11 . . . .**153** C3
Keelings La CM0 . . . .**85** E8
Keelings Rd CM0 . . . .**85** F8
Keene Way CM2 . . . .**54** B3
Keer Ave SS8 . . . .**164** D2
Keighley Mews SS3 . . . . . .**149** D2
Keighley Rd RM3 . . . .**114** E3
Keir Hardie Ho RM16 . . . . .**173** D5
Keir Hardie Way IG11 . . . . .**153** A5
Keir Hardy Ho 6 DA17 . . . .**169** A3
Keith Ave SS11 . . . .**99** D2
Keith Lauder Ho RM6 . . . . .**134** E6
Keith Rd IG11 . . . .**152** D3
Keith Way
Hornchurch RM11 . . . .**136** E4
Southend-on-S SS2 . . . . . .**147** E5
Kelburn Way RM13 . . . . . .**155** A2
Kellington Rd SS8 . . . .**164** C5
Kelly Ho RM15 . . . .**171** C5
Kelly Rd SS13 . . . .**143** E6
Kelly Way RM6 . . . .**134** E5
Kelsie Way IG6 . . . .**111** E4
Kelso Lodge E18 . . . .**110** E1
Kelston Rd IG6 . . . .**111** B1
Kelvedon CI
Billericay CM11 . . . .**97** C2
Brentwood CM13 . . . .**95** E3
Chelmsford CM1 . . . .**32** A6
Rayleigh SS6 . . . .**123** A3
Kelvedon Gn CM15 . . . .**71** F2
Kelvedon Hall La CM14 . . . .**71** B4
Kelvedon Hatch Com Prim
Sch CM15 . . . .**71** E2
Kelvedon Hatch Nuclear
Bunker✷ CM14 . . . .**71** C3
Kelvedon Ho IG9 . . . .**88** E2
Kelvedon Rd CM11 . . . .**97** C2
Kelvedon Way IG8 . . . .**110** F4
Kelvedon Wlk RM13 . . . . . .**154** F4
Kelvin Ho 3 DA17 . . . .**169** A3
Kelvin Rd
South Benfleet SS7 . . . . . .**144** D7
Tilbury RM18 . . . .**179** A5
Kelvinside SS17 . . . .**160** E4
Kembles SS6 . . . .**123** E4
Kemp Ho E6 . . . .**152** A6
Kemp Rd RM8 . . . .**134** D3
Kempley Ct RM17 . . . .**178** D8
Kempton Ave RM12 . . . . . .**136** F1
Kempton CI SS7 . . . .**145** B7
Kempton Rd E6 . . . .**152** A4
Kemsley CI DA9 . . . .**177** B1
Kendal Ave Barking IG11 . . .**152** E4
Epping CM16 . . . .**68** A8
Kendal CI Hullbridge SS5 . . .**101** E1
Rayleigh SS6 . . . .**123** A3
Woodford IG8 . . . .**109** F8
Kendal Croft RM12 . . . . . .**155** A7
Kendal Ct 9 Chingford E4 . .**87** C1
Wickford SS12 . . . .**122** A5
Kendal Rd EN9 . . . .**65** C4
Kendal Way SS6 . . . .**146** E7
Kendale RM16 . . . .**174** B3
Kendon CI E11 . . . .**132** B6
Kenholme SS9 . . . .**146** E4
Kenilworth Ave
Chingford E17 . . . .**109** A1
Romford RM3 . . . .**115** B4
Kenilworth CI CM12 . . . .**96** E2
Kenilworth Ct
7 Chingford E4 . . . .**109** C8
8 Dartford DA2 . . . .**176** B1
Kenilworth Gdns
Hornchurch RM12 . . . .**136** D1
Ilford IG3 . . . .**133** F2
Loughton IG10 . . . .**88** F3
Rayleigh SS6 . . . .**123** C3
Southend-on-S SS0,SS9 . . .**147** A3
Kenilworth PI SS15 . . . . . .**119** E1
Kenley CI SS11 . . . .**122** B6
Kenley Gdns RM12 . . . . . .**136** F2
Kenmar CI SS16 . . . .**146** A8
Kenmore CI SS8 . . . .**164** E2
Kennedy Ave SS15 . . . . . .**140** F6
South Benfleet SS7 . . . . . .**144** B7
Kennedy CI Rayleigh SS6 . .**146** A8
South Benfleet SS7 . . . . . .**144** B7
Kennedy Rd IG11 . . . .**152** E4
Kennel La CM12,CM11 . . . .**119** C7
Kennet CI RM14 . . . .**137** E5
Kennet Gn RM15 . . . .**172** B6
Kennet Way CM1 . . . .**31** D5
Kenneth Ave IG1 . . . .**152** B8
Kenneth Chambers Ct
IG8 . . . .**110** E4

Kenneth Gdns SS17 . . . .**160** F5
Kenneth More Rd 4
IG1 . . . .**133** B1
Kenneth Rd
Basildon SS13 . . . .**143** C7
Dagenham RM6 . . . .**134** E4
Thundersley SS7 . . . .**144** F5
Kenning Rd EN11 . . . .**21** B8
Kennington Ave SS7 . . . . .**144** C6
Kenningtons Prim Sch
RM15 . . . .**171** C7
Kennylands Rd IG6 . . . . . .**112** A3
Kensington Ct RM17 . . . . .**178** C8
Kensington Dr IG8 . . . .**110** D1
Kensington Gdns
Billericay CM12 . . . .**97** A4
East Tilbury RM18 . . . . . .**175** C2
Redbridge IG1 . . . .**132** F3
Kensington Ho 7 IG8 . . . .**111** A3
Kensington Rd
Pilgrims Hatch CM15 . . . . . .**94** A3
Romford RM7 . . . .**135** C5
Southend-on-S SS1 . . . . . .**167** D7
Kensington Way SS5 . . . . .**124** C6
Kent Ave
Canvey Island SS8 . . . . . .**164** B5
Dagenham RM9 . . . .**154** A1
Southend-on-S SS9 . . . . . .**146** F3
Kent CI SS15 . . . .**141** B6
Kent Dr RM12 . . . .**155** D8
Kent Elms CI SS2 . . . .**146** F5
Kent Elms Cnr SS9 . . . . . .**146** F5
Kent Green CI SS5 . . . . . .**124** F5
Kent Ho RM7 . . . .**113** A2
Kent Kraft Ind Est
Northfleet DA11 . . . .**178** A2
Swanscombe DA10 . . . . . .**177** A2
Kent Rd Dagenham RM10 . .**154** B7
Grays RM17 . . . .**173** C1
Kent View Aveley RM15 . . .**171** C4
Rainham RM13 . . . .**170** D6
Kent View Ave SS9 . . . . . .**166** A8
Kent View Ct SS8 . . . .**164** B1
Kent View Gdns IG3 . . . . . .**133** E2
Kent View Rd SS16 . . . . . .**142** F4
Kent Way SS6 . . . .**146** A8
Kentish Rd DA17 . . . .**169** A2
Kenton Way SS16 . . . .**140** F5
Kents Farm La CM2 . . . . . .**76** D4
Kents Hill Jun & Inf Sch
SS7 . . . .**144** D4
Kents Hill Rd SS7 . . . .**144** D4
Kents Hill Rd N SS7 . . . . . .**144** D6
Kents La CM15 . . . .**25** D2
Kentwell Ct SS7 . . . .**144** C3
Kenway Rainham RM13 . . .**155** D2
Romford RM5 . . . .**113** C1
Southend-on-S SS2 . . . . . .**148** A2
Kenway CI RM13 . . . .**155** C2
Kenway Wlk RM13 . . . . . .**155** D2
Kenwood Gdns
Ilford IG2 . . . .**133** A6
2 Wanstead E18 . . . .**132** B8
Kenwood Rd SS17 . . . .**161** B5
Keppel Rd RM9 . . . .**153** E8
Kerby Rise CM2 . . . .**32** F2
Kernow Ct RM12 . . . .**136** E2
Kerril Croft CM20 . . . .**10** A1
Kerry Ave RM15 . . . .**170** F4
Kerry CI RM14 . . . .**137** F4
Kerry Dr RM14 . . . .**137** F4
Kerry Rd RM16 . . . .**173** D5
Kersbrooke Way SS17 . . . .**161** B5
Kersey Gdns RM3 . . . .**114** F3
Kershaw CI Grays RM16 . . .**172** C2
Hornchurch RM11 . . . .**136** E4
Kershaw Rd RM10 . . . .**135** A1
Kershaws CI SS12 . . . .**121** C6
Kesteven CI IG6 . . . .**111** F4
Kestral Pk CM13 . . . .**95** E4
Kestrel CI
Hornchurch RM12 . . . .**155** B5
Redbridge IG6 . . . .**112** C6
Kestrel Gr SS6 . . . .**123** B3
Kestrel Ho SS3 . . . .**149** F1
Kestrel Mews CM9 . . . .**59** B8
Kestrel Rd EN9 . . . .**66** A5
Kestrel Wlk CM2 . . . .**54** B5
Keswick Ave
Hornchurch RM11 . . . .**136** E2
Hullbridge SS5 . . . .**101** E2
Keswick CI SS6 . . . .**123** E2
Keswick Gdns IG4 . . . .**132** E2
Keswick Ho 14 RM3 . . . . . .**114** D4
Keswick Rd SS7 . . . .**144** E7
Ketleys CM2 . . . .**54** C3
Kettering Rd RM3 . . . .**114** E3
Kettlebury Way CM5 . . . . . .**48** F1
Kevin CI CM11 . . . .**119** D7
Keyes CI SS3 . . . .**149** E1
Keyes Rd DA1 . . . .**176** A3
Keynsham Ave IG8 . . . . . .**109** E6
Keys The CM13 . . . .**116** C4
Keysers Rd EN10 . . . .**21** B1
Keysland SS7 . . . .**145** B7
Khartoum PI DA12 . . . .**179** C1
Khartoum Rd IG1 . . . .**152** B7
Kibcaps SS16 . . . .**141** F4
Kidd Ho RM9 . . . .**153** F8
Kidman Ct RM2 . . . .**136** C8
Kielder CI IG6 . . . .**111** F4
Kilbarry Wlk CM11 . . . .**97** D6
Kildown Rd IG3 . . . .**134** A3
Kilmartin Rd IG3 . . . .**134** A3
Kilmartin Way RM12 . . . . .**155** B7
Kilmington CI CM13 . . . . . .**117** B8
Kiln Cotts CM3 . . . .**56** D6

Kiln La CM17 . . . .**24** C7
Kiln Rd Hadleigh SS7 . . . . .**145** B4
North Weald Bassett CM16 . .**47** A4
Kiln Shaw SS16 . . . .**141** C4
Kiln Way RM17 . . . .**172** F1
Kiln Wood La RM4 . . . .**113** D5
Kilnfield
Chipping Ongar CM5 . . . . . .**48** F2
Wyatts Green CM15 . . . . . .**72** D3
Kilnwood Ave SS5 . . . .**124** D5
Kilowan CI SS16 . . . .**140** F4
Kilsby Wlk RM9 . . . .**153** B6
Kilworth Ave
Brentwood CM15 . . . .**95** A3
Southend-on-S SS1 . . . . . .**167** B8
Kimberley Ave
Ilford IG2 . . . .**133** E4
Romford RM7 . . . .**135** C5
Kimberley Ct SS7 . . . .**144** C3
Kimberley Rd
Chingford E4 . . . .**87** E1
Little Wakering SS3 . . . . . .**149** E6
South Benfleet SS7 . . . . . .**144** C3
Rayleigh SS6 . . . .**123** E2
Southminster CM0 . . . .**84** D4
Kimberley Way E4 . . . .**87** E1
Kimberly Dr SS15 . . . .**119** F2
Kimpton Ave CM15 . . . .**94** C2
Kimpton's CI CM5 . . . .**48** F5
Kinfauns Ave RM11 . . . . . .**136** C5
Kinfauns Rd IG3 . . . .**134** B3
King Alfred Rd RM3 . . . . . .**114** F1
King Edmund Sch The
SS4 . . . .**125** E5
King Edward Ave
Burnham-on-C CM0 . . . . . .**106** B6
Rainham RM13 . . . .**155** D2
King Edward Ct CM1 . . . . . .**32** A3
King Edward Dr RM16 . . . . .**173** E3
King Edward Rd
Basildon SS15 . . . .**141** B8
Brentwood CM14 . . . .**116** C7
Greenhithe DA9 . . . .**177** A2
Romford RM1 . . . .**135** F5
King Edward Terr SS15 . . . .**141** B8
King Edward VI Gram Sch
CM1 . . . .**32** A3
King Edward's Rd
Barking IG11 . . . .**152** D3
South Woodham Ferrers
CM3 . . . .**101** D8
Stanford-le-H SS17 . . . . . .**175** D8
King George Ave IG2 . . . . .**133** D5
King George Ct RM7 . . . . . .**135** C8
King George Hospl IG3 . . . .**134** A6
King George Rd EN9 . . . . . .**65** C5
King George VI Ave
RM18 . . . .**175** B2
King George's CI SS6 . . . . .**123** D1
King George's CI SS6 . . . . .**123** D1
King George's PI CM9 . . . . .**37** A2
King George's Rd CM15 . . . .**94** B3
King Harold Ct EN9 . . . .**65** C6
King Harold Sch EN9 . . . . . .**65** E6
King Henry's Dr SS4 . . . . . .**147** F7
King Henry's Mews EN3 . . . .**65** A2
King Henrys Ct EN9 . . . .**65** C3
King John Sch The SS7 . . . .**145** B3
King Solomon High Sch
IG6 . . . .**111** D1
King St
Gravesend DA12 . . . .**179** B1
High Ongar CM5 . . . .**50** B3
Maldon CM9 . . . .**37** A1
Stanford-le-H SS17 . . . . . .**160** C1
King Williams Ct EN9 . . . . . .**65** C4
King's Ave
Buckhurst Hill IG9 . . . .**110** D8
Woodford IG8 . . . .**110** C5
King's Chase CM14 . . . . . .**116** C7
King's Gn IG10 . . . .**88** E6
King's Hill IG10 . . . .**88** E7
King's Rd Barking IG11 . . . .**152** C5
Brentwood CM14 . . . .**116** C7
Chingford E4 . . . .**87** D1
Romford RM1 . . . .**136** A6
South Benfleet SS7 . . . . . .**144** E2
Southend-on-S SS0 . . . . . .**147** B1
King's Wood Sch RM3 . . . .**115** A6
Kingaby Gdns RM13 . . . . . .**155** A5
Kingfisher Ave E11 . . . . . .**132** B5
Kingfisher CI
Brentwood CM13 . . . .**95** A2
Heybridge CM9 . . . .**37** C5
Southend-on-S SS3 . . . . . .**168** E8
Stansted Abbotts SG12 . . . . .**8** C3
Kingfisher Cres SS6 . . . . . .**123** B3
Kingfisher Dr
Greenhithe DA9 . . . .**177** A1
South Benfleet SS7 . . . . . .**144** C2
Kingfisher Lodge CM2 . . . . .**54** F7
Kingfisher Rd RM14 . . . . . .**137** F3
Kingfisher Way CM19 . . . . . .**9** A1
Kingfishers
Basildon SS16 . . . .**142** C4
Ingatestone CM4 . . . .**74** C5
Kingfishers The 1
SS11 . . . .**122** A5
Kingley CI SS12 . . . .**121** B7
Kingley Dr SS12 . . . .**121** B7
Kings Ave RM6 . . . .**134** C5
Kings CI
Canvey Island SS8 . . . . . .**163** C3
Rayleigh SS6 . . . .**123** E2
Kings Cres SS15 . . . .**119** B1
Kings Croft CM0 . . . .**84** D4
Kings Ct
2 Buckhurst Hill IG9 . . . . .**110** D8
Burnham-on-C CM0 . . . . . .**106** B4
Kings Eight CM14 . . . .**116** C7

Kings Farm
Chingford E17 . . . .**109** B2
Rayleigh SS6 . . . .**123** D1
Kings Gdns Ilford IG1 . . . . .**133** D2
Upminster RM14 . . . .**137** E4
Kings Gr RM1 . . . .**136** A6
Kings Head Hill E4 . . . .**87** B2
Kings Head Wlk 6 CM2 . . . .**32** C5
Kings Keep SS0 . . . .**166** C3
Kings Lodge SS7 . . . .**145** C3
Kings Lynn Dr RM3 . . . . . .**114** D4
Kings Meadow CM CM9 . . . .**66** A5
Kings Mews IG7 . . . .**111** C8
Kings Oak RM7 . . . .**135** A8
Kings Par SS17 . . . .**160** C5
Kings Pk SS7 . . . .**144** F5
Kings PI Buckhurst Hill IG9 .**110** D8
Loughton IG10 . . . .**88** D2
Kings Rd Basildon SS15 . . .**119** B1
Burnham-on-C CM0 . . . . . .**106** B4
Canvey Island SS8 . . . . . .**163** C3
Chelmsford CM1 . . . .**31** F4
Rayleigh SS6 . . . .**123** E2
Southminster CM0 . . . .**84** D4
Kings Road Prim Sch
CM1 . . . .**31** F4
Kings Way
Billericay CM11 . . . .**119** D6
South Woodham F CM3 . . . .**79** C1
Kingsbridge Cir 6 RM3 . . . .**114** E4
Kingsbridge CI RM3 . . . . . .**114** E4
Kingsbridge Ind Est
IG11 . . . .**152** E2
Kingsbridge Rd
Barking IG11 . . . .**152** D3
Romford RM3 . . . .**114** E4
Kingscroft SS2 . . . .**148** B1
Kingsdale Ct
Swanscombe DA10 . . . . . .**177** E1
Waltham Abbey EN9 . . . . . .**66** A5
Kingsdale Ind Est The
CM1 . . . .**32** C3
Kingsdon La CM17 . . . .**24** C7
Kingsdown CI SS13 . . . . . .**143** C6
Kingsdown SS2 . . . .**146** F6
Kingsdown Wlk SS8 . . . . . .**164** A5
Kingsfield EN11 . . . .**21** A8
Kingsford Dr CM2 . . . .**33** B4
Kingsgate Ct E18 . . . .**132** B8
Kingshawes SS7 . . . .**145** B6
Kingshill Ave RM5 . . . .**113** C5
Kingsland CM18 . . . .**23** C6
Kingsley Ave DA1 . . . .**176** A2
Kingsley CI RM10 . . . .**154** B8
Kingsley Cres SS7 . . . .**145** C8
Kingsley Ct RM2 . . . .**136** B5
Kingsley Gdns
Chingford E4 . . . .**109** A5
Hornchurch RM11 . . . .**136** D7
Kingsley Grange 1 E11 . . . .**132** A6
Kingsley La SS7 . . . .**145** B8
Kingsley Mdws SS12 . . . . .**121** D5
Kingsley Mews RM9 . . . . . .**153** D6
Kingsley Rd
Brentwood CM13 . . . .**95** D2
Chingford E17 . . . .**109** C1
Loughton IG10 . . . .**89** D6
Redbridge IG6 . . . .**111** C2
Kingsley Wlk RM16 . . . . . .**174** A2
Kingsman Dr RM16 . . . . . .**173** B6
Kingsman Rd SS17 . . . . . .**160** B5
Kingsmans Farm Rd
SS5 . . . .**102** A4
Kingsmead
Lower Nazeing EN9,EN10 . . .**21** C1
Sawbridgeworth CM21 . . . . . .**1** E1
Kingsmead Ave RM1 . . . . . .**135** C4
Kingsmead Ct RM16 . . . . . .**22** B7
Kingsmead Hill CM19 . . . . . .**22** B7
Kingsmead Lodge 9
E4 . . . .**109** C8
Kingsmead Mans 4
RM1 . . . .**135** C5
Kingsmere SS7 . . . .**145** C5
Kingsmill Gdns RM9 . . . . . .**153** F7
Kingsmill Rd RM9 . . . .**153** F7
Kingsmoor Jun & Inf Sch
CM18 . . . .**23** C4
Kingsmoor Rd CM19 . . . . . .**23** B5
Kingspark Ct E18 . . . .**132** A8
Kingsteignton SS3 . . . .**168** B8
Kingston Chase CM9 . . . . . .**36** F5
Kingston CI RM6 . . . .**134** E8
Kingston Cres CM2 . . . .**32** E3
Kingston Ct Grays RM17 . . .**173** B3
Northfleet DA11 . . . .**178** B2
Kingston Hill SS16 . . . .**141** D2
Kingston Hill Ave RM6 . . . . .**134** E8
Kingston Prim Sch SS7 . . . .**144** E6
Kingston Rd Ilford IG1 . . . . .**152** C8
Romford RM1 . . . .**135** F5
Kingston Ridge SS16 . . . . .**141** D3
Kingston Way SS7 . . . .**144** E6
Kingsview Ct SS11 . . . .**121** F6
Kingsway
Hullbridge SS5 . . . .**123** D8
Southend-on-S SS3 . . . . . .**147** A2
Woodford IG8 . . . .**110** C5
Kingsway Mews SS3 . . . . . .**147** B2
Kingswood Chase SS9 . . . .**146** D3
Kingswood CI CM11 . . . .**97** C2
Kingswood Cres SS6 . . . . .**123** B1
Kingswood Ct
Basildon SS14 . . . .**142** F8
Bradwell-on-S CM0 . . . . . .**42** B2

Kingswood Ct continued
Chingford E4 . . . .**109** A5
Kingswood Inf Sch
SS16 . . . .**142** B5
Kingswood Lodge SS9 . . . .**146** D3
Kingswood Rd
Basildon SS16 . . . .**142** C5
Ilford IG3 . . . .**134** A4
Kinnaird Way IG8 . . . .**110** F4
Kipling Ave RM18 . . . .**179** C6
Kipling CI
Brentwood CM14 . . . .**116** B5
Chelmsford CM1 . . . .**32** A5
Kipling Mews SS2 . . . .**148** A2
Kipling Rd DA1 . . . .**176** B2
Kipling Twrs RM3 . . . .**114** D3
Kirby CI Loughton IG10 . . . . .**88** E2
Redbridge IG6 . . . .**111** E4
Romford RM3 . . . .**115** A5
Kirby Rd SS14 . . . .**142** F6
Kirkham Ave SS16 . . . .**159** F7
Kirkham Ho 9 RM3 . . . . . .**114** D4
Kirkham Rd SS17 . . . .**159** F8
Kirkham Shaw SS17 . . . . . .**159** F8
Kirkland Ave IG5 . . . .**111** A1
Kirklees CM1 . . . .**31** F4
Kirklees Rd RM8 . . . .**153** C7
Kirkmans Rd CM2 . . . .**54** D3
Kirton CI RM12 . . . .**155** C6
Kitchener Rd
Chingford E17 . . . .**109** B2
Dagenham RM10 . . . .**154** B6
North Fambridge CM3 . . . . .**81** A1
Kitkatts Rd SS8 . . . .**164** A3
Kitson Way CM20 . . . .**10** C3
Kittiwake Dr CM9 . . . .**37** C5
Knapton CI CM1 . . . .**32** D7
Knares The SS16 . . . .**141** B8
Knebworth Ave E17 . . . . . .**109** A2
Knebworth Ho E17 . . . .**109** A2
Knight CI RM8 . . . .**134** C2
Knight 1 E4 . . . .**87** C1
Knight Ho IG10 . . . .**89** D5
Knight St
Sawbridgeworth CM21 . . . . . .**1** E2
South Woodham Ferrers
CM3 . . . .**101** E7
Knight's Ct
4 Basildon SS14 . . . .**142** F8
Sawbridgeworth CM21 . . . . . .**1** E2
Knight's Way CM13 . . . . . .**117** A7
Knightbridge Wlk CM12 . .**97** A4
Knighton CI
Romford RM7 . . . .**135** D5
Woodford IG8 . . . .**110** B6
Knighton Dr IG8 . . . .**110** B6
Knighton Gn IG9 . . . .**110** B8
Knighton La IG9 . . . .**110** B8
Knighton Rd
Romford RM7 . . . .**135** C5
Wanstead E7 . . . .**132** A1
Knights SS15 . . . .**141** D8
Knights Manor Way
DA1 . . . .**176** A2
Knights Way IG6 . . . .**111** C4
Knights Wlk RM4 . . . .**90** B6
Knightsbridge Gdns 5
RM7 . . . .**135** D6
Knightsmead Sch RM15 . . .**172** A6
Knightswick Ctr SS8 . . . . . .**164** C4
Knightswick Rd SS8 . . . . . .**164** B4
Knightswood Rd RM13 . . . .**155** A3
Knivet CI SS6 . . . .**123** E4
Knockhall Chase DA9 . . . . .**177** C2
Knockhall Cty Prim Sch
DA9 . . . .**177** C2
Knockhall Rd DA9 . . . .**177** C2
Knole CI CM3 . . . .**101** D5
Knoll The Billericay CM12 . . .**97** B4
Rayleigh SS6 . . . .**123** D2
Knollcroft SS3 . . . .**168** D6
Knowle Ho EN11 . . . .**21** A5
Knowle The
Basildon SS16 . . . .**142** C4
Hoddesdon EN11 . . . .**21** A5
Knowlton Cotts RM15 . . . . .**172** C8
Knox CI RM7 . . . .**59** A8
Knox Ct SS12 . . . .**121** F5
Kolburg Rd SS8 . . . .**164** D2
Kollum Rd SS8 . . . .**164** F3
Koln CI SS8 . . . .**163** C3
Komberg Cres SS8 . . . .**164** C5
Konnybrook SS7 . . . .**145** A4
Korndyk Ave SS8 . . . .**164** C4
Kursaal Way SS1 . . . .**167** C7
Kyme Rd RM11 . . . .**135** F5
Kynance CI RM3 . . . .**114** C6
Kynoch Ct SS17 . . . .**160** E1
Kyrkly Ct 11 RM19 . . . . . .**171** B1

L

La Plata Gr CM14 . . . .**116** B7
La Salette RC Prim Sch
RM13 . . . .**154** F2
Laars Ave SS8 . . . .**164** C5
Laburnham CI CM14 . . . . . .**138** A4
Laburnham Ct SS3 . . . .**168** F5
Laburnham Gdns RM14 . . . .**137** F4
Laburnum Ave
Hornchurch RM12 . . . .**136** A2
Wickford SS12 . . . .**121** C6

Laburnum Cl
Hockley SS5 . . . . .124 C6
Sheering CM22 . . . . . . .12 C3
Wickford SS12 . . . . . . .121 C6
Laburnum Dr
Chelmsford CM2 . . . . . . .54 C6
Corringham SS17 . . . . . .161 B4
Laburnum Gr
Canvey Island SS8 . . . . .163 D3
Hockley SS5 . . . . .124 B6
South Ockendon RM15 . . .157 C1
Laburnum Ho
3 Basildon SS13 . . . . . .143 B8
3 Dagenham RM10 . . . .135 A2
Laburnum Rd
Coopersale CM16 . . . . . .46 C2
Hoddesdon EN11 . . . . . .21 B8
Laburnum Way SS6 . . . .123 B6
Laburnum Wlk RM12 . . .155 C6
Labworth Rd SS8 . . . . .164 C2
Lacey Dr RM8 . . . . . . .134 C1
Ladram Cl SS1 . . . . . .168 C8
Ladram Rd SS1 . . . . . .168 C8
Ladram Way SS1 . . . . .168 B8
Lady Hamilton Ct SS1 . .168 B8
Lady La CM2 . . . . .54 C8
Lady's Hill CM14 . . . . . .70 F1
Ladyfields IG10 . . . . . . .89 C5
Ladyfields IG10 . . . . . . .89 C5
Ladygate Ctr SS12 . . . .121 D7
Ladyshot CM20 . . . . . . .11 B1
Ladysmith Ave IG2 . . . .133 E4
Ladysmith Way SS15 . . .119 F2
Ladywell La CM2 . . . . . .55 B5
Ladywell Prospect CM21 . .2 A1
Lagonda Ave IG6 . . . . .111 F4
Laindon Common Rd
CM12 . . . . .119 A6
Laindon Ctr SS15 . . . . .141 B6
Laindon Link SS15,SS16 .141 D5
Laindon Park Prim Sch
SS15 . . . . .141 E8
Laindon Rd CM12 . . . . .119 C8
Laindon Sta SS15 . . . . .141 C5
Laing Cl IG6 . . . . .111 D4
Laird Ave RM16 . . . . . .173 D4
Lake Ave Billericay CM12 .97 B3
Rainham RM13 . . . . . . .155 D3
Lake Cl RM8 . . . . .134 D1
Lake Dr SS7 . . . . .144 F4
Lake Gdns RM10 . . . . .154 A4
Lake House Rd E11 . . . .132 C4
Lake Meadows Office Village
CM12 . . . . .96 F3
Lake Rd Dagenham RM9 .154 B2
Ilford RM6 . . . . .134 D7
Lower Nazeing EN9 . . . . .21 A1
Lake Rise Grays RM20 . .172 A2
Romford RM1 . . . . .135 F8
Lake Rise Trad Est
RM20 . . . . .172 A2
Lake View SS16 . . . . . .140 F4
Lakefields Cl RM13 . . . .155 D5
Lakeland Cl IG7 . . . . . .112 B6
Lakenham Ho SS2 . . . . .147 E5
Lakes Ct SG12 . . . . .8 B4
Lakeside Billericay CM12 . .97 A4
Rainham RM13 . . . . . . .155 E3
Rayleigh SS6 . . . . .123 D4
Lakeside Cl IG7 . . . . . .111 F6
Lakeside Ave IG4 . . . . .132 D7
Lakeside Cres
Brentwood CM14 . . . . . .116 D4
Canvey Island SS8 . . . . .164 D5
Lakeside Path SS8 . . . .164 A5
Lakeside Ret Pk RM20 . .172 A2
Lakeside Sh Ctr RM20 . .172 B3
Lakeview SS8 . . . . . . .164 A5
Lakeview Ct E4 . . . . . .109 D4
Lakeview Cvn Pk RM3 . .114 C8
Lakin Cl CM2 . . . . .33 A3
Lamb Cl RM18 . . . . . . .179 C5
Lamb's La RM13 . . . . . .155 D5
Lamb's La N RM13 . . . .155 D1
Lamb's La S RM13 . . . .155 C1
Lamberhurst Rd RM8 . . .134 F3
Lambert Ct RM7 . . . . . .135 A6
Lambeth Mews SS5 . . . .124 C6
Lambeth Rd
South Benfleet SS7 . . . . .144 C6
Southend-on-S SS9 . . . .146 E6
Lambley Rd RM9 . . . . . .153 B6
Lambourne
Canvey Island SS8 . . . . .164 A2
East Tilbury RM18 . . . . .175 C2
Lambourne Cl IG7 . . . . .112 B7
Lambourne Cres
Basildon SS14 . . . . . . .142 F5
Chigwell IG7 . . . . .112 B8
Lambourne Ct **5** IG8 . . .110 C3
Lambourne Dr CM13 . . . .95 E3
Lambourne Gdns
4 Barking IG11 . . . . . .152 F5
Chingford E4 . . . . .109 A8
Hornchurch RM12 . . . . .136 D2
Lambourne Gr CM9 . . . . .58 F8
Lambourne Hall Rd SS4 .104 F2
Lambourne Mead Cotts
SS4 . . . . .105 A1
Lambourne Prim Sch
RM4 . . . . .90 B5
Lambourne Rd
Barking IG11 . . . . .152 F5
Chigwell IG7 . . . . .111 F7
Ilford IG3 . . . . .133 E2

Lambourne Sq RM4 . . . . .90 C1
Lambourni Cl SS3 . . . . .149 E2
Lambs Mdw IG8 . . . . . .110 D1
Lamerton Rd IG6 . . . . . .111 B3
Lamont Cl **1** SS12 . . . .121 E5
Lamorna Cl E17 . . . . . .109 C2
Lampern Cl CM12 . . . . . .97 B6
Lampern Cres CM12 . . . .97 B6
Lampern Mews CM12 . . . .97 B6
Lampeter Ho **4** RM3 . . .114 E3
Lampetsdowne SS17 . . . .161 B4
Lampits EN11 . . . . .21 B6
Lampits Hill SS17 . . . . .161 B5
Lampits Hill Ave SS17 . .161 A5
Lampits La SS17 . . . . . .161 A5
Lamplighters Cl EN9 . . . .66 A5
Lamson Rd RM13 . . . . .154 F1
Lancaster Ave
Barking IG11 . . . . .152 A4
Wanstead E18 . . . . . . .132 B7
Lancaster Bsns Pk SS2 .147 C2
Lancaster Cl CM15 . . . . .94 A4
Lancaster Cres **3** SS1 . .167 B8
Lancaster Dr
Basildon SS16 . . . . . . .140 F5
Hornchurch RM12 . . . . .155 C6
Loughton IG10 . . . . .88 E3
Lancaster Gdns
Rayleigh SS6 . . . . .146 A8
Southend-on-S SS1 . . . .167 B8
Lancaster Pl IG1 . . . . . .152 C8
Lancaster Rd
Grays RM16 . . . . .172 D2
North Weald Bassett CM16 .47 A5
Rayleigh SS6 . . . . .124 A1
Southend-on-S SS1 . . . .147 C3
Lancelot Rd IG6 . . . . . .111 E3
Lancer Way CM12 . . . . . .96 F3
Lancing Rd Ilford IG2 . . .133 D5
Romford RM3 . . . . .114 E3
Landau Way DA8 . . . . . .170 D1
Lander Rd RM17 . . . . . .173 D1
Landermere SS14 . . . . .142 B7
Landers Ct CM1 . . . . . . .31 E5
Landisdale CM3 . . . . . . .57 A7
Landsburg Rd SS4 . . . . .164 D5
Landscape Rd IG8 . . . . .110 B3
Landseer Ave E12 . . . . .152 D5
Landseer Cl RM11 . . . . .136 B3
Landshill Ct SS0 . . . . . .147 C1
Landview Gdns CM5 . . . .49 A1
Landwick Cotts SS3 . . . .150 D4
Landwick La CM0 . . . . . .85 F7
Lane Ave DA9 . . . . . . .177 C1
Lane End CM17 . . . . . . .24 C7
Lane Mews CM12 . . . . .132 F1
Laneside Ave RM8 . . . . .134 F4
Langdale Cl RM8 . . . . . .134 C3
Langdale Ct **9** IG1 . . . .133 B1
Langdale Gdns
Chelmsford CM2 . . . . . . .54 D8
Hornchurch RM12 . . . . .155 A7
Langdale Ho SS6 . . . . . .123 D2
Langdon Conservation Ctr ★
SS16 . . . . .140 E3
Langdon Cres E6 . . . . . .152 A3
Langdon Hills Ctry Pk ★
SS17 . . . . .160 F8
Langdon Mews CM11 . . . .97 B3
Langdon Nature Reserve ★
SS16 . . . . .141 D4
Langdon Rd Rayleigh SS6 123 B3
Wallend E6 . . . . .152 A4
Langdon Sch E6 . . . . . .152 B4
Langdon Way SS17 . . . .161 B5
Langemore Way CM11 . . .97 B3
Langenhoe SS12 . . . . . .121 E6
Langfield Cl RM4 . . . . . .21 E1
Langford Cres SS7 . . . . .144 F6
Langford Gn SG13 . . . . .143 C8
Langford Rd
Heybridge CM9 . . . . .36 F6
Langford CM9 . . . . .36 D8
Woodford IG8 . . . . .110 C4
Langfords IG9 . . . . .110 D8
Langham Cres CM12 . . . .119 C7
Langham Ct RM11 . . . . .136 D4
Langham Dr Ilford RM6 . .134 B5
Rayleigh SS6 . . . . .123 A3
Langhorne Rd RM10 . . . .154 A5
Langland Cl SS1 . . . . . .161 A4
Langley Cl Romford RM3 .114 D3
Southend-on-S SS9 . . . .146 B7
Langley Cres
Dagenham RM9 . . . . . .153 D5
Wanstead E11 . . . . . . .132 C4
Langley Dr
Brentwood CM14 . . . . . .116 A7
Wanstead E11 . . . . . . .132 B4
Langley Gdns RM9 . . . . .153 D5
Langley Gn EN9 . . . . . . .21 D1
Langley Mdw IG10 . . . . .89 D7
Langley Pl CM12 . . . . . . .96 E3
Langleys SS16 . . . . . . .142 B4
Langport Dr SS0 . . . . . .147 C2
Langport Ho **3** RM3 . . .114 E3
Langside Cl SS15 . . . . .141 B8
Langston Rd IG10 . . . . . .89 D5
Langthorne Cres RM17 . .173 C2
Langthornes **1** CM11 . . .97 B2
Langton Ave
Chelmsford CM1 . . . . . . .31 E5
Wallend E6 . . . . .152 A2
Langton Way RM16 . . . .174 C2
Langtons Jun & Inf Sch
RM11 . . . . .136 E3
Lanham Pl **7** SS13 . . . .143 B8

Lanhams SS13 . . . . . . .143 C8
Lanhams Ct **5** SS13 . . . .143 B8
Lansbury Ave
Barking IG11 . . . . .153 A5
Dagenham RM6 . . . . . . .134 E6
Lansbury Cres DA1 . . . .176 A2
Lansdown Ave SS7 . . . . .145 B6
Lansdown Rd RM18 . . . .179 A5
Lansdowne Ave SS9 . . . .147 A1
Lansdowne Ct EN10 . . . . .21 A3
Lansdowne Dr SS6 . . . .123 C3
Lansdowne Prim Sch
RM18 . . . . .178 F5
Lansdowne Rd
Chingford E4 . . . . .109 A8
Ilford IG3 . . . . .133 F4
Wanstead E18 . . . . . . .132 A8
Lansdowne Sq DA11 . . . .178 F1
Lantern Stps **18** SS1 . . .167 C7
Lappmark Rd SS8 . . . . .164 D3
Lapwater Ct SS9 . . . . . .146 C2
Lapwater Ct SS9 . . . . . .146 C2
Lapwing Dr CM9 . . . . . . .37 C5
Lapwing Rd SS11 . . . . . .99 C2
Larch Cl SS15 . . . . . . .119 C1
Larch Gr CM2 . . . . .54 C6
Larch Wlk CM9 . . . . .37 C6
Larches The Boreham CM3 33 E8
South Benfleet SS7 . . . . .144 C2
Larchwood Ave RM5 . . . .113 B4
Larchwood Cl
Romford RM5 . . . . .113 C4
Southend-on-S SS9 . . . .146 D6
Larchwood Gdns CM15 . . .94 A3
Lark Cl CM14 . . . . .116 B6
Lark Hill Rd SS4 . . . . . .104 B1
Lark's La Broomfield CM3 . .19 A6
Great Waltham CM3 . . . . .18 F5
Larke Rise SS2 . . . . . . .147 D5
Larkfield SS17 . . . . . . .161 B5
Larkfield Cl SS4 . . . . . .125 D4
Larkhill Ave SS4 . . . . . .104 A2
Larkin Ct CM13 . . . . . . .95 C2
Larkrise Prim Sch CM13 . .95 C3
Larkshall Bsns Ctr E4 . . .109 C6
Larkshall Cres E4 . . . . .109 C6
Larkshall Ct Chingford E4 .109 C5
Romford RM7 . . . . .113 C1
Larkshall Rd E4 . . . . . .109 C6
Larkspur Cl RM15 . . . . .157 C2
Larkspur Ct **3** CM1 . . . . .32 F6
Larkswood CM17 . . . . . . .24 C6
Larkswood Ct E4 . . . . . .109 B6
Larkswood Jun & Inf Sch
E4 . . . . .109 B6
Larkswood Rd
Chingford E4 . . . . .109 B6
Corringham SS17 . . . . . .161 B4
Larkswood Wlk **2** SS12 121 D6
Larsen Dr EN9 . . . . .65 D5
Larup Ave SS8 . . . . . . .164 C4
Larup Gdns SS8 . . . . . .164 C4
Lascelles Cl CM15 . . . . . .94 A4
Lascelles Gdns SS4 . . . .125 D6
Latchett Rd E18 . . . . . .110 B2
Latchetts Shaw SS16 . . .142 B4
Latchford Pl IG7 . . . . . .112 B6
Latching Cl RM3 . . . . . .114 D6
Latchingdon CE Prim Sch
CM3 . . . . .82 B6
Latchingdon Cl SS6 . . . .123 A3
Latchingdon Gdns IG8 . .110 E4
Latchingdon Rd CM3 . . . .81 B5
Latchmore Bank CM22 . . . .2 B8
Lathcoates Cres CM2 . . . .54 C8
Lathom Rd E6 . . . . .152 A5
Latimer Dr Basildon SS15 119 B1
Hornchurch RM12 . . . . .136 D1
Latton Bush Ctr The
CM18 . . . . .23 F5
Latton Gn CM18 . . . . . . .23 F4
Latton Green Prim Sch
CM18 . . . . .23 F4
Latton Hall Cl CM20 . . . . .11 A1
Latton Ho CM18 . . . . . . .24 B5
Latton St
Harlow, Brays Grove CM20 .24 B7
Harlow, Potter Street CM17 24 C5
Launceston Cl RM3 . . . . .114 C2
Launder's La RM13 . . . . .155 F1
Laundry Cotts RM13 . . . .170 D6
Laundry La
Lower Nazeing EN9 . . . . .43 E6
Mountnessing CM15 . . . . .95 D8
Laura Cl E11 . . . . .132 C6
Laurel Ave SS12 . . . . . .121 C7
Laurel Cl Brentwood CM13 .95 B4
Redbridge IG6 . . . . . . .111 D4
Southend-on-S SS9 . . . .165 D8
Laurel Cres RM7 . . . . . .135 E3
Laurel Ct **6** CM15 . . . . . .95 C3
Laurel Dr RM15 . . . . . . .157 D1
Laurel Gdns E4 . . . . . . .87 B2
Laurel Gr **4** CM2 . . . . . .54 A8
Laurel La RM12 . . . . . . .155 C6
Laurel Mead Ct **8** E18 . .110 A2
Laurels The Rayleigh SS6 145 F8
South Woodham Ferrers
CM3 . . . . .101 D8
8 Belvedere DA17 . . . . .169 A1
Laurence Croft CM1 . . . . .31 B1
Laurence Ind Est SS2 . . .147 B6
Laurie Wlk RM1 . . . . . . .135 E6
Lauriston Bglws CM9 . . . .39 C6
Lauriston Pl **1** SS1 . . . .167 B8
Lavehham Ho E17 . . . . .109 B2

Lavender Ave CM15 . . . . .94 B3
Lavender Cl Harlow CM20 . .10 E1
Romford RM3 . . . . .114 D1
South Ockendon RM15 . . .157 E1
Lavender Ct **1** CM1 . . . . .32 F5
Lavender Dr CM0 . . . . . . .84 C3
Lavender Gr SS0 . . . . . .147 D3
Lavender Mews
Canvey Island SS8 . . . . .163 F2
Southend-on-S SS0 . . . .147 D3
Lavender Pl IG1 . . . . . . .152 B7
Lavender Way SS5 . . . . .121 C7
Lavenham Ct CM15 . . . . .94 D1
Lavers Ct SS6 . . . . .123 E3
Law Ho IG11 . . . . .153 A3
Lawford Cl RM12 . . . . . .155 C8
Lawford La
Chelmsford CM1 . . . . . . .31 D3
Writtle CM1 . . . . .31 D1
Lawford Mead Inf Sch
CM1 . . . . .31 D5
Lawford Mead Jun Sch
CM1 . . . . .31 D5
Lawling Ave CM9 . . . . . . .37 C5
Lawlinge Rd CM3 . . . . . .82 B5
Lawn Ave SS2 . . . . .148 B2
Lawn Farm Gr RM6 . . . .134 E7
Lawn La CM1 . . . . .32 D6
Lawn Prim Sch DA11 . . . .178 C1
Lawn Rd DA11 . . . . .178 C2
Lawn The CM20 . . . . . . .11 B3
Lawns Cres RM17 . . . . .178 D8
Lawns Ct SS7 . . . . .144 B7
Lawns Pl RM17 . . . . . . .178 D8
Lawns The
Chelmsford CM1 . . . . . . .32 D5
Chingford E4 . . . . .109 A5
East Hanningfield CM3 . . . .78 C7
South Benfleet SS7 . . . . .144 C7
Brentwood CM14 . . . . . .116 E5
Lawns Way RM5 . . . . . .113 C3
Lawrence Ave
Little Ilford E12 . . . . . . .152 A8
Sawbridgeworth CM21 . . . .1 E4
Stanstead Abbotts SG12 . . .8 C4
Lawrence Cres RM10 . . .135 B1
Lawrence Gdns RM18 . . .179 E5
Lawrence Hill E4 . . . . . .109 A8
Lawrence Moorings CM21 .1 F2
Lawrence Rd
Basildon SS13 . . . . . . .143 F8
Romford RM3 . . . . .114 E6
Lawton Rd IG10 . . . . . . .89 B6
Laxtons SS17 . . . . .160 D3
Laxtons The SS4 . . . . . .125 D5
Layborne Ave RM3 . . . . .114 C8
Lea Ct **1** E4 . . . . .109 C8
Lea Hall Bglws CM22 . . . .3 B3
Lea Rd Grays RM16 . . . .174 A1
Hoddesdon EN11 . . . . . .21 A1
Holdbrook EN9 . . . . .65 A5
South Benfleet SS7 . . . . .144 C5
Lea Road Ind Pk EN9 . . . .65 A5
Lea Valley Rd E4 . . . . . . .87 A3
Lea Way CM2 . . . . .119 B8
Leach Cl CM2 . . . . .55 B7
Leadale Ave E4 . . . . . . .109 A8
Leaden Cl CM6 . . . . .15 D8
Leader Ave E12 . . . . . . .152 A7
Leafy Way CM13 . . . . . . .95 D1
Leamington Cl RM3 . . . .115 A4
Leamington Gdns IG3 . . .133 F2
Leamington Rd
Hockley SS5 . . . . .124 F7
Romford RM3 . . . . .115 A5
Southend-on-S SS3 . . . .167 C8
Leapingwell Cl CM2 . . . . .33 A3
Leas Cl SS0 . . . . .166 B8
Leas Ct CM0 . . . . .106 C6
Leas Gdns SS0 . . . . . . .166 B8
Leas The
Burnham-on-C CM0 . . . . .106 C6
Ingatestone SS4 . . . . . . .74 A2
Southend-on-S SS0 . . . .166 C7
Upminster RM14 . . . . . .137 D4
Leaside SS7 . . . . .144 B6
Leaside Bsns Ctr EN3 . . .87 A7
Leaside Lodge **6** EN11 . .21 B4
Leasway
Brentwood CM14 . . . . . .116 D7
Grays RM16 . . . . .173 D7
Rayleigh SS6 . . . . .123 C2
Upminster RM14 . . . . . .156 C8
Wickford SS12 . . . . . . .121 B6
Leasway The SS0 . . . . .166 B8
Leat Cl CM21 . . . . .1 F3
Leathart Rd RM12 . . . . .155 B5
Leather La
Hornchurch RM11 . . . . .136 D1
Southend-on-S SS1 . . . .167 A8
Leatherbottle Hill CM4 . . .65 B6
Leaview E4 . . . . .65 C1
Leaview Ct E4 . . . . .87 C1
Lechmere App IG8 . . . . .110 D1
Lechmere Ave
Chigwell IG7 . . . . .111 C6
Woodford IG8 . . . . .110 D1
Leconfield Wlk RM12 . . . .155 C6
Lede Rd SS8 . . . . .164 B4
Lee Ave RM6 . . . . .134 E5
Lee Chapel La SS16 . . . .141 D3
Lee Chapel Prim Sch
SS16 . . . . .141 F4
Lee Cl SG12 . . . . .8 C4
Lee Ct CM2 . . . . .54 A8
Lee Gardens Ave RM11 . .137 A3
Lee Gr IG7 . . . . .111 B8
Lee Lotts SS3 . . . . .150 A4

Lee Rd SS13 . . . . .143 F6
Lee Valley Ctry Pk ★
EN10 . . . . .21 B2
Lee Valley Ho EN9 . . . . . .66 A5
Lee Valley Park Vst Ctr ★
EN9 . . . . .65 C6
Lee Valley Pk ★ EN3 . . . .87 A8
Lee Wlk SS16 . . . . .141 E5
Lee Woottens La SS16 . . .142 A4
Leecon Way SS4 . . . . . .125 E3
Leeds Rd IG1 . . . . .133 D3
Leeford CM1 . . . . .31 F6
Leeholm Ho RM15 . . . . .171 C4
Lees Manor Ct RM11 . . .136 F2
Lees The SS8 . . . . .164 A6
Leeward Rd CM3 . . . . . .101 E5
Leeway The CM3 . . . . . . .56 F7
Legg St CM1 . . . . .32 B3
Legon Ave RM7 . . . . . . .135 D5
Legra Ave EN11 . . . . . . .21 A6
Leicester Ave SS4 . . . . .147 F8
Leicester Gdns IG3 . . . .133 E4
Leicester Rd
Tilbury RM18 . . . . .178 F6
Wanstead E11 . . . . . . .132 B6
Leige Ave SS8 . . . . . . .164 A6
Leige Ave IG4 . . . . .132 B7
Leigh Beck Jun & Inf Schs
SS8 . . . . .164 E3
Leigh Beck La SS8 . . . . .164 E2
Leigh Beck Rd SS8 . . . . .164 E3
Leigh Ct **8** RM3 . . . . . .110 A1
Leigh Dr RM3 . . . . .114 A6
Leigh Fells SS13 . . . . . .143 C6
Leigh Gdns SS9 . . . . . .146 A5
Leigh Hall Rd SS9 . . . . .146 E1
Leigh Heath Ct SS9 . . . .146 A2
Leigh Heritage Ctr ★
SS9 . . . . .165 D8
Leigh Hill SS9 . . . . .165 E8
Leigh Hill Cl SS9 . . . . . .165 E8
Leigh Hts SS9 . . . . .145 F3
Leigh Jun & Inf Schs
SS9 . . . . .146 E1
Leigh Park Cl SS9 . . . . .146 A4
Leigh Park Ct SS9 . . . . .165 D8
Leigh Park Rd SS9 . . . . .165 D8
Leigh Rd
Canvey Island SS8 . . . . .164 B4
Southend-on-S SS9 . . . .146 F1
Wallend E6 . . . . .152 A6
Leigh View Dr SS9 . . . . .146 F4
Leigh-on-Sea Sta SS9 . . .165 C8
Leigham Court Dr SS9 . . .146 F1
Leighams Rd CM3 . . . . . .78 E7
Leighcliff Rd SS9 . . . . . .165 E7
Leighcroft Gdns SS9 . . . .146 D4
Leighfields SS7 . . . . . . .145 B6
Leighfields Ave SS9 . . . .146 D6
Leighfields Rd SS9 . . . . .146 D6
Leighlands Rd CM3 . . . .101 E7
Leighs Rd CM3 . . . . .19 E6
Leighs Rifleman CM12 . . .96 F3
Leighton Ave
Little Ilford E12 . . . . . . .152 A7
Southend-on-S SS9 . . . .146 F1
Leighton Gdns RM18 . . . .179 B7
Leighton Rd SS7 . . . . . .144 C2
Leighville Gr SS9 . . . . . .146 D1
Leighwood Ave SS9 . . . .146 D6
Leinster Rd SS15 . . . . . .141 D6
Leitrim Ave SS3 . . . . . .168 C5
Lekoe Rd SS8 . . . . .163 F6
Lena Kennedy Cl E4 . . . .109 C4
Lenham Way SS13 . . . . .143 C6
Lenmore Ave RM17 . . . .173 C3
Lennard Row RM15 . . . .171 C5
Lennox Ave DA11 . . . . . .179 A1
Lennox Cl Grays RM16 . .172 C2
Romford RM1 . . . . .135 F5
Lennox Dr SS12 . . . . . .121 F5
Lennox Gdns IG1 . . . . . .132 F3
Lennox Ho **7** DA17 . . . .169 A4
Lennox Rd DA11 . . . . . .178 F1
Lenthall Ave RM17 . . . . .173 A4
Lenthall Rd IG10 . . . . . . .89 C5
Leon Dr SS16 . . . . .142 D3
Leonard Ave RM7 . . . . .135 D3
Leonard Dr SS6 . . . . . . .123 A4
Leonard Rd
Basildon SS16 . . . . . . .142 B2
Chingford E4 . . . . .109 A4
Southend-on-S SS0 . . . .166 D7
Leonard Way CM14 . . . .115 E6
Leslie Cl SS9 . . . . .146 D6
Leslie Dr SS9 . . . . .146 D6
Leslie Gdns SS6 . . . . . .123 F1
Leslie Newnham Ct **1**
CM9 . . . . .37 A1
Leslie Pk CM0 . . . . . . .106 C4
Leslie Rd SS6 . . . . .123 F1
Lesney Gdns SS4 . . . . . .125 D3
Lessingham Ave IG5 . . . .133 A8
Lessington Ave RM7 . . . .135 C5
Lessness Heath Prim Sch
DA17 . . . . .169 A1
Lessness Pk DA17 . . . . .169 A1
Lessness Rd
Belvedere DA17 . . . . . . .169 A1
15 Erith DA17 . . . . . . .169 A1
Lester Ho IG8 . . . . .109 D3
Lettons Chase SS3 . . . . .101 E6
Letzen Rd SS8 . . . . . . .164 A4
Leveller Row CM12 . . . . .96 F3
Leventhorpe Sch The
CM21 . . . . .1 A3
Lever La SS4 . . . . .125 F1

Lever Sq RM16 174 A2
Leverton Jun & Inf Schs The EN9 65 F5
Leverton Way EN9 65 C6
Leveson Rd RM16 174 B3
Levett Gdns IG3 152 F8
Levett Rd Barking IG11 152 E6
Stanford-le-H SS17 160 E2
Levine Gdns IG11 153 D3
Lewes Cl RM17 178 A8
Lewes Rd Romford RM3 114 D6
Southend-on-S SS2 148 C3
Lewes Way SS7 145 B7
Lewin Pl CM3 33 E8
Lewis Ave E17 109 A2
Lewis Cl CM15 94 F2
Lewis Dr CM2 54 B6
Lewis Rd
Hornchurch RM11 136 C5
Swanscombe DA10 177 E1
Lewis Way RM10 154 B6
Lexden Dr RM6 134 B5
Lexham Ho 9 IG11 152 D4
Lexington Way RM14 137 F5
Ley St IG1,IG2 133 D3
Leybourne Dr CM1 32 E7
Leyburn Cres RM3 114 E3
Leyburn Rd RM3 114 E3
Leycroft Cl IG10 89 A4
Leyland Ct SS1 167 B8
Leyland Gdns IG8 110 C5
Leys Ave RM10 154 C5
Leys Cl RM10 154 D5
Leys Prim Sch The RM10 154 C5
Leys The Basildon SS16 142 C4
Chelmsford CM2 32 F5
Leysings SS16 141 E4
Leyswood Dr IG2 133 E6
Liberty Cotts RM4 113 E8
Liberty Ct IG11 153 C3
Liberty II Ctr RM1 135 F7
Liberty The RM1 135 E6
Library Hill CM14 116 D8
Libro Ct E4 109 A6
Lichen Ct IG6 133 B8
Lichfield Cl CM1 31 E4
Lichfield Rd
Dagenham RM8 134 C1
Woodford IG8 109 E6
Lichfield Terr RM14 137 F2
Lichfields The SS14 142 F7
Lifstan Way SS1 167 E7
Lilac Ave
Canvey Island SS8 164 C4
Wickford SS12 121 C7
Lilac Cl Chelmsford CM2 54 C6
Pilgrims Hatch CM15 94 B4
Lilac Gdns RM7 135 E3
Lilac Rd EN11 21 B8
Lilford Rd CM11 97 C4
Lilian Cres CM13 117 C8
Lilian Gdns IG8 110 B2
Lilian Pl SS6 146 A8
Lilian Rd CM0 106 C5
Lillechurch Rd RM8 153 C6
Lilley Cl CM14 115 F6
Lilliard Cl EN11 8 B2
Lilliput Rd RM7 135 D4
Lillyputts Equestrian Ctr RM11 137 A5
Lillyville Wlk SS6 124 A1
Lily Alton Ct RM9 153 F8
Lily Cl CM1 32 F6
Lilystone Cl CM4 75 D1
Limberg Rd SS8 163 D4
Limbourne Ave RM8 134 F4
Limbourne Dr CM9 37 D5
Limburg Rd SS8 163 D4
Lime Ave
Brentwood CM13 116 F7
Southend-on-S SS9 146 C2
Upminster RM14 156 A8
Lime Cl
Buckhurst Hill IG9 110 D8
Romford RM7 135 C7
South Ockendon RM15 157 C2
Lime Ct Hockley SS5 124 E6
Hornchurch RM11 136 C4
Lime Gr
Doddinghurst CM15 72 D1
Redbridge IG6 111 F4
Lime Lodge SS9 146 C2
Lime Pl SS15 119 C1
Lime Rd SS7 144 E4
Lime Way CM0 106 A5
Lime Wlk CM2 54 C6
Limebrook Way CM9 58 E7
Limerick Gdns RM14 137 F4
Limes Ave Chigwell IG7 111 C4
Wanstead E11 132 B7
Limes Ct Brentwood CM15 94 D1
Hoddesdon EN11 21 A6
Limes Farm Jun & Inf Sch IG7 111 D5
Limes The
Brentwood CM13 116 F7
Galleywood CM2 54 B2
Ingatestone CM4 74 C4
Purfleet RM19 171 A1
Rayleigh SS6 123 F1
Romford RM11 136 D8
Limeslade Cl SS17 161 A4
Limetree Ave SS7 144 B4
Limetree Rd SS8 164 E4
Lincefield SS16 141 B3
Lincewood Prim Sch
Basildon SS16 141 B3
Lincewood Prim Sch *continued*
Basildon SS16 141 C4
Lincoln Ave RM7 135 E3
Lincoln Chase SS2 148 E3
Lincoln Cl RM11 137 A6
Lincoln Ct 2 Ilford IG2 133 C5
Redbridge IG1 132 F4
Lincoln Gdns IG1 132 E4
Lincoln Ho 12 RM3 114 D4
Lincoln Rd Basildon SS14 142 F7
Rochford SS4 125 C5
Woodford E18 110 A2
Lincoln Way SS8 163 E4
Lincolns Field CM16 45 F1
Lincolns La CM14 93 C3
Linda Gdns CM12 96 E4
Lindal Ct 1 E18 110 A2
Linde Rd SS8 164 B4
Linden Cl Chelmsford CM2 54 C7
Purfleet RM19 176 C8
Rayleigh SS6 123 F1
South Benfleet SS7 144 C6
Linden Cres IG8 110 B4
Linden Ct SS9 147 A2
Linden Leas SS7 144 C6
Linden Rd SS7 144 C6
Linden Rise CM14 116 D5
Linden St RM7 135 D6
Linden Way SS8 163 F4
Lindens The
Basildon SS16 141 A5
Loughton IG10 88 F4
Stock CM4 75 F2
Lindfield Rd RM3 114 E5
Lindhurst Dr CM11 98 C4
Lindisfarne Ave SS9 147 A2
Lindisfarne Ct
Basildon SS12 122 A5
Maldon CM9 58 E8
Lindisfarne Rd RM8 134 C1
Lindon Rd SS11 99 C3
Lindsell Gn SS14 142 E5
Lindsell La SS14 142 E5
Lindsey Cl CM14 116 A6
Lindsey Ct Rayleigh SS6 123 A3
14 Wickford SS12 121 E5
Lindsey Rd
Dagenham RM8 134 C1
Great Wakering SS3 150 B4
Lindsey St CM16 46 A2
Lindsey Way RM11 136 C6
Lindum SS1 168 A6
Linford Cl CM19 23 C6
Linford Dr SS14 142 F6
Linford End CM19 23 C6
Linford Mews CM9 58 E8
Linford Rd RM16 174 C1
Lingcroft SS16 142 A4
Lingfield Ave RM14 137 A1
Lingfield Dr SS4 126 A3
Lingmere Cl IG7 111 C8
Lingrove Gdns IG9 110 B8
Lingwood Cl CM3 56 E7
Link Rd
Canvey Island SS8 163 F4
Dagenham RM9 154 B3
Rayleigh SS6 123 D3
Stanford-le-H SS17 160 D3
Link Way RM11 136 E3
Linkdale CM12 119 B8
Links Ave RM2 114 B1
Links Ct SS1 167 F7
Links Dr CM2 53 F7
Links Rd IG8 110 A5
Links The CM12 96 E4
Links Way SS7 145 F3
Linkside IG7 111 C5
Linksway SS9 146 C4
Linkway Basildon SS14 142 B6
Dagenham RM8 153 C8
Linkway Rd CM14 115 F7
Linley Cl RM18 180 D7
Linley Cres RM7 135 C8
Linne Rd SS8 164 C5
Linnet Cl SS3 168 E8
Linnet Dr Chelmsford CM2 54 B6
South Benfleet SS7 144 C2
Linnet Terr IG5 133 A8
Linnet Way RM19 171 B1
Linnets SS16 142 A3
Linnett Cl E4 109 C6
Linroping Ave SS8 164 F3
Linsdell Rd IG11 152 C4
Linton Ct RM1 113 E1
Linton Rd Barking IG11 152 C5
Southend-on-S SS3 168 E6
Lintons The
1 Barking IG11 152 C5
Chelmsford CM2 55 D6
Linwood CM21 1 E2
Lion & Lamb Ct 6 CM14 116 C8
Lion Fields SS3 150 B3
Lion Hill SS17 161 D4
Lion La CM12 97 A2
Lionel Oxley Ho RM17 178 B8
Lionel Rd SS8 164 B3
Lionfield Terr CM1 32 D3
Liphook Cl RM12 154 F8
Lippits Hill SS16 141 C3
Lippitts Hill IG10 87 F7
Lisa Cl CM12 97 B6
Lisle Pl RM17 173 A3
Lister Ave RM3 114 E1
Lister Rd RM18 179 A5
Lister Tye CM2 54 C7
Liston Way 1 IG8 110 C3
Listowel Rd RM10 135 A1
Litchborough Pk CM3 56 F8
Littell Tweed CM2 33 A3
Little & Great Sir Hughes La CM2 55 B2
Little Aston Rd RM3 115 A3
Little Baddow Rd
Danbury CM3 56 E7
Woodham Walter CM9 35 C3
Little Belhus Cl RM15 157 A1
Little Bentley SS14 142 B7
Little Berry La SS16 141 A4
Little Brays CM18 24 A6
Little Brook Hospl The DA2 176 C1
Little Brook Rd CM19 22 C8
Little Cattins CM19 22 F4
Little Charlton SS13 143 C6
Little Chittock SS14 142 E6
Little Dodden SS16 141 F4
Little Dorrit CM1 31 E7
Little Dragons IG10 88 D5
Little Fields CM3 57 A7
Little Fretches SS9 146 E4
Little Friday Rd E4 109 E8
Little Garth SS13 143 A5
Little Gaynes Gdns RM14 156 B8
Little Gaynes La RM14 156 B8
Little Gearies IG6 133 B7
Little Gregories La CM16 67 D5
Little Grove Field CM19 23 C8
Little Gypps Cl SS8 163 F4
Little Gypps Ct SS8 163 F4
Little Gypps Rd SS8 163 F3
Little Hallingbury CE Prim Sch CM22 2 C7
Little Hayes Chase
Hullbridge CM3 102 C8
South Woodham F CM3 80 C1
Little Hays SS9 146 B6
Little Heath
Hatfield Heath CM22 3 A3
Ilford RM6 134 B7
Little Heathl Sch RM6 134 B7
Little Hills CM9 36 D8
Little Holt 8 E11 132 A6
Little Hyde La CM4 74 B6
Little Kingston SS16 141 D2
Little Laver Rd CM5 26 F7
Little London La CM9 35 D4
Little Lullaway SS15 141 F7
Little Malgraves Ind Est RM14 140 F1
Little Mdw CM1 31 A1
Little Mdws CM9 57 E6
Little Nell CM1 31 E7
Little Norsey Rd CM11 97 C4
Little Oaks SS14 142 A6
Little Oxcroft SS15 141 B6
Little Parndon Sch CM20 10 B1
Little Pluckett's Way IG9 88 D1
Little Pound CM15 72 C3
Little Pynchons CM18 24 A5
Little Russets CM13 95 E2
Little Searles SS13 143 B7
Little Spenders SS14 142 D8
Little St EN9 65 C3
Little Stambridge Hall Rd SS4 126 B3
Little Stile CM1 53 A8
Little Thorpe SS1 149 B1
Little Thurrock Prim Sch RM17 173 D3
Little Totham Rd CM9 38 D8
Little Wakering Hall La SS3 150 A4
Little Wakering Rd SS3 149 E6
Little Waltham CE Prim Sch CM3 19 B7
Little Waltham Rd CM1 19 D1
Little Warley Hall La CM13,RM14 138 E6
Little Wheatley Chase SS6 123 A4
Little Wlk CM20 23 D8
Littlebrook Manor Way DA1 176 A2
Littlebury Ct
Basildon SS13 143 A8
Kelvedon Hatch CM15 71 F2
Littlebury Gn SS13 143 A8
Littlecroft CM3 101 D6
Littlehurst La SS15 119 F2
Littlemoor Rd IG1 133 D1
Littlethorpe SS16 142 F4
Littleton Ave E4 87 F1
Livingstone Cl CM5 49 A2
Livingstone Cotts CM5 49 A2
Livingstone Terr RM13 154 E4
Llewellyn Cl CM1 32 D3
Lloyd Mews EN3 65 A1
Lloyd Rd RM9 153 F5
Lloyd Wise Cl SS2 148 D3
Lobelia Cl CM1 33 A6
Locarno Ave SS11 99 E2
Lock Hill CM9 37 E2
Lock View CM21 1 F2
Locke Cl Rainham RM13 154 F6
Stanford-le-H SS17 160 C3
Lockhart Lodge E4 87 E2
Locks Hill SS4 125 F1
Lockside Marina CM2 32 D1
Locksley Cl SS2 148 F2
Lockwood Wlk RM1 135 E6
Lockyer Rd RM19 176 C8
Lodden Ho 5 RM3 115 A4
Lodge Ave
Dagenham RM8 153 B6
Lodge Ave *continued*
Great Baddow CM2 54 F7
Romford RM2 136 A7
Lodge Cl Brentwood CM13 95 E2
Chigwell IG7 112 A7
Rayleigh SS6 123 E1
Thundersley SS7 145 A5
Lodge Cres CM3 33 E7
Lodge Ct RM12 136 E2
Lodge Farm Cl SS9 146 D5
Lodge Hall CM18 23 E4
Lodge Hill IG4 132 E7
Lodge La
Grays RM16,RM17 173 B3
Purleigh CM3 58 C2
Romford RM5 113 A4
Waltham Abbey EN9 65 D4
Lodge Rd Loughton CM16 67 A5
Maldon CM9 36 F3
Woodham Ferrers CM3 78 F6
Woodham Mortimer CM3, CM9 58 B5
Writtle CM1 53 A8
Lodge The Epping CM16 46 A1
2 Hornchurch RM11 136 B3
Redbridge IG6 111 E3
Lodge Villas IG8 109 F4
Lodgelands Cl SS6 123 F1
Lodwick SS3 168 C5
Loewen Rd RM16 174 A3
Loftin Way CM2 54 D7
Logan Ct 3 RM1 135 E6
Logan Link SS12 121 F5
Logan Mews 2 RM1 135 E6
Loman Path RM15 171 F7
Lombard Ave IG3 133 E3
Lombard Ct RM7 135 C7
Lombards Chase CM13 139 D5
Lombards The RM11 136 F4
Lombardy Cl 3 SS13 143 C6
Lombardy Pl CM1 32 B3
London Hill
Chelmsford CM2 53 F2
Galleywood CM2 54 A2
Rayleigh SS6 123 D3
London Rd Abridge RM4 90 A6
Aveley RM15 171 A4
Barking IG11 152 C5
Basildon, Crays Hill CM11, SS12 120 E6
Basildon,Vange SS16 142 D3
Billericay CM12 96 E2
Brentwood CM14 116 A7
Chelmsford CM2 53 E6
Chipping Ongar CM5 70 C4
Grays RM17,RM20 177 D8
Greenhithe DA9,DA2 177 C2
Hadleigh SS7 145 D3
Harlow CM17 11 C2
Harlow, Latton Bush CM17 24 C4
Maldon CM9 36 D3
Northfleet RM17 178 E1
Romford RM7 135 B5
Sawbridgeworth CM21 1 E2
South Benfleet SS7 144 D5
Southend-on-S SS9 146 D2
Southend-on-S,Westcliff-on-S SS1 166 F8
Stanford-le-H SS17 160 B1
Stapleford Tawney RM4 91 D8
Tilbury RM18 179 B5
Wickford SS11,SS6 122 D5
London Road Purfleet RM19 176 C8
London Road Ret Pk SS0 166 F8
London Road West Thurrock RM20 177 A8
London Southend Airport SS2 147 E7
Londons Cl RM14 156 C7
Long Acre Basildon SS14 142 C7
Harlow CM17 11 B4
Long Banks CM18 23 D5
Long Brandocks CM1 31 A1
Long Comm CM9 36 F5
Long Croft Dr EN8 65 A5
Long Ct RM19 171 A2
Long Deacon Rd E4 87 E1
Long Gages SS14 142 B7
Long Gn IG7 111 E5
Long Gr RM3 114 E1
Long Ho CM18 23 F6
Long La
Chadwell St M RM16 173 F5
Grays RM16 173 C5
Hullbridge SS5 101 F3
Long Ley CM20 23 F8
Long Leys E4 109 C4
Long Lynderswood SS15 141 F6
Long Mdw
Brentwood CM13 117 C8
Romford RM3 114 C8
Long Meadow Dr SS11 121 E8
Long Rd SS8 164 A3
Long Reach Rd IG11 152 F1
Long Riding SS14 142 D6
Long Ridings Ave CM13 95 C4
Long Ridings Prim Sch CM13 95 B4
Long St EN9 66 E7
Long Wlk EN8 43 A1
Long Wood CM18 23 D3
Longacre CM1 53 E8
Longacre Rd E17 109 D2
Longaford Way CM13 95 C1
Longborough Cl 2 SS13 121 A1
Longbow SS2 148 E2
Longbridge Ho RM8 153 B8
Longbridge Rd
Barking IG11 152 E7
Dagenham RM8 153 B8
Longcroft Rise IG10 89 B4
Longcrofts EN9 65 E5
Longdon Ct RM1 135 F6
Longfellow Dr CM13 95 C2
Longfellow Rd CM9 37 A1
Longfield Harlow CM18 24 A6
Loughton IG10 88 D4
Longfield Ave RM11 135 F4
Longfield Cl SS11 122 A7
Longfield Cotts IG10 89 A7
Longfield Rd
Great Baddow CM2 54 E8
South Woodham Ferrers CM3 101 D8
Wickford SS11 122 A7
Longfields CM5 49 A1
Longhams Dr CM3 101 D8
Longhayes Ave RM6 134 D7
Longhayes Ct RM6 134 D7
Longhouse Rd RM16 174 B3
Longland Bridge CM22 12 C8
Longleat Cl CM1 31 F7
Longmans SS3 168 G6
Longmead SS13 143 C8
Longmead Ave CM2 54 F8
Longmead Cl CM15 94 E1
Longmeads Cl CM1 31 A1
Longmore Ave CM2 54 E8
Longport Cl IG6 112 A4
Longreach Ct IG11 152 D3
Longrise CM12 119 B8
Longsands SS3 168 D7
Longshaw Prim Sch E4 109 D7
Longshaw Rd E4 109 D7
Longship Way CM9 58 E8
Longshots Cl CM1 19 A1
Longstomps Ave CM2 54 A7
Longtail CM11 97 D5
Longtown Cl RM3 114 C5
Longtown Ct 21 DA2 176 B1
Longtown Rd RM3 114 C5
Longview Way RM5 113 D2
Longwick SS16 141 C4
Longwood Cl RM14 156 C7
Longwood Ct RM14 156 C7
Longwood Gdns
Ilford IG5,IG6 133 A8
Redbridge IG5 132 F7
Longwood Par IG6 133 B8
Lonsdale Ave
Brentwood CM13 95 D3
Romford RM7 135 C5
Lonsdale Cres IG2 133 B5
Lonsdale Ct SS2 148 D3
Lonsdale Rd
Southend-on-S SS2 148 D2
Wanstead E11 132 A4
Looe Gdns IG6 133 B8
Loop Rd EN9 65 B7
Lord Ave IG5 132 F8
Lord Gdns IG5 132 F7
Lord Roberts Ave SS9 146 F1
Lord St EN11 21 A6
Lords Way SS13 121 B2
Lordship Cl CM13 95 D2
Lordship Rd CM1 31 B3
Lordswood View CM6 15 D7
Lorien Gdns CM3 101 C6
Lorimar Bsns Ctr RM13 169 E8
Lorne Gdns E11 132 C7
Lorne Rd CM14 116 C6
Lornes Cl SS2 148 D3
Lorraine Cl CM11 119 D6
Lorraine Ct 4 RM1 135 F6
Lorrimore Cl CM12 96 F5
Loten Rd SS7 144 B2
Lottem Rd SS8 164 D2
Loudoun Ave IG6 133 B6
Loughton Ct EN9 66 B6
Loughton La CM16 67 D2
Loughton Seedbed Ctr IG10 89 D5
Loughton Sta IG10 88 E4
Loughton Way IG9 88 E1
Louis Cl SS6 123 A3
Louis Ct 3 RM10 154 B6
Louis Dr SS6 123 A4
Louis Dr E SS6 123 B4
Louis Dr W SS6 123 A4
Louisa Ave SS7 144 B6
Louise Ct 4 E11 132 B6
Louise Gdns RM13 154 E2
Louise Graham Ho 5 IG11 152 D4
Louise Rd SS6 123 E2
Louvain Dr CM1 32 F7
Louvaine Ave SS12 121 B7
Love La Aveley RM15 171 C4
Chigwell IG8 110 F4
Chipping Ongar CM5 49 A3
East Tilbury RM18 180 C8
Rayleigh SS6 123 C2
Lovelace Ave SS1 167 D8
Lovelace Gdns
Barking IG11 153 A8
Southend-on-S SS2 148 D1
Lovelace Villas SS2 148 D1
Loveland Mans 6 IG11 152 F5

Lovell Rise SS9 ....147 A6
Lovell Wlk RM12 ......155 A6
Lovens Cl SS8 ....164 C2
Lover's La DA9 ....177 D3
Loves Wlk CM1 ....31 A7
Lovet Rd RM19 ....23 A7
Lovibond Pl **4** CM2 ....32 F4
Low Cl DA9 ....177 A2
Low Hall Cl E4 ....87 B2
Low Street La
  East Tilbury RM18 ....179 F8
  West Tilbury RM18 ...174 F1
Lowbrook Rd IG1 ......152 B8
Lowe Cl IG7 ....112 A5
Lowe The IG7 ....112 A5
Lowen Rd RM13 ....154 D3
Lower Alderton Hall La
  IG10 ....89 A4
Lower Anchor St CM2 ...32 A1
Lower Ave SS13 ....143 E8
Lower Bedfords Rd
  RM1,RM3 ....114 A4
Lower Broad St RM10 ..154 A4
Lower Burnham Rd CM3 .81 C2
Lower Bury La CM16 ....67 E8
Lower Chase CM3 ....82 F4
Lower Church Hill DA9 .176 B2
Lower Church Rd SS7 ..144 B6
Lower Cloister CM11 ....97 B2
Lower Cres SS17 ....175 A3
Lower Dunton Rd SS17,
  RM14,CM13 ....140 D4
Lower Gn CM2 ....54 C2
Lower Lambricks SS6 ..123 D4
Lower Mardyke Ave
  RM13 ....154 C3
Lower Mdw CM18 ....23 E4
Lower Noke Cl RM3,
  CM14 ....114 F8
Lower Park Rd
  Belvedere DA17 ......169 A2
  Loughton IG10 ....88 E4
  Wickford SS12 ....121 C4
Lower Queen's Rd IG9 .110 D8
Lower Rd
  Belvedere DA17 ......169 B3
  Great Amwell SG12 ....8 A3
  Hullbridge SS5 ....101 F1
  Little Hallingbury CM22 ..1 C2
  Loughton IG10 ....89 A8
  Mountnessing CM15 ....95 D6
  Northfleet DA11 ......178 A3
  Rochford SS4 ....102 D2
  Tilbury RM18 ....179 A3
Lower Sheerings CM21 ..2 A3
Lower Southend Rd
  SS11 ....121 D8
Lower St SS15 ....119 E1
Lower Stock Rd CM4 ....76 C4
Lower Swaines CM16 ....45 F1
Lowewood Mus★ EN11 ..21 A5
Lowfield CM21 ....1 E1
Lowfield Ct EN11 ......21 A6
Lowfield La EN11 ......21 A6
Lowland Gdns RM7 ....135 B5
Lowlands Rd RM15 ....171 C5
Lowry Cl SS3 ....149 F1
Lowry Rd RM8 ....153 B7
Lowshoe La RM5 ......113 B2
Loxdon Ct RM6 ....134 B5
Loxford SS13 ....143 A8
Loxford Rd IG1 ....152 B6
Loxford Sch of Science &
  Tech IG1 ....152 D7
Loxham Rd E4 ....109 B3
Loxley Ct RM3 ....114 B3
Loyola Prep Sch IG9 ...88 C1
Lubbards Cl SS6 ......123 D5
Lubbins Park Com Prim Sch
  SS8 ....164 C2
Lucam Lodge SS4 .....125 F2
Lucas Ave CM2 ....54 C6
Lucas Cres DA9 ....177 C3
Lucas Ct
  Doddinghurst CM15 ....72 C3
  Romford RM2 ....114 D1
  Waltham Abbey EN9 ....65 F6
Lucas Rd RM17 ....173 A3
Lucerne Dr SS11 ......122 A7
Lucerne Way
  Romford RM3 ....114 D4
  Writtle CM1 ....53 B8
Lucerne Wlk SS11 ....122 A7
Lucksfield Way CM2 ....54 F5
Luckyn La SS14 ......141 F8
Lucton Mews IG10 .....89 B5
Luctons Ave IG9 ....88 C1
Lucy Gdns RM8 ....134 E1
Lucy Rd SS1 ....167 B7
Ludgores La CM3 ....56 D5
Ludgrove CM3 ....82 A6
Ludham Cl IG6 ....111 C2
Ludlow Mews SS13 ....143 B6
Ludlow Pl RM17 ......173 B3
Lugg App E12 ....133 A1
Luker Rd SS1 ....167 A8
Lukin Cres E4 ....109 D7
Lukinstone Cl IG10 .....88 E3
Lullington Rd RM9 ....153 E5
Lulworth Cl SS17 .....175 B8
Lulworth Dr RM5 .....113 B5
Lumley Cl SS3 ....149 F1
Luncies Rd SS14 .....142 F5
Lundy Cl SS2 ....147 B7

Lupin Cl RM7 ....135 D2
Lupin Dr CM1 ....32 F6
Lupin Mews **1** CM1 ....32 F6
Lupin Cres IG11 ......152 B6
Luppits Cl CM13 ....95 A1
Lushes Ct IG10 ....89 B4
Lushes Rd IG10 ....89 B4
Lutea Cl SS15 ....119 D1
Luthers Ct CM15 ......71 E2
Luton Ho **9** RM3 .....114 E5
Luxborough RM10 ....110 F6
Luxborough La IG7 ...110 F6
Luxford Pl **4** CM21 ....1 F1
Lych Gate SS15 ....141 C6
Lychgate Ind Est SS6 .122 E1
Lydford Ct **25** DA2 ...176 B1
Lydford Rd SS0 ......166 E7
Lylt Rd SS8 ....164 A3
Lyme Rd SS2 ....148 C1
Lymington Ave SS9 ...146 E1
Lymington Rd RM8 ...134 D3
Lympstone Cl SS0 ....147 A5
Lynbrook Cl RM13 ...154 D3
Lynceley Grange CM16 .46 A2
Lynch The EN11 ....21 B6
Lyndale Ave CM2 ......32 C5
Lyndale Ave SS2 .....148 B3
Lyndale Est RM20 ....177 B8
Lyndbourne Ct SS7 ..144 C5
Lyndene CM3 ....82 A6
Lyndhurst Ct **11** E18 ..110 A2
Lyndhurst Dr
  Bicknacre CM3 ....56 F1
  Hornchurch RM12 ....136 C4
Lyndhurst Gdns
  Barking IG11 ....152 E6
  Ilford IG2 ....133 D5
Lyndhurst Rd
  Chingford E4 ....109 C3
  Corringham SS17 .....160 F4
  Rochford SS4 ....103 C1
Lyndhurst Rise IG7 ...111 A6
Lyndhurst Way RM13 ..95 C2
Lyndon Rd DA17 .....169 A2
Lynfold Gdns IG3 ....133 F2
Lynfords Ave SS11 ...100 A3
Lynfords Dr
  Wickford SS11 ....100 A3
  Wickford, Runwell SS11 .99 F2
Lynmouth Ave CM2 ....32 C5
Lynmouth Gdns CM2 ..32 C5
Lynmouth Ho **8** RM3 .114 E5
Lynn Rd IG2 ....133 D4
Lynn View Cl SS7 ....144 C5
Lynnett Rd RM8 ......134 D2
Lynross Cl RM3 ......114 F1
Lynstede SS14 ....143 A5
Lynton Ave RM7 .....113 B2
Lynton Cres IG2 .....133 D5
Lynton Dr CM1 ....32 E5
Lynton Ho IG1 ....133 C2
Lynton Rd Chingford E4 .109 B5
  Hadleigh SS7 ....145 C3
  Southend-on-S SS1 ..167 F6
Lynwood Cl
  Romford RM5 ....113 B4
  Woodford E18 ....110 C2
Lynwood Dr RM5 ....113 B3
Lynwood Gn SS5 ....146 A8
Lyon Cl CM2 ....54 B3
Lyon Rd RM1 ....135 F4
Lyster Ave CM2 ....55 A7
Lytton Cl IG10 ....89 D6
Lytton Rd
  Chadwell St M RM16 ..173 F2
  Grays RM16 ....174 A3
  Romford RM2 ....136 B6
Lyttons Way EN11 ......8 A1

M
Mabey's Wlk CM21 .....1 B1
Macaulay Rd SS16 ...141 A5
Macclesfield Ho **7**
  RM3 ....114 E5
Macdonald Ave
  Dagenham RM10 .....135 B1
  Hornchurch RM11 ...136 F7
  Southend-on-S SS0 ..147 E2
Macdonald Rd E17 ...109 C1
Macdonald Way RM11 .136 E7
Mace Ct RM17 ....178 E8
Mace Wlk CM1 ....31 F3
Macgregor Dr SS12 ..121 E5
Macintyres Wlk SS4 .125 C6
Mackenzie Cl SS12 ..121 E6
Mackley Dr SS17 ....160 F5
Maclaren Way **5** SS12 .121 E5
Maclennan Ave RM13 .155 D2
Macleod Ct RM17 ...173 D2
Macmillan Ct **4** CM2 ..32 B1
Macmillan Gdns DA1 .176 A3
Macmurdo Cl SS9 ....146 D7
Macmurdo Rd SS9 ...146 D7
Macon Way RM14 ...137 F5
Madden Cl DA10 ....177 E1
Maddox Ct **1** E4 ....87 D1
Maddox Rd CM20 .....23 E8
Madeira Ave SS9 ....146 E2
Madeira Gr IG1 ......152 D7
Madeleines Flats CM19 .23 B7
Madeline Gr IG1 .....152 D7
Madeline Pl CM1 .....31 E6
Madells E11 ....67 F8
Madles La CM4 ....75 F1
Madras Ho IG1 ......152 B8

Madras Rd IG1 ......152 B8
Madrid Ave SS6 .....123 B7
Mafeking Ave IG2 ...133 D4
Magazine Rd SS3 ....168 E6
Magdalen Gdns E6 ..152 A1
Magdalene Gdns E6 .152 A1
Magenta Cl CM12 .....96 E3
Magna Mead SS3 ...149 D7
Magnet Rd RM20 ....177 C8
Magnolia Cl
  Canvey Island SS8 ...164 A2
  Chelmsford CM2 .....54 B6
  South Ockendon RM15 .157 E1
Magnolia La SS15 ...119 C1
Magnolia Lodge E4 ..109 B7
Magnolia Pl SS17 ...160 E4
Magnolia Rd SS4 ....125 B5
Magnolia Way
  Pilgrims Hatch CM15 ..94 B4
  Rochford SS4 ....148 A8
Magnolias CM11 .....119 C6
Magnum Cl RM13 ...155 C5
Magpie La CM13 ....116 E2
Magpies CM16 ....45 A7
Magwitch Cl CM1 ....31 F7
Mahonia Dr SS16 ...140 F5
Maida Ave E4 ....87 B2
Maida Rd DA17 .....169 A3
Maida Way E4 ....87 B2
Maidstone Ave RM5 .113 C1
Maidstone Rd RM17 .178 A8
Main Rd Bicknacre CM3 .79 A6
  Boreham CM3 ....20 F1
  Broomfield CM1 ......19 B2
  Danbury CM3 ....56 A7
  Danbury CM3 ....56 D7
  East Hanningfield CM3 .78 C5
  Hawkwell SS5 ......124 F4
  Hockley SS5 ....124 D6
  Rettendon CM3,SS11 .100 B6
  Romford RM1 ....136 A8
  St Lawrence CM0 ....62 D7
Maine Cres SS6 ......123 B4
Maitland Pl SS3 .....149 E1
Maitland Rd SS12 ...121 E5
Maitlands IG10 ....88 F6
Maizey Ct CM15 ......94 A4
Makepeace Rd E11 ..132 A7
Makinen Ho IG9 ......88 C1
Malan Sq RM12 .....155 B6
Malby Lodge SS0 ...166 C8
Malcolm Way E11 ...132 A7
Maldon Court Sch CM9 .36 F7
Maldon Ct E6 ....152 A4
Maldon District Mus★
  CM9 ....37 B2
Maldon Ho IG9 ....88 C2
Maldon Prim Sch CM9 .37 A2
Maldon Rd
  Bradwell Waterside CM0 .41 F1
  Bradwell-on-S CM0 ...42 A1
  Bradwell-on-S, Mill End
    CM0 ....63 C7
  Burnham-on-C CM0 ..105 E8
  Dagenham RM7 ......135 C4
  Danbury, Gay Bowers CM3 .57 B5
  Danbury, Runsell Green
    CM3 ....57 B7
  Goldhanger CM9 ......38 E7
  Great Baddow CM2 ...55 C7
  Langford CM9 ....36 A8
  Langford CM9 ....36 D6
  Latchingdon CM3 .....81 F6
  Margaretting CM4 ....75 B8
  Mayland CM3,CM0 ...61 D1
  Southend-on-S SS2 ..148 A1
  Woodham Mortimer CM9 .37 F7
Maldon Wlk IG8 .....110 C4
Malford Ct E18 ......110 A1
Malford Gr E18 .....110 A1
Malgraves SS13 ....143 B7
Malgraves Pl SS13 .143 B7
Malkin Dr CM17 ......24 E7
Mall The RM11 ......136 B3
Mallard Cl RM14 ....137 F4
Mallard Ct Chingford E4 .87 D2
  Ilford IG1 ....133 C2
  3 Southend-on-S SS1 .167 C8
Mallard Rd SS2 ......54 A5
Mallard Way CM13 ...95 B2
Mallards Mayland SS3 .83 A8
Mallards Rd
  Barking IG11 ....153 A1
  Woodford IG8 ....110 B3
Mallards Rise SS17 ...24 D8
Mallards The SS3 ...150 A4
Mallinson Cl RM12 ..155 C7
Mallion Ct EN9 ....65 F6
Mallories CM20 ....10 F2
Mallory Way CM12 ...97 A1
Mallow Ct RM17 ....178 E8
Mallow Gdns CM12 ...96 F5
Mallows Gn CM19 ...23 A3
Malmesbury Rd E18 .109 F2
Malmsmead SS3 ....168 C8
Malpas Rd
  Dagenham RM9 .....153 D6
  Grays RM16 ....174 C3
Malsters Lodge **9** EN11 .21 D8
Malta Rd RM18 .....178 F5
Maltese Rd CM1 .....32 A4
Malthouse Pl **6** RM1 .135 E6
Malting La RM16 ....159 A1
Malting Villas Rd SS4 .125 F2
Maltings Chase CM4 .74 B3

Maltings Dr CM16 .....46 A2
Maltings Hill CM5 .....26 E3
Maltings Ind Est The SG12 .8 D4
Maltings La CM16 .....46 A2
Maltings Rd
  Battlesbridge SS11 ..100 E2
  Great Baddow CM2 ...55 A5
Maltings The
  Gravesend DA11 ....179 A1
  Romford RM1 ....135 F4
  Southminster CM0 ....84 A4
Malvern SS2 ....148 B1
Malvern Ave
  Canvey Island SS8 ...163 D3
  Chingford E4 ....109 D3
Malvern Cl
  Chelmsford CM1 .....31 D6
  Rayleigh SS6 ....123 D4
Malvern Dr Ilford IG3 .152 F8
  Woodford IG8 ....110 C6
Malvern Gdns IG10 ...88 F3
Malvern Ho DA11 ...178 D1
Malvern Rd Grays RM17 .173 E2
  Hockley SS5 ....124 F8
  Hornchurch RM11 ...136 A5
Malwood Dr SS7 ....144 B5
Malwood Rd SS7 ....144 B5
Malyon Court Cl SS7 .145 B4
Malyons SS13 ....143 B8
Malyons Cl SS13 ...143 B8
Malyons Gn SS13 ...143 B8
Malyons La SS5 ....101 D2
Malyons Mews SS13 .143 B8
Malyons Pl SS13 ...143 B8
Malyons The SS7 ...145 B4
Manbrough Ave E6 ..152 A2
Manchester Dr SS9 .146 F2
Manchester Way RM10 .154 B8
Mandeville Cl CM17 ..24 C6
Mandeville Prim Sch
  CM21 ....1 D3
Mandeville Way
  Basildon SS15,SS16 ..141 B5
  Broomfield CM1 ......19 B3
  South Benfleet SS7 ..144 C7
Mandeville Wlk CM13 .95 E2
Manford Cl IG7 .....112 B6
Manford Cross IG7 ..112 A5
Manford Ct Chigwell IG7 .111 F5
  Redbridge IG7 ......112 A5
Manford Prim Sch IG7 .111 F5
Manford Way
  Chigwell IG7 ....111 E5
  Redbridge IG7 ......112 A5
Mangapp Chase CM0 .106 A8
Mangapps Farm Rly Mus★
  CM0 ....106 A8
Manilla Rd SS1 .....167 C2
Mannering Gdns SS0 .147 A3
Manners Cnr SS2 ...147 E5
Manners Way SS2 ..147 E5
Mannin Rd RM6 ....134 B5
Manning Gr SS16 ...141 C4
Manning Rd RM10 ..154 A5
Manning St RM15 ..171 C5
Mannock Dr IG10 ....89 C7
Manns Way SS6 ....145 D8
Manor Ave Basildon SS13 .143 C7
  Hornchurch RM11 ...136 C6
Manor Cl Aveley RM15 .171 C5
  Dagenham RM10 ...154 D6
  Ramsden Heath CM11 .98 C3
  Rayleigh SS6 ....145 D8
  Romford RM1 ....136 A6
Manor Cl S RM15 ...171 C5
Manor Cotts RM14 .159 A4
Manor Cres
  Hornchurch RM11 ...136 C6
  Little Waltham CM3 ..19 B5
Manor Ct **3** Barking IG11 .152 F5
  Chingford E4 ....87 E1
  South Benfleet SS7 ..144 D7
  Southend-on-S SS1 ..167 D7
  Waltham Abbey EN9 ...65 C6
Manor Dr CM2 ....54 E7
Manor Farm Dr E4 ..109 E7
Manor Hatch CM18 ..24 A7
Manor Hatch Cl CM18 .24 B7
Manor Ho CM3 ....57 A7
Manor House Gdns **2**
  E11 ....132 B5
Manor Inf Sch IG11 .152 F6
Manor Jun Sch IG11 .152 F6
Manor Prim Sch The
  RM1 ....135 F6
Manor Rd Abridge RM4 .90 E2
  Barking IG11 ....152 F6
  Basildon SS15 ......141 B7
  Chelmsford CM2 .....32 C1
  Chigwell IG7 ....111 C5
  Dagenham RM10 ...154 D6
  Dengie CM0 ....63 D1
  Grays, West Thurrock
    RM20 ....177 C8
  Grays,Little Thurrock Marshes
    RM17 ....178 C8
  Harlow CM17 ....11 C5
  High Beach IG10 ......88 B8
  Hockley SS5 ....124 C6
  Hoddesdon EN11 ....21 A7
  Ilford RM6 ....134 D5
  Loughton IG10 ....88 C1
  Maldon CM9 ....36 A4
  Romford RM1 ....136 A6
  South Benfleet SS7 ..144 D6
  South Woodham Ferrers
    CM3 ....101 C8

Manor Rd continued
  Southend-on-S SS0 ..166 C5
  Stanford-le-H SS17 ..160 D1
  Swanscombe DA10 ..177 D1
  Tilbury RM18 ....179 A5
  Waltham Abbey EN9 ...65 D6
  Woodham Walter CM9 ..35 E5
Manor Sq RM8 ......134 C2
Manor Trad Est SS7 .144 D7
Manor Way
  Brentwood CM14 ...116 A7
  Chingford E4 ....109 D6
  Corringham SS17 ...161 A2
  Grays RM17 ....178 C7
  Northfleet RM17 ....178 A3
  Rainham RM13 .....154 E1
  Swanscombe DA10 ..177 E3
Manor Way Bsns Ctr
  RM13 ....169 D8
Manorway IG8 ......110 C5
Manorway The
  Corringham SS17 ...161 D2
  Stanford-le-H SS17 ..160 D2
Mansard Cl RM12 ..136 A2
Manse Chase CM9 ...37 A1
Mansel Cl SS9 .....146 E6
Mansel Gr E17 .....109 A2
Manser Rd RM13 ...154 E3
Mansfield CM21 ....1 A4
Mansfield Gdns RM12 .136 D2
Mansfield Hill E4 .....87 B1
Mansfield Rd Ilford IG1 .133 A2
  Wanstead E11 ......132 B5
Mansfields CM1 ......30 F1
Manstead Gdns
  Dagenham RM6 ....134 C4
  Rainham RM13 .....170 B2
Mansted Gdns SS4 .125 D5
Manston Rd CM20 ...23 D8
Manston Way RM12 .155 B6
Manton Rd EN3 ......65 A1
Maple Ave Heybridge CM9 .37 C3
  Southend-on-S SS9 .165 F8
  Upminster RM14 ...156 B8
Maple Cl
  Brentwood CM13 ...116 C7
  Buckhurst Hill IG9 ..110 D7
  Hornchurch RM12 ..136 B1
  8 Redbridge IG6 ..111 E5
  Theydon Bois CM16 ..67 D2
Maple Ct
  7 Dagenham RM8 .134 C4
  Southend-on-S SS3 .168 F8
  Stansted Abbotts SG12 ..8 B3
Maple Dr Chelmsford CM2 .54 B6
  Rayleigh SS6 ....123 C2
  South Ockendon RM15 .157 D1
Maple Gate IG10 .....89 A7
Maple Lodge IG9 .....88 D1
Maple Mead CM12 ..119 C6
Maple Rd RM17 ....178 C6
Maple River Ind Est
  CM20 ....11 B6
Maple Springs EN9 ..66 C3
Maple Sq SS2 ......148 B2
Maple St RM7 ......135 C5
Maple Tree La SS16 .140 F5
Maple Way
  Burnham-on-C CM0 .106 A6
  Canvey Island SS8 ..163 E3
Maplecroft La EN9 ...21 E2
Mapledene Ave SS5 .101 E2
Mapleford Sweep SS16 .142 B4
Mapleleaf Gdns SS12 .121 B6
Mapleleafe Gdns IG6 .133 B8
Maples SS17 ....160 E2
Maples The Harlow CM19 .23 B4
  4 Wickford SS12 ..121 C5
Maplesfield SS7 ....145 B4
Maplestead SS14 ..142 B4
Maplestead Rd RM9 .153 B4
Mapleton Rd E4 ....109 C7
Mapletree La CM4 ...73 E8
Maplin Cl SS7 .....144 C7
Maplin Ct SS3 .....168 A6
Maplin Gdns SS14 .142 E5
Maplin Mews SS3 ..168 E6
Maplin Way SS1 ...168 A6
Maplin Way N SS1 ..149 C1
Mapperley Pl **3** E11 .132 A5
Mapperley Dr IG8 ..109 E3
Mar Rd RM15 ......157 C1
Marchmant Rd RM12 .136 C5
Marconi Gdns CM15 .94 C4
Marconi Rd CM1 .....32 B5
Marcos Rd SS8 ....164 D3
Marcus Ave SS1 ...168 B7
Marcus Chase SS1 .168 B7
Marcus Gdns SS1 .168 B7
Marden Ash **7** SS15 .141 E4
Marden Cl IG7 .....112 B8
Marden Rd **5** RM1 .135 C6
Mardyke Ho RM13 .154 D3
Mardyke Rd CM20 ...11 A2
Maresby Ho E4 ....109 B8
Margaret Ave
  Brentwood CM15 ....95 A3
  Chingford E4 ....109 F3
Margaret Bondfield Ave
  IG11 ....153 A5
Margaret Cl Epping CM16 .45 E2
  Romford RM2 ......136 B6
  Waltham Abbey EN9 ..65 C6
Margaret Dr SS2 ...147 E4
Margaret Rd Epping CM16 .46 A2
  Romford RM2 ......136 B6
Margaret Way IG4 ..132 C5

Margaretting CE Prim Sch
CM4 ....74 F8
Margaretting Rd
Chelmsford CM2 ....53 F1
Galleywood CM2 ....54 A2
Wanstead E12 ....132 C3
Writtle CM1 ....53 A6
Margarite Way SS12 ....121 B7
Margery Rd RM8 ....134 D1
Margeth Rd CM12 ....119 C3
Margherita Pl EN9 ....66 A5
Margherita Rd EN9 ....66 A5
Margraten Ave SS8 ......164 D2
Marguerite Dr SS9 ....146 F1
Mariam Gdns RM12 ......136 F2
Marian Rd RM16 ....172 E5
Marian Lawson Ct IG7 ..112 A5
Marie Cl SS17 ....161 A8
Marien Ct E4 ....109 D5
Marigold Cl CM1 ....32 F6
Marigold Pl CM17 ....11 B4
Marina Ave SS6 ....123 C3
Marina Cl SS2 ....147 E4
Marina Dr DA11 ....178 F1
Marina Gdns RM7 ....135 C6
Marine App SS8 ....164 B2
Marine Ave
Canvey Island SS8 ......164 E2
Southend-on-S SS9 ......146 D1
Southend-on-S,Clifftown
SS0 ....166 E7
Marine Cl SS9 ....146 A1
Marine Cotts RM13 ......170 D6
Marine Ct RM19 ....170 F2
Marine Dr IG11 ....153 B2
Marine Par
Canvey Island SS8 ......164 F2
Mayland CM3 ....60 E1
Southend-on-S SS1 ......167 B7
Southend-on-S, Leigh-on-S
SS9 ....146 B1
Mariner Rd E12 ....152 A8
Mariners Ct
Great Wakering SS3 ....150 C3
Greenhithe DA9 ....177 B3
Mariners Way CM9 ....59 A8
Marion Cl IG6 ....111 D3
Marion Gr IG8 ....109 E6
Marionette Stps [7] SS1 167 C7
Marisco Cl RM16 ....174 B2
Mariskals SS13 ....143 A6
Maritime Ave CM9 ....37 C3
Maritime Cl DA9 ....177 B2
Marjorams Ave IG10 ....89 A7
Mark Ave E4 ....87 B3
Mark Hall Cycle Mus &
Gdns* CM20 ....11 B3
Mark Hall Moors CM20 ..11 B3
Mark Hall Sch CM17 ......11 C3
Mark La DA12 ....179 E4
Mark Rd CM0 ....63 F6
Mark Wade Cl E12 ....132 D2
Mark's Ave CM5 ....49 A4
Market Ave SS12 ....121 C8
Market Hill CM9 ....37 A3
Market Hill Ct CM9 ....37 A3
Market Ho CM20 ....10 D1
Market Link RM1 ....135 E7
Market Pavement [2]
SS14 ....142 A5
Market Pl Abridge RM4 ..90 B6
Ingatestone CM4 ....74 B4
Maldon CM9 ....36 F2
Romford RM1 ....135 E6
Southend-on-S SS1 ......167 A7
Market Rd
Chelmsford CM1 ....32 B2
Wickford SS12 ....121 C7
Market Sq Basildon SS14 142 A5
[6] Chelmsford CM1 ......32 B2
Rochford SS4 ....125 F2
South Woodham Ferrers
CM3 ....101 E7
Waltham Abbey EN9 ......65 C6
Market St Harlow CM17 ..11 C4
Wallend E6 ....152 A3
Markfield Gdns E4 ....87 B2
Markham Ho [1] RM10 ..135 A1
Markhams SS17 ....160 F3
Markhams Chase SS15 .141 D7
Markland Cl CM2 ....54 C3
Markland Dr CM9 ....36 E1
Marklay Dr CM3 ....101 C7
Marks Cl Billericay CM12 ..96 F4
Ingatestone CM4 ....73 F1
Marks Ct SS1 ....167 C7
Marks Gate Inf Sch
RM6 ....134 E8
Marks Gate Jun Sch
RM6 ....134 E8
Marks Hall La CM6 ....15 F1
Marks La CM3 ....99 F8
Marks Rd RM7 ....135 D6
Markwell Wood CM19 ....23 B2
Markyate Rd RM8 ....153 B7
Marlands Rd
Redbridge IG5 ....132 E8
Woodford IG5 ....110 F1
Marlborough Ave CM0 ...63 E3
Marlborough Cl
Grays RM16 ....173 C4
South Benfleet SS7 ......144 D4
Upminster RM14 ....137 E4
Marlborough Ct [7] IG9 .110 C8
Marlborough Dr IG5 .....132 E8
Marlborough Gdns
RM14 ....137 E4

Marlborough Ho CM16 .116 B6
Marlborough Pl SS1 .....166 F7
Marlborough Rd
[2] Chelmsford CM2 ....32 A1
Chingford E4 ....109 B4
Dagenham RM8 ....153 C8
Pilgrims Hatch CM15 ....94 A3
Romford RM7 ....135 B7
Southend-on-S SS1 ......167 D8
Wanstead E18 ....132 A8
[9] Woodford E18 ....110 A1
Marlborough Terr CM2 ...32 A1
Marlborough Way CM12 ..97 A5
Marlborough Wlk SS5 ...124 C6
Marle Gdns EN9 ....65 C7
Marlescroft Way IG10 ....89 B4
Marlin Cl SS7 ....145 E6
Marlow Ave RM19 ....171 A2
Marlow Gdns SS2 ....147 E4
Marlowe Cl
Billericay CM12 ....97 B5
Maldon CM9 ....59 A8
Redbridge IG6 ....111 C2
Marlowe Gdns RM3 .....114 C2
Marlowe Ho [12] IG8 ....111 A3
Marlpits Rd CM3,CM9 ....57 C4
Marlyon Rd IG6 ....112 B5
Marmaduke Ave SS6 ....123 B4
Marmion App E4 ....109 A6
Marmion Ave E4 ....109 A6
Marmion Ct E4 ....109 A6
Marney Cl CM2 ....54 E8
Marney Dr SS14 ....142 F5
Marquis Ct IG11 ....152 E7
Marram Ct RM17 ....178 E8
Marriotts CM17 ....11 C5
Marsden Ho [1] RM3 ....114 F4
Marsh Farm Country Pk*
CM3 ....101 E5
Marsh Farm Rd CM3 ...101 D4
Marsh Green Prim Sch
RM10 ....154 A3
Marsh Green Rd RM10 .154 A4
Marsh Hill EN9 ....43 D4
Marsh La Fobbing SS17 .161 D6
Harlow CM17 ....11 E5
Mountnessing CM13 ......96 A7
Stanstead Abbotts SG12 ..8 D4
Marsh Rd
Burnham-on-C CM0 .....107 B7
Tillingham CM0 ....64 B4
Marsh St Dartford DA1 ..176 A3
Dartford DA1 ....176 A5
Marsh View St SS16 ....142 E3
Marsh Way RM13 ....169 D8
Marshall Cl SS9 ....146 A3
Marshalls SS4 ....125 D4
Marshalls Cl SS6 ....123 F2
Marshalls Dr RM1 ....135 E8
Marshalls Park Sch
RM1 ....113 E1
Marshalls Rd RM7 ....135 D7
Marshfoot Rd RM16,
RM17 ....173 F1
Marston Ave RM10 ......135 A1
Marston Bay Ind Est
RM2 ....114 D1
Marston Beck CM2 ....33 A2
Marston Cl RM10 ....135 A1
Marston Ho RM17 ....178 A8
Marston Rd
Hoddesdon EN11 ....21 B7
Woodford IG5 ....110 E1
Marten Rd E17 ....109 A1
Martham Cl IG6 ....111 B2
Martin Cl CM11 ....97 B1
Martin Dr Dartford DA2 ..176 C1
Rainham RM13 ....155 B1
Martin Gdns RM8 ....153 D8
Martin Rd Aveley RM15 .171 D5
Dagenham RM8 ....153 D8
Martin Wlk SS5 ....124 F4
Martin's Ct SS2 ....148 A1
Martina Terr [9] IG6 .....111 E5
Martindale Ave SS15 ...119 D2
Martingale Cl CM11 ....97 D5
Martingale Dr CM1 ....32 F7
Martingale Rd CM11 ......97 D5
Martini Dr EN3 ....65 A2
Martins Cl SS17 ....160 D3
Martins Mews SS7 ....144 C4
Martinsfield Cl IG7 ....111 E6
Martlesham Cl RM12 ....155 C7
Martley Dr IG2 ....133 B6
Martock Ave SS0 ....147 A5
Martyns Gr SS0 ....147 B2
Marvens CM2 ....54 D3
Marwell Cl RM1 ....136 A6
Mary Macarthur Ho
[8] Belvedere DA17 .....169 A3
[11] Dagenham RM10 ...135 A1
Mary Rose Cl RM16 .....172 C2
Marylands Ave SS5 .....124 D7
Mascalls Gdns CM14 ...115 F6
Mascalls La
Brentwood CM14 ....115 F6
Great Warley CM14 .....116 A4
Mascalls The CM2 ....54 E8
Mascalls Way CM2 ....54 E8
Masefield Cl RM3 ....114 C2
Masefield Cres RM3 .....114 C2
Masefield Ct [2] CM14 .116 C6
Masefield Dr RM14 ......137 C4
Masefield Gdns E6 ......152 A1
Masefield Rd
Dartford DA1 ....176 B2
Grays RM16 ....173 E4

Masefield Rd continued
Maldon CM9 ....59 A8
Mashbury Rd CM1 ....17 D6
Mashiters Hill RM1 ......113 D2
Mashiters Wlk RM1 .....135 E8
Mason Dr RM3 ....114 E1
Mason Rd IG8 ....109 E6
Mason Way EN9 ....65 F6
Masthead Cl DA12 ....176 C3
Matching Field CM15 .....71 F2
Matching Gn SS14 ....120 D1
Matching Green CE Prim Sch
CM17 ....13 D1
Matching La CM6 ....14 C6
Matching Rd
Harlow, Matching CM22 ..13 B8
Harlow,Harlow Tye CM17 ..12 B4
Hatfield Heath CM22 ....3 B2
Matfield Cl CM1 ....32 D7
Mathart Ct E4 ....109 D4
Mathews Ave E6 ....152 A3
Mathews Villas CM19 ....22 E6
Mathieson Ho E4 ....87 E2
Matlock Gdns RM12 ....136 E1
Matlock Ho [13] RM3 ...114 D4
Matlock Rd SS8 ....163 F3
Matson Ct IG8 ....109 E3
Matthews Rd CM17 .....114 F2
Maud Gdns IG11 ....152 F3
Maugham Cl SS12 ....121 D5
Maunder Ct RM16 ....172 D2
Maunds Farm CM18 ......23 E4
Maunds Hatch CM18 .....23 E4
Maurice Ct SS8 ....164 D2
Maurice Ho [5] CM14 ..116 C6
Maurice St SS8 ....164 D3
Mavis Gr RM12 ....136 E2
Mawney Cl RM7 ....113 B1
Mawney Prim Sch RM7 135 B6
Mawney Rd RM7 ....135 C7
Maxey Gdns RM9 ....153 E8
Maxey Rd RM9 ....153 E8
Maxim Rd DA8 ....169 D2
Maximfeldt Rd DA8 ......169 E1
May Ave
Canvey Island SS8 ......164 D2
Canvey Island SS8 ......164 C3
May Ct RM17 ....178 E8
May Rd E4 ....109 A4
May Terr IG1 ....152 B8
May Villa RM2 ....114 D1
May Wlk CM2 ....54 C7
Maya Angelou Ct E4 ....109 C6
Maya Cl SS3 ....168 E7
Mayall Cl EN3 ....65 A1
Maybank Ave
Hornchurch RM12 ....155 C7
Woodford E18 ....110 B1
Maybank Rd E18 ....110 A1
Maybells Commercial Est
IG11 ....153 D3
Maybrick Rd RM11 ......136 C5
Maybrook Ct E11 ....132 B3
Maybury Cl IG10 ....89 B5
Maybury Rd IG11 ....153 A3
Maybush Rd RM11 ......136 E4
Maycroft Ave RM17 ....173 D1
Maycroft Gdns RM17 ..173 D1
Maydeb Ct RM6 ....134 F5
Maydells SS13 ....143 B5
Maydells Ct SS13 ....143 B5
Maydene CM3 ....101 D7
Mayer Rd EN9 ....65 B3
Mayes La Chelmsford CM2 ..55 E5
Danbury CM3 ....56 E6
Mayesbrook Rd
Barking IG11 ....152 F4
Dagenham IG3,RM8 ....134 B1
Mayesford Rd RM6 ......134 C4
Mayespark Prim Sch
IG3 ....134 A1
Mayfair Ave
Basildon SS13 ....143 C8
Dagenham RM6 ....134 D5
Ilford IG1 ....133 A4
Mayfair Gdns IG8 ....110 A5
Mayfair Ind Area CM3 ..81 F6
Mayfield
Swanscombe DA10 .....177 E1
Waltham Abbey EN9 ......65 D5
Mayfield Ave
Hullbridge SS5 ....101 E2
Southend-on-S SS2 .....147 E4
Woodford IG8 ....110 A4
Mayfield Cl CM17 ....11 F4
Mayfield Ct EN9 ....66 A5
Mayfield Ctr CM0 ....106 A5
Mayfield Gdns CM14 ....94 C1
Mayfield Rd
Belvedere DA17 ....169 C2
Chingford E4 ....109 D8
Dagenham RM8 ....134 C3
Writtle CM1 ....31 A2
Mayfield Sch & Coll
RM8 ....134 C3
Mayfields RM16 ....173 C4
Mayflower Cl
Lower Nazeing EN9 ....43 E8
South Ockendon RM15 .157 C1
Southend-on-S SS2 .....147 B6
Mayflower Ct
Canvey Island SS8 ......164 D2
Chipping Ongar CM5 ....49 A4
Harlow CM19 ....23 B4
Mayflower Dr CM9 ....59 A7
Mayflower High Sch
CM12 ....97 C5

Mayflower Ho
[2] Barking IG11 ....152 D4
Brentwood CM13 ....116 C4
Mayflower Rd
[5] Billericay CM11 ....97 B2
Grays RM16 ....172 C1
Mayflower Ret Pk SS14 120 D2
Mayflower Way CM5 .....49 A4
Mayflowers SS7 ....144 B7
Maygreen Cres CM11 ..136 A4
Mayhew Cl E4 ....109 A7
Mayland Ave SS8 ....164 A2
Mayland Cl
Heybridge CM9 ....37 D4
Mayland CM3 ....83 A7
Mayland Gn CM3 ....83 B8
Mayland Hill CM3 ....83 C5
Mayland Mans [4] SS2 .152 B5
Maylands Ave RM12 ....155 B8
Maylands Way RM3 .....115 C4
Maylandsea Prim Sch
CM3 ....82 F8
Maylins Dr CM21 ....1 D2
Maynard Ct
[2] Holbrook EN3 ....65 A1
Waltham Abbey EN9 .....65 F5
Maynards RM11 ....136 E4
Mayne Crest CM1 ....32 E6
Maypole Cres IG6 ....111 D3
Maypole Dr IG7 ....112 A7
Maypole Rd CM9 ....36 F7
Maypole St CM17 ....11 C1
Mayswood Gdns RM10 154 C1
Maytree Cl RM13 ....154 E3
Maytree Wlk SS7 ....144 C6
Mayville Rd IG1 ....152 B7
Maywin Dr RM11 ....136 F3
Maze The SS9 ....146 D7
McAdam Cl EN11 ....21 A8
McCalmont Dr SS6 ......123 C7
McClintock Pl EN3 ....65 B2
McDivitt Wlk SS9 ....147 A6
McEntee Sch The E17 ..109 A2
McGrail Cl CM11 ....164 F2
McIntosh Cl RM1 ....135 E8
McIntosh Rd RM1 ....135 E8
McKenzie Rd EN10 ....21 A3
Mead Cl Grays RM16 ...173 B4
Loughton IG10 ....89 B7
Romford RM2 ....114 A1
Mead Cres E4 ....109 C6
Mead Ct EN9 ....65 B5
Mead Gr RM6 ....134 D4
Mead Lodge [3] EN11 ....21 D8
Mead Park Ind Est CM20 .10 F4
Mead Pastures CM9 ......35 D3
Mead Path CM2 ....53 F8
Mead Prim Sch RM3 ....114 F4
Mead The Basildon SS15 141 B8
Hoddesdon EN10 ....21 B2
Mead Way SS12 ....152 E8
Mead Wlk CM5 ....48 F1
Meade Cl CM11 ....97 D5
Meadgate SS13 ....143 C8
Meadgate Ave
Great Baddow CM2 ......54 D8
Woodford IG8 ....110 E5
Meadgate Prim Sch CM2 54 E8
Meadgate Rd EN9 ....21 C3
Meadgate Terr CM2 ....54 D8
Meadow Cl Chingford E4 .87 B1
Linford SS17 ....175 A3
Thundersley SS7 ....145 B6
Meadow Ct
Billericay CM11 ....97 C2
Canvey Island SS8 ......163 B8
Harlow CM18 ....23 E4
Wickford SS11 ....121 E8
Meadow Dr
Basildon SS16 ....160 B8
Southend-on-S SS1 .....167 E7
Meadow La SS1 ....99 E3
Meadow Mews CM3 ....101 B8
Meadow Rd
Barking IG11 ....153 A5
Dagenham RM9 ....153 F6
Epping CM16 ....45 F2
Grays RM16 ....173 C5
Hadleigh SS7 ....145 E2
Hullbridge SS5 ....101 E2
Loughton IG10 ....89 B1
Rettendon CM3 ....100 C5
Romford RM7 ....135 C3
Meadow Rise
Billericay CM11 ....97 C2
Blackmore CM4 ....72 E8
Meadow Side CM1 ....32 B3
Meadow View
Basildon SS16 ....140 E4
Bicknacre CM3 ....56 E1
Epping CM16 ....46 A4
Pilgrims Hatch CM15 ....94 C3
Meadow View Wlk SS8 .163 E4
Meadow Way
Burnham-on-C CM0 .....106 A7
Chigwell IG7 ....111 C8
Hockley SS5 ....124 E6
Latchingdon CM3 ....82 A6
Sawbridgeworth CM21 ....2 A1
Upminster RM14 ....137 D2
Wickford SS12 ....121 E3
Meadow Way The CM11 .97 C2
Meadow Wlk
[5] Chelmsford CM2 .....32 C2
Dagenham RM9 ....153 F6
Wanstead E18 ....132 A7
Meadowcross EN9 ....65 E5

Meadowgate CM4 ....75 F2
Meadowland Rd SS11 ..122 A6
Meadowlands RM11 .....136 E4
Meadows Cl CM13 ....117 C4
Meadows The
[3] Chelmsford CM2 .....32 C2
Ingrave CM13 ....117 C5
Sawbridgeworth CM21 ...2 A2
Meadowside
Chelmsford CM2 ....32 C3
Rayleigh SS6 ....123 D2
South Benfleet SS7 .....144 A1
Meadowside Ct CM1 .....20 C1
Meadowside Rd RM14 .156 C4
Meads Ct CM4 ....74 B4
Meads Cl CM15 ....116 E8
Meads La IG3 ....133 F4
Meads The
Basildon SS16 ....143 A4
Chelmsford CM2 ....32 A1
Ingatestone CM4 ....74 A4
Upminster RM14 ....137 E2
Meadsway CM13 ....116 E4
Meadway
Canvey Island SS8 ......164 C2
Grays RM17 ....173 D2
Hoddesdon EN11 ....21 A1
Maldon CM9 ....37 B1
Rayleigh SS6 ....123 E1
Romford RM2 ....114 A1
South Benfleet SS7 .....144 C7
Woodford IG8 ....110 C5
Meadway Ct RM8 ....134 F2
Meadway The
Buckhurst Hill IG9 ....88 D1
Loughton IG10 ....88 F1
Southend-on-S SS0 .....166 B8
Meakins Cl SS9 ....147 A7
Mearns Pl [3] CM2 ....32 C4
Meath Rd IG1 ....133 C4
Medebridge Rd
Grays RM5,RM16 ....173 A8
South Ockendon RM16 .158 A4
Medick Ct RM17 ....178 E8
Medina Rd RM11 ....173 C5
Medlar Dr RM15 ....157 E1
Medlar Rd RM17 ....178 E8
Medlars Mead CM22 ......3 F5
Medoc Cl SS13 ....143 C8
Medora Rd RM7 ....135 C7
Medway CM0 ....106 A6
Medway Cl
Chelmsford CM1 ....31 D4
Ilford IG1 ....152 D4
Medway Cres SS9 ....146 B1
Meeson Bglws CM3 .....100 D3
Meeson Mdws CM9 ....58 E8
Meeson's La RM17 ......172 F1
Meesons Mead SS4 ....125 D6
Meggison Way SS7 ......144 C3
Meggy Tye CM2 ....33 B5
Meister Cl IG1 ....133 D3
Melanie Ct SS4 ....125 D6
Melba Ct CM1 ....31 C1
Melba Gdns RM18 ....179 D1
Melbourne Ave CM1 ......31 E5
Melbourne Ct
Chelmsford CM1 ....31 E5
Tilbury RM18 ....178 E6
Melbourne Gdns RM6 ..134 E6
Melbourne Par CM1 ......31 E5
Melbourne Park Prim Sch
CM1 ....31 F6
Melbourne Quay [8]
DA11 ....179 B1
Melbourne Rd Ilford IG1 133 B3
Tilbury RM18 ....178 E6
Melcombe Rd SS7 ....144 C3
Meldrum Rd IG3 ....134 A2
Melford Ave IG11 ....152 F6
Melford Pl CM14 ....94 C1
Melford Rd IG1 ....133 D2
Melksham Cl RM3 ....114 F3
Melksham Dr RM3 ....114 F3
Melksham Gdns RM3 ..114 F3
Melksham Gn RM3 ......114 F3
Mell Rd CM9 ....40 E8
Mellis Cl IG11 ....152 F4
Mellish Gdns IG8 ....110 A5
Mellish Way RM11 ......136 C5
Mellor Cl CM4 ....74 B4
Mellow Mead SS15 .....141 B8
Mellow Purgess SS15 .141 C6
Mellow Purgess Cl
SS15 ....141 C6
Mellow Purgess End
SS15 ....141 C6
Mellows Rd IG5 ....132 F8
Melstock Ave RM14 ....156 C8
Melton Gdns RM1 ....135 F4
Melville Ct Romford RM3 114 C4
Southend-on-S SS1 .....167 D6
Melville Dr SS12 ....121 C4
Melville Heath CM3 .....101 E6
Melville Rd
Rainham RM13 ....155 B1
Romford RM5 ....113 B2
Memory Cl CM9 ....59 A7
Mendip Cl Rayleigh SS6 123 D4
Wickford SS11 ....121 C6
Mendip Cres SS0 ....147 A4
Mendip Rd
Chelmsford CM1 ....31 D6
Hornchurch RM11 ....136 A4
Ilford IG2 ....133 E6

Mendip Rd continued
Southend-on-S SS0 ......147 A4
Mendips The SS9 ......146 F5
Mendoza Cl RM11 ......136 E6
Menish Way CM2 ......33 A3
Menthone Pl RM11 ......136 D4
Mentmore SS16 ......141 B4
Menzies Ave SS15 ......140 F6
Meon Cl CM1 ......32 C6
Meppel Ave SS8 ......164 A6
Mercer Ave SS3 ......150 A4
Mercer Rd CM11 ......97 D5
Mercers CM19 ......23 A5
Merchant St CM3 ......101 E7
Mercia Cl CM2 ......55 A5
Mercury Cl SS11 ......121 F8
Mercury Ct 8 RM1 ......135 F8
Mercury Gdns RM1 ......135 F6
Mercury Pl CM9 ......36 F5
Merdle Sq CM1 ......31 F6
Merebridge Rd RM16 ......172 B6
Meredene SS14 ......142 F5
Meredith Rd RM16 ......174 A4
Merefield CM21 ......1 E1
Meresmans RM1 ......171 D7
Mereworth Rd CM3 ......101 C5
Meriadoc Dr CM3 ......101 D6
Meriden Cl IG6 ......111 C2
Meridian Way SG12 ......8 B5
Meridien RM1 ......135 F4
Meriel Wlk DA9 ......177 B3
Merilies Cl SS0 ......147 B4
Merilies Gdns SS0 ......147 B3
Merino Cl E11 ......132 C2
Merlin Cl Grays RM16 ......172 E3
Redbridge IG6 ......112 C6
Romford RM5 ......113 D4
Waltham Abbey EN9 ......66 A5
Merlin Ct SS8 ......164 B3
Merlin Gdns RM5 ......113 D4
Merlin Gr IG6 ......111 C3
Merlin Pl CM1 ......31 F5
Merlin Rd Romford RM5 ......113 D4
Wanstead E12 ......132 D2
Merlin Way
North Weald Bassett CM16 ......47 A6
Wickford SS11 ......99 D1
Mermagen Dr RM13 ......155 B5
Mermaid Way CM9 ......59 B8
Merriam Cl E4 ......109 C5
Merricks La IG4 ......142 E3
Merrielands Cres RM9 ......153 F3
Merrielands Ret Pk
RM9 ......153 F3
Merring Way CM19 ......22 F7
Merritt Ho RM1 ......135 F4
Merrivale SS7 ......144 C2
Merrivale Ave IG4 ......132 D7
Merry Fiddlers RM8 ......134 F2
Merryfield App SS9 ......146 E4
Merryfields Ave SS5 ......124 D7
Merryhill Cl E4 ......87 B2
Merrylands SS15 ......141 B4
Merrylands Chase
CM13 ......140 D7
Merrylands Prim Sch
SS15 ......141 A6
Merrymead Chase CM15 ......94 D1
Mersea Cres SS12 ......121 F6
Mersea Ho IG11 ......152 B6
Mersey Ave RM14 ......137 D5
Mersey Way CM1 ......31 C5
Merten Rd RM6 ......134 E4
Merton Pl Grays RM16 ......174 A2
South Woodham Ferrers
CM3 ......101 F6
Merton Rd Barking IG11 ......152 F5
Hockley SS5 ......124 A8
Ilford IG3 ......133 F4
South Benfleet SS7 ......144 C4
Mess RM SS3 ......168 F5
Messant Cl RM3 ......114 D1
Meteor Rd SS0 ......166 D8
Meteor Way CM1 ......31 F2
Metford Cres EN3 ......65 A1
Methersgate SS14 ......142 C7
Methuen Rd DA17 ......169 B2
Metsons La CM1 ......51 E2
Metz Ave SS8 ......164 A4
Mews Ct CM2 ......32 B1
Mews Pl IG8 ......110 A6
Mews The Grays RM17 ......173 C2
Harlow CM18 ......23 E4
Hockley SS5 ......124 C6
Redbridge IG4 ......132 D6
Romford RM1 ......135 E7
Sawbridgeworth CM21 ......1 E3
Mey Wlk SS5 ......124 C6
Meyel Ave SS8 ......164 C2
Meynell Ave SS8 ......164 C2
Meynell Rd RM3 ......114 B3
Micawber Way CM1 ......31 D7
Michael Gdns RM11 ......136 D7
Michael's Cotts SS3 ......168 D6
Mid Colne SS16 ......142 D4
Midas Bsns Ctr RM10 ......154 B8
Middle Boy RM4 ......90 C6
Middle Cloister 3 CM11 ......97 B2
Middle Crockerford
SS16 ......142 E4
Middle Gn CM15 ......72 C2
Middle Mead
Rochford SS4 ......125 F2
Wickford SS11 ......121 F6
Middle Mead Cl CM2 ......76 F4

Middle Rd Ingrave CM13 ......117 C6
Waltham Abbey EN9 ......65 B7
Middle St EN9 ......44 A8
Middlefield Ave EN11 ......21 A8
Middlefield Cl EN11 ......21 A8
Middlefield Gdns IG2 ......133 B5
Middleham Ct 14 DA2 ......176 B1
Middlemead
South Hanningfield CM3 ......99 C8
West Hanningfield CM2 ......77 C3
Middlesborough Ho 7
RM3 ......114 E3
Middlesburg SS8 ......163 E5
Middlesex Ave SS9 ......146 E3
Middleton Ave E4 ......109 A4
Middleton Gdns IG2 ......133 B5
Middleton Hall (Brentwood
Prep Sch) CM15 ......94 E1
Middleton Hall La CM15 ......116 E8
Middleton Rd CM15 ......94 F1
Middleton Row CM3 ......101 E6
Midguard Way CM9 ......58 F8
Midhurst Ave SS0 ......147 D4
Midhurst Cl RM12 ......155 A8
Midland Ct RM1 ......135 F6
Midsummer Mdw SS3 ......149 E1
Mighell Ave IG4 ......132 D6
Milbank CM2 ......33 B4
Milbanke Cl SS3 ......149 E1
Milbourn Ct SS4 ......125 F2
Milburn Cres CM1 ......31 D1
Mildenhall Ho RM3 ......115 A5
Mildmay Ct 2 CM2 ......32 B1
Mildmay Ind Est CM0 ......106 B5
Mildmay Jun & Inf Schs
CM2 ......54 B5
Mildmay Rd
Burnham-on-C CM0 ......106 C5
Chelmsford CM2 ......32 B1
Ilford IG1 ......133 B1
Romford RM7 ......135 C5
Mildmayes SS16 ......141 C4
Mildmays CM3 ......56 C7
Mildred Cl DA1 ......176 A1
Mildred Rd DA8 ......169 E1
Mile Cl EN9 ......65 C6
Miles Cl CM19 ......23 B7
Miles Gray Rd SS14 ......119 F1
Milestone Rd DA2 ......176 B1
Milford Rd RM16 ......173 D5
Milkwell Gdns IG8 ......110 B3
Mill Cl Roxwell CM1 ......30 A5
Tillingham CM0 ......63 E4
Mill Cotts
Corringham SS17 ......161 D5
Great Baddow CM2 ......55 C8
Mill Field CM17 ......11 C4
Mill Gn Basildon SS13 ......143 A7
Burnham-on-C CM0 ......106 B4
Mill Gr CM5 ......49 D4
Mill Grange CM0 ......106 B7
Mill Green Ct SS13 ......143 B7
Mill Green Pl SS13 ......143 B7
Mill Green Rd CM4 ......73 F7
Mill Hill Chelmsford CM2 ......53 F2
Purleigh CM3 ......58 C1
Shenfield CM15 ......94 F2
South Benfleet SS7 ......163 E8
Mill Hill Dr CM12 ......97 B5
Mill Ho IG8 ......109 F5
Mill La Broomfield CM1 ......19 C1
Corringham SS17 ......161 C6
Dagenham RM6 ......134 C5
Danbury CM3 ......57 A6
Fobbing SS17 ......161 C7
Grays RM16 ......172 D1
Harlow CM17 ......11 E4
Hatfield Heath CM22 ......2 F3
High Ongar CM5 ......49 D2
Hoddesdon EN10 ......21 A2
Horndon-on-t-H SS17 ......159 F3
Ingatestone CM4 ......74 A6
Kelvedon Hatch CM15 ......71 C2
Little Baddow CM3 ......34 E3
Maldon CM9 ......37 A3
Moreton CM5 ......26 C5
Navestock Heath RM4 ......92 B8
Orsett RM16 ......174 A7
Purleigh CM3 ......58 C1
Ramsden Heath CM11 ......98 B5
Rochford SS4 ......126 B2
Sawbridgeworth CM21 ......1 F3
Sewardstone E4 ......87 B6
Stock CM4 ......75 F2
Toot Hill CM5 ......47 E2
Woodford IG8 ......109 F5
Wyatts Green CM15 ......72 D4
Mill Lodge SS3 ......168 E6
Mill Park Ave RM12 ......136 E2
Mill Race SG12 ......8 C4
Mill Rd Aveley RM15 ......171 C6
Billericay CM11 ......119 D6
Burnham-on-C CM0 ......106 C7
Ilford IG1 ......133 A1
Maldon CM9 ......37 B2
Margaret Roding CM1 ......16 D5
Mayland CM3 ......83 B8
Stock CM4 ......75 F2
Tillingham CM0 ......63 E4
Mill St CM17 ......24 F5
Mill View CM17 ......173 E7
Mill View Ct CM1 ......30 A5
Mill Vue Rd CM2 ......32 F2
Millais Ave E12 ......152 A7
Millais Pl RM18 ......179 B7
Millard Terr RM10 ......154 A6
Millars CM3 ......101 E8

Millars The CM1 ......19 A3
Millbank Ave CM5 ......48 F2
Millbank CM5 ......48 F2
Millbrook Chigwell IG7 ......111 D5
1 Wanstead E18 ......132 A8
3 Woodford E18 ......110 A1
Millbrook Gdns
Dagenham RM6 ......134 E5
Romford RM2 ......113 D2
Millennium Wlk CM14 ......116 D8
Miller Ave EN3 ......65 A1
Miller's La IG7 ......90 B1
Millers Cl IG7 ......112 B8
Millers Croft CM2 ......54 F6
Millers Green Rd CM5 ......28 B3
Millers La SG12 ......8 C4
Millers Mews CM4 ......74 C4
Millersdale CM19 ......23 B4
Millfield
Burnham-on-C CM0 ......106 B4
High Ongar CM5 ......49 D3
Millfield Cl SS6 ......123 E3
Millfields Danbury CM3 ......57 A6
Sawbridgeworth CM21 ......1 F3
Writtle CM1 ......31 A1
Millhaven Cl RM6 ......134 B5
Millhead Way SS4 ......126 B5
Millhoe Ct EN9 ......65 F5
Millhouse Inf Sch SS15 ......141 C8
Millhouse Jun Sch
SS15 ......141 C8
Millhurst Mews CM17 ......11 E4
Millicent Preston Ho 4
IG11 ......152 D4
Milligans Chase CM2 ......54 B1
Millom Ho 1 RM3 ......114 D4
Mills Way IG7 ......111 C5
Millsmead Way IG10 ......88 F7
Millson Bank CM1 ......33 A4
Millview Mdws SS4 ......125 F1
Millwell Cres IG7 ......111 D5
Milne Ct 4 E18 ......110 A2
Milner Pl CM12 ......96 F5
Milner Rd RM8 ......134 C2
Milton Ave Basildon SS16 ......140 F4
Hornchurch RM12 ......135 F2
Southend-on-S SS0 ......166 F2
Milton Cl Rayleigh SS6 ......124 A2
Southend-on-S SS2 ......148 A1
Milton Cres
Chipping Ongar CM5 ......48 F7
Ilford IG2 ......133 C5
Milton Ct Dagenham RM6 ......134 C4
Southend-on-S SS0 ......166 F2
Waltham Abbey EN9 ......65 C5
Milton Gdns RM18 ......179 B6
Milton Hall Cl SS3 ......150 A3
Milton Hall Prim Sch
SS0 ......166 B8
Milton Pl Chelmsford CM1 ......32 A5
Gravesend DA12 ......179 C1
Southend-on-S SS1 ......166 F7
Milton Rd
Belvedere DA17 ......169 A4
Brentwood CM14 ......116 C6
Corringham SS17 ......160 F6
Gravesend DA12 ......179 C1
Grays RM17 ......173 B1
Maldon CM9 ......59 A8
Romford RM1 ......136 A5
Southend-on-S SS0 ......166 E8
Swanscombe DA10 ......177 E1
Milton St
Southend-on-S SS2 ......148 A1
Swanscombe DA10 ......177 D1
Waltham Abbey EN9 ......65 C5
Miltsin Ave SS8 ......164 C5
Milverton Gdns IG3 ......133 F2
Milwards CM19 ......23 B4
Milwards Prim Sch CM19 ......23 B4
Mimosa Cl Basildon SS16 ......140 F4
Chelmsford CM1 ......32 F6
Pilgrims Hatch CM15 ......94 B4
Romford RM3 ......114 C3
Minchen Rd CM20 ......11 A1
Minehead Ho 6 RM3 ......114 E5
Minerva Rd E4 ......109 B3
Minster Cl SS6 ......124 A1
Minster Ct RM11 ......137 A3
Minster Rd SS15 ......141 C6
Minster Way
Hornchurch RM11 ......137 A3
Maldon CM9 ......58 E8
Minton Hts SS4 ......125 C6
Minton La CM17 ......24 C8
Miramar Ave SS8 ......163 E3
Miramar Way RM12 ......155 D7
Miranda Ho 6 DA17 ......169 A1
Mirosa Dr CM9 ......37 B1
Mirosa Reach CM9 ......59 A8
Mirravale Ct 5 IG9 ......110 C8
Mirravale Trad Est RM6 ......134 E4
Mirror Stps 1 SS1 ......167 C7
Mistley End SS16 ......142 C5
Mistley Path SS16 ......142 C5
Mistley Rd CM20 ......11 A2
Mistley Side SS16 ......142 C5
Mistley Thorn IG1 ......133 A4
Mistral Ct E4 ......109 B7
Mitcham Rd IG3 ......133 F4
Mitchell Cl Erith DA17 ......169 C3
Rainham RM13 ......155 C3
Mitchell Way CM3 ......101 D8
Mitchells Ave SS8 ......164 D4
Mitchells Wlk SS8 ......164 D4
Mitre Bldgs CM20 ......10 C1
Mitre Ct Belvedere DA17 ......169 A2
9 Dagenham RM6 ......134 B4
8 Woodford E18 ......110 A2

Mitre Ho RM7 ......135 B7
Mitton Vale CM2 ......32 F2
Moat Cl
Doddinghurst CM15 ......72 C3
Ramsden Heath CM11 ......98 C3
Moat Edge Gdns CM12 ......97 A4
Moat End SS1 ......149 B1
Moat Field SS14 ......142 C8
Moat Lodge Ho SS14 ......142 C7
Moat Rise SS6 ......123 D1
Moat The CM5 ......47 F2
Moblin Lodge IG9 ......88 C1
Molesworth EN11 ......8 A2
Mollands CM3 ......142 F4
Mollands Ct RM15 ......157 E1
Mollands La RM15 ......157 D1
Mollison Ave EN3 ......65 A3
Molrams La CM2 ......55 B6
Momples Rd CM20 ......11 B1
Monarch Cl
Rainham RM13 ......155 A3
Tilbury RM18 ......179 B5
Monarch Pl IG9 ......110 C8
Monarch Rd DA17 ......169 A3
Monastery Rd SS15 ......141 C6
Monkchester Cl IG10 ......89 A8
Monkham's Ave IG8 ......110 B5
Monkham's Dr IG8 ......110 B5
Monkham's La IG8 ......110 B6
Monkhams Hall EN9 ......43 C2
Monks Chase CM13 ......117 C5
Monks Cl EN10 ......21 A3
Monks Haven SS17 ......160 E2
Monks Mead CM3 ......56 F2
Monks Well DA9 ......177 C3
Monksbury CM18 ......24 A5
Monksford SS5 ......101 D1
Monksgrove IG10 ......89 A4
Monkside SS14 ......142 D7
Monkswick Rd CM20 ......10 F1
Monkswood Ave EN9 ......65 D6
Monkswood Gdns IG5 ......133 B8
Monkwood Cl RM1 ......136 A6
Monmouth Ave E18 ......132 B8
Monmouth Mews SS16 ......140 F5
Monmouth Rd RM9 ......153 F7
Monnow Gn RM15 ......171 C6
Monnow Rd RM15 ......171 C6
Monoux Cl CM11 ......97 D1
Monoux Gr E17 ......109 A2
Mons Ave RM11 ......97 D2
Montagu Gdns CM1 ......32 F7
Montague Bldgs 2 SS1 ......167 B8
Montague Ho 13 IG8 ......111 A3
Montague Pl SS8 ......163 E5
Montague Way CM12 ......97 A4
Montalt Ho IG8 ......109 F6
Montalt Rd IG8 ......109 F5
Montbazon Ct CM14 ......94 B1
Monteagle Ave IG11 ......152 C6
Monteagle Prim Sch
RM9 ......153 B4
Montefiore Ave SS6 ......123 D8
Montfort Ave SS17 ......161 A4
Montfort Gdns IG6 ......111 C4
Montgomery Inf & Jun Sch
SS7 ......144 B7
Montgomery Cl
Chelmsford CM1 ......32 E7
Grays RM17 ......173 C2
Montgomery Cres RM3 ......114 D5
Montgomery Ct SS3 ......149 E1
Montpelier Gdns RM6 ......134 B1
Montpelier Cl CM12 ......97 A5
Montpellier Ct 3 CM14 ......116 C7
Montpellier Ho IG7 ......111 C5
Montreal Rd Ilford IG1 ......133 C4
Tilbury RM18 ......179 A5
Montrose Ave RM2 ......114 C1
Montrose Cl IG8 ......110 A6
Montrose Rd CM2 ......33 A4
Montsale SS13 ......143 C8
Montserrat Ave IG8 ......109 D3
Moons Cl SS4 ......125 D7
Moor Hall La CM3 ......56 E2
Moor Hall Rd CM17 ......12 A4
Moor La RM14 ......137 F4
Moor Park Cl SS9 ......146 C5
Moor Park Gdns SS9 ......146 C5
Moorcroft SS4 ......125 D6
Moorcroft Ave SS7 ......145 E6
Moore Ave Grays RM20 ......172 E1
Tilbury RM18 ......179 B5
Moore Cl CM11 ......97 D5
Moore Cres RM9 ......153 B4
Moore Ho RM11 ......136 A5
Moore Rd DA10 ......177 E1
Moore Twr CM18 ......23 F7
Moore's Pl CM14 ......116 D8
Moores Ave SS17 ......142 C1
Moorescroft CM15 ......71 E2
Moorfields CM18 ......23 C4
Moorhen Ave CM0 ......62 C8
Moorhen Way CM19 ......9 A1
Moorland Cl RM5 ......113 B2
Moorlands Reach CM21 ......2 A1
Mopsies Rd SS14 ......142 E6
Moran Ave CM1 ......32 B7
Morant Gdns RM5 ......113 B5
Morant Rd RM16 ......174 B3
Moray Cl RM1 ......113 C4
Moray Way RM1 ......113 C4
Mordaunt Gdns RM9 ......153 E5
Morden Rd RM6 ......134 C4
Mordon Rd IG3 ......133 F4
Morecambe Cl RM12 ......155 B7

Morecambe Ho 5 RM3 ......114 E5
Moreland Ave SS7 ......144 C7
Moreland Cl
Great Wakering SS3 ......150 A4
South Benfleet SS7 ......144 C6
Moreland Rd SS11 ......99 C2
Moreland Way E4 ......109 C7
Morelands Ave RM16 ......173 C4
Moremead EN9 ......65 D6
Mores La CM14 ......93 D5
Moreton Bridge SS5 ......26 D1
Moreton CE Prim Sch
CM5 ......26 C3
Moreton Gdns IG8 ......110 E5
Moreton Rd
Chipping Ongar CM5 ......48 F7
Fyfield CM5 ......27 B2
Moreton CM5 ......26 C5
Moretons Basildon SS13 ......143 A6
Galleywood CM2 ......54 B2
Moretons Ct SS13 ......143 A6
Moretons Mews SS13 ......143 A6
Moretons Pl SS13 ......143 A6
Morgan Cl RM10 ......154 A5
Morgan Cres SS4 ......67 C3
Morgan Terr RM6 ......134 C6
Morgan Way
Rainham RM13 ......155 C2
Woodford IG8 ......110 E4
Morland Rd
Dagenham RM10 ......154 A5
Ilford IG1 ......133 B2
Morland Road Day Hospl
RM10 ......154 A4
Morley Ave E4 ......109 D3
Morley Gr CM20 ......10 C2
Morley Hill SS17 ......160 F5
Morley Link SS17 ......160 F5
Morley Rd Barking IG11 ......152 D4
Dagenham RM6 ......134 C6
Morley Sq RM16 ......174 A2
Mornington Ave
Ilford IG1 ......133 A4
Rochford SS4 ......126 A2
Mornington Cl IG8 ......110 A6
Mornington Cres
Canvey Island SS8 ......164 C4
Hadleigh SS7 ......145 F3
Mornington Ho SS0 ......166 E3
Mornington Rd
Canvey Island SS8 ......164 C4
Chingford E4 ......87 D2
Loughton IG10 ......89 C6
Woodford IG8 ......109 F6
Morningtons CM19 ......23 C4
Morpeth Ho 8 RM3 ......114 D4
Morrab Gdns IG3 ......133 F1
Morrells SS14 ......141 F4
Morrin's Chase SS3 ......150 D3
Morrins Cl SS3 ......150 D3
Morris Ave CM11 ......97 D1
Morris Ct Basildon SS15 ......141 B7
Chingford E4 ......109 B7
Holdbrook EN3 ......65 A2
Waltham Abbey EN9 ......65 F5
Morris Gdns DA1 ......176 A2
Morris Ho CM18 ......23 C5
Morris Rd Chelmsford CM2 ......32 D2
Dagenham RM8 ......134 F2
Romford RM3 ......114 B3
Morrison Ho RM16 ......173 D4
Morrison Rd IG11 ......153 E2
Morris Way SS6 ......123 E5
Mortimer Rd SS6 ......123 E5
Mortlake Rd IG1 ......152 D8
Mosbach Gdns CM13 ......117 B8
Moseley St SS2 ......148 C1
Moss Cl SS16 ......142 E3
Moss Dr SS16 ......142 E3
Moss La
Hornchurch RM11 ......136 A5
Romford RM1 ......135 F5
Moss Path CM2 ......54 B8
Moss Rd Dagenham RM10 ......154 A5
South Ockendon RM15 ......172 C8
Moss Wlk CM2 ......54 B6
Mossdown Cl DA17 ......169 A2
Mossford Ct Ilford IG6 ......133 B8
Redbridge IG6 ......111 B1
Mossford Gn IG6 ......133 C8
Mossford Green Prim Sch
IG6 ......111 C1
Mossford La IG6 ......111 C1
Motehill SS16 ......142 E3
Motherwell Way RM20 ......172 A1
Mott St High Beach IG10 ......88 A8
Sewardstone IG10 ......87 E8
Moulsham Chase CM2 ......54 C8
Moulsham Dr CM2 ......54 B8
Moulsham High Sch CM2 ......54 B7
Moulsham Jun & Inf Schs
CM2 ......54 B7
Moulsham St
Chelmsford CM1 ......32 B2
Chelmsford CM2 ......32 B1
Moulsham Thrift CM2 ......54 A6
Moultrie Way RM14 ......137 E5
Mount Ave
Brentwood CM13 ......95 B2
Chingford E4 ......109 B7
Hockley SS5 ......124 E7
Rayleigh SS5 ......123 C3
Romford RM3 ......115 C4
Southend-on-S SS0 ......166 D3
Mount Bovers La SS5 ......124 E3
Mount Cl Rayleigh SS6 ......123 C2
Wickford SS11 ......121 F6

Mount Cres
Brentwood CM14 ....116 D6
Hockley SS5 ....124 D6
South Benfleet SS7 .....144 E4
Mount Echo Ave E4 ....87 B1
Mount Echo Dr E4 ....87 B1
Mount Pleasant
Ilford IG1 ....152 C7
Maldon CM9 ....36 F2
Mount Pleasant Ave
CM13 ....95 E4
Mount Pleasant Cotts
CM15 ....95 A4
Mount Pleasant Rd
Chigwell IG7 ....111 D6
Romford RM5 ....113 D4
South Woodham Ferrers
CM3 ....101 D7
Mount Rd
Dagenham RM8 ....134 F3
Epping CM16 ....68 E6
South Benfleet SS7 .....144 F4
Wickford SS11 ....121 E8
Mount The Billericay CM11 97 E3
Brentwood CM14 ......116 C7
Romford RM3 ....114 C7
Stanford-le-H SS17 ....160 F3
Mount View
Billericay CM11 ....97 E2
Brentwood CM14 ......116 C6
Mount View Rd E4 .....87 D2
Mount Way SS11 ......121 E8
Mountain Ash Ave SS9 .146 B6
Mountain Ash Cl SS9 ...146 B6
Mountbatten Ct IG9 ...110 D8
Mountbatten Dr SS3 ...149 E1
Mountbatten Ho 4
RM2 ....136 C7
Mountbatten Way CM1 ..32 E7
Mountdale Gdns SS9 ...146 F4
Mountfield Cl SS17 .....160 E3
Mountfield Rd E6 ......152 A2
Mountfields SS13 ......143 C4
Mounthill Ave CM2 .....32 D3
Mountnessing SS7 .....145 D2
Mountnessing CE Prim Sch
CM15 ....95 E7
Mountnessing La CM15 .72 E1
Mountnessing Rd
Billericay CM12 ....96 E4
Blackmore CM4 ....72 F6
Mountnessing CM15,CM4 .73 A4
Mountney Cl CM4 ......73 F1
Mounts Rd DA9 ....177 B1
Mountview Cl SS16 .....142 E3
Mountview Cres CM0 ...62 C8
Movers La IG11 ....152 E4
Mowbray Rd CM20 .....11 A3
Mowbrays Cl RM5 .....113 C1
Mowbrays Rd RM5 .....113 C1
Mowbrey Gdns IG10 ...89 C8
Mowden Hall La CM3 ...35 A8
Mucking Hall Cotts SS3 149 B8
Mucking Hall Rd SS3 ..149 C8
Mucking Wharf Rd
SS17 ....175 C7
Muckingford Rd RM18,
SS17 ....174 E2
Mudlands Ind Est RM13 154 F2
Muggeridge Rd RM10 ..154 B8
Muir Pl SS12 ....121 D5
Muirway SS7 ....144 B7
Mulberry Ave Chingford E4 109 A8
Romford RM2 ....136 C7
Mulberry Ct IG11 .....152 F5
Mulberry Dr RM19 ....170 F2
Mulberry Gn CM17 ....11 D4
Mulberry Hill CM15 ....94 F2
Mulberry Rd SS8 ......163 C3
Mulberry Terr CM17 ...11 B4
Mulberry Way
Belvedere DA17 ....169 C4
Chelmsford CM1 ......32 C4
Ilford IG6 ....133 C7
Woodford E18 ....110 B1
Mulberrys The SS2 ....148 A3
Mullberry Gdns SS16 ..141 B5
Mullein Ct RM17 ......178 E8
Mullions The CM12 ....96 F3
Multon Lea CM1 ....33 A7
Mundon Ct SS14 ......142 F5
Mundon Gdns IG1 .....133 D3
Mundon Rd CM9 ......59 C7
Mungo Park Rd RM13 ..155 A6
Munro Ct 15 SS12 ....121 E5
Munsons Alley CM0 ....84 D4
Munster Ct CM12 ......96 F5
Munsterburg Rd SS8 ...164 D5
Murchison Cl CM1 .....31 E5
Murchison Rd EN11 ....8 B1
Murfitt Way RM14 ....156 A8
Murray Ho SS1 ....167 F6
Murray Way SS12 .....121 D5
Murrell Lock CM2 .....33 A4
Murrels La SS5 ....124 A7
Murthering La
Navestock Heath RM4 ...92 B5
Stapleford Abbotts RM4 ..91 F3
Murtwell Dr IG7 ....111 C4
Mus of Power✶ CM9 ....36 D6
Musket Gr SS9 ....146 B7
Muskham Rd CM20 ....11 B3
Mutton Row CM5 ......70 C4
Mygrove Cl RM13 .....155 D3
Mygrove Gdns RM13 ..155 D3
Mygrove Rd RM13 .....155 D3
Myln Mdw CM4 ....75 F2
Mylne Ct EN11 ....8 A1

Mynards Way CM3 .....56 C7
Mynchens SS15 ......141 E6
Myrtle Gr RM15 ......171 C4
Myrtle Rd
Brentwood CM14 ......116 C6
Ilford IG1 ....133 B2
Romford RM3 ....114 C4

N

Nabbott Rd CM1 ....31 E2
Nadir Ct E11 ....132 A4
Naffenton Rise IG10 ...88 D4
Nag's Head La CM14 ..115 D4
Nagle Cl E17 ....109 D1
Nairn Ct RM18 ....178 F5
Nairn Ho CM14 ....116 C6
Nalla Gdns CM1 ....32 A6
Namur Rd SS8 ....164 C5
Nansen Ave SS4 ......125 D6
Nantwich Ho 4 RM3 ..114 E5
Napier Ave 9 SS1 ....167 A8
Napier Cl Basildon SS14 142 D6
Hornchurch RM11 ......136 B3
Napier Cres SS12 .....121 E5
Napier Ct RM1 ....31 E5
Napier Ct W SS1 ......166 F8
Napier Gdns SS7 ......145 C6
Napier Ho RM13 ......154 F7
Napier Ho Rayleigh SS6 .123 F3
Wallend E6 ....152 A3
Narboro Ct RM1 ......136 A5
Nare Rd RM15 ....171 C6
Narvik Cl CM9 ....58 E8
Naseby Rd
Dagenham RM10 ......135 A1
Woodford IG5 ....110 F2
Nash Dr CM1 ....19 A3
Nash Rd RM6 ....134 D7
Natal Rd IG1 ....152 B8
Natasha Ct RM1 ......114 C3
Nathan Cl RM14 ......137 E3
Nathan's La CM5 ......52 E5
Nation Way E4 ....87 C1
National Motor Boat Mus✶
SS16 ....143 B2
National Sea Training Coll
DA12 ....180 A1
Naunton Way RM12 ...136 D1
Navarre Gdns RM5 ....113 B5
Navestock Cl
Chingford E4 ....109 C7
Rayleigh SS6 ....123 A3
Navestock Cres IG8 ...110 C2
Navestock Gdns SS1 ..148 F1
Navestock Ho IG11 ...153 B3
Navestock Side CM14 ..93 C7
Navigation Pl CM9 ....37 B4
Navigation Rd CM2 ....32 C2
Nayland Cl SS12 ......121 E7
Nayland Ho SS2 ......147 E5
Nazeing Comm EN9 ...44 D8
Nazeing Ho IG9 ....88 D7
Nazeing New Rd EN10 ..21 B2
Nazeing Prim Sch EN9 .43 E8
Nazeing Rd EN9 ....21 D1
Nazeing The SS14 ....142 E6
Nazeing Wlk RM13 ....154 C5
Nazeingbury Cl EN9 ...21 D1
Nazeingbury Par EN9 ..21 D1
Neal Ct EN9 ....65 F6
Neale Ct RM11 ....136 F2
Neasham Rd RM8 .....153 B7
Neave Cres RM3 ......114 D2
Nectar Ct 1 EN11 ....21 D8
Needham Cl CM11 ....97 B3
Neil Armstrong Way
SS9 ....147 A6
Nelmes Cl RM11 ......136 F6
Nelmes Cres RM11 ....136 F6
Nelmes Ct RM11 ......136 D7
Nelmes Prim Sch RM11 136 F7
Nelmes Rd RM11 .....136 E5
Nelmes Way RM11 ....136 E7
Nelson Cl
Brentwood CM14 ......116 D5
Rayleigh SS6 ....123 F4
Romford RM7 ....113 B2
Nelson Cres CM9 .....59 B8
Nelson Ct 2 CM0 .....106 C4
Nelson Dr SS9 ....146 F1
Nelson Gdns SS6 .....123 F4
Nelson Gr CM1 ....31 F3
Nelson Ho
Greenhithe DA9 ....177 D2
3 Romford RM3 ......114 E5
Nelson Mews SS1 ....167 A7
Nelson Pl CM3 ....101 E6
Nelson Prim Sch E6 ...152 A3
Nelson Rd Basildon SS14 142 E6
Chingford E4 ....109 B4
Orsett RM16 ....174 D7
Rainham RM13 ....154 F3
Rayleigh SS6 ....123 F4
Rochford SS4 ....125 C6
South Ockendon RM15 ..157 C3
Southend-on-S SS9 ....147 A4
Wanstead E11 ....132 B7
Nelson St
Southend-on-S SS1 ....167 A7
Wallend E6 ....152 A4
Nelwyn Ave RM11 ....136 F6
Neptune Cl RM13 .....154 F3
Neptune Ct Barking IG11 153 B2
Chelmsford CM1 ......31 F4
Neptune Wlk DA8 ....169 D2
Nesbit Cl SS12 ....121 C5

Ness Rd SS3 ....168 E6
Nesta Rd IG8 ....109 F4
Nestuda Way SS2 ....147 B5
Nethan Dr RM15 .....171 C6
Nether Mayne SS16 ..142 B3
Nether Priors SS14 ...142 C4
Netherfield SS7 ......145 A4
Netherfield Ct SG12 ...8 D3
Netherfield Gdns IG11 .152 D5
Netherfield La SG12 ...8 E3
Netherhall Rd DA19 ...21 F5
Netherpark Dr RM2 ..113 F1
Nethewode Ct DA17 ..169 B3
Netley Ct IG2 ....133 D6
Netley Rd IG2 ....133 D6
Netteswell Cross 10 E2
Netteswell Orch CM20 .10 D3
Netteswell Rd CM20 ...10 F3
Netteswell Rectory CM20 23 E8
Netteswell Twr CM20 ..10 D1
Nettleton Ho 23 F7
Nevada Rd SS8 ......164 C5
Nevell Rd RM16 ......174 B3
Nevendon Grange SS12 121 C6
Nevendon Mews SS13 .121 A2
Nevendon Rd
Basildon SS13 ....121 A2
Wickford SS12 ....121 B4
Nevern Cl SS6 ....145 F8
Nevern Rd SS6 ......145 E8
Nevill Way IG10 ......88 E3
Neville Gdns RM8 ....134 D1
Neville Rd
Dagenham RM8 ....134 D1
Redbridge IG6 ....111 C2
Neville Shaw SS14 ...142 B6
Nevin Dr E4 ....87 B1
Nevis Cl RM1 ....113 E4
Nevyll Ct SS1 ....168 B8
New Ave SS16 ....141 A4
New Barns Way SS7 ..111 B7
New Bowers Way CM1 .32 F6
New Bury Mdw CM22 .3 F5
New Century Rd SS15 .141 B6
New Cotts Basildon SS13 143 D5
Rainham RM13 ....170 C7
Rochford SS4 ....127 F5
New Court Bsns Pk
CM18 ....23 C4
New Dukes Way CM2 ..32 F4
New England Cl CM3 ..56 F1
New England Cres SS3 .150 C2
New England Est IG11 .152 C3
New Farm Dr RM4 ....90 C6
New Ford Rd EN8 .....65 A4
New Forest La IG7 ....111 A4
New Hall Dr RM3 .....114 E2
New Hall La CM9 .....59 E4
New Hall Rd SS4 .....103 B1
New Hall Sch CM3 ....20 A1
New Hall Vineyard✶
CM3 ....58 D2
New Jubilee Ct 1 IG8 .110 A3
New Lodge Chase CM3 .34 B2
New London Rd CM2 ..32 A1
New Maltings RM15 ...171 D5
New Moor Cl CM0 ....84 D4
New Moor Cres CM0 ..84 E4
New Nabbotts Way CM1 .32 E4
New North Rd IG6 ....111 E4
New Park Rd
Rochford SS5 ....103 A1
South Benfleet SS7 ....144 C5
New Place Gdns RM14 .137 D2
New Plymouth Ho RM13 154 F2
New Rd Abridge RM4 ..90 D3
Basildon SS14 ....119 A3
Brentwood CM14 ......116 D8
Broomfield CM1 ....19 B1
Burnham-on-C CM0 ...106 C5
Canvey Island SS8 ....163 E3
Chingford E4 ....109 C6
Dagenham RM9,RM10,
RM13 ....154 C2
Gravesend DA11 ......179 B1
Grays RM17 ....178 B8
Great Baddow CM2 ....55 A6
Great Wakering SS3 ...150 C3
Hadleigh SS7 ....145 D3
Harlow CM17 ....11 D4
Hoddesdon EN10 ......21 A4
Ilford IG3 ....133 E2
Ingatestone CM4 ......74 C4
Rainham RM13 ....155 B2
Southend-on-S SS9 ....165 D8
New River Ave SG12 ...8 B4
New River Cl EN11 ....21 B7
New Row
Paglesham Eastend SS4 .128 A5
Sheering CM22 ....12 C6
New Rush Hall Sch IG6 111 C3
New St Chelmsford CM1 .32 B3
Maldon CM9 ....36 F2
Sawbridgeworth CM21 ..1 C3
New Swan Yd DA11 ..179 B1
New Tavern Fort✶
DA12 ....179 C1
New Wanstead E11 ...132 A5
New Waverley Rd SS15 .119 E1
New Way La CM17 ....12 D1
New Writtle St CM2 ...32 B1
New Zealand Way RM13 154 F2
Newbery Side SS15 ...141 C5
Newburgh Rd RM17 ..173 D1
Newbury Cl RM3 .....114 D4
Newbury Cotts 4 IG2 .133 C5
Newbury Ct 7 E11 ...132 A7

Newbury Gdns
Romford RM3 ....114 D4
Upminster RM14 ......136 F1
Newbury Park Prim Sch
IG2 ....133 D5
Newbury Park Sta IG2 .133 D5
Newbury Rd
Chingford E4 ....109 C4
Ilford IG2 ....133 E5
Romford RM3 ....114 D4
Newbury Wlk RM3 ....114 D5
Newcastle Ave IG6 ...112 A4
Newcourt Rd CM2 ....32 D3
Newell Ave SS3 ......168 G8
Newgate St E4 ....109 E7
Newhall SS4 ....125 C6
Newhall Ct EN9 ......65 F6
Newham Ho IG10 ....88 D3
Newham Way E6 .....152 A1
Newhouse Ave
Ilford RM6 ....134 D8
Wickford SS12 ....120 F7
Newhouse La CM5 ...26 C1
Newington Ave SS2 ..148 E2
Newington Cl SS2 ....148 F2
Newington Gdns SS2 ..148 E2
Newlands Cl
Billericay CM12 ....97 B4
Brentwood CM14 ......95 D2
Newlands End SS15 ..141 B8
Newlands Rd
Billericay CM12 ....97 A3
Canvey Island SS8 ....164 D5
Wickford SS12 ....121 D4
Woodford IG8 ....109 F8
Newlands Spring Prim Sch
CM1 ....31 B2
Newman Cl RM11 .....136 E6
Newman Ct IG10 .....89 B6
Newmans Dr CM13 ...95 C2
Newmans La IG10 ....89 B6
Newmarket Ho 2 RM3 114 E5
Newmarket Way RM12 .155 E8
Newnham Cl IG10 ....88 D3
Newnham Gn CM9 ...36 E3
Newnham Lodge 10
DA17 ....169 A1
Newnham Pl RM16 ...174 A1
Newpiece IG10 ....89 B6
Newport Ave CM3 ....81 B5
Newport Cl CM2 .....55 B6
Newport Ct SS6 ......123 B4
Newports CM21 ......1 C1
Newstead Ho RM13 ..114 D6
Newstead Rd SS3 ....150 B4
Newsum Gdns SS6 ...123 A3
Newteswell Dr EN9 ..65 D7
Newton Cl
Corringham SS17 ......161 A5
Hoddesdon EN11 ......8 B2
Newton Dr CM21 .....1 D1
Newton Hall Gdns SS4 .125 C4
Newton Park Rd SS7 .145 B2
Newton Rd
Redbridge IG7 ....112 B5
Tilbury RM18 ....179 A5
Newton's Ct DA2 ....176 D3
Newtons Prim Sch
RM13 ....154 D3
Nicholas Cl
South Ockendon RM15 .157 C2
Writtle CM1 ....31 B1
Nicholas Ct CM1 .....31 D6
Nicholas Rd RM8 .....134 F1
Nicholl Rd Basildon SS15 141 C7
Epping CM16 ....67 F8
Nicholls Field CM18 ...24 B7
Nichols Ct CM2 ......32 A1
Nicholson Cres SS7 ..145 C5
Nicholson Ct EN11 ...21 B6
Nicholson Gr 15 SS12 .121 E5
Nicholson Ho SS1 ....167 B8
Nicholson Pl CM3 ....78 B7
Nicholson Rd SS7 ....145 B3
Nickleby Rd CM1 .....31 D6
Nicola Mews IG6 .....111 B4
Nicolas Wlk RM16 ...174 B4
Nigel Mews IG1 ......152 B8
Nightingale Ave
Chingford E4 ....109 E5
Upminster RM14 ......137 F3
Nightingale Cl
Chingford E4 ....109 E6
Rayleigh SS6 ....123 B3
Southend-on-S SS2 ....147 B5
Nightingale Cnr 2 CM9 .37 A1
Nightingale Cl 1 E11 .132 B6
Nightingale Gr DA1 ...176 A3
Nightingale La E11 ...132 B6
Nightingale Prim Sch
E18 ....132 C2
Nightingale Rd SS8 ...164 C3
Nightingales
Basildon SS16 ....140 F5
Waltham Abbey EN9 ...65 E6
Nine Ashes Farm Cotts
CM4 ....50 C2
Nine Ashes Rd
Blackmore CM4 ....50 D1
Stondon Massey CM15 ..72 B6
Ninefields EN9 ....65 D1
Nipsells Chase CM3 ...61 A1
Nita Ct SS16 ....116 C5
Niton Ct SS17 ....175 C8
Niven Cl SS12 ....121 E5
Noak Bridge Prim Sch
SS15 ....119 F1
Noak Hill Cl CM12 ....119 C4

Noak Hill Cl CM12 ....119 B4
Noak Hill Rd
Basildon CM12 ....119 B4
Romford RM3 ....114 D7
Noakes Ave CM2 .....54 E6
Nobel Sq SS13 ....121 C2
Nobel Villas EN9 .....65 D5
Nobles Green Cl SS9 .146 E7
Nobles Green Rd SS9 .146 E7
Noel Sq RM8 ....153 C8
Nonsuch Cl IG6 ......111 B4
Nook The SG12 ......8 B4
Norbury Gdns RM6 ...134 D6
Norbury Rd E4 ......109 A5
Nordenfeldt Rd DA8 ..169 D1
Nordic Lodge CM9 ...58 F8
Nordland Rd SS8 .....164 D5
Nordmann Pl RM15 ..157 C1
Nore Rd SS9 ....146 C8
Nore View SS16 .....140 F4
Noredale SS3 ....168 D5
Norfolk Ave SS9 .....146 F3
Norfolk Cl Basildon SS15 141 C1
Canvey Island SS8 ....164 A5
Dartford DA1 ....176 A1
Maldon CM9 ....36 E1
Norfolk Ct SS4 ......125 D5
Norfolk Dr CM1 ......32 A7
Norfolk Ho RM7 .....113 A2
Norfolk Pl RM16 .....172 C1
Norfolk Rd Barking IG11 152 E5
Dagenham RM10 ......154 B7
Gravesend DA12 ......179 E1
Ilford IG3 ....133 E1
Norfolk Way SS8 ....163 F5
Norhan Ct 16 CM9 ...176 B1
Norman Cl Romford RM5 113 B1
Waltham Abbey EN9 ...65 D6
Norman Cres
Brentwood CM13 ......117 A7
Rayleigh SS6 ....123 E5
Norman Ct Ilford IG1 ..133 D4
Woodford IG8 ....110 B5
Norman Pl SS9 ......165 E8
Norman Rd
Belvedere DA17 ....169 B3
Hornchurch RM11 ....136 B4
Ilford IG1 ....152 B7
Norman Terr SS9 ....165 E8
Normandy Ave CM0 ..106 C5
Normandy Way EN11 .21 D3
Normanhurst CM13 ...95 C3
Normanhurst Sch E4 ..87 D2
Normans Rd SS8 .....164 D4
Normanton Ave E4 ...109 B6
Normanton Pk E4 ....109 E8
Norris La EN11 ......21 A7
Norris Rd EN11 ......21 A6
Norris Rise 4 EN11 ..21 A7
Norseman Ct 3 IG3 ..134 B3
Norsey Cl CM11 .....97 B3
Norsey Dr CM11 .....97 D3
Norsey Rd CM11 .....97 C4
Norsey View Dr CM12 .97 B6
Norsey Wood Nature
Reserve✶ CM11 ....97 D4
North Ave
Canvey Island SS8 ....164 A3
Chelmsford CM1 ......31 F5
Southend-on-S SS2 ...148 C3
North Barn RM10 ....21 B1
North Benfleet Hall Rd
Basildon SS12 ....122 A1
North Benfleet SS12 ...121 F1
North Circular Rd
Chingford E17 ....109 B2
Ilford IG1,E12 ....133 A1
Wallend E6, E12 ......152 A5
Wanstead IG1 ....132 D5
Woodford E18 ....110 C1
North Cl Dagenham RM10 154 A4
Redbridge IG7 ....112 A5
North Colne SS16 ....142 A4
North Cres
Southend-on-S SS2 ...147 D5
Wickford SS12 ....121 D7
North Crescent Prim Sch
SS12 ....121 D7
North Crockerford SS16 142 E4
North Cross Rd IG6 ..133 C7
North Dell CM1 ......32 E7
North Dr Brentwood CM13 .96 C2
Great Baddow CM2 ....54 F7
Mayland CM3 ....60 F1
Romford RM2 ....136 C8
North End
Buckhurst Hill IG9 ....88 C2
Romford RM3 ....114 C8
Southminster CM0 ....84 C5
North Gate CM20 ....10 C1
North Gr CM18 ......24 C7
North Gunnels SS14 .142 B6
North Hill
Horndon-on-t-H SS17 .160 A3
Little Baddow CM3 ...34 D5
North Hill Dr RM3 ....114 D6
North Hill Farm SS17 .159 F4
North Hill Gn RM3 ...114 D6
North Ho CM18 ......23 F6
North Kent Ave DA11 .178 C1
North Pl Harlow CM20 .11 B5

North Pl *continued*
4 Waltham Abbey EN9 ....**65** B6
North Rd Basildon CM11 .**120** D5
Belvedere DA17 ....**169** B4
Dagenham RM6 ....**134** E6
Havering-atte-B RM4 ....**91** F1
Hoddesdon EN11 ....**21** A7
Ilford IG3 ....**133** E2
Purfleet RM19 ....**171** C2
Romford RM4 ....**113** E7
South Ockendon RM15 ..**157** D4
Southend-on-S SS0 ....**147** E1
North Residence IG3 ..**134** B6
North Road Ave CM14 .**116** C8
North Service Rd 4
CM14 ....**116** C8
North Shoebury Rd SS3 **149** D1
North St Barking IG11 ..**152** C5
Great Wakering SS3 ....**150** B4
Hornchurch RM11 ......**136** D4
Lower Nazeing EN9 ......**21** E1
Maldon CM9 ....**37** B2
Rochford SS4 ....**125** F2
Romford RM1 ....**135** D7
Southend-on-S SS9 ....**165** E8
Southminster CM0 ......**84** D4
Tillingham CM0 ....**63** E4
North View Caravan Site★
IG6 ....**112** A3
North Weald Cl SS11 ..**122** B6
Northallerton Way 15
RM3 ....**114** D5
Northampton Gr SS16 **140** F4
Northampton Ho 4
RM3 ....**114** E6
Northbank Rd E17 ....**109** C5
Northbrook Rd IG1 ..**133** A2
Northbrooks CM19 ....**23** C7
Northbury Jun & Inf Sch
IG11 ....**152** C6
Northdene IG7 ....**111** C6
Northdown Gdns IG2 **133** E6
Northdown Rd RM11 .**136** M4
Northend CM14 ......**116** C5
Northern Ave SS7 ....**144** C5
Northern Relief Rd
IG11 ....**152** C6
Northfalls Rd SS8 ....**164** F3
Northfield IG10 ......**88** D5
Northfield Cl CM11 ....**97** C2
Northfield Cres SS3 ..**150** B4
Northfield Gdns RM9 .**153** F8
Northfield Path RM9 ..**153** F8
Northfield Rd
Dagenham RM9 ......**153** F8
Sawbridgeworth CM21 ....**1** E4
Northfields RM17 ....**173** D2
Northfleet Ind Est DA11 **177** F3
Northfleet Sta DA11 ..**178** B1
Northgate Ind Pk RM5 **112** F1
Northlands App SS16 .**141** C1
Northlands Cl SS17 ..**160** E5
Northlands Farm Chase
SS17 ....**160** E2
Northlands Jun & Inf Sch
SS13 ....**143** B6
Northlands Pavement 3
SS13 ....**143** B5
Northlime RM16 ....**173** C3
Northolt Way RM12 ..**155** C7
Northumberland Ave
Basildon SS15 ....**141** C5
Hornchurch RM11 ......**136** C6
Southend-on-S SS1 ....**167** D6
Wanstead E11 ....**132** C3
Northumberland Cres
SS1 ....**167** D7
Northumberland Ct 1
CM2 ....**32** F4
Northumberland Ho 11
IG8 ....**111** A3
Northumberland Rd
SS17 ....**175** A4
Northview Ave RM18 ..**179** A6
Northview Dr
Southend-on-S SS0 ....**147** D2
Woodford IG8 ....**110** D1
Northville Dr SS0 ....**147** C4
Northwick Park Jun & Inf
Schs SS8 ....**163** E4
Northwick Rd SS8 ....**163** B4
Northwick Ret Pk SS8 .**163** E4
Northwood RM16 ....**174** B4
Northwood Ave RM12 .**155** E4
Northwood Gdns IG5 ..**133** A4
Norton Ave SS8 ......**164** E3
Norton Cl Chingford E4 **109** A5
Corringham SS17 ......**161** A4
Norton Ct IG2 ....**133** D5
Norton Heath Rd CM5 ..**50** E8
Norton La High Ongar CM5 49 D5
High Ongar, Norton Mandeville
CM4,CM5 ....**50** C6
Norton Rd
Chelmsford CM1 ......**32** A3
Dagenham RM10 ......**154** D6
Ingatestone CM4 ......**74** B4
Norway Wlk RM13 ....**155** C1
Norwich Ave SS2 ....**148** C2
Norwich Cl SS2 ......**148** C2
Norwich Cres SS6 ....**123** C5
Norwich Ho SS4 ....**125** D5
Norwich Mews IG3 ..**134** A3
Norwich Wlk SS14 ..**142** F7
Norwood Ave RM7 ..**135** D4

Norwood Ct DA1 ....**176** A3
Norwood Dr SS7 ....**144** E1
Norwood End
Basildon SS14 ....**142** D7
Fyfield CM5 ....**27** D5
Nottage Cl SS17 ....**160** E4
Nottingham Way SS16 **140** F5
Nuneaton Rd RM9 ....**153** E5
Nunns Way RM17 ....**173** D2
Nursery Cl Ilford RM6 **134** D5
Rayleigh SS6 ....**123** D1
South Ockendon RM15 .**157** C1
Woodford IG8 ....**110** B5
Nursery Fields CM21 ....**1** D2
Nursery Gdns SS15 ..**141** D8
Nursery La CM3 ......**56** F8
Nursery Rd
Chelmsford CM2 ......**54** B8
Hoddesdon EN11 ....**8** B1
Hook End CM15 ....**72** C5
Loughton IG10 ....**88** D5
Lower Nazeing EN9 ....**21** D2
Stanford-le-H SS17 ..**160** E3
Nursery Wlk RM7 ....**135** D5
Nutberry Ave RM16 ..**173** B4
Nutberry Cl RM16 ....**173** A4
Nutbrowne Rd RM9 ..**154** A4
Nutcombe Cres SS4 ..**125** D4
Nutfield Gdns IG3 ..**134** A2
Nuthatch Cl CM11 ..**119** C8
Nutter La E11 ......**132** C6
Nuxley Rd DA17 ....**169** A1
Nyall Ct RM2 ....**136** D8
Nyssa Cl IG8 ....**110** F4
Nyth Cl RM14 ......**137** D5

O

O'Donoghue Ho SS17 .**160** E2
Oak Ave Basildon CM11 **120** C4
Upminster RM14 ......**156** B8
Wickford SS11 ....**122** C7
Oak Chase SS12 ....**121** E5
Oak Cl Maldon CM9 ..**59** B8
Waltham Abbey EN9 ....**65** D5
Oak Cnr CM9 ....**57** D6
Oak Cotts CM3 ....**33** E8
Oak Ct Chingford E4 ..**109** B4
Hadleigh SS7 ....**145** E2
South Ockendon RM15 .**157** C3
Oak Dene Cl RM11 ..**136** B5
Oak End CM18 ......**23** F6
Oak Farm Rd CM9 ....**35** E1
Oak Glade CM16 ......**46** D2
Oak Glen RM11 ......**136** B8
Oak Gn RM11 ....**90** D1
Oak Hall Rd E11 ....**132** B5
Oak Hill Cl IG8 ......**109** D3
Oak Hill Cres IG8 ..**109** E3
Oak Hill Gdns IG8 ..**109** F2
Oak Hill Rd RM4 ......**91** E1
Oak Ho SS3 ....**168** F8
Oak La Basildon CM11 **120** C3
Woodford IG8 ....**109** F6
Oak Lodge E11 ......**132** A4
Oak Lodge Ave IG7 ..**111** D5
Oak Lodge Tye CM1 ..**33** A6
Oak Piece CM16 ......**47** C6
Oak Rd Basildon CM11 **120** C4
Canvey Island SS8 ....**164** C3
Epping CM16 ....**45** F1
Grays RM17 ....**178** C4
Greenhithe DA9 ......**176** E1
Heybridge CM9 ....**37** B6
Ramsden Heath CM11 ..**98** D5
Rochford SS4 ....**125** E2
Romford RM3 ....**114** F2
Oak Rd N SS7 ......**145** E2
Oak Rd S SS7 ......**145** E2
Oak Rise IG9 ......**110** D7
Oak St RM7 ....**135** C6
Oak Tree Cl IG10 ....**89** C8
Oak Wlk Hockley SS5 ..**124** E7
South Benfleet SS7 ..**144** B8
Southend-on-S SS9 ..**146** D4
Oakbank CM13 ......**95** E4
Oakdale Ct E4 ......**109** C5
Oakdale Gdns E4 ....**109** C5
Oakdale Inf Sch E18 .**110** B1
Oakdale Jun Sch E18 **110** B1
Oakdale Rd E18 ....**110** B1
Oakdene RM3 ......**114** F1
Oakdene Rd SS13 ..**143** C8
Oakdown Ho IG7 ....**111** F5
Oaken Grange Dr SS2 **147** E5
Oakfield E4 ....**109** B5
Oakfield Cl SS7 ....**144** C3
Oakfield Ho 2 IG1 ..**133** B1
Oakfield Lodge 8 IG1 **133** B1
Oakfield Prim Sch SS12 **121** E5
Oakfield Rd Ilford IG1 **133** B1
Rochford SS4 ....**103** A1
South Benfleet SS7 ..**144** C3
Oakfields Chigwell IG7 **111** C5
Loughton IG10 ....**89** A4
Oakhall Ct E11 ......**132** B5
Oakham Cl SS16 ....**140** F5
Oakham Ct SS9 ....**146** E2
Oakhill Prim Sch E18 **109** E4
Oakhill Rd RM19 ....**171** E4
Oakhurst Cl
Redbridge IG6 ......**111** C2
Wickford SS11 ......**121** C5
Oakhurst Dr SS12 ..**121** C5

Oakhurst Gdns E4 ......**87** F1
Oakhurst Rd
Enfield EN3 ....**145** F8
Southend-on-S SS2 ..**148** A2
Oakland Farm Ind Est
CM4 ....**97** F6
Oakland Gdns CM13 ..**95** F8
Oakland Pl IG9 ....**110** A8
Oaklands Ave RM1 ..**135** F7
Oaklands Cres CM2 ..**54** B8
Oaklands Dr Harlow CM17 **24** C7
South Ockendon RM15 **172** C8
Oaklands Inf Sch CM2 **54** B8
Oaklands Mews SS4 **125** D4
Oaklands Park Ave IG1 **133** C2
Oaklands Sch IG10 ..**88** D4
Oaklands Way CM3 ..**34** C2
Oaklea Ave CM2 ......**32** E3
Oakleafe Gdns IG6 ..**133** B8
Oakleigh Ave
Hullbridge SS5 ......**101** E2
Southend-on-S SS1 ..**167** D8
Oakleigh Lodge SS4 ..**125** D4
Oakleigh Park Dr SS9 **146** E1
Oakleigh Rise CM16 ..**68** A7
Oakleighs SS7 ....**144** C4
Oakley Ave Barking IG11 **152** F5
Rayleigh SS6 ....**122** F3
Oakley Cl Chingford E4 **109** C8
Grays RM20 ....**177** C8
Oakley Ct IG10 ......**89** A7
Oakley Dr Billericay CM12 **96** F4
Romford RM3 ....**115** A5
Oakmoor Way IG7 ..**111** E5
Oaks Ave RM5 ......**113** C1
Oaks Gr E4 ....**109** E8
Oaks La IG2 ....**133** E7
Oaks Park High Sch
IG2 ....**133** E6
Oaks Ret Pk CM20 ....**10** F3
Oaks The Billericay CM11 **119** C6
Chingford E4 ....**109** E3
Dartford DA2 ....**176** B1
Oaktree Cl CM13 ....**116** F7
Oaktree Gr IG1 ......**152** D7
Oakway RM16 ......**173** C5
Oakwood EN9 ......**65** E5
Oakwood Ave
Brentwood CM13 ......**95** E3
Southend-on-S SS9 ..**146** E5
Oakwood Chase RM11 **136** F4
Oakwood Cl
South Benfleet SS7 ..**144** B5
Woodford IG8 ....**109** E6
Oakwood Ct Althorne CM3 **83** A3
Chingford E4 ....**87** E2
Romford RM2 ....**136** C8
Southend-on-S SS9 ..**146** E5
Oakwood Dr CM12 ..**97** C5
Oakwood Est CM20 ....**11** B4
Oakwood Gdns IG3 ..**133** F2
Oakwood Gr SS13 ..**143** B6
Oakwood Hill IG10 ..**89** B4
Oakwood Hill Ind Est
IG10 ....**89** B4
Oakwood Rd
Corringham SS17 ....**161** B4
Rayleigh SS6 ....**123** C4
Oakwood Villas SS9 ..**146** C7
Oasis Ct CM1 ....**32** F5
Oast Way SS4 ......**125** F2
Oates Rd RM5 ......**113** B5
Oban Cl SS11 ......**122** B5
Oban Ho IG11 ......**152** D3
Oban Rd SS2 ....**148** C1
Occasio Ho CM20 ....**23** C8
Ockendon Rd RM14 ..**157** C2
Ockendon Sch The
RM15 ....**172** A8
Ockendon Sta RM15 **157** B2
Octave Ho CM16 ....**67** E3
Odell Cl IG11 ......**152** F5
Odeon The IG11 ....**152** D5
Odessa Rd SS8 ....**164** D3
Odin Lodge CM9 ....**58** F8
Ogard Rd EN11 ......**21** C8
Ogilvie Ct SS12 ....**121** E5
Oglethorpe Rd RM10 **135** A1
Okehampton Rd RM3 **114** C4
Okehampton Sq RM3 **114** C4
Old Barn Cl CM3 ......**77** F2
Old Barns La CM3 ....**51** C3
Old Bell La SS4 ......**78** B1
Old Brickworks The
RM3 ....**115** A3
Old Church Hill SS16 **141** A1
Old Church La CM13 ..**96** B6
Old Church Rd
Basildon SS13 ......**143** F5
Chingford E4 ....**109** A7
East Hanningfield CM3 ..**78** B6
Old Coastguard Cotts
CM0 ....**41** E4
Old Court Rd CM2 ....**32** D3
Old Croft Cl CM1 ....**16** D5
Old Crown La CM14 ..**93** D7
Old Ct CM2 ....**32** D3
Old Farm Ct CM12 ..**97** A4
Old Forge Rd CM3 ..**33** E8
Old Forge The SS6 ..**123** C4
Old Hall Cl SS3 ....**150** A4
Old Hall Rise CM17 ..**24** D8
Old Heath Rd CM3,CM0 **84** A2
Old Highway EN11 ..**21** C8
Old Hill Ave SS16 ..**160** B8
Old House La
Lower Nazeing EN9 ....**43** F8

Old House La *continued*
Roydon CM19 ....**22** E6
Old Jenkins Cl SS17 ..**160** B1
Old Leigh Rd SS9 ..**147** A1
Old London Rd
Rawreth SS11 ......**122** D6
Woodham Walter CM9 ..**35** E1
Old Macdonald's
Educational Farm Pk**★**
CM14 ....**92** F1
Old Market Ret Pk 10
SS3 ....**143** B5
Old Mead SS2 ......**147** A7
Old Mill Ct E18 ....**132** C8
Old Mill La CM22 ......**2** B6
Old Mill Par 2 RM1 .**135** E5
Old Mill Pl RM7 ....**135** D5
Old Nazeing Rd EN10 **21** C1
Old Oaks EN9 ......**65** E7
Old Orch CM18 ......**23** D6
Old Rd Harlow CM17 ..**11** D5
Navestock Heath RM4 ..**92** D5
Old Rectory Ct SS2 **148** E1
Old Rectory Rd CM5 ..**70** B5
Old Rectory The CM3 ..**78** B7
Old School Field CM1 ..**32** E4
Old School Mdw SS3 **149** E4
Old Ship La SS4 ....**125** F2
Old Shire La EN9 ....**66** B3
Old Southend Rd
Southend-on-S SS1 ..**167** B7
West Hanningfield CM2 ..**77** D8
Old Station Rd IG10 ..**88** E4
Old Street Hill CM22 ..**3** D5
Old Vicarage Cl CM1 ..**6** C2
Old Wickford Rd CM3 **101** B8
Oldbury Ave CM2 ....**54** F8
Oldbury Cotts SS2 ..**149** D3
Oldchurch Gdns RM7 **135** D4
Oldchurch Hospl RM7 **135** D5
Oldchurch Rise RM7 **135** E4
Oldfields CM14 ....**116** C6
Oldhouse Croft CM20 **10** E2
Oldmead Ho 8 RM10 **154** B6
Oldwyk SS16 ......**142** E4
Olive Ave SS9 ......**146** A2
Olive St RM7 ......**135** D6
Oliver Cl RM20 ....**176** F7
Oliver Rd Brentwood CM15 95 A4
Grays RM20 ....**177** A7
Rainham RM13 ......**154** F4
Oliver Way CM1 ....**31** F7
Olivers Cres SS3 ..**150** B4
Olivia Dr SS9 ......**146** A2
Ollard's Gr IG10 ....**88** D5
Ollards Ct IG10 ....**88** D5
Olympic Bsns Ctr SS14 **120** F7
Omnibus Way E17 ..**109** A1
One Tree Hill SS16,SS17 **141** F1
Ongar Cl RM6 ......**134** C6
Ongar Ent Ctr CM5 ..**49** A5
Ongar Pl CM14 ....**116** D8
Ongar Rd Abridge RM4 ..**90** D7
Brentwood CM15 ......**94** B2
Fyfield CM5 ....**27** C2
Kelvedon Hatch CM15 ..**71** D4
Margaret Roding CM6 ..**15** D3
Pilgrims Hatch CM15 ..**94** A3
Stondon Massey CM15 ..**71** E8
Writtle CM1 ....**30** F1
Ongar War Meml Hospl
CM5 ....**49** A5
Ongar Way RM13 ..**154** E4
Onslow Cl E4 ......**109** D8
Onslow Gdns
Chipping Ongar CM5 ..**49** A4
Wanstead E18 ......**132** C8
Opal Mews 2 IG1 ..**133** B2
Optima Bsns Pk EN11 **21** C7
Orange Gr IG7 ......**111** C4
Orange Rd SS8 ....**164** D4
Orange Tree Cl CM2 ..**54** C6
Orange Tree Hill RM4 **113** E6
Orchard Ave
Billericay CM12 ......**97** C5
Brentwood CM13 ....**116** F7
Downham CM11 ......**98** E2
Hockley SS5 ....**124** E7
Rainham RM13 ......**155** C1
Rayleigh SS6 ....**145** C8
Orchard Bglws SS4 ..**104** F1
Orchard Cl Billericay CM12 96 F4
Chelmsford CM2 ......**54** C6
Chingford E4 ....**109** A6
Great Wakering SS3 ..**150** B4
Hockley SS5 ....**124** F7
Maldon CM9 ....**36** F2
Sheering CM22 ......**12** C8
South Ockendon RM15 **157** C1
Southminster CM0 ....**84** D4
Stanstead Abbotts SG12 ..**8** C4
Wanstead E11 ......**132** B7
Writtle CM1 ....**31** B1
Orchard Croft CM20 ..**11** A2
Orchard Dr Grays RM17 **173** A4
Theydon Bois CM16 ..**67** E3
Orchard Gdns EN9 ..**65** C5
Orchard Gr SS9 ....**146** F6
Orchard La
Pilgrims Hatch CM15 ..**93** F4
Woodford IG8 ......**110** C6
Orchard Lea CM21 ....**1** C1
Orchard Mead SS9 ..**146** E5
Orchard Piece CM2 ..**72** F8
Orchard Rd
Belvedere DA17 ......**169** A2
Burnham-on-C CM0 ..**106** C4

Orchard Rd *continued*
Dagenham RM10 ....**154** A6
Maldon CM9 ....**36** F2
Mayland CM3 ....**61** A1
Romford RM7 ......**113** B6
South Benfleet SS7 ..**144** B7
South Ockendon RM15 **172** C8
Southminster CM0 ....**84** E4
Swanscombe DA10 ..**177** E2
Orchard Side SS12 ..**146** F6
Orchard St CM2 ......**32** B1
Orchard Terr DA9 ..**176** E1
Orchard The SS12 ..**121** B7
Orchard Way IG7 ..**112** A7
Orchards The
Epping CM16 ....**68** A7
Sawbridgeworth CM21 ..**1** E3
Orchid Cl RM4 ......**90** B6
Orchid Pl CM3 ......**101** D8
Orchill Dr CM3 ....**145** E4
Orchis Gr RM17 ....**172** F1
Orchis Way RM3 ....**114** F4
Ordnance Rd DA12 ..**179** C1
Orestes Ct 8 E18 ..**132** A8
Oreston Rd RM13 ..**155** D2
Orford Cres CM1 ....**32** C5
Orford Ct 5 DA2 ..**176** B1
Orford Rd E18 ......**132** B8
Oriel Gdns IG5 ......**132** F8
Orion Ct SS14 ......**121** A1
Orkney Gdns SS12 ..**121** F5
Orlando Dr SS13 ..**121** C1
Ormesby Chine CM3 **101** C5
Ormond Cl RM3 ....**114** D1
Ormonde Ave
Rochford SS4 ....**125** C3
South Benfleet SS7 ..**146** A2
Ormonde Cl RM1 ..**135** F4
Ormonde Gdns SS9 **146** A2
Ormonde Rise IG9 ..**88** C1
Ormonds Cres CM3 ..**79** B4
Ormsby Rd SS8 ....**163** D3
Orplands Cotts CM0 ..**41** F1
Orsett Ave SS9 ....**146** C5
Orsett CE Prim Sch
RM16 ....**174** A4
Orsett End SS14 ..**142** D7
Orsett Heath Cres
RM16 ....**174** A8
Orsett Hospl RM16 **174** A8
Orsett Ind Pk RM16 **174** F8
Orsett Rd Grays RM17 **173** B1
Horndon-on-t-H SS17 ..**159** D2
Orsett Terr IG8 ....**110** C3
Orton Cl CM4 ....**75** A8
Orton Gr RM7 ......**135** D6
Orton Ho 2 RM3 ..**114** E3
Orwell RM18 ......**175** C2
Orwell Cl SS11 ....**122** B5
Orwell Ct SS11 ....**122** B5
Orwell Lodge 2 E18 **132** A7
Orwell Way CM0 ..**106** A6
Osborne Cl RM11 ..**136** B5
Osborne Ho 10 IG8 **111** A3
Osborne Hts CM14 ..**116** B6
Osborne Rd
Basildon,Barstable SS16 **142** C5
Basildon,North Benfleet
SS13 ....**143** E8
Buckhurst Hill IG9 ..**88** B2
Dagenham RM9 ......**153** F7
Hoddesdon EN10 ......**21** A4
Hornchurch RM11 ....**136** C5
Pilgrims Hatch CM15 ..**94** B3
Southend-on-S SS0 ..**147** E1
Osborne Sq RM9 ..**153** F8
Osbourne Ave SS5 ..**124** C6
Osbourne Ho SS0 ..**147** C1
Osbourne Rd DA2 ..**176** B1
Osea Rd CM9 ....**38** B3
Osea Way CM1 ......**32** F5
Osprey Cl
Southend-on-S SS3 ..**149** E5
Wanstead E11 ......**132** A7
Osprey Ct
Brentwood CM14 ....**116** B7
Waltham Abbey EN9 ..**66** A5
Osprey Rd EN9 ......**66** A5
Osprey Way CM2 ....**54** A5
Ospreys The SS9 ..**146** F1
Ostell Cres EN3 ......**65** A1
Osterley Dr SS16 ..**140** F5
Osterley Pl CM3 ....**101** D5
Otley App IG2 ......**133** B3
Otley Dr IG2 ....**133** B5
Ottawa Gdns RM10 ..**154** D5
Ottawa Rd RM18 ..**179** A5
Otterbourne Rd E4 ..**109** D7
Ouida Rd SS8 ......**164** D3
Oulton Ave SS8 ....**163** F5
Oulton Cres IG11 ..**152** F7
Oundle Ho 8 RM3 ..**114** D6
Our Lady Immaculate RC
Prim Sch CM4 ......**32** A1
Our Lady of Lourdes Prim
Sch SS9 ....**147** A2
Our Lady of Lourdes RC Prim
Sch E11 ....**132** A4
Our Lady of Ransom RC Prim
Sch SS6 ....**123** A4
Outing Cl SS1 ......**167** C2
Outing's La CM15 ....**72** B3
Outwood Common Rd
CM11 ....**97** C3
Outwood Farm Cl CM11 **97** C2
Outwood Farm Rd CM11 **97** C3
Oval Gdns RM17 ..**173** C3

Oval Rd N RM10 ......154 B4
Oval Rd S RM10 ......154 B3
Overcliff Flats SS0 ...166 D7
Overcliff Rd RM17 ....173 D1
Overcliffe DA11 ......179 A1
Overmead Dr CM3 .....101 E8
Overstrand Ho RM12 ..136 B2
Overton Cl SS7 ....144 C6
Overton Ct E11 ....132 A4
Overton Dr
  Dagenham RM6 ......134 C4
  South Benfleet SS7 ..144 C6
  Wanstead E11 ....132 B4
Overton Rd SS7 ....144 C6
Overton Way SS7 ......144 B6
Ovingdean Gdns CM12 ..97 A5
Owen Cl RM5 ....113 B4
Owen Gdns IG8 ....110 E4
Owen Waters Ho IG5 ..111 A2
Owlets Hall Cl RM3 ...136 F8
Oxcroft Ct SS15 ......141 B6
Oxendon Dr EN11 ......21 A5
Oxford Ave Grays RM16 174 A2
  Hornchurch RM11 ....137 A4
Oxford Cl SS16 ....140 F5
Oxford Ct
  Brentwood CM14 ....116 D6
  Chelmsford CM2 .....32 E4
Oxford Rd
  Canvey Island SS8 ...164 D3
  Horndon-on-t-H SS17 .159 E4
  Ilford IG1 ....152 C7
  Rochford SS4 ....125 E4
  Romford RM3 ....114 F4
  Stanford-le-H SS17 ..160 B1
  Woodford IG8 ....110 D5
Oxley Cl RM2 ....114 C1
Oxley Gdns SS17 ......160 E5
Oxleys Rd EN9 ....66 A7
Oxleys The CM17 ......11 E4
Oxlow La RM10 ....154 A8
Oxney Mead CM1 ......52 F8
Oxted Ho RM3 ....114 F1
Oxwich Cl SS17 ......161 A4
Oyster Catcher Terr
  IG5 ....133 A8
Oyster Cotts CM0 .....40 C1
Oyster Pl CM2 ....32 F4
Ozonia Ave SS12 ......121 C5
Ozonia Cl SS12 ....121 B5
Ozonia Way SS12 .....121 C5
Ozonia Wlk 3 SS12 ...121 C5

P

Paarl Rd SS8 ....164 B4
Paceheath Cl RM5 ....113 D4
Pacific Cl DA10 ......177 E2
Paddock Cl
  Billericay CM11 .....119 C7
  Orsett RM16 ....174 B8
  Southend-on-S SS9 ..146 E7
Paddock Ct CM1 ......32 E8
Paddock Mead CM18 ..23 C3
Paddock The
  Hoddesdon EN10 ....21 A3
  Stock CM4 ....75 E3
Paddocks The
  High Roding CM6 ....5 E7
  Ingatestone CM4 ....74 B3
  Orsett RM16 ....174 B8
  Rayleigh SS6 ....123 F2
  Stapleford Abbotts RM4 .91 F3
Padfield Ct 2 RM1 ...135 F5
Padgets The EN9 .....65 E5
Padgetts Way SS5 ....101 D3
Padham's Green Rd CM4 96 D8
Padnall Ct RM6 ......134 D7
Padnall Rd RM6 ......134 D7
Page Cl RM9 ....153 E7
Page Rd SS13 ....143 F7
Pageant Cl RM18 .....179 C6
Pages La Romford RM3 .115 B1
  Tollesbury CM9 .....39 F8
Paget Dr CM12 ....97 A5
Paget Rd IG1 ....152 B8
Pagette Way RM17 ....173 A2
Paglesfield 4 CM13 ..95 D4
Paglesham Rd
  Paglesham Eastend SS4 128 A5
  Rochford SS4 ....127 C6
Paignton Ave CM1 ....32 D5
Paignton Cl SS6 .....123 D5
Paines Brook Rd RM3 .114 F4
Paines Brook Way RM3 114 F4
Painswick Ave SS17 ...160 F5
Painters Rd IG2,RM6 ..134 A8
Pakes Way CM16 .....67 E2
Palace Gdns IG9 .....88 D1
Palace Gr SS15 ......141 E8
Palace View Rd E4 ...109 B5
Palatine Pk SS15 .....140 F6
Palepit CM3 ....81 C5
Paley Gdns IG10 .....89 B6
Palin Ho RM16 ....173 A5
Palins Way RM16 .....173 A5
Pall Mall SS9 ....146 E1
Palliser Dr RM13 .....170 A8
Palm Cl CM2 ....54 C6
Palm Mews SS15 .....119 D1
Palm Rd RM7 ....135 C6
Palmeira Ave SS0 ....166 D7
Palmeira Mans SS0 ...166 D7
Palmer Cl SS15 ......141 D6
Palmer Ct RM1 ....136 A6
Palmer Rd RM8 ......134 D3
Palmer's Ave RM17 ...173 C1

Palmers 3 SS17 ......160 F3
Palmers Coll RM17 ....173 E2
Palmers Croft CM2 ....33 A2
Palmers Dr RM17 .....173 C2
Palmers Gr EN9 ......21 F1
Palmers Hill CM16 ....46 A2
Palmerston Ct 2 IG9 ..110 C8
Palmerston Gdns RM20 172 D1
Palmerston Lodge CM2 .54 F7
Palmerston Rd
  Buckhurst Hill IG9 ...88 C1
  Grays RM20 ....172 D1
  Southend-on-S SS0 ..166 D7
Palmerstone Rd
  Canvey Island SS8 ...163 D3
  Rainham RM13 ......155 C3
Pamela Ct 5 RM1 ....135 F6
Pamplins SS15 ....141 F6
Pan La CM3 ....77 F5
Pan Wlk CM1 ....31 D5
Panadown SS15 ......141 F6
Pancroft RM4 ....90 B6
Panfield Mews IG2 ...133 A5
Panfields SS15 ......141 A6
Pantile Ave SS2 .....148 C3
Pantile Cotts RM14 ...137 D6
Pantile Ct CM0 ......84 C4
Pantile Hill CM0 .....84 C4
Pantiles The CM12 ....97 A4
Panventon Ct RM18 ...179 A5
Papenburg Rd SS8 ....164 A6
Paprills SS16 ....141 E5
Parade The
  8 Basildon SS13 ....143 B5
  Brentwood CM14 ....116 C7
  Romford RM4 ....113 E7
  Swanscombe DA10 ...177 F2
  Aveley RM15 ....171 C4
  Romford RM3 ....115 B4
Paradise Dr
  Waltham Abbey EN9 ..65 C5
  Writtle CM1 ....53 B8
Pargat Dr SS9 ....146 C7
Pargetters Hyam SS5 .124 F6
Parham Dr IG2 ....133 B6
Paringdon Jun Sch
  CM18 ....23 D4
Paringdon Rd CM18,CM19 23 C3
Parish Cl RM11 ......136 B2
Parish Way SS15 .....141 C7
Park Ave Barking IG11 .152 C6
  Brentwood CM13 ....95 D1
  Canvey Island SS8 ...164 F2
  Chelmsford CM1 .....31 F4
  Grays RM20 ....177 B8
  Harlow CM17 ......24 C5
  Ilford IG1 ....133 A3
  Southend-on-S SS9 ..146 E6
  Upminster RM14 ....137 E4
  Wallend E6 ....152 A3
  Woodford IG8 ....110 B5
Park Bvd RM2 ....113 F2
Park Chase SS7 ......145 E2
Park Cl
  North Weald Bassett CM16 .47 A4
  Wickford SS12 ......121 C6
Park Cres
  Hornchurch RM11 ....136 A4
  Southend-on-S SS0 ..166 F8
Park Ct 2 Chingford E4 109 C8
  Harlow CM20 ......10 D2
Park Dr Dagenham RM10 135 C1
  Hatfield Heath CM22 ..3 B2
  Ingatestone CM4 ....74 C4
  Maldon CM9 ....37 B1
  Romford RM1 ....135 D7
  Upminster RM14 ....156 C8
  Wickford SS12 ......121 D6
Park End Rd RM1 .....135 E7
Park Farm Rd
  Hornchurch RM14 ....155 F7
  Upminster RM14 ....156 A6
Park Fields CM19 .....22 B7
Park Gate Rd SS17 ...161 A8
Park Gdns Erith DA8 ..169 D2
  Hockley SS5 ....124 F3
Park Grange IG7 .....111 D5
Park Hill Harlow CM17 .11 B4
  Loughton IG10 ......88 D4
Park Ho SS17 ....160 F3
Park La Aveley RM15 ..171 D5
  Canvey Island SS8 ...164 F3
  Harlow CM20 ......10 D2
  Hornchurch RM11 ....136 A4
  Hornchurch, Elm Park
  RM12 ....155 B6
  Ilford RM6 ....134 D5
  Ingrave CM13 ......117 D3
  Pleshey CM3 ....7 F4
  Ramsden Heath CM11 .98 C3
  Southend-on-S SS1 ..167 C8
  Southend-on-S,Clifftown
  SS0 ....166 F8
Park Mdw CM15 ......72 D1
Park Mead CM20 ......10 B1
Park Mews 6 RM13 ...155 A6
Park Rd Brentwood CM14 116 B8
  Burnham-on-C CM0 ..106 B5
  Canvey Island SS8 ...164 D3
  Chelmsford CM1 .....32 B2
  Corringham SS17 ....161 A3
  Grays RM17 ....173 B1
  Hoddesdon EN11 ....21 A6
  Ilford IG1 ....133 D1
  Maldon CM9 ....36 F2
  Pleshey CM3 ....7 E4
  Southend-on-S SS9 ..146 B1

Park Rd continued
  Southend-on-S,Clifftown
  SS0 ....166 F8
  Stanford-le-H SS17 ..160 B1
  Swanscombe DA10 ...177 E1
  Thundersley SS7 ....144 F6
  Wanstead E12 ......132 B2
Park Sch for Girls IG1 133 B3
Park Sch The SS6 ....123 B6
Park Side Basildon SS13 143 A7
  Billericay CM11 .....97 C2
  Buckhurst Hill IG9 ...110 B8
  Southend-on-S SS0 ..147 A1
Park Sq RM4 ....90 E3
Park St SS0 ....166 F8
Park Terr Greenhithe DA9 177 B2
  Southend-on-S SS0 ..166 F8
Park Vale Ct CM1 ....94 C1
Park View Aveley RM15 171 D5
  Canvey Island SS8 ...164 E2
  Hoddesdon EN11 ....21 A5
Park View Cres CM2 ..54 F5
Park View Ct
  Southend-on-S SS9 ..146 E6
  Wickford SS11 ......99 C1
Park View Dr SS9 ....146 B5
Park View Gdns
  Grays RM17 ....173 B1
  Redbridge IG5 ......132 F7
Park Villas RM6 .....134 D5
Park Way RM15 ......94 F1
Parkanaur Ave SS1 ...168 B7
Parkdale CM3 ....56 C7
Parker Ave RM18 .....179 C6
Parker Ct CM0 ......41 F4
Parker Rd Chelmsford CM2 32 C1
  Grays RM17 ....177 F8
Parker's Farm Rd RM16 158 F5
Parkes Rd IG7 ....111 E5
Parkfields SS7 ......145 C4
Parkgate SS0 ....166 F8
Parkhill Cl RM12 .....136 C2
Parkhill Jun Sch
  Ilford IG5 ....133 A8
  Redbridge IG5 ......132 F8
Parkhill Rd E4 ......87 C2
Parkhurst Dr SS6 ....123 C7
Parkhurst Rd
  Basildon SS13 ......143 B5
  Little Ilford E12 ....152 A8
Parkinson Dr CM1 ....31 F1
Parkland Ave
  Romford RM1 ....113 F1
  Upminster RM14 ....156 B7
Parkland Cl Chigwell IG7 111 C7
  3 Hoddesdon EN11 ..8 B1
Parkland Rd IG8 .....110 B3
Parkland Way CM2 ...54 C2
Parklands Billericay CM11 97 B3
  Canvey Island SS8 ...164 A5
  Chigwell IG7 ....111 C7
  Coopersale CM16 ....46 D2
  Rochford SS4 ....125 D3
  Waltham Abbey EN9 ..65 D7
Parklands Ave SS6 ...123 E2
Parklands Cl IG2 .....133 C4
Parklands Dr CM1 ....32 D3
Parklands Jun & Inf Sch
  RM1 ....113 D1
Parklands Jun Sch RM1 135 D8
Parkmead IG10 ......89 A4
Parkmill Cl SS17 .....161 A4
Parkmore Cl RM8 ....110 A6
Parkside Grays RM16 ..173 E3
  Sheering CM17 .....12 E3
Parkside Ave
  Romford RM1 ....135 D8
  Tilbury RM18 ....179 B5
Parkside Ct 2 E11 ...132 A5
Parkside Ctr SS2 ....147 F5
Parkside Ho RM10 ...135 C1
Parkside Lodge DA8 ..169 C1
Parkside Rd DA17 ...169 C2
Parkside Terr IG1 ....152 C7
Parkstone Ave
  Hadleigh SS7 ......145 A4
  Hornchurch RM11 ....136 E5
  Wickford SS12 ......120 F8
Parkstone Dr SS2 ....147 E4
Parkview Ho RM12 ...136 B2
Parkway
  Chelmsford CM1 CM2 .32 B2
  Corringham SS17 ....161 C5
  Harlow CM19 ......22 E8
  Ilford IG3 ....133 F1
  Orsett RM16 ....174 A8
  Rainham RM13 ......155 A1
  Rayleigh SS6 ....145 F8
  Romford RM2 ....113 F1
  Sawbridgeworth CM21 .1 F1
  Woodford IG8 ....110 C5
Parkway Cl SS9 ......146 F7
Parkway The SS6 ....164 B2
Parnall Rd CM18 .....23 D4
Parndon Ho IG10 ....88 D2
Parndon Mill La CM20 .10 B3
Parndon Wood Nature
  Reserve* CM19 .....23 D2
Parndon Wood Rd CM18,
  CM19 ....23 C3
Parnell Cl RM16 .....172 C1
Paroma Rd DA17 .....169 A3
Parr Cl RM16 ....172 C2
Parrock St 18 DA12 ...179 B1
Parrotts Field EN11 ...21 B7
Parry Cl SS17 ....160 D3
Parsloe Rd CM19 ....23 B3

Parsloes Ave RM9 ....153 E7
Parsloes Prim Sch RM9 153 F6
Parsonage Chase CM9 .81 D8
Parsonage Cl CM1 ...19 A1
Parsonage Farm Prim Sch
  RM13 ....155 C2
Parsonage Field CM15 .72 D2
Parsonage La
  Basildon SS15 ......141 C6
  Little Baddow CM3 ..34 C3
  Margaretting CM4 ...75 A7
Parsonage Leys CM20 .23 A8
Parsonage Rd
  Grays RM20 ....177 C2
  Rainham RM13 ......155 C2
Parsons Cnr SS3 ....149 D2
Parsons Lawn SS3 ...149 D1
Parsons Rd SS7 .....144 D7
Partridge Ave CM1 ...31 F6
Partridge Ct CM18 ...23 E6
Partridge Gn SS13 ...143 A5
Partridge Rd CM18 ...23 D5
Parvills EN9 ....65 D7
Paschal Way CM2 ....54 F8
Pasfield EN9 ....65 D6
Paslow Hall Cotts CM5 .49 F4
Pasloes SS15 ....142 F4
Passingham Ave CM11 .119 C6
Passingham Ct CM11 ..119 C7
Passmores Comp Sch
  CM18 ....23 D6
Pasteur Dr RM3 .....114 D1
Pastoral Way CM14 ..116 B5
Pasture Rd RM9 .....153 F7
Patching Hall La CM1 .32 A6
Paternoster Cl EN9 ..65 F7
Paternoster Hill EN9 ..65 F7
Paternoster Row RM4 ..92 C1
Pathways SS14 .....142 E5
Patmore Rd EN9 .....65 C5
Patmore Way RM5 ...113 B5
Patricia Dr
  Corringham SS17 ....161 C6
  Hornchurch RM11 ....136 E3
Patricia Gdns CM11 ..119 D7
Patrick Gr EN9 ......65 B6
Patterdale SS7 .....144 B7
Patterson Ct DA1 ....176 A2
Pattiswick Cnr SS14 ..142 E7
Pattiswick Sq SS14 ..142 E7
Pattocks SS14 ......142 E6
Paul Ct RM7 ....135 C5
Paul Robeson Ct E6 ..152 A2
Paul's Rd SS15 .....141 C8
Pauline Gdns CM12 ..96 F4
Pauls Cl SS8 ....164 A6
Pauls La EN11 ......21 A6
Paulson Ho 7 IG11 ..152 B5
Pavement Mews 1
  RM6 ....134 D4
Pavet Cl RM10 ......154 B6
Pavilion Cl SS14 .....148 E1
Pavilion Dr SS9 .....146 F2
Pavilion Rd IG1 .....132 F4
Pavilion Terr IG2 ....133 D6
Pavilions The
  North Weald Bassett CM16 .47 C6
  Southend-on-S SS1 ..166 F2
Pavillion Pl CM12 ....96 F4
Pavitt Mdw CM2 ....54 C2
Pawle Cl CM2 ....55 A7
Paxfords SS15 ......140 F6
Paycock Rd CM19 ...23 A6
Paycocke Cl SS14 ...120 E2
Paycocke Mews SS14 .120 E2
Paycocke Rd SS14 ...120 D2
Payne Cl IG11 ....152 F5
Payne Pl CM3 ....78 B6
Paynes La EN9 ......43 C7
Paynters Mead SS16 .142 E3
Payzes Gdns IG8 ....109 F5
Pea La RM14 ....157 A6
Peabody Ct EN3 ....65 A2
Peach Ave SS5 .....124 E8
Peacock Cl
  Dagenham RM8 .....134 C2
  Hornchurch RM11 ....136 E7
Peacock St 7 DA12 ..179 C1
Peacocks CM19 .....22 F6
Peaketon Ave IG4 ...132 D6
Pear Tree Cl SS15 ...119 C1
Pear Tree Ct E18 ....110 B2
Pear Tree Mead CM18 ..24 A5
Pear Tree Mead Prim Sch
  CM18 ....24 A5
Pear Trees SS7 .....144 F4
Pearce Manor CM2 ...53 F8
Pearcy Cl RM3 ......114 E3
Pearl Ct EN11 ......21 A6
Pearlstones Ct RM10 .154 A4
Pearmain Cl SS11 ...99 D1
Pearsons 2 SS17 ...160 F3
Pearsons Ave SS6 ...123 B4
Peartree Cl
  Doddinghurst CM15 ..72 D1
  Goldhanger CM9 ....38 E6
  South Ockendon RM15 157 C3
  Southend-on-S SS2 ..148 C3
Peartree Gdns
  Dagenham RM8 .....153 B8
  Romford RM7 ....113 B1
Peartree La Bicknacre CM3 56 F3
  Bulphan CM14 ......139 F1
  Doddinghurst CM15 ..72 D2
Peartree Wlk CM12 ..97 A4
Peartrees CM13 .....117 C4
Peas Mead Terr E4 ...109 C6

Ova – Per **213**

Pease Cl RM12 ......155 B5
Pease Pl CM5 ....78 B6
Pebmarsh Dr SS12 ...121 E6
Peck's Hill EN9 .....21 E2
Pedlars Cl CM3 .....57 A6
Pedlars End CM5 ....26 C2
Pedlars Path CM3 ...57 A6
Pedley Rd RM8 .....134 C3
Peel Ave SS3 ....168 G8
Peel Cl E4 ....109 B8
Peel Dr IG5 ....110 E1
Peel Pl IG5 ....110 E1
Peel Rd Chelmsford CM2 .32 F4
  Woodford E18 ......109 F2
Peel Way RM3 ......114 F1
Peerage Way RM11 ..136 F5
Peers Sq CM2 ......33 A4
Pegelm Gdns RM11 ..136 F4
Peggotty Cl CM1 ....31 F6
Pegrams Ct CM18 ...23 C5
Pegrams Rd CM18 ...23 C5
Peldon Pavement SS14 142 D8
Peldon Rd CM19 ....23 A6
Pelham Ave IG11 ...152 F4
Pelham Pl SS17 .....160 E4
Pelham Rd Ilford IG1 .133 D2
  Southend-on-S SS2 ..148 E1
  Wanstead E18 ......132 B8
Pelly Ct CM16 ......67 F8
Pemberton Ave
  Ingatestone CM4 ....74 B4
  Romford RM2 ....136 B8
Pemberton Ct CM4 ..74 B4
Pemberton Field SS4 .103 B4
Pemberton Gdns RM6 .134 E6
Pembrey Way RM12 ..155 C6
Pembridge Ct 5 SS1 .167 C8
Pembroke Ave
  Corringham SS17 ....161 A4
  Maldon CM9 ....36 F1
Pembroke Bsns Ctr
  SS14 ....120 E2
Pembroke Cl
  Billericay CM12 .....97 B5
  Erith DA8 ....169 D1
  Hornchurch RM11 ....137 A4
Pembroke Gdns RM10 135 B5
Pembroke Ho SS4 ...147 F7
Pembroke Mews SS13 143 C8
Pembroke Par DA8 ..169 C1
Pembroke Pl CM1 ...32 B7
Pembroke Rd Erith DA8 169 D2
  Ilford IG3 ....133 F4
Pembury Rd SS0 ....166 C7
Pendine Cl SS17 ....161 A4
Pendle Cl SS14 .....121 A1
Pendle Dr SS14 .....120 F1
Pendlestone SS7 ....145 C4
Pendower SS6 ......123 B1
Penerley Rd RM13 ...170 B8
Penhurst Ave SS2 ...147 F2
Penhurst Rd IG6 ....111 B3
Peniel Acad CM15 ...71 E1
Penistone Wlk RM3 ..114 C4
Penlow Rd CM18 ....23 D5
Penn Cl RM16 ......159 B1
Penn Gdns RM5 ....113 B4
Pennial Rd SS8 .....164 A4
Pennine Rd CM1 ....31 D5
Pennington Cl RM5 ..113 A4
Penny Cl RM13 .....155 B2
Penny Ct RM13 .....155 B2
Penny Fields CM14 ..116 C6
Penny La SS17 .....160 E4
Penny Royal Rd RM3 .56 D6
Penny Stps 14 SS1 ..167 C7
Penny's La CM4 .....74 F8
Pennymead CM20 ...11 A1
Penrhyn Ave E17 ....109 A2
Penrhyn Cres E17 ...109 A2
Penrhyn Gr E17 .....109 A2
Penrith Cres RM13 ..155 A2
Penrith Rd Redbridge IG6 111 F4
  Romford RM3 ....115 A4
Penrose Mead CM1 ..53 B8
Penshurst CM17 ....11 C3
Penshurst Dr CM3 ..101 D5
Penson's La
  Chipping Ongar CM5 ..48 D4
  Toot Hill CM5 ......48 E5
Penstemon Dr DA10 ..177 E2
Pentire Cl RM14 ....137 E5
Pentire Rd E17 .....109 D2
Pentland Ave
  Chelmsford CM1 .....32 A6
  Southend-on-S SS3 ..168 A6
Pentlow Way IG9 ...88 E2
Pentney Rd 5 E4 ...87 D1
Penwood Cl CM11 ..97 D6
Penzance Cl CM1 ...32 E5
Penzance Gdns RM3 .115 A4
Penzance Rd RM3 ..115 A4
Peony Cl CM15 ......94 B3
Peony Ct IG8 ....109 E3
Pepper Alley IG10 ...88 A8
Pepper Hill SG12 ....8 A4
Pepys Cl Dartford DA1 176 A3
  Tilbury RM18 ....179 C6
Pepys Ct 4 EN11 ....21 D8
Percival Gdns RM6 ..134 D5
Percival Rd RM11 ...136 C5
Percy Cottis Rd SS4 ..125 E4
Percy Rd Ilford IG3 ..134 A4
  Romford RM7 ....135 C8
  Southend-on-S SS9 ..146 D1

Percy St RM17 ....178 C8
Peregrin Rd EN9 ....66 A5
Peregrine Cl
 Basildon SS16 ....142 B4
 Southend-on-S SS3 ...149 E1
Peregrine Dr
 Chelmsford CM2 ....54 A4
 South Benfleet SS7 ...144 C2
Peregrine Gdns SS6 ...123 B3
Peregrine Rd IG6 ......112 C5
Peregrine Wlk 6 RM12 .155 B6
Perkins Cl DA9 ....176 F2
Perkins Rd IG2 ....133 D6
Perriclose CM1 ....32 D7
Perrin Pl CM2 ....32 A1
Perry Cl RM13 ....154 C3
Perry Gn SS14 ....142 B8
Perry Hill Chelmsford CM1 32 D3
 Lower Nazeing EN9 .....43 F8
Perry Ho RM13 ....154 C3
Perry Rd Harlow CM18 ...23 C4
 South Benfleet SS7 ...144 B3
Perry Spring
 Basildon SS16 ....142 D5
 Harlow CM17 ....24 D6
Perry St CM12 ....97 B5
Perry Way RM15 ....171 C6
Perryfield CM17 ....13 C2
Perryfield La CM5 ......27 E5
Perryfields Jun & Inf Sch
 CM1 ....32 D6
Perryman Ho IG11 ......152 C4
Perrymans Farm Rd
 IG2 ....133 D6
Pershore Cl IG2 ....133 B6
Perth Ho RM18 ....179 A5
Perth Rd Barking IG11 ..152 C4
 Ilford IG1,IG2 ....133 B4
Perth Terr IG2 ....133 C4
Pertwee Dr
 Great Baddow CM2 .....54 F6
 South Woodham Ferrers
 CM3 ....101 D7
Petands Ct RM12 ......136 D1
Peter Bradley Ct RM9 .153 F5
Peter St CM4 ....97 F8
Peterborough Ave
 RM14 ....137 F3
Peterborough Gdns IG1 132 E4
Peterborough Way 5
 SS14 ....142 F8
Peters Cl RM18 ....134 D3
Peters Ct SS15 ....141 B6
Petersfield CM1 ....32 B7
Petersfield Ave RM3 ...114 C4
Petersfield Cl RM3 ....115 A4
Peterswood CM18 ......23 D4
Peterswood Inf Sch
 CM18 ....23 D4
Petre Cl Ingatestone CM4 .74 A2
 West Horndon RM13 ...139 C5
Petrebrook CM2 ....33 A3
Petrel Way CM2 ....33 A3
Petresfield Way CM13 .139 C5
Pett Cl RM11 ....136 B2
Petticrow Quays CM0 ..106 C3
Pettit's Pl RM10 ......154 A7
Pettit's Rd RM10 .....154 A7
Pettits Bvd RM1 ......113 E2
Pettits Cl RM1 ....113 E1
Pettits La
 Doddinghurst CM15 ....72 E2
 Romford RM1 ....135 F8
Pettits La N RM1 .....113 E2
Pettley Gdns RM7 .....135 D6
Petunia Cres CM1 ......32 F6
Petworth Gdns SS2 ...148 F2
Petworth Way RM12 ...154 F8
Pevensey Ct 10 E18 ...110 A2
Pevensey Gdns SS5 ...101 F1
Pevensey Way SS3 ....143 B6
Peverel Ho 4 RM10 ...135 A2
Peveril 26 DA2 ....176 B1
Pewsey Cl E4 ....109 A5
Phelips Rd CM19 ....23 B3
Philan Way RM5 ....113 D4
Philbrick Cres E SS6 ..123 C3
Philbrick Cres W SS6 .123 C3
Philip Ave RM7 ....135 D3
Philip Cl
 Pilgrims Hatch CM15 ...94 C3
 Romford RM7 ....135 D3
Philip Rd RM13 ....154 E2
Philip Sydney Rd RM20 .172 D1
Philippa Way RM16 ...174 B2
Phillida Rd RM3 ......115 A1
Phillips Ho RM16 .....174 A8
Philmead Rd SS7 .....144 B2
Philpott Ave SS2 .....148 E2
Phoenix Bldgs 1 RM13 .155 B1
Phoenix Ct E4 ....109 B7
Phoenix Gr CM2 ....54 A8
Phoenix Prim Sch SS15 141 C6
Phoenix Way SS7 .....145 C7
Picador Ho 1 RM10 ...154 B6
Picardy Manorway
 DA17 ....169 B4
Picardy Rd DA17 .....169 A2
Picardy St DA17 .....169 A3
Picasso Way SS3 .....150 A1
Pick Hill EN9 ....66 A7
Pickering Ave E6 .....152 A2
Pickering Ct 13 DA2 ..176 B1
Picketts SS8 ....163 D4

Picketts Ave SS9 .....146 E4
Picketts Cl SS9 ......146 E4
Pickwick Ave CM1 ......31 D6
Pickwick Cl SS15 ....141 D7
Picton Cl SS6 ....123 E1
Picton Gdns SS6 .....123 E1
Pier Hill SS1 ....167 A7
Pier Rd Gravesend DA11 .178 F1
 Greenhithe DA9 ......177 B3
Piercing Hill CM16 .....67 D4
Piercys SS13 ....143 B5
Pierrot Stps 5 SS1 ..167 C7
Pigeon Ct E4 ....109 C4
Piggs Corner Complex
 RM17 ....173 C3
Pigstye Green Rd CM5 ..51 A8
Pike Way CM16 ....47 A4
Pilgrim Way SS15 ....141 C6
Pilgrims La
 Pilgrims Hatch CM14 ...93 E4
 Pilgrims Hatch, Bentley
 CM14 ....93 D5
Pilgrims Cl Billericay CM11 97 B2
 Pilgrims Hatch CM15 ...93 F4
 Southend-on-S SS2 ...148 E1
Pilgrims Ct DA1 ......176 A2
Pilgrims Hatch Prim Sch
 CM15 ....94 A3
Pilgrims La RM16 ....172 C5
Pilgrims View DA9 ...177 C1
Pilgrims Way SS7 ....145 F3
Pilgrims Wlk 4 CM11 ..97 B2
Pilgrims' Rd DA10 ...177 E3
Pilkingtons CM17 ......24 D8
Pilot Cl SS11 ....122 A5
Pilots Pl 6 DA12 ....179 C1
Pimpernel Way RM3 ..114 D4
Pincey Mead SS13 ....143 A5
Pinceybrook Rd CM18 ..23 C4
Pindar Rd EN11 ....21 C7
Pine Cl Canvey Island SS8 163 E4
 Ingatestone CM4 ......74 C4
 Southend-on-S SS2 ...146 B5
 7 Wickford SS12 ....121 C5
Pine Cres CM13 ....95 D5
Pine Ct RM14 ....156 B8
Pine Dr CM4 ....74 C4
Pine Lodge SS3 ......168 F8
Pine Rd SS7 ....145 D2
Pine Tree Pl SS4 ....125 E2
Pine View Manor CM16 ..46 A1
Pinecroft Brentwood CM13 95 B2
 Romford RM2 ....136 C7
Pines Rd CM1 ....31 D5
Pines The Basildon SS15 .119 C5
 Grays RM16 ....173 B5
 Woodford IG8 ....110 A7
Pinetrees SS7 ....145 C3
Pineview Ct E4 ....87 C1
Pinewood Ave
 Rainham RM13 ....155 B1
 Southend-on-S SS9 ..146 D5
Pinewood Cl
 Harlow CM17 ....24 C7
 Hullbridge SS5 ......101 E2
Pinewood Prim Sch
 RM5 ....113 B5
Pinewood Rd RM4 ....113 D6
Pinewood Way CM13 ...95 D4
Pinfolds RM15 ....171 D7
Pinley Gdns RM9 ....153 B4
Pinmill SS14 ....142 B6
Pinnacles E6 ....65 E5
Pinners Cl CM0 ......105 F7
Pintail Rd IG8 ....110 B3
Pintails 4 SS13 .....143 C6
Pintolls CM3 ....101 A4
Pioneer Sch
 Basildon SS14 ....142 C7
 Basildon SS14 ....142 C8
Pipchin Rd CM1 ....31 F6
Piper's Tye CM2 ......54 D3
Pippin Ct SS11 ......121 F3
Pippins Rd CM0 .....106 C6
Pipps Hill Rd N CM11 ..120 B3
Pishiobury Dr CM21 ...11 D8
Pitcairn Cl RM7 .....135 A7
Pitmans Cl SS1 ......167 A8
Pitsea Jun & Inf Sch
 SS13 ....143 A5
Pitsea Rd SS14 ......143 A5
Pitsea Sta SS13 .....143 B4
Pitsea View Rd CM11 .120 D4
Pitseaville Gr SS16 ..142 E5
Pitt Chase CM2 ....54 E5
Pittfields SS13 .....141 B5
Pittman Cl CM13 ....117 C5
Pittman Gdns IG1 ...152 C7
Pittman's Field CM20 ..10 F1
Place Farm La CM15 ...72 A2
Pladda Mews SS12 ...121 F5
Plain The CM16 ......46 B3
Plains The E4 ....87 E2
Plaistow Cl SS17 ....160 D2
Plane Tree Cl
 Burnham-on-C CM0 ...106 B6
 Chelmsford CM2 ......54 B6
Plantagenet Pl 8 EN9 ..65 B6
Plantaganet Gdns RM6 .134 D4
Plantaganet Pl RM6 ..134 D4
Plantation Cl DA9 ...176 F1
Plantation Rd CM3 ...20 F1
Plas Newydd SS1 ....167 E6
Plas Newydd Cl SS1 ..167 E6
Plashet Cl SS17 .....160 D2

Plashets CM22 ....2 D1
Plashetts SS14 ......142 D7
Platford Gn RM11 ...136 E7
Platinum Ct RM7 ....135 B8
Playfield Ave RM5 ...113 C2
Playhouse Sq CM20 ...23 C8
Plaza Way SS1 ......167 B8
Pleasant Cl SS1 ....167 B7
Pleasant Dr CM12 ....96 E3
Pleasant Mews SS1 .167 B7
Pleasant Rd SS1 ....167 B7
Pleasant Terr SS1 ..165 E8
Pleasant View DA8 .169 E1
Pleshey Cl
 Southend-on-S SS1 ..167 F8
 6 Wickford SS12 ...121 C6
Plotters Ct 7 EN11 ..21 D8
Plough Rise RM14 ...137 F3
Plover Gdns RM14 ...137 F3
Plover Wlk CM2 ......54 B5
Plovers Mead CM15 ..72 D3
Plovers The CM0 .....62 D7
Plowman Way RM8 ..134 C3
Plowmans SS6 ....123 E4
Ployters Rd CM18 ....23 C4
Plumberow SS15 ....141 E6
Plumberow Ave SS5 .124 E7
Plumberow Mount Ave
 SS5 ....124 E8
Plumberow Prim Sch
 SS5 ....124 E7
Plume Ave CM9 ......36 F1
Plume Sch (Lower) CM9 .37 A2
Plume Sch (Upper) CM9 .36 F2
Plumleys SS13 ......143 B7
Plumpton Ave RM12 .136 F5
Plumpton Rd EN11 ..21 C8
Plumptre La CM3 ....56 D5
Plumtree Ave CM2 ...54 F6
Plumtree Cl RM10 ..154 C6
Plumtree Mead IG10 ..89 A6
Plymouth Ho 10 IG11 .153 A5
Plymouth Rd
 Chelmsford CM1 ......32 E5
 Grays RM16 ....172 E5
Plymtree SS1 ....149 C1
Pocklington Cl CM2 ..33 A3
Point Cl SS8 ....164 F3
Point Rd SS8 ....164 F3
Pole Hill Rd E4 .....87 C2
Polegate Cotts RM7 .177 E8
Polesworth Rd RM9 .153 D5
Poley Rd SS7 ....160 C1
Police Hos RM13 ....155 C2
Pollard Cl IG7 ......112 A5
Pollard Hatch CM19 ..23 B5
Pollard's Gn CM2 ....32 F2
Pollards Cl Loughton IG10 88 C4
 Rochford SS4 ....125 F2
Pollards St CM2 .....125 E2
Polstead Cl SS6 ....123 A3
Polsteads SS16 .....142 E3
Polsten Mews EN3 ..65 A2
Pomfret Mead SS14 .142 A6
Pompadour Cl CM14 .116 C5
Pond La CM22 ....3 A2
Pond Lees Cl RM10 .154 D5
Pond Wlk RM14 .....137 E2
Pondfield La CM13 ..117 A3
Pondfield Rd RM10 .154 B7
Ponds Rd CM2 ....54 B1
Pontypool Wlk RM3 .114 C4
Pool's La SS7 ....51 F4
Poole Ho RM16 .....174 C4
Poole Rd RM11 .....137 A4
Pooles Ct IG3 ......134 A1
Pooles La SS5 ......101 E3
Poors La SS7 ....145 E4
Poors La N SS7 ....146 A5
Poors' Piece Nature Trail*
 CM3 ....34 F1
Popes Cres SS13 ...143 B5
Popes Wlk SS6 .....124 A5
Poplar Cl Blackmore CM4 72 E8
 Chelmsford CM2 .....54 C6
 Ingatestone CM4 ....74 A2
 South Ockendon RM15 .157 D1
 South Woodham Ferrers
 CM3 ....101 C8
Poplar Cotts CM17 ...24 E5
Poplar Ct Chingford E4 .109 B4
 Hockley SS5 ....124 E6
Poplar Dr SS13 .....95 C3
Poplar Gr CM0 ......106 C6
Poplar Grove Chase CM9 37 B8
Poplar Mount DA17 .169 C2
Poplar Rd
 Canvey Island SS8 ..164 C3
 Rayleigh SS6 ......145 F8
Poplar Row CM16 ...67 E2
Poplar Shaw EN9 ..65 F6
Poplar St RM7 .....135 C7
Poplar Way IG6 ....133 C7
Poplars Ave RM4 ...124 F4
Poplars The Abridge RM4 90 B6
 12 Basildon SS13 ...143 C6
Poppy Cl Erith DA17 .169 B3
 Pilgrims Hatch CM15 ..94 B4
Poppy Gn CM1 ......33 A6
Poppyfield Ct SS9 .146 D6
Porchester Cl RM11 .136 E5
Porchester Rd RM12 ..97 A5
Porlock Ave SS0 ....147 A4
Port Ave DA9 ......177 B1

Portchester Ct SS9 .146 F1
Porter Cl RM20 ....177 C8
Porters SS13 ......143 C8
Porters Ave RM8 ..153 C7
Porters Cl CM11 ...94 A1
Porters Grange Prim Sch
 SS1 ....167 B8
Portia Ct 12 IG11 ..153 A5
Portland Ave SS1 ..167 B8
Portland Cl RM6 ...134 E6
Portland Commercial Est
 IG11 ....153 C3
Portland Gdns RM6 .134 D6
Portland Rd DA11 ..178 D1
Portmadoc Ho 2 RM3 .114 E6
Portman Dr
 Billericay CM12 .....97 B5
 Woodford IG8 ......110 D1
Portmore Gdns RM5 .113 A5
Portnoi Cl RM1 ....113 D1
Portreath Pl CM1 ...32 A7
Portsea Rd RM18 ..179 C6
Portway Chelmsford CM2 .33 B4
 Rainham RM13 .....155 A4
Poseidon Ct IG11 ..153 B2
Post Mdw CM11 ...119 D6
Post Office Cotts CM22 ..2 C8
Post Office Rd
 Chelmsford CM1 ....32 B8
 Harlow CM20 ....10 D1
 Ingatestone CM4 ....74 B3
 Woodham Mortimer CM9 .57 E6
Postman's La CM3 .34 E3
Postway Mews 1 IG1 .133 B1
Potash Rd Billericay CM11 97 D6
 Matching Green CM17 .13 D4
Potiphar Pl CM14 ..116 B6
Potter St CM17 .....24 C6
Potter Street Prim Sch
 CM17 ....24 C6
Potters Cl Danbury CM3 .57 A6
 Loughton IG10 .....88 F7
Potters Field CM17 ..24 D6
Potters La CM3 ....78 D2
Potters Way SS2 ..147 F5
Pottery La CM1 ....32 A5
Potton Dr SS12 ...121 F6
Poulton Cl CM9 ....59 B8
Pound Cl EN9 .....43 E8
Pound Fields CM1 .53 B8
Pound La
 Basildon,Laindon SS15 .141 D8
 Basildon,North Benfleet
 SS12 ....143 F7
 Orsett RM16 ....159 A1
Pound La N SS11 ...119 D1
Pound Lane Central
 SS15 ....119 D1
Poundfield Rd IG10 ..89 A4
Powdermill La EN9 ..65 B6
Powdermill Mews 2
 EN9 ....65 B6
Powdermill Way EN9 .65 B6
Powell Ct SS4 .....125 F1
Powell Gdns RM10 .154 A8
Powell Rd Basildon SS15 141 B7
 Buckhurst Hill IG9 ..88 C2
Powle Terr IG1 ....152 D7
Pownsett Terr IG1 .152 C7
Poynder Rd RM18 ..179 B6
Poynings Ave SS2 .148 E2
Poynings Way RM3 .114 E2
Poyntens SS6 .....123 C1
Poynters La SS3 ..150 B2
Pratts Farm La CM3 ..19 D4
Preaching Cross CM4 .97 F6
Precinct The SS17 .160 D1
Premier Ave RM16 .173 C4
Prentice Cl SS4 ...125 F2
Prentice Hall La CM9 .40 B8
Prentice Pl CM17 ..24 C6
Prescott SS16 ....141 C3
Prescott Cl RM11 .136 B3
Prescott Gn IG10 ..89 C6
Presidents Ct SS15 .140 F6
Preston Ave E4 ...109 D4
Preston Dr E11 ...132 C6
Preston Gdns
 Rayleigh SS6 ......123 D4
 Redbridge IG1 .....132 E5
Preston Ho 3 RM10 .135 A1
Preston Rd Romford RM3 114 D6
 Southend-on-S SS0 .166 D8
Prestwood Cl SS7 .144 F7
Prestwood Dr
 Romford RM5 ......113 C6
 Thundersley SS7 ...145 A7
Pretoria Cl SS15 ..119 F1
Pretoria Cres E4 ..87 C1
Pretoria Rd Chingford E4 .87 C1
 Ilford IG1 ....152 B7
 Romford RM7 ......135 C4
Priest's La
 Brentwood CM15 ...116 C1
 Shenfield CM15 ....94 F1
Priestley Ct RM17 .173 C2
Priestley Gdns RM6 .134 B5
Priests Ave RM1 ...113 C6
Priests Field CM13 .117 C5
Primley La SS6 ....2 C1
Primrose Ave RM6 .134 C4
Primrose Cl
 Basildon SS16 .....141 B4
 Canvey Island SS8 .164 A6
Primrose Ct 1 CM14 .116 C7
Primrose Field CM18 .23 F5
Primrose Glen RM11 .136 E7

Primrose Hill
 Brentwood CM14 ...116 C7
 Chelmsford CM1 ....31 F3
Primrose Rd E18 ...110 B1
Primrose Wlk
 Maldon CM9 ....37 B1
 Southminster CM0 ..84 C3
Primula Way CM1 ..33 A6
Prince Ave SS2, SS0 .147 C4
Prince Avenue Prim Sch
 SS0 ....147 D5
Prince Charles Ave
 RM16 ....159 B1
Prince Cl SS0 .....147 C5
Prince Edward Rd CM11 .97 C2
Prince Philip Ave RM16 .173 B6
Prince William Ave SS8 163 F6
Prince's Rd
 Navestock Heath CM14,RM4 92 A3
 Navestock Side CM14 .93 A7
Princes Ave
 Corringham SS17 ..161 A3
 Mayland CM3 ......83 A8
 Southminster CM0 ..84 C3
 Thundersley SS7 ..144 F6
 Woodford IG8 .....110 C5
Princes Cl Basildon SS15 141 E8
 Billericay CM12 ....97 C6
 North Weald Bassett CM16 97 C6
Princes Ct Billericay CM12 .97 C6
 Southend-on-S SS2 .147 C5
Princes Gate
 Harlow CM20 ......10 A1
 Southminster CM0 ..84 C4
Princes Lodge SS0 .166 B2
Princes Mews SS12 ..97 C6
Princes Pk RM13 ..155 F5
Princes Rd
 Buckhurst Hill IG9 .110 C8
 Burnham-on-C CM0 .106 C6
 Canvey Island SS8 .163 F3
 Chelmsford CM2 ...54 B7
 Ilford IG6 ....133 D7
 Maldon CM9 ....37 A2
 Romford RM3 ......136 A6
Princes St
 Gravesend DA11 ...179 B1
 Southend-on-S SS1 .166 F8
Princes Way
 Brentwood CM13 ...95 A4
 Buckhurst Hill EN9 .110 C8
Princesfield Rd EN9 .66 B6
Princess Alexandra Hospl
 CM20 ....10 C1
Princess Ave RM18 .175 D4
Princess Ct SS11 ..122 A8
Princess Gdns SS4 .125 C5
Princess Margaret Rd
 RM18 ....180 C3
Princess Par RM10 .154 A3
Princess Rd SS6 ..123 F3
Printers Way CM20 ..11 A5
Prior Chase RM17 .172 F2
Prior Rd IG1 ....133 E4
Prior's Way CM0 ..84 E4
Prioress Cres DA9 .177 C2
Priories The SS5 ..101 D1
Priors Cl SS14 ....142 C6
Priors Ct
 Sawbridgeworth CM22 .2 A1
 Southminster CM0 ..84 E4
Priors E SS14 .....142 C6
Priors Pk RM12 ...136 C1
Priory Ave Chingford E4 .109 A7
 Harlow CM17 ......11 C5
 Southend-on-S SS2 .147 F3
Priory Cl Chelmsford CM1 .31 E2
 Hoddesdon EN11 ..21 A5
 Pilgrims Hatch CM15 .94 A3
 Woodford E18 .....110 A2
Priory Cres SS2 ..147 E4
Priory Ct Harlow CM18 .24 B5
 Ilford RM6 ....134 B5
Priory Gr RM3 ....114 C6
Priory Ind Pk SS2 .148 A4
Priory La CM3 ....56 F1
Priory Mead CM15 .72 C3
Priory Mews 1 RM11 .136 B3
Priory Path RM3 ..114 E7
Priory Prim Sch CM3 .56 F2
Priory Rd Barking IG11 .152 D5
 Bicknacre CM3 .....56 E1
 Loughton IG10 ....88 E5
 Romford RM3 .....114 E7
 Stanford-le-H SS17 .160 E3
Priory Sch SS2 ...147 E3
Priory The Billericay CM12 .97 C6
 Writtle CM1 ....53 B8
Priory View Rd SS9 .146 E5
Priory Wood Cres SS9 .146 E5
Priorywood Dr SS9 .146 E5
Pritchett Cl EN3 ..65 A2
Prittle Ct SS7 ....145 C5
Prittlebrook Ind Est
 SS2 ....147 F3
Prittlewell CE Jun & Inf Sch
 SS2 ....147 F2
Prittlewell Chase SS0 147 D3
Prittlewell Mews SS2 .147 F2
Prittlewell Priory Mus*
 SS2 ....147 F3
Prittlewell Sch The SS0 147 C3
Prittlewell Sq SS1 .166 F7
Prittlewell St SS2 .148 A1
Prittlewell Sta SS2 .148 A3
Professional Pl 2 SS11 122 A5
Progress Rd SS5 ...124 C6
Promenade CM3 ...60 C1

Promenade The
Burnham-on-C CM0 ......106 C4
Southend-on-S SS3 ......168 C5
Prospect Ave SS17 .....160 B1
Prospect Bsns Pk IG10 ..89 D5
Prospect Cl
Belvedere DA17 ....169 A2
Southend-on-S SS1 ......167 C7
Prospect Pl
Gravesend DA12 ....179 D1
Grays RM17 ....178 B8
Romford RM5 ....113 C1
Prospect Rd
Hornchurch RM11 ....136 F8
Woodford IG8 ....110 C5
Prospect Way CM13 .....95 E5
Prospero Ho 7 DA17 ....169 A1
Protea Way SS8 ....164 B4
Providence CM0 ....106 C4
Providence Pl RM5 .....112 F2
Providence St DA9 .....177 A2
Prower Cl CM11 ....97 B1
Prudhoe Ct 15 DA2 ......176 B1
Prykes Dr CM1 ....32 A2
Pryors Rd CM2 ....54 C2
Puck La SS16 ....142 C5
Puckleside SS16 ....141 C4
Pudding La IG7 ....89 F2
Pudsey Hall La SS4 ....104 A2
Puffin Cl Barking IG11 ...153 B2
Wickford SS12 ....121 F5
Puffin Pl SS3 ....149 E1
Puffin Terr IG5 ....133 A8
Pugh Pl SS17 ....160 D4
Pulborough Ho 1 RM3 ..114 E3
Pullman Ct SS11 ....121 D8
Pulpits Cl SS5 ....124 F7
Pulteney Gdns 9 E18 ..132 B8
Pulteney Rd E18 ....132 B8
Pump Hill
Great Baddow CM2 ....54 F6
Loughton IG10 ....88 F7
Pump La Chelmsford CM1 .32 E6
Danbury CM3 ....56 D5
Epping Green CM16 ....45 B7
Pleshey CM3 ....7 E1
Purleigh CM3 ....58 D1
Pump Mead Cl CM0 .....84 D4
Pump St SS17 ....160 A2
Punchard Cres EN3 .....65 B1
Punchbowl Cotts SS4 ..127 D7
Purbeck Ct CM2 ....54 E6
Purbeck Rd RM11 ....136 A4
Purcell Cl Basildon SS15 .141 D8
Stanford-le-H SS17 ......160 C3
Writtle CM1 ....31 A1
Purcell Way SS17 ......160 C3
Purdeys Way SS4 ......148 A8
Purfleet By-Pass RM19 .171 C1
Purfleet Ind Pk RM15 ..170 F4
Purfleet Prim Sch
RM19 ....171 A2
Purfleet Rd RM15 ......171 B5
Purford Gn CM18 ....24 A7
Purford Green Jun & Inf Schs
CM18 ....24 A6
Purland Cl RM8 ....134 F3
Purleigh Ave IG8 ......110 E4
Purleigh Cl SS13 ....121 C1
Purleigh Gr CM3 ....81 A5
Purleigh Prim Sch CM3 ..58 D1
Purleigh Rd SS6 ....123 B3
Purleigh St CM9 ....59 A1
Purleigh Wash CM9 ......59 B2
Purley Cl IG5 ....111 A1
Purley Way SS0 ....147 C5
Purlieu Way CM16 ....67 E4
Putney Gdns RM6 ......134 B6
Pye Cnr CM20 ....10 D5
Pyenest Rd CM19 ....23 C6
Pym Pl RM17 ....173 A2
Pyms Rd CM2 ....54 B3
Pynchon Mews CM1 ......32 D3
Pynchon Paddocks CM22 .2 D7
Pyne Gate CM2 ....54 B1
Pynest Green La EN9 ....66 B2
Pypers Hatch CM20 .....23 F8
Pyrgo Priory Sch RM3 ..115 A6
Pyrles Gn IG10 ....89 B8
Pyrles La IG10 ....89 B7
Pytt Field CM17 ....24 B7

Q

Quadrant Arc RM1 .....135 E6
Quadrant The RM19 ....171 C2
Quaker La EN9 ....65 C5
Quale Rd CM2 ....33 B4
Quantock 6 SS1 ....167 A8
Quarles Cl RM5 ....113 A3
Quarry Hill RM17 ......173 A1
Quarry Hill Inf Sch
RM17 ....173 B1
Quarry Hill Jun Sch
RM17 ....173 B1
Quarry Mews RM19 .....171 A2
Quarry Spring CM20 .....24 A8
Quarter Gate CM3 ......101 E5
Quatro Pk SS14 ....121 A2
Quattro Pk SS14 ....120 F2
Quay La DA9 ....177 B3
Quay The CM0 ....106 C4
Quayside Ind Est CM9 ...37 A4
Quebec Ave 4 SS1 .....167 B8
Quebec Gdns CM3 ......101 D6
Quebec Rd Ilford IG1 ...133 C4
Tilbury RM18 ....179 A5
Queen Anne's Dr SS0 ..147 C4
Queen Anne's Mews
SS0 ....147 C4
Queen Anns Gr SS5 ....123 D8
Queen Elizabeth Ave
RM18 ....175 B2
Queen Elizabeth Chase
SS4 ....147 F7
Queen Elizabeth Ct EN9 .65 C3
Queen Elizabeth Dr
SS17 ....160 F4
Queen Elizabeth II Sq 4
CM3 ....101 E7
Queen Elizabeth's Hunting
Lodge* E4 ....87 F2
Queen Mary Ave RM18 .175 C2
Queen Mary Cl RM1 ....135 F5
Queen Mary Ct RM18 ...175 C2
Queen Marys Ct EN9 ....65 C4
Queen St
Brentwood CM14 ....116 C5
Chelmsford CM2 ....32 A1
Fyfield CM5 ....27 E2
Gravesend DA12 ....179 B1
Maldon CM9 ....37 A2
Romford RM7 ....135 D5
Southminster CM0 ....84 C4
Queen's Ave Maldon CM9 .37 A1
Southend-on-S SS9 ......146 E1
Woodford IG8 ....110 B5
Queen's Cl CM21 ....1 F4
Queen's Dr EN8 ....65 A5
Queen's Gate Mews
CM12 ....96 F5
Queen's Grove Rd E4 ...87 D1
Queen's Park Ctry Pk*
CM12 ....97 B6
Queen's Rd Barking IG11 152 C6
Brentwood CM14 ....116 D8
Buckhurst Hill IG9 .....110 C8
Burnham-on-C CM0 ......106 C5
Chelmsford CM2 ....32 D2
South Benfleet SS7 .....144 D2
Queenborough Gdns
IG2 ....133 A7
Queenborough Rd CM0 ..84 D4
Queens Ct
Burnham-on-C CM0 ......106 B4
Southend-on-S SS9 ......146 E1
Southend-on-S,Chalkwell
SS9 ....165 F8
Queens Gate IG4 ......132 F7
Queens Gdns
Rainham RM13 ....154 D3
Upminster RM14 ....137 F5
Queens Lodge SS7 .....145 C3
Queens Park Ave CM12 ..97 B5
Queens Park Ct CM12 ...96 F5
Queens Park Rd RM3 ..115 A2
Queens Rd
Basildon, Crays Hill CM11 .120 B4
Basildon, Steeple View
SS15 ....119 C1
Loughton IG10 ....88 F6
North Weald Bassett CM16 .47 B6
Rayleigh SS6 ....123 E2
Southend-on-S,Chalkwell
SS9 ....165 F8
Southend-on-S,Clifftown
SS1 ....166 F8
Queens Wlk E4 ....87 D1
Queensbridge Ind Est
RM20 ....177 A8
Queensbury IG9 ....88 B1
Queensgate Ctr
Grays RM17 ....173 A1
Harlow CM20 ....10 F4
Queenside Ct RM7 .....135 C7
Queensland Ave SS4 ....147 F7
Queensland Cres CM1 ...31 E5
Queensmere SS7 ....145 B5
Queenstown Gdns
RM13 ....154 F2
Queensway
Chipping Ongar CM5 ......48 F5
Southend-on-S SS1 .....167 B8
Queensway Ho SS8 .....163 D3
Queensway Lodge SS1 ..167 B7
Queenswood Ave
Brentwood CM13 ....95 D4
Chingford E17 ....109 C2
Queenswood Gdns E11 .132 B2
Quendon Dr EN9 ....65 D6
Quendon Rd SS14 ....142 E8
Quennell Way CM13 .....95 D2
Quilp Dr CM1 ....31 F7
Quilters Cl SS14 ....142 D8
Quilters Dr CM12 ....119 A8
Quilters Inf & Jun Schs
CM12 ....97 A1
Quilters Straight SS14 .142 E8
Quince Tree Cl RM15 ...157 C1
Quinion Cl CM1 ....31 D7
Quorn Gdns SS9 ....146 A1
Quorn The CM4 ....74 A3

R

Rachael Clarke Cl SS17 .160 E4
Rachael Ct 1 CM2 ....32 B1
Rachel Cl IG6 ....133 D8
Rackenford SS3 ....168 D8
Radbourne Cres E17 ...109 D1
Radburn Cl CM18 ....24 A4
Radburn Pl DA10 ....177 E2
Radford Bsns Ctr CM12 ..96 F3
Radford Cres CM12 ....97 A3
Radford Ct CM12 ....97 B3
Radford Ho CM12 ....97 B3
Radford Way
Barking IG11 ....152 F2
Billericay CM12 ....97 A3
Radley Ave IG3 ....153 A8
Radley Ct IG7 ....111 E6
Radley Green Rd CM4,
CM5 ....51 C7
Radley's La E18 ....110 A1
Radleys Mead RM10 ....154 B6
Radnor Cres IG4 ....132 F6
Radnor Rd SS4 ....103 C1
Radstock Ho 11 RM3 ....114 D5
Radstocks CM12 ....97 B3
Radwinter Ave SS12 ...121 D6
Rahn Rd CM16 ....68 A8
Raider Cl RM7 ....113 B2
Railway App SS15 ......141 A6
Railway Cotts Ilford IG6 133 D8
Redbridge IG6 ....111 D2
Railway Pl
Belvedere DA17 ....169 A3
12 Gravesend DA11 .....179 B1
Railway Sq
Brentwood CM14 ....116 C7
Chelmsford CM1 ....32 A3
Railway St
Chelmsford CM1 ....32 A3
Dagenham RM6 ....134 C4
Northfleet DA11 ....178 A2
Railway Terr
Chingford E17 ....109 C2
Southend-on-S SS2 .....148 A3
Rainbow Ave SS8 ......164 C4
Rainbow La SS17 ....160 F1
Rainbow Mews CM9 .....36 F5
Rainbow Rd
Canvey Island SS8 ......164 C4
Grays RM16 ....172 C2
Sheering CM17 ....12 E3
Rainham Rd RM13 ......154 F4
Rainham Rd N RM10 ...135 B2
Rainham Rd S RM10 ...154 C7
Rainham Sta RM13 ......155 A1
Rainham Trad Est RM13 .154 F1
Rainham Village Prim Sch
RM13 ....155 A1
Rainsford Ave CM1 ......31 F3
Rainsford La CM1 ....31 F2
Rainsford Rd CM1 ....31 F3
Rainsford Way RM12 ...136 A3
Raleigh Dr SS15 ....141 D5
Ram Gorse CM20 ....10 B2
Ramblers Way CM0 .....106 D4
Rampart St SS3 ....168 G6
Rampart Terr SS3 ......168 G6
Ramparts The SS6 ......123 F2
Rampton Cl E4 ....109 A7
Rams Gr RM6 ....134 E7
Ramsay Dr SS16 ....142 E3
Ramsay Gdns RM3 ......114 C2
Ramsay Rd E7 ....152 A1
Ramsden Dr RM5 ....113 A3
Ramsden Hall Sch CM11 .97 F3
Ramsden Park Rd CM11 .98 D1
Ramsden View Rd SS12 .120 F6
Ramsey Chase
Latchingdon CM3 ....82 A6
Wickford SS12 ....121 F6
Ramsey Cl CM9 ....37 D4
Ramsey Ct SS0 ....147 B3
Ramsgill App IG2 ......133 F7
Ramsgill Dr IG2 ....133 F7
Ramshaw Dr CM2 ....32 F3
Ramuz Dr SS0 ....147 D2
Randall Ct RM13 ....155 B2
Randall Dr RM12 ....155 D8
Randalls Dr CM13 ....95 E3
Randolph Cl Maldon CM9 .58 F8
Southend-on-S SS9 .....146 E3
Randolph Gr RM6 ....134 C6
Rands Rd CM6 ....5 F8
Randulph Terr CM1 ......32 D3
Randway SS6 ....123 D1
Ranelagh Gdns
Ilford IG1 ....133 A3
Redbridge IG1 ....132 F3
Wanstead E11 ....132 C6
Ranelagh Rd E6 ....152 A3
Ranger's Rd
Buckhurst Hill E4,IG9,IG10 .88 A2
Chingford E4 ....87 F2
Ransomes Way CM1 .....32 B4
Rantree Fold SS16 ......141 F4
Ranulf Cl CM17 ....11 C6
Ranworth Ave EN11 ....8 B2
Raphael Ave
Romford RM1 ....135 F8
Tilbury RM18 ....179 B7
Raphael Dr
Chelmsford CM1 ....32 F7
Southend-on-S SS3 .....150 A1
Raphael Ind Sch RM11 .136 A5
Raphaels SS15 ....141 E6
Raphaels Ct RM1 ....135 F7
Rapier Cl RM19 ....171 A2
Rat La SS6 ....145 C8
Rat's La IG10 ....66 B1
Ratsborough Chase CM0 84 C2
Rattwick Dr SS8 ....164 F3
Ratty's La EN11 ....21 D6
Ravel Gdns RM15 ....171 C7
Ravel Rd RM15 ....171 D7
Raven Cl CM12 ....96 F4
Raven Cres CM12 ....96 F4
Raven Dr SS7 ....144 C2
Raven La CM12 ....96 F4
Raven Rd E18 ....110 C1
Ravencroft RM16 ....174 B4
Ravendale Way SS3 ....149 D1
Ravenings Par IG3 .....134 A3
Ravenoak Way IG7 .....111 E5
Ravens Ct SS1 ....166 F7
Ravensbourne Cres
RM3 ....136 F8
Ravensbourne Dr CM1 ...31 E2
Ravensbourne Gdns
IG5 ....111 B2
Ravensbourne Sch RM3 114 D2
Ravenscourt CM15 ....94 D1
Ravenscourt Cl RM12 ..136 E1
Ravenscourt Dr
Basildon SS16 ....142 E5
Hornchurch RM12 ....136 E1
Ravenscourt Gr RM12 ..136 E2
Ravensdale SS16 ....142 B4
Ravensfield
Basildon SS14 ....142 F6
Dagenham RM9 ....153 D8
Ravensmere CM16 ....46 A1
Ravenswood Chase SS4 147 F7
Ravenswood Cl RM5 ....113 B5
Rawdon Dr EN11 ....21 A5
Rawlyn Cl RM16 ....172 C1
Rawreth Gdns SS11 ....100 E1
Rawreth Ind Est SS6 ...123 B5
Rawreth La SS11 ....123 B6
Ray Cl Canvey Island SS8 .164 A2
Southend-on-S SS9 .....146 B1
Ray Ct IG8 ....110 D4
Ray Gdns IG11 ....153 A3
Ray Lodge Prim Sch
IG8 ....110 D4
Ray Lodge Rd IG8 ......110 D4
Ray Mead CM3 ....18 F7
Ray Rd RM5 ....113 B5
Ray The CM1 ....32 E5
Ray Wlk SS9 ....146 B1
Rayburn Rd RM11 ......137 A4
Rayburne Ct IG9 ....88 C1
Raydons Gdns RM9 .....153 E7
Raydons Rd RM9 ....153 E7
Rayfield CM16 ....46 A2
Rayleigh Ave
Rayleigh SS9 ....146 B8
Southend-on-S SS0 .....147 E1
Rayleigh Cl CM13 ....95 C3
Rayleigh Downs Rd SS6 146 B7
Rayleigh Dr SS9 ....146 D3
Rayleigh Ho SS6 ....123 C1
Rayleigh Par 8 CM13 ....95 C3
Rayleigh Prim Sch SS6 .123 C2
Rayleigh Rd
Brentwood CM13 ....95 D3
Southend-on-S SS9 .....146 D6
Stanford-le-H SS17 .....160 B1
Thundersley SS7 ....145 C6
Woodford IG8 ....110 C3
Rayleigh Sta SS6 ....123 C3
Rayley La CM16 ....47 A8
Rayment Ave SS8 ....164 D3
Raymond Ave E18 ....109 F1
Raymond Gdns IG7 .....112 B7
Raymond Rd IG2 ....133 D4
Raymonds Cl CM3 ......101 C7
Raymonds Dr SS7 ......144 F6
Rayners Ct DA11 ....178 B1
Raynes Ave E11 ....132 C4
Rayside SS14 ....142 C5
Reaburn Ct CM1 ....32 E6
Read Cl SS5 ....125 A4
Read Ct EN9 ....66 A6
Reader's Cnr CM2 ....54 E5
Readers Ct CM2 ....54 E6
Reading Cl SS16 ....140 F5
Readings The CM18 ......23 F5
Reads Cl IG1 ....133 B1
Rebels La SS3 ....148 F3
Recreation Ave
Corringham SS17 ....161 C4
Romford RM7 ....135 C6
Romford, Harold Wood
RM3 ....114 F1
Southend-on-S SS9 .....146 F2
Recreation Ct SS9 ......146 F2
Recreation Wlk CM11 ....98 C5
Rectory Ave SS4 ....125 C6
Rectory Chase
Doddinghurst CM15 ......72 C2
Little Warley CM13 .....138 E7
Southend-on-S SS2 .....148 E1
Rectory Cl Chingford E4 .109 A7
Hadleigh SS7 ....145 E3
Hunsdonbury SG12 ....9 D8
Ingatestone CM4 ....74 B4
Little Waltham CM3 ......19 C6
Stock CM4 ....75 D2
Rectory Cres E11 ......132 C5
Rectory Ct Basildon SS13 143 C7
Grays RM17 ....178 D8
Loughton IG10 ....89 A7
Woodford E18 ....109 F2
Rectory Field CM19 ......23 B6
Rectory Garth SS6 ......123 D3
Rectory Gdns
Basildon SS13 ....143 C6
Upminster RM14 ....137 E2
Rectory Gr
Southend-on-S SS9 .....165 D8
Wickford SS11 ....121 F7
Rectory La
Chelmsford CM1 ....32 B4
Harlow CM19 ....23 B6
Ingrave CM13 ....117 E3
Latchingdon CM3 ....82 B3
Rectory La *continued*
Loughton IG10 ....89 B6
Rettendon SS11 ....100 E6
Woodham Mortimer CM9 ...57 F6
Rectory Park Dr SS13 ..143 B5
Rectory Rd
Basildon SS13 ....143 C6
Dagenham RM10 ....154 B5
Grays RM17 ....173 D2
Hadleigh SS7 ....145 E3
Hockley SS5 ....125 B4
Little Burstead CM12 ....119 A2
Little Ilford E12 ....152 A7
North Fambridge CM3 ...103 A8
Orsett RM16 ....174 B8
Stanford-le-H SS17 .....160 C1
West Tilbury RM18 ......179 D8
Woodham Walter CM9 ....35 D3
Writtle CM1 ....53 B8
Rectory Terr
Hockley SS5 ....125 B4
Stanford-le-H SS17 .....160 C1
Rectory Wood CM20 ......10 C1
Red Cotts CM22 ....12 D8
Red Lion Cres CM17 .....24 C6
Red Lion La CM17 ....24 D6
Red Oaks Mead CM16 ...67 D2
Red Rd CM14 ....116 B6
Red Willow CM19 ....22 F5
Redbrick Row CM22 ....2 B8
Redbridge Coll RM6 ....134 B6
Redbridge Ct IG4 ......132 D5
Redbridge Ent Ctr IG1 .133 C2
Redbridge Foyer IG1 ...133 C2
Redbridge Inf Sch IG4 .132 E6
Redbridge Inst IG2 .....133 B6
Redbridge Jun Sch IG4 132 E6
Redbridge La E IG4 ....132 E6
Redbridge La W E11 ...132 C5
Redbridge Sports Ctr
IG6 ....111 D2
Redbridge Sta IG4 .....132 D5
Redbrook Ct SS17 ......175 A3
Redbury Cl RM13 ....155 B1
Redcar Rd RM3 ....114 F5
Redcliff Dr SS9 ....165 F8
Redcliffe Gdns
Ilford IG1 ....133 A3
Redbridge IG1 ....132 F3
Redcliffe Rd 3 CM2 .....32 A1
Redden Court Comp Sch
RM3 ....136 F8
Redden Court Rd RM3 ..136 F8
Reddings La CM0 ....63 C3
Redfern Gdns RM2 .....114 D1
Redgate Cl SS11 ....122 A8
Redgates Pl CM2 ....32 D4
Redgrave Rd SS16 ......142 E4
Redgrove Ho CM16 ....46 A2
Redhills Rd CM3 ....101 E8
Redif Ho RM10 ....154 B8
Redinge The CM11 ......119 D7
Redlie Cl SS17 ....160 D4
Redmans Ind Est RM18 .180 A8
Redmayne Dr CM2 ....53 F8
Redo Ho 2 E12 ....152 A7
Redricks La CM21 ....11 A6
Redriff Rd RM7 ....113 B1
Redrose La CM4 ....50 E1
Redruth Cl CM1 ....32 E5
Redruth Gdns RM3 ......114 F5
Redruth Rd RM3 ....114 F5
Redruth Wlk RM3 ....114 F5
Redshank Cres CM3 .....79 D1
Redshank Dr CM9 ....37 C5
Redstock Rd SS2 ....148 A2
Redwing Ct RM3 ....114 D3
Redwing Dr CM11 ....119 C8
Redwood Chase RM15 ..157 D1
Redwood Cl IG9 ....110 B8
Redwood Ct DA1 ....176 A1
Redwood Dr
Basildon SS15 ....119 D1
Writtle CM1 ....30 F1
Redwood Gdns
Chingford E4 ....87 B3
Redbridge IG7 ....112 A5
Redwoods The SS8 .....163 E3
Ree Lane Cotts IG10 ....89 A7
Reed Mans 7 E11 ....132 A5
Reed Pond Wlk
Basildon SS16 ....141 B4
Romford RM2 ....113 F1
Reede Gdns RM10 ......154 B7
Reede Rd RM10 ....154 B6
Reede Way RM10 ....154 B6
Reedings Jun Sch CM21 ...1 E3
Reedings Way CM21 ....1 F4
Reeds Way SS12 ....121 C8
Reesland Cl E12 ....152 A6
Reeves Cl Basildon SS16 .140 F4
Stondon Massey CM15 ....72 B5
Reeves La CM19 ....22 D5
Reeves Way CM3 ....101 E7
Regal Cl CM2 ....54 D8
Regan Cl SS17 ....160 E4
Regarder Rd IG7 ....112 B5
Regarth Ave RM1 ....135 E5
Regatta Ct SS9 ....165 F8
Regency Cl
Chelmsford CM2 ....32 D3
Chigwell IG7 ....111 C5
Rochford SS4 ....125 E2
Wickford SS11 ....99 D2

Regency Ct
Brentwood CM14 . . . . . .**116** C8
Harlow CM18 . . . .**24** A5
Heybridge CM9 . . . .**37** A5
Hockley SS5 . . . .**124** E6
Regency Gdns RM11 . . .**136** C4
Regency Gn SS2 . . . . . .**147** F3
Regency Lodge ■ IG9 . .**110** D8
Regent Cl Grays RM16 . .**173** C4
Rayleigh SS6 . . . .**123** B4
Regent Ct Basildon SS15 .**121** A1
Romford RM2 . . . .**136** B8
Regent Dr CM12 . . . .**96** F5
Regent Gdns IG3 . . . . . .**134** A5
Regent Rd CM16 . . . .**45** F1
Regent Sq DA17 . . . .**169** B2
Regents Cl CM0 . . . .**84** D4
Regents Ct
Burnham-on-C CM0 . . . .**106** B4
■ Gravesend DA11 . . . .**179** B1
Regents Dr IG8 . . . .**111** A3
Regents Pl IG10 . . . .**88** D2
Regina Rd CM1 . . . .**32** C3
Reginald Mews CM17 . . .**11** C1
Reginald Rd RM3 . . . . .**115** A2
Reigate Rd IG3 . . . .**133** F2
Rembrandt Cl
■ Canvey Island SS8 . .**164** A3
Southend-on-S SS3 . . . .**168** G8
Rembrandt Gr CM1 . . . . .**32** E6
Remembrance Ave CM0 .**106** B4
Renacres SS16 . . . .**141** F4
Rennie Ct ■ EN3 . . . . . .**65** A1
Rennie Pl CM2 . . . .**33** B3
Renoir Pl CM1 . . . .**32** F7
Renown Cl RM7 . . . .**113** B2
Renown The SS3 . . . . . .**168** F8
Renwick Rd IG11 . . . . . .**153** B2
Repton Ave RM2 . . . . . .**136** A8
Repton Cl SS13 . . . .**121** A1
Repton Ct Basildon SS13 .**121** A1
Woodford IG5 . . . .**110** F2
Repton Dr RM2 . . . .**136** A7
Repton Gdns RM2 . . . . .**136** A8
Repton Gr
Southend-on-S SS2 . . . .**147** A7
Woodford IG5 . . . .**110** F2
Repulse Cl RM5 . . . .**113** B2
Reservoir Cl DA9 . . . . . .**177** C1
Rest Cotts SS4 . . . .**104** E1
Retford Cl RM3 . . . .**115** A4
Retford Path RM3 . . . . .**115** A4
Retford Rd RM3 . . . .**115** A4
Retingham Way E4 . . . . .**109** B8
Retreat Rd Hockley SS5 .**124** E6
Southend-on-S SS0 . . . .**166** E7
Retreat The
Brentwood CM14 . . . . . .**94** B1
Grays RM17 . . . .**178** B8
Shenfield CM13 . . . .**95** B3
Retreat Way IG7 . . . . . .**112** B7
Rettendon Cl SS6 . . . . .**123** A3
Rettendon Gdns SS11 . . .**99** E1
Rettendon Prim Sch
CM3 . . . .**100** C5
Rettendon Turnpike
SS11 . . . .**100** C3
Reubens Rd CM13 . . . . . .**95** B3
Review Rd RM10 . . . . . .**154** B4
Rex Par ■ IG8 . . . .**110** C4
Reydon Ave E11 . . . .**132** C5
Reynard Ct CM2 . . . .**54** F6
Reynolds Ave
Dagenham RM6 . . . . . .**134** C4
Little Ilford E12 . . . . . .**152** A7
Reynolds Ct RM6 . . . . . .**134** D8
Reynolds Gate SS14 . . . .**101** E6
Reynolds Ho SS2 . . . . . .**147** F2
Rhapsody Cres CM14 . . .**116** B5
Rhoda Rd SS7 . . . .**144** E4
Rhoda Rd N SS7 . . . .**144** E5
Rhum Mews SS12 . . . . .**122** A4
Ribble Cl RM4 . . . .**110** C4
Richard Alibon Prim Sch
RM10 . . . .**154** A7
Richard Blackburn Ho
RM7 . . . .**135** E2
Richard Burton Ct ■
IG9 . . . .**110** C8
Richard Fell Ho ■ E12 . .**152** A8
Richards Ave RM7 . . . . .**135** C5
Richardson Cl DA9 . . . . .**176** F2
Richardson Gdns ■
RM10 . . . .**154** B6
Richardson Pl CM1 . . . . .**31** F4
Riches Rd IG1 . . . .**133** C2
Richmond Ave
Chingford E4 . . . .**109** D5
South Benfleet SS7 . . . .**144** C2
Southend-on-S SS1 . . . .**167** A7
Southend-on-S, Cambridge Town
SS3 . . . .**168** D6
Southend-on-S, Westcliff-on-S
SS0 . . . .**166** E8
Richmond Ave Prim Sch
SS3 . . . .**168** D6
Richmond Cres E4 . . . . .**109** D5
Richmond Ct
■ Romford RM1 . . . . .**135** F5
Southend-on-S SS3 . . . .**168** D6
Southend-on-S, Chalkwell
SS9 . . . .**165** F8
Richmond Dr
Rayleigh SS6 . . . .**145** D8

Richmond Dr *continued*
■ Redbridge IG8 . . . . .**111** A3
Southend-on-S SS0 . . . .**147** C4
Richmond Pk IG10 . . . . . .**88** D2
Richmond Rd
Chelmsford CM2 . . . . . .**33** A4
Chingford E4 . . . .**87** D1
Grays RM17 . . . .**173** C1
Ilford IG1 . . . .**133** C1
Romford RM1 . . . .**135** F5
Wickford SS11 . . . .**99** C2
Richmond St SS2 . . . . . .**148** B1
Richmond Way E11 . . . . .**132** A2
Ricketts Dr CM12 . . . . . .**96** F3
Rickling SS16 . . . .**142** F4
Riddiford Ct CM1 . . . . . .**31** F4
Riddings La CM18 . . . . . .**24** A4
Ridge The CM3 . . . .**34** E2
Ridgemount SS7 . . . . . .**144** E4
Ridges The E4 . . . .**109** A6
Ridgeway Billericay CM12 **119** A8
Brentwood CM13 . . . . . .**95** B1
Grays RM17 . . . .**173** E2
Ingatestone CM4 . . . . . .**74** A2
Maldon CM9 . . . .**59** A8
Rayleigh SS6 . . . .**123** C1
Woodford IG8 . . . .**110** C6
Ridgeway Gdns
Redbridge IG4 . . . .**132** E6
Southend-on-S SS0 . . . .**166** B8
Ridgeway The
Chingford E4 . . . .**87** C1
Romford RM2 . . . .**136** A7
Romford, Harold Wood
RM3 . . . .**114** F2
Southend-on-S SS0 . . . .**166** B8
Ridgeways CM17 . . . .**24** E8
Ridgewell Ave CM1 . . . . .**31** F4
Ridgewell Cl RM10 . . . . .**154** B4
Ridgmont Pl RM11 . . . . .**136** D5
Ridgwell Ave RM16 . . . . .**159** A1
Ridings The
Canvey Island SS8 . . . .**164** A5
Great Baddow CM2 . . . . .**54** D7
Rochford SS4 . . . .**125** F1
Redbridge IG7 . . . .**112** B6
Ridley Cl Barking IG11 . . .**152** F5
Romford RM3 . . . .**114** B2
Ridley Cotts CM3 . . . .**80** C3
Ridley Rd Basildon SS13 .**121** C1
Chelmsford CM1 . . . . . .**32** B8
Riffams Ct SS13 . . . . . .**143** C8
Riffams Dr SS13 . . . . . .**143** C8
Riffhams CM13 . . . .**117** B7
Riffhams Chase CM3 . . . .**34** D2
Riffhams Dr CM3 . . . .**34** D2
Riffhams La Danbury CM3 .**56** C8
Little Baddow CM3 . . . . .**34** C1
Rigby Gdns RM16 . . . . .**174** B2
Rigby Mews IG1 . . . . . .**133** A2
Rigby Pl EN3 . . . .**65** A2
Rignal's La CM2 . . . .**54** D3
Ringwood Ave CM2 . . . . .**136** D2
Ringwood Dr SS9 . . . . . .**146** C7
Ringwood Ho ■ RM3 . . .**114** D4
Ripley Rd
Belvedere DA17 . . . . . .**169** A2
Ilford IG3 . . . .**133** F2
Ripley View IG10 . . . .**67** B1
Ripon Gdns IG1 . . . .**132** E4
Ripon Ho ■ RM3 . . . . . .**114** D4
Ripple Ct ⑩ IG11 . . . . .**152** D4
Ripple Jun Sch IG11 . . . .**152** E4
Ripple Prim Sch IG11 . . .**152** E5
Ripple Rd Barking IG11 . .**152** C5
Barking IG11 . . . .**152** E4
Dagenham IG11 . . . . . .**153** D4
Rippleside SS14 . . . . . .**142** F6
Rippleside Commercial Est
IG11 . . . .**153** C4
Risdens CM18 . . . .**23** D5
Rise Park Bvd RM1 . . . .**113** F2
Rise Park Jun & Inf Sch
RM1 . . . .**113** D2
Rise Park Par RM1 . . . . .**113** E1
Rise Pk SS15 . . . .**141** F6
Rise The
Buckhurst Hill IG9 . . . . .**88** D1
Chingford E4 . . . .**87** D1
Wanstead E11 . . . .**132** A6
Risebridge Chase RM1 . .**113** F3
Risebridge Rd RM2 . . . .**114** A2
Riseway CM15 . . . .**116** E7
Rising The CM11 . . . .**97** D1
Risings Terr RM11 . . . . .**136** F8
Rivendell Vale CM3 . . . . .**101** C4
Rivenhall
Thundersley SS7 . . . . . .**145** B8
Wickford SS11 . . . .**122** A6
River Ave EN11 . . . .**21** B7
River Blackwater Chalet Site
CM9 . . . .**37** C3
River Cl Holdbrook EN8 . . .**65** A5
Rainham RM13 . . . .**170** B8
Wanstead E11 . . . .**132** C5
River Cotts CM3 . . . .**33** F8
River Ct Purfleet RM19 . .**170** F2
Sawbridgeworth CM21 . . .**1** F3
Wanstead E11 . . . .**132** C5
River Dr RM14 . . . .**137** D5
River Lee Ctry Pk★ EN9 .**43** B1
River Meads SG12 . . . . . .**8** C4
River Rd Barking IG11 . . .**152** E2
Barking IG11 . . . .**153** B1
Brentwood CM14 . . . . . .**115** F6
Buckhurst Hill IG9 . . . . .**88** E1
River Road Bsns Pk
IG11 . . . .**152** F2

River View Althorne CM3 . .**82** E2
Dartford DA1 . . . .**176** A3
Grays RM16 . . . .**174** A1
River View Cl SS15 . . . .**119** C1
River View Rd SS7 . . . . .**144** E2
River Way Harlow CM20 . . .**11** B5
Loughton IG10 . . . .**89** A3
Riverdale SS9 . . . .**146** D7
Riverdale Rd DA8 . . . . . .**169** C1
Riverdene Rd IG1 . . . . . .**133** B1
Riverfield La CM21 . . . . . .**1** C1
Rivermead Gate CM1 . . . .**32** B4
Rivermead Ind Est CM1 . .**32** B4
Rivermill CM21 . . . .**1** C1
Riversdale Rd RM5 . . . . .**113** B3
Riverside CM1 . . . .**32** C3
Riverside Ave EN10 . . . . .**21** A1
Riverside Cotts
Barking IG11 . . . .**152** D3
North Fambridge CM3 . .**103** A6
Stanstead Abbotts SG12 . .**8** C4
Riverside Ct Chingford E4 .**87** B3
Harlow CM20 . . . .**11** C6
Riverside Ho SS12 . . . . .**121** D8
Riverside Ind Est
Barking IG11 . . . .**153** A2
Rochford SS4 . . . .**125** F1
Riverside Jun & Inf Schs
SS5 . . . .**101** E3
Riverside Pk CM1 . . . . . .**32** C3
Riverside Rd CM0 . . . . . .**106** C4
Riverside Wlk SS12 . . . .**121** B8
Riverside Works IG11 . . .**152** B5
Riversmead EN11 . . . . . .**21** A5
Riverton Dr CM0 . . . .**40** B1
Rivertons SS16 . . . .**142** F4
Riverview SS16 . . . .**143** F4
Riverview Ct
Basildon SS16 . . . .**142** E4
⑭ Belvedere DA17 . . . .**169** A1
Greenhithe DA9 . . . . . .**176** F1
Riverview Flats ⑬
RM19 . . . .**171** D1
Riverview Gdns SS5 . . . .**101** C3
Riverview Rd DA9 . . . . . .**177** A2
Riverview Terr ■ RM19 . .**171** B1
Riviera Dr SS1 . . . .**167** D8
Rivington Ave IG8 . . . . . .**110** D1
RJ Mitchell Prim Sch The
RM12 . . . .**155** B6
Roach RM18 . . . .**175** C2
Roach Ave SS6 . . . .**123** C4
Roach Vale SS9 . . . .**146** F4
Robert Cl Billericay CM12 . .**96** F2
Chelmsford CM2 . . . . . .**32** F4
Chigwell IG7 . . . .**111** F5
Robert Clack Lower Sch
RM8 . . . .**134** F2
Robert Clack Sch RM8 . .**135** A3
Robert Daniels Ct CM16 . .**67** E2
Robert Drake Prim Sch The
SS7 . . . .**144** D7
Robert Leonard Ind Est
SS2 . . . .**147** F5
Robert Way SS11 . . . . . .**121** F6
Roberts Cl RM3 . . . .**114** B2
Roberts Ct RM3 . . . .**54** E7
Roberts Rd
Basildon SS15 . . . .**141** B7
Belvedere DA17 . . . . . .**169** A1
Chingford E17 . . . .**109** B2
North Fambridge CM3 . .**103** A7
Robertson Cl RM17 . . . .**173** B2
Robertson Dr SS12 . . . .**121** E5
Robin Cl Billericay CM12 . .**97** C6
Romford RM5 . . . .**113** C3
Stanstead Abbotts SG12 . .**8** C3
Robin Hood Rd CM15 . . . .**94** C2
Robin Way CM2 . . . .**54** B5
Robin's La CM16 . . . .**67** C3
Robinia Cl Basildon SS15 **119** D1
Redbridge IG6 . . . .**111** E4
Robins The CM15 . . . . . .**72** D4
Robinson Cl RM12 . . . . .**155** B5
Robinson Rd
Dagenham RM10 . . . . .**154** A8
Horndon-on-t-H SS17 . . .**159** A4
Robinsons Cl CM0 . . . . . .**84** D3
Robinsway EN9 . . . .**65** E5
Robjohns Rd CM1 . . . . . .**53** E8
Roborough Wlk RM12 . . .**155** C6
Roche Ave SS4 . . . .**125** C2
Rochefort Dr SS4 . . . . . .**147** F8
Rochehall Way SS4 . . . .**148** B8
Rochester Dr SS0 . . . . . .**147** C4
Rochester Gdns IG1 . . . .**132** F4
Rochester Mews SS0 . . .**147** C4
Rochester Way
Basildon SS14 . . . .**142** F7
⑥ Chelmsford CM1 . . . .**32** B1
Rainham RM13 . . . .**154** D3
Rocheway SS4 . . . .**126** A2
Rochford Ave
Brentwood CM15 . . . . . .**95** A4
Ilford RM6 . . . .**134** C6
Loughton IG10 . . . .**89** C6
Southend-on-S SS0 . . . .**147** E1
Waltham Abbey EN9 . . . .**65** D6
Rochford Cl
Hornchurch RM12 . . . . .**155** B6
Wickford SS11 . . . .**121** F6
Rochford Cty Prim Sch
SS4 . . . .**125** E2
Rochford Garden Way
SS4 . . . .**125** E3
Rochford Gn IG10 . . . . . .**89** C6
Rochford Hall Cl SS4 . . .**125** D1

Rochford Hall Cotts
SS4 . . . .**125** D1
Rochford Ho EN9 . . . .**65** D6
Rochford Rd
Canvey Island SS8 . . . .**164** D3
Chelmsford CM2 . . . . . .**32** C1
Southend-on-S SS2 . . . .**147** E5
Rochford Sta SS4 . . . . . .**125** E1
Rock Gdns RM10 . . . . . .**154** B7
Rockall SS2 . . . .**147** A7
Rockchase Gdns RM11 . .**136** E5
Rockingham Ave RM11 . .**136** E5
Rocklands Ct RM17 . . . .**173** C1
Rockleigh Ave SS9 . . . . .**147** A1
Rockleigh Ct CM15 . . . . .**95** A2
Rockwell Rd RM10 . . . . .**154** B7
Rockwood Gdns IG10 . . . .**89** C6
Rodbridge Dr SS1 . . . . . .**167** E8
Roden Cl CM17 . . . .**11** F4
Roden St IG1 . . . .**133** A1
Roden Terr CM5 . . . .**15** A1
Roding Ave IG8 . . . .**110** E4
Roding Cl Fyfield CM5 . . . .**27** D2
Great Wakering SS3 . . . .**150** B4
Roding Dr CM15 . . . .**71** F2
Roding Gdns IG10 . . . . . .**88** E3
Roding Hall RM4 . . . .**90** B6
Roding Hospl IG4 . . . . . .**132** D8
Roding La
Buckhurst Hill IG9, IG7 . .**88** E1
Chigwell IG7 . . . .**89** A1
Roding La N IG8 . . . . . .**110** E2
Roding La S IG4 . . . . . .**132** D7
Roding Leigh CM3 . . . . .**101** E2
Roding Lodge IG1 . . . . .**132** D5
Roding Prim Sch
Barking RM8 . . . .**153** C7
Woodford IG8 . . . .**110** E3
Roding Rd IG10 . . . .**88** F3
Roding The CM14 . . . . . .**94** B1
Roding Valley High Sch
IG10 . . . .**88** E4
Roding Valley Meadows
(Nature Reserve)★
IG10 . . . .**89** A2
Roding Valley Sta IG9 . .**110** D6
Roding View
Buckhurst Hill IG9 . . . . .**88** D1
Chipping Ongar CM5 . . . .**49** B4
Roding Way
Rainham RM13 . . . .**155** D3
Wickford SS12 . . . .**121** E7
Rodings Ave SS17 . . . . .**160** D4
Rodings Ct E4 . . . .**109** D5
Rodings Prim Sch CM6 . .**15** C8
Rodings The
Southend-on-S SS9 . . . .**146** D7
Upminster RM14 . . . . . .**137** D5
■ Woodford IG8 . . . . .**110** C4
Rodney Cres EN11 . . . . . .**21** A8
Rodney Rd
Chipping Ongar CM5 . . . .**48** F2
Wanstead E11 . . . .**132** B7
Rodney Way
Chelmsford CM1 . . . . . .**53** E7
Romford RM7 . . . .**113** B2
Rodwells SS13 . . . .**149** E4
Roebuck Ct E4 . . . .**109** C3
Roebuck La IG9 . . . .**88** C1
Roebuck Rd IG6 . . . .**112** B4
Roebuck Trad Est IG6 . . .**112** B4
Roedean Cl SS2 . . . .**148** F1
Roedean Dr RM1 . . . . . .**135** E7
Roedean Gdns SS2 . . . . .**148** F2
Roger Reede's Almshouses
RM1 . . . .**135** E7
Rogers Gdns RM10 . . . .**154** A7
Rogers Ho ■ RM10 . . . .**135** A1
Rogers Rd
Dagenham RM10 . . . . .**154** A7
Grays RM17 . . . .**173** C2
Roggel Rd SS8 . . . .**164** D2
Rohan Ct SS6 . . . .**101** D6
Rokeby Gdns IG8 . . . . . .**110** A2
Rokells SS14 . . . .**142** A7
Rokescroft SS13 . . . . . .**143** A5
Roland La SS8 . . . .**164** B4
Rolands Cl CM1 . . . .**32** B7
Roles Gr RM6 . . . .**134** E7
Roll Gdns IG2 . . . .**133** A6
Rollestons CM1 . . . .**52** F8
Rolls Park Ave E4 . . . . .**109** B5
Rolls Park Rd E4 . . . . . .**109** B5
Rom Cres RM7 . . . .**135** F4
Rom Valley Way RM7 . . .**135** C4
Romagne Cl SS17 . . . . . .**159** F3
Romainville Way SS8 . . .**163** C3
Roman RM18 . . . .**175** C2
Roman Cl Maldon CM9 . . . .**36** F4
Mountnessing CM15 . . . .**95** E8
Roman Ct ⑧ SS11 . . . . .**122** A5
Roman Ho
⑧ Chelmsford CM2 . . . .**32** B1
Rainham RM13 . . . .**154** D3
Roman Mews ⑦ EN11 . . .**21** A7
Roman Rd Ilford IG1 . . . .**152** B6
Ingatestone CM4 . . . . . .**73** F1
Little Waltham CM3 . . . . .**19** B5
Mountnessing CM15 . . . .**95** E8
Roman Rise CM21 . . . . . .**1** D2
Roman St ⑧ EN11 . . . . . .**21** A7
Roman Vale CM17 . . . . . .**11** C5
Roman Way
Billericay CM12 . . . . . .**119** A8
Burnham-on-C CM0 . . . .**106** D4
Waltham Abbey EN9 . . . .**65** B4

Romans Farm Chase
CM0 . . . .**106** C2
Romans Pl CM1 . . . .**31** B1
Romans Way CM1 . . . . . .**31** B1
Romanshurst CM9 . . . . . .**37** A4
Romany Stps ⑰ SS1 . . .**167** C7
Romeland EN9 . . . .**65** C6
Romford Rd
Aveley RM15 . . . .**171** C7
Chipping Ongar CM5 . . . .**70** F7
Ilford E12 . . . .**133** A1
Redbridge IG6 . . . .**112** C5
Upminster RM15 . . . . . .**156** C5
Romford Sta RM1 . . . . .**135** E5
Romney Chase RM11 . . .**137** A6
Romney Ho SS4 . . . .**125** F2
Romney Rd CM12 . . . . . .**96** F3
Romsey Cl Hockley SS5 . .**124** D6
South Benfleet SS7 . . . .**144** A5
Stanford-le-H SS17 . . . .**160** B1
Romsey Cres SS7 . . . . .**144** B5
Romsey Dr SS7 . . . .**144** B5
Romsey Gdns RM9 . . . . .**153** C2
Romsey Rd
Dagenham RM9 . . . . . .**153** D4
South Benfleet SS7 . . . .**144** A5
Romsey Way SS7 . . . . . .**144** B5
Romside Commercial Ctr
RM7 . . . .**135** D7
Ronald Dr SS6 . . . .**123** A4
Ronald Hill Gr SS9 . . . . .**146** D7
Ronald Park Ave SS0 . . .**147** C2
Ronald Rd RM3 . . . .**115** C4
Roneo Cnr RM12 . . . . . .**135** F3
Roneo Link RM12 . . . . . .**135** F2
Ronnie La E12 . . . .**152** A8
Ronver Lodge E4 . . . . . .**109** F4
Roodegate SS14 . . . . . .**142** A6
Rook Cl RM13 . . . .**155** C6
Rook Lodge IG1 . . . .**132** D5
Rookery Cl Rayleigh SS6 .**123** C2
Stanford-le-H SS17 . . . .**160** B1
Rookery Cres RM10 . . . .**154** B5
Rookery Hill SS17 . . . . .**161** C3
Rookery La CM3 . . . .**80** C3
Rookery Mead CM3 . . . . .**101** D8
Rookery Rd CM4 . . . .**50** D4
Rookery The RM20 . . . . .**177** A8
Rookery View RM17 . . . .**173** D1
Rookes Cres CM1 . . . . . .**31** F1
Rookley Ct ⑮ RM9 . . . . .**171** B1
Rookwood Ave IG10 . . . . .**89** C6
Rookwood Ct RM17 . . . .**173** B2
Rookwood Gdns E4 . . . .**109** F5
Rookwood Ho IG11 . . . . .**152** D3
Rookyards SS16 . . . . . .**142** F5
Roosevelt Ave SS8 . . . . .**164** A4
Roosevelt Rd ■ SS15 . . .**141** A4
Roosevelt Way RM10 . . .**154** D6
Roothings The CM9 . . . . .**37** B5
Roots Hall Ave SS2 . . . .**147** C3
Roots Hall Dr SS2 . . . . .**147** C2
Rope Wlk CM9 . . . .**37** A4
Roper's Chase CM1 . . . . .**53** A7
Ropers Ave E4 . . . .**109** C5
Rosalind Ct ⑥ IG11 . . . .**153** A5
Rosary Gdns SS0 . . . . . .**147** B4
Rosbach Rd SS8 . . . . . .**164** D3
Rosberg Rd SS8 . . . . . .**164** E5
Roscommon Way SS8 . . .**163** C3
Rose & Crown Mews
CM0 . . . .**84** D4
Rose Ave E18 . . . .**110** B1
Rose Bank CM14 . . . . . .**116** D7
Rose Cl ⑩ SS12 . . . . . .**121** C5
Rose Cotts Harlow CM17 . .**24** F5
Willingale CM5 . . . .**28** D3
Rose Ct IG1 . . . .**152** B6
Rose Dr CM0 . . . .**84** D3
Rose Glen Chelmsford CM2 **54** C7
Romford RM7 . . . .**135** E3
Rose Hatch Ave RM6 . . .**134** D4
Rose La Billericay CM12 . . .**97** A2
Dagenham RM6 . . . . . .**134** E7
Rose Park Ct IG5 . . . . . .**110** F1
Rose St DA11 . . . .**178** B1
Rose Tree Mews IG8 . . .**110** E4
Rose Vale EN11 . . . .**21** A4
Rose Valley CM14 . . . . .**116** D7
Rose Valley Cres SS17 . .**160** E4
Rose Way SS4 . . . .**148** A8
Roseacre Cl RM11 . . . . .**136** F4
Roseacres CM21 . . . .**1** D3
Rosebank EN9 . . . .**65** C6
Rosebank Ave RM12 . . . .**155** C7
Rosebay Ave CM12 . . . . .**96** F5
Roseberry Ave
Basildon SS16 . . . .**141** B4
South Benfleet SS7 . . . .**144** C7
Roseberry Ct SS7 . . . . .**144** C7
Roseberry Gdns RM14 . .**137** F5
Roseberry Wlk SS7 . . . .**144** C7
Rosebery Rd
Chelmsford CM2 . . . . . .**54** B8
Grays RM17 . . . .**177** E8
Rosebury Ct CM13 . . . . . .**95** D3
Rosebury Sq ② IG8 . . . .**111** A3
Rosecroft Cl SS16 . . . . .**141** A4
Rosedale Gdns RM9 . . . .**153** B5
Rosedale Rd
Dagenham RM9 . . . . . .**153** B5
Grays RM17 . . . .**173** D1
Romford RM1 . . . .**135** C8
Rosedene Gdns IG2 . . . .**133** C4

Roselaine SS14 ....142 B7
Roselands Ave EN11 ......8 A1
Roselawn Fields CM1 ....32 B8
Roseley Cotts CM20 .....10 B4
Rosemary Ave RM1 ......135 F8
Rosemary Cl Harlow CM17 11 C4
South Ockendon RM15 ....157 C2
Rosemary Cotts CM3 .....20 E1
Rosemary Dr IG4 ......132 D6
Rosemary Gdns RM8 ....134 F3
Rosemary Lodge SS2 ....147 F1
Rosemead SS7 ....144 C7
Rosemead Gdns CM13 ....95 D5
Rosemount CM19 ....23 A5
Rosemount Cl IG8 .....110 F4
Roserna Rd SS8 ....164 D3
Roses The IG8 ....109 F3
Rosetti Terr RM8 ......153 B8
Rosewood Ave RM12 ....155 A7
Rosewood Ct RM15 ....157 E2
Rosewood Ct RM6 .....134 C6
Rosewood La SS3 ......168 F7
Rosherville CE Prim Sch
DA11 ....178 E1
Rosherville Way DA11 ...178 E1
Rosilian Dr SS5 ......102 C1
Roslings Cl CM1 ......31 D5
Roslyn Gdns RM2 .....113 F1
Ross Ave RM8 ....134 F3
Ross Way SS16 ....141 B3
Rossall Cl RM11 ......136 A5
Rossdene Gdns CM6 ....15 D7
Rossendale CM1 ......31 E1
Rosshill Ind Pk SS2 ...148 A4
Rossiter Rd SS3 ......168 H8
Rosslyn Ave Chingford E4 109 F8
Dagenham RM8 ....135 A4
Romford RM3 ....114 F1
Rosslyn Cl SS5 ......124 E7
Rosslyn Ct SS17 ......160 C1
Rosslyn Rd Barking IG11 152 D5
Billericay CM12 ....96 F2
Hockley SS5 ....124 E7
Roth Dr CM13 ....117 B8
Rothbury Ave RM13 ....170 B8
Rothbury Ho RM3 ....114 D4
Rothbury Rd CM1 .....31 D1
Rothesay Ave CM2 ....54 A8
Rothmans Ave CM2 ....54 E6
Rothwell Cl SS9 ......146 C6
Rothwell Gdns RM9 ...153 C4
Rothwell Rd RM9 .....153 C4
Rotunda The RM7 ....135 D6
Rough Hill Farm Cotts
CM3 ....78 C7
Roughtallys CM16 .....46 F4
Roughtons CM2 ......54 C3
Round Hill Rd SS7 ....145 A2
Roundacre SS14 ......142 A6
Roundaway Rd IG5 ....110 F1
Roundbush Bglws CM9 ..81 C8
Roundbush Rd CM9 ....81 A8
Rounders Ct RM10 ....154 B6
Roundhills EN9 ....65 E4
Roundmead Ave IG10 ..89 A6
Roundmead Cl IG10 ...89 A7
Roundwood Ave CM3 ..95 B2
Roundwood Gr CM13 ..95 B2
Roundwood Lake CM13 .95 B2
Rounton Rd EN9 ......65 E6
Rous Chase CM2 ......54 B1
Rous Rd IG9 ....88 E1
Rover Ave IG6 ....111 F4
Rowallen Par RM8 ....134 C3
Rowan Cl Ilford IG1 ...152 D7
Rayleigh SS6 ....123 B6
Rowan Dr CM9 ....37 C5
Rowan Gr RM5 ......171 C6
Rowan Green E CM13 ..116 F7
Rowan Green W CM13 .116 F7
Rowan Ho
Basildon SS13 ....143 B8
Ilford IG1 ....152 D7
Rowan Way
Canewdon SS4 ....104 E1
Ilford RM6 ....134 C8
South Ockendon RM15 ..157 C1
Rowan Wlk
Hornchurch RM11 .....136 D7
Southend-on-S SS9 ...146 D6
Rowans The
Aveley RM15 ....171 C6
Billericay CM11 ......119 D8
Rayleigh SS9 ....146 B6
Rowans Way
Loughton IG10 ......88 F5
Wickford SS11 ....121 E8
Rowden Par E4 ......109 A4
Rowden Park Gdns E4 ..109 A4
Rowden Rd E4 ......109 B4
Rowdowns Rd RM9 ....153 F5
Rowe Gdns IG11 .....153 A3
Rowenhall SS16 ......140 F6
Rowhedge CM13 ......117 B7
Rowhedge Cl SS13 ....121 D2
Rowland Cres IG7 ....111 E6
Rowland Wlk RM4 ....113 E7
Rowlands Rd RM8 ....134 F2
Rowlands The SS7 ....144 E3
Rowley Mead CM16 ....46 C6
Rowley Rd RM16 .....174 A8
Rowney Gdns
Dagenham RM9 ......153 C6
Sawbridgeworth CM21 ..11 C8
Rowney Rd RM9 ......153 B6
Rowney Wood CM21 ....1 C1
Rows The CM20 ......10 D1
Roxburgh Ave RM14 ...137 C1

Roxwell Ave CM1 ......31 D3
Roxwell CE Prim Sch
CM1 ....30 A6
Roxwell Gdns CM13 ...95 C4
Roxwell Ho IG10 .....88 E2
Roxwell Rd Barking IG11 153 A3
Chelmsford CM1 ......31 C4
Roxwell CM1 ....30 E5
Writtle CM1 ....31 A4
Roxwell Way IG8 .....110 C3
Roxy Ave RM6 ....134 C4
Roy Gdns IG2 ....133 F6
Royal Artillery Way SS2 148 F2
Royal Cl Ilford IG3 ....134 A4
Rochford SS4 ....125 D5
Royal Ct Basildon SS15 141 B7
Brentwood CM14 .....116 C7
Maldon CM9 ....37 A1
Royal Docks Rd E6 ...152 B1
Royal Gunpowder Mills★
EN9 ....65 B7
Royal Jubilee Ct RM2 .136 A8
Royal Liberty Sch The
RM2 ....136 C8
Royal Mews SS1 .....167 A7
Royal Oak Chase SS15 .141 E8
Royal Oak Ct RM8 ....134 C2
Royal Oak Dr SS11 ...122 A8
Royal Par RM10 .....154 B6
Royal Pier Rd DA12 ..179 C1
Royal Terr SS1 ......167 A7
Royals The SS1 ......167 A7
Roycraft Ave IG11 ...152 F3
Roycroft Cl E18 .....110 B2
Roydon Bridge SS14 ..142 D8
Roydon Cl IG10 .....88 E2
Roydon Lodge Chalet Est
CM19 ....9 C1
Roydon Mill CM19 .....9 A1
Roydon Prim Sch CM19 .22 B8
Roydon Rd Harlow CM19 .9 E1
Stanstead Abbotts SG12 ..8 E4
Roydon Sta CM19 .....9 B2
Royer Cl SS5 ....125 A4
Royle Cl RM2 ....136 B6
Royston Ave
Basildon SS15 ....119 D1
Chingford E4 ....109 B5
Southend-on-S SS2 ...148 B3
Royston Ct IG1 .....132 D5
Royston Gdns IG1 ....132 D5
Royston Par IG1 ....132 D5
Royston Rd RM3 .....115 A3
Rubens Cl SS3 ......168 G8
Rubens Gate CM1 .....32 F7
Rubicon Are SS11 ....121 F8
Rubin Pl EN3 ....65 A2
Ruby Ct
Rainham RM13 ....155 A1
Southend-on-S SS9 ...146 E5
Rue De St Lawrence EN9 65 C5
Ruffles Cl SS6 ......123 E4
Rugby Gdns RM9 .....153 C6
Rugby Rd RM9 ......153 C6
Rumbold Rd EN11 .....21 C8
Rumbullion Dr CM12 ..96 F3
Rumford Sh Hall The
RM1 ....135 E7
Rumsey Fields CM3 ...56 F7
Rumsey Row CM1 ....31 B1
Runcorn Ho RM3 ....114 E4
Rundells CM18 ......24 A4
Rundells Wlk SS14 ...142 E7
Rundels Cotts SS7 ...145 A6
Rundels The SS7 ....145 A6
Running Mare La CM3 ..54 A3
Running Waters CM13 .117 A6
Runnymede Chase SS7 .145 A5
Runnymede Ct SS17 ..160 C1
Runnymede Rd
Canvey Island SS8 ...164 C6
Stanford-le-H SS17 ..160 C1
Runsell Ct CM3 ......56 F7
Runsell La CM3 .....56 F8
Runsell View CM3 ....57 A7
Runwell Gdns SS11 ...99 C3
Runwell Hospl SS11 ..100 A5
Runwell Prim Sch SS11 .99 D2
Runwell Rd SS11 ....100 B3
Runwell Terr SS1 ....166 F7
Runwood Rd SS8 ....163 C4
Rupert Rd CM0 ......84 C4
Rural Cl RM11 ......136 B3
Rural Vale DA11 ....178 E1
Rurik Ct CM9 ....58 F8
Rush Cl
South Benfleet SS7 ..144 B6
Stanstead Abbotts SG12 ..8 C4
Rush Croft Sch E4 ...109 B3
Rush Dr EN9 ....65 C3
Rush Green Gdns RM7 .135 C3
Rush Green Inf Sch
RM7 ....135 D3
Rush Green Rd RM7 ..135 D3
Rushbottom La SS7 ..144 B7
Rushcroft Rd E4 ....109 B3
Rushden Gdns
Ilford IG5 ....133 A8
Redbridge IG5 ......111 A1
Rushdene Rd
Billericay CM12 ......96 F1
Brentwood CM15 .....94 C2
Rushdon Cl Grays RM17 173 A3
Romford RM1 ....136 A6
Rushes La CM0 ......63 A1
Rushes Mead CM18 ...23 E6
Rushfield CM21 ......1 E2
Rushley SS13 ....121 D1

Rushley Cl Grays RM16 .173 D5
Great Wakering SS3 ..150 A4
Rushleydale CM1 ....32 E5
Rushmere Ave RM14 ..137 C1
Rusholme Rd RM10 ...135 A1
Rushton Ct RM1 .....136 A6
Rushton Gr CM17 ....24 E8
Ruskin Ave
Southend-on-S SS2 ..148 B2
Upminster RM14 ....137 C1
Waltham Abbey EN9 ..65 E5
Ruskin Dene CM12 ...97 A3
Ruskin Gdns RM3 ....114 B3
Ruskin Gr RM1 ......176 A2
Ruskin Path SS12 ...121 D5
Ruskin Rd
Belvedere DA17 .....169 A2
Chelmsford CM2 .....32 E2
Grays RM16 ....174 A2
Stanford-le-H SS17 ..160 C1
Ruskoi Rd SS8 ......163 F5
Rusper Rd RM9 .....153 C6
Russel Rd RM17 ....173 A2
Russell Cl Basildon SS15 141 B6
Brentwood CM15 ....94 B2
Russell Ct SS11 .....121 F7
Russell Gdns
Chelmsford CM2 .....54 A4
Ilford IG1 ....133 D4
Wickford SS11 ......121 F7
Russell Gr SS4 .....126 A2
Russell Lodge E4 ...109 C8
Russell Quay DA11 ..179 A1
Russell Rd
Buckhurst Hill IG9 ...88 C1
Gravesend DA12 ....179 D1
North Fambridge CM3 ..81 B1
Tilbury RM18 ....178 F5
Russell Way SS11 ....53 E7
Russet Cl SS17 .....160 D3
Russet Ho RM17 ....178 C7
Russet Way
Burnham-on-C CM0 ..106 C6
Hockley SS5 ....124 F8
Russets Galleywood CM2 .54 C3
Hornchurch RM11 ...136 E7
Russets Cl E4 ......109 D6
Russets The SS4 ....125 D5
Russetts SS16 ......141 A5
Rustic Cl RM14 .....137 E3
Rutherford Cl
Billericay CM12 ......97 A5
Southend-on-S SS9 ..146 C6
Rutherfords CM1 .....19 B1
Ruthven Cl SS12 ....121 D6
Rutland App RM11 ...137 A6
Rutland Ave SS1 ....167 E7
Rutland Cl SS15 ....141 A6
Rutland Dr
Hornchurch RM11 ...137 A6
Rayleigh SS6 ....123 C7
Rutland Gate DA17 ..169 B1
Rutland Gdns
Dagenham RM8 .....153 C7
Rochford SS4 ....125 C5
Rutland Ho RM7 ....113 A1
Rutland Rd
Chelmsford CM2 .....32 A7
Ilford IG1 ....133 D4
North Fambridge CM3 .103 A7
Wanstead E11 ......132 B6
Rutley Cl RM3 .....114 D1
Rydal Cl Hullbridge SS5 .101 D3
Rayleigh SS6 ....123 E2
Rydal Dr CM9 ......59 B8
Ryde Cl SS9 ....146 B5
Ryde Dr SS17 ......175 C8
Ryde The SS9 ......146 B5
Ryder Gdns RM13 ...154 F6
Ryder Way SS13 ....121 D2
Rye Cl RM12 ......155 C7
Rye Field The CM3 ...34 D3
Rye Hill Rd CM18 ....23 E2
Rye House Gatehouse★
EN11 ....21 D8
Rye House Sta EN11 ..21 C8
Rye Mead SS16 .....141 C4
Rye Mead Cotts EN11 ..21 C8
Rye Rd EN11 ....21 C8
Rye Wlk CM4 ......74 A2
Ryecroft CM19 ......23 B8
Ryecroft Ave IG5 ....111 B1
Ryedene SS16 ......142 F3
Ryedene Cl SS16 ....142 E3
Ryedene Com Prim Sch
SS16 ....142 F3
Ryedene Pl SS16 ....142 F3
Ryefield Cl EN11 .....8 B2
Ryelands Prim Sch EN11 21 B7
Ryes La CM22 ....3 B7
Rykhill RM16 ....174 B3
Rylands Rd SS2 ....148 D2
Ryle The CM1 ......53 A8
Rysley CM3 ....34 D4

S

Sabina Rd RM16 .....174 C2
Sabines Rd RM4 .....92 E6
Sable Way SS15 ....140 F7
Sackville Cl CM1 ....31 E4
Sackville Cres RM3 ..114 E2
Sackville Gdns IG1 ..132 F3
Sackville Rd SS2 ...148 E1
Sacred Heart of Mary RC
Girls Sch RM14 .....137 B2

Sacred Heart RC Sch
SS1 ....167 C8
Saddle Rise CM1 ....32 E8
Saddleworth Rd RM3 .114 C4
Sadlers SS7 ....144 B6
Sadlers Cl CM1 .....97 D5
Sadlers Mead CM18 ..24 A7
Saffery Cl SS9 ......146 C7
Saffron Cl
Horndon-on-t-H SS17 .160 A3
West Horndon CM13 .139 D5
Saffron Croft CM9 ....36 E2
Saffron Ct SS15 ....140 F6
Saffron Gdns SS17 ..159 F5
Saffron Rd Grays RM16 172 C2
Romford RM5 ......113 D1
Saffron Wlk CM11 ...97 B2
Saint's Wlk RM16 ...174 C2
SS Peter & Paul's Prim Sch
CM1 ....133 D1
St Agnes Dr SS8 ....163 D4
St Agnes Rd CM2 ...119 C3
St Aidan's RC Prim Sch
CM1 ....133 D3
St Aidans Ct IG11 ...153 B3
St Alban's Ave E6 ...152 A2
St Alban's Cres IG8 .110 A2
St Alban's RC Prim Sch
RM12 ....155 B5
St Alban's Rd
Coopersale CM16 ....46 D2
Woodford IG8 ......110 A3
St Albans Ave RM14 .137 E2
St Albans RC Prim Sch
CM20 ....10 F2
St Albans Rd IG3 ...133 F4
St Andrew's CE Prim Sch
SG12 ....8 D4
St Andrew's Ho CM20 .10 F2
St Andrew's Mdw CM18 .23 F7
St Andrew's Rd
Redbridge IG1 ......132 F4
Rochford SS4 ....125 E4
Tilbury RM18 ....178 E5
St Andrews Ave
Hornchurch RM12 ...155 A8
Rainham RM12 .....154 F7
St Andrews CE Prim Sch
CM16 ....47 C6
St Andrews Cl
Canvey Island SS8 ..163 D4
North Weald Bassett CM16 .47 D7
St Andrews Ct DA11 .179 B1
St Andrews Dr CM1 ..97 B3
St Andrews La SS15 .141 C7
St Andrews Pl CM15 .116 F8
St Andrews Rd
Boreham CM3 ......20 F1
Romford RM7 ......135 D5
Southend-on-S SS3 ..168 D6
St Ann's IG11 ......152 C4
St Ann's Rd
Barking IG11 ....152 C4
Southend-on-S SS2 ..148 A1
St Anne Line RC Jun & Inf
Schs SS15 ....141 F6
St Anne's Pk EN10 ...21 A4
St Anne's Rd CM15 ..95 C8
St Anne's Sch CM2 ..32 A1
St Annes RM16 .....173 B5
St Annes Ct CM16 ...173 B5
St Annes Ct CM1 ....32 C3
St Annes Rd SS8 ...164 E3
St Annes Terr IG6 ..111 E5
St Anns Cl SS15 ....141 C7
St Anselm's RC Prim Sch
DA1 ....176 A2
St Anthony's Ave IG8 110 C3
St Anthony's Dr CM2 .54 C3
St Antony's RC Prim Sch
IG8 ....110 A6
St Aubyn's Sch IG8 ..109 F3
St Audrey's Rd CM16 174 B2
St Augustine Rd RM8 .174 B2
St Augustine's Ave SS1 168 B7
St Augustine's RC Prim Sch
Hoddesdon EN11 ....21 B6
Ilford IG2 ....133 B6
St Awdry's Rd IG11 .152 D5
St Barnabas Rd IG8 .110 C3
St Bede's RC Prim Sch
RM6 ....134 C6
St Benet's Rd SS7 ...147 F3
St Bernard's High Sch
SS0 ....166 B8
St Catharine's Rd EN10 .21 A4
St Catherine's Hoddesdon CE
Prim Sch EN11 .....21 B6
St Catherine's Rd CM1 .31 E2
St Catherines Cl SS11 121 F8
St Catherines Rd E4 .109 A8
St Cecilia Rd RM2 ..174 B2
St Cedd's CE Prim Sch
CM0 ....42 B2
St Cedd's Sch CM1 ..32 A4
St Cedds Ct RM16 ...173 B5
St Chad's Gdns RM6 .134 C4
St Chad's Rd
Dagenham RM6 .....134 C4
Tilbury RM16,RM18 ..179 A7
St Chad's Sch RM18 .179 A6
St Chads Cl SS15 ...141 C4
St Charles Dr SS11 ..121 E7
St Charles Rd CM14 ..94 B3
St Christopher Sch The
SS9 ....146 F4
St Christophers Cl SS8 163 D4

St Clair Cl IG5 ......110 F1
St Clare Mdw SS4 ...125 F3
St Clement's Ave
Grays RM16 ....177 B8
Southend-on-S SS9 ..146 A3
St Clement's Cl SS7 .144 D5
St Clement's Cres SS7 144 D5
St Clement's Ct SS9 .165 D8
St Clement's Dr SS9 .146 E3
St Clement's Rd
Grays RM16 ....177 C7
South Benfleet SS7 ..144 D5
St Clements Cl SS5 ..125 A4
St Clements Ct
Grays RM17 ....177 F8
Purfleet RM19 .....171 A2
Waltham Abbey EN9 ..65 C6
St Clere's Comp Sch
SS17 ....175 C8
St Cleres Cres SS11 .121 F7
St Cleres Way CM3 ...56 D7
St Cross Ct SS11 ....21 A4
St Cross RC Prim Sch
EN11 ....21 A4
St Cuthberts Rd EN11 ..8 C1
St David's Ct RM1 ...135 F4
St David's Rd SS16 ..141 B4
St David's Way SS11 .121 E7
St Davids Cl SS11 ..132 B6
St Davids Dr SS9 ...146 A3
St Davids Terr SS9 ..146 A3
St Davids Wlk SS8 ..163 D4
St Dunstan's Rd SG12 ..9 D8
St Edith's Cl CM12 ..97 A1
St Ediths La CM12 ...97 A1
St Edmund's Cl SS2 .148 C3
St Edmund's Rd IG1 .132 F5
St Edmund's Way CM17 .11 C4
St Edmunds Rd DA1 .176 A3
St Edward's CE Comp Sch
RM7 ....135 A5
St Edward's CE Prim Sch
RM1 ....135 E8
St Edwards Way RM1,
RM7 ....135 D6
St Egberts Way E4 ...87 C1
St Erkenwald Mews
IG11 ....152 D4
St Erkenwald Rd IG11 152 D4
St Erkenwelds Ct SS1 167 C8
St Ethelburga Ct RM3 .115 A1
St Fabian's Dr CM1 ..31 E4
St Fidelis' Rd DA8 ..169 D1
St Francis Ct SS2 ...148 C1
St Francis RC Prim Sch
CM9 ....36 E2
St Francis Way
Grays RM16 ....174 C3
Ilford IG1 ....152 D8
St Francis' Rd DA8 ..168 B3
St Gabriel's Cl E11 ..132 B3
St Gabriels Ct SS13 .143 B5
St George's Ave
Grays RM17 ....173 C2
Hornchurch RM11 ...136 B5
St George's Ct CM14 ..94 B2
St George's Ctr DA11 179 B1
St George's Dr SS0 .147 E3
St George's Hospl
RM12 ....155 D7
St George's La SS3 ..168 F6
St George's Park Ave
SS0 ....147 B2
St George's RC Prim Sch
SS3 ....168 E8
St George's Rd IG1 ..132 F5
St Georges Ct
Heybridge Basin CM9 .37 D3
Hook End CM15 ....72 B4
St Georges Ct
Romford RM1 ......135 F5
Romford RM7 ......135 C7
St Georges Rd RM9 .153 E8
St Georges Wlk
Canvey Island SS8 ..163 D4
South Benfleet SS7 ..144 B6
St Giles Ave RM10 ..154 B5
St Giles Cl
Dagenham RM10 ....154 B5
Maldon CM9 ....36 E2
Orsett RM16 ....174 A8
St Giles Cres CM9 ...36 E2
St Gregorys Ho CM16 ..68 A8
St Guiberts Rd SS8 ..163 E5
St Helen's Ct CM16 ..46 A1
St Helen's RC Inf Sch
CM14 ....116 D8
St Helen's RC Prim Sch
SS1 ....166 F8
St Helen's Rd
Redbridge IG1 ......132 F5
Southend-on-S SS0 ..166 E8
St Helens Rd CM13 ..155 A1
St Helens Wlk CM12 ..96 F4
St Hildas Sch SS0 ...147 C1
St Ives Cl RM3 .....114 F3
St Ivians Dr RM2 ...136 A8
St Jame's Ho RM1 ..135 F6
St James Ave SS16 ..163 B7
St James Ave E SS17 160 E3
St James Ave W SS17 .160 E3
St James CE Prim Sch
CM18 ....23 D4
St James Cl
Canvey Island SS8 ..163 D4

St James Cl *continued*
Southend-on-S SS0 ......147 A3
St James Ct
Canvey Island SS8 ......164 B1
Greenhithe DA9 ....176 F1
Romford RM1 ....135 F7
Wanstead E12 ....132 C2
St James Ctr CM20 ....11 A4
St James Gate IG9 .....88 B1
St James Gdns
Ilford RM6 ....134 B7
Southend-on-S SS0 ......147 A3
St James Mews CM12 ....97 A2
St James Pk CM1 ....31 D4
St James Rd SS16 ......142 D5
St James' Ave CM5 ......49 A1
St James's Ave DA11 ...179 A1
St James's Rd
Brentwood CM14 ....116 C7
Gravesend DA11 ....179 A1
St James's St DA11 .....179 A1
St James's Wlk SS5 ....124 C6
St John Fisher RC Jun Sch
IG10 ....89 C7
St John Payne RC Comp Sch
CM1 ....31 F6
St John The Baptist CE Prim Sch IG2 ....8 A5
St John's Ave
Brentwood CM14 ....116 D6
Chelmsford CM2 ....54 B8
Harlow CM17 ....11 C4
St John's CE Prim Sch
IG9 ....88 B1
St John's CE Sec Sch
CM16 ....45 E1
St John's Cl RM13 .....155 A5
St John's Ct IG9 ....88 B1
St John's Danbury CE Prim Sch CM3 ....56 F2
St John's Gn CM1 ....31 B1
St John's Hospl CM2 ....53 F6
St John's Lodge IG10 ...88 F7
St John's Rd
Barking IG11 ....152 E4
Billericay CM11 ....97 B3
Chelmsford CM2 ....54 B8
Chingford, Chingford Hatch E4 ....109 B6
Chingford, Highams Park E17 ....109 C1
Epping CM16 ....45 F1
Erith DA8 ....169 D1
Great Wakering SS3 ....150 B3
Hadleigh SS7 ....145 C3
Loughton IG10 ....88 F7
Southend-on-S SS0 .....166 E8
Writtle CM1 ....31 B1
St John's Sch CM2 ......97 B3
St John's Way SS17 ....160 F4
St Johns Cl
Basildon SS15 ....141 C7
Great Wakering SS3 ....150 B3
St Johns Cres SS8 ......163 D3
St Johns Ct Erith DA8 ..169 D1
Mayland CM3 ....83 A8
Southend-on-S SS1 .....166 F7
St Johns Dr SS6 ....122 F4
St Johns La SG12 ....8 A1
St Johns Mews SS17 ...160 F4
St Johns Pl CM11 ....98 B4
St Johns RC Sch IG8 ...111 A5
St Johns Rd Grays RM16 .174 B1
Ilford IG2 ....133 E4
Romford RM5 ....113 C5
St Johns Wlk CM17 ......11 C4
St Joseph The Worker RC Prim Sch CM13 ......95 C3
St Joseph's Convent Sch
E11 ....132 A5
St Joseph's Ct E4 ....87 D2
St Joseph's RC Prim Sch
Canvey Island SS8 .....164 B4
Dagenham RM9 ....153 F8
South Woodham Ferrers CM3 ....101 E7
Stanford-le-H SS17 .....160 D2
Upminster RM14 ....137 B2
St Josephs RC Prim Sch
IG11 ....152 C4
St Judes Ct IG8 ....110 A3
St Katherine's CE Prim Sch
SS8 ....164 A1
St Katherines Ct SS8 ...163 E3
St Kathryns Pl RM14 ...137 C2
St Kilda's Rd CM15 ......94 C2
St Lawrence Ct SS9 ....146 E6
St Lawrence Dr
St Lawrence CM0 ....40 B1
Steeple CM0 ....62 B8
St Lawrence Gdns
Blackmore CM4 ....72 C4
Southend-on-S SS9 ....146 E6
St Lawrence Hill CM0 ....62 E5
St Lawrence Rd
Tillingham CM0 ....63 D5
Upminster RM14 ....137 C2
St Leonard's Ave E4 ...109 D4
St Leonard's CE Jun Sch
CM0 ....84 D4
St Leonard's Rd SS1 ...167 B7
St Leonards Cl RM17 ...177 F8
St Leonards Gdns IG1 ..152 C7
St Leonards Rd EN9 .....43 D6

St Leonards Way RM11 ..136 B2
St Luke's Ave IG1 ......152 B7
St Luke's Path ∎ IG1 ..152 B7
St Luke's RC Prim Sch
CM19 ....23 C6
St Lukes Rd SS2 ....148 C2
St Lukes Sch IG10 ......89 A6
St Lukes Cl
Basildon SS15 ....141 C7
Canvey Island SS8 .....163 D4
St Lukes Pl SS4 ....125 E2
St Margaret's Ave SS17 .175 C8
St Margaret's CE Prim Sch
SS13 ....143 E5
St Margaret's Hospl
CM6 ....46 B2
St Margaret's Rd
Chelmsford CM2 ....32 E3
Hoddesdon SG12 ....8 B2
Wanstead E12 ....132 C2
St Margarets IG11 .....152 D4
St Margarets CE Prim Sch
IG11 ....152 C5
St Margarets Sta SG12 ...8 C4
St Mark's Ave DA11 ....178 F1
St Mark's Field SS4 ....125 F2
St Mark's Rd SS7 ......145 C3
St Mark's West Essex CE Sch
CM18 ....23 E7
St Marks Rd SS8 ....163 D4
St Martin's Cl
Brentwood CM13 ....117 C8
Rayleigh SS6 ....145 C8
St Martin's Mews CM5 ...49 A2
St Martin's Sch CM13 ...95 C1
St Martins Cl
South Benfleet SS7 ....144 B7
White Roding CM6 ......14 C7
St Martins Sq SS14 ....142 A6
St Mary's Ave
Billericay CM12 ....97 A2
Brentwood CM15 ....95 A4
Wanstead E11 ....132 B4
St Mary's Bglws CM1 ....6 B2
St Mary's Cath✶ CM1 ...32 B2
St Mary's CE Prim Sch
Burnham-on-C CM0 ....106 C6
Hatfield Broad Oak CM22 ..3 F1
Shenfield CM15 ....94 F3
Woodham Ferrers CM3 ...79 B4
St Mary's Cl Grays RM17 .178 D8
Great Baddow CM2 .....54 F6
St Mary's Cres SS13 ...143 E1
St Mary's Ct CM9 ....37 B2
St Mary's Ct SS2 ....147 F2
St Mary's Dr SS7 ....144 E1
St Mary's Hare Jun Sch
RM2 ....136 C8
St Mary's Ho 6 CM0 ...106 C4
St Mary's La Maldon CM9 ..37 B2
Upminster RM14 ....138 D3
West Horndon CM13 ...139 B4
St Mary's Lodge E11 ...132 B5
St Mary's Path SS13 ...143 C7
St Mary's Prittlewell CE Prim Sch SS2 ....147 F1
St Mary's RC Prim Sch
Chingford E4 ....87 D1
Hornchurch RM12 ......136 A3
Tilbury RM18 ....178 F5
St Mary's Rd
Burnham-on-C CM0 ....106 B6
Grays RM16 ....174 B2
Greenhithe DA9 ....176 E2
South Benfleet SS7 ....163 E8
Southend-on-S SS2 ....147 F2
St Marys IG11 ....152 C6
St Marys Cl
South Benfleet SS7 ....144 D1
Southend-on-S SS9 ....149 D1
St Marys Mead CM1 .....19 A1
St Marys Rd Ilford IG1 ..133 D2
Wickford SS12 ....121 B5
St Marys Way IG7 ......111 A5
St Matthew's Cl RM13 ..155 A5
St Michael's Dr CM1 .....30 A5
St Michael's Prep Sch
SS9 ....146 C1
St Michael's Rd
Chelmsford CM2 ....54 B8
Hadleigh SS7 ....145 F6
Hoddesdon EN10 ....21 A3
St Michaels Ave SS13 ..143 C4
St Michaels Cl
Aveley RM15 ....171 C6
Harlow CM20 ....10 E1
Latchingdon CM3 ....82 A5
St Michaels Rd
Canvey Island SS8 .....163 D4
Grays RM16 ....174 B1
St Michaels Wlk CM2 ....54 C2
St Mildreds Rd CM2 .....54 B8
St Nazaire Rd CM1 ......31 E6
St Neot's Rd RM3 ......114 F4
St Nicholas Ave RM12 ..136 A1
St Nicholas CE Prim Sch
Rawreth SS11 ....122 E7
Tillingham CM0 ....63 E4
St Nicholas Gn CM17 ....11 D1
St Nicholas La SS13 ...141 C7
St Nicholas La SS15 ...141 D1
St Nicholas Pl IG10 .....89 A5
St Nicholas Rd CM0 .....63 E4
St Nicholas Sch
Harlow CM17 ....11 F3
Southend-on-S SS2 ....148 E2
St Olave's Rd E6 ....152 A4
St Omar Cl SS12 ....121 E4

St Patrick's Pl RM16 ...174 C2
St Patrick's RC Prim Sch
RM7 ....113 B2
St Paul's Cl RM15 ......171 C6
St Paul's Ct SS0 ....166 E8
St Paul's Pl RM15 ......171 C6
St Pauls Gdns CM12 ....97 A4
St Pauls Rd Barking IG11 152 C4
Canvey Island SS8 .....163 D4
St Pauls Way EN9 ......65 D6
St Peter's Ave
Chipping Ongar CM5 ....49 A5
Maldon CM9 ....36 F2
St Peter's CE Prim Sch
CM14 ....115 E8
St Peter's Chapel✶ CM0 .42 F5
St Peter's Ct CM0 ......63 E8
St Peter's Flat Nature Reserve✶ CM0 ....42 F5
St Peter's High Sch & Tech Coll CM0 ....106 B6
St Peter's Hospl CM9 ...36 F2
St Peter's Pavement
SS14 ....120 F1
St Peter's RC Prim Sch
Dagenham RM9 ....153 F4
Romford RM1 ....135 E8
St Peter's Rd
Brentwood CM14 ......116 B6
Chelmsford CM1 ....31 E2
St Peter's Terr SS12 ...121 C7
St Peters CE Prim Sch
CM2 ....76 F4
St Peters Cl
Goldhanger CM9 ....38 E6
Ilford IG2 ....133 F7
St Peters Ct SS3 ......168 G7
St Peters Field CM0 ...106 A7
St Peters RC Prim Sch
CM11 ....119 E6
St Peters Rd
Canvey Island SS8 .....163 D4
Grays RM16 ....174 B2
Hockley SS5 ....124 B7
St Peters Wlk CM12 .....96 F4
St Philip's Priory Sch
CM2 ....54 A8
St Pius X RC Prim Sch
CM1 ....31 D4
St Ronans Cres IG8 ....110 A3
St Stephens Cres CM13 117 A6
St Stephens Ct CM3 .....83 A8
St Stephens Rd CM3 .....81 A4
St Swithins Cotts CM2 ...55 C3
St Teresa RC Prim Sch The
RM8 ....153 C8
St Teresa Wlk RM16 ....174 B3
St Teresa's RC Prim Sch
Basildon SS14 ....142 F6
Rochford SS4 ....125 E3
St Theresa Ct E4 ....87 D2
St Thomas Gdns IG1 ....152 C6
St Thomas More High Sch for Boys SS0 ....147 A3
St Thomas of Canterbury CE Jun & Inf Schs CM15 ..94 D2
St Thomas of Canterbury RC Prim Sch RM17 ......173 B2
St Thomas Rd
Belvedere DA17 ....169 C4
Brentwood CM14 ......116 B6
Rochford SS4 ....103 B4
St Thomas' Ct CM14 ...116 D8
St Thomas's Cl CM9 .....66 B6
St Thomas's Pl RM17 ...178 C8
St Thomas's Prim Sch
RM4 ....114 E8
St Thomas's Row CM0 ...42 B2
St Ursula's RC Jun & Inf Schs
RM3 ....114 B4
St Vincent's RC Prim Sch
RM8 ....134 C2
St Vincent's Rd SS0 ....166 E7
St Vincents Ave DA1 ...176 A2
St Vincents Dr
Chelmsford CM2 ....54 B8
Dartford DA1 ....176 A1
St Winifred's Cl IG7 ....111 C5
Sairard Cl SS9 ....146 D7
Sairard Gdns SS9 ......146 D7
Sakins Croft CM18 ......23 F5
Saladin Dr RM19 ....171 A2
Salamons Way RM13 ...169 E7
Salcombe Dr RM6 ......134 F5
Salcombe Pk IG10 ....88 D4
Salcott Cres SS12 ......121 F6
Salem Wlk SS6 ....123 B4
Salerno Way CM1 ....31 E6
Salesbury Dr CM11 ......97 C2
Salforal Cl CM3 ....78 B1
Saling Gn SS15 ....119 F2
Salisbury Ave
Barking IG11 ....152 E5
Basildon SS15 ....141 D5
Southend-on-S SS0 ....147 E1
Stanford-le-H SS17 ....160 D1
Salisbury Cl RM14 ......137 F2
Salisbury Ct SS9 ....146 D2
Salisbury Gdns IG9 .....110 D8
Salisbury Hall Gdns E4 ..109 A4
Salisbury Rd
Chingford E4 ....109 A2
Dagenham RM10 ......154 A6
Grays RM17 ....173 C1
Hoddesdon EN11 ....21 C3
Ilford IG3 ....133 E2
Romford RM2 ....136 B6
Southend-on-S SS9 ....146 D1

Salix Rd RM17 ....178 E8
Sally Murray Cl E12 ....152 A8
Salmon Par CM1 ....32 B3
Salmon Rd DA17 ....169 A1
Salmond's Gr CM13 ....117 C5
Salt's Gn CM1 ....16 D2
Saltash Rd IG6 ....111 D3
Saltcoats CM3 ....101 D8
Saltcoats Pk✶ CM3 ....101 F8
Saltcote Maltings CM9 ...37 E4
Salter Pl CM2 ....32 F2
Saltern Ct IG11 ....153 B2
Saltford Cl DA8 ....169 E1
Saltings The SS7 ....145 D3
Salway Cl IG8 ....110 A3
Salway Lodge 4 IG8 ...110 A3
Samantha Mews RM4 ...113 E7
Samian Ct CM2 ....36 F5
Samphire Ct RM17 .....178 E8
Samson Ho SS15 ....119 B1
Samuel Manor CM2 ......32 F3
Samuel Rd SS16 ....141 B4
Samuel's Cnr SS3 ......150 A5
Samuels Dr SS1 ....168 B8
San Juan PR RM16 ......172 C2
San Luis Dr RM16 ......172 C2
San Marcos Dr RM16 ...172 C2
San Remo Mans SS0 ....166 E7
San Remo Par SS0 .....166 E7
San Remo Rd SS8 ......164 D3
Sanctuary Gdn SS17 ...160 E2
Sanctuary Rd SS9 ......146 A3
Sandbanks SS7 ....145 D2
Sandcliff Rd DA8 ....169 D1
Sanderling Gdns CM9 ....37 C5
Sanderling Way DA9 ...177 A1
Sanderlings SS7 ....144 C2
Sanders Draper Sch The
RM12 ....155 D8
Sanders Rd SS8 ....164 A6
Sanderson Cl CM13 ....139 C5
Sanderson Ct SS7 .....144 C5
Sandford Ave IG10 ......89 C6
Sandford Mill Rd
Chelmsford CM2 ....32 F2
Chelmsford CM2 ....33 B2
Great Baddow CM2 .....55 C8
Sandford Rd CM2 ....32 E3
Sandgate Cl RM7 ......135 C4
Sandhill Rd SS9 ....146 C4
Sandhurst SS8 ....163 C3
Sandhurst Cl SS9 ......146 F4
Sandhurst Cres SS9 ....146 F4
Sandhurst Dr IG3 ......152 F8
Sandhurst Rd RM18 ....179 C5
Sandleigh Rd SS9 .....146 F4
Sandon Brook Pl CM2 ...55 E8
Sandon Cl Basildon SS14 142 F5
Rochford SS4 ....125 D3
Sandon Ct Basildon SS14 142 F5
Ilford IG3 ....134 A1
Sandon Hall Bridleway
CM2 ....55 D4
Sandon Pl CM5 ....49 A1
Sandon Rd SS14 ....142 F5
Sandon Sch The CM2 ...55 B6
Sandown Ave
Dagenham RM10 ......154 C6
Hornchurch RM12 ......136 D2
Southend-on-S SS0 ....147 B2
Sandown Cl SS11 ......122 A7
Sandown Rd CM10 .....154 C6
Sandown Rd
Orsett RM16 ....174 E7
Thundersley SS7 ......145 B7
Wickford SS11 ....122 A7
Sandpiper Cl
Greenhithe DA9 ....177 A1
Heybridge CM9 ....37 C5
Southend-on-S SS3 ...168 E8
Sandpiper Terr IG5 ....133 B8
Sandpiper Wlk CM2 .....54 C6
Sandpipers SS3 ....168 G6
Sandpit La
Burnham-on-C CM0 ....106 C5
Pilgrims Hatch CM14 ...93 F2
Sandpit Rd SS3 ....168 H8
Sandringham Ave
Harlow CM19 ....22 E8
Hockley SS5 ....124 D6
Sandringham Cl
Ilford IG6 ....133 C8
Stanford-le-H SS17 ....160 E3
Sandringham Gdns IG6 .133 C8
Sandringham Pl CM2 ....32 C2
Sandringham Rd
Barking IG11 ....152 F6
Basildon SS15 ....141 E8
Pilgrims Hatch CM15 ...94 B3
Southend-on-S SS1 ....167 D7
Sands Way IG8 ....110 F4
Sandy La Aveley RM15 ..171 A6
Grays, Chadwell St Mary RM16 ....174 C1
Grays, West Thurrock RM20 ....177 B8
Sandyhill Rd IG1 ....152 B8
Sangster Ct SS6 ....123 F2
Sans Souci SS9 ....165 D8
Santiago Way RM16 ....172 D1
Sappers Ct CM21 ....1 F2
Sapphire Cl RM8 ....134 C3
Sapphire Ct SS1 ....167 D6
Sapphire Ho 4 RM13 ..155 D7
Sara Cres DA9 ....177 B3
Sarbir Ind Pk CM17 ......1 F5
Sark Gr SS12 ....121 F5
Sarre Ave RM12 ....155 C6

Sassoon Way 3 CM9 ....37 A1
Satanita Rd SS0 ....166 D8
Saunton Rd RM12 ......136 A2
Savannah Hts SS9 .....147 A1
Saverake Rd CM1 ....31 E1
Savill Row IG8 ....109 F4
Savill's Cotts IG7 ......111 C8
Saville Rd RM6 ....134 F4
Savoy Cl SS16 ....141 A5
Savoy Wood CM19 ......23 B2
Sawbridgeworth Rd
Hatfield Heath CM22 .....2 E3
Little Hallingbury CM22 ..2 B6
Sawbridgeworth Sta
CM21 ....2 A3
Sawkins Ave CM2 ......54 D6
Sawkins Cl CM2 ....54 D6
Sawkins Gdns CM2 ....54 D6
Sawney Brook CM1 .....31 A1
Sawston Dr 10 CM19 ..171 B1
Sawyer's Chase RM4 ...90 B6
Sawyer's Hall La CM15 ..94 D1
Sawyers Ct CM15 ......94 D1
Sawyers Gr CM15 ......94 D1
Saxham Rd IG11 ......152 E3
Saxlingham Rd E4 .....109 C7
Saxon Cl
Brentwood CM13 ......117 C8
Rayleigh SS6 ....123 E5
Romford RM3 ....114 F1
Wickford SS11 ....99 E1
Saxon Ct Maldon CM9 ...37 A3
South Benfleet SS7 ...144 C5
Saxon Gdns SS3 ......168 D7
Saxon Ho RM14 ....138 D4
Saxon Pl SS4 ....125 F4
Saxon Rd IG1 ....152 B7
Saxon Way
Chelmsford CM1 ....32 B7
Maldon CM9 ....37 B1
South Benfleet SS7 ...144 C2
Waltham Abbey EN9 ....65 C6
Saxonville SS7 ....144 B4
Sayer Cl DA9 ....177 A2
Sayers CM21 ....1 A7
Sayers Gdns CM21 ......1 F2
Sayesbury Ave CM21 ....1 E4
Sayesbury Rd CM21 .....1 E4
Saywell Brook CM2 .....33 A2
Scalby Rd CM0 ....84 A3
Scaldhurst SS13 ......143 C4
Scarborough Rd
Southend-on-S SS9 ...146 E2
Southminster CM0 ......84 A3
Scargill Jun & Inf Sch
RM13 ....155 A6
Scarles Croft CM3 .....78 C5
Scarletts SS14 ....142 C8
Scholars Ho 6 E4 ......87 D1
Scholars Rd E4 ....87 D1
School Green La CM16 ..47 C6
School La
Abbess Roding CM5 ....14 F3
Basildon SS12 ....122 A2
Beauchamp Roding CM5 .28 A7
Broomfield CM1 ....19 B1
Chelmsford CM1 ....31 F8
Chigwell IG7 ....111 F6
Harlow CM20 ....10 E2
High Easter CM1 ....6 B3
Ingrave CM13 ....117 C4
Orsett RM16 ....174 A8
South Benfleet SS7 ...163 D8
Stock CM4 ....75 D2
Tilgate Green CM5 .....25 D6
School Rd
Billericay CM12 ....119 A8
Chipping Ongar CM5 ...70 B2
Dagenham RM10 ......154 B4
Downham CM11 ....98 F5
Kelvedon Hatch CM15 ..71 F2
Margaret Roding CM1 ..16 C5
School View Rd CM1 ....31 F3
School Villas CM6 ....5 B4
School Way
Dagenham RM8 ....134 C1
Southend-on-S SS9 ...146 F3
Schoolfield Rd RM20 ...177 A8
Schoolhouse Gdns IG10 .89 B5
Schooner Cl IG11 .....153 B2
Schooner Ct DA2 ......176 C3
Schooner Ho DA8 .....169 E1
Scilla Ct RM17 ....178 D8
Scimitar Pk SS13 .....121 D2
Scoter Cl IG8 ....110 B3
Scotland Rd IG9 ....88 C1
Scotney Wlk RM12 ....155 D7
Scott Ave SG12 ....8 B4
Scott Dr SS12 ....121 E5
Scott Ho Romford RM11 .136 A5
Southend-on-S SS9 ...147 A7
Scott Rd RM16 ....174 A2
Scottes La RM8 ....134 D3
Scotts Cl RM12 ....155 C7
Scotts Hall Cotts SS4 ..126 D8
Scotts Hall Rd SS4 ....126 D7
Scotts Hill CM0 ....84 B4
Scotts Prim Sch RM12 .155 C7
Scotts Wlk
Chelmsford CM1 ....31 F5
Rayleigh SS6 ....124 C2
Scraley Rd CM9 ....37 C8
Scratton Rd
Southend-on-S SS1 ....166 F7
Stanford-le-H SS17 ....160 D2
Scrattons Terr IG11 ...153 D4
Scrub La SS7 ....145 F3
Scrub Rise CM12 ......118 F8

Scurvy Hall La CM3 19 B8
Scylla Cl CM9 37 C6
SE Essex Coll
Southend-on-S SS1 166 F8
Southend-on-S SS2 147 F1
Sea Reach SS9 165 E8
Sea View Par
Mayland CM3 60 F2
St Lawrence CM0 40 C1
Sea View Prom CM0 40 B1
Sea View Rd SS9 165 E8
Sea Watch SS1 167 B7
Seaborough Rd RM16 174 C3
Seabrink SS9 166 A8
Seabrook Gdns
Boreham CM3 20 F1
Romford RM7 135 A4
Seabrook Rd
Dagenham RM8 134 D1
Great Baddow CM2 55 A6
Seabrooke Rise RM17 178 B8
Seaburn Cl RM13 154 E3
Seaforth Ave SS2 148 C2
Seaforth Cl RM1 113 E3
Seaforth Gdns IG8 110 C5
Seaforth Gr SS2 148 D2
Seaforth Rd SS0 166 D7
Seagry Rd E11 132 B4
Seagull Cl IG11 153 A2
Seally Rd RM17 173 A1
Seamans La CM4 76 C2
Seamer Rd CM0 84 A3
Seamore Ave SS7 144 C7
Seamore Cl SS7 144 C6
Seamore Wlk SS7 144 C7
Seaton Ave IG3 152 F7
Seaview Ave SS16 142 D3
Seaview Dr SS3 150 C3
Seaview Rd
Canvey Island SS8 164 E2
Southend-on-S SS9 168 E6
Seaview Terr SS7 145 D1
Seaway
Canvey Island SS8 164 B2
Southend-on-S SS1 167 B7
St Lawrence CM0 62 C8
Seax Ct SS15 140 F7
Seax Way SS15 140 F7
Sebastian Ave CM15 95 A3
Sebastian Ct 10 IG11 152 F5
Sebert Cl CM11 119 D7
Second Ave
Basildon SS16 140 E4
Billericay CM12 118 F7
Canvey Island SS8 163 E4
Chelmsford CM1 32 B5
Dagenham RM10 154 B3
Grays RM20 177 A8
Harlow CM18,CM20 23 F8
Hook End CM15 72 C5
Hullbridge SS5 101 F1
Ilford RM6 134 C6
Southend-on-S SS0 166 B7
Stanford-le-H SS17 160 D3
Wickford SS11 122 A6
Seddons Wlk SS5 124 E6
Sedge Ct RM17 178 E7
Sedge Gn EN9 21 E3
Sedgefield Cl RM3 114 F6
Sedgefield Cres RM3 114 F6
Sedgemoor SS3 149 D1
Sedgemoor Dr RM10 154 A8
Sedley Rise IG10 88 F7
Seedbed Ctr SS3 168 F7
Seedbed Ctr The RM7 135 E4
Seeleys The CM17 11 C4
Sejant Ho RM17 178 B8
Selborne Ave E12 152 A8
Selborne Rd IG1 133 A2
Selbourne Rd
Hockley SS5 124 E6
South Benfleet SS7 144 D6
Southend-on-S SS2 148 C3
Seldon Cl SS0 147 B3
Selinas La RM8 134 F4
Selsdon Cl RM5 113 C2
Selsdon Rd E11 132 A4
Selwood Rd CM14 115 F7
Selworthy Cl
Billericay CM11 119 C7
Wanstead E11 132 A6
Selwyn Ave Chingford E4 109 C4
Ilford IG3 133 F5
Selwyn Inf Sch E4 109 C4
Selwyn Jun Sch E4 109 C4
Selwyn Rd
Southend-on-S SS2 148 C2
Tilbury RM18 178 F5
Semper Rd RM16 174 C4
Semples SS17 160 F2
Serena Ct RM12 136 C2
Sergeants Green La EN9 66 C6
Service Industry Bays
CM20 10 F2
Seton Gdns RM9 153 C5
Settle Rd RM3 115 A6
Seven Acres SS11 121 F8
Seven Arches Rd CM14 116 E7
Seven Ash Gn CM1 32 C5
Seven Kings High Sch
IG1 133 D4
Seven Kings Rd IG3 133 F2
Seven Kings Sta IG3 133 E3
Seven Ways Par IG2 133 A6
Sevenoaks Cl RM3 114 C6
Seventh Ave
Canvey Island SS8 163 E4
Chelmsford CM1 32 B6
Severn RM18 175 B3
Severn Ave RM2 136 B8
Severn Dr RM14 137 D5
Severn Rd RM15 171 C7
Severns Field CM16 46 A2
Sewards End SS12 121 E6
Sewardstone Gdns E4 87 B4
Sewardstone Rd
Chingford E4 87 B5
Sewardstone E4 65 D3
Sewardstone St EN9 65 C5
Sewell Cl RM16 172 C1
Sewell Harris Cl CM20 10 F1
Sexton Cl RM13 154 F4
Sexton Rd RM18 178 F6
Seymer Rd RM1 135 D8
Seymour Cl
Basildon SS15 141 D6
Loughton IG10 88 E3
Seymour Ct E4 109 F8
Seymour Gdns IG1 132 F3
Seymour Mews CM21 11 E7
Seymour Pl RM11 136 D4
Seymour Rd Chingford E4 87 B1
Hadleigh SS7 145 F3
Southend-on-S SS0 147 C1
Tilbury RM18 178 F6
Seymour St CM2 32 A1
Seymour's IG10 89 A8
Seymours Harlow CM19 22 F5
Harlow CM19 23 A5
Shafter Rd RM10 154 C6
Shaftesbury IG10 88 D6
Shaftesbury Ave SS1 167 E6
Shaftesbury Ct RM6 134 C4
Shaftesbury La DA1 176 B3
Shaftesbury Rd
Chingford E4 87 D1
Epping CM16 45 F2
Romford RM1 135 F5
Shaftesburys The IG11 152 C3
Shaftsbury Ct SS13 143 B7
Shakespeare Ave
Basildon SS16 141 A5
Billericay CM11 97 D2
Rayleigh SS6 124 A2
Southend-on-S SS0 147 E2
Tilbury RM18 179 B6
Shakespeare Ct EN11 8 A2
Shakespeare Dr
Maldon CM9 59 A8
Southend-on-S SS0 147 E2
Shakespeare Rd
Dartford DA1 176 B3
8 Romford RM1 135 F5
Shakespeare Sq IG6 111 C4
Shakeston Cl CM1 53 B8
Shakletons CM5 49 A3
Shalford 3 IG8 110 C4
Shalford Lodge CM1 32 B8
Shalford Rd CM11 97 D2
Shanklin Ave CM12 97 A2
Shanklin Dr SS0 147 B2
Shannon Ave SS6 123 D1
Shannon Cl SS9 146 E4
Shannon Way
Aveley RM15 171 C6
Canvey Island SS8 163 D3
Shardelow Ave CM1 33 A8
Sharlands Cl SS11 121 F8
Sharnbrook SS3 149 D2
Sharpecroft CM19 23 C8
Sharpington Cl CM2 54 C3
Shaw Ave IG11 153 E3
Shaw Cl
Hornchurch RM11 136 B3
Wickford SS12 121 D5
Shaw Cres
Brentwood CM13 95 D5
Tilbury RM18 179 C6
Shaw Gdns IG11 153 E3
Shaw Prim Sch RM15 172 B7
Shaw The CM22 3 A3
Shawbridge CM19 23 C5
Shearers Way CM3 20 F1
Shearwater Cl IG11 153 A2
Sheepcotes CM2 33 B5
Sheepcotes La
Heybridge CM9 37 F8
Little Waltham CM3 19 C7
Southminster CM0 84 D5
Sheepcotes Rd RM6 134 E7
Sheering CE Prim Sch
CM22 12 D8
Sheering Ct SS6 123 A3
Sheering Dr CM17 11 E4
Sheering Lower Rd CM21 2 A2
Sheering Mill La CM21 1 F2
Sheering Rd CM17 11 F4
Sheerwater Cl CM0 106 B5
Sheffield Dr RM3 115 A5
Sheffield Gdns RM3 115 A5
Sheila Cl RM5 113 B3
Sheila Rd RM5 113 B3
Sheilings The RM11 136 F6
Sheldon Ave IG5 111 B1
Sheldon Cl
Corringham SS17 161 B5
Harlow CM17 24 E8
Sheldon Ct CM13 95 B3
Sheldon Ho E4 109 E4
Sheldon Rd
Canvey Island SS8 164 E3
Dagenham RM9 153 E5
Sheldrick Link CM2 33 B4
Shellbeach Rd SS8 164 D2
Shelley Ave RM12 135 F2
Shelley Cl
Chipping Ongar CM5 48 F5
Maldon CM9 59 A8
Shelley Ct
Waltham Abbey EN9 65 F6
8 Wanstead E11 132 A7
Shelley Gr IG10 88 F5
Shelley Pl Rayleigh SS6 123 A3
Tilbury RM18 179 B6
Shelley Prim Sch CM5 48 F5
Shelley Rd
Brentwood CM13 95 D2
Chelmsford CM2 32 D2
Shelley Sq SS2 148 B2
Shellow Rd CM5 28 D4
Shelly Ave SS16 141 A5
Shelsley Dr SS16 141 C3
Shen Place Almhouses
CM15 94 D1
Shenfield Cres CM15 116 E7
Shenfield Ct CM18 23 C5
Shenfield Gdns CM13 95 B3
Shenfield Gn CM15 95 A2
Shenfield High Sch
CM15 95 A4
Shenfield Pl CM15 94 E2
Shenfield Rd
Brentwood CM15 94 E1
Woodford IG8 110 B3
Shenfield Sta CM15 95 A2
Shenley Rd DA1 176 A1
Shenstone Gdns
Ilford IG2 133 F6
Romford RM3 114 C2
Shenval Ho CM20 11 A4
Shenval Ind Est CM20 11 A4
Shepard Cl SS9 147 A6
Shepeshall SS15 141 E5
Shephards Ct SS5 124 E5
Shepherds Cl
Hadleigh SS7 145 E4
Ilford RM6 134 D7
Shepherds Hill RM3 115 B1
Shepherds Wlk SS7 145 E4
Shepley Mews EN3 65 A2
Sheppard Dr CM2 33 A4
Sheppards CM19 22 F5
Sheppey Gdns RM9 153 C5
Sheppey Rd RM9 153 C5
Sherards Orch CM19 23 B6
Sherborne Gdns RM5 113 A5
Sherborne Rd CM1 32 D5
Sherbourne Cl SS2 147 E6
Sherbourne Dr SS13 121 A1
Sherbourne Gdns SS2 147 F6
Shere Rd IG2 133 A6
Sheredan Rd E4 109 E5
Sherfield Rd RM17 178 B8
Sheridan Ave SS7 145 B3
Sheridan Cl Rayleigh SS6 123 F2
Romford RM3 114 C3
Sheridan Ct DA1 176 A3
Sheridan Mews 3 E11 132 B5
Sheridan Rd DA17 169 A2
Sheringham Ave
Little Ilford E12 152 A7
Romford RM7 135 C5
Sheringham Cl SS17 160 E3
Sheringham Dr IG11 153 A7
Sheriton Sq SS6 123 D4
Sherman Gdns RM6 134 C5
Shernbroke Rd EN9 65 F5
Shernwood Ho 1 E18 132 A7
Sherry Mews IG11 152 D5
Sherry Way SS7 145 E6
Sherwood RM16 172 E5
Sherwood Ave E18 132 B8
Sherwood Cl SS16 141 A4
Sherwood Cres SS7 145 E4
Sherwood Dr CM1 31 D1
Sherwood Gdns IG11 152 D5
Sherwood Ho CM18 23 F6
Sherwood Rd IG6 133 D7
Sherwood Way SS2 148 E2
Shevon Way CM14 115 F6
Shillibeer Wlk IG7 111 F7
Shillingstone SS3 149 D1
Shingle Ct EN9 66 A6
Ship Cotts CM2 76 B6
Ship La RM15 171 E4
Ship Rd
Burnham-on-C CM0 106 C4
West Hanningfield CM2 76 C5
Shipton Cl RM8 134 D1
Shipwrights Cl SS7 145 B2
Shipwrights Dr SS7 145 B3
Shire Cl Billericay CM11 97 D5
Chelmsford CM1 32 F7
Shirebourn Vale CM3 101 D6
Shirley Ct Ilford IG2 133 D6
Loughton IG10 88 F7
Shirley Gdns
Barking IG11 152 E6
Basildon SS13 143 C8
Hornchurch RM12 136 C2
Shirley Lodge SS9 146 E5
Shirley Rd SS9 146 E5
Shoebury Ave SS3 168 F7
Shoebury Common Rd
SS3 168 C5
Shoebury Rd
Great Wakering SS3 150 C3
Southend-on-S SS1 149 B1
Shoeburyness Comp Sch
SS3 168 D7
Shoeburyness Sta SS3 168 F7
Shonks Mill Rd RM4 70 C1
Shooters Dr EN9 21 E1
Shop Row SS4 128 A5
Shopland Hall Rd SS4 148 D6
Shopland Rd SS4 148 C7
Shore Rd CM0 106 C4
Shore The DA11 178 C2
Shorefield SS7 144 B3
Shorefield Gdns SS0 166 E7
Shorefield Rd SS0 166 D7
Short Acre SS14 142 C6
Short La CM11 98 C4
Short Rd
Canvey Island SS8 164 B4
Hadleigh SS7 145 D2
Short St SS2 148 A1
Shortcroft CM15 71 F2
Shortcrofts Rd RM9 153 F6
Shorter Ave CM15 94 F2
Shortlands SS14 142 B6
Shortlands Ave CM5 48 F5
Shorwell Ct 18 RM19 171 B1
Shrewsbury Cl SS16 140 F5
Shrewsbury Dr SS7 144 D7
Shropshire Cl CM2 54 F5
Shrubberies The
Chigwell IG7 111 C5
Ilford IG2 133 F6
Woodford E18 110 A1
Writtle CM1 52 F8
Shrubbery Cl SS15 141 D8
Shrubbery The
Upminster RM14 137 C1
7 Wanstead E11 132 B6
Shrublands Cl
Chelmsford CM2 32 C2
Chigwell IG7 111 C4
Sibley Row EN9 22 E2
Sibneys Gn CM18 23 E4
Sidings The IG10 88 E3
Sidmouth Ave SS0 147 D5
Sidmouth Rd CM1 32 E6
Sidney Elson Way E6 152 A3
Sidney Pl CM1 33 A7
Sidney Rd
Theydon Bois CM16 67 D3
Wanstead E7 132 A1
Sidwell Ave SS7 144 E1
Sidwell Chase SS7 144 E1
Sidwell La SS7 144 E1
Sidwell Pk SS7 144 E1
Sierra Dr RM9 154 C3
Silchester Cnr SS3 149 B3
Silchester Ct SS3 149 B3
Silva Island Way SS12 121 F5
Silver Birch Ave CM16 46 E4
Silver Birch Mews IG6 111 C4
Silver Birches CM13 95 A1
Silver La CM5 29 A2
Silver Rd CM0 106 C4
Silver Spring Cl DA8 169 B1
Silver St Abridge RM4 90 B6
Maldon CM9 36 F3
Waltham Abbey EN9 65 C6
Silver Way Romford RM7 135 B8
Wickford SS11 121 C8
Silverdale Rayleigh SS6 145 E8
Stanford-le-H SS17 160 D4
Thundersley SS7 144 F7
Silverdale Ave Ilford IG3 133 F6
Southend-on-S SS0 147 E2
Silverdale Dr RM12 155 B7
Silverdale E SS17 160 D4
Silverdale Par IG3 133 F6
Silverdale Rd E4 109 D4
Silverlocke Rd RM17 178 D8
Silvermead 7 E18 110 A2
Silvermere SS16 141 A5
Silvermere Ave RM5 113 B4
Silverpoint Marine SS8 165 A3
Silvers IG9 88 C1
Silversea Dr SS0 147 B2
Silverthorn Cl SS4 125 D4
Silverthorn Gdns E4 109 A8
Silverthorne SS8 163 F3
Silvertown Ave SS17 160 D2
Silvertree Cl SS5 124 B6
Silverwood Cl
Grays RM16 173 A6
Harlow EN9 22 E3
Silvester Way CM2 33 B4
Simmonds La CM9 59 A1
Simmonds Way CM3 56 F8
Simmons La E4 109 D8
Simmons Pl RM16 173 A5
Simon Campion Ct CM16 46 A1
Simpson Rd RM13 154 F6
Sims Cl RM1 135 F7
Sinclair Rd E4 109 A5
Sinclair Wlk SS12 121 D5
Singleton Cl RM12 154 F8
Singleton Rd RM9 153 F7
Sippetts Ct IG1 133 D3
Sir Francis Way CM14 116 B8
Sir George Monoux Sixth
Form Coll E17 109 B1
Sir Walter Raleigh Dr
SS6 123 C4
Sirdar Rd SS6 145 D8
Sisley Rd IG11 152 F4
Siviter Way RM10 154 B5
Sixth Ave
Canvey Island SS8 163 E4
Chelmsford CM1 32 B6
Skarnings Ct EN9 66 A6
Skeale's Ct RM12 136 C1
Skelter Stps 9 SS1 167 C7
Skerry Rise CM1 32 B7
Skinner's La CM2 54 B3
Skipper Ct 4 IG11 152 C4
Skippers Cl DA9 177 B2
Skipsey Ave E6 152 A1
Skreens Ct CM1 31 D4
Sky Peals Rd IG8 109 D3
Skylark Cl CM11 97 C1
Skylark Wlk CM2 54 B5
Slacksbury Hatch CM19 23 B8
Slade End CM16 67 F3
Slade's La CM2 54 A3
Slades The SS16 142 E3
Slaney Rd RM1 135 E6
Sleepers Farm Rd RM16 174 B4
Slewins Cl RM11 136 C6
Slewins La RM11 136 C6
Slipe La EN10 43 A7
Sloane Mews CM12 96 F5
Slough La CM3 57 D3
Slough Rd Danbury CM3 57 C3
High Easter CM1 6 B2
Smallgains Ave SS8 164 E4
Smallgains La CM4 97 E8
Smallholdings SS2 147 D6
Smarden Cl DA17 169 A1
Smart Cl RM3 114 B2
Smart's La IG10 88 E5
Smartt Ave SS8 164 A4
Smeaton Cl EN9 65 E7
Smeaton Rd Chigwell IG8 110 F5
Holdbrook EN3 65 A2
Smith St SS3 168 F6
Smither's Chase SS2 148 B5
Smithers Dr CM2 55 A6
Smiths Ave CM3 83 A8
Smugglers Wlk DA9 177 B2
Smyatts Cl CM0 84 D3
Smythe Cl CM11 97 D5
Smythe Rd CM11 97 D5
Smythe Row CM3 80 C4
Snakes Hill CM14 93 C6
Snakes La
Southend-on-S SS2 147 A6
Woodford IG8 110 D4
Snakes La E IG8 110 C4
Snakes La W IG8 110 B4
Snaresbrook Hall 11
E18 132 A8
Snaresbrook Prim Sch
E18 132 A7
Snaresbrook Sta E11 132 A6
Snelling Gr CM2 54 F6
Snoreham Gdns CM3 82 B5
Snowdon Ct 5 RM2 136 C7
Snowdonia Cl SS13 143 C8
Snowdrop Cl CM1 32 E7
Snowdrop Path RM3 114 D3
Soames Mead CM15 72 A6
Soane St SS13 121 B1
Softwater La SS7 145 E3
Solar Ct RM12 136 C2
Solid La CM15 93 F8
Solway RM18 175 C3
Somerby Cl EN10 21 A2
Somerby Rd IG11 152 D5
Somercotes SS15 141 C5
Somercotes Ct SS15 141 C5
Somerdean 2 SS13 143 C6
Somers Heath Prim Sch
RM15 172 A6
Somersby Gdns IG4 132 F6
Somerset Ave
Rochford SS4 125 E3
Southend-on-S SS0 147 B4
Somerset Cl IG8 110 A2
Somerset Cres SS0 147 B4
Somerset Gdns
Basildon SS13 143 B6
Hornchurch RM11 137 A3
Somerset Pl CM1 32 A7
Somerset Rd
Basildon SS15 141 B6
Holdbrook EN3 65 A1
Linford SS17 175 A4
Somerton Ave SS0 147 B5
Somerville Gdns SS9 165 F8
Somerville Rd RM6 134 C6
Somnes Ave SS8 163 E6
Sonning Way SS3 149 D1
Sonters Down CM3 100 C5
Soper Mews 6 EN3 65 A1
Soper Sq CM17 11 C1
Sopwith Cres SS11 122 B5
Sorrel Ct RM17 178 D8
Sorrel Wlk RM1 135 F8
Sorrell Cl Goldhanger CM9 38 E7
Little Waltham CM3 19 B6
Sorrells The SS17 160 F3
Sorrels The SS7 144 D7
South Ave Basildon SS16 160 B7
Chingford E4 87 C2
Hullbridge SS5 101 E1
Southend-on-S SS2 148 C1
South Beech Ave SS12 121 D7
South Benfleet Foundation
Prim Sch SS7 144 D2
South Block CM21 1 F2
South Charlton Mead La
EN11 21 D5
South Cl RM10 154 A4
South Colne SS16 142 D4
South Cres SS2 147 D5
South Crockerford
SS16 142 E4
South Cross Rd IG6 133 C6
South Dr
Brentwood CM14 116 D6

South Dr continued
Romford RM2 . . . .**136** C8
South East Essex Sixth Form
Coll SS7 . . . .**145** A5
South End Rd RM12,
RM13 . . . .**155** B5
South Gate Harlow CM20 . .**23** D8
Purfleet RM19 . . . .**171** C2
South Green Cty Jun & Inf
Schs CM11 . . . .**119** C7
South Gunnels SS14 . . . . . .**142** B6
South Hall Dr RM13 . . . .**170** B8
South Hanningfield Rd
CM3,SS11,CM11 . . . .**99** C8
South Hanningfield Way
SS11 . . . .**99** D3
South Hill
Basildon SS16,SS17 . . . .**160** A7
Horndon-on-t-H SS17 . . . . . .**160** A3
South Hill Cl CM3 . . . .**56** D6
South Hill Cres SS17 . . . . . .**160** A3
South House Chase CM9 **59** C7
South Kent Ave DA11 . . . . . .**178** C1
South Mayne SS14 . . . .**143** A5
South Ordnance Rd EN3 . .**65** A2
South Par
Canvey Island SS8 . . . .**164** E2
South Ockendon RM15 . . . . .**172** C8
South Park Bsns Ctr
IG3 . . . .**133** E2
South Park Cres IG1 . . . . . .**133** E1
South Park Dr
Barking IG11 . . . .**152** E8
Ilford IG3 . . . .**133** E1
South Park Inf Sch IG3 .**133** E1
South Park Prim Sch
IG1 . . . .**133** E1
South Park Rd IG1 . . . .**133** D1
South Park Terr IG1 . . . . . .**133** E1
South Park Villas IG1 . . . .**152** E8
South Pl Harlow CM20 . . . . . .**11** A4
Waltham Abbey EN9 . . . .**65** C6
South Primrose Hill CM1 **31** F3
South Rd
Basildon, Crays Hill CM11 . . .**120** D5
Basildon,Vange SS17 . . . . . .**142** C1
Dagenham RM6 . . . .**134** E5
Harlow CM20 . . . .**11** A4
Ilford RM6 . . . .**134** C6
South Ockendon RM15 . . . . .**172** C4
South Residence IG3 . . . .**134** B6
South Ridge CM11 . . . .**97** C2
South Riding SS14 . . . .**142** E6
South St
Bradwell-on-S CM0 . . . .**42** A2
Brentwood CM14 . . . .**116** E8
Great Waltham CM3 . . . .**18** E7
Rainham RM13 . . . .**154** D3
Rochford SS4 . . . .**125** F1
Romford RM1 . . . .**135** E6
Romford RM1 . . . .**135** F5
Stanstead Abbotts SG12 . . . . .**8** C4
Tillingham CM0 . . . .**63** B3
South View RM16 . . . .**174** B8
South View Cl SS6 . . . .**145** F8
South View Cres IG2 . . . . .**133** B5
South View Dr RM14 . . . . . .**137** B5
South View Rd
Grays RM20 . . . .**177** C8
Loughton IG10 . . . .**88** F3
Rettendon SS4 . . . .**100** C5
South Benfleet SS7 . . . .**144** C3
South Wash Rd SS15 . . . . .**119** E1
South Way Purfleet RM19 **171** C3
Waltham Abbey EN9 . . . .**65** C3
South Weald Dr EN9 . . . .**65** D6
South Weald Rd CM14 . . . .**116** A7
South Wlk SS14 . . . .**142** B5
South Woodford Sta
E18 . . . .**110** B1
Southall Ho 4 RM3 . . . .**114** E4
Southall Way CM14 . . . .**115** F6
Southborough Dr SS0 . . . .**147** B2
Southborough Rd CM2 . . . .**54** A8
Southbourne Gdns
Ilford IG1 . . . .**152** C7
Southend-on-S SS0 . . . .**147** B4
Southbourne Gr
Hockley SS5 . . . .**125** A6
Southend-on-S SS0 . . . .**147** B3
Wickford SS12 . . . .**121** A8
Southbrook CM21 . . . .**1** E1
Southbury Cl RM12 . . . .**155** D7
Southchurch Ave
Southend-on-S SS1 . . . .**167** B8
Southend-on-S, Shoeburyness
SS3 . . . .**168** G7
Southchurch Bvd SS2 . . . .**148** F1
Southchurch Hall Cl
SS1 . . . .**167** C8
Southchurch Hall Mus★
SS1 . . . .**167** C8
Southchurch Rd SS1 . . . . .**167** C8
Southcliff SS7 . . . .**144** C4
Southcote Cres SS14 . . . . .**142** E8
Southcote Row 2 SS14 **142** F8
Southcote Sq SS14 . . . .**142** F8
Southdale IG7 . . . .**111** D4
Southdown Cres IG2 . . . . .**133** E6
Southdown Rd RM11 . . . . . .**136** B4
Southend Arterial Rd
Basildon SS2,SS6,SS7 . . . . . .**122** B2
Basildon, Steeple View
CM12,SS15 . . . .**119** D1
Great Warley CM13,RM14 . . .**138** C6

Southend Arterial Rd continued
Rayleigh SS6 . . . .**145** E8
Romford RM2 . . . .**114** D1
Upminster RM14,RM11 . . . . .**137** C7
West Horndon RM13 . . . .**139** D7
Southend High Sch for Boys
SS0 . . . .**147** C7
Southend High Sch for Girls
SS2 . . . .**148** F1
Southend Ho SS17 . . . .**160** E3
Southend La RM9 . . . .**66** C5
Southend Pier Mus★
SS1 . . . .**167** A7
Southend Rd
Billericay CM11 . . . .**119** D7
Grays RM17 . . . .**173** C2
Great Baddow CM2 . . . .**55** B4
Great Wakering SS3 . . . .**149** C3
Hockley SS5 . . . .**124** E5
Howe Green CM2 . . . .**55** D2
Rochford SS4 . . . .**147** F1
Stanford-le-H SS17 . . . .**160** E4
Wallend E6 . . . .**152** A6
Wickford SS11 . . . .**122** B4
Woodford IG8 . . . .**110** D1
Woodham Mortimer CM9 . . . . .**57** C5
**Southend Road (North
Circular)** E17, E18 . . . . . .**109** F1
Southend-on-Sea (Victoria)
Sta SS2 . . . .**148** A1
**Southend-on-Sea Central
Mus &Planetarium★**
SS2 . . . .**148** A1
Southend-on-Sea Central
Sta SS1 . . . .**167** A8
Southend-on-Sea East Side
SS1 . . . .**167** C8
Southend-on-Sea Sea Life
Ctr★ SS1 . . . .**167** A7
Souther Cross CM1 . . . .**16** E5
Souther Cross Cotts
CM1 . . . .**16** D5
Souther Cross Rd CM1 . .**16** D5
Southern Dr
Loughton IG10 . . . .**88** F3
South Woodham Ferrers
CM3 . . . .**101** C7
Southern Lodge CM19 . . . .**23** C5
Southern Terr 2 EN11 . . . .**8** B1
Southern Way
Harlow CM18 . . . .**23** E5
Romford RM7 . . . .**135** A5
Southernhay
Basildon SS14 . . . .**142** B5
Basildon SS14 . . . .**142** B6
Loughton IG10 . . . .**88** D4
Southend-on-S SS9 . . . .**146** E5
Southey Cl CM3 . . . .**37** C4
Southey Wlk RM18 . . . .**179** B6
Southfalls Rd SS8 . . . .**164** F3
Southfield Chase CM12 . . .**118** E1
Southfield Cl SS7 . . . .**145** E5
Southfield Dr SS7 . . . .**145** E5
Southfield Rd EN11 . . . .**21** A4
Southfield Way CM0 . . . .**84** C4
Southfleet Rd DA10 . . . .**177** F1
Southgate Ho 1 SS14 . . . .**142** A6
Southgate Mews SS3 . . . .**150** B3
Southland Terr 3
RM19 . . . .**171** B1
Southlands Chase CM2 . .**55** E2
Southlands Rd CM11 . . . . . .**120** E6
Southminster Cty Inf Sch
CM0 . . . .**84** D4
Southminster Rd
Althorne SS4 . . . .**83** C4
Asheldham CM0 . . . .**85** A7
Burnham-on-C CM0 . . . .**106** B8
St Lawrence CM0 . . . .**62** F3
Southminster Sta CM0 . . . .**84** E4
Southsea Ave SS9 . . . .**146** B1
Southsea Ho 13 RM3 . . . . .**114** D5
Southview Ave RM18 . . . . . .**179** A6
Southview Cl CM3 . . . .**101** D8
Southview Dr
Southend-on-S SS0 . . . .**147** C2
Wanstead E18 . . . .**132** B8
Southview Hts RM20 . . . . . .**177** C8
Southview Rd
Basildon SS16 . . . .**142** E5
Danbury CM3 . . . .**56** D6
Hockley SS5 . . . .**124** F7
Southview Terr CM3 . . . .**56** D6
Southwalters SS14 . . . .**163** F4
Southwark Path SS14 . . . . .**142** F7
Southway SS16 . . . .**141** D2
Southwell Cl RM16 . . . .**172** C1
Southwell Rd SS7 . . . .**144** E4
Southwick Gdns SS8 . . . . .**163** F3
Southwick Rd SS8 . . . .**163** F3
Southwold Cres SS7 . . . . . .**144** C5
Southwold Dr IG11 . . . .**153** A7
Southwood Chase CM3 . .**57** A4
Southwood Ct SS14 . . . .**142** D8
Southwood Gdns
Ilford IG2 . . . .**133** B7
Rayleigh SS9 . . . .**146** B8
Southwood Prim Sch
RM9 . . . .**153** E8
Sovereign Cl SS4 . . . .**125** E2
Sovereign Ct
5 Brentwood CM14 . . . . . .**116** C7
Harlow CM19 . . . .**23** B5
Southend-on-S SS9 . . . .**146** E2
Sovereign Ho RM13 . . . .**155** B2
Sovereign Mews SS6 . . . . . .**60** C8
Sovereign Pk SS14 . . . .**120** E1
Sovereign Pl SS3 . . . .**168** E7

Sovereign Rd IG11 . . . .**153** C2
Sowerberry Cl CM1 . . . .**31** F7
Sowrey Ave RM13 . . . .**155** A6
Spa Cl SS5 . . . .**124** E6
Spa Ct SS5 . . . .**124** E6
Spa Dr CM0 . . . .**40** B1
Spa Rd SS5 . . . .**124** E6
Spains Hall Pl SS16 . . . . . .**142** C5
Spains Hall Rd CM5 . . . .**28** E2
Spalding Ave CM1 . . . .**31** E5
Spalding Ct CM1 . . . .**32** A3
Spalding Way CM2 . . . .**54** F8
Spalt Cl CM13 . . . .**117** B8
Spanbeek Rd SS8 . . . .**164** B5
Spar La CM3 . . . .**58** C3
Spareleaze Hill IG10 . . . . . .**88** F5
Sparkbridge 8 SS15 . . . . .**141** E6
Sparks Cl RM8 . . . .**134** D2
Sparrow Ct E4 . . . .**109** C4
Sparrow Rd RM10 . . . .**135** B1
Sparrow's La
Hatfield Heath CM22 . . . .**3** F1
White Roding CM22 . . . .**13** E6
Sparrows CM1 . . . .**52** A5
Sparrows Herne SS16 . . . .**142** B4
Sparsholt Rd IG11 . . . .**152** E4
Spearpoint Gdns IG2 . . . .**133** F7
Speedwell Ct RM17 . . . .**178** E2
Spellbrook Cl SS12 . . . .**121** F6
Spellbrook La E CM22 . . . . . .**1** F8
Spellbrook La W CM23 . . . . .**1** E7
Spellbrook Prim Sch
CM23 . . . .**1** F7
Spells Cl CM0 . . . .**84** D4
Spencer Cl Billericay CM12 **96** F5
Maldon CM9 . . . .**59** A8
Woodford IG8 . . . .**110** C5
Spencer Ct
Hornchurch RM12 . . . .**136** A1
South Woodham Ferrers
CM3 . . . .**101** E7
Spencer Gdns SS4 . . . .**125** E5
Spencer Ho SS0 . . . .**147** A1
Spencer Rd
Chingford E17 . . . .**109** C1
Ilford IG3 . . . .**133** F3
Rainham RM13 . . . .**154** D3
South Benfleet SS7 . . . .**144** D6
Spencer Wlk RM18 . . . .**179** B6
Spencers SS5 . . . .**124** E4
Spencers Croft CM18 . . . . .**24** B6
Spencers Ct SS12 . . . .**121** C7
Spenders Cl SS14 . . . .**142** D8
Spenlow Dr CM1 . . . .**31** D7
Spenser Cres RM14 . . . . . .**137** C4
Spey Way RM1 . . . .**113** E3
Speyside Wlk 2 SS12 . . . . .**121** E5
Spilbutters CM15 . . . .**72** B3
Spilsby Rd RM3 . . . .**114** E3
Spindle Beams SS4 . . . . . .**125** F1
Spindles RM18 . . . .**179** A7
Spingate Cl RM12 . . . .**155** D7
Spinnaker Cl IG11 . . . .**153** B2
Spinnaker Dr CM9 . . . .**37** E3
Spinnaker The CM3 . . . . . .**101** E5
Spinnakers The SS7 . . . . . .**144** B4
Spinney Cl
Rainham RM13 . . . .**154** E3
Wickford SS11 . . . .**121** F7
Spinney Ct CM21 . . . .**1** E2
Spinney Gdns RM9 . . . .**153** E7
Spinney Jun & Inf Schs
CM20 . . . .**11** A1
Spinney The
Billericay CM12 . . . .**97** B4
Brentwood CM13 . . . .**95** C3
Chipping Ongar CM5 . . . .**48** F1
Orsett RM16 . . . .**159** A1
Loughton IG10 . . . .**89** B5
Spinneys The
Hockley SS5 . . . .**124** D5
Rayleigh SS6 . . . .**124** A1
Southend-on-S SS9 . . . .**146** F7
Spinneywood SS15 . . . .**141** A8
Spinning Wheel Mead
CM18 . . . .**24** A5
Spire Green Ctr CM19 . . . .**22** E7
Spire Rd SS15 . . . .**141** C7
Spires The CM2 . . . .**54** F6
Spital La CM14 . . . .**115** F6
Spital Rd Maldon CM9 . . . .**36** F2
Maldon CM9 . . . .**58** D7
Sporehams La
Danbury CM3 . . . .**56** C4
Howe Green CM2,CM3 . . . . . .**55** F4
Sporhams SS16 . . . .**141** F4
Spots Wlk CM2 . . . .**54** D3
Spratt Hall Rd E11 . . . .**132** A5
Spread Eagle Pl CM4 . . . . . .**74** C4
Spriggs La CM4 . . . .**51** A2
Spriggs Oak CM4 . . . .**51** A2
Spring Cl Dagenham RM8 **134** D3
Little Baddow CM3 . . . .**34** D5
Spring Ct 10 E18 . . . .**132** B8
Spring Elms La CM3 . . . .**34** F3
Spring Gdns
Hornchurch RM12 . . . .**155** B8
Rayleigh SS6 . . . .**123** C2
Romford RM7 . . . .**135** C5
Spring Gr IG10 . . . .**88** D3
Spring Hills CM20 . . . .**10** B1
Spring La CM9 . . . .**37** B4
Spring Mews CM1 . . . .**31** E5
Spring Pond Cl CM2 . . . .**54** E8
Spring Pond Mdw CM15 **72** C4
Spring Rise CM2 . . . .**54** F6
Spring Vale DA9 . . . .**177** C1

Springbank Ave RM12 . . . .**155** C7
Springbok Ho CM2 . . . .**54** F5
Springfarm Cl RM13 . . . . . .**155** D2
Springfield Epping CM16 . . . .**67** F7
Hadleigh SS7 . . . .**145** C8
Springfield Ave CM13 . . . . . .**95** E2
Springfield Basin CM2 . . . .**32** C2
Springfield Cl CM5 . . . .**48** F5
Springfield Cotts CM9 . . . . .**37** B5
Springfield Ct
2 Ilford IG1 . . . .**152** B7
Rayleigh SS6 . . . .**123** A4
Upminster RM14 . . . .**137** B1
Springfield Dr Ilford IG2 **133** C5
Southend-on-S SS0 . . . .**147** D3
Springfield Gdns
Upminster RM14 . . . .**137** C1
Woodford IG8 . . . .**110** C3
Springfield Gn CM1 . . . .**32** E4
Springfield Ind Est CM0 **106** A5
Springfield Lyons App
CM2 . . . .**33** A5
Springfield Nursery Est
CM0 . . . .**106** A5
Springfield Park Ave
CM2 . . . .**32** E2
Springfield Park Hill
CM2 . . . .**32** D2
Springfield Park La CM2 **32** E2
Springfield Park Par
CM2 . . . .**32** D2
Springfield Park Rd CM2 **32** E2
Springfield Pl CM1 . . . .**32** E5
Springfield Rd
Billericay CM12 . . . .**97** B5
Burnham-on-C CM0 . . . .**106** A6
Canvey Island SS8 . . . .**164** F3
Chelmsford CM1 . . . .**32** E4
Chingford E4 . . . .**87** E2
Grays RM16 . . . .**173** E4
Wickford SS11 . . . .**121** F8
Springfields
Basildon SS16 . . . .**142** F4
Waltham Abbey EN9 . . . .**65** E5
Springhall Ct CM21 . . . .**1** E1
Springhall La CM21 . . . .**1** E1
Springhall Rd CM21 . . . .**1** F2
Springhead Rd DA11 . . . . . .**178** D1
Springhouse La SS17 . . . . .**161** A3
Springhouse Rd SS17 . . . . .**160** F4
Springleigh Pl SS0 . . . .**147** D2
Springpond Rd CM2 . . . .**53** E7
Springwater Cl SS9 . . . . . .**146** C7
Springwater Gr SS9 . . . . . .**146** C7
Springwater Rd SS9 . . . . . .**146** C8
Springwell Ct SS12 . . . .**8** C2
Springwood Way RM1 . . . .**136** A6
Spruce Cl SS15 . . . .**119** C1
Spruce Hill CM18 . . . .**23** E3
Spruce Hills Rd E17 . . . . . .**109** C1
Sprundel Ave SS8 . . . .**164** D2
Spur Cl RM4 . . . .**90** B6
Spur Rd SS11 . . . .**152** C2
Spurgate CM13 . . . .**95** B1
Spurling Rd RM9 . . . .**153** F6
Spurway Par 2 IG2 . . . .**132** F6
Squadrons App RM12 . . . .**155** D6
Square St CM17 . . . .**11** C1
Square The
7 Brentwood CM14 . . . . . .**116** C8
Heybridge CM9 . . . .**37** A5
Horndon-on-t-H SS17 . . . . . .**159** F3
Ilford IG1 . . . .**133** A4
Sawbridgeworth CM21 . . . .**1** E2
Stock CM4 . . . .**75** E2
Tillingham CM0 . . . .**63** E4
Woodford IG8 . . . .**110** E5
Squire St CM3 . . . .**101** E7
Squires Ct EN11 . . . .**21** A5
Squires The RM7 . . . .**135** B5
Squirrel's Chase RM16 **174** A4
Squirrel's Heath Ave
RM2 . . . .**136** B8
Squirrel's La IG9 . . . .**110** D7
Squirrells Ct CM1 . . . .**31** F5
Squirrels SS16 . . . .**141** B3
Squirrels Ct SS16 . . . .**141** C5
Squirrels Heath Jun & Inf
Sch RM2 . . . .**136** B6
Squirrels Heath La
RM11,RM2 . . . .**136** D7
Squirrels Heath Rd RM3 **137** F1
Stable Mews SS2 . . . .**147** E4
Stablecroft CM1 . . . .**32** E8
Stables The
Sawbridgeworth CM21 . . . .**2** B3
Buckhurst Hill IG9 . . . .**88** C2
Stacey Dr SS16 . . . .**141** C2
Stacey's Mount CM11 . . . .**120** C5
Stackfield CM20 . . . .**11** A3
Staddles CM22 . . . .**2** B8
Stadium Rd SS2 . . . .**148** A1
Stadium Trad Est SS7 . . . .**145** C7
Stadium Way Harlow CM19 **9** F1
Thundersley SS7 . . . .**145** C7
Staffa Cl SS12 . . . .**121** F5
Stafford Ave RM11 . . . .**136** D8
Stafford Cl Grays RM16 . . . .**172** C2
Greenhithe DA9 . . . .**176** F2
Linford SS17 . . . .**175** A3
Southend-on-S SS9 . . . .**147** A6
Stafford Ct EN10 . . . .**21** A3
Stafford Dr EN10 . . . .**21** A3
Stafford Gn SS16 . . . .**140** F4
Stafford Ho EN10 . . . .**21** A3
Stafford Wlk SS16 . . . .**164** A5
Staffords CM17 . . . .**11** E4
Stag La IG9 . . . .**110** B8

Stagden Cross SS14 . . . .**142** F5
Stagden Cross Villas CM1 .**6** E2
Staggart Gn IG7 . . . .**111** F4
Staines Rd IG1 . . . .**152** D8
Stainforth Rd IG2 . . . .**133** D5
Stairs Rd SS3 . . . .**150** F4
Stalham Way IG6 . . . .**111** B2
Stambridge Prim Sch
SS4 . . . .**126** C2
Stambridge Rd SS4 . . . . . .**126** C2
Stamford Gdns RM9 . . . . . .**153** C5
Stamford Rd RM9 . . . .**153** C5
Stammers Ct CM0 . . . .**84** D4
Standard Rd DA17 . . . .**169** A1
Standen Ave
Hornchurch RM12 . . . .**136** E1
South Woodham Ferrers
CM3 . . . .**101** C5
Standfield Gdns RM10 . . . .**154** A6
Standfield Rd RM10 . . . .**154** A7
Standingford CM19 . . . .**23** B3
Stanetta Ct 3 RM6 . . . . . .**134** B4
Staneway SS14 . . . .**141** D3
Stanfield Rd SS2 . . . .**148** A1
Stanfields Ct CM20 . . . .**10** E1
Stanford Cl
Romford RM7 . . . .**135** B5
Woodford IG8 . . . .**110** E5
Stanford Ct EN9 . . . .**66** A6
Stanford Gdns RM15 . . . . . .**171** C5
Stanford Hall 1 SS17 . . . .**160** F3
Stanford Ho SS17 . . . .**153** B3
Stanford Marshes★
SS17 . . . .**175** E7
Stanford Rd
Canvey Island SS8 . . . .**164** A3
Grays RM16 . . . .**173** E4
Orsett SS17,RM16 . . . .**174** E8
Stanford-le-H SS17 . . . .**160** B1
Stanford Rivers Rd CM5 **71** A8
Stanford-Le-Hope By-Pass
Basildon SS16,SS17 . . . .**142** B1
Orsett RM16 . . . .**174** D8
Stanford-le-H SS17 . . . .**160** D4
Stanford-le-Hope Jun & Inf
Schs SS17 . . . .**160** D1
Stanford-le-Hope Sta
SS17 . . . .**160** E1
Stanhope Gdns
1 Dagenham RM8 . . . .**134** F1
Redbridge IG1 . . . .**132** C5
Stanhope Rd
Dagenham RM8 . . . .**134** F1
Rainham RM13 . . . .**155** A3
Swanscombe DA10 . . . .**177** F1
Stanier Cl SS1 . . . .**168** C7
Stanley Ave Barking IG11 **152** F3
Dagenham RM8 . . . .**134** F3
Romford RM2 . . . .**136** A7
Stanley Cl
Greenhithe DA9 . . . .**176** E2
Hornchurch RM12 . . . .**136** C2
Romford RM2 . . . .**136** A7
Stanley Pl CM5 . . . .**49** A2
Stanley Rd Bulphan RM14 **158** F8
Canvey Island SS8 . . . .**164** D4
Chingford E4 . . . .**87** D1
Grays RM17 . . . .**178** B8
Hornchurch RM12 . . . .**136** D2
Ilford IG1 . . . .**133** D2
Rochford SS4 . . . .**125** C7
South Benfleet SS7 . . . .**144** D6
Southend-on-S SS1 . . . .**167** B7
Swanscombe DA10 . . . .**177** F1
Woodford E18 . . . .**109** F2
Stanley Rd N RM13 . . . .**154** E4
Stanley Rd S RM13 . . . .**154** F3
Stanley Rise CM2 . . . .**32** F3
Stanley Terr CM12 . . . .**97** A1
Stanmore Rd
Belvedere DA17 . . . .**169** C4
Wickford SS11 . . . .**122** B6
Stanmore Way IG10 . . . .**89** A8
Stannetts SS15 . . . .**141** B8
Stansfield Ct SS7 . . . .**144** B7
Stansfield Rd SS7 . . . .**144** B5
Stansgate Rd
Dagenham RM10 . . . .**135** A1
Steeple CM0 . . . .**61** F5
Stanstead Dr EN11 . . . .**21** B8
Stanstead Rd
Hoddesdon EN11 . . . .**8** B1
Wanstead E11 . . . .**132** B6
Stansted Cl
Billericay CM11 . . . .**97** D2
Chelmsford CM1 . . . .**31** E1
Hornchurch RM12 . . . .**155** B6
Stanton Gate RM7 . . . .**135** D6
Stantons CM20 . . . .**10** E1
Stanway Cl 2 IG7 . . . .**111** C5
Stanway Rd
South Benfleet SS7 . . . .**144** C4
Waltham Abbey EN9 . . . .**66** A6
Stanwyck Dr IG7 . . . .**111** C5
Stanwyck Gdns RM3 . . . . . .**114** B5
Staple Tye CM18 . . . .**23** C5
Staple Tye Sh Mews
CM18 . . . .**23** C5
Stapleford Abbotts Prim Sch
RM4 . . . .**91** C4
Stapleford Ave IG2 . . . .**133** E6
Stapleford Cl
Chelmsford CM2 . . . .**32** A1
Chingford E4 . . . .**87** C1
Stapleford End SS11 . . . . .**122** B5
Stapleford Gdns RM5 . . . . .**113** A4
Stapleford Rd RM4 . . . .**91** B5
Stapleford Way IG11 . . . . . .**153** B2

Staplegrove SS3 ......168 D8
Staples Rd IG10 ......88 E6
Staples Road Jun & Inf Sch
  IG10 ......88 E6
Stapleton Cres RM13 ...155 A6
Stapley Rd DA17 ......169 A1
Star Bsns Ctr RM13 ...169 D8
Star La Epping CM16 ...46 A1
  Great Wakering SS3 ...149 E3
  Ingatestone CM4 ......74 C4
Starboard Ave DA9 ....177 B1
Starboard View CM3 ...101 E6
Starch House La IG6 ...111 D1
Starling Cl IG9 ......88 A1
Starmans Cl RM9 .....153 E4
State Mans IG6 ......111 C1
State Par IG6 ......111 C1
Station App
  Basildon,Laindon SS15 ...141 C5
  Basildon,Pitsea SS16 ...143 B4
  Burnham-on-C CM0 ....106 B5
  Canvey Island SS8 ....163 F6
  Grays RM17 ......178 A8
  Harlow CM20 ......11 C5
  Hockley SS5 ......124 E6
  North Fambridge CM3 ...103 B8
  North Woodham Ferrers
    CM3 ......101 C8
  Southend-on-S SS1 ...167 A8
  Southend-on-S, Prittlewell
    SS2 ......147 F2
  Theydon Bois CM16 ...67 E3
  Wanstead E11 ......132 A6
  Wickford SS11 ......121 D8
  Woodford IG8 ......110 B4
  2 Woodford, South Woodford
    E18 ......110 B1
  Woodford, Woodford Wells
    IG9 ......110 D6
Station Ave Rayleigh SS6 123 C3
  Southend-on-S SS2 ...148 A3
  Wickford SS11 ......121 D8
Station Cres
  Cold Norton CM3 ......80 F5
  Rayleigh SS6 ......123 D3
Station Ct SS12 ......121 D8
Station Est 1 E18 ....110 B1
Station Gate SS15 ....141 C5
Station Ind Est CM0 ...106 B5
Station La Basildon SS13 143 B5
  Hornchurch RM12 .....136 E2
  Ingatestone CM4 ......74 B3
Station Par Barking IG11 152 C5
  Dagenham RM10 ......154 A6
  Hornchurch RM12 .....155 B8
  3 Romford RM1 ......135 E5
  Wanstead E11 ......132 A6
  Woodford IG9 ......110 D6
Station Pas E18 ......110 B1
Station Rd Althorne CM3 ..82 F1
  Belvedere DA17 ......169 A3
  Billericay CM12 ......96 F2
  Burnham-on-C CM0 ...106 B6
  Canvey Island SS8 ....164 E2
  Chigwell IG7 ......111 B7
  Chingford E4 ......87 D1
  Cold Norton CM3 ......81 A5
  East Tilbury RM18 ....180 B7
  Epping CM16 ......68 A8
  Greenhithe DA9 ......177 A2
  Greenhithe DA9 ......177 A3
  Harlow CM17 ......11 C4
  Hockley SS5 ......124 E6
  Hoddesdon EN10 ......21 A3
  Holdbrook EN9 ......65 A5
  Ilford IG11 ......133 B1
  Ilford, Barkingside IG6 ...133 D8
  Loughton IG10 ......88 E4
  Maldon CM9 ......37 A3
  North Weald Bassett CM16 ..47 B4
  Northfleet DA11 ......178 B1
  Rayleigh SS6 ......123 C3
  Romford RM2 ......136 C7
  Romford, Chadwell Heath
    RM6,RM8 ......134 D4
  Romford, Harold Wood
    RM3 ......114 F2
  Sawbridgeworth CM21 ...1 F3
  South Benfleet SS7 ....163 D8
  Southend-on-S, Leigh-on-S
    SS9 ......146 E1
  Southend-on-S, Leigh-on-S
    SS9 ......146 E3
  Southend-on-S, Thorpe Bay
    SS1 ......168 B8
  Southend-on-S,Westcliff-on-S
    SS0 ......166 D7
  Southminster CM0 .....84 E4
  Stansted Abbotts SG12 ...8 C4
  Upminster RM14 ......137 C2
  West Horndon CM13 ...139 D5
  Wickford SS11 ......99 C2
Station Rd N DA17 ....169 B3
Station Sq RM2 ......136 B7
Station Way
  Basildon SS14,SS16 ...142 A5
  Buckhurst Hill IG9 ...110 D6
Staveley Cl 4 E11 ....132 A6
Staverton Rd RM11 ...136 D5
Stays La CM5 ......29 A3
Steadman Ho 4 RM10 ...135 A1
Steamer Terr 2 CM1 ...32 A3
Stebbing Way IG11 ...153 E3
Stebbings SS16 ......141 C4
Stebbings Ct 5 CM0 ...106 C4
Steed Cl RM11 ......136 F2
Steeds Way IG10 ......88 E6
Steel App IG11 ......153 D3

Steele Ave DA9 ......177 A2
Steen Cl CM4 ......74 B4
Steeple Cl Heybridge CM9 ..37 D5
  Rochford SS4 ......125 D3
Steeple Hts SS7 ......144 B6
Steeple Mdws CM0 ....84 B4
Steeple Rd
  Latchingdon CM3 .....82 D7
  Southminster CM0 ....62 C4
  Steeple CM0 ......84 B7
Steeple View CM17 ...173 A1
Steeple Way CM15 ....72 B2
Steeplefield SS9 ......146 E6
Steeplehall SS13 ......143 A5
Steerforth Cl CM1 ....31 D7
Steli Ave SS8 ......163 F5
Stella Maris Cl SS8 ...164 F3
Sten Cl EN3 ......65 A2
Stenning Ave SS17 ...175 B2
Stephen Ave RM13 ...155 A6
Stephens Cl RM3 ......114 C5
Stephens Cres SS17 ...159 F3
Stephenson Rd
  North Fambridge CM3 ...103 A8
  Southend-on-S SS9 ...146 C6
Sterling Ind Est RM10 ...154 B8
Stern Cl IG11 ......153 C3
Sterry Cres RM10 ....154 A7
Sterry Gdns RM10 ....154 A6
Sterry Ho RM13 ......155 F1
Sterry Rd Barking IG11 ...152 F4
  Dagenham RM10 ......154 A7
Stevanne Ct 1 DA17 ...169 A1
Stevenage Rd E6 ......152 A6
Stevens Cl SS8 ......164 D4
Stevens Rd RM8 ......134 C1
Stevens Way IG7 ......111 E6
Stevenson Way SS12 ...121 C5
Stewards Cl CM16 ....68 A6
Stewards Elm Farm La
  CM16 ......126 D4
Stewards Green Rd
  CM16 ......68 B6
Stewards Sch CM18 ...23 D4
Stewards Wlk RM1 ...135 E6
Stewart Ave RM14 ...137 B1
Stewart Pl CM3 ......121 F5
Stewart Rainbird Ho 1
  E12 ......152 A7
Stewart Rd CM2 ......54 A6
Steyning Ave SS2 ....148 E1
Stickland Rd DA17 ....169 A2
Stifford Clays Jun & Inf Schs
  RM16 ......173 B5
Stifford Clays Rd
  Grays RM16 ......173 B6
  Orsett RM16 ......173 B7
Stifford Hill RM16 ....172 C5
Stifford Prim Sch RM17 172 F1
Stifford Rd Aveley RM15 ...171 E5
  South Ockendon RM15 ...172 B6
Stile Croft CM18 ......24 A6
Stile La SS6 ......123 D2
Stilemans SS11 ......121 D8
Stiles Cl DA8 ......169 B1
Stiles The CM9 ......37 E3
Stilwells SS4 ......126 A2
Stirling Ave SS9 ......146 B2
Stirling Cl Rainham RM13 155 B2
  Rayleigh SS6 ......123 B5
Stirling Pl SS13 ......143 B8
Stirrup Cl CM1 ......32 E7
Stivvy's Rd CM9 ......35 C3
Stock CE Prim Sch CM4 ...75 D3
Stock Chase CM9 ......37 B5
Stock Cl SS2 ......147 F4
Stock Ind Pk SS2 ....148 A4
Stock La CM4 ......74 D3
Stock Park Ct SS9 ....146 E6
Stock Rd Billericay CM12 ...97 C5
  Galleywood CM2 ......54 B2
  Southend-on-S SS2 ...147 F4
  Stock CM4 ......76 B6
Stock Terr CM9 ......37 B5
Stockdale Rd RM8 ....134 F2
Stocker Gdns RM9 ...153 C5
Stockfield Ave EN11 ...21 B8
Stockland Rd RM7 ....135 D5
Stocksfield CM15 ......71 F2
Stockwell Cl CM11 ...119 D7
Stockwood SS7 ......145 B7
Stoke Ave IG6 ......112 A4
Stoke Rd RM13 ......155 D2
Stokefelde SS13 ......143 B8
Stokes Cotts IG6 ......111 C2
Stokes Ct SS2 ......148 E2
Stokesay Ct 11 DA2 ...176 B1
Stonard Rd RM8 ......135 A4
Stonards Hill Epping CM16 68 C8
  Loughton IG10 ......88 F4
Stondon Rd CM5 ......49 B1
Stone Cl RM8 ......134 F2
Stone Cross CM20 ....10 D1
Stone Crossing Halt
  DA9 ......176 E2
Stone Ct DA8 ......169 F1
Stone House Hospl DA2 176 C1
Stone Lodge Farm Pk★
  DA2 ......176 C1
Stone Place Rd DA9 ...176 E2
Stone St DA11 ......179 B1
Stonebridge Rd DA11 ...178 B2
Stonechat Rd CM2 ...54 C3
Stonegate CM4 ......74 C3
Stonehall Ave IG1 ....132 C4
Stonehill Cl SS9 ......146 F4
Stonehill Ct E4 ......87 B2

Stonehill Rd Roxwell CM1 ..29 F3
  Southend-on-S SS9 ...146 F5
Stonehouse Cnr RM19 ...176 E8
Stoneleigh CM21 ......1 D3
Stoneleigh Dr EN11 ...8 B1
Stoneleigh Rd IG5 ....132 F8
Stoneleighs SS7 ......144 F6
Stoneness Rd RM20 ...177 C2
Stonewood Rd DA8 ...169 E1
Stoney Bridge Dr EN9 ...66 A5
Stoney Hills
  Burnham-on-C CM0 ...106 C8
  Ramsden Heath CM11 ...98 B5
Stoneycroft RM IG8 ...110 E4
Stony La CM5 ......48 C8
Stony Path IG10 ......88 F8
Stony Wood CM18 ....23 E7
Stonyshotts EN9 ......65 E6
Storas Ct 9 RM19 ...171 B1
Stormonts Way SS16 ...141 D2
Storms Way CM2 ......33 B2
Stornoway Rd SS2 ...148 D1
Storr Gdns CM13 ......95 D4
Stort Mill CM20 ......11 B6
Stortford Rd
  Hatfield Heath CM22 ...2 E4
  Hoddesdon EN11 ......21 C7
  Leaden Roding CM6 ...15 E7
Stour Cl SS3 ......168 E6
Stour Rd
  Dagenham RM10 .....135 A2
  Grays RM17 ......174 A1
Stour Way RM14 ......137 E5
Stow Rd CM3 ......80 D5
Stow The CM20 ......10 F2
Stow Villas CM3 ......80 C4
Stowe Ct SS0 ......147 E1
Stowe Pl SS2 ......148 C2
Stowe Villas SS2 ......167 C8
Stowe's La CM0 ......63 D4
Stradbroke Dr IG7 ....111 B4
Stradbroke Gr
  Buckhurst Hill IG9 ....88 D1
  Ilford IG5 ......133 A4
  Redbridge IG5 ......132 F8
  Woodford IG5 ......110 E1
Stradbroke Pk IG7 ....111 B4
Strafford Ave IG5 ....111 A4
Straight Rd RM3 ......114 C3
Straits The EN9 ......65 B7
Strangman Ave SS7 ...145 B4
Strasbourg Rd SS8 ...164 D5
Stratford Cl
  Barking IG11 ......153 A5
  Dagenham RM10 .....154 A5
Stratford Gdns SS17 ...160 D3
Stratford Ho
  Rayleigh SS6 ......123 D2
  6 Romford RM3 ......114 C4
Strathfield Gdns IG11 ...152 D6
Strathmore RM18 ....175 C2
Strathmore Gdns RM12 135 B4
Strathmore Rd CM3 ...103 B8
Stratton Dr IG11 ......152 F6
Stratton Ho SS1 ......166 F7
Stratton Rd RM3 ......115 A5
Stratton Wlk RM3 ....115 A5
Street The
  Galleywood CM2 ......54 B2
  High Ongar CM5 ......49 D4
  High Roding CM6 ......5 E7
  Latchingdon CM3 .....82 A5
  Little Waltham CM3 ...19 B6
  Mashbury CM1 ......17 B8
  Pleshey CM3 ......7 F2
  Purleigh CM3,CM9 ...58 F1
  Roxwell CM1 ......30 B6
  Sheering CM22 ......12 C8
  Steeple CM0 ......61 F2
  Stow Maries CM3 ......80 C4
  Willingale CM5 ......28 D3
  Woodham Ferrers CM3 ...79 B4
  Woodham Walter CM9 ...35 D2
Stroma Ave SS8 ......163 F6
Stroma Gdns SS3 ....168 D6
Stromburg Rd SS8 ...163 F5
Stromness Pl 7 SS2 ...167 C8
Stromness Rd SS2 ...148 C1
Strood Ave RM7 ......135 D3
Stroud Ho 8 RM3 ...114 D5
Strouds Cl RM6 ......134 B6
Struan Ave SS7 ......160 E5
Struan Ho 11 E11 ....132 A4
Stuart Cl
  Canvey Island SS8 ...164 B4
  Great Baddow CM2 ...55 B6
  Great Wakering SS3 ...149 F4
  Pilgrims Hatch CM15 ...94 B4
  Southend-on-S SS2 ...148 A2
Stuart Ct E4 ......109 F8
Stuart Ho EN9 ......65 F6
Stuart Rd Barking IG11 ...152 F4
  Gravesend DA11 ......179 A1
  Grays RM17 ......173 B1
  Southend-on-S SS2 ...148 B2
Stuart St SS2 ......148 A3
Stuart Way CM11 ......97 E1
Stuarts RM11 ......136 E3
Stubbers La RM14 ...156 E5
Stubbs Mews RM8 ...153 B8
Stublands SS14 ......142 F6
Studland Ave SS12 ...120 F8
Studley Ave E4 ......109 D3
Studley Cl IG4 ......132 D5
Studley Dr IG4 ......132 D5
Studley Rd RM9 ......153 D5
Stump La CM1 ......32 C4
Sturge Ave E17 ......109 B1

Sturrocks SS16 ......142 E3
Sudbrook Cl SS12 ...121 D6
Sudbury Cl SS5 ......124 D6
Sudbury Rd Barking IG11 152 F7
  Canvey Island SS8 ...163 F5
  Downham CM11 ......99 A5
Sudburys Farm Rd
  CM12 ......118 C6
Sudeley Gdns SS5 ....124 D6
Sudicamps Ct EN9 ...66 A6
Suffield Rd E4 ......109 B6
Suffolk Ave SS9 ......146 F3
Suffolk Cres CM9 ......36 E1
Suffolk Ct Ilford IG3 ...133 E5
  Rochford SS4 ......125 E2
Suffolk Dr Basildon SS15 141 B6
  Chelmsford CM2 ......33 A4
Suffolk Ho RM7 ......113 A2
Suffolk Rd Barking IG11 ...152 D5
  Dagenham RM10 .....154 C7
  Gravesend DA12 ......179 D1
  Ilford IG3 ......133 E5
  Maldon CM9 ......36 E1
Suffolk Way
  Canvey Island SS8 ...163 E4
  Hornchurch RM11 ...137 A7
Suffolk Wlk SS8 ......163 E4
Sugden Ave SS12 ....121 A7
Sugden Way IG11 ...152 F3
Sullivan Rd RM18 ....179 A6
Sullivan Way SS16 ...141 A5
Sultan Rd E11 ......109 E8
Summercourt Rd SS0 ...166 E8
Summerdale
  Althorne CM3 ......83 A3
  Billericay CM12 ......97 A2
Summerfield Rd IG10 ...88 D3
Summerfields CM4 ...74 C3
Summerhill CM3 ......83 A3
Summerlands SS8 ...163 F5
Summerwood Cl SS7 ...145 C8
Summit Dr IG8 ......110 D1
Summit The IG10 ......88 F8
Sumners Farm Cl CM19 23 A3
Sumpners Link SS15 ...140 E6
Sumpters Way SS2 ...147 F5
Sun Ray Ave CM13 ...95 E3
Sun Rd DA10 ......177 F1
Sun St Billericay CM12 ...97 A1
  Sawbridgeworth CM21 ...1 F1
  Waltham Abbey EN9 ...65 C6
Sunbury Ct SS3 ......149 E2
Sunbury Way CM9 ...58 F8
Sunderland Way E12 ...132 D2
Sundew Ct RM17 ......178 D8
Sundridge Cl DA1 ....176 A1
Sunflower Cl 5 CM1 ...32 F6
Sunflower Way RM3 ...114 D2
Sunnedon SS16 ......142 D5
Sunningdale SS8 ......164 C4
Sunningdale Ave
  Barking IG11 ......152 D5
  Rainham RM13 ......155 B1
  Southend-on-S SS9 ...147 A1
Sunningdale Rd
  Althorne CM3 ......82 E2
  Chelmsford CM1 ......31 E4
  Rainham RM13 ......155 A5
Sunninghill Gdns IG2 ...133 F6
Sunnings La RM14 ...156 D5
Sunny Ct CM18 ......23 F5
Sunny Mews RM5 ...113 C3
Sunny Rd SS5 ......124 E5
Sunny Way CM0 ......62 C8
Sunnybank Cl SS9 ...146 F6
Sunnycroft Gdns RM14 137 F4
Sunnydene Ave E4 ...109 D5
Sunnydene Cl RM3 ...114 F3
Sunnyfield Gdns SS5 ...124 B6
Sunnymead Flats 10
  CM0 ......106 C4
Sunnymede SS7 ......112 B7
Sunnymede Cl SS7 ...145 A6
Sunnymede Dr IG6 ...133 B7
Sunnymede Inf Sch
  CM11 ......97 D1
Sunnyside Basildon SS16 140 F4
  Lower Nazeing EN9 ...21 F1
Sunnyside Dr E4 ......87 C2
Sunnyside Gdns RM14 137 C1
Sunnyside Rd
  Epping CM16 ......67 F7
  Ilford IG1 ......133 D1
Sunnyway Cotts CM3 ...56 E3
Sunray Ho SS0 ......166 D8
Sunrise Ave
  Chelmsford CM1 ......32 A5
  Hornchurch RM12 ...136 C1
Sunrise Lodge RM12 ...136 C1
Sunset Ave Chingford E4 ...87 B1
Sunset Ct 4 IG8 ......110 C3
Surbiton Ave SS1 ...167 D4
Surbiton Rd SS2 ......148 D1
Surig Rd SS8 ......164 C4
Surman Cres CM13 ...95 C2
Surman Terr RM11 ...136 C1
Surmans Cl RM9 ......153 C4
Surrey Ave SS9 ......146 F3
Surrey Dr RM11 ......137 A3
Surrey Ho RM7 ......113 A2
Surrey Rd Barking IG11 ...152 E5
  Dagenham RM10 .....154 C7
Surrey Way SS15 ......141 B6
Surridge Cl RM13 ...155 C2
Susan Cl RM7 ......135 C8

Susan Fielder Cotts 3
  SS8 ......164 A3
Susan Lawrence Ho 4
  E12 ......152 A8
Sussex Ave RM3 ......114 F3
Sussex Cl Basildon SS15 141 B5
  Boreham CM3 ......33 F8
  Canvey Island SS8 ...164 A5
  Hoddesdon EN11 ......21 A7
  Redbridge IG4 ......132 F6
Sussex Ct CM12 ......97 B6
Sussex Ho RM7 ......113 A2
Sussex Rd
  Brentwood CM14 ....116 B6
  Walland E6 ......152 A4
Sussex Terr 2 RM19 ...171 B1
Sussex Way
  Billericay CM12 ......97 B6
  Canvey Island SS8 ...164 A5
Sutcliffe Cl SS12 ......121 D6
Sutherland Bvd SS9 ...146 B2
Sutherland Cl DA9 ...176 F2
Sutherland Ho
  Chelmsford CM1 ......32 A4
  5 Redbridge IG8 ...111 A3
Sutherland Pl SS12 ...121 D5
Sutherland Rd DA17 ...169 A6
Sutton Acres CM22 ...2 D7
Sutton Cl IG10 ......88 E2
Sutton Court Dr SS4 ...147 F7
Sutton Ct SS2 ......148 C2
Sutton Ford Cotts SS4 148 B8
Sutton Gdns IG11 ...152 E3
Sutton Gn IG11 ......152 E4
Sutton Mead CM2 ...33 A4
Sutton Rd Barking IG11 ...152 E4
  Rochford SS3,SS4 ...148 B6
  Southend-on-S SS2 ...148 B2
Suttons Ave RM12 ...136 D1
Suttons Bsns Pk RM13 154 E2
Suttons Gdns RM12 ...136 D1
Suttons La RM12 ......155 D7
Suttons Prim Sch RM12 155 D8
Suttons Rd SS3 ......168 A8
Swale Cl RM15 ......171 C7
Swale Rd SS7 ......145 B5
Swallow Cl Grays RM16 ...171 C7
  Greenhithe DA9 ......176 F2
  Rayleigh SS6 ......123 B3
Swallow Ct
  6 Brentwood CM14 ...116 C7
  Chingford IG8 ......109 D3
  Ilford IG2 ......133 B6
Swallow Dale SS16 ...142 C4
Swallow Dr SS7 ......144 C2
Swallow Path CM2 ...54 B5
Swallow Rd SS11 ......99 C2
Swallow Wlk 5 RM15 ...155 B6
Swallowcliffe SS3 ...149 D1
Swallows CM17 ......11 C4
Swallows The CM11 ...119 C8
Swan & Pike Rd EN3 ...65 A1
Swan Ave RM14 ......137 F5
Swan Cl SS15 ......141 E6
Swan Ct Maldon CM9 ...37 B4
  South Benfleet SS7 ...144 B5
Swan La
  Kelvedon Hatch CM15 ...71 E2
  Loughton IG10 ......88 C2
  Stock CM4 ......75 C5
  Wickford SS11 ......99 D1
Swan Mead SS16 ......142 D4
Swan Paddock 3 CM14 116 C8
Swan Wlk RM1 ......135 E6
Swanage Rd
  Chingford E4 ......109 C3
  Southend-on-S SS2 ...148 B1
Swanbourne Dr RM12 ...136 C1
Swans Green Cl SS7 ...145 A6
Swans Pasture CM1 ...32 D6
Swanscombe Bsns Ctr
  DA10 ......177 E2
Swanscombe Cross
  DA10 ......177 D2
Swanscombe St DA10 ...177 F1
Swanscombe Sta DA10 ...177 F2
Swanshope IG10 ......89 B7
Swanstead SS16 ......142 E4
Swatchways SS1 ......167 C6
Sweet Briar Ave SS7 ...144 D2
Sweet Briar Dr SS15 ...119 D1
Sweetbriar Lodge SS8 163 E4
Sweyne Ave Hockley SS5 125 A4
  Southend-on-S SS2 ...147 F1
Sweyne Cl SS6 ......123 B4
Sweyne Ct SS2 ......147 F1
Sweyne Park Sch The
  SS6 ......123 C4
Sweyne Rd DA10 ......177 F1
Sweyns CM17 ......24 C6
Swift Cl
  Stanstead Abbotts SG12 ...8 C4
  Upminster RM14 ......137 E3
Swift Ho 8 E18 ......132 B8
Swiftsure Rd RM16 ...172 C2
Swinborne Ct SS13 ...121 B2
Swinborne Rd SS13 ...121 C1
Swindon Cl Ilford IG3 ...133 E3
  Romford RM3 ......114 F5
Swindon Gdns RM3 ...114 F5
Swindon La RM3 ......114 F5
Swingboat Terr 3 SS1 ...167 C7
Swiss Ave CM1 ......32 A4

Sycamore Cl
Canvey Island SS8 ......163 F3
Loughton IG10 ....89 B7
Rayleigh SS6 ....123 B6
Tilbury RM18 ......179 A5
Sycamore Ct Erith DA8 ..169 D1
Southend-on-S SS3 ....168 F7
Wickford SS12 ....121 D8
Sycamore Dr CM14 ....94 C1
Sycamore Field CM19 ..23 A5
Sycamore Gr SS2 ......148 B2
Sycamore Ho
4 Buckhurst Hill IG9 ..110 D8
Wickford SS11 ......121 E7
Sycamore Mews DA8 ..169 D1
Sycamore Rd CM9 .....37 C6
Sycamore Way
Canewdon SS4 ....104 D1
Chelmsford CM2 ....54 C6
South Ockendon RM15 .157 D1
Sycamore Wlk IG6 ....133 C7
Sycamores The
14 Basildon SS13 ....143 C6
Aveley RM15 ....171 D5
Sydenham Cl RM1 ....135 F7
Sydervelt Rd SS8 .....164 A4
Sydner Cl CM2 ....55 A5
Sydney Rd Redbridge IG6 111 C1
South Benfleet SS7 ...144 C4
Southend-on-S SS9 ...146 B2
Tilbury RM18 ....179 A5
Wanstead E11 ......132 B5
Woodford IG8 ....110 A4
Sydney Russell Sch The
RM9 ....153 D7
Sykes Mead SS6 ......123 D1
Sylvan Ave
Dagenham RM6 ......134 F5
Hornchurch RM11 ....136 F5
Sylvan Cl Basildon SS15 141 B6
Canvey Island SS8 ....164 B2
Chelmsford CM2 ......54 B6
Grays RM16 ....172 A5
Sylvan Ct SS15 ......140 F7
Sylvan Mews DA9 ....177 B3
Sylvan Rd Ilford IG1 ...133 C2
Wanstead E11 ......132 A6
Sylvan Tryst CM12 ....97 B4
Sylvan Way
Basildon SS15 ......140 F7
Chigwell IG7 ....112 B7
Dagenham RM8 ......134 B1
Southend-on-S SS9 ...146 A4
Sylvester Gdns IG6 ...112 B5
Sylvesters CM19 ......22 F6
Sylvia Ave CM13 .....117 C8
Sylvia Pankhurst Ho 10
RM10 ....135 A1
Symons Ave SS9 .....146 E7
Syracuse Ave RM13 ...155 E2
Syringa Ct RM17 .....178 D8

T

Tabor's Hill CM2 ......54 F7
Tabora Ave SS8 ......163 F6
Tabors Ave CM2 ......54 F8
Tabors Ct CM15 ......94 F2
Tabrums The CM3 .....79 C1
Tabrums Way RM14 ...137 E6
Tadlows Cl SS11 .....156 B7
Tadworth Par RM12 ...155 B8
Taffrail Gdns CM3 ....101 C5
Tailors Ct SS2 ....147 F5
Tait Mews CM9 ....37 A2
Taits SS17 ....160 F7
Takeley Cl Romford RM5 113 D1
Waltham Abbey EN9 ....65 D6
Takely End SS16 .....142 A5
Takely Ride SS16 .....142 A5
Talbot Ave SS6 ......123 C3
Talbot Gdns IG3 .....134 A2
Talbot Rd Dagenham RM9 153 D5
Wallend E6 ....152 A3
Talbrook CM14 ......115 F7
Talgarth Ho 3 RM3 ...114 E4
Talisman Cl 2 IG3 ....134 B3
Talisman Wlk CM11 ...97 D6
Tall Trees Cl RM11 ...136 E5
Tallis Cl SS17 ......160 C3
Tallis Ct RM2 ....136 C8
Tallis Rd SS15 ......141 D8
Tallis Way CM14 .....116 B5
Tallon Rd CM13 ......95 E4
Tallow Gate CM3 .....101 E6
Tally-Ho Dr CM13 ....96 C1
Talus CM19 ....171 D2
Tama Cotts RM14 ....137 F2
Tamar Cl RM14 ......137 E6
Tamar Dr RM15 .....171 C7
Tamar Rise CM1 .....32 C6
Tamar Sq IG8 ....110 B4
Tamarisk SS7 ....144 C4
Tamarisk Rd RM15 ...157 C1
Tamworth Ave IG8 ...109 C4
Tan House La
Navestock Heath CM14 ..92 F5
Navestock Side CM14 ..93 A6
Tanfield Dr CM14 ....92 A2
Tanfield Tye Cotts CM2 76 C7
Tangent Link RM3 ....114 D2
Tangent Rd RM1 .....114 D2
Tangham Wlk SS14 ...142 C7

Tangmere Cl SS11 ....122 B6
Tangmere Cres RM12 .155 B6
Tank Hill Rd RM19 ...171 A2
Tank La RM19 ......171 B2
Tankerville Dr SS9 ...146 B3
Tanner St IG11 ......152 C6
Tanners La IG6 ......133 C8
Tanners Way
Hunsdonbury SS12 ......9 D8
South Woodham Ferrers
CM3 ....101 C8
Tannery Cl RM10 ....135 B1
Tanswell Ave SS13 ...143 B6
Tanswell Cl SS13 ....143 B6
Tanswell Ct SS13 ....143 B7
Tansy Cl RM3 ....114 E4
Tantelen Rd SS8 .....163 F5
Tantony Gr RM6 .....134 D8
Tany's Dell CM20 .....11 A3
Tany's Dell Com Prim Sch
CM20 ....11 A3
Tapley Rd CM1 ......31 F7
Tara Ct 9 IG9 ......110 C8
Taranto Rd SS8 .....164 D3
Tarlings CM3 ....10 F3
Tarnworth Rd RM3 ...115 A4
Tasker Ho IG11 .....152 D3
Tasker Rd RM16 .....174 B3
Tasman Cl SS17 .....160 F4
Tasman Ct CM1 .....31 D5
Tasmania Ho RM18 ...179 A6
Tatsfield Ave EN9 ....43 E8
Tattenham Rd SS15 ..141 B7
Tattersall Gdns SS9 ..146 A1
Tattersall Way CM1 ..53 E7
Tattersalls Chase CM0 84 E4
Tattershall Ct 19 DA2 176 B1
Taunton Cl IG6 ......111 F4
Taunton Dr SS0 .....147 B4
Taunton Ho RM3 ....114 F5
Taunton Rd
Chelmsford CM1 .....32 E5
Northfleet DA11 .....178 A2
Romford RM3 ......114 C6
Taveners Green Cl SS12 121 E6
Taverners Way
Chingford E4 ....87 E1
Hoddesdon EN11 ......21 A6
Tavistock Cl RM3 ....114 D2
Tavistock Dr CM12 ...96 F5
Tavistock Gdns IG3 ..152 E8
Tavistock Ho 1 IG8 ..111 A3
Tavistock Rd
Basildon SS15 ......141 C8
Chelmsford CM1 .....32 E5
Wanstead E18 ......132 A8
Tawney Comm CM16 ..69 B7
Tawney La RM4 .....69 D4
Tawneys Rd CM18 ....23 F6
Tawny Ave E14 ......156 B7
Tay Way RM1 ....113 F2
Taylifers CM19 ......23 A3
Taylor Ave CM1 .....31 E5
Taylor Cl RM5 ......113 A3
Taylor Gdns RM3 ....114 C8
Taylors Ave EN11 ....21 A5
Tayside Wlk 6 SS12 ..121 E5
Teagles SS15 ....141 E6
Teal Ave CM3 ....83 A8
Teal Ct CM3 ....83 A8
Teale Ho 5 EN11 ....21 D8
Ted Hennem Ho RM10 135 B1
Tees Cl RM14 ......137 D5
Tees Dr RM3 ....114 D2
Tees Rd CM1 ....32 C6
Teigngrace SS3 .....168 D8
Teignmouth Dr SS6 ..123 D5
Telegraph Mews
Ilford,Goodmayes IG3 ..134 A3
Ilford, Seven Kings IG3 .133 F3
Telese Ave SS8 .....164 B3
Telford Ho 2 DA17 ...169 A3
Telford Pl CM1 ......32 C4
Telham Rd E6 ......152 A3
Tempest Mead CM16 ..47 B4
Tempest Way RM13 ..155 A6
Templar Ct RM7 .....135 B7
Templar Ho RM3 ....154 D3
Temple Ave RM8 ....135 A3
Temple Bank CM20 ...11 B5
Temple Cl Basildon SS15 141 C7
Billericay CM12 .....96 F5
Hadleigh SS7 ....145 F3
Temple Ct SS2 ......148 C3
Temple Farm Trad Est
CM2 ....76 C6
Temple Gate Cotts SS2 148 B5
Temple Gdns RM8 ...134 D1
Temple Hall Ct E4 ...109 D8
Temple Hill Prim Sch
DA1 ....176 A2
Temple Mead CM19 ...9 B1
Temple Sutton Prim Sch
SS2 ....148 C3
Temple Way CM9 ....36 F5
Templefields Ent Ctr
CM20 ....11 A3
Templer Ave RM16 ...174 A2
Templeton Ave E4 ...109 B6
Templewood Ct SS7 ..145 D3
Templewood Rd SS7 .145 D3
Temptin Ave SS8 ....164 E4
Ten Acre App CM9 ...36 F5
Tenby Cl RM6 ......134 E5
Tenby Rd RM6 .....134 E5
Tendring Ave SS6 ....123 B4
Tendring Ct CM13 ....95 D4

Tendring Rd CM18 ....23 E6
Tendring Way RM6 ...134 C6
Tenney Ho RM17 ....178 C7
Tennyson Ave
Grays RM17 ....173 C3
Southend-on-S SS2 ..148 B2
Waltham Abbey EN9 ...65 E5
Wanstead E11 ......132 A4
Tennyson Cl SS9 ....146 A2
Tennyson Dr 9 SS13 .143 B5
Tennyson Ho CM16 ...68 A8
Tennyson Rd
Brentwood CM13 ....95 D2
Chelmsford CM1 .....31 F5
Dartford DA1 ......176 A2
Maldon CM9 ....59 A8
Romford RM3 ......114 C3
Tennyson Way RM12 .135 F2
Tensing Gdns CM12 ..97 A1
Tenterden Rd RM8 ...134 F2
Tenterfield Rd CM9 ...37 A2
Tenterfields SS13 ....121 C1
Teramo Rd SS8 .....164 D3
Tercel Path IG7 .....112 B6
Terence Webster Rd
SS12 ....121 E6
Terling SS16 ....142 B5
Terling Rd RM8 .....135 A2
Terlings Pk CM20 ....10 A3
Terlings The CM14 ...116 A7
Terminal Cl SS3 .....168 F7
Terminus Dr SS16 ...143 B4
Terminus St CM20 ...10 D1
Terms Ave SS8 .....164 A5
Tern Cl CM3 ....83 A8
Tern Ct CM14 ......115 F6
Tern Gdns RM14 ....137 E3
Tern Way CM14 .....115 E6
Terni Rd SS8 ....164 D3
Terr The SS7 ....163 D8
Terrace St DA12 ....179 B1
Terrace The
Chingford E4 ....109 E7
2 Gravesend DA12 ..179 C1
Rayleigh SS6 ....123 C7
Southend-on-S SS3 ..168 F6
Southend-on-S,Chalkwell
SS9 ....165 E8
1 Woodford IG8 ....110 A4
Terrace Wlk RM9 ....153 E2
Teviot Ave RM15 ....171 C7
Tewkes Rd SS8 .....164 D5
Tewkesbury Cl IG10 ..88 E3
Thackeray Ave RM18 .179 B6
Thackeray Rd CM14 ..134 B4
Thackerey Row 1 SS12 121 C5
Thal Massing Cl CM13 117 B8
Thames Ave
Chelmsford CM1 .....31 D4
Dagenham RM9 .....154 C2
Thames Cl
Corringham SS17 ....161 A3
Rainham RM13 .....170 B7
Rayleigh SS6 ....123 C1
Southend-on-S SS9 ..146 B1
Thames Cres SS17 ...161 C5
Thames Ct SS8 .....164 B1
Thames Dr Grays RM16 174 A1
Southend-on-S SS9 ..146 A1
Thames Gate DA1 ...176 A3
Thames Gateway Pk
RM9 ....153 F2
Thames Haven Rd SS17 161 B3
Thames Ind Pk RM18 .175 B1
Thames Rd Barking IG11 153 A2
Canvey Island SS8 ...163 F2
Grays RM17 ....178 B7
Thames View
Basildon SS16 ......141 C1
Grays RM16 ....174 A1
Greenhithe DA9 ....177 C2
Thames View Inf Sch
IG11 ....153 A3
Thames View Jun Sch
IG11 ....152 F3
Thames View Lodge
IG11 ....152 E2
Thames Way
Burnham-on-C CM0 ..106 A6
Gravesend DA11 ....179 A1
Thameshill Ave CM3 ..113 C1
Thameside Cres 6 SS8 164 A3
Thameside Inf Sch
RM17 ....178 C8
Thameside Jun Sch
RM17 ....178 C8
Thameswater Ct SS7 .145 F2
Thamley RM19 .....171 A2
Thanet Grange SS0 ..147 C5
Thatchers Cl IG10 ....89 C7
Thatchers Croft CM3 ..81 F6
Thatches Gr RM6 ....134 E7
Thaxted Bold CM13 ..95 D4
Thaxted Gn CM13 ....95 C4
Thaxted Ho RM10 ...154 B5
Thaxted Lodge 3 E18 132 B8
Thaxted Rd IG9 .....88 E2
Thaxted Way EN9 ....65 D6
Thaxted Wlk RM13 ..154 E5
Thear Cl SS0 ....147 C4
Thele Av SG12 ....8 D4
Thele Est SG12 ......8 E4
Theleway Cl EN11 ....8 B1
Thelma Ave SS8 ....164 A4
Theobalds Ave RM17 .173 C1
Theobalds Cl SS9 ...146 C1
Theobalds Rd SS9 ...146 C1

Thetford Ct CM1 .....31 E1
Thetford Gdns RM9 ..153 E4
Thetford Pl SS15 ....119 D1
Thetford Rd RM9 ....153 D5
Theydon Bois Prim Sch
CM16 ....67 E3
Theydon Bois Sta CM16 67 F3
Theydon Bold CM13 ..95 D4
Theydon Bower CM16 .68 A8
Theydon Cres SS14 ..120 F1
Theydon Ct EN9 .....66 A6
Theydon Gdns RM13 .154 F5
Theydon Gr Epping CM16 46 A1
Woodford IG8 ......110 A2
Theydon Park Rd CM16 67 E1
Theydon Pl CM16 ....67 F8
Theydon Rd CM16 ...67 D6
Thicket Gr RM9 .....153 C6
Thielen Rd SS8 .....164 A4
Thieves' Cnr CM1 ....31 A4
Third Ave Basildon SS16 140 E3
Canvey Island SS8 ...163 E4
Chelmsford CM1 .....32 B5
Dagenham RM10 ....154 B3
Grays RM20 ....177 A8
Harlow CM18,CM19 ..23 C7
Ilford RM6 ....134 C5
Stanford-le-H SS17 ..160 E4
Wickford SS11 .....122 A6
Third Wlk SS8 .....163 E4
Thirlmere Rd SS7 ...144 E7
Thirslet Dr CM9 .....37 C6
Thisselt Rd SS8 .....164 B4
Thistle Cl SS15 .....119 F1
Thistle Mead IG10 ...89 A6
Thistledene Ave RM5 .113 B5
Thistledown SS14 ...142 C6
Thistledown Ct SS14 .142 C6
Thistley Cl
Goldhanger CM9 .....38 E6
Southend-on-S SS9 ..146 E4
Thoby La CM15 .....73 C1
Thomas Arnold Prim Sch
RM9 ....153 F5
Thomas Bata Ave RM18 175 B2
Thomas Cl
Brentwood CM15 ....116 E7
Chelmsford CM2 .....32 E7
Thomas Ct RM8 .....134 C2
Thomas Dr SS8 .....163 E5
Thomas England Ho
RM7 ....135 D5
Thomas Rd SS13 ....143 E7
Thomas Sims Ct RM12 155 B7
Thomas Willingale Sch
IG10 ....89 C6
Thomasin Rd SS13 ..121 C1
Thompson Ave SS8 ..164 F3
Thompson Cl IG1 ...133 C2
Thompson Rd RM9 ..134 F1
Thorin's Gate CM3 ..101 C6
Thorington Ave SS7 .145 D6
Thorington Rd SS6 ..124 A1
Thorley Rd RM16 ...173 A5
Thorn La RM13 .....155 D8
Thornborough Ave CM3 101 F7
Thornbridge SS7 ....144 B4
Thornbury Cl EN11 ...8 B2
Thornbury Ho 3 RM3 .114 D5
Thornbush SS15 ....141 E6
Thorncroft RM11 ....136 B5
Thorndale SS7 .....145 B7
Thorndales CM14 ...116 D6
Thorndon App SS13 ..117 D4
Thorndon Ave CM13 .139 C6
Thorndon Country Pk★
CM13 ....117 D1
Thorndon Countryside Ctr★
CM13 ....116 F3
Thorndon Ct CM13 ..116 C4
Thorndon Ctry Pk★
CM13 ....116 F3
Thorndon Gate CM13 116 F3
Thorndon Park Cl SS9 146 C5
Thorndon Park Cres
SS9 ....146 B5
Thorndon Park Dr SS9 146 B5
Thorney Bay Rd SS8 .164 A2
Thorneycroft Dr EN3 ..65 A2
Thornford Gdns SS2 .147 F5
Thornhill
North Weald Bassett CM16 47 C5
Purleigh CM3 ......58 D1
Southend-on-S SS9 ..146 E4
Thornhill Gdns IG11 .152 E5
Thornridge CM14 ....94 B1
Thornton Ho 8 E11 ..132 A4
Thornton Pl CM4 ....75 E2
Thornton Rd
Belvedere DA17 ....169 B2
Ilford IG1 ....152 B8
Thornton Way SS15 ..141 A6
Thorntons CM13 ....117 D4
Thorntons Farm Ave
RM7 ....135 D2
Thornwood Cl E18 ...110 B1
Thornwood Gr SS9 ..146 D6
Thornwood Ho IG9 ..88 E2
Thornwood Rd CM16 ..46 B3
Thorogood Way RM13 154 C4
Thorold Rd IG1 .....133 C3
Thorolds SS16 .....142 B3
Thorp Leas SS8 .....164 B4
Thorpe Bay Gdns SS1 168 B6
Thorpe Bay Sch The
SS2 ....148 F1
Thorpe Bay Sta SS1 .168 B8

Thorpe Bold CM13 ...95 D4
Thorpe Cl Hockley SS5 124 F4
Wickford SS12 .....121 F6
Thorpe Espl SS1 ....168 B6
Thorpe Gdns SS5 ...124 F4
Thorpe Greenways Jun & Inf
Sch SS1 ....167 E7
Thorpe Hall Ave SS1 .168 A7
Thorpe Hall Cl SS1 ..168 A8
Thorpe Hall Prim Sch
E17 ....109 C2
Thorpe Hall Rd E17 ..109 C2
Thorpe Hall Sch SS1 .149 A2
Thorpe Lodge
Romford RM11 .....136 D5
Southend-on-S SS1 ..167 D6
Thorpe Rd Barking IG11 152 D5
Chingford E17 .....109 C1
Hockley SS5 ....124 F3
Hockley SS5 ....124 F4
Wanstead E7 ......132 A1
Thorpedale Gdns IG1,
IG6 ....133 B7
Thorpedene Ave SS5 .101 E2
Thorpedene Gdns SS3 .168 D6
Thorpedene Inf Sch
SS3 ....168 C7
Thorpedene Jun Sch
SS3 ....168 C7
Thorrington Bold CM13 95 D4
Thorrington Cross SS14 142 C6
Thors Oak SS17 ....160 C2
Thrapston Ho 10 RM3 114 E5
Threadneedle St 2 CM1 32 B2
Three Horseshoes Rd
CM19 ....23 B6
Three Mile Hill CM4 ..53 C2
Threshelford SS16 ..141 F4
Thrift Gn CM13 .....117 A7
Thrift Wood CM3 ....56 F1
Thrifts Mead CM16 ..67 E2
Thriftwood Sch CM2 .54 B3
Throwley Cl SS13 ...143 C5
Thunderer Rd RM9 ..153 C1
Thundersley Church Rd
SS7 ....144 D5
Thundersley Gr SS7 .144 D4
Thundersley Jun & Inf Schs
SS7 ....145 A4
Thundersley Park Rd
SS7 ....144 E3
Thurgood Rd EN11 ..21 A8
Thurlby Cl IG8 .....110 F5
Thurlby Ho IG8 .....110 F5
Thurlestone Ave IG3 .152 F8
Thurloe Gdns RM1 ..135 F5
Thurlow Cl E4 .....109 B4
Thurlow Ct 6 E11 ...132 A6
Thurlow Dr SS1 ....167 F8
Thurlow Gdns IG6 ..111 D4
Thurlstone SS7 .....145 C5
Thurrock & Basildon Coll
(Nethelmayne) Campus
SS16 ....141 F4
Thurrock & Basildon Coll
(Woodview Campus)
RM16 ....173 F2
Thurrock Bsns Ctr
RM20 ....176 F8
Thurrock Com Hospl
RM16 ....173 C5
Thurrock Commercial Ctr
RM15 ....170 F4
Thurrock Ent Ctr RM17 178 A8
Thurrock Local History Mus★
RM17 ....173 B1
Thurrock Park Way
RM18 ....178 D7
Thurso Cl RM3 .....115 B4
Thurstans CM19 ....23 C3
Thurston Ave SS2 ...148 E1
Thynne Rd CM11 ....97 C2
Tickenhall Dr CM17 ..24 D7
Tickfield Ave SS2 ...147 F2
Tideway Maldon CM9 ..59 B8
Southend-on-S SS1 ..167 D6
Tidworth Ave SS11 ..99 E2
Tidy's La CM16 .....46 B2
Tighfield Wlk CM3 ..101 C5
Tilburg Rd SS8 .....164 A4
Tilbury Fort★ RM18 ..179 C2
Tilbury Manor Inf Sch
RM18 ....179 B7
Tilbury Manor Jun Sch
RM18 ....179 B7
Tilbury Mead CM18 ..24 A6
Tilbury Rd CM13 ....139 E4
Tilbury Town Sta RM18 178 F5
Tilegate Ho CM18 ....23 E6
Tilegate Rd Harlow CM18,23 F6
Tilgate Green CM5 ...25 D5
Tillingham Bold CM13 95 D4
Tillingham Ct EN9 ...66 A6
Tillingham Gn 6 SS15 141 B4
Tillingham Rd
Southminster CM0 ...84 F6
Tillingham CM0 .....63 B2
Tillingham Way SS6 .123 B3
Tillotson Rd IG1 ....133 A4
Tillwicks Rd CM18 ..24 A6
Tilney Ct SS3 ....110 A8
Tilney Dr IG9 ......110 A8
Tilney Rd
Buckhurst Hill IG9 ..110 A8
Dagenham RM9 ....153 F6
Tilney Turn SS16 ...142 F4
Timber Ct RM17 ....178 A4

Timber Wharf Cotts
SS11 ....100 E2
Timberdene Ave IG6 ...111 C2
Timberlog Cl SS14 .....142 E6
Timberlog La SS14,SS16 142 E6
Timbermans View SS16 .142 F4
Time Sq SS14 ....142 A5
Timsons La CM2 ....32 A5
Tindal Sq **3** CM1 ......32 B2
Tindal St CM1 ....32 B2
Tindall Cl RM3 ....114 F1
Tine Rd **1** Chigwell IG7 .111 E5
  Chigwell IG7 ....111 F5
Tinker's La SS4 ....125 F1
Tinkler Side SS14 .....142 B6
Tinnocks La CM0 ....40 B1
Tintagel Ct RM11 .....137 A3
Tintagel Way CM9 ......58 E8
Tintern Ave SS0 ......147 C5
Tintern Mews SS0 .....147 C1
Tiplers Bridge CM11 ...98 D5
Tippersfield SS7 .....144 E4
Tipps Cross CM15 .....72 B5
Tipps Cross La CM15 ...72 B4
Tipps Cross Mead CM15 .72 B4
Tiptree Cl Chingford E4 .109 C7
  Hornchurch RM11 .....137 A3
  Southend-on-S SS9 ...146 F4
Tiptree Cres Ilford IG5 .133 A8
  Redbridge IG5 ....111 A1
Tiptree Ct CM13 ......95 D4
Tiptree Gr SS12 ......121 D7
Tiree Chase SS12 .....121 F5
Titan Rd RM17 ....173 A1
Tithe Barn Agricultural &
  Folk Mus The★ RM11 .137 D4
Tithe The SS12 ....121 B6
Tithelands CM19 ......23 A5
Titley Cl E4 ....109 A5
Tiverton Ave IG5 .....133 A8
Tiverton Gr RM3 ......115 A5
Tobruk Rd CM1 ....31 F6
Todd Cl RM13 ....155 D1
Toddbrook CM19 ....23 B7
Toft Ave RM17 ....173 D2
Tofts Chase CM3 ......34 E5
Tolbut Ct **5** RM1 .....135 F5
Tolcairn Ct **2** DA17 ..169 A1
Toledo Cl SS1 ....167 B8
Toledo Rd SS1 ....167 B8
Tollesbury Cl **1** CM13 .121 E6
Tollesbury Ct CM13 ...95 D4
Tollesbury Gdns IG6 ..133 D8
Tollgate SS7 ....145 C6
Tollgate Rd DA2 .....176 D1
Tolworth Gdns RM6 ...134 D6
Tolworth Par RM6 ....134 E6
Tom Mann Cl IG11 ....152 E4
Tom Tit La CM9 ......57 E7
Tomkins Cl SS17 .....160 C3
Tomkyns La
  Romford RM14 ....115 D1
  Upminster RM14 .....137 D7
Tomlins Orch IG11 ...152 C4
Tomlyns Cl CM13 .....95 E3
Tomswood Ct IG6 .....111 C4
Tomswood Hill IG6 ...111 C3
Tomswood Rd IG7 ....111 A4
Tonbridge Rd
  Hockley SS5 ....124 F8
  Romford RM3 ....114 D3
Tongres Rd SS8 ......164 A4
Took Dr CM3 ....101 C6
Toot Hill Rd CM5 ....47 F1
Top House Rise E4 ...87 C2
Top Rd CM9 ....35 D2
Topaz Ct **3** RM13 ....155 A1
Toplands Ave RM15 ...171 C5
Toppesfield Ave SS12 .121 C5
Tor Bryan CM4 ....74 B2
Torbitt Way IG2 .....133 F6
Torells Sch RM16 ....173 F4
Torfell **5** E18 ......109 F1
Torney Cl SS16 ......140 F4
Toronto Cl Ilford IG1 .133 C3
  Tilbury RM18 ....179 A6
Torquay Cl SS6 ......123 D5
Torquay Dr SS9 ......146 E1
Torquay Gdns IG4 ....132 D7
Torquay Rd CM1 ......32 D5
Torrance Cl RM11 ....136 C3
Torrell's Hall Cotts CM5 .28 E4
Torridge RM18 ....175 C2
Torrington SS3 ......168 D8
Torrington Cl CM1 ...32 D5
Torrington Dr IG10 ..89 C5
Torrington Gdns IG10 .89 C5
Torrington Rd
  Dagenham RM8 ......134 F3
  Wanstead E18 ....132 A8
Torsi Rd SS8 ....164 D3
Totman Cl SS6 ....145 D8
Totman Cres SS6 .....145 D8
Totnes Wlk CM1 .....32 E6
Toucan Cl SS3 ......149 E1
Toucan Way SS16 ....142 A3
Tovey Ave EN11 .....21 A8
Tovey Cl EN9 ....43 E8
Tower Ave Basildon SS15 141 C7
  Chelmsford CM1 ....31 F4
Tower Cl
  North Weald Bassett CM16 .47 D7
  Redbridge IG6 ......111 B4
Tower Court Mews SS0 .166 E7
Tower Ct
  Brentwood CM14 ....116 C8
  Chipping Ongar CM5 .49 A2
  Southend-on-S SS0 .166 E7

Tower Ctr EN11 ......21 A6
Tower Cvn Pk SS5 ....101 E4
Tower Hill CM14 .....116 C8
Tower Ho CM13 ....95 D2
Tower Hts **10** EN11 ...21 A7
Tower Rd
  Belvedere DA17 .....169 C2
  Epping CM16 ....45 F1
  Writtle CM1 ....30 F1
Towerfield Cl SS3 ...168 E7
Towerfield Rd SS3 ...168 E7
Towers Jun & Inf Schs
  RM11 ....136 C4
Towers Rd Grays RM17 .173 C4
  Heybridge CM9 ......37 C5
Town Croft CM1 ......32 A5
Town Mead Rd EN9 ...65 C5
Town Pier Sq DA11 ..179 B1
Town Quay IG11 .....152 B4
Town Quay Wharf IG11 .152 B4
Town Sq SS14 ....142 A6
Towneley Cotts RM4 .91 E1
Townfield St CM1 ...32 B3
Townfield Wlk SS3 ..149 E4
Townfields SS2 .....148 A2
Townsend CM2 ......33 B5
Tracyes Rd CM18 ....24 B6
Traddles Ct CM1 ....31 F6
Trafalgar Bsns Ctr IG11 152 F1
Trafalgar Ct E6 ....152 A4
Trafalgar Ho RM13 ..153 B2
Trafalgar Pl E11 ...132 A7
Trafalgar Rd
  Rainham RM13 ......154 F3
  Southend-on-S SS3 ..168 D7
Trafalgar Way CM12 .97 B5
Trafford Cl E15 ....111 F4
Tranquil Rise DA8 ..169 E1
Trap's Hill IG10 ...88 F5
Trasa Ct RM17 .....178 C8
Travers Way SS13 ..143 A6
Trayford Ct **8** RM19 .171 B1
Trebble Rd DA10 ...177 E1
Tree Cl RM4 ....90 B6
Tree Top Mews RM10 .154 D6
Tree Tops
  Brentwood CM15 ....94 C1
  1 Romford RM2 ...110 A6
Treebeard Copse CM3 .101 C6
Treeby Ct EN3 .....65 A2
Treecot Dr SS9 ....147 A4
Treelawn Dr SS9 ..146 F4
Treelawn Gdns SS9 .146 F4
Treetops Sch RM17 .173 B2
Treetops View IG10 .88 D2
Trefgarne Rd RM10 .135 A2
Trefoil Ho RM7 ....178 B7
Tregaron Ho **3** RM3 .114 D4
Trehearn Rd IG6 ...111 D3
Trelawn CM3 ......33 E3
Trelawney Rd IG6 ..111 D3
Trenance Gdns IG3 .134 A1
Trenchard Cres CM1 .32 D8
Trenchard Lodge CM1 .32 D7
Trenders Ave SS6 ..123 B6
Trenham Ave SS13 ..143 D7
Trent Ave RM14 ....137 D5
Trent Cl
  Burnham-on-C CM0 ..106 A6
  Wickford SS12 .....121 D6
Trent Ct E11 ....132 A6
Trent Rd Buckhurst Hill IG9 88 B1
  Chelmsford CM1 ....31 D5
Trentbridge Cl IG6 .111 F4
Tresco Gdns IG3 ...134 A2
Tresco Way SS12 ...121 F5
Trescoe Gdns RM5 ..113 C5
Tresham Rd IG11 ...152 F5
Treswell Rd RM9 ...153 E4
Trevera Ct EN11 ...21 A7
Trevor Cl RM12 ....118 F7
Trevor Rd IG8 .....110 A3
Trevose Rd E17 ...109 D2
Trewithen Ct SS6 .146 A8
Triangle Garage CM9 .37 B5
Triangle The
  Barking IG11 ......152 C6
  Basildon SS16 .....141 B4
Trianon Ct **10** SS13 .143 C6
Trident Ind Est EN11 .21 C7
Trienna Ct CM13 ...117 B7
Trillo Ct IG1 .....133 E4
Trimble Cl CM4 ...74 B4
Trimley Cl SS14 ...142 C7
Trindehay SS15 ...141 E5
Trinder Way SS12 .121 B6
Tring Cl Ilford IG2 .133 D6
  Romford RM3 ......114 F6
Tring Gdns RM3 ...114 F6
Tring Gn RM3 .....114 F6
Tring Wlk RM3 ...114 E6
Trinidad Gdns RM10 .154 D5
Trinity Ave SS0 ...166 E7
Trinity Cl Basildon SS15 .141 C6
  Billericay CM11 ....119 C6
  Chelmsford CM2 ....32 D3
  Rayleigh SS6 ......123 E1
Trinity Ct **8** E4 ....109 C8
Trinity Gdns **11** E18 .132 B8
Trinity Lodge SS2 .148 D1
Trinity RC High Sch (Lower)
  IG8 ....110 A6
Trinity RC High Sch (Upper
  Sch) IG8 ....109 F6
Trinity RC High Sch (Upper)
  IG8 ....110 A6

Trinity Rd
  Billericay CM11 ....119 C6
  Chelmsford CM2 ....32 D2
  Ilford IG1 ....133 C8
  Rayleigh SS6 ......123 E1
  Southend-on-S SS2 .148 D1
Trinity Road Prim Sch
  CM2 ....32 D2
Trinity Sch
  Belvedere DA17 ....169 C2
  Dagenham RM10 ....154 A8
Trinity Sq CM3 .....101 E7
Trinity St Mary's CE Prim Sch
  CM3 ....101 E7
Trinity Terr IG9 ...88 B2
Trinity Wood Rd SS5 .125 A8
Tripat Cl SS17 ....161 D5
Tripton Rd CM18 ...23 E7
Triton Ct IG9 .....110 A8
Triton Lodge DA8 .169 E1
Triton Way SS7 ...145 B6
Triumph Cl RM16 ..172 C2
Triumph Ho IG11 ..153 A2
Trivett Cl DA9 ...177 A2
Trojan Terr CM21 ..1 E3
Troopers Dr RM3 ..114 D6
Trotter's Gap SG12 .8 E4
Trotters Rd CM18 ..24 A5
Trotwood IG7 .....111 D4
Trotwood Cl
  Brentwood CM15 ...94 C1
  Chelmsford CM1 ...31 E7
Troubridge Cl CM3 .101 F7
Trowbridge Rd RM3 .114 E4
Trueloves La CM4 ..73 E2
Truman Ct SS15 ...141 A6
Trumpeter Ct CM12 .96 F3
Trunnions The SS4 .125 F1
Truro Cres SS6 ...123 C5
Truro Gdns IG1 ...132 E4
Truro Wlk RM3 ...114 C4
Trusses Rd
  Bradwell Waterside CM0 ..41 F3
  Bradwell-on-S CM0 .42 A3
Trust The RM2 ....136 F2
Trustons Gdns RM11 .136 A4
Tryfan Cl IG4 ....132 D6
Tuck Rd RM13 ....155 A6
Tudor Ave Romford RM2 .136 A8
  Stanford-le-H SS17 .160 E4
Tudor Cl Brentwood CM15 .95 A3
  Chigwell IG7 ......111 A6
  Hunsdonbury SG12 .9 D8
  Ingatestone CM4 ...74 A2
  Rayleigh SS6 ......123 F2
  Southend-on-S SS9 .146 C7
  Thundersley SS7 ...144 F5
  Woodford IG8 .....110 B5
Tudor Court Prim Sch
  RM16 ....172 F4
Tudor Cres IG6 ...111 C4
Tudor Ct Basildon SS15 .119 F2
  Romford RM3 ......115 B4
  Sawbridgeworth CM21 ..1 E3
Tudor Dr RM2 ....136 A7
Tudor Gdns
  Romford RM2 ......136 A7
  Southend-on-S SS9 .146 D3
  Southend-on-S, Cambridge Town
    SS3 ....168 D6
  Upminster RM14 ...137 C1
Tudor Mews RM1 ..135 F6
Tudor Par RM6 ...134 D4
Tudor Pl CM3 ....83 A8
Tudor Rd Barking IG11 .152 F5
  Canvey Island SS8 .163 D3
  Chingford E4 ......109 B4
  Southend-on-S SS0 .147 E2
Tudor Way Hockley SS5 .124 F4
  Waltham Abbey EN9 .65 D6
  Wickford SS12 .....121 B7
Tudor Wlk SS12 ...121 A7
Tufter Rd IG7 ....111 F5
Tufton Rd E4 ....109 A6
Tugby Pl CM1 ....31 E6
Tulip Cl Chelmsford CM1 .32 E7
  Pilgrims Hatch CM15 .94 B4
  Romford RM3 ......114 D4
Tulip Gdns Chingford E4 .109 D7
  Ilford IG1 ....152 B6
Tumbler Rd CM18 ..24 B7
Tunbridge Rd SS2 .147 F2
Tunfield Rd EN11 ..8 B1
Tunnel Cotts RM20 .177 A8
Tunnel Est RM20 ..171 F2
Tunnmeade CM20 ..11 A1
Tunstall Ave IG6 .112 A4
Tunstall Cl SS13 ..143 C5
Tupman Cl CM1 ...31 D6
Turkey Oaks CM1 .32 D3
Turnage Rd RM8 ..134 E3
Turner Cl SS3 ....168 F8
Turner Rd RM12 ..135 F2
Turners Cl CM5 ...48 F2
Turners Ct RM4 ..90 B6
Turnors CM20 ....23 C8
Turnpike La RM18 .174 D1
Turold Rd SS17 ..160 E4
Turp Ave RM16 ...173 C4
Turpin Ave RM5 ..113 B4
Turpin Cl EN3 ...65 A2
Turpin's La IG8 ..110 F5
Turpins The SS14 .142 C7
Tusser Ct CM2 ...54 D8
Tutors Way CM3 ..101 E7
Tuttlebee La IG9 .110 A6

Tuttleby Cotts RM4 ..90 E2
Twain Terr **2** SS12 .121 C5
Tweed RM18 ....175 C2
Tweed Glen RM1 ..113 D3
Tweed Gn RM1 ...113 D3
Tweed Way RM1 ..113 D3
Twelve Acre Ho **5** E12 .133 A1
Twentyman Cl IG8 .110 A3
Twin Oaks CM2 ...33 A4
Twine Cl IG11 ....153 B2
Twinstead SS12 ..121 F6
Twitten La CM2 ..54 B2
Twitty Fee CM3 ..57 A8
Two Tree Island Nature
  Reserve★ SS9 ...165 B7
Twyford Ave SS3 .150 A4
Twyford Rd IG1 ..152 C5
Twyzel Rd SS8 ...164 C5
Tyburns The CM13 .117 D3
Tycehurst Hill IG10 .88 F5
Tye Common Rd CM12 .118 C2
Tye Green Village CM18 .23 F5
Tye The 78 C7
Tyefields SS13 ..143 C7
Tyelands CM12 ..118 F8
Tyle Gn RM11 ...136 F7
Tylehurst Gdns IG1 .152 C7
Tyler Ave SS15 ..141 E4
Tyler Way CM14 .94 E3
Tylers Ave Billericay CM12 .97 C5
  Southend-on-S SS1 .167 A8
Tylers Cl Chelmsford CM2 .54 B6
  Loughton IG10 ....88 E2
Tylers Cres RM12 .155 C5
Tylers Ct **9** CM14 .116 C6
Tylers Rd CM19 ..22 D3
Tylers Ride CM3 .101 E7
Tylewood SS7 ...145 C3
Tylney Ave SS4 ..125 E3
Tylney Croft CM19 .23 B6
Tyms The RM11 .123 E4
Tyndale Cl SS5 ..101 D3
Tyndale Ho SS5 .101 D3
Tyndales La CM3 .57 B5
Tyne Cl RM14 ....137 D5
Tyne Gdns RM15 .171 C6
Tyne Way CM1 ...31 D5
Tyrel Dr SS1 ....167 B8
Tyrell Rise CM14 .116 C5
Tyrells SS5 ......124 D5
Tyrells Cl Chelmsford CM2 .32 E4
  Upminster RM14 ..137 B2
Tyrells The SS17 .161 A3
Tyrells Way CM2 .54 F7
Tyrells Hall Cl RM17 .178 D8
Tyrells Rd CM11 ..119 D6
Tyrells Sch The CM1 .32 E5
Tysea Cl CM18 ...23 F5
Tysea Hill RM4 ..91 F2
Tysea Rd CM18 ..23 F5
Tyssen Mead CM3 .33 E8
Tyssen Pl RM15 .157 C2
Tythe Barn Way CM3 .101 C8
Tythe Cl CM1 ....32 E8

U

Udall Gdns RM5 .....113 A4
Ullenden Rd **6** E18 .110 A1
Ullswater Rd SS7 ..144 E7
Ullswater Way RM12 .155 A7
Ulster Ave SS3 ....168 D6
Ulting Hall Rd CM9 .35 E7
Ulting La CM9 ....35 E6
Ulting Rd CM9 ...35 C8
Ulting Way SS11 .122 A8
Ulverston Ho **1** RM3 .114 E4
Ulverston Rd
  Chingford E17 ....109 D1
  Rochford SS4 .....103 C1
Una Rd SS13 .....143 F6
Underhill Rd SS7 .144 E3
Underwood Rd
  Chingford E4 ......109 B5
  Woodford IG8 ....110 D3
Underwood Sq SS9 .146 C6
Unicorn Wlk DA9 .176 F2
Union La SS4 ....125 E2
Univ of East London
  RM8 ....153 A8
University Way DA1 .176 A4
Unwin Pl CM4 ...75 E2
Uphall Rd IG1 ...152 B7
Uphall Sch IG1 .152 B7
Uphavering Ho RM12 .136 C2
Upland Cl CM2 ..96 F4
Upland Court Rd RM3 .114 F1
Upland Dr RM3 ..96 F4
Upland Rd Billericay CM12 .96 F4
  Southend-on-S SS9 .166 A8
  Thornwood CM16 ..45 F5
Uplands Hockley SS5 .124 F5
  South Benfleet SS7 .144 B3
Uplands Dr CM1 ..32 D7
Uplands Park Ct SS6 .123 B3
Uplands Park Rd SS6 .123 B3
Uplands Rd
  Brentwood CM14 ..116 E6
  Hockley SS5 ......124 F5
  Ilford RM6 ....134 D8
  South Benfleet SS7 .144 B3

Uplands Rd continued
  Woodford IG8 .....110 E3
Uplands The IG10 ..88 F6
Upminster Bridge Sta
  RM12 ....136 F2
Upminster Inf & Jun Schs
  RM14 ....137 C2
Upminster Mill★ RM14 .137 B2
Upminster Rd Hornchurch RM11 .136 F2
Upminster Rd N RM13 .155 D2
Upminster Rd S RM13 .155 B1
Upminster Sta RM14 .137 C2
Upminster Trad Pk
  RM14 ....138 D4
Upney Ct RM12 ...155 D2
Upney La IG11 ...152 F5
Upney Sta IG11 ..152 F5
Uppark Dr IG2 ..133 C5
Upper Abbey Rd DA17 .169 A2
Upper Ave SS13 ..143 E8
Upper Brentwood Rd
  RM2 ....136 C8
Upper Bridge Rd CM2 .32 A1
Upper Chase
  Althorne CM3 .....82 F3
  2 Chelmsford CM2 .54 A8
Upper Church Hill DA9 .176 E2
Upper Cornsland CM16 .116 D7
Upper Holly Hill Rd
  DA17 ....169 B1
Upper Hook CM18 .23 F6
Upper Lambricks SS6 .123 E4
Upper Market Rd SS11 .121 C8
Upper Marsh La EN11 .21 A1
Upper Mayne SS14,SS15 .141 F7
Upper Mealines CM18 .24 A5
Upper Moors CM3 .18 F7
Upper Park Rd
  Belvedere DA17 ...169 B2
  Wickford SS12 ....121 D4
Upper Pk Harlow CM20 .10 B1
  Loughton IG10 ....88 D4
Upper Rainham Rd
  Hornchurch RM12 ..135 F2
  Rainham RM12 ....154 D2
Upper Rd CM11 ..120 D5
Upper Roman Rd CM2 .32 B1
Upper Ryle CM14 .94 B2
Upper Sheridan Rd
  DA17 ....169 A2
Upper Stonyfield CM19 .23 B8
Upper Swaines CM16 .45 F1
Upshire Prim Foundation Sch
  EN9 ....66 B6
Upshire Rd EN9 ..66 A6
Upton Cl SS17 ...160 D2
Upton Ho **5** RM3 .114 D5
Upway SS6 ......123 D3
Upway The SS14 .142 C8
Upwood Ct RM1 ..135 F7
Urban Ave RM12 .136 C1
Urmond Rd SS8 ..164 A4
Urswick Gdns RM9 .153 E5
Urswick Rd RM9 .153 E5
Usk Rd RM15 ...171 D7
Uttons Ave SS9 ..165 D8
Uvedale Rd RM10 .135 A1
Uxbridge Cl SS11 .121 F6

V

Vaagen Rd SS8 ....164 B4
Vadsoe Rd SS8 ...164 B5
Valance Ave E4 ...87 F1
Valance Way SS16 .141 C4
Vale Ave SS2 ....148 A2
Vale Cl CM15 ....93 F4
Vale Ct CM4 ....97 D6
Vale End CM2 ...54 C3
Vale The Basildon SS16 .142 D3
  Brentwood CM14 ..94 C1
  Stock CM4 ....97 D7
  Woodford IG8 ...110 A3
Valence Ave RM8 .134 D2
Valence Cir RM8 .134 D1
Valence House Mus★
  RM8 ....134 D2
Valence Inf Sch RM8 .134 D2
Valence Jun Sch RM8 .134 D2
Valence Wood Rd RM8 .134 E1
Valentine The IG2 .133 A5
Valentines Stock CM4 .75 F2
  6 Wickford SS12 .121 D6
Valentines High Sch
  IG2 ....133 A5
Valentines Rd IG1 .133 B3
Valentines Way RM7 .135 E2
Valerie Ho SS9 ..146 E2
Valiant Cl RM7 ..113 B1
Valkyrie Rd SS0 .166 D8
Vallance Cl SS2 .148 E3
Valletta Cl CM1 .32 A3
Valley Bridge CM1 .32 B6
Valley Cl Loughton IG10 .88 F3
  Waltham Abbey EN9 .65 C7
Valley Ct IG8 ...110 B3
Valley Dr DA9 ..177 B1
Valley Hill IG10 .88 E3
Valley Rd Billericay CM11 .97 C2
  Erith DA8 ....169 D2
Valley Side E4 ..87 A1
Valley Side Par E4 .109 A8
Valley View DA9 .177 B1
Valmar Ave SS17 .160 B1

Van Dieman's La CM2 . . .54 C8
Van Dieman's Rd CM2 . . .54 C8
Van Diemens Pass SS8 .164 F3
Vanderbilt Ave SS6 . . . . .123 C8
Vanderwalt Ave SS8 . . . .164 C3
Vanessa Cl DA17 . . . . . . .169 A1
Vange Com Prim Sch
SS17 . . . . .142 D2
Vange Corner Dr SS16 .142 B1
Vange Hill Ct SS16 . . . . .142 E3
Vange Hill Dr SS16 . . . . .142 E4
Vange Park Rd SS16 . . . .142 B1
Vange Riverview Ctr
SS16 . . . . .142 F4
Vanguard Cl RM7 . . . . . . .113 B1
Vanguard Way SS3 . . . . .168 F7
Vanguards The SS3 . . . . .168 F7
Vanryne Ho IG10 . . . . . . .88 C6
Vantorts Cl CM21 . . . . .1 E2
Vantorts Rd CM21 . . . . .1 E2
Varden Cl CM1 . . . . .31 F6
Vardon Dr SS9 . . . . .146 B3
Vaughan Ave
Hornchurch RM12 . . . . . . .155 E8
Southend-on-S SS2 . . . . . .148 E1
Vaughan Cl SS4 . . . . . . .125 E5
Vaughan Gdns
Ilford IG1 . . . . .133 A4
Redbridge IG1 . . . . .132 F4
Vaughan Williams Rd
SS15 . . . . .141 C8
Vaughan Williams Way
CM14 . . . . .116 B6
Vaulx Rd SS8 . . . . .164 B4
Velizy Ave CM20 . . . . . . .10 D1
Vellacotts CM1 . . . . .32 B7
Venables Cl
Canvey Island SS8 . . . . . . .164 C4
Dagenham RM10 . . . . .154 B8
Venette Cl RM13 . . . . . . .170 B8
Venlo Rd SS8 . . . . .164 B5
Venmead Ct DA17 . . . . . .169 A2
Venta Way CM9 . . . . .59 B8
Ventnor Gdns IG11 . . . . .152 E6
Ventnor Mans IG11 . . . . .152 E6
Veny Cres RM12 . . . . . . .155 D7
Vera Rd CM11 . . . . .99 A3
Verbena Cl RM15 . . . . . .172 C7
Verderers Rd IG7 . . . . . .112 A6
Vere Rd IG10 . . . . .89 C5
Vermeer Cres SS3 . . . . . .168 G8
Vermeer Ride CM1 . . . . . .32 F7
Vermont Cl SS13 . . . . . . .143 C8
Verney Gdns RM9 . . . . . .153 E8
Verney Rd RM9 . . . . .153 E8
Vernon Ave Rayleigh SS6 .123 B4
Woodford IG8 . . . . .110 B3
Vernon Cnr CM4 . . . . . . .75 D2
Vernon Cres CM13 . . . . .117 A7
Vernon Ct SS9 . . . . .146 C1
Vernon Rd Ilford IG3 . . . .133 F3
North Fambridge CM3 . . . . .81 A1
Romford RM5 . . . . .113 C5
Southend-on-S SS9 . . . . . .146 C1
Swanscombe DA10 . . . . . .177 F1
Vernons Wlk 4 SS13 . . . .121 A1
Veronica Cl RM3 . . . . . . .114 C3
Veronique Gdns IG6 . . . .133 C6
Vert Ho RM17 . . . . .178 C7
Vesey Gdns RM10 . . . . . .135 A1
Vestry Cl SS15 . . . . .141 C7
Vexil Cl RM19 . . . . .171 D2
Vi & John Rubens Ho
IG2 . . . . .133 A5
Viaduct Cl CM1 . . . . .32 A2
Viaduct The E18 . . . . . . .110 B1
Viborg Gdns CM9 . . . . . . .58 E8
Vica Cotts CM3 . . . . .34 D5
Vicar's Wlk RM8 . . . . . . .134 B1
Vicarage Cl
Basildon SS15 . . . . .141 C6
Brentwood CM14 . . . . .115 E6
Canvey Island SS8 . . . . . . .163 D3
Roxwell CM1 . . . . .30 B5
Vicarage Ct
Billericay CM12 . . . . .97 B2
Waltham Abbey EN9 . . . . . .66 A5
Woodford IG8 . . . . .110 E3
Vicarage Dr
Barking IG11 . . . . .152 C5
Northfleet DA11 . . . . .178 C1
Vicarage Field Sh Ctr
IG11 . . . . .152 C5
Vicarage Hill SS7 . . . . . .144 E2
Vicarage La Chigwell IG7 .111 D7
Great Baddow CM2 . . . . . . .54 F5
Ilford IG1 . . . . .133 D3
Mundon CM9 . . . . .59 E2
North Weald Bassett CM16 . .47 B7
North Weald Bassett CM16 . .47 C7
Tillingham CM0 . . . . .63 E4
Wallend E6 . . . . .152 A2
Vicarage Mdw CM0 . . . . . .84 D3
Vicarage Mews CM2 . . . . .54 F6
Vicarage Rd
Chelmsford CM2 . . . . .54 B8
Coopersale CM16 . . . . .46 C2
Dagenham RM10 . . . . .154 B5
Hornchurch RM12 . . . . . . .136 A3
Pleshey CM3 . . . . .7 E2
Roxwell CM1 . . . . .30 D5
Woodford IG8 . . . . .110 E3
Vicarage Sq RM17 . . . . . .178 A8
Vicarage Wood CM20 . . . .11 A7

Viceroy Ct
Horndon-on-t-H SS17 . . . . .159 F3
Southend-on-S SS0 . . . . . .166 B7
Vickers Rd Erith DA8 . . . .169 D1
Southend-on-S SS2 . . . . . .147 D6
Victor App RM12 . . . . . . .136 D3
Victor Ave SS13 . . . . .143 D6
Victor Cl RM12 . . . . .136 D3
Victor Ct
Hornchurch RM12 . . . . . . .136 D3
Rainham RM13 . . . . .154 D3
Victor Dr SS9 . . . . .165 F8
Victor Gdns Hockley SS5 .124 F5
Hornchurch RM12 . . . . . . .136 D3
Victor Mew Cl SS12 . . . . .121 D5
Victor Wlk RM12 . . . . . . .136 D3
Victor's Cres CM13 . . . . .117 B8
Victoria Ave
Basildon SS16 . . . . .141 C3
Grays RM16 . . . . .173 C4
Rayleigh SS6 . . . . .123 B4
Romford RM5 . . . . .113 B4
Southend-on-S SS2 . . . . . .147 F2
Wickford SS12 . . . . .121 C7
Victoria Cl Basildon SS15 .141 C3
Grays RM16 . . . . .173 C4
Victoria Cotts
Heybridge CM9 . . . . .37 A5
Ilford IG1 . . . . .133 C6
Victoria Cres
Basildon SS15 . . . . .141 B8
Chelmsford CM1 . . . . .32 A3
Wickford SS12 . . . . .121 B7
Victoria Dr
Great Wakering SS3 . . . . . .150 C2
Southend-on-S SS9 . . . . . .146 E1
Victoria Ho
1 Romford RM1 . . . . .135 F5
2 Romford, Ardleigh Green
RM2 . . . . .136 C7
Victoria Lanes Sh Ctr
SS1 . . . . .167 A7
Victoria Plaza 4 SS1 . .167 A8
Victoria Plaza Sh Ctr 1
SS1 . . . . .167 A8
Victoria Rd Barking IG11 .152 B6
Basildon,Laindon SS15 . . . .141 A4
Basildon,Vange SS16 . . . . .142 D2
Brentwood CM14 . . . . .116 C6
Buckhurst Hill IG9 . . . . . . .110 D8
Bulphan RM14 . . . . .158 F8
Chelmsford CM1 . . . . .32 B3
Chingford E4 . . . . .87 E1
Chingford, Highams Park
E17 . . . . .109 C1
Cold Norton CM3 . . . . .80 F6
Dagenham RM10 . . . . .154 C7
Horndon-on-t-H SS17 . . . . .159 F3
Maldon CM9 . . . . .37 A2
Rayleigh SS6 . . . . .123 E3
Romford RM1 . . . . .135 F5
South Woodham Ferrers
CM3 . . . . .101 D6
Southend-on-S SS1 . . . . . .167 D7
Southend-on-S,Chalkwell
SS9 . . . . .165 E8
Stanford-le-H SS17 . . . . . .160 C2
Waltham Abbey EN9 . . . . . .65 C5
Wanstead E18 . . . . .132 B8
Writtle CM1 . . . . .30 F1
Victoria Rd S CM1 . . . . . .32 B2
Victory Cl Grays RM16 . . .172 D2
Wickford SS12 . . . . .122 A5
Victory Ct IG11 . . . . .153 B2
Victory La SS4 . . . . .125 D6
Victory Lodge DA8 . . . . . .169 E1
Victory Rd
Rainham RM13 . . . . .155 A3
Wanstead E11 . . . . .132 B7
Victory Way
Dartford DA2 . . . . .176 C3
Romford RM7 . . . . .113 B1
Vienna Cl IG5 . . . . .110 D1
View Cl IG7 . . . . .111 D5
Vigerons Way RM16 . . . . .174 B2
Vignoles Rd RM7 . . . . . . .135 A4
Viking Bsns Ctr RM7 . . . .135 C4
Viking Cl SS3 . . . . .168 C7
Viking Rd CM9 . . . . .36 E1
Viking Way
Belvedere DA8 . . . . .169 C3
Pilgrims Hatch CM15 . . . . . .94 B3
Rainham RM13 . . . . .155 A1
Wickford SS11 . . . . .99 E2
Vikings Way SS8 . . . . . . .163 D3
Villa Rd SS7 . . . . .144 C4
Village Arc The 2 E4 . . .87 D1
Village Cl Chingford E4 . .109 C5
Hoddesdon EN11 . . . . .21 D8
Village Dr SS8 . . . . .163 E3
Village Gate CM2 . . . . . . .33 A2
Village Gn SS4 . . . . .104 D1
Village Hall Cl SS8 . . . . .163 D3
Village Home The IG6 . . .133 C8
Village Hts IG8 . . . . .109 F5
Village Inf Sch RM10 . . . .154 A5
Village Sq CM22 . . . . .33 A3
Villiers Pl CM3 . . . . .33 E8
Villiers Way SS7 . . . . . . .144 E5
Vincent Ave SS17 . . . . . .159 F3

Vincent Cl
Corringham SS17 . . . . .161 B3
Redbridge IG6 . . . . .111 C4
Southend-on-S SS3 . . . . . .168 C7
Vincent Ct CM14 . . . . . . .116 B8
Vincent Lodge CM3 . . . . .101 E6
Vincent Mews SS13 . . . . .143 E7
Vincent Rd Chingford E4 .109 D4
Dagenham RM9 . . . . .153 E5
Rainham RM13 . . . . .155 C1
Rochford SS4 . . . . .103 B1
Vincent Way CM12 . . . . . .97 A5
Vine Cl SS14 . . . . .142 E6
Vine Ct 10 DA11 . . . . . . .179 B1
Vine Gdns IG1 . . . . .152 C7
Vine Gr CM20 . . . . .10 E5
Vine St RM7 . . . . .135 C2
Vineries Cl RM9 . . . . .153 F6
Vineway CM14 . . . . .94 C1
Vineyards The CM2 . . . . . .54 F7
Vintners The SS2 . . . . . . .147 F5
Viola Cl RM15 . . . . .157 C2
Violet Cl CM1 . . . . .32 E7
Violet Rd E18 . . . . .110 B1
Virginia Cl Romford RM5 .113 C3
South Benfleet SS7 . . . . . . .144 B7
Virginia Gdns IG6 . . . . . .111 D1
Virley Cl CM9 . . . . .37 D4
Vista Dr IG4 . . . . .132 D6
Vista Rd SS11 . . . . .121 F7
Voluntary Pl E11 . . . . . . .132 A5
Volwycke Ave CM9 . . . . . .58 F8
Voorburg Rd SS8 . . . . . . .164 D4
Vowler Rd SS16 . . . . .141 B4
Voysey Gdns SS13 . . . . . .121 B1

W

Waalwyk Dr SS8 . . . . . . .164 C4
Waarden Rd SS8 . . . . . . .164 B4
Waarem Ave SS8 . . . . . . .164 B4
Wadeville Ave RM6 . . . . .134 F4
Wadeville Cl DA17 . . . . . .169 A1
Wadham Ave E17 . . . . . . .109 B3
Wadham Cl CM4 . . . . .74 A4
Wadham Park Ave SS5 . . .102 A1
Wadham Rd E17 . . . . .109 B2
Wadhurst Ct E6 . . . . .152 A3
Wagon Mead CM22 . . . . . .3 A3
Wagstaff Gdns RM9 . . . . .153 C5
Wagtail Dr CM9 . . . . .37 C5
Waikato Lodge IG9 . . . . . .88 C1
Wainfleet Ave RM5 . . . . .113 C1
Wainwright Ave CM13 . . . .95 D3
Wake Arms Rdbt IG10 . . . .66 F1
Wakefield Ave CM12 . . . . .97 A2
Wakefield Gdns IG1 . . . . .132 E5
Wakefield Rd DA9 . . . . . .177 C2
Wakelin Chase CM4 . . . . .74 A3
Wakerfield Cl RM11 . . . . .136 F6
Wakering Ave SS3 . . . . . .168 G7
Wakering Rd
Barking IG11 . . . . .152 C5
Great Wakering SS3 . . . . . .150 B1
Southend-on-S SS1,SS3 . . .149 A2
Wakerings The IG11 . . . . .152 C6
Wakescolne SS11 . . . . . . .122 A6
Walace Ct EN3 . . . . .65 A2
Walbrook 9 E18 . . . . . . .132 A8
Waldeck Rd DA1 . . . . . . .176 A1
Waldegrave SS16 . . . . . . .142 B4
Waldegrave Ct
11 Barking IG11 . . . . .152 D4
Upminster RM14 . . . . .137 B3
Waldegrave Gdns RM14 .137 B2
Waldegrave Rd RM8 . . . . .134 C2
Walden Ave RM13 . . . . . .154 D3
Walden Rd RM11 . . . . . . .136 D5
Walden Way
Hornchurch RM11 . . . . . . .136 D5
Redbridge IG6 . . . . .111 E3
Waldon M18 . . . . .175 C3
Waldringfield SS14 . . . . . .142 B7
Walford Pl CM2 . . . . .32 F2
Walfords Cl CM17 . . . . . . .11 C3
Walfrey Gdns RM9 . . . . . .153 E5
Walk The Billericay CM12 . .97 A1
Hornchurch RM11 . . . . . . .136 F2
Hullbridge SS5 . . . . .101 D3
Walker Ave CM5 . . . . .27 D2
Walker Dr SS9 . . . . .146 A2
Walkers Cl CM1 . . . . .32 D7
Walkers Sq SS17 . . . . . . .160 D1
Walkey Way SS3 . . . . . . .168 H7
Walkways SS8 . . . . .163 F5
Wall Chase CM6 . . . . .7 F7
Wall End Ct E6 . . . . .152 A4
Wall End Rd E6 . . . . .152 A5
Wall Rd SS8 . . . . .164 F3
Wallace Binder Cl CM9 . . .36 F1
Wallace Cl SS5 . . . . .101 D3
Wallace Cres CM2 . . . . . . .54 D8
Wallace Dr SS12 . . . . . . .121 C5
Wallace Gdns DA10 . . . . .177 E1
Wallace Rd RM17 . . . . . . .173 A2
Wallace St SS3 . . . . .168 F7
Wallace's La CM3 . . . . . . .20 D4
Wallasea Gdns CM1 . . . . .32 F5
Wallenger Ave RM2 . . . . .136 B8
Waller's Hoppet IG10 . . . .88 F7
Wallers Cl
Dagenham RM9 . . . . .153 F4
Woodford IG8 . . . . .110 A4
Wallers Way EN11 . . . . . . .8 B1
Wallflower St 11 CM1 . . . .32 F6
Wallington Ho 2 RM3 . . .114 C4
Wallington Rd IG3 . . . . . .133 F4

Wallis Ave SS2 . . . . .147 F2
Wallis Cl RM11 . . . . .136 B3
Wallis Pk DA11 . . . . .178 B2
Walmer Cl Chingford E4 . .109 B1
Romford RM7 . . . . .113 B1
Walnut Cl IG6 . . . . .133 C7
Walnut Cotts CM21 . . . . . .1 E4
Walnut Ct SS5 . . . . .124 E7
Walnut Gr RM12 . . . . . . .136 D3
Walnut Tree Ave CM21 . . .1 E4
Walnut Tree Cl EN11 . . . . .21 A6
Walnut Tree Cotts CM3 . .18 E5
Walnut Tree Cres CM21 . .1 E3
Walnut Tree Rd
Dagenham RM8 . . . . .134 E2
Erith DA8 . . . . .169 E1
Walnut Way IG9 . . . . .110 D7
Walpole Cl RM17 . . . . . . .173 C2
Walpole Rd E18 . . . . .109 F2
Walpole Wlk SS6 . . . . . . .123 B4
Walsham Ent Ctr RM17 . .173 C1
Walsingham Cl SS15 . . . .141 C7
Walsingham Ho E4 . . . . . .87 D2
Walsingham Rd SS2 . . . .148 B2
Walsingham Way CM12 . . .97 B5
Walter Hurford Par 5
E12 . . . . .152 A8
Walters Cl
Galleywood CM2 . . . . .54 C3
Southend-on-S SS9 . . . . . .146 E6
Waltham Abbey* EN9 . . . .65 C6
Waltham Cl 11 SS13 . . . . .95 C3
Waltham Cres SS2 . . . . . .148 B3
Waltham Ct E17 . . . . .109 C2
Waltham Forest Coll
E17 . . . . .109 B1
Waltham Glen CM2 . . . . . .54 C7
Waltham Holy Cross Jun &
Inf Schs EN9 . . . . .65 D6
Waltham Park Way E17 . .109 A3
Waltham Pk E17 . . . . .109 A3
Waltham Rd Boreham CM3 20 F4
Lower Nazeing EN9 . . . . . . .44 A6
Rayleigh SS6 . . . . .123 B3
Woodford IG8 . . . . .110 E4
Waltham Way E4 . . . . .87 A1
Walthams SS13 . . . . .143 B7
Walthams Pl SS13 . . . . . .143 B7
Walthamstow Ave E4 . . . .109 A3
Walthamstow Ave (North
Circular Rd) E4 . . . . . . .109 A3
Walthamstow Bsns Ctr
E17 . . . . .109 C1
Walton Cl Basildon SS15 .141 C8
Hoddesdon EN11 . . . . .21 C8
Walton Gdns
Brentwood CM13 . . . . .95 C4
Waltham Abbey EN9 . . . . . .65 B6
Walton Rd
Hoddesdon EN11 . . . . .21 C8
Little Ilford E12 . . . . .152 A8
Romford RM5 . . . . .112 F3
Southend-on-S SS1 . . . . . .167 F6
Walton's Hall Rd SS17 . . .175 B5
Wambrook SS3 . . . . .149 D1
Wambrook Cl CM13 . . . . . .95 C1
Wamburg Rd SS8 . . . . . . .164 E4
Wanderer Dr IG11 . . . . . .153 C2
Wangey Rd RM6 . . . . . . .134 D4
Wannock Gdns IG6 . . . . .111 B3
Wansfell Coll CM16 . . . . . .67 D4
Wansfell Gdns SS1 . . . . .167 F8
Wansford Cl CM14 . . . . . .115 F7
Wansford Rd IG8 . . . . . . .110 C2
Wanstead Church Sch
E11 . . . . .132 A6
Wanstead High Sch
E11 . . . . .132 C5
Wanstead Hospl E11 . . . .132 B7
Wanstead La IG1 . . . . . . .132 E5
Wanstead Park Ave
E12 . . . . .132 D2
Wanstead Park Rd
Ilford IG1 . . . . .133 A2
Redbridge IG1 . . . . .132 E3
Wanstead Pl E11 . . . . . . .132 A6
Wanstead Sta E11 . . . . . .132 B5
Wantage Ho 10 RM3 . . . .114 D4
Wantfield Cotts CM4 . . . . .74 F8
Wantz Chase CM9 . . . . . .37 A2
Wantz Cnr CM2 . . . . .76 E5
Wantz Haven CM9 . . . . . .37 A2
Wantz La RM13 . . . . .155 B1
Wantz Rd
Dagenham RM10 . . . . .154 B7
Maldon CM9 . . . . .37 A2
Margaretting CM4 . . . . .75 A8
Warboys Cres E4 . . . . . . .109 C5
Warburton Terr E17 . . . . .109 B1
Warburtons SS17 . . . . . . .161 A3
Ward Ave RM17 . . . . .173 B2
Ward Gdns RM3 . . . . .114 E1
Ward Hatch CM20 . . . . . . .11 A7
Ward Path CM2 . . . . .33 B4
Warden Ave RM5 . . . . . . .113 C5
Wardle Way CM1 . . . . . . .31 E7
Wardona Ct DA10 . . . . . .177 F1
Wardour Ct 9 DA2 . . . . .176 B1
Wards Rd IG2 . . . . .133 D4
Ware Rd EN11 . . . . .8 A1
Waremead Rd IG2 . . . . . .133 D3
Wares Rd
Margaret Roding CM1 . . . . .16 C5
Mashbury CM1 . . . . .17 A4
Warescot Cl CM15 . . . . . .94 B2

Warescot Rd CM15 . . . . . .94 B2
Warley Ave RM8 . . . . . . .134 F4
Warley Gap CM13 . . . . . .116 C3
Warley Hall La CM14 . . . .138 F4
Warley Hill CM13,CM14 . .116 C5
Warley Hill Bsns Pk The
CM13 . . . . .116 C4
Warley Hospl CM14 . . . . .116 B5
Warley Mount CM14 . . . . .116 C4
Warley Prim Sch CM14 . .116 C5
Warley Rd
Great Warley CM13 . . . . . .116 B3
Redbridge IG5 . . . . .111 A2
Romford RM3 . . . . .115 E1
Woodford IG8 . . . . .110 B3
Warley St CM13,RM14 . . .138 C5
Warleywoods Cres
CM14 . . . . .116 B6
Warlow Cl EN3 . . . . .65 A2
Warminster Ho RM3 . . . .114 F5
Warner Cl CM11 . . . . .97 D1
Warners Bridge Chase
SS4 . . . . .147 F6
Warners Cl IG8 . . . . .110 A5
Warners Gdns SS4 . . . . . .147 E6
Warren Chase SS7 . . . . . .145 A4
Warren Cl Broomfield CM1 .19 E3
Rayleigh SS6 . . . . .145 C8
Stanford-le-H SS17 . . . . . .160 D1
Warren Ct IG7 . . . . .111 D6
Warren Dr Basildon SS14 .142 E6
Hornchurch RM12 . . . . . . .136 B1
Wickford SS11 . . . . .122 A8
Warren Dr The E11 . . . . . .132 C4
Warren Farm Cotts
RM6 . . . . .134 F7
Warren Field CM16 . . . . . .68 A7
Warren Hastings Ct
DA11 . . . . .178 F1
Warren Hill IG10 . . . . .88 C4
Warren Hts Grays RM16 . .172 E2
Loughton IG10 . . . . .88 C4
Warren Jun Sch RM6 . . . .134 F6
Warren La
Doddinghurst CM15 . . . . . . .94 A8
Grays RM16 . . . . .172 D2
Warren Pond Rd E4 . . . . . .87 F2
Warren Prim Sch RM6 . . .172 C3
Warren Rd Chingford E4 . .109 C8
Ilford IG6 . . . . .133 D6
South Hanningfield CM3 . . . .99 D7
Southend-on-S SS9 . . . . . .146 A3
Wanstead E11 . . . . .132 C4
Warren Sch The RM6 . . . .134 F6
Warren Terr Grays RM16 .172 D4
Ilford RM6 . . . . .134 D7
Warren The CM12 . . . . . . .96 E4
Warriner Ave RM12 . . . . .136 D2
Warrington Gdns RM11 . .136 D5
Warrington Rd RM8 . . . . .134 D4
Warrington Sq
Billericay CM12 . . . . .96 F3
Dagenham RM8 . . . . .134 D2
Warrior Ho 7 SS1 . . . . . .167 A8
Warrior Sq
Little Ilford E12 . . . . .152 A8
Southend-on-S SS1 . . . . . .167 A8
Warrior Sq E SS1 . . . . . .167 A8
Warrior Sq N SS1 . . . . . .167 A8
Warrior Square Rd SS3 . .168 F5
Warwick Cl
Canvey Island SS8 . . . . . . .164 A5
Maldon CM9 . . . . .37 A1
Rayleigh SS6 . . . . .123 F1
South Benfleet SS7 . . . . . . .144 A5
Warwick Cres CM9 . . . . . .37 A1
Warwick Ct CM13 . . . . . .117 A7
Warwick Dr Maldon CM9 . .37 A1
Rochford SS4 . . . . .147 F7
Warwick Gdns Ilford IG1 133 B3
Rayleigh SS6 . . . . .123 F1
Romford RM2 . . . . .136 C8
Warwick Gn SS6 . . . . . . .124 A1
Warwick La RM13,RM14 . .156 B3
Warwick Par CM3 . . . . . .101 C2
Warwick Pl
Basildon SS16 . . . . .140 F4
Northfleet DA11 . . . . .178 B2
Pilgrims Hatch CM14 . . . . . .93 C3
Warwick Rd
Chingford E4 . . . . .109 A5
Rainham RM13 . . . . .155 D2
Rayleigh SS6 . . . . .124 A1
Southend-on-S SS1 . . . . . .167 F6
Wanstead E11 . . . . .132 B6
Warwick Sq CM1 . . . . .31 F4
Wash La CM9 . . . . .38 B7
Wash Rd Basildon SS15 . .119 E2
Brentwood CM13 . . . . .95 E4
Washington Ave SS15 . . .141 A6
Washington Ct CM9 . . . . . .36 E1
Washington Ct CM9 . . . . . .36 E1
Washington Rd
Maldon CM9 . . . . .36 F1
2 Woodford E18 . . . . . . .109 F1
Wat Tyler Ctry Pk*
SS16 . . . . .143 B2
Watchfield La SS6 . . . . . .123 C1
Watchouse Rd CM2 . . . . . .54 C3
Water La Harlow CM19 . . .23 A5
Ilford IG3 . . . . .133 F1
Purfleet RM19 . . . . .171 A2
Roydon CM19 . . . . .22 C4
Water Lane Prim Sch
CM19 . . . . .23 A4
Water Mdws
Basildon SS13 . . . . .143 A4
Linford SS17 . . . . .175 A3

Waterbeach Rd RM9 153 C6
Waterdene SS8 163 F5
Waterfalls The SS16 141 B3
Waterfield Cl DA17 169 A3
Waterford Rd SS3 168 D5
Waterfront Wlk SS14 120 B1
Waterglade Ind Pk
RM20 176 F8
Waterhale SS1 149 A1
Waterhall Ave E4 109 E6
Waterhouse La CM1 31 F1
Waterhouse Moor CM18 23 F7
Waterhouse St CM1 31 F1
Waterloo Gdns RM7 135 E5
Waterloo La CM1 32 C2
Waterloo Rd
Brentwood CM14 94 C1
Redbridge IG6 111 C1
Romford RM7 135 E5
Southend-on-S SS3 168 D7
Watermans RM1 135 F6
Watermans Way
Greenhithe DA9 177 B3
North Weald Bassett CM16 47 A4
Waters Edge SS0 166 D7
Waters Edge Ct DA8 169 F1
Waters Gdns RM10 154 A7
Waters Mead SS1 168 A6
Waters Villas CM22 4 A6
Waterside SS1 167 D6
Waterside Cl
Barking IG11 153 A8
Romford RM3 115 A3
Waterside Ind Est EN11 21 D5
Waterside Mead SS8 163 F6
Waterside Pl CM22 2 A2
Waterside Rd
Bradwell Waterside CM0 41 F3
Paglesham Eastend SS4 128 A5
Watersmeet CM19 23 B4
Waterson Rd RM16 174 C2
Waterson Vale CM2 54 C8
Waterville Dr SS16 143 A4
Waterworks La SS17 161 D6
Watery La
Battlesbridge SS11 101 C1
Matching Green CM17 26 D8
Wates Way CM15 94 D1
Watford Ho RM3 114 F5
Watkin Mews EN3 65 A2
Watkins Cl SS13 121 D1
Watkins Way SS3 149 F1
Watlington Rd
Harlow CM17 11 D4
South Benfleet SS7 144 B2
Watson Ave E6 152 A5
Watson Cl Grays RM20 177 A6
Southend-on-S SS3 168 D7
Watson Gdns RM3 114 D1
Watsons Lodge 4
RM10 154 B6
Watt's La SS4 125 F1
Watts Cres RM19 171 C2
Wavell Cl CM1 32 D8
Waveney Dr CM1 32 C6
Waverley Bridge Ct CM9 37 B5
Waverley Cl E18 110 C1
Waverley Cres
Romford RM3 114 C3
Wickford SS11 99 C3
Waverley Gdns
Barking IG11 152 E3
Grays RM16 173 A4
Redbridge IG6 111 C1
Waverley Rd
Basildon SS15 119 E1
Rainham RM13 155 B2
South Benfleet SS7 144 C6
Woodford E18 110 C2
Wavertree Rd
South Benfleet SS7 144 B4
Woodford E18 110 A1
Waxwell Rd SS5 101 E2
Waycross Rd RM14 137 E5
Wayfarer Gdns CM0 106 A5
Wayfaring Gn RM17 172 F1
Waylands Ct IG1 152 D8
Wayletts Basildon SS15 141 A8
Southend-on-S SS9 146 B6
Waymans RM15 171 D7
Wayre St CM17 11 C4
Wayre The CM17 11 C4
Wayside CM3 56 E8
Wayside Ave RM12 136 D2
Wayside Cl RM1 135 F8
Wayside Commercial Est
IG11 153 A3
Wayside Gdns RM10 154 A7
Wayside Mews IG2 133 A6
Weald Bridge Rd CM16 25 E2
Weald Cl CM14 116 A7
Weald Ctry Pk★ CM14 93 E2
Weald Ctry Pk Visitor Ctr★
CM14 93 D1
Weald Hall La CM16 46 E6
Weald Hall Lane Ind Est
CM16 46 C6
Weald Park Way CM14 115 F7
Weald Pl CM14 116 C8
Weald Rd
South Weald CM14 93 C1
South Weald CM14 93 F1
Weald The SS8 163 E4
Weald Way RM7 135 B5
Wealden Ho CM15 94 B3
Weale Rd E4 109 D7
Wear Dr CM1 32 D6
Weare Gifford SS3 168 C8
Weaverdale SS3 149 E1
Weavers SS16 143 A4
Weavers Cl 2 CM11 97 B2
Weavers Ho 5 E11 132 A5
Webb Cl CM2 33 B3
Webb Ho 2 RM10 135 A1
Webber Ho 6 IG11 152 B5
Webbscroft Rd RM10 154 B8
Webley Ct EN3 65 A2
Webster Cl
Hornchurch RM12 136 D1
Waltham Abbey EN9 66 A6
Webster Ct SS6 123 D2
Webster Pl CM4 75 E2
Webster Rd SS17 160 E2
Websters Way SS6 123 D2
Wedderburn Rd IG11 152 E4
Wedds Way SS3 150 B4
Wedgewood Cl CM16 46 A1
Wedgewood Ct SS4 125 D6
Wedgewood Dr CM17 24 E7
Wedgwood Way SS4 125 C6
Wedhey CM19 23 C8
Wedlake Cl RM11 136 E3
Wedmore Ave IG5 111 A2
Wednesbury Gdns RM3 114 F3
Wednesbury Gn RM3 114 F3
Wednesbury Rd RM3 114 F3
Weel Rd SS8 164 D2
Weelkes Cl SS17 160 C3
Weight Rd CM2 32 C2
Weind The CM16 67 E3
Weir Farm Rd SS6 145 C8
Weir Gdns SS6 123 C1
Weir Pond Rd SS4 125 F2
Weir Wynd CM12 97 B1
Weirbrook SS7 145 B8
Welbeck Cl SS5 124 F5
Welbeck Dr SS16 141 A4
Welbeck Rd SS8 164 B3
Welbeck Rise SS16 141 A4
Welch Cl SS2 148 E2
Well Cottage Cl E11 132 C4
Well Field CM1 31 A1
Well La Danbury CM3 56 C7
Galleywood CM2 54 B2
Harlow CM19 10 A1
Harlow CM20 23 A8
Pilgrims Hatch CM15 93 F6
South Ockendon RM16 172 E5
Stock CM4 75 E1
Well Mead CM12 119 C7
Well Terr CM9 37 B5
Well's St 3 CM1 32 A3
Welland RM18 175 C2
Welland Ave CM1 31 C5
Welland Rd CM0 106 A6
Weller Gr CM1 31 E7
Wellesley CM19 23 A3
Wellesley Hospl SS2 148 C3
Wellesley Rd
Brentwood CM14 94 C1
Ilford IG1 133 B3
Wanstead E11 132 A6
Wellfields IG10 89 A6
Welling Rd RM16 174 D7
Wellingborough Ho
RM3 114 F5
Wellingbury SS7 144 C5
Wellington Ave
Chingford E4 109 B8
Hullbridge SS5 123 D8
Southend-on-S SS0 147 B1
Wellington Cl
Chelmsford CM1 31 D5
Dagenham RM10 154 C5
Wellington Ct RM16 173 B5
Wellington Dr RM10 154 C5
Wellington Hill IG10 66 B1
Wellington Mews CM12 97 A5
Wellington Pl CM14 116 C5
Wellington Prim Sch
E4 109 B8
Wellington Rd
Hockley SS5 102 F1
Maldon CM9 36 F2
North Weald Bassett CM16 47 A4
Rayleigh SS6 123 F4
Tilbury RM18 179 A5
Wanstead E11 132 A6
Wellington St 1 IG11 152 C4
Wellingtonia Ave RM4 113 E7
Wellingtons The CM0 84 D3
Wellmead IG3 134 A4
Wellmeads CM2 54 B8
Wells Ave SS2 147 D6
Wells Ct Chelmsford CM1 32 D5
6 Romford RM1 135 E5
Wells Gdns
7 Basildon SS14 142 F8
Dagenham RM10 154 B7
Rainham RM13 154 F6
Redbridge IG1 132 E4
Wells Ho 4 IG11 153 A5
Wells Park Sch IG7 111 F6
Wells Prim Sch IG8 110 A6
Wellsfield SS6 123 E4
Wellstead Gdns SS0 147 B3
Wellstead Rd E6 152 A3
Wellstye Gn SS14 142 E8
Wellwood Rd IG3 134 A4
Welton Way SS4 126 A1
Wembley Ave CM3 83 A8
Wendene SS16 142 F4
Wendon Cl SS4 125 C4
Wendover Ct SS17 160 D1
Wendover Gdns CM13 117 B7
Wendover Way RM12 155 C7
Wenham Dr SS0 147 E2
Wenham Gdns CM13 95 C3
Wenlocks La CM4 72 E6
Wennington Rd RM13 170 C7
Wensley Ave IG8 110 A3
Wensley Cl RM5 113 A5
Wensley Rd SS7 145 B5
Wensleydale Ave IG5 110 E1
Wentworth Ct 5 E4 109 D5
Wentworth Ho 6 IG8 111 A3
Wentworth Mdws CM9 36 F2
Wentworth Pl RM16 173 D3
Wentworth Prim Sch
CM9 36 F1
Wentworth Rd SS2 148 B3
Wentworth Way RM13 155 B2
Werneth Hall Rd
Ilford IG5 133 A8
Redbridge IG5 132 F8
Wesley Ct SS1 167 B8
Wesley Gdns CM12 96 F5
Wesley Rd SS1 167 B7
Wessem Rd SS8 164 B5
Wessex Cl IG3 133 E5
Wessley Cl CM0 63 E4
West Ave Althorne CM3 82 E2
Basildon SS16 140 E4
Chelmsford CM1 31 F5
Hullbridge SS5 101 D2
Mayland CM3 60 E1
West Bank IG11 152 B4
West Beech Ave SS11 121 E7
West Beech Cl SS11 121 E7
West Beech Mews SS12 121 D7
West Belvedere CM3 56 F7
West Bowers Rd CM9 35 C4
West Chase Maldon CM9 36 F3
Mundon CM9 59 E1
West Cl Hoddesdon EN11 21 A8
Rainham RM13 155 B1
West Cloister CM11 97 B2
West Cres SS8 163 F4
West Crescent Rd 1
DA12 179 C1
West Croft CM11 97 B1
West Ct CM21 1 E3
West Dene Dr RM3 114 D5
West Gate CM20 23 C8
West Gn SS7 144 B5
West Gr IG8 110 C5
West Hanningfield Rd
Great Baddow CM2 55 A3
West Hanningfield CM2 76 E7
West Hatch High Sch
IG7 110 F5
West Hayes CM22 3 A3
West Ho IG11 152 B6
West Hook SS16 140 F4
West Horndon Prim Sch
CM13 139 D6
West Horndon Sta
CM13 139 C5
West House Est CM0 84 D4
West Kent Ave DA11 178 C1
West Lawn CM2 54 C2
West Leigh Jun & Inf Schs
SS9 146 D2
West Ley CM0 106 C5
West Lodge RM17 173 B2
West Malling Way
RM12 155 C7
West Mayne SS15 140 E6
West Mill DA11 178 F1
West Park Ave CM12 97 A3
West Park Cl RM6 134 E6
West Park Cres CM12 97 A2
West Park Dr CM12 97 A2
West Park Hill CM14 116 A7
West Pl CM20 11 A3
West Point Pl SS8 163 C3
West Rd Dagenham RM6 134 E5
Harlow CM20 11 A4
Romford RM7 135 D4
Sawbridgeworth CM21 1 C3
South Ockendon RM15 157 B2
Southend-on-S SS0 147 E1
Southend-on-S, Cambridge Town
SS3 168 D6
West Ridge CM12 119 A8
West Sq Harlow CM20 10 C1
Maldon CM9 36 F3
West St Erith DA8 169 E1
Gravesend DA11 179 B1
Grays RM17 178 A8
Rochford SS4 125 E2
Southend-on-S SS0,SS2 147 E2
Southend-on-S,Chalkwell
SS9 165 E8
West Station Ind Est
CM9 58 E8
West Station Rd CM9 36 E1
West Thorpe SS16 142 B6
West Thurrock Prim Sch
RM20 177 A8
West Thurrock Way
Grays RM20 172 B2
Purfleet RM20 171 F2
West View Ilford RM6 134 C6
Loughton IG10 88 F6
West View Cl RM13 155 C2
West View Dr SS6 123 B1
West Way CM14 116 A7
West Wlk CM20 23 C8
West Wood Cl SS7 145 C4
Westall Rd IG10 89 C6
Westborough Prim Sch
SS0 147 E2
Westborough Rd SS0 147 D2
Westbourne Cl
Hadleigh SS7 145 D5
Hockley SS5 125 A7
Westbourne Ct SS0 147 B2
Westbourne Dr CM14 115 F6
Westbourne Gdns CM12 97 B5
Westbourne Gr
Chelmsford CM2 54 D7
Southend-on-S SS0 147 B3
Westbury SS4 125 D4
Westbury Ct
3 Barking IG11 152 D4
1 Buckhurst Hill IG9 110 C8
Westbury Dr CM14 116 C8
Westbury Ho SS2 148 C2
Westbury La IG9 110 C8
Westbury Rd
Barking IG11 152 D4
Brentwood CM14 116 C8
Buckhurst Hill IG9 88 C1
Ilford IG1 133 A2
Redbridge IG1 132 F2
Southend-on-S SS2 148 C2
Westbury Rise CM17 24 D7
Westbury Terr RM14 137 E2
Westcliff Ave SS0 166 E7
Westcliff Dr SS9 146 D1
Westcliff Gdns SS8 164 E2
Westcliff High Sch (Boys)
SS0 147 A3
Westcliff High Sch (Girls)
SS0 147 A3
Westcliff Par SS0 166 E7
Westcliff Park Dr SS0 147 D2
Westcliff Sta SS0 166 D8
Westcroft Ct EN10 21 A4
Westerdale CM1 32 D7
Westerings Bicknacre CM3 56 F2
Purleigh CM3 58 D1
Westerings Prim Sch The
SS5 124 E4
Westerings The
Great Baddow CM2 54 F5
Hockley SS5 124 E5
Westerland Ave SS8 164 D3
Western Approaches
SS2 147 A7
Western Ave
Brentwood CM14 94 C1
Dagenham RM10 154 D6
Epping CM16 67 F7
Romford RM2 114 C1
Western Cross Cl DA9 177 C1
Western Ct 10 RM1 135 E6
Western Espl
Canvey Island SS8 164 B1
Southend-on-S SS0,SS1 166 E7
Western Gdns 2 CM14 116 C8
Western Mews CM12 97 A2
Western Rd
Billericay CM12 97 A2
Brentwood CM14 116 C8
Burnham-on-C CM0 106 C4
Hadleigh SS7 145 E6
Lower Nazeing EN9 21 E1
Rayleigh SS6 123 B1
Romford RM1 135 F6
Southend-on-S SS9 146 B1
Western Terr 1 EN11 8 B1
Westernville Gdns IG2 133 C4
Westfield Basildon SS15 141 A8
Harlow CM18 23 E7
Loughton IG10 88 C4
Westfield Ave CM1 32 A4
Westfield Bglws CM9 59 E1
Westfield Cl
Rayleigh SS6 123 B5
Wickford SS11 121 F8
Westfield Park Dr IG8 110 E4
Westfield Rd
Dagenham RM9 153 F8
3 Hoddesdon EN11 21 A7
Westfields Gdns RM6 134 C5
Westgate Basildon SS14 142 A6
Southend-on-S SS3 168 E6
Westgate Pk SS14 142 A5
Westlake Ave SS13 143 E6
Westland Ave RM11 136 E3
Westland View RM16 173 A5
Westlands Com Prim Sch
CM1 31 E2
Westleigh Ave SS9 146 D1
Westleigh Ct
Southend-on-S SS9 146 D1
12 Wanstead E11 132 A6
Westley Rd SS16 141 C2
Westlyn Cl RM13 155 C1
Westman Rd SS8 164 E3
Westmarch CM3 101 C6
Westmayne Ind Pk
SS15 140 E6
Westmede Basildon SS16 141 C5
Chigwell IG7 111 C4
Westminster Ct 4 E11 132 B5
Westminster Dr
Hockley SS5 124 D6
Southend-on-S SS0 147 B2
Westminster Gdns
Barking IG11 152 E3
Chingford E4 87 E1
Redbridge IG6 111 D1
Westminster Mans SS0 147 B2
Westmoreland Ave
RM11 136 C6
Westmorland Cl E12 132 D2
Weston Ave RM20 171 F1
Weston Cl CM13 95 C2
Weston Gn RM9 153 F8
Weston Rd
Dagenham RM9 153 E8
Southend-on-S SS1 167 A7
Westone Mans 5 IG11 152 F5
Westray Wlk SS12 122 A5
Westrow Dr IG11 153 A7
Westrow Gdns IG3 133 F1
Westside Bsns Ctr CM19 22 F7
Westview Dr IG8 110 D1
Westward Ho SS1 166 F7
Westward Rd E4 109 A5
Westwater SS7 144 B4
Westway Chelmsford CM1 53 E8
South Woodham Ferrers
CM3 101 C7
Westwood Ave CM14 116 A6
Westwood Gdns SS7 145 D5
Westwood Lodge SS7 145 C5
Westwood Prim Sch
SS7 145 D4
Westwood Rd
Canvey Island SS8 164 B3
Ilford IG3 134 A4
Wetherland SS16 141 F5
Wetherly Cl CM17 11 F4
Wethersfield Cl SS6 123 A3
Wethersfield Way SS11 122 B5
Weybourne Cl SS2 148 B3
Weybourne Gdns SS2 148 B3
Weybridge Wlk SS3 149 E1
Weydale SS17 161 B5
Weylond Rd RM8 134 F1
Weymarks SS15 141 D7
Weymouth Rd CM1 32 E6
Whadden Chase CM4 74 A3
Whalebone Ave RM6 134 F5
Whalebone Gr RM6 134 F5
Whalebone La N RM6 134 E8
Whalebone La S RM6,
RM8 134 F4
Wharf Cl SS17 160 D1
Wharf Rd
Brentwood CM14 116 C7
Chelmsford CM2 32 C2
Fobbing SS17 161 D4
Gravesend DA12 179 E1
Grays RM17 177 F8
Heybridge Basin CM9 37 F4
Hoddesdon EN10 43 A7
Stanford-le-H SS17 175 E7
Wharf Rd S RM17 177 F8
Wharfside Cl DA8 169 F1
Wharley Hook CM18 24 A5
Wharnecliffe DA9 177 B1
Wharton Dr CM1 33 A7
Wheatear Pl CM11 97 C1
Wheatfield Way
Basildon SS16 141 A4
Chelmsford CM1 31 F3
Wheatfields
3 Brentwood CM14 116 C6
Harlow CM17 11 D6
Rochford SS4 126 D4
Wheatley Cl
Greenhithe DA9 177 A2
Hornchurch RM11 136 D6
Rochford SS4 125 D4
Sawbridgeworth CM21 1 C1
Wheatley Mans 8 IG11 153 A5
Wheatley Rd SS17 161 B5
Wheatsheaf Rd RM1 135 F5
Wheatstone Rd DA8 169 D1
Wheel Farm Dr RM10 135 C1
Wheeler Cl IG8 110 F5
Wheeler's Hill CM3 19 D6
Wheelers CM16 46 A2
Wheelers Cl EN9 21 F1
Wheelers Cross IG11 152 D3
Wheelers Farm Gdns
CM16 47 B5
Wheelers La
Fobbing SS17 161 D5
Pilgrims Hatch CM14 93 B6
Wheelwrights The SS2 148 A5
Whernside Ave SS8 164 C5
Whieldon Gr CM17 24 E7
Whinhams Way CM12 96 F3
Whist Ave SS11 99 F1
Whistler Mews RM8 153 B7
Whistler Rise SS3 168 G8
Whitakers Way IG10 88 F8
Whitby Ave CM13 117 D4
Whitby Cl DA9 177 A2
Whitby Rd CM0 84 B2
Whitchurch Rd RM3 114 E6
Whitcroft SS16 141 C3
White Bridge Jun & Inf Schs
The IG10 88 E2
White Elm Rd CM3 57 A2
White Gates RM12 136 C3
White Gdns RM10 154 A6
White Hall RM4 90 B6
White Hall Rd SS3 150 B4
White Hart Cotts CM2 33 A6
White Hart La
Brentwood CM14 116 C8
Chelmsford CM1 32 F8
Hockley SS5 124 F5
Romford RM7 113 A1
White Hart Yd DA11 179 B1
White Horse La CM9 36 F2
White House Chase SS6 123 E1
White House Rd SS9 147 A6
White Lyons Rd CM14 116 C7
White Mead CM1 19 B2

White Post Field CM21 ....1 D2
White Tree Ct CM3 ......101 B6
White's Hill CM4 ....75 F1
Whitebarn La RM10 ....154 A4
Whitebeam Cl CM2 ......53 F7
Whitebeam Dr RM15 ...157 C2
Whitefield Ct CM3 ......83 A8
Whitefield Sch E17 ....109 D1
Whitefriars Cres SS0 ..166 C8
Whitegate Rd SS1 ......167 A8
Whitehall Cl
  Chigwell IG7 ....112 A7
  Lower Nazeing EN9 .....21 E1
Whitehall Cotts SG12 ...9 D8
Whitehall Est CM19 ....22 E7
Whitehall Gdns E4 .....87 C5
Whitehall La
  Corringham SS17 .....161 C7
  Grays RM17 ....173 C1
  Woodford IG9 ....110 A8
Whitehall Lodge IG8 ..110 A7
Whitehall Prim Sch E4 .109 E8
Whitehall Rd
  Chingford E4 ....109 E8
  Grays RM17 ....173 C1
  Woodford IG8 ....110 A7
Whitehead Cl CM1 ......53 B8
Whitehills Rd IG10 .....89 A6
Whitehouse Cres CM2 ..54 D8
Whitehouse Rd CM3 ...101 D8
Whitelands CM15 ....72 D4
Whitelands Cl SS11 .....99 E1
Whitelands Way RM3 ..114 D2
Whites Ave IG2 ....133 E5
Whites Cl DA9 ....177 C1
Whitesbridge La CM4 ...53 D1
Whiteshott SS16 ....142 A4
Whitesmith Dr CM12 ...96 E3
Whitethorn Gdns
  Chelmsford CM2 ....54 C7
  Hornchurch RM11 ....136 C5
Whitewaits CM20 ....10 E1
Whiteways Billericay CM11 97 E3
  Canvey Island SS8 ....164 D1
  Southend-on-S SS9 ...146 F6
Whitfield Ct IG1 ....132 F4
Whitfield Link CM2 .....54 D7
Whitfields SS17 ....160 F2
Whiting Ave IG11 .....152 B5
Whitings The IG2 ......133 E6
Whitings Way E6 ......152 A1
Whitley Ct EN11 ....21 B8
Whitley Rd EN11 ....21 B8
Whitmore Ave
  Grays RM16 ....173 B6
  Romford RM3 ....114 E1
Whitmore Cl RM16 ....174 E7
Whitmore Cres CM2 ....33 B4
Whitmore Ct SS14 ....142 E8
Whitmore Jun & Inf Sch
  SS14 ....120 E1
Whitmore Way SS14 ..142 D8
Whitney Ave IG4 ......132 D7
Whittingham Ave SS2 .148 E2
Whittingstall Rd EN11 ..21 C8
Whittington Rd CM13 ..95 D4
Whitwell Ct SS17 .....175 C8
Whitworth Cres EN3 ...65 A2
Whybrews SS17 ....160 F2
Whybridge Cl RM13 ...154 F4
Whybridge Inf Sch
  RM13 ....155 A4
Whybridge Jun Sch
  RM13 ....154 F4
Whytewaters SS16 ....142 F4
Whyverne Cl CM1 ......32 E6
Wick Beech Ave SS11 .121 E7
Wick Chase SS2 ......148 F1
Wick Cres SS12 ......121 E5
Wick Dr Wickford SS12 .121 D7
  Wickford SS12 ....121 E5
Wick Farm Rd CM0 .....62 C8
Wick Glen CM12 ....96 F4
Wick La SS11 ....121 E7
Wick Rd CM0 ....106 D4
Wickets Way IG6 ......111 F4
Wickford Ash CM1 .....31 D6
Wickfields IG7 ....111 D4
Wickford Ave SS13 ...143 B5
Wickford Bsns Pk **6**
  SS11 ....122 A5
Wickford CE Inf Sch
  SS11 ....121 E8
Wickford Ct RM3 .....114 F5
Wickford Ct **9** SS13 ..143 A6
Wickford Dr RM3 .....114 F5
Wickford Hall 121 F8
Wickford Inf Sch The
  SS12 ....121 C8
Wickford Jun Sch SS12 121 C8
Wickford Mews **7**
  SS13 ....143 A6
Wickford Pl **8** SS13 ..143 A6
Wickford Rd
  South Woodham Ferrers
  CM3 ....101 B8
  Southend-on-S SS0 ...166 E7
Wickford Sta SS12 ...121 C8
Wickham Cres CM1 ....31 F6
Wickham Pl SS16 .....142 C4
Wickham Rd
  Chingford E4 ....109 C3
  Grays RM16 ....174 C4
Wickham's Chase CM3 .57 C2

Wickhay SS15 ....141 F5
Wickhay Cotts CM3 ....34 D5
Wicklands Rd SG12 .....9 D8
Wicklow Ave CM1 ......31 D6
Wicklow Wlk SS3 .....168 C7
Wickmead Cl SS2 .....148 E2
Wid Cl CM13 ....95 D4
Wid Terr CM15 ....72 C3
Widbrook CM15 ....72 C3
Widecombe Cl RM3 ...114 D2
Widecombe Gdns IG4 ..132 E2
Widford Chase CM2 ....53 F7
Widford Cl CM2 ....53 F7
Widford Gr CM2 ....53 F7
Widford Ind Est CM1 ..53 E8
Widford Lodge Sch CM2 53 F7
Widford Park Pl CM2 ..53 F7
Widford Rd CM2 ....53 F7
Widgeons SS13 ....143 C6
Widworthy Hayes CM13 .95 B1
Wiggin's La CM12 .....118 E7
Wiggins La CM12 .....118 E7
Wiggins View CM2 .....33 B4
Wigham Ho IG11 .....152 C5
Wigley Bush La CM14 .115 E7
Wigram Rd E11 ......132 C5
Wigton Rd RM3 ......114 E6
Wigton Way RM3 .....114 E6
Wilde Cl RM18 ....179 C5
Wilfred Ave RM13 ....170 A8
Wilfred St **13** DA11 ..179 B1
Wilkes Rd CM13 ....95 D4
Wilkinson Cl DA1 ....176 A3
Wilkinsons Mead CM2 ..33 A4
Willetts Mews EN11 ...21 A7
William Bellamy Jun & Inf
  Schs RM10 ....135 A2
William Cl RM5 ......113 D2
William Cl IG6 ....133 D7
William de Ferrers Sch
  CM3 ....101 E7
William Edwards Sch
  RM16 ....173 B6
William Ford CE Jun Sch
  RM10 ....154 A5
William Hunter Way
  CM14 ....116 C8
William Martin CE Jun & Inf
  Schs CM18 ....23 F4
William Pike Ho RM7 .135 D5
William Rd SS13 .....143 F6
William Read Prim Sch
  SS8 ....163 F3
William Smith Ho **10**
  DA17 ....169 A3
William St Barking IG11 152 C5
  Grays RM17 ....178 C4
William Tansley Smith Ho
  RM12 ....136 F2
William Torbitt Inf Sch
  IG2 ....133 F6
William Torbitt Prim Sch
  IG2 ....133 F6
Williams Rd CM1 .....119 B1
Williamsons Way SS17 160 F5
Willingale Ave SS6 ...123 A4
Willingale Cl
  Brentwood CM13 ......95 B3
  Loughton IG10 ....89 C7
  Woodford IG8 ....110 C4
Willingale Ct SS13 ....67 E3
Willingale Rd Fyfield CM5 .27 F2
  Loughton IG10 ....89 D7
  Willingale CM4,CM5 ...50 E6
Willingale Way SS1 ...149 A1
Willingales The **9** SS15 141 A6
Willinghall Cl EN9 ....65 D7
Willis Ho **2** E12 ....133 A1
Willis Rd DA8 ....169 D2
Willmott Rd SS2 .....147 D6
Willoughby Dr
  Chelmsford CM2 ....32 F2
  Rainham RM13 ......154 E5
Willow Cl Brentwood CM13 95 B3
  Broomfield CM1 ......19 B1
  Buckhurst Hill IG9 ...110 D7
  Burnham-on-C CM0 ..106 B6
  Canvey Island SS8 ...163 F3
  Doddinghurst CM15 ...72 D1
  Hockley SS5 ....124 F6
  Hornchurch RM12 ....136 B1
  Rayleigh SS6 ....123 D4
  Southend-on-S SS9 ..146 F6
Willow Cotts CM3 .....79 A6
Willow Ct Barking IG11 152 C7
  8 Dagenham RM8 ..134 D4
Willow Dr SS6 ....123 C4
Willow Gn CM4 ....74 B4
Willow Gr CM3 ....79 A1
Willow Ho **1** SS13 ..143 B8
Willow Lodge SS3 ....168 F8
Willow Mead CM21 .....1 E2
Willow Par RM14 ....137 E3
Willow Path EN9 ......65 E5
Willow Pl CM17 ....25 A4
Willow Rd RM6 ......134 E5
Willow St Chingford E4 .87 D2
  Romford RM7 ....135 C7
Willow Way RM3 .....115 B4
Willow Wlk
  Canewdon SS4 ....104 D1
  Hadleigh SS7 ....145 D1
  Heybridge CM9 ....37 C6
  Hockley SS5 ....124 F6
  Upminster RM14 ....137 E3
Willowbank CM2 ....54 D4

Willowbrook Prim Sch
  CM13 ....95 D3
Willowdale Ctr SS12 ..121 D8
Willowdene CM15 ......93 F4
Willowdene Ct CM14 ..116 C6
Willowfield
  Basildon SS13 ....119 C1
  Harlow CM18 ....23 D6
Willowherb Wlk RM3 .114 C3
Willowhill SS17 ......160 E5
Willowmead
  Chigwell IG7 ....112 A7
  Ramsden Heath CM11 ..98 C5
Willows Prim Sch SS14 142 C8
Willows The
  13 Basildon SS13 ..143 C6
  Billericay CM11 ......119 D7
  Boreham CM3 ....33 F8
  Chelmsford CM1 ......32 A2
  Grays RM17 ....178 E8
  South Benfleet SS7 ..144 B4
  Southend-on-S SS1 ..149 A1
  Wallend E12 ....152 A5
  Loughton IG10 ....88 D4
Wills Hill SS17 ......160 D3
Wilmington Gdns IG11 152 E5
Wilmot Gn CM13 .....116 C4
Wilmot Ho CM13 .....116 C4
Wilmslow Ho **3** RM3 114 C6
Wilmslowe SS6 ....164 E5
Wilnett Ct **4** RM6 ..134 B4
Wilnett Villas **5** RM6 134 B4
Wilrich Ave SS8 .....164 D3
Wilshire Ave CM2 .....32 F3
Wilsman Rd RM15 ...157 C3
Wilsner SS13 ....143 C7
Wilson Cl SS17 ......175 C8
Wilson Ct SS12 ......121 A8
Wilson Rd Redbridge IG1 132 F4
  Southend-on-S SS1 ..166 F7
Wilson's Ct CM9 ......37 B2
Wilthorne Gdns RM10 154 B5
Wilton Cl **7** IG8 ...110 A4
Wilton Dr RM5 ....113 D3
Wiltshire Ave RM11 ..136 F7
Wiltshire Cl IG11 ....152 C6
Wimarc Cres SS6 ....123 B4
Wimbish SS13 ....143 B6
Wimbish End SS13 ..143 B6
Wimbish Mews SS13 .143 B6
Wimborne Cl
  Buckhurst Hill IG9 ...110 C8
  Sawbridgeworth CM21 ..1 D2
Wimborne Rd SS2 ...148 B1
Wimbourne SS15 .....141 A7
Wimhurst Cl SS5 ....124 E7
Winbrook Cl SS6 ....145 E8
Winbrook Rd SS6 ....145 E8
Wincanton Gdns
  Ilford IG6 ....133 B8
  Redbridge IG6 ....111 B1
Wincanton Rd RM3 ..114 D7
Winchcombe Cl SS9 .146 E3
Winchelsea Dr CM2 ...54 E7
Winchelsea Rd E7 ...132 A1
Winchester Ave RM14 137 F2
Winchester Cl SS9 ...146 E3
Winchester Gdns SS15 119 C1
Winchester Ho **5** IG11 153 A5
Winchester Rd
  Chingford E4 ....109 C3
  Ilford IG1 ....133 D1
Winckford Cl CM3 .....19 B6
Wincoat Cl SS7 ......144 C3
Wincoat Dr SS7 .....144 C3
Wind Hill CM17 ....26 A4
Windermere Ave
  Hornchurch RM12 ...155 A8
  Hullbridge SS5 ......101 C3
Windermere Gdns IG4 132 E6
Windermere Rd
  South Benfleet SS7 ..144 E7
  Southend-on-S SS1 ..167 C8
Winding Way RM8 ...134 C1
Windley Tye CM1 ......31 E3
Windmill Cl
  Upminster RM14 ....137 A2
  Waltham Abbey EN9 ..65 E5
Windmill Fields CM17 ..11 F4
Windmill Hts CM12 ..119 B8
Windmill Mdws CM6 ...5 C2
Windmill St DA12 ....179 B1
Windmill Stps **6** SS1 167 C7
Windmill Way CM15 ...71 E2
Windmills The CM1 ....19 B3
Windrush Ct DA8 ....169 E1
Windrush Dr CM1 .....32 C6
Windsor Ave
  Corringham SS17 ....161 A5
  Grays RM16 ....173 B4
Windsor Cl
  Canvey Island SS8 ...164 B3
  Southend-on-S SS9 ..146 E3
Windsor Gdns
  Hadleigh SS7 ....145 C4
  Hockley SS5 ....125 B4
  Wickford SS11 ....99 D1
Windsor Mews SS6 ..123 C1
Windsor Rd
  Basildon SS13, CM11 .143 B8
  Chingford E4 ....109 B6
  Dagenham RM8 ......134 E1
  Hornchurch RM11 ...136 C4
  Ilford IG1 ....152 C8
  Pilgrims Hatch CM15 ..94 B3
  Ramsden Heath CM11 ..98 D4
  Southend-on-S SS0 ..147 E1
  Wanstead E11 ....132 A2

Windsor Trad Est CM11 .98 D4
Windsor Way
  Chelmsford CM1 ......31 E1
  Rayleigh SS6 ....123 E1
Windsor Wood EN9 ....65 E6
Windsors The IG9 ....110 E8
Windward Way CM3 ..101 F6
Windy Hill CM13 ......95 C1
Winfields SS13 ....143 C7
Winford Dr EN10 ......21 A1
Wingate Rd IG1 .....152 B7
Wingfield RM17 ......172 F1
Wingfield Cl CM13 ...117 A7
Wingfield Gdns RM14 137 F5
Wingletye La RM11 ..137 A5
Wingrave Cres CM14 .115 E6
Wingrove Ct
  Brentwood CM14 ....115 E6
  Chelmsford CM1 ......32 A6
Wingrove Dr **6** RM19 171 B1
Wingway CM1 ....94 C1
Winifred Ave RM12 ..155 E8
Winifred Rd
  Basildon SS13 ....143 B6
  Dagenham RM8 .....134 E3
  Erith DA8 ....169 E1
Winmill Rd RM8 .....134 F1
Winningales Ct IG5 ..132 E8
Winns Ave E17 ....109 A1
Winns Terr E17 ......109 A1
Winsbeach E17 ......109 D1
Winsford Gdns SS0 ..147 A4
Winsford Way SS0 ....33 C6
Winslow Gr E4 ......109 E8
Winstanley Way SS14 142 A8
Winstead Gdns RM10 154 C7
Winston Cl
  Greenhithe DA9 .....176 F1
  Romford RM7 ....135 B7
Winston Way IG1 ....133 B8
Winstree SS13 ....143 B8
Winstree Rd CM0 ....106 B5
Winter Folly SS11 ...141 E5
Winter Gardens Jun & Inf
  Schs SS8 ....164 A5
Winter Gardens Path
  SS8 ....163 E7
Winter's Ct E4 ......109 B7
Winterbourne Rd RM8 134 C2
Winters Way EN9 .....66 A6
Winterscroft Rd **5** EN11 21 A7
Winterswyk Ave SS8 164 E3
Winton Ave
  Southend-on-S SS0 ..166 E7
  Wickford SS12 ....121 A8
Winton Lodge SS14 ..147 C1
Wiscombe Hill SS16 ..141 C3
Wisdons Cl RM10 ....135 B3
Wisemans Gdns CM21 ..1 C1
Wissants CM19 ....23 C4
Wistaria Cl CM15 ....94 B4
Wisteria Cl IG1 ......152 B6
Wisteria Lodge **7** CM1 .32 F6
Witchards SS16 .....142 B5
Witham Cl IG10 ......88 E3
Witham Gdns CM13 ..139 D5
Witham Rd
  Dagenham RM10 ....154 A7
  Langford CM9 ....36 D7
  Romford RM2 ....136 B6
Witherings The RM11 136 F6
Withy Mead E4 ....109 D7
Withypool SS3 ....149 D1
Withywindle The CM3 101 C6
Witney Rd CM0 ......106 C4
Wittem Rd SS8 ......164 B5
Wittenham Way E4 ..109 D7
Wittering Wlk RM12 .155 C6
Witterings The SS8 .164 A5
Wivenhoe Rd IG11 ...153 B3
Wix Rd RM9 ....153 D4
Woburn Ave
  Hornchurch RM12 ...155 A8
  Theydon Bois CM16 ...67 E2
Woburn Ct
  Chelmsford CM2 ......32 A1
  5 Woodford E18 ..110 A1
Woburn Pl CM12 ......96 F5
Wodehouse Rd DA1 ..176 A3
Wokindon Rd RM16 ..174 B3
Wollaston Cres SS13 121 D2
Wollaston Way SS13 121 D2
Wolmers Hey CM3 .....18 F7
Wolseley Rd
  Chelmsford CM2 ......32 A1
  Romford RM7 ....135 D4
Wolsey Ave E6 ......152 A2
Wolsey Gdns IG6 ....111 C4
Wolverton Ho **1** RM3 114 C5
Wonston Rd CM0 .....84 C4
Wood Ave Hockley SS5 124 E8
  Purfleet RM19 ....171 C2
Wood Cnr CM9 ....36 B2
Wood Dale CM2 ....54 E6
Wood End SS5 ......124 D5
Wood Farm Cl SS9 ..146 D4
Wood Gn SS13 ......121 B1
Wood La
  Aythorpe Roding CM6 ..5 D1
  Dagenham RM8,RM9,
  RM10 ....134 F1
  Heybridge CM9 ....37 A5
  Hockley SS5 ....124 D8
  Hornchurch RM12 ...155 A7
  Mundon CM9 ....59 E1
  Willingale CM5 ....28 F3
  Woodford IG8 ....109 F5
Wood Meads CM16 ....46 B2

Wood Rd CM9 ....37 B6
Wood St Chelmsford CM2 .54 A2
  Grays RM17 ....178 C3
Wood View RM16,RM17 173 E2
Woodacre RM15 .....172 A8
Woodberry Cl
  Canvey Island SS8 ...164 A6
  Southend-on-S SS5 ..146 C5
Woodberry Down CM16 46 A3
Woodberry Rd SS11 .122 A6
Woodberry Way E4 ...87 C2
Woodbine Cl CM19 ....23 C6
Woodbine Close Cvn Pk
  EN9 ....66 C4
Woodbine Pl E11 ....132 A6
Woodbridge Cl CM3 ..114 D6
Woodbridge Ct IG8 ..110 E3
Woodbridge High Sch
  IG8 ....110 B3
Woodbridge La CM3 .114 D6
Woodbridge Rd IG11 .152 F7
Woodbrook Cres CM12 .96 F3
Woodbrook Gdns EN9 ..65 E6
Woodbrooke Way SS17 161 B5
Woodburn Cl SS7 ....145 B4
Woodbury Cl E11 ....132 B7
Woodbury Hill IG10 ...88 E7
Woodcote App RM12 ..155 E8
Woodcote Ave RM12 .155 E8
Woodcote Cres **7** SS13 143 C6
Woodcote Mews IG10 ..88 D4
Woodcote Rd
  Southend-on-S SS9 ..147 A2
  Wanstead E11 ....132 A4
Woodcote Way SS7 ..144 B7
Woodcotes SS3 .....149 E1
Woodcroft CM18 ......23 D6
Woodcroft Ave SG12 ...8 C4
Woodcroft Cl SS7 ...145 C4
Woodcutters Ave
  Grays RM16 ....173 C4
  Southend-on-S SS9 ..146 F6
Woodedge Cl E4 ......87 F1
Woodend Rd E17 ....109 C1
Woodfield **5** SS12 ..121 D6
Woodfield Cotts
  Heybridge CM9 ....37 C6
  Ingatestone CM4 .....74 D5
Woodfield Dr RM2 ...136 A7
Woodfield Gdns SS9 .165 E8
Woodfield Park Dr SS9 147 A1
Woodfield Rd
  Hadleigh SS7 ....146 A3
  Southend-on-S SS9 ..166 A4
Woodfield Terr CM16 ..46 C6
Woodfield Way RM12 .136 C3
Woodfines The RM11 .136 D5
Woodford Ave Ilford IG2 133 C4
  Redbridge IG4 ......132 C5
Woodford Bridge Rd
  IG4 ....132 E2
Woodford Ct EN9 .....66 C4
Woodford Cty High Sch for
  Girls IG8 ....109 F4
Woodford Green Prep Sch
  IG8 ....110 A4
Woodford Green Prim Sch
  IG8 ....110 A5
Woodford Ho **5** E18 .132 A7
Woodford New Rd
  Chingford E17 ....109 E1
  Woodford IG8,E17 ...109 F3
Woodford Rd E18 ....132 A8
Woodford Sta IG8 ...110 B3
Woodford Trad Est
  Redbridge IG8 ......132 D8
  Woodford IG8 ......110 D1
Woodgrange Cl SS1 .167 B8
Woodgrange Ct EN11 ..21 A5
Woodgrange Dr SS1 .167 E7
Woodgreen Rd EN9 ...66 C5
Woodhall Cres RM11 .136 F3
Woodhall Hill CM1 ....18 C2
Woodhall Par CM1 ....32 A7
Woodhall Rd CM1 ....32 A7
Woodham Ct **2** CM3 101 C7
Woodham Ferrers Sta
  CM3 ....101 C8
Woodham Halt CM3 ..101 C8
Woodham Ley Prim Sch
  SS7 ....144 B6
Woodham Mortimer Rd
  CM9 ....57 E8
Woodham Park Dr SS7 144 C2
Woodham Rd
  Battlesbridge SS11 ..100 E4
  South Benfleet SS7 ..144 B2
  South Woodham Ferrers
  CM3 ....101 F8
  Stow Maries CM3 .....80 B3
Woodham Walter CE Prim
  Sch CM9 ....35 D3
Woodham Way SG12 ...8 C4
Woodhaven Gdns IG6 133 C2
Woodhays **1** SS13 .143 C6
Woodhill CM18 ....23 E5
Woodhill Common Rd
  CM3 ....56 B5
Woodhill Rd
  Chelmsford CM2 ......55 E6
  Danbury CM3 ....56 B6
Woodhouse La CM3 ...19 A4
Woodhurst Rd SS8 ..163 E3
Wooding Gr CM19 ....23 B8
Woodland Ave CM13 ..95 D4
Woodland Cl
  Brentwood CM13 .....95 C4

Woodland Cl continued
Ingatestone CM4 . . . . .74 C4
South Benfleet SS7 . . . . .146 A3
Woodford IG8 . . . . .110 B7
Woodland Ct 10 E11 . . .132 A6
Woodland Gr CM16 . . . .68 A7
Woodland Park Chase
CM3 . . . . .83 A7
Woodland Rd
Chelmsford CM1 . . . . . . .32 A4
Chingford E4 . . . . .87 C1
Loughton IG10 . . . . .88 E6
Woodland Way
Chipping Ongar CM5 . . . . .48 F1
Greenhithe DA9 . . . . . . .177 A3
Theydon Bois CM16 . . . . .67 E4
Woodford IG8 . . . . .110 B7
Woodlands Althorne CM3 . .83 A3
Broomfield CM1 . . . . .19 A4
Epping CM16 . . . . .68 A8
Great Waltham CM1 . . . . .18 F4
Woodlands Ave
Dagenham RM6 . . . . .134 E4
Hornchurch RM11 . . . . . .136 E6
Rayleigh SS6 . . . . .145 E8
Wanstead E11 . . . . .132 B3
Woodlands Cl
Basildon SS16 . . . . .142 F4
Grays RM16 . . . . .173 E3
Hockley SS5 . . . . .124 D5
Hoddesdon EN11 . . . . . . .21 A5
Rayleigh SS6 . . . . .145 D8
Woodlands Dr
Basildon SS17 . . . . .142 C1
Hoddesdon EN11 . . . . . . .21 A4
Woodlands Inf Sch IG1 . . .152 D7
Woodlands Jun Sch
IG1 . . . . .152 D7
Woodlands Par SS5 . . . .124 D5
Woodlands Pk SS9 . . . . .146 A3
Woodlands Prep Sch
CM13 . . . . .138 D7
Woodlands Rd
Hockley SS5 . . . . .124 D5
Ilford IG1 . . . . .133 C1
Romford RM1 . . . . .135 F8
Romford,Harold Wood
RM3 . . . . .115 A2
Wickford SS12 . . . . .121 D7
Woodlands Sch
Basildon SS16 . . . . .142 A4
Chelmsford CM1 . . . . . . .31 F6
Woodlands The SS3 . . . .168 E8
Woodleigh 3 E18 . . . . .110 A2
Woodleigh Ave SS9 . . . .146 D3
Woodley Wlk SS3 . . . . .149 E2
Woodlow SS7 . . . . .145 B6
Woodleys CM20 . . . . . . .11 A1
Woodman La E4 . . . . . . .87 E4
Woodman Path IG6 . . . .111 E4
Woodman Rd
Brentwood CM14 . . . . . . .116 D5
Redbridge IG7 . . . . .111 F5
Woodmanhurst Rd
SS17 . . . . .160 F5
Woodmill Mews EN11 . . .21 B8
Woodpond Ave SS5 . . . .124 E5
Woodredon Cl CM19 . . . .22 B7

Woodredon Farm La
CM16 . . . . .66 D4
Woodridden Hill EN9,
CM16 . . . . .66 E3
Woodroffe Cl CM2 . . . . .33 A3
Woodrose Lodge 6 CM1 .32 F6
Woodrush Way RM6 . . . .134 D7
Woods The SS7 . . . . . . .145 F3
Woodshire Rd RM10 . . . .135 B1
Woodside
Buckhurst Hill IG9 . . . . . .110 C8
Little Baddow CM3 . . . . . .34 F1
Mundon CM9 . . . . .59 E2
Southend-on-S SS9 . . . . .146 B5
Southminster CM0 . . . . . .84 C4
Thornwood CM16 . . . . . . .46 D5
Woodside Ave SS7 . . . .144 C8
Woodside Chase SS5 . . .124 E4
Woodside Cl
Brentwood CM13 . . . . . . .95 D4
Rainham RM13 . . . . .155 C1
Southend-on-S SS9 . . . . .146 B6
Woodside Cotts
Edney Common CM1 . . . . .52 C5
Ingatestone CM4 . . . . . . .73 F7
Woodside Ct SS9 . . . . . .146 B5
Woodside Gdns E4 . . . .109 B4
Woodside Prim Sch
RM16 . . . . .173 F3
Woodside Rd
Hockley SS5 . . . . .124 B5
Hockley,South Fambridge
SS5 . . . . .102 F1
Woodford IG8 . . . . .110 A6
Woodside Sch DA17 . . . . .169 B2
Woodside View SS7 . . . .144 D8
Woodstock Ave RM3 . . .115 B4
Woodstock Cres
Basildon SS15 . . . . .140 F6
Hockley SS5 . . . . .124 D6
Woodstock Gdns
Basildon SS15 . . . . .140 F6
Ilford IG3 . . . . .134 A2
Woodstock Pl CM2 . . . . .54 F5
Woodstock Rd E17 . . . .109 D1
Woodview SS16 . . . . . . .140 E4
Woodview Ave E4 . . . . .109 C6
Woodville Cl SS4 . . . . . .125 D3
Woodville Gdns IG6 . . . .133 B7
Woodville Prim Sch The
CM3 . . . . .79 D1
Woodville Rd
Canvey Island SS8 . . . . . .164 D3
Woodford E18 . . . . .110 B1
Woodward Cl RM17 . . . .173 B2
Woodward Gdns RM9 . . .153 C5
Woodward Hts RM17 . . .173 B2
Woodward Rd RM9 . . . .153 C5
Woodward Terr DA9 . . . .176 E1
Woodwards CM19 . . . . . .23 C6
Woodway CM13 . . . . . . .95 A1
Woodyards
Bradwell Waterside CM0 . . .41 F3
Bradwell-on-S CM0 . . . . . .42 A3
Woolards Way CM3 . . . .101 D7
Woolden Ho E4 . . . . . . .87 E2
Woolf Wlk RM18 . . . . . .179 C5
Woolhampton Way IG7 .112 B7
Woolifers Ave SS17 . . . .161 B4

Woollard St EN9 . . . . . .65 C5
Woollard Way CM4 . . . . .72 E8
Woolmer Gn SS15 . . . . .141 E7
Woolmers Mead CM3 . . . .7 F2
Woolmonger's La CM4 . . .72 A8
Woolpack SS3 . . . . .168 D7
Woolshotts Rd SS12 . . . .120 F7
Woolwich Manor Way
E6 . . . . .152 A1
Woolwich Rd DA17 . . . . .169 A1
Wootton Rd RM11 . . . . .136 D6
Worcester Ave RM14 . . .137 F2
Worcester Cl
Basildon SS16 . . . . .140 F5
Greenhithe DA9 . . . . . . .177 B3
Mayland CM3 . . . . .61 A1
Stanford-le-H SS17 . . . . .160 D3
Worcester Cres IG8 . . . .110 C6
Worcester Ct CM2 . . . . . .55 A5
Worcester Dr SS6 . . . . .123 F1
Worcester Gdns IG1 . . . .132 E4
Worcester Rd CM0 . . . . .106 C6
Wordsworth Ave
Maldon CM9 . . . . .59 A8
Woodford E18 . . . . .109 F1
Wordsworth Cl
Romford RM3 . . . . .114 C2
Southend-on-S SS2 . . . . .148 B2
Tilbury RM18 . . . . .179 C5
Wordsworth Ct CM1 . . . .32 A5
Wordsworth Way DA1 . .176 A3
Workhouse La CM3 . . . . .79 B2
Wormley Ct EN9 . . . . . . .66 A6
Wormyngford Ct EN9 . . .66 A6
Worrin Cl CM15 . . . . . . .94 F1
Worrin Rd CM15 . . . . . . .94 F1
Worthing Cl RM17 . . . . .177 E8
Worthing Rd SS15 . . . . .141 B6
Wouldham Rd RM17 . . . .177 D8
Wr Twr Rd CM14 . . . . . .116 C5
Wrackhall Ct SS8 . . . . . .164 E2
Wrangley Ct EN9 . . . . . . .66 A6
Wray Ave IG5 . . . . .133 A8
Wray Cl RM11 . . . . .136 D4
Wraysbury Dr SS15 . . . .119 D1
Wren Ave SS9 . . . . .146 D7
Wren Cl Billericay CM11 . .97 C1
South Benfleet SS7 . . . . .144 B6
Southend-on-S SS9 . . . . .146 D7
Wren Dr EN9 . . . . .66 A5
Wren Gdns
Dagenham RM9 . . . . .153 D7
Hornchurch RM12 . . . . . .135 F3
Wren Pl CM14 . . . . .116 D7
Wren Rd RM9 . . . . .153 D7
Wren Terr Ilford IG5 . . . .133 A8
Loughton IG10 . . . . .89 B8
Wren Wlk RM18 . . . . . . .179 B7
Wrens The CM19 . . . . . . .23 B8
Wrexham Rd
Basildon SS15 . . . . .141 B5
Romford RM3 . . . . .114 D7
Wright Cl DA10 . . . . . . .177 D1
Wright Mead CM2 . . . . . .33 B4
Wright's Green La CM22 . .2 D8
Wrights Cl RM10 . . . . . .154 B8
Wrights Ct CM17 . . . . . . .24 C6
Wrights Green La CM22 . . .2 D7
Wrights La CM15 . . . . . . .72 D3

Wrightsbridge Rd
Brentwood CM14 . . . . . . .92 F1
South Weald CM14 . . . . . .93 A1
Wrigley Cl E4 . . . . .109 D5
Wrington Ho RM3 . . . . . .114 F5
Writtle Coll CM1 . . . . . . .31 B3
Writtle Coll (Cow Watering
Campus) CM1 . . . . .30 E2
Writtle Jun & Inf Schs
CM1 . . . . .53 A8
Writtle Rd Chelmsford CM1 53 E8
Margaretting CM4 . . . . . .52 F2
Writtle Wlk
Basildon SS14 . . . . .142 E7
Rainham RM13 . . . . .154 C5
Wroths Path IG10 . . . . . .88 F8
Wroxall Ct 14 RM19 . . .171 B1
Wroxall Rd RM9 . . . . . . .153 C6
Wroxham Cl SS9 . . . . . .146 B6
Wroxham Way IG6 . . . . .111 B2
Wyatt's Green Rd CM15 . .72 E2
Wyatts Dr SS1 . . . . .167 F8
Wyatts Green La CM15 . . .72 D3
Wyburn Rd SS7 . . . . . . .145 E6
Wyburns Ave SS6 . . . . .145 E8
Wyburns Ave E SS6 . . . .145 E8
Wyburns Prim Sch SS6 . .145 F8
Wych Elm CM20 . . . . . . .10 C1
Wych Elm Cl RM11 . . . . .137 A4
Wych Elm Rd RM11 . . . .137 A5
Wych Mews SS15 . . . . . .119 D1
Wychford Dr CM21 . . . . . .1 C1
Wychwood Gdns
Ilford IG5 . . . . .133 A7
Redbridge IG5 . . . . .132 F7
Wycke Hill CM9 . . . . .58 D8
Wycke Hill Bsns Pk CM9 .58 E8
Wycke La CM9 . . . . .40 E8
Wycombe Ave SS7 . . . . .144 B6
Wycombe Rd IG2 . . . . . .132 F6
Wyemead Cres E4 . . . . .109 E8
Wyfields IG5 . . . . .111 B2
Wyhill Wlk RM10 . . . . . .154 C6
Wykeham Ave
Dagenham RM9 . . . . .153 C6
Hornchurch RM11 . . . . . .136 D5
Wykeham Gn RM9 . . . . .153 C6
Wykeham Prim Sch
RM12 . . . . .136 A3
Wykeham Rd CM1 . . . . . .31 B1
Wykes Gn SS14 . . . . . . .142 D7
Wyldwood Cl CM17 . . . . .11 C6
Wymark Cl RM13 . . . . . .155 A3
Wynn Bridge Cl IG8 . . . .110 D2
Wynndale Rd E18 . . . . . .110 B2
Wynters SS16 . . . . .142 B4
Wyse's Rd
Edney Common CM1 . . . . .52 A6
Roxwell CM1 . . . . .51 F7
Wythams SS13 . . . . .143 C7
Wythefield SS13 . . . . . . .143 A6
Wythenshawe Rd RM10 . 135 A1
Wyvern Ho RM17 . . . . . .178 B8

Y

Yale Way RM12 . . . . . . .155 A8
Yamburg Rd SS8 . . . . . .164 D3

Woo – Zid 227

Yantlet SS9 . . . . .146 E2
Yardeley SS15 . . . . .141 E6
Yardley Bsns Pk SS14 . .141 F8
Yardley Cl E4 . . . . .87 B4
Yardley La E4 . . . . .87 B4
Yardley Prim Sch E4 . . . .87 C3
Yarnacott SS3 . . . . .168 D8
Yarnton Way DA17 . . . . .169 A3
Yarwood Rd CM2 . . . . . . .32 E2
Yeldham Lock CM2 . . . . . .33 A2
Yellowpine Way IG7 . . . .112 B6
Yelverton Cl RM3 . . . . . .114 D2
Yeomen Way IG6 . . . . . .111 C4
Yeovil Chase SS0 . . . . . .147 B4
Yeovil Ct SS2 . . . . .148 D2
Yevele Way RM11 . . . . . .136 E4
Yew Cl Basildon SS15 . . .119 D1
Buckhurst Hill IG9 . . . . . .110 D8
Yew Tree Cl CM13 . . . . . .95 B3
Yew Tree Gdns
Chelmsford CM2 . . . . .54 C6
Dagenham RM6 . . . . .134 E6
4 Romford RM7 . . . . . . .135 D6
Yew Wlk EN11 . . . . .21 A5
Yewlands Hoddesdon EN11 21 A5
Sawbridgeworth CM21 . . . . .1 E1
Yewlands Dr EN11 . . . . . .21 A5
Yonge Cl CM3 . . . . .20 E1
York Ave SS17 . . . . .161 A5
York Cl Rayleigh SS6 . . . .146 A8
Shenfield CM15 . . . . .94 F2
York Cres IG10 . . . . .88 E6
York Hill IG10 . . . . .88 E6
York Ho Chingford E4 . . .109 A6
1 Ilford IG1 . . . . .133 B2
Loughton IG10 . . . . .89 D5
York Mews IG1 . . . . .133 A1
York Pl IG1 . . . . .133 A2
York Rd Billericay CM12 . .97 A5
Burnham-on-C CM0 . . . . .106 C4
Chelmsford CM2 . . . . .54 A8
Chingford E4 . . . . .109 A6
Horndon-on-t-H SS17 . . . .159 F4
Ilford IG1 . . . . .133 A2
North Weald Bassett CM16 .47 A4
Rainham RM13 . . . . .154 D5
Rayleigh SS1 . . . . .146 A8
Rochford SS4 . . . . .125 C7
Shenfield CM15 . . . . .94 F2
Southend-on-S SS1 . . . . .167 B7
York Rise SS6 . . . . .146 A8
York St IG11 . . . . .152 C4
Yorkes CM18 . . . . .23 F5
Young Cl SS9 . . . . .147 A7
Youngs Rd IG2 . . . . .133 D6
Yoxley App IG2 . . . . .133 C5
Yoxley Dr IG2 . . . . .133 C5

Z

Zandi Rd SS8 . . . . .164 D2
Zealand Dr SS8 . . . . . . .164 E3
Zelham Dr SS8 . . . . .164 F3
Zider Pass SS8 . . . . .164 F3

NG	NH	NJ	NK
NM	NN	NO	NP
NR	NS	NT	NU
NX	NY	NZ	
SC	SD	SE	TA
SH	SJ	SK	TF	TG
SM	SN	SO	SP	TL	TM
SR	SS	ST	SU	TQ	TR
SW	SX	SY	SZ	TV

Any feature in this atlas can be given a unique reference to help you find the same feature on other Ordnance Survey maps of the area, or to help someone else locate you if they do not have a Street Atlas.

The grid squares in this atlas match the Ordnance Survey National Grid and are at 500 metre intervals. The small figures at the bottom and sides of every other grid line are the National Grid kilometre values (**00** to **99** km) and are repeated across the country every 100 km (see left).

To give a unique National Grid reference you need to locate where in the country you are. The country is divided into 100 km squares with each square given a unique two-letter reference. Use the administrative map to determine in which 100 km square a particular page of this atlas falls.

The bold letters and numbers between each grid line (**A** to **F**, **1** to **8**) are for use within a specific Street Atlas only, and when used with the page number, are a convenient way of referencing these grid squares.

Example   The railway bridge over DARLEY GREEN RD in grid square B1

Step 1: Identify the two-letter reference, in this example the page is in **SP**

Eastings (read from left to right along the bottom) come before Northings (read from bottom to top). If you have trouble remembering say to yourself "Along the hall, THEN up the stairs"!

Step 2: Identify the 1 km square in which the railway bridge falls. Use the figures in the southwest corner of this square: Eastings **17**, Northings **74**. This gives a unique reference: **SP 17 74**, accurate to 1 km.

Step 3: To give a more precise reference accurate to 100 m you need to estimate how many tenths along and how many tenths up this 1 km square the feature is (to help with this the 1 km square is divided into four 500 m squares). This makes the bridge about **8** tenths along and about **1** tenth up from the southwest corner.

This gives a unique reference: **SP 178 741**, accurate to 100 m.

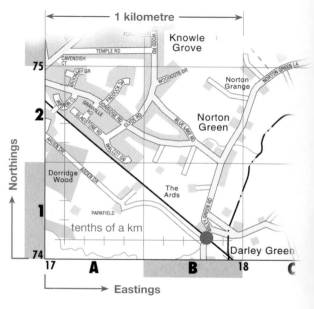

Addresses

Name and Address	Telephone	Page	Grid reference

Name and Address	Telephone	Page	Grid reference

Street Atlases from Philip's

Philip's publish an extensive range of regional and local street atlases which are ideal for motoring, business and leisure use. They are widely used by the emergency services and local authorities throughout Britain.

Key features include:

◆ Superb county-wide mapping at an extra-large scale of 3½ inches to 1 mile, or 2½ inches to 1 mile in pocket editions

◆ Complete urban and rural coverage, detailing every named street in town and country

◆ Each atlas available in two handy sizes – standard spiral and pocket paperback

'The mapping is very clear... great in scope and value'

★★★★ BEST BUY　　　AUTO EXPRESS

PHILIP'S STREET ATLAS Cambridgeshire With complete coverage of Peterborough BEST BUY Auto Express

PHILIP'S STREET ATLAS Glasgow and West Central Scotland

PHILIP'S STREET ATLAS Cardiff, Swansea and the Valleys Unique comprehensive coverage

PHILIP'S STREET ATLAS London The definitive London atlas

PHILIP'S STREET ATLAS East Sussex With complete coverage of Brighton and Hove. The definitive East Sussex atlas

PHILIP'S STREET ATLAS North Yorkshire Unique comprehensive coverage BEST BUY Auto Express

PHILIP'S STREET ATLAS Wiltshire and Swindon Unique comprehensive coverage

PHILIP'S STREET ATLAS Devon Unique comprehensive coverage BEST BUY Auto Express. Includes Lyme Regis, Saltash and Wellington, plus Exeter and Plymouth city centres at extra-large scale. with time-saving through-routes

1 Bedfordshire
2 Berkshire
3 Birmingham and West Midlands
4 Bristol and Bath
5 Buckinghamshire
6 Cambridgeshire
7 Cardiff, Swansea and The Valleys
8 Cheshire
9 Cornwall
10 Derbyshire
11 Devon
12 Dorset
13 County Durham and Teesside
14 Edinburgh and East Central Scotland
15 North Essex
16 South Essex
17 Glasgow and West Central Scotland
18 Gloucestershire
19 North Hampshire
20 South Hampshire
21 Herefordshire and Monmouthshire
22 Hertfordshire
23 East Kent
24 West Kent
25 Lancashire
26 Leicestershire and Rutland
27 Lincolnshire
28 London
29 Greater Manchester
30 Merseyside
31 Norfolk
32 Northamptonshire
33 Nottinghamshire
34 Oxfordshire
35 Shropshire
36 Somerset
37 Staffordshire
38 Suffolk
39 Surrey
40 East Sussex
41 West Sussex
42 Tyne and Wear and Northumberland
43 Warwickshire
44 Worcestershire
45 Wiltshire and Swindon
46 East Yorkshire and Northern Lincolnshire
47 North Yorkshire
48 South Yorkshire
49 West Yorkshire

How to order

The Philip's range of street atlases is available from good retailers or directly from the publisher by phoning 01903 828503